# food
## the definitive guide

# FOOD THE DEFINITIVE GUIDE

Published by Murdoch Books®
First published 2001
© Text, design, photography and illustrations Murdoch Books® 2001.
ISBN 1-85391-174-7

A catalogue record of this book is available from the British Library.

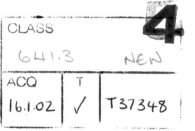
Publishing Manager: Kay Halsey
Food Editor: Lulu Grimes
Editor: Kim Rowney
Designer and Cover Design: Vivien Valk
Design Concept and Art Direction: Juliet Cohen
Consultant Editor: John Newton
Food Consultant: C. J. Jackson
Photographers: Ben Dearnley, Jared Fowler
Stylists: Michaela Le Compte, Justine Poole
Additional Styling: Katy Holder, Sarah de Nardi
Stylists' Assistants: Jo Glynn, Rodney Dunn, Michelle Thrift, Saskia Hay, Kim Passenger,
Michelle Lawton, Valli Little, Kerrie Mullins, Kate Murdoch
Additional Research: Michelle Earl, Katy Holder, Anna Waddington
Recipes: Jo Glynn, Michelle Earl, Katy Holder
Illustrations: Stephen Pollitt
Cover Photography: Chris Jones
Cover Styling and Art Direction: Juliet Cohen
Publisher: Kay Scarlett
Production Manager: Liz Fitzgerald
Group General Manager: Mark Smith

Printed by Kyodo Printing Co. (S'pore) Pte Ltd.
PRINTED IN SINGAPORE

Published by:
AUSTRALIA
Murdoch Books® Australia
GPO Box 1203, Sydney, NSW 1045
Phone: (02) 8220 2000   Fax: (02) 8220 2558

UK
Murdoch Books® UK
Ferry House, 51–57 Lacy Road, London SW15 1PR
Phone: (020) 8355 1480   Fax: (020) 8355 1499

IMPORTANT: Those who might be at risk from the effects of salmonella food poisoning (the elderly, pregnant women, young children and those suffering from immune deficiency diseases) should consult their GP with any concerns about eating raw eggs.

Pictured right: physalis, page 295.

# food
## the definitive guide

**Consultant editor**

**John Newton**

Written and researched by
Kim Rowney, Lulu Grimes, Kay Halsey

## MURDOCH
### B O O K S

# contents

# introduction

## How to use this book

To find a particular piece of information, first look to see if it appears under one of the A–Z entry headings, which are ordered alphabetically.

If it does not have a main entry, it may come under a general grouping, such as bread, fish or vinegar.

If the information is not listed under a general grouping, check the index at the back—this will direct you towards all the key words in the book. Where there are alternative names or spellings for an entry, they will be found here as well.

Many entries contain cross-references under the categories *see also* and *goes with*. This can lead you to additional information.

At the back of the book are reference pages with lots of basic information about your kitchen and cooking. The first section looks at kitchen equipment, what to buy and how to use it.

Following this is a section of kitchen terms. These supplement the information in the book with an explanation of common cooking and food terms. If an unusual word appears in a recipe or a menu, this is the place to check its meaning.

Lastly, there is a section of cooking information pages. Here you will find international conversion charts for weights and measures, quick reference material for oven temperatures and catering quantities, as well as information on food safety and correct refrigeration, freezing, defrosting and microwaving.

In addition to the index, there is a recipe index, which can be used if you are just looking for a classic sauce or ideas for what to do with a bunch of fresh asparagus.

*Publisher's note*

Every effort has been made to ensure that all the information in this book was correct when the book went to press. However, guidelines for the preparation and cooking of food are constantly changing and some foods can potentially be harmful or are now prohibited in certain countries. Reasonable care should therefore be taken, particularly when eating wild foods such as mushrooms. This book is not intended to be the definitive guide to food preparation and the Publisher cannot be held liable for any action or claim arising from the use of this book.

Any of a variety of single-shelled marine molluscs, abalone is highly prized as a seafood delicacy in Japan and China. It has cream-coloured flesh and a mild meaty flavour, similar to a clam. In many countries, abalone has been over-harvested and, as it needs to be picked off the rocks by hand, it can be very expensive: farming, currently in progress in many countries, may help bring the price down. In New Zealand abalone are called paua and are most commonly deep-fried as fritters and served with chips. In the Channel Islands a smaller European variety of abalone are called ormer; these are often made into a stew.

Abalone clings to the rock with a large muscular foot, and it is this foot that is the edible part. Contrary to popular belief, fresh abalone need not be beaten to tenderize the flesh, though the hard base of the foot does need to be trimmed away. The flesh can be cooked in many ways: sliced, then dipped in egg and breadcrumbs and fried (about 30–40 seconds each side); steamed in the shell; used in stir-fries or Chinese braised dishes; or served raw as sashimi. It is particularly good in garlic butter. Sprinkled with the juice of half a lemon and extra virgin olive oil it will keep for many days.

Dried abalone is also much prized in Asia and can be bought at Asian shops. Tinned abalone is the easiest to use as it is cleaned and already very tender. Some of it is sold already cut into steaks. Abalone can be bought canned, dried, salted or frozen, although fresh *(pictured)* is best.

**Also known as — *awabi, ormer, paua***

## PREPARATION

*When using fresh abalone you will need to first release the muscular foot from its shell. Do this by running a sharp knife between the flesh and shell. Next, scrape off any slime and trim off the horned pad at the base of the foot.*

Native to South America, but also grown in Australia and Florida, abiu is a round fruit, about the size of an orange, with shiny, thick yellow skin. The flesh tastes of sweet caramel when fully ripe, and is high in vitamin C. The fruit can be peeled and eaten in segments; chilled and eaten with a spoon; cut into cubes and added to fruit salad; or puréed for drinks and sorbets. Ripen by storing at room temperature.

**Also known as — *abi, caimo, cauje***

Acerola berries are exceptionally high in vitamin C—two or three berries will meet daily vitamin C requirements. For this reason the fruit is often used commercially in vitamin C tablets and baby food. The fruit, which is similar in appearance to a cherry but with three lobes, is available in those countries in which it grows, but is more commonly found as a powder in health food shops.

**Also known as — *Barbados cherry, Brazilian cherry, West Indian cherry***

The food of Saharan Africa is a melting pot of native ingredients mixed with the flavours of European colonialists and traders, foods brought by the slave ships of the New World and the cooking of Asian immigrants. North African cooking is also part of a Mediterranean heritage and can be found under 'Middle Eastern food'.

African food is based on starch derived from such native tubers as cassava, yam, and numerous varieties of the introduced sweet potato. These are accompanied by a meat or vegetable stew. Leafy greens, peas and beans are steamed or boiled, but rarely eaten raw in salads. Cereals, peanuts, corn, bananas and plantains are widely eaten, while dairy products and eggs provide protein in the village diet.

## EAST AFRICA

Less influenced by Europe than much of Africa, East African food is based on the starches of millet, sorghum and bananas. *Irio*, a Kenyan corn and potato dish, *ugali*, a cornmeal mush, and fritters are all eaten with stews. Little meat is eaten, as cattle confer status (the Masai live on the milk and blood, but not the meat, of their cattle). Along the coast, the Swahili culture absorbed Arabic saffron, cloves and pilaffs from Arab settlers. Later, Indian workers brought curries.

*Mozambique is well known for its seafood. This dish is piri piri prawns, a fiery hot dish made using piri piri chillies.*

*Doro wat (chicken stew) is usually served with injera, a large type of flatbread.*

Sudanese cuisine has more European and Arab influences than the rest of East Africa—they speak Arabic and eat lamb and chicken, such as *bamia*, an okra lamb stew, with rice, breads and a pancake called *kisra*. The coffee is excellent.

Surrounded by mountains, Ethiopia has one of the most unusual cuisines in Africa. Traders introduced chillies and spices and the food is uncharacteristically meat-based: there is even a version of steak tartare—*kifto leb leb*. *Berbere* is a red spice paste that forms the basis of dishes such as *wat*, a stew of hard-boiled eggs, meat, fish or vegetables. *Doro wat*, chicken stew, is the national dish. The taste of *niter kibbeh*, spiced butter, is in many dishes either as a seasoning or cooking oil. Traditionally, meals are eaten with a huge flat bread, *injera*, made from the nutritious teff grain. The bread is torn up to scoop up the *wat*. The meal may finish with *tej*, a honey-based wine and coffee, which was first discovered here.

The island of Madagascar is mostly Malaysian/Polynesian, with a mix of Indian, Arab, African and European, especially French, influences. Here, rice is the staple, and the island is famous for its fish, mild curries and vanilla.

The Portuguese techniques of spicing, roasting and marinating, as well as ingredients from their colonies, greatly influenced African cuisine, particularly in their colonies of Angola (West Africa) and Mozambique. Both are renowned for their spicy *piri piri*—a lemon and chilli paste used on meat, chicken and shellfish. Mozambique's seafood, especially prawns, is outstanding.

*Irio, a stewed vegetable dish from Kenya. The ingredients are mashed together before eating.*

## WEST AFRICA

The most important foreign culinary influence comes from the swap of ingredients during the slave trade, when ships brought okra, coconuts, plantains, chillies, peppers, beans, peanuts, corn and tomatoes from the New World.

*White bean fritters are a popular Nigerian dish.*

As their meat is of poor quality, West Africans eat a lot of seafood and, unusually, meat and dried fish are often combined in stews. High rainfall means the main starch, unlike the rest of Africa, is rice, along with couscous from North Africa. Yams are very important (yam festivals are held regularly) and are made into dishes like *foo-foo*—a mashed pudding that goes with stews, and *iyan*, a yam porridge. Sweet potatoes, plantain, root vegetables, potato and cassava provide dietary bulk. Black-eyed peas are a staple and peanuts are found everywhere: in the stew called *mafé*, and processed for cooking oil. Deep-frying is a traditional cooking technique, used to make *akara*—Nigerian white bean fritters—and banana fritters.

*Also from Senegal, chicken yassa. The chicken is marinated in a mixture of lemon juice, oil and flavoured with a habanero chilli.*

Senegal, one of the most French-influenced countries in West Africa, makes much use of onion and garlic. Seafood is the mainstay and *thiebou dienn* and *kaldou* are fish stews served with rice. There is little meat and no pork, so their famous stew, *yassa*, is usually made with chicken, or sometimes with fish or lamb marinated in lemon juice.

## SOUTH AFRICA

South African food is as diverse as its people—a fusion of African, Malay, Indian, Dutch and English cooking. Traditional meals revolve around *mealies* (cornmeal), an indigenous sorghum and millet, served with spicy meat and vegetable stews. The Dutch brought their baking, such as *soetkoekies*—spice cookies—and rice dishes from Indonesia; the British introduced meat pies; and the French cultivated the vineyards that have today become South Africa's growing and acclaimed wine industry.

*Mafé is a peanut stew and a Senegalese classic. It can be made with lamb, as here, beef or chicken.*

Malay and Indian workers brought curries, *breyani* (meaning biryani—a spicy dish of rice and meat or fish, usually coloured with saffron) and dhals, which became part of Cape Malay cooking. British meat pies became curried *boboties*, and *sosaties* (the name comes from the Malay for 'satay') are meat skewers integral to the great South African barbecue, or *braaivleis*. Curries are served with sambals, chutneys and *achars* (pickles), a legacy of immigrants from India and Southeast Asia, while little German burgers, *frikkadels*, are served with yellow rice. *Bredies* have a more African influence and are one-pot stews, often served with *mealies*. *Biltong* is dried smoked pieces of meat. Seafood is widely eaten, with rock lobster a speciality. Pickled fish such as *snoek* is popular and was originally prepared for Dutch sailors. The cooking also makes use of good game and lamb.

*Lamb sosaties and lime achar (pickles)*

*See also* **bobotie, piri piri, teff**

# agar-agar

Agar-agar is a flavourless vegetarian gelling agent made from seaweed. It is used to set ice cream, Asian desserts and jellies *(pictured)*. Foods set with agar-agar will set at room temperature, unlike those containing gelatine, which set on chilling. Desserts that have a high acidic content, such as lemon jelly, may need more agar-agar before they will set. Agar-agar flakes, strands, powder or blocks are sold in health food and Asian shops.

**Also known as — agar, Japanese gelatine, kanten, seaweed gelatine**

Agar-agar strands can be used to make Asian-style jellies.

# aïoli

## AIOLI

*Put 6 peeled garlic cloves, 2 egg yolks and a pinch of salt into a blender and blend the ingredients until a thick paste forms. With the motor running, add about 250 ml olive oil, drop by drop, until the aïoli is thick and creamy; however, if it gets too thick, add a little lemon juice. Season to taste. This recipe can also be made using a mortar and pestle. Serves 6.*

A classic of Provençal cuisine, aïoli is a strongly flavoured garlic mayonnaise made with egg yolks, garlic and olive oil. The name is formed from the Provençal *ail*, meaning 'garlic' and *oli*, meaning 'oil'. Serve aïoli with salads, egg dishes, fish soup, cold poached fish or as an accompaniment to hot or cold vegetables. The *grand aïoli*, a festive Provençal platter, may consist of poached salted cod, boiled chicken, hard-boiled eggs, vegetables and snails, all of which are served with large dollops of aïoli.

# alfalfa

Alfalfa seeds are sprouted to give a fine, crisp plant stem, and it is these sprouts that are eaten in salads, sandwiches or stir-fries (toss them in at the last minute or they will wilt quickly when heated). Alfalfa belongs to the legume family and is closely related to beans and peas.

Buy crisp alfalfa sprouts with a fresh smell and roots that are moist and white. Avoid sprouts with brown tips or those that are starting to look a bit slimy. To keep the sprouts crisp and fresh, put them in a bowl filled with water and keep them in the fridge, changing the water daily.

**alligator** — see Cajun

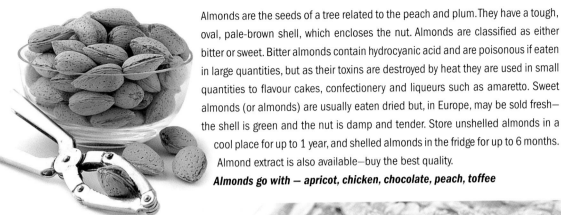

Almonds are the seeds of a tree related to the peach and plum. They have a tough, oval, pale-brown shell, which encloses the nut. Almonds are classified as either bitter or sweet. Bitter almonds contain hydrocyanic acid and are poisonous if eaten in large quantities, but as their toxins are destroyed by heat they are used in small quantities to flavour cakes, confectionery and liqueurs such as amaretto. Sweet almonds (or almonds) are usually eaten dried but, in Europe, may be sold fresh—the shell is green and the nut is damp and tender. Store unshelled almonds in a cool place for up to 1 year, and shelled almonds in the fridge for up to 6 months. Almond extract is also available—buy the best quality.

*Almonds go with — apricot, chicken, chocolate, peach, toffee*

## COOKING

**Blanching** - *Pour boiling water over almonds and stand for 2 minutes. Drain and slip off the skins using your fingers. Chop the almonds when they are warm and damp as the nut is softer.*

**Toasting** - *Spread almonds in an even layer on a baking tray. Put the tray in a 180°C oven and cook for 8–10 minutes. Use a timer as the almonds will burn very quickly after they start to brown.*

**Grinding** - *For fresh, ground almonds, grind them with a food processor or mortar and pestle. Use either blanched almonds or those with their skins on. As almonds are high in oil, add a little sugar to help absorb the oil and prevent an oily paste forming.*

## TYPES OF SWEET ALMONDS

| | |
|---|---|
| **Whole** | Sold in shells with their skins on or blanched (skins removed). Roasting stops them going soggy. Whole almonds may also be salted, smoked or honey-roasted. |
| **Nibbed and slivered** | Sprinkle nibbed (chopped) or slivered almonds onto salads, mix into pasta sauces or use to decorate fish (good with trout) or vegetables. |
| **Flaked** | Toast flakes and decorate trifles, crumbles, cakes, ice cream or tarts (pictured) or add to salads. |
| **Ground** | Also called almond meal or powder, ground almonds can be used in baking to add texture, richness and flavour. Freshly ground almonds have a better flavour. |

## ALMOND MILK

*Almond milk is drunk in the Middle East to celebrate special occasions, it is considered a nourishing drink in India, and is widely drunk in Europe. Use as a lactose-free ingredient in ice cream, rice pudding, milk shakes or in fruit smoothies (try it with peaches or strawberries). To make almond milk, grind 250 g blanched almonds and 100 g sugar in a blender with 400 ml water to make a thick paste. Leave for 1 hour, add 400 ml water, then sieve the mixture through muslin into a jug. Press hard on the solids to squeeze out any excess liquid. Serve chilled. Makes 750 ml.*

*See also  amaretti, amaretto, macaroon, marzipan, ratafia*

## amaranth

Amaranth is a leafy vegetable cultivated for both its leaves and seeds. There are many types, but the ones grown for eating are commonly known as green and red amaranth (the latter is not entirely red: the leaf is edged in green and the middle is tinged a deep red). The leaves have a slightly pungent flavour and are used in the same way as spinach, either raw in salads, in stir-fries, or as an ingredient in soups. Amaranth is best used on the day of purchase as the leaves become limp very quickly. A pickled version is also available from Asian supermarkets.

Amaranth seeds, which are very high in protein, are used in soups and cereals, or ground into a gluten-free flour and used in baking. Both seeds and flour can be purchased from health food shops.

*Also known as — African spinach, bhaji, callaloo, Chinese spinach, een choy, elephant's ear, Indian spinach, sag*

*See also* **Caribbean food**

## amaretti

Amaretti are light, macaroon biscuits made with sweet and bitter almonds. The bitter almonds give amaretti their characteristic flavour—and their name, which means 'little bitter things'. There are many varieties of amaretti, but they are often seen wrapped in pairs and served with coffee. Amaretti can also be eaten with a dessert wine, crumbled as a topping for trifles, or they give a special flavour to savoury dishes such as *tortelli di zucca*, a pumpkin ravioli that is a speciality of northern Italy.

## amaretto

Amaretto is an Italian liqueur flavoured with almonds and apricots. *Amaretto di Saronno* is the original brand produced in Italy, but amaretto is now used as the generic term. *Amaretto* means 'slightly bitter', and refers to the bitter almonds that were traditionally used as its main flavouring ingredient.

Amaretto was once best known as an after-dinner liqueur, but it is now used widely as an ingredient in cakes, sauces and cocktails.

*Amaretto goes with — almond, apricot, chocolate, peach*

Culinarily as well as economically, America has had an extraordinary impact on the world diet since the second half of the twentieth century. The hot dog, the hamburger and black fizzy drinks are hard to escape in any corner of the globe. The Italian Slow Food movement began as a protest against the onslaught of fast food in Europe. But American food history is richer and more complex than the hamburger, and begins well before the twentieth century.

## NATIVE AMERICAN FOOD

When the pilgrims arrived in America in the 1600s they found no familiar foods. The Native Americans helped them survive in those first years by introducing them to the 'sacred sisters' of Indian cooking—corn, beans and squash. Until the late 1700s, almost all settlers were farmers with a diet of cornmeal and salt pork. Later, immigrants brought their own food and cooking to America to create a truly global cuisine, with many famous American dishes having their roots in the food of the Old World.

## THE EAST

The pilgrims' first Thanksgiving in New England celebrated a new food—corn, later made into Johnny cakes, succotash and hasty pudding. The second Thanksgiving introduced turkey, cranberries and pumpkin pie. New England is now famous for its seafood: clambakes, lobster and chowder. Boiled dinners, codfish cakes and fruit pies (grunts, slumps and pandowies), are all made from foods stored for the winter.

The Dutch and Germans who settled in Pennsylvania brought coleslaw, waffles, pancakes, doughnuts and *koekjes* (cookies).

In New York, immigration led to much new food, which today can be found in the Jewish delis with corned beef or hot pastrami sandwiches on rye, in Italian

pizza and pasta joints, and the egg rolls and fortune cookies of Chinatown.

## THE SOUTH

The settlers first relied on corn, which they made into fritters, cornbread, hominy and grits. Later, rice planted in Carolina was used in dishes such as hopping John. Many regional specialities are based on seafood: Maryland crab cakes, Louisiana crawfish *étouffée* and Mississippi fried catfish. Fried chicken and fried green tomatoes are truly Southern, while pork, especially ribs, is the choice for Southern barbecues.

Influences on cooking have ranged from the soul food of the slaves to Creole and Cajun. In the Southwest, Indians grew chillies, which, with Spanish and Mexican influences, created Tex Mex and Southwestern cooking.

In Florida, Spanish settlers imported citrus fruits and used limes to make the famous key lime pie. Now, Florida has had another wave of Spanish influence, mixed with Caribbean flavours, in the form of Cuban immigrants.

## THE WEST AND HAWAII

Immigration to the Midwest was strongly Scandinavian and German—especially Milwaukee with its beer and sausages, including the original frankfurter.

Pacific Rim cooking, a multicultural cuisine, has Mexican influences from over the border, while the Chinese labourers who settled in San Francisco introduced egg foo yung, chop suey and chow mein. Recently, the American wine industry has grown enormously.

■ *See also* **Cajun, chowder, Creole, hominy, hopping John, succotash, Tex-Mex**

*From top: Key lime pie (the natural yellow colour of the limes shows through in this traditional recipe, but some pies may be coloured with green food colouring); barbecue pork spareribs with coleslaw; bell pepper and goat's cheese wrap; Philadelphia cheese steak sandwich.*

## anchoïade

At its most basic, anchoïade, a Provençal spread or paste, is made by processing anchovies with garlic, olive oil and vinegar in a food processor or a mortar and pestle. Typically, it is used as a spread on toast or bread, or as a dip to be served with raw vegetables. It is also excellent in pizza toppings or pasta sauces. Ready-made anchoïade can be bought at supermarkets and delicatessens.

ANCHOIADE

*In a food processor, blend 160 g anchovy fillets, 2 garlic cloves, 1 teaspoon thyme, 3 teaspoons chopped parsley and enough olive oil to make a thick paste. Season well with pepper and lemon juice and serve with toasted bread. Serves 6.*

## angel food cake

Angel food cake is a light sponge cake made with egg whites but no yolks or fats. The cake relies on air beaten into the egg whites (usually 10 to 12) to make it rise. Traditionally, it is baked in an angel cake tin or ring mould as this allows the cake to cook evenly. In contrast to the delicate colour and texture of angel food cake is devil's food cake—a dense, rich chocolate cake. Bicarbonate of soda is used in the cake mixture, causing the chocolate to turn a deep red-brown colour.

**Also known as — angel cake**

## angelica

The angelica variety of most interest to cooks is *Angelica archangelico*, an aromatic herb that resembles a tall parsley plant. It is native to the northern hemisphere and grows well in Scotland, Germany, Scandinavia and Russia, but can be cultivated in warmer climes. In medieval times, it was thought to be an antidote to poison. According to one legend, the Archangel Raphael revealed in a dream that angelica was a cure for the plague.

Today, angelica is regarded more for its culinary qualities. The fresh stems and leaves are used as a flavouring for confectionery, pastries and liqueurs; oil from the seeds and roots is used in the preparation of liqueurs; and the leaves are used fresh in salads. Its most popular use is in cake decoration, where its green stalks are blanched, peeled and boiled, then candied in sugar to produce a vivid green colour.

*Cup cakes decorated with strips of angelica*

## ANGELS-ON-HORSEBACK

*Stretch out rashers of rindless bacon, then wrap each rasher around a clean, shucked oyster. Place seam side down on a baking tray and cook under a hot grill until the bacon is brown and crisp.*

## DEVILS-ON-HORSEBACK

*Stuff stoned prunes with mango chutney. Wrap in bacon and cook, following the method above.*

*Angels-on-horseback (front) and devils-on-horseback (back).*

Angels-on-horseback are oysters that are wrapped in bacon and secured with a toothpick, then fried, baked or grilled and served on small pieces of buttered toast. Traditionally they were served at the end of a meal, but today you are likely to encounter them as a canapé served without the toast. The angels are the oysters, which curl as they cook to resemble angel wings riding on slices of toast, and it was this imagery that gave this canapé its interesting name. Devils-on-horseback are similar, but are made with prunes instead of oysters.

# Anna potatoes

A classic French dish, Anna potatoes is a type of potato 'cake'. To prepare it, thinly sliced, patted-dry potatoes are arranged in circles in a dish and, as each layer is added, the potatoes are buttered and seasoned. The dish is covered with foil and the top weighted down to force the layers together, baked until golden brown, then turned out. A heavy-based baking dish, a cast-iron frying pan, or a special copper 'cocotte Anna' dish will conduct heat well, giving the potato cake an even, brown crust.

**Also known as — pommes Anna**

# annatto

Annatto is a bright-orange food colouring, which is extracted from the dark red, triangular seeds of a small tree native to South America. Although the seed is edible, it has little flavour and its culinary value lies more in its colouring properties. Annatto is used in Filipino, South American, Southeast Asian and Caribbean cooking as a colouring agent. Usually the seeds are fried in oil or lard and then discarded, and the remaining yellow lard is used to fry vegetables or meat to give them a golden yellow coating.

When ground into a powder or paste, annatto is used to colour butter, margarine and smoked fish. Washed-rind cheeses, such as Livarot, are sometimes dipped in annatto colouring to deepen the colour of their rind, while the colouring of some cheeses, such as Red Leicester, is also enhanced with annatto.

**Also known as — achuete, anatto, anchiote**

# antipasto

Antipasto is a selection of appetizers served before a meal. The word is derived from the Italian *ante*, meaning 'before' and *pasto* meaning 'meal'. Common elements of an antipasto platter are cured meats and salamis, anchovies, cold fish, olives, tomatoes, marinated vegetables and frittata, but this may vary depending on the region. In most areas of Italy, antipasto are vegetable and meat based, but in coastal areas you are more likely to encounter an antipasto of fish, mussels, anchovies and calamari. Bruschetta, arancini and crostini may also be served as antipasto.

## GIARDINIERA
This mixed vegetable pickle is made with raw, chopped cauliflowers, carrots and green beans, which are marinated in vinegar.

## SUN-DRIED TOMATOES
These sun-dried tomatoes have been marinated in olive oil and herbs.

## CIPOLLINI
Baby onions in a sweet and sour dressing made with balsamic vinegar and sugar.

## OLIVA ALL'ASCOLONA
These olives (on platter) are stuffed with salami and cheese, then coated in egg and breadcrumbs and deep-fried.

## AUBERGINES
Fry thin slices of aubergine in oil, then dress with olive oil and chilli.

## INSALATA ALLA CAPRESE
Cut tomatoes into slices, top with mozzarella and dress with olive oil and basil leaves.

## MARINATED COURGETTES
Slice grilled courgettes into strips, then marinate them in vinegar, garlic, mint and oregano.

## OLIVES

Black *oliva di gaeta* olives are excellent for antipasto. These are cured in water, then salted and kept in a mild brine. Other olives include the green *cergnola* or dried black olives—these have a more concentrated flavour.

## ROASTED PEPPERS

Cut roasted and skinned red and yellow peppers into strips, then marinate them in olive oil.

## BROAD BEAN PUREE

*Use 500 g fresh or frozen broad beans or soak 250 g dried broad bean in cold water overnight. Put the beans in a saucepan and cover with cold water. Bring to the boil and simmer the beans until tender. Purée with 4 tablespoons olive oil and enough cooking water to make a spreadable paste. Season well. Serves 4.*

## BROAD BEAN PUREE

Boil, then purée broad beans with olive oil (see recipe above). Serve the purée with chicory or pieces of bread.

## SWEET AND SOUR SARDINES

These sardines are dusted with flour, and fried, then marinated in olive oil, wine vinegar and sugar with fried onion, raisins and pine nuts.

## OCTOPUS

These baby octopuses are boiled, then dressed with olive oil, parsley and lemon juice.

## MUSSELS

Top mussels with breadcrumbs, garlic and parsley, then bake them in their half shells.

## MARINATED ANCHOVIES

Serve anchovy fillets marinated in olive oil, lemon juice, garlic and parsley.

# apple

Apples were one of the earliest cultivated fruits, and today there are around 8,000 varieties to choose from. Apples range in colour from red to yellow; their texture from firm to soft; and their taste from tart to sweet. High in vitamin C and fibre, apples are a healthy snack, a useful ingredient in both sweet and savoury dishes, and because of their high pectin content, are often used in jams and jellies.

*Apples go with — brown sugar, Calvados, chicken, cinnamon, cream, lemon, orange, pork*

## BAKED APPLES

*Remove the cores from 4 eating apples. Mix 4 tablespoons sultanas with 4 teaspoons softened butter and a large pinch of mixed spice. Stuff the cores and bake at 180°C for 30 minutes, or until tender. Serves 4.*

## TYPES OF APPLES

Granny Smith

Fuji

Red Delicious

Pink Lady

Golden Delicious

Jonathan

Royal Gala

Lady William

Bramley

**Eating**

Good eating (dessert) apples are sweet and often slightly acidic. They can be sliced and tossed in salads, or served with a cheese platter. As these apples have a high sugar content, they hold their shape well and are perfect for use in baked pies and tarts, or if fried and caramelized, are excellent with a pork or chicken dish. Good eating apples include: Braeburn, Fuji, Discovery, Empire, Red Delicious, Royal Gala, Russet and Lady William.

**Cooking and eating**

Apples suitable for cooking, such as those used to make purées or crumbles, are more acidic and become soft and break up when stewed or baked. Some apples are good for both cooking and eating: Spartan, Golden Delicious (good for purée), Cox's Orange Pippin, Rome, Granny Smith (hold their shape well), Pink Lady, Jonagold and Jonathan.

**Cooking**

Bramley, Grenadier and Newton Wonder are usually very sour and are best used as cooking apples. These apples make excellent purées as their flesh breaks down easily.

## STORAGE

*Don't store apples with ethylene-sensitive vegetables and fruit because the ethylene given off by apples causes these vegetables and fruit to deteriorate.*

*Apples will store well at room temperature, but they will maintain their crisp texture for longer if kept in the vegetable crisper of the fridge.*

## COOKING

*To stop apple slices turning brown, brush them with lemon juice or use them as soon as you slice them.*

*See also **Calvados, cider***

A relative of the peach, apricots have a velvety, golden-orange skin and an aromatic, sweet flesh. Apricots are now grown in most temperate climates throughout the world, but their original habitat was in northern China where they grew wild more than 2,000 years ago.

Fresh apricots are excellent when eaten raw or in fruit salads, but they also cook beautifully in sauces, jams, pies or tarts, or they can be poached with sweet wine and vanilla. Their rich flavour complements savoury dishes, and they are used widely in Middle Eastern cooking (particularly in lamb and rice dishes) and tagines. Apricot stones can be cracked to obtain the kernel, which tastes similar to a bitter almond, and may be used with the flesh to add flavour when cooking (though the kernels do contain hydrocyanic acid and are poisonous if eaten in large quantities).

**Apricots go with — almond, amaretto, cheese, cherry, cinnamon, honey, pork, walnut**

MAKING APRICOT GLAZE

*1 Melt apricot jam with a little water and lemon juice. Pass through a sieve to produce a pale glaze. Brush over fruit tarts and pastries.*

STORAGE

*Ripe apricots are best eaten on the day of purchase. They should have a strong aroma: colour is not an indication of ripeness.*

*Unripe fruit will develop full flavour by ripening at room temperature. To speed this up, place them in a brown paper bag and close it. Ripe apricots will keep for 1 week in the fridge.*

*Dry apricots by splitting, stoning and placing in a 120°C oven for 4–5 hours, or until ready.*

### arancini

A speciality of Sicily, arancini are savoury rice balls wrapped around a filling, coated in breadcrumbs and deep-fried. The filling is usually tomatoes mixed with chicken livers, meat or mozzarella; ham and peas; or chicken and herbs *(pictured)*. Arancini means 'little oranges', referring to their size, shape and their lovely golden colour, which may be enhanced by mixing saffron with the rice.

 *See also* **suppli**

see brandy — **Armagnac**

# arrowroot

A starch powder obtained from the root of a tropical plant used as a thickening agent. Arrowroot is tasteless and the fine powder becomes clear when cooked and is therefore useful for thickening clear sauces. Arrowroot must be slaked (mixed with a small amount of water to form a smooth paste) before it is mixed with a hot liquid for use in sauces, puddings or pie fillings. Heat the sauce until thick and remove it immediately as overcooking will cause it to thin again.

# artichoke

The globe artichoke is the unopened bud of a brilliant blue flower. As a tiny baby, it may be eaten whole, even raw in salads; a more mature bud may be stuffed, quartered, boiled or fried; and finally, as a large artichoke, it may be boiled and eaten one leaf at a time (suck or scrape the flesh off the fibrous base with your teeth), dipped into vinaigrette or hollandaise sauce. In all but the baby artichoke, care must be taken to discard the prickly choke, above the fleshy (and delicious) base, known also as the heart. Choose heavy artichokes with firm heads and stems, and leaves that are tightly overlapping.

**Artichokes go with — anchovy, basil, egg, lemon, Parmesan, tomato**

*See also* **Jerusalem artichoke**

## STORAGE

*Will keep in the vegetable crisper of the fridge for 1 week if sprinkled with water and sealed in a plastic bag. Alternatively, store them upright in water, like flowers, for several days.*

## PREPARATION

*Rub the cut surfaces with lemon or vinegar to stop them turning brown.*

*Always cut with a stainless steel knife to avoid staining the flesh.*

*Wash your hands after handling the stem as it gives off a bitter flavour.*

## COOKING

*Cook in stainless steel, glass or enamel pots, as aluminium pots can impart a metallic flavour and will discolour the artichoke.*

*If serving cold, plunge artichokes in iced water for 3 minutes to stop the cooking process, then drain them upside down.*

*If frying artichokes, first boil them in a blanc (boiling water with a little flour and lemon juice mixed in) so they keep their colour.*

*Artichokes contain cynarin, which makes everything you eat or drink with, or after, them taste sweet. This makes artichokes difficult to match with wine.*

## PREPARING AND COOKING ARTICHOKES

1 Hold the artichoke head in one hand, snap off the stem and remove any tough fibres. Cut off the top third of the artichoke and any sharp leaf ends.

2 Remove any tough outer leaves, then simmer in boiling water (add a squeeze of lemon) for 20–30 minutes, or until an outer leaf pulls off easily. Drain well.

**arugula** — see rocket

## BITTER MELON

Used in Chinese, Southeast Asian and Indian cooking, bitter melon is usually sliced and salted to remove the bitter juices, then braised or stuffed with pork and served with black bean sauce or cooked in curries.

***Also known as — bitter gourd***

## BOK CHOY

A member of the cabbage family with a slightly mustardy taste. Separate the leaves, wash well and use both leaf and stem in soups and stir-fries, steam and serve with oyster sauce or fry in sesame oil with garlic and ginger. A smaller type is Shanghai bok choy, or baby bok choy *(pictured)*, used in the same way.

***Also known as — Chinese chard, Chinese white cabbage, pak choy***

## CHINESE CABBAGE

A versatile vegetable with a mild, sweet flavour. It can be shredded and eaten raw, steamed, used in stir-fries, soups and curries, or used to make cabbage rolls. Chinese cabbage is also used to make Korean kimchi.

***Also known as — celery cabbage, Chinese leaves, napa cabbage, Peking cabbage, wong bok***

## CHINESE KEYS

A member of the ginger family, Chinese keys is a reddish brown root vegetable with thick, tapering roots that grow in a cluster, resembling a bunch of keys. Its spicy flavouring is used mainly in curries and pickles in Thai and Indonesian cooking. Chinese keys may also be sold under the name 'rhizome powder'. As well as being sold fresh, it is also available in bottles and cans.

***Also known as — kiachi***

*The curious cook will discover new and fascinating vegetables in Asian markets and greengrocers.*
*This is a guide to some of the most common.*
*As with any vegetables, choose crisp-leaved, firm-stemmed healthy specimens. At home, wash and store in a cool place or wrap in foil and store in the vegetable crisper.*

## CHINESE CELERY

The celery stalks are thin and hollow and they have a stronger taste and smell than Western celery. It is used in stir-fries and soups or blanched and used in salads. Make sure the leaves are green and the stems are firm.

## CHINESE BROCCOLI

Chinese broccoli is distinguished by its small white flowers. It can be steamed whole and served with oyster sauce, or cut up the leaves and stems and add to soups and stir-fries. Young stalks are crisp and mild; thicker stalks need to be peeled and halved.

***Also known as — Chinese kale, gai lan***

## CHOY SUM

Related to bok choy, choy sum has mild mustard-flavoured leaves and small, yellow flowers. Steam or stir-fry whole and serve with oil and garlic and oyster sauce, or chop and add the leaves to soups.

***Also known as — Chinese flowering cabbage***

## CHRYSANTHEMUM GREENS

The young leaves are used in salads and stir-fries and the edible flowers are used in Chinese cooking.

*Also known as — chop suey greens, garland chrysanthemum*

## GAI CHOY

A strong, bitter cabbage that is generally pickled as Sichuan pickled cabbage or used in pork-based soups. Another variety, jook gai choy, can be used in soups and stir-fries.

*Also known as — mustard greens, Oriental mustard, swatow mustard cabbage*

## HAIRY MELON

A relative of the winter melon that looks like a cucumber covered in tiny hairs. It is used in Cantonese cookery. Remove the hairs by scrubbing or peeling it, then bake or boil the flesh; cut it into strips and stir-fry; cut into large pieces, core and fill with a meat stuffing; or use in braised dishes.

*Also known as — fuzzy melon*

## ONG CHOY

An aquatic plant popular in Southeast Asia, which is cooked like spinach and used in soups, curries and stir-fries. It is sometimes steamed and served as a side dish.

*Also known as — kang kong, swamp cabbage, water spinach, water convolvulus*

## SHISO

Widely used in Japanese cooking, shiso leaves can be red, green or purple. Green leaves are used in sushi, battered and fried in tempura, wrapped around meat or fish and added to salads; the red leaves are used to give colour and flavour to umeboshi (pickled plums).

*Also known as — beefsteak plant, perilla*

## SIN QUA

Similar to a cucumber in shape, but with ridges, this vegetable tastes similar to okra and courgette. To buy, choose deep green specimens with firm ridges. To use, peel off the ridges and some of the skin. It can then be baked, boiled or used in curries and braised dishes.

*Also known as — angled loofah, angled luffa, Chinese okra, ridged loofah, vegetable gourd*

## TARO SHOOTS

The edible shoots of a Southeast Asian and Pacific Island vegetable. The root should be washed well, peeled and sliced for use in soups and in stir-fries. Thin slices may be deep-fried.

*Also known as — pak ha*

## TATSOI

Small, dark-green, shiny leaves with a white stem. The leaves need to be thoroughly washed and can be steamed or stir-fried and often used in soups. Baby tatsoi can be used raw in salads.

*Also known as — rosette pak choy*

## WINTER MELON

A very large vegetable used like a squash and stir-fried or used in braised dishes or soups, especially the famous dish Winter Melon Pond where it is hollowed out and elaborately carved.

*Also known as — Chinese bitter melon, wax gourd, white gourd*

*See also  amaranth*

A member of the lily family, these delicately flavoured shoots need to be cooked with care so as not to damage the fragile tips: stand upright in a special asparagus steamer (which allows the spears to cook in water and the tips to cook in steam), or lie flat in a large saucepan or frying pan filled with lightly salted water. Once cooked, serve asparagus with melted butter and Parmesan, or add to risottos, quiches, stir-fries or salads. When buying asparagus, choose firm, bright-green spears with tight tips. Check the cut ends are not split or dried out.

***Asparagus goes with — egg, ham, hollandaise, lemon, soy sauce***

## TYPES OF ASPARAGUS

| | |
|---|---|
| ***Green*** | This is the most common type of asparagus and is cut above ground when the shoots are 15 cm long. |
| ***White*** | White asparagus is cut while the asparagus is below the ground (the lack of light prevents it from producing chlorophyll and turning green). It is more tender than the green variety and is popular in parts of Europe. Before cooking, white asparagus needs to be peeled up to the tip as the skin is tough. Generally more expensive. |
| ***Purple*** | Purple when fresh, this type of asparagus turns green when cooked. |
| ***Sprue*** | Young, thin asparagus. |

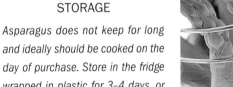

## STORAGE

*Asparagus does not keep for long and ideally should be cooked on the day of purchase. Store in the fridge wrapped in plastic for 3–4 days, or stand the bundle in a container of water and cover with a plastic bag.*

## COOKING

*To give extra flavour to a risotto, use vegetable or chicken stock instead of water to cook the asparagus. Use the stock to make the risotto.*

## PREPARING AND COOKING ASPARAGUS

*1  Snap off the woody bottom of the asparagus spear at its natural breaking point. Peel any thick, woody stems.*

*2  Lay the asparagus flat in a frying pan filled with simmering water. Cook until tender when pierced with the tip of a knife.*

*3  A well-cooked spear of asparagus should be tender and bend when you pick it up with a fork; it should not droop over.*

# aspic

A savoury jelly made with clarified stock set with gelatine, aspic is used to glaze cold fish, meat, poultry, vegetables, eggs and pâtés. Aspic may also be cubed or cut decoratively into shapes as a garnish, or served separately as a relish for cold meat. Clear aspics can be used as a base for moulded dishes, such as *oeufs en gelée* (eggs in aspic) or to fill the gaps between meat and the pastry in cold meat pies. It can also be used as a setting agent for glazes, such as those used for *chaudfroid*—an important centrepiece at French buffets during the nineteenth century where dishes, often whole cooked turkeys, salmon, chicken or ham, were cooked and covered with a glaze of white sauce and aspic. Aspic is now available as granules, which need to be mixed with water. It can also be made by adding 3 teaspoons or 6 sheets of gelatine to 500 ml of clarified stock.

*Aspic is used to fill the gap between the meat and the pastry in a pork pie.*

# aubergine

Aubergines are often thought of as a vegetable, but they are actually a fruit and a member of the same family as the tomato and potato. The aubergine is a native of Southeast Asia, but its versatility has made it a widely used ingredient in Mediterranean, Italian, French and Middle Eastern cuisines. Aubergines can be served hot or cold, puréed, fried, stuffed or battered, and they are the main ingredient of many famous dishes such as moussaka, imam bayildi, baba ghanoush and ratatouille.

## PESTO AUBERGINES

*Fry round slices of aubergine in olive oil until brown and crisp, then transfer them to a baking tray. Top each one with a teaspoon of pesto and grill until bubbling.*

Aubergines vary in size and shape: from small, round pea shapes to large, fat pumpkin-shaped fruit. Their colour too can range from green, cream or yellow to pale or dark purple. Look for firm, heavy aubergines that have shiny, smooth skins with no brown patches and a distinct cleft in the wider end.

**Aubergines go with — basil, cheese, coriander, cumin, garlic, ginger, lamb, mint, olive oil, parsley, sour cream, tomato, yoghurt**

**Also known as — eggplant, brinjal, Guinea squash, garden egg**

*Aubergines, including white (centre back) and pea (centre) varieties.*

## PREPARATION

*Most aubergines don't need peeling or degorging (salting and draining) to reduce their bitterness, but this can reduce the amount of oil they absorb as they cook. Blanching in boiling water also helps stop this. To degorge, cut into slices and put in a colander. Sprinkle heavily with salt and weight down with a plate (to speed up the removal of liquid). Leave for 30 minutes, then rinse in cold water. Dry well with paper towels. Always cut with a stainless steel knife to stop them discolouring.*

The vast island continent of Australia stretches (north/south) from Asia to the Antarctic, and (east/west) from the Pacific to the Indian oceans: in size, it is large enough to contain Italy—including Sicily and Sardinia—23 times. It contains every conceivable terrain and climate for the cultivation of crops and livestock and an enormous range of seafood in its waters. From durian in the north to apples from Tasmania in the south; from beef to buffalo; from Sydney rock oysters to Atlantic salmon, all are available in profusion. However, since the arrival of the English in 1788, almost until the present day, the wide variety of indigenous food stuffs (except seafood) was largely ignored. Only now are Australians beginning to utilize such foods as kangaroo and finger limes.

*Lamingtons—squares of sponge dipped in chocolate and coconut.*

*Barbecued prawns and octopus*

By the 1830s, European settlers had largely re-created European farming methods—albeit on an industrial scale—and the national diet of 'meat and three veg' was firmly established, with some 'bush' variations like fire-baked damper bread and billy tea. The gold rushes of the 1850s brought the first non-European migrants, the Chinese, whose food was, for most Australians, up until the 1960s, the only variation from a monotonous English diet. Then, after World War II, a huge influx of mainly Mediterranean refugees and migrants changed forever the Australian diet. The steak was joined by pasta, and wine sales rapidly caught up with beer. In the 1970s, an increase in Asian migration (especially post Vietnam war) accelerated the introduction of new tastes and ingredients, which, along with a willingness by more Australians to experiment, became the foundations of a new Australian cuisine. This has blossomed in the last decades, with young chefs, and cooks at home, utilizing the ever-increasing range of ingredients to create a cuisine that borrows from other cultures, while making food that is uniquely Australian. The wine industry has grown up as swiftly as the food, and great wines are being produced right around the country.

*Meat pie and tomato sauce*

*Pumpkin soup topped with sour cream*

Apart from macadamias and seafood, until recently, few native ingredients were cultivated commercially. Kangaroo, wallaby and crocodile can be found in restaurants, but are rarely used in home cooking. The best-known culinary inventions are damper, Anzac biscuits and lamingtons. The sweet dessert pavlova; Vegemite, a yeast extract spread on bread; and the Australian meat pie are still, despite Modern Australian cooking, national icons.

■ *See also* **crocodile, damper, pavlova**

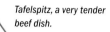

Tafelspitz, a very tender beef dish.

Its geographical position, with borders on seven countries including Italy, and an empire that, at various times, spilt over all seven, has left Austria with a rich and diverse table that could lay claim to be the first multi-cultural cuisine in Europe, owing a particular debt to the Italians, an influence most obvious in the cuisine of the South Tyrol. Proof can be found in dishes such as *Nockerln*, Austrian gnocchi; *Fiaker* goulash, the local version of the Hungarian classic; and *Wiener Schnitzel*, borrowed from the Italians while they were at war in that country. Other classics include *Tafelspitz*, braised beef served with chive sauce; and *Liptauer*, soft cheese with paprika served with pretzels and sausages at wine taverns called '*Heurigers*'.

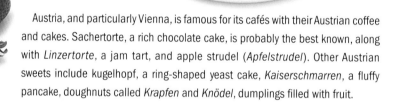

Linzertorte, served with mélange coffee (made with equal parts of coffee and milk).

Knödels filled with strawberries

Austria, and particularly Vienna, is famous for its cafés with their Austrian coffee and cakes. Sachertorte, a rich chocolate cake, is probably the best known, along with *Linzertorte*, a jam tart, and apple strudel (*Apfelstrudel*). Other Austrian sweets include kugelhopf, a ring-shaped yeast cake, *Kaiserschmarren*, a fluffy pancake, doughnuts called *Krapfen* and *Knödel*, dumplings filled with fruit.

See also **Sachertorte, schnitzel, strudel**

## avocado

Avocados have soft, buttery flesh and a mild, slightly nutty flavour, and are the only fruit that contains fat (monounsaturated fat). Because of their pear shape, avocados are sometimes called 'avocado pear' or 'alligator pear', referring to the rough skin texture of some varieties, such as Sharwill and Hass (also Haas). Other varieties have thin, smooth skin, such as Fuerte, and the small, stoneless Fuerte (cocktail avocado).

Avocados are best eaten raw—cut in half and serve with a vinaigrette; slice and add to salads; purée for use in dips or guacamole; or use as a base for sweet dishes such as ice cream. Cut avocado turns brown, so cut it just before use or brush with lemon juice to stop it discolouring. Avocados don't ripen well on the tree, but firm, unripe avocados will ripen at room temperature after 3–4 days. To speed this up, put them in a bowl with fruit that gives off ethylene (such as apples). They should feel tender or give slightly at the stem end when ripe.

**Avocados go with — bacon, blue cheese, chilli, coriander, crab, lemon, lime, mayonnaise, onion, sour cream, tomato**

Avocados, including Hass (front) and Fuerte (centre).

# b

## baba

There is some controversy over the baba and its origins. The Slavic version is a yeasted cake baked in a tall mould; the Polish or Ukrainian version is baked in a fluted mould, giving it the appearance of a woman's skirt; and the rum baba, the French version, is thought to have been invented by the Polish king Leszczyinski who, upon declaring his cake to be too dry, soaked it in rum, and named it after the story of Ali Baba. All are made from the same mixture.

■ *See also* **savarin**

## baba ghanoush

A creamy dip or appetizer of Middle Eastern origin, baba ghanoush is made with roasted and mashed aubergine, garlic and tahini. Baba ghanoush is served cold and may be presented in many ways: in a bowl accompanied by triangles of pitta bread; as a dip for raw vegetables; or served with grilled vegetables or meats.
*Also known as — baba gannoujh, baba ganouje, baba ganoush, moutabal*

### BABA GHANOUSH

*Roast a large aubergine at 200°C for 30 minutes, or until soft. Allow to cool, then peel and cut into cubes and process with 1 tablespoon tahini, 1 crushed garlic clove and plenty of lemon juice. Season well. Serves 6.*

see papaya — **babaco**

## babka

Babka is a rich yeast bread from Eastern Europe. There are two types of babka: the Polish make a soft yeast bread, similar to kugelhopf, sometimes adding raisins and grated citrus peel; the Jewish version is made from a dough that is rolled out, spread with a filling, usually cheese, chocolate, raspberry or almond paste, then rolled up and baked in a loaf tin. Babka is traditionally baked at Easter time in Poland and Russia.

# b a c o n

Although the word 'bacon' comes from the old German, meaning 'back', bacon is English, and does not come from a pig's back. When every English family owned at least one pig, bacon was a staple in their diet. Originally it was made from the cured sides of a pig; the legs were cured separately to make ham. Now the whole side, including the back leg, is cured. Bacon is sold in rashers, joints and steaks, and the different cuts vary in their fat and meat content. It is available smoked, unsmoked (green) or tendersweet (a mild cure). Bacon rashers can be grilled or fried. Bacon joints can be baked, roasted or braised.

*Clockwise from top left: rolled pancetta, lard (rendered pork fat), bacon rashers, speck, pancetta.*

## CURING BACON

*Curing bacon was once an annual task of all farmers, when all parts of the animal were cured or preserved for eating during the winter. On some farms, the traditional process of curing bacon is still used today: the carcass is scalded, scraped and dry-salted, then air-dried or smoked to produce a good-quality bacon. Factory bacon is often cured in brine, as this is a quicker, easier and more controllable process, but the flavour of the bacon then tends to come from artificial additives (such as monosodium glutamate) rather than the ageing process.*

*A BLT (bacon, lettuce and tomato) sandwich.*

**See also  ham, pancetta**

## ENGLISH/AMERICAN BACON

| | |
|---|---|
| **Back** | Sold as rashers, chops or rolled joints. Back rashers tend to be rounded and have a lot of meat on them. |
| **Canadian** | A cured bacon with little fat. The curing liquid is low in salt and high in sugar. |
| **Collar** | Sold cut into small joints of bacon or rashers. |
| **Gammon** | Cured leg of pork, which can be cooked as a ham, cut into rashers or steaks, or cooked as a bacon joint. Gammon hock is used for soups. |
| **Middle** | Divided into back rashers and streaky rashers, or cut as a long middle cut rasher to include both back and streaky. |
| **Streaky** | These rashers are cut from the pig's belly. Front rashers are leaner than the ones from the back. They may be used to wrap food as a protective layer or to help baste it. |

## EUROPEAN BACON

| | |
|---|---|
| **Guanciale** | The cured jaw and cheek of a pig. A speciality of Italy, this is the bacon used to make pasta carbonara and *all'amatriciana*. |
| **Lard** | Lard is the French word for bacon, as well as being the name for rendered down pork fat. *Lard de poitrine* is a type of streaky bacon. |
| **Pancetta** | Salt-cured belly of pork, sold rolled or as a thick strip to be sliced. |
| **Speck** | German word for bacon. |
| **Tocino** | A Spanish bacon that is salt-cured and unsmoked. It is often sold covered with a layer of crystalline salt. |

Chewy and dense in texture, bagels are unlike most breads in that they are first boiled and then baked. Bagel means 'bracelet' in German and because of its shape, with no clear beginning or end, they are thought to be a symbol of the eternal cycle of life. Bagels are made with strong or high-gluten flour, the dough is shaped into rings, boiled in water, then baked. Bagels may be sprinkled with sesame seeds or poppy seeds, salt or onions before they are baked. Traditionally, bagels are made without eggs, but a lighter, less chewy bagel is made by adding an egg to the dough. An unboiled bagel is called a bialy.

Jewish immigrants introduced the bagel to America and, typically, they are served with lox (smoked salmon) and cream cheese. Now, they may be eaten in an endless variety of ways: filled, with ham and lettuce; scrambled eggs, salmon and chives; chopped eggs; fried bacon; or toasted and spread with butter and jam.

A speciality of Piedmont in northern Italy, bagna caôda (meaning 'hot bath') is a dip made with olive oil, butter, chopped anchovies and garlic. Bagna caôda is served warm, accompanied by strong red wine. Vegetables are dipped into the hot 'bath'—celery, cardoons, fennel, endives, spring onions and artichokes—whatever is in season, and transferred to the mouth over a piece of bread.

*Also known as — bagna cauda*

### BAGNA CAODA

*In a saucepan, combine 6 tablespoons butter, 125 ml olive oil, 4 crushed garlic cloves and 6 finely chopped anchovy fillets. Stir over low heat until the mixture is blended and creamy, not liquid. Serve bagna caôda warm with raw vegetables cut into pieces or strips. Serves 4.*

A long, thin loaf of bread whose name, translated from the French, means 'little rod'. The French have such a fondness for their baguette, with its crunchy golden-brown crust and snow-white crumb, that it appears daily or twice daily on every table throughout France. Traditionally, baguettes were not baked in a tin but shaped into a thin loaf and left to rise between the folds of a floured cloth. Before baking, the loaf is slashed in its characteristic diagonal pattern.

*Also known as — French stick, pistolet*

## baked Alaska

Made of a layer of cake topped with ice cream, coated with uncooked meringue and baked in the oven just long enough to allow the meringue to become crisp before the ice cream melts. When cooked, the meringue may be doused in brandy and set alight. It's thought that the idea was invented by the Chinese, who baked ice cream wrapped in pastry. The French adapted the idea, but replaced the pastry with meringue to make *omelette norvégienne*, but it was the Americans who coined the name 'baked Alaska'.

### MINI BAKED ALASKAS

*Lay 6 slices of a small swiss roll on a lightly oiled baking tray. Whisk 2 egg whites until soft peaks form, then add 90 g caster sugar and beat until stiff and shiny. Put a scoop of vanilla ice cream on each slice of swiss roll and cover with a thick layer of the meringue. Bake at 230 °C for 2–3 minutes, or until the meringue is nicely browned and crisp. Serves 6.*

## baked beans

Baked beans are made from haricot beans cooked in a tomato sauce. The recipe is a derivation of the original Boston baked beans, a traditional American dish made using haricot beans cooked in a sauce of molasses, sugar, salt pork and mustard (some versions add onions and spices). In America, the haricot bean is called the navy bean, so called because it has been a staple of the US navy since the 1800s.

Baked beans are widely recognized as being a good source of fibre and protein. The tinned version is popular and makes a handy snack when heated and served on toast or serve them at breakfast with sausages and eggs. They are a quick and convenient food for campers—heat on the fire and eat from the tin. Home-made baked beans don't often give the same result as the tinned version because the beans used by manufacturers are grown to have a tender skin.

## Bakewell tart

Bakewell tart is made from shortcrust pastry filled with a thin layer of jam and topped with almond cake. Traditionally, almond essence was used to give the Bakewell tart its characteristic flavour, but nowadays it's more usual to see recipes that use ground almonds instead. The tart can be finished in a variety of ways: with a pastry lattice topping, with a sugar glaze or icing, or decorated with flaked almonds. The tart is named after the town of Bakewell in Derbyshire, England.

*Bicarbonate of soda*

Baking powder is a mixture of cream of tartar and sodium bicarbonate. In baking, when liquid is added, cream of tartar (an acid) reacts with sodium bicarbonate (an alkali), and releases bubbles of carbon dioxide, causing the cake to rise. Most commercial brands are double-acting: they produce bubbles when activated first by liquid, then by heat. To make a single-acting version, mix ½ teaspoon of cream of tartar and ¼ teaspoon of sodium bicarbonate to equal about 1 teaspoon of baking powder in a recipe. Don't be too heavy-handed when using baking powder as too much will taint the cake with a slight soapy flavour. Replace every 6 months—to see if it's still active, stir some into a cup of hot water—it should bubble vigorously.

Bicarbonate of soda is also a rising agent, but needs an acid such as buttermilk, yoghurt or sour cream to activate it. Bicarbonate of soda starts acting as soon as liquid is added, so cook the mixture quickly.

■ *See also* **cream of tartar**

*Baking powder*

## baklava

A Middle Eastern favourite, baklava is made with layers of buttered filo pastry filled with chopped nuts (walnuts, almonds or pistachios), sugar and spices. The pastry is cut into triangles or squares, baked, then doused in honey or lemon juice syrup. Baklava is thought to have been introduced by the Armenian Christians—the 40 sheets of filo used to make it were said to symbolize the 40 days of Lent. Serve with a strong coffee and a glass of water or as a dessert.

***Also known as — baklawa***

## balsamic vinegar

### SERVING SUGGESTIONS

*To make a salad dressing, mix a few drops of balsamic vinegar with a little olive oil.*

*Drizzle balsamic vinegar over cooked vegetables, meat or fish.*

*Toss a few drops of balsamic vinegar with sliced strawberries and serve with cream or ice cream.*

*Add two or three drops of vinegar to vanilla ice cream.*

A rich, sweet and fragrant vinegar made from white *Trebbiano di Spagna* grapes in Modena, Italy. The best balsamic vinegars, *Aceto Balsamico Tradizionale de Modena*, are made by blending very old (up to 100 years) vinegars with progressively younger vinegars (no younger than 12 years) from barrels of different woods. Each 100 ml bottle of this rare and precious liquid is certified by the consortium that was set up to approve its quality. The commercial variety, labelled simply *Aceto Balsamico de Modena*, varies considerably in price and quality.

**31**

## balti

A cooking style named, apparently, for its origin in Baltistan in Northern Pakistan, and the vessel (also known as a *karahi*), a two-handled cast iron wok-like utensil in which it is cooked. Its popularity spread from Birmingham after one Baltistani immigrant opened a restaurant there. It comprises freshly cooked aromatically spiced curries, not overly spiked with chilli. Balti is eaten with freshly baked balti bread, not rice.

## bamboo

Bamboo trees grow mainly in Asia, sometimes up to 30 m tall. Bamboo leaves are used to wrap food prior to cooking and the young shoots are widely used in Asian cooking. The shoots are crunchy in texture and have a mild flavour, and are often added to stir-fries and soups. Bamboo shoots are sold in tins, bottles or fresh (these are seasonal and expensive and need to be boiled to remove the toxins).

## banana

### BANANAS FOSTER

*Fry 2 thickly sliced bananas in 1 tablespoon unsalted butter until golden. Add 1 tablespoon soft brown sugar and fry until bananas are caramelized. Sprinkle with 1 tablespoon rum and serve with vanilla ice cream. Serves 2.*

Bananas do not grow on trees or palms and are actually a giant herb. Bananas are thought to be one of the world's oldest cultivated fruits, and evidence of their existence dates back to the sixth century BC in India. Bananas grow in bunches called a 'hand' and each hand has about 15–20 fingers (or fruit). They are harvested when green and ripen best after picking.

Bananas are used both as a fruit and a vegetable. To prevent discolouration of the flesh, cut with a stainless steel knife and toss the slices in lemon juice. Bananas for cooking should be firmer than the ones eaten raw. Cooking brings out their full flavour: lightly fry in butter and brown sugar or coat with batter and deep-fry and serve with cream or ice cream. Banana leaves are useful too and can be used to wrap rice, fish or chicken: the parcel can be steamed or grilled. Banana flowers are also edible. They can be sliced thinly and added to salads or used in a vegetable stir-fry.

**Bananas go with — bacon, chocolate, coconut, curry, rum, sugar, yoghurt**

■ *See also* **plantain**

*From left: Cavendish bananas, sliced banana sitting in banana flower, Lady's fingers (all sitting on banana leaves).*

### STORAGE

*Do not keep bananas in the fridge as the skin will turn black (though this doesn't actually affect the taste). If possible, store bananas on a banana hook if you have one (or any hook will do). Bananas produce ethylene, which will cause other fruit or vegetables sitting near them to ripen prematurely.*

## Banbury cake — see Eccles cake

'Bangers and mash' is a British colloquial term for sausages and mashed potatoes, and is usually served smothered with thick, brown gravy. The exploding noise made by an unpricked sausage as it cooks is probably how the term 'banger' was coined, a banger being the slang for 'firecracker'.

see chicken — **bantam**

## barbecue

A barbecue is either a meal cooked outside over an open fire, or the grill or fireplace it is cooked on. Flavours are enhanced by basting the meat, fish or vegetables with marinades during cooking, or throwing aromatic woods onto the coals. The etymology of the word is vague: it may have come from the Spanish American *barbacoa*, meaning 'a frame made of sticks', or the French *barbe à queue*, 'from beard to tail', referring to the method of cooking the whole animal.

*A hibachi, a Japanese style of barbecue, can be used inside or outside.*

### CHICKEN SKEWERS

*Marinate pieces of chicken and vegetables, such as mushrooms and sliced courgettes, in a mixture of olive oil and crushed garlic and lemon juice. Leave to marinate for at least 1 hour or overnight, then thread chicken and vegetables onto skewers. Season and grill on both sides.*

## barley

Barley is the earliest known cultivated cereal and in the past was often mixed with wheat to make a nutritious bread. Barley contains little gluten, so it is rarely used to make bread now (except unleavened), and has found wider usage as a basic ingredient in malting and beer brewing, or to thicken and add flavour to soups and stews. Barley has a slightly nutty flavour and is a popular substitute for rice in risotto or pilaff dishes. Barley can also be boiled and mixed with cream and eaten as a dessert.

Barley water, prepared from the grain, is a health drink and was once considered a good remedy for fever. When combined with sugar, barley water can be used to make barley sugar, though nowadays most barley sugar is commercially produced.

**Barley goes with — bacon, fatty meats, game, soup**

### TYPES OF BARLEY

| | |
|---|---|
| **Pearl** | This has been processed to remove both the husk and germ. Pearl barley is particularly good in meat stews and soups. |
| **Pot** | Unlike pearl barley, pot barley has only had the outer husk removed. It is also called milled barley and is nuttier in flavour than pearl barley. It is used in the same way as pearl barley, but requires longer cooking to soften it. Scotch barley is unhusked. |
| **Flakes** | Partially cooked barley that has been flattened and dried. It can be used like rolled oats in muesli or to make porridge. |

## Bath Oliver

A plain, unsweetened biscuit, Bath Olivers were originally thought to have slimming properties. In the centre of the biscuit is an impression of the man credited as their inventor, Dr William Oliver of Bath (1695-1764). Today you would more likely eat a Bath Oliver with butter and a slice of cheese—perhaps not quite as slimming!

## Battenburg

A rectangular cake baked in an oblong tin, the Battenburg was named in honour of the marriage of Queen Victoria's granddaughter to Prince Louis of Battenburg in the 1800s. The cake is famous for its chequerboard pattern, made by using two differently coloured sponge cakes—typically one is coloured pink and the other white. The cake is covered with marzipan.

## Bavarian cream

A classic creamy dessert, Bavarian cream is made from rich vanilla-flavoured custard, lightened with whipped cream to produce a creamy and velvety-smooth dessert. Vanilla, chocolate, orange, coffee and fruit purées are popular flavours and these are added to the egg-custard base before it is poured into a decorative mould to set. To serve, the dessert is turned out of its mould onto a plate.

*Also known as — bavarois, crème bavaroise*

## bay leaf

The glossy green leaves of an evergreen tree, used to add a strong, slightly peppery flavour to many dishes. The bay leaf was probably introduced into Europe by the Romans, who held the bay in high esteem—they used it to make laurel wreaths to crown their poets, athletic and military victors. The berries of the bay tree and the leaves of other laurels (such as the bay rum berry) are poisonous.

Bay leaves can be used fresh or dried, and are usually removed before the dish is served. Add one or two to enhance stews or stuffings; add to a bouquet garni; insert a leaf under chicken skin; use to flavour rice while it is cooking; or add to the milk infusions used in baked custards or béchamel sauce. Fresh bay leaves have a stronger flavour than dried. Wash fresh leaves well and store them in the fridge for up to 3 days. Dried bay leaves will keep in an airtight container for up to 6 months.

*Bay leaves go with — fish, lamb, marinades, pork, potato, soup, tomato*
*Also known as — bay laurel, laurel leaf, sweet bay*

A white, cheese-like curd made from soya beans, bean curd was invented by the Chinese about 2,000 years ago. The Chinese call it *doufu*, meaning 'rotten beans', and the Japanese name is *tofu*. To make it, soya beans are liquidized to form soya milk. A coagulating agent is added, causing the whey and protein to separate. The whey is drained off and the curd is pressed into blocks.

Bean curd is bland in taste, but its soft, silken texture absorbs the flavour of the ingredients it is cooked with. It is an excellent source of protein, is low in fat, high in vitamins B and E and useful in a meatless diet. Bean curd is usually sold in blocks, either fresh, vacuum-packed or in small tubs or cartons of water.

**Bean curd goes with — chilli, garlic, ginger**

**Also known as — tofu**

## STORAGE

*Store fresh bean curd covered in water in the fridge for up to 5 days and change the water daily.*

## PREPARATION

*Dry bean curd before use by sitting on paper towels. Don't squeeze the water out as this will make it chewy.*

## AGEDASHI TOFU

*Cube 600 g firm bean curd and dust with cornflour. Deep-fry in batches until golden and drain well. In a saucepan, add 2 teaspoons dashi granules and 4 teaspoons light soy sauce to 400 ml water and boil. Divide the bean curd among 4 bowls and add chopped spring onions and grated ginger. Pour over a little liquid and garnish with bonito flakes. Serves 4.*

## TYPES OF BEAN CURD

| | |
|---|---|
| **Soft (silken)** | Soft bean curd needs to be handled carefully. It can be added to soups (at the end of cooking) or gently steamed or scrambled and piled on top of noodles. Use it as a dairy substitute in ice cream or cheesecakes. |
| **Firm and silken firm** | This is more robust and can be stir-fried or deep-fried without it breaking up, added to miso soup, or eaten as a side dish. Dust cubes of bean curd in rice flour before frying to give them a crisp coating. Firm bean curd can also be flavoured, preserved in rice wine, chilli or brine. |
| **Sheets (yuba, skins, wrappers)** | Sheets can be bought dried, frozen or vacuum-packed. If dried, they need to be softened before use with a little water. Fill them with rice (*inari-zushi*), use to wrap food parcels, or cut into strips and use as a garnish. They can be fried, braised or steamed. |
| **Deep-fried (puffs)** | Sold as large cubes, usually in plastic bags, and used in stir-fries and soups. If using in soup, such as laksa, prick the skin a few times to help them to absorb the flavours. Add at the last minute or they will soak up all the soup. |

■ *See also* **soya beans, tempe**

## bean pastes and sauces

A seasoning made from yellow or black fermented and salted soya beans, bean pastes have been used by the Chinese to flavour food for thousands of years. Bean pastes appear in many guises on the supermarket shelf and the labels vary enormously. Don't be discouraged by the pungent aroma when you open the jar as a spoonful or two of paste of any type will flavour a stir-fry perfectly.

*Stir-fried calamari and bok choy with black bean sauce.*

### TYPES OF BEAN PASTES AND SAUCES

**Black bean sauce**　　Made from puréed, fermented black soya beans and flavoured with garlic and star anise. The salty flavour works well with fish, squid, crab or beef. Use in dipping sauces, marinades or toss with stir-fried chicken or beef.

**Yellow bean sauce**　　Made from fermented yellow soya beans but brown in colour. Used in southern Chinese cooking when a lighter coloured sauce is required.

**Chilli bean paste**　　Red or brown in colour and sometimes called hot bean paste. This is a thick bean sauce mixed with chilli and sometimes fermented black beans, garlic and spices. Some are extremely hot, so use with caution. Use with bland ingredients like bean curd, noodles and vegetables.

**Red bean paste**　　Made from adzuki beans, red bean paste is sweet and used in cakes such as moon cakes and steamed buns.

▨ *See also* **hoisin, miso, soy sauce, soya beans**

## bean sprouts

### GROWING SPROUTS

*Wash the mung beans thoroughly, then put them in a large jar and fill it with tepid water. Cover the top with muslin or cheesecloth, secure it with a rubber band, then drain the water out through the cloth. Leave the jar on its side in a dark, warm place (light causes the sprouts to turn green). Repeat this rinsing process morning and evening. Sprouting will begin after 2–3 days and they will be ready to eat after 4–6 days.*

Bean sprouts are the edible, crisp young shoots of mung beans. They are high in vitamin C and are used as a vegetable in stir-fries, eaten raw in salads or added to sandwich fillings. Bean sprouts are sold in tins, or fresh in bags or containers, but can be easily sprouted at home. Keep fresh bean sprouts in cold water in the fridge and change the water daily. Bean sprouts may also refer to sprouts of the soya bean—these are larger and take longer to germinate than mung beans.

▨ *See also* **mung beans, sprouts**

Green beans are native to tropical America and were cultivated in Mexico and Peru over 7,000 years ago. There are hundreds of varieties and they can be steamed, boiled, stir-fried or cooked for use in salads. Green beans are known as *fagiolino* in Italian and *haricot* in French. Cook beans in lots of lightly salted water until they are just tender.

***Beans go with — almond, bacon, butter, cheese, garlic, herbs, olive oil, tomato, vinaigrette***

## TYPES OF BEANS

*Broad*

*Runner*

*Yard long*

*French*

*Borlotti*

### Broad beans

Also known as fava beans, these young broad beans can be eaten in their pods like mangetout, but as they get older, the pods become tougher and the beans inside develop a grey, leathery skin. Older beans need to be removed from their pods before cooking and should also be double podded to remove the grey skins. To do this, blanch them for a couple of minutes, drain and cool under running cold water, then slip off the skins. When buying broad beans, remember that most of the weight is the pods, which you will be throwing away. Frozen broad beans are also available.

### Runner beans

These flat beans should snap crisply when fresh, and most need to be stringed down each side unless they are very young. Though it is common to chop or slice the beans before cooking, this will cause most of the nutrients to leach out during cooking.

### Yard long beans

Also known as snake beans, these long beans are like French beans and are generally sold in bundles. Make sure any swellings in the pods are small—this will mean the beans are young and fresh.

### French beans

Also known as green beans and string beans, these are usually fine, thin green beans, but they are also available in yellow waxy pods, purple or cream pods, and green and purple pods. Make sure the pods snap crisply when you buy them.

### Borlotti beans

Popular whether dried or fresh, borlotti beans have distinguishable cream and red pods with beans the same colour. Borlotti beans are popular in Italy where they are mainly used in soups or stewed with olive oil and garlic as a side dish.

## BRAISED GREEN BEANS

*In a large frying pan, fry 1 chopped onion with 1 crushed garlic clove in 3 tablespoons olive oil until soft. Add 500 g green beans and fry. Add 400 g tin chopped tomatoes and simmer until the beans are tender. Season well. Serves 4.*

*See also* **legumes, pulses**

## BEARNAISE SAUCE

*In a saucepan, boil 3 tablespoons tarragon vinegar, 1 chopped shallot, ½ bay leaf, a sprig of chervil and tarragon. Reduce by 2/3; strain and return to pan. Beat 2 egg yolks, add to pan and whisk over low heat until thick. Add 110 g unsalted, softened butter, a little at a time, beating continuously. Increase heat until sauce is thick, add 1 tablespoon chopped tarragon and season well.*

Named after the French province of Béarn, Béarnaise is a thick, creamy pungent sauce made with butter, egg yolks, vinegar and tarragon. Classically, it also contains a little meat glace. To make it, the vinegar is reduced over heat and mixed with butter. Use a non-reactive pan so there is no danger of the sauce discolouring or being tainted with a metallic flavour. Serve over fillets of beef, lamb chops, grilled fish, or try it with vegetables and eggs.

## béchamel sauce

This basic of European cooking, which may well have started life in Italy, is first mentioned during the reign of Louis XIV in the seventeenth century. It is made by adding milk to a roux. Unlike a basic white sauce, the milk is infused with flavourings such as onions, cloves, bay leaves and nutmeg, with many variations on the theme. Use béchamel as a topping for lasagne, cannelloni and gratin, as a binding sauce for soufflés and pasta bakes, and as a base for onion sauce. Béchamel can be browned under the grill after it has been poured over food, or use it as a pouring sauce for vegetables, fish or chicken. A white sauce is made in exactly the same way, using just flour, butter and milk, and without any flavourings.

### COOKING

*For a smooth sauce, whisk the milk gradually into the flour. If the sauce does becomes lumpy, pass it through a sieve, then reheat it. To prevent a raw, floury taste, the flour should be fully cooked out so the starch grains burst.*

*When the sauce is cooling, cover the surface to stop a skin forming.*

### MAKING BECHAMEL SAUCE

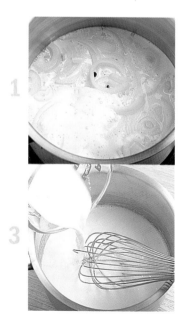

1  Scald 250 ml milk with a sliced onion, 3 peppercorns and a bay leaf and leave to infuse.

2  To make a roux, melt 1 tablespoon butter, then add 1 tablespoon plain flour and cook for 2 minutes over low heat until foaming.

3  Strain, then slowly whisk in the hot milk off the heat.

4  Bring to the boil, whisking constantly until thick. Season with salt, pepper and nutmeg and simmer for 20 minutes.

Beef refers to the meat of cattle such as heifers, cows, bullocks and bulls that have been raised and fattened for meat production. The quality of the beef varies according to breed, diet and farming technique. Specialist beef, such as organic, grass-fed or Shimotun beef from Kobe in Japan (reared on beer and grains and massaged daily) produce higher-quality meat than mass-produced beef reared on grain. Often beef is hung for 2–3 weeks to allow it to mature in flavour and become more tender (in countries such as in South America, beef is eaten freshly killed). Prime cuts of beef are more expensive and have been aged to improve both flavour and texture, while cuts for stewing are sold younger. Classic beef dishes include beef Wellington, *boeuf bourguignonne*, *beef en croute*, roast beef, goulash and beef Stroganoff.

## STORAGE

*Wipe any blood off the beef, put it on a plate, cover with clingfilm and store in the fridge. Put larger cuts on a rack on a plate to allow the juices to escape. Keep raw meat away from cooked to stop cross contamination. To ensure beef cooks evenly, remove from fridge half an hour before use.*

*Oil small cuts of meat before storing to help stop the meat oxidizing.*

*Freeze beef either vacuum-packed or well wrapped in freezer wrap. It will keep for up to 1 year.*

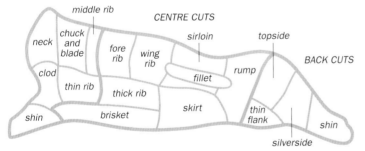

## CUTS OF MEAT

**Front cuts**   Cuts from the front contain the muscles that do the most work and are the toughest. Therefore, they need long, slow cooking (pot roasting, braising or stewing). Cuts include neck, clod, chuck, blade and shin.

**Centre cuts**   Cuts from the top and centre are tender and can be cooked quickly (roasting, grilling or frying). Cuts include fore rib, wing rib, sirloin, fillet and rump. Cuts from the underside, like brisket and skirt, need long, slow cooking

**Back cuts**   The back of the animal falls in between the first two cuts and needs a reasonably long cooking time (casseroling, braising or pot roasting). Cuts include topside, silverside and shin.

## BUYING

*A beef carcass is divided into sections from which numerous cuts are made (the names of these cuts vary from country to country). Choose cuts of meat that will suit your recipe and the cooking method. Don't buy expensive cuts of meat if you are going to use the meat in a stew or casserole: a less-expensive cut of meat will suffice.*

*Buy dark-red, moist meat with creamy white fat (bright red meat usually indicates that it has not been aged sufficiently).*

*Because of limited storage space, meat bought from the butcher will rarely have been hung for more than 1 week. If you intend buying a joint, if possible, order it ahead and ask the butcher to hang it for you.*

### Roasting

Choose joints from the back, ribs, fillet or sirloin for roasting. Meat should be well marbled with fat and slightly larger than needed, as it will shrink slightly when cooked. A covering of fat will baste the meat well as you cook it. Beef cooked on the bone cooks faster than a rolled joint and the bones also add extra flavour. If you ask your butcher to chine (loosen the backbone from the ribs) your joint, it will be easier to carve it when cooked. Season and sear the joint before cooking.

To roast beef on the bone to medium, allow 20 minutes cooking per 500 g plus 20 minutes; for beef off the bone, 25 minutes per 500 g plus 25 minutes. Cook at 200°C or start your roasting at 240°C for 15 minutes, then reduce the temperature to 180°C for the remaining time. When cooking is complete, rest for 15 minutes.

### Slow cooking

Less expensive or tougher cuts of meat can benefit greatly from slowly cooking in liquid on a low temperature as the connective tissue melts, tenderizing the meat. Dishes such as *boeuf bourguignonne* and Hungarian goulash are slow-cooked to produce a rich, tender meat. Methods of slow cooking include pot-roasting, braising, casseroling and stewing. Use a heavy ovenproof dish that comfortably holds the meat but is not too big. Stews are traditionally cooked on the stovetop; casseroles on either the stovetop or in the oven. Pot-roasting is useful when cooking less tender cuts such as topside, silverside and top rump, which are best left whole. Braising generally involves less liquid than casseroling or stewing and the meat is left whole. It is done in the oven in a dish with an airtight seal made by putting a piece of greaseproof paper between the lid and dish.

## BEEF WELLINGTON

*In a frying pan, brown a 1 kg beef fillet on all sides in oil. Place the beef in a 220°C oven and roast for 20 minutes. Allow to cool. Cook 3 chopped shallots and 1 crushed garlic clove in 100 g butter until soft. Add 350 g trimmed chicken livers and cook for 5 minutes. Put the livers in a food processor with 1 tablespoon brandy and process to form a smooth paste, then season well. Roll 450 g puff pastry out into a rectangle large enough to enclose the beef. Centre the beef in the pastry and spread the paste over the beef. Wrap the pastry around the beef, folding the ends under, then place it seam side down on a baking tray. Brush the pastry with beaten egg and bake at 220°C for 30 minutes (rare) or 40 minutes (medium). Serves 6.*

## CORNED BEEF

*Corned beef is made by curing pieces of brisket or silverside in brine. The beef is so named because, originally, the meat was covered in large grains or 'corns' of salt to cure it. When cured, the beef is boiled and served hot or cold. Corned beef is also sold in tins.*

**Beef goes with — Asian vegetables, capers, carrot, celeriac, celery, cheese, garlic, gherkin, herbs, horseradish, mustard, olive, parsnip, potato**

▉ *See also* **mince, steaks, veal**

Beer, the most widely drunk alcoholic beverage in the world, is made by brewing malted cereals, mostly barley, with yeast and flavouring them with hops. There are two main types of beer: ale and lager. Lager is usually fermented for 1 week at low temperatures to produce a lightly flavoured beer. Ale is fermented for 3 days at higher temperatures to give it a fruitier flavour. Stout is a maltier type of ale in which roasted cereals are added to the brew to produce a dark beer with a strong flavour.

Beer can be used as an ingredient in cooking. Most meat recipes that call for beer refer to dark brown ale, rather than the lighter-flavoured lager. Beer is used instead of yeast in some pancakes and breads, in batters to produce a light, crispy texture, or with red meats.

■ *See also* **stout**

*From left: stout, lager, ale.*

Native to the Mediterranean, beetroot is a root vegetable originally cultivated for its young leaves, but now grown for its sweet, purple-red root. Not all beetroot are deep red, but there are golden and white varieties. Chioggia, an Italian variety, has alternating red and white rings.

When cooking beetroot, take care to prevent it from bleeding. Don't cut or peel before they are cooked, and wash them carefully to prevent the skin breaking. Beetroot is remarkably versatile: grate it raw and add to salads; bake, steam or boil it; purée it with oil and spices to make a dip; or as in Eastern European kitchens, use it to make the soup, borscht. Cook and use the leaves as you would spinach: blanch them and add to soups, salads or pasta sauces. Store beetroot in the crisper drawer of the fridge for up to 2 weeks, and 1 to 2 days for the leaves. Beetroot is also sold in tins.

**Beetroot goes with — balsamic vinegar, chives, orange, potato, sherry, sour cream**
**Also known as — beet, gold beet (golden variety), harvard beets**

### BEETROOT MASH

*To prepare the beetroot, cut off the leaves, leaving 3 cm of stalk above the bulb. Wash thoroughly, but don't peel: the skin and root must be intact when cooked or the beetroot will 'bleed' and lose its colour. Boil until tender (this can take up to 2 hours), rub off the skins and mash with an equal quantity of cooked potatoes. Season. Add chopped chives and a knob of butter. Serve with fish, chicken or meat. Serves 4.*

# beignet

Basically French for fritter, a beignet is any deep-fried batter-coated food (such as aubergine, pineapple, apple). In New Orleans, it is a ball of choux pastry, deep-fried and sprinkled with icing sugar. A beignet soufflé is the same, but may be filled with jam or cheese or chopped ham and cheese.

***Also known as — beignet soufflé buñelo, French puff***

# Belgian food

Sandwiched between France and Holland, the tiny nation of Belgium covers 30,000 square kilometres divided into nine provinces. The surprisingly Belgian cuisine has been influenced through invasion and war by both the Germanic cultures of the north and the Latin cultures of the south, and is also reflected in the division within Belgium itself: from the German-speaking Flemish in the north to the French-speaking Walloons in the south. Generally speaking, the Walloons are said to be more interested in food; the Flemish in finances.

The best-known food of Belgium is hardly an original, but is a superb example of its type: the crisp, perfectly cooked Belgian French fry can be bought at stalls on almost every corner, served in a paper cone and usually eaten with a mayonnaise. Another potato dish, *Stoemp*, is a potato and vegetable purée often made with Brussels sprouts. Chicory (or Belgian endive) is widely used and is usually eaten hot.

Seafood is an important part of Belgian cuisine, particularly enjoyed by the Flemish because of their proximity to the sea. *Waterzooi* (roughly translated as 'hodgepodge') is a stew

made from North Sea fish, traditionally those the fishermen were unable to sell at the market. Mussels, too, are a speciality, often steamed in their own juices and served in the pot or cooked with flavourings such as wine, cream, tomatoes or herbs. They are usually served with a plate of chunky French fries. Belgians also love chicken and game and there is a chicken version of *Waterzooi*. Other specialities include Ardennes ham and *Herve* cheese.

Belgium boasts a great brewing tradition that dates back thousands of years. The most famous are trappist beers, brewed in monasteries by monks and lambic beers, which spontaneously ferment from the wild yeast in the air. Beer is also used innovatively in cooking, most notably in the Flemish beef stew, *Carbonade à la flamande*.

For dessert, Liège waffles are a treat, sold warm in outdoor markets, and Belgian chocolates, especially that from Bruges, are famous the world over.

**See also  *carbonade à la flamande, stoemp***

*From top: mussels with French fries (moules et frites) and beer, Waterzooi, Belgian waffles.*

Berries are small, juicy fruit rich in vitamin C. Different species grow worldwide: some are well known; others less so (such as bilberries, huckleberries, cloudberries and lingonberries). Select plump, ripe berries with an even colour, and discard any crushed or mouldy ones. Wash gently in a colander, drain, then dry on paper towels. Store in the fridge on a plate lined with paper towel, covered with clingfilm.

Berries freeze well, ensuring year-round availability. If freezing soft berries (such as raspberries and strawberries), space them apart on a tray lined with baking paper. Freeze for a few hours, transfer into freezer bags and return to the freezer. Firm berries (such as blackcurrants, gooseberries and cranberries) can be placed directly into bags and frozen.

▓ *See also*  **blackberry, blueberry, cranberry, gooseberry, loganberry, mulberry, raspberry, strawberry**

*Clockwise from left: raspberries, strawberries, blueberries.*

### BESAN TEMPURA

*Sift 145 g besan flour, 75 g rice flour and a pinch of salt into a bowl. Add 1 teaspoon turmeric, 1 teaspoon chilli powder and ½ teaspoon nigella. Add 250 ml water, stirring all the time to make a smooth batter. Leave to stand for 10 minutes. Dip sliced vegetables and baby spinach leaves into the batter and deep-fry until golden. Serve with a chilli sauce.*

Made from finely ground chickpeas, besan is a nutritious high-protein flour. Besan makes an excellent batter for fish; can be used to thicken curries and soups; is used in dumplings and noodles; is used as a batter for Indian pakoras; and is found in the Indian sweet, *barfi*. Buy besan flour in Asian markets or supermarkets. Buy it already ground as domestic blenders can't cope with the hard chickpeas.

***Also known as — besan, chickpea flour, channa powder***

This classic North American dessert, in its many guises, usually consists of sliced fruit mixed with spices and brown sugar and layered with buttered breadcrumbs. Apple Betty is one of the most popular, but peach or apricot can also be used. Their main characteristic is that the breadcrumbs are layered in with the fruit and not just sprinkled over the top.

***Also known as — apple brown Betty, brown Betty***

### APPLE BETTY

*Cook 5 peeled, cored and chopped apples with 50 g butter and 1 tablespoon sugar until the apples are soft. Fry 200 g fresh breadcrumbs in 50 g butter until crisp, then add 1 tablespoon brown sugar. Layer the apples and breadcrumbs in an ovenproof dish, starting and finishing with a layer of breadcrumbs, and bake at 180 °C for 20 minutes, or until golden brown. Serves 4.*

## beurre blanc

A classic French sauce made by beating butter into a reduction of wine and vinegar. Traditionally served with fish, but also good with chicken, eggs, asparagus or artichokes. When making the sauce, form an emulsion quickly so you can add the butter with less risk of the sauce separating. Prepare just before serving and keep warm in a bain-marie as reheating will cause the sauce to split. You can enhance the flavour with chives or citrus zest.

### BEURRE BLANC

*Bring to the boil 50 ml white wine vinegar, 125 ml white wine and 2 finely chopped shallots. Simmer and reduce to 3 tablespoons. Strain and return to saucepan. Whisk in 250 g unsalted cubed butter, a cube at a time over low heat, so the butter melts into the sauce and doesn't split. Season to taste.*

## bicarbonate of soda — see baking powder

## bird's nest

An exotic and expensive delicacy with a delicate flavour and texture, bird's nest is an ingredient used mainly in Chinese cooking. The nest is made from the saliva excreted by swallows and is hand-picked off high rocky outcrops or caves. Black nests are cheaper as they need to have the debris picked out of them by hand before they are clean enough to eat; white nests are cleaner and therefore more expensive. The Chinese believe them to be good for the blood and the complexion.

## biscotti

The plural of biscotto. In Italy, biscotti refers to any small biscuits, but elsewhere, it usually means those small biscuits traditionally served dipped in *vin santo*, a Tuscan dessert wine. Biscotto means 'twice baked', referring to the method of baking the loaf of dough, slicing it, then baking it again to produce a very hard, crunchy biscuit. The most recognized versions are *cantucci* (or *biscotti di Prato*), Tuscan almond biscuits. Biscotti can also be flavoured with aniseed, fennel or sesame seeds.

## biscuit

The word 'biscuit' originally referred to a tough, dry rusk. French for 'twice cooked', biscuits were baked in long rolls, sliced and baked again so they would last a long time. Today, biscuits come in all forms—sweet or savoury (sometimes called 'crackers'), chewy, soft or crisp, plain or flavoured, coated in icing or chocolate—and are eaten as a snack or used as an ingredient in desserts. Confusingly, in North America, a biscuit refers to a scone.

A rich, creamy shellfish soup flavoured with white wine or cognac and cream. Typically, a bisque is made using crab, lobster or oysters. Today, bisque is misused to mean any smooth, creamy soup, including vegetables or chicken. A shellfish bisque is not difficult to make, but it takes time: shellfish are sautéed in their shells, then simmered in wine and seasonings. The meat is removed from the shells and puréed with butter and thickened with cream and dressed with diced pieces of shellfish. Originally, bisques were made from game birds.

## bitters

A highly alcoholic aromatic bitter flavouring made from a distillation of rum, herbs, roots and spices. Angostura bitters, named after the Venezuelan town of the same name, is one of the most recognized brands and was originally used to reduce fever and to improve the appetite. Bitters is used in small quantities to flavour cocktails (it adds the 'pink' to pink gin), fruit salads and ice cream, and can be added to the creamy sauces used on chicken or fish.

### CHAMPAGNE COCKTAIL

*Put a sugar cube at the bottom of each champagne glass and soak with a few drops of bitters. Top up the glass with champagne.*

see shrimp paste — **blachan**

## black bottom pie

A traditional American dessert, black bottom pie consists of a crumb or pastry crust filled with a thin layer of dark chocolate custard. The custard is topped with a thicker layer of rum chiffon (made by folding beaten egg whites into a rum-flavoured custard), finished with sweetened whipped cream and sprinkled with chocolate shavings. The pie is cut into wedges to serve.

## Black Forest gateau

The famous Black Forest gateau hails from Germany's Black Forest region. The cake consists of three layers of Kirsch-flavoured chocolate sponge, which is filled with sour cherries (usually morello) and whipped cream.

**Also known as — Black Forest cake, Black Forest cherry torte**

see treacle — **black treacle**

# blackberry

Fruit of the *Rubus* genus, found growing on prickly, highly invasive bushes. High in vitamin C and fibre, blackberries can be eaten fresh or stewed with yoghurt, cream or ice cream, or sprinkled over cereal. They are an essential in summer pudding or can be used in jams, pies or liqueurs. There are many blackberry hybrids, including the loganberry, youngberry, boysenberry and olallieberry.

**Blackberries go with — apple, brandy, lemon, soft or fresh cheese**
**Also known as — bramble**

■ *See also* **berries, loganberry, raspberry**

## BLACKBERRIES WITH PORT

*Sprinkle 250 g hulled blackberries with 3 tablespoons caster sugar and leave them to rest in the fridge. Simmer 50 ml water, 1 tablespoon sugar, 2 tablespoons port and the zest of half an orange in a small saucepan for 5 minutes. Pour the hot syrup over the blackberries and leave them to chill for 20 minutes in the fridge. Serve with cream or ice cream. Serves 4.*

## BUYING

*Choose plump, dark-purple, shiny blackberries. Inspect the bottom of punnets for any signs of crushed or leaking fruit. Blackberries that still have their stems attached indicate that the berries are immature and were picked too early.*

*If making jam, select some less ripe berries, as these contain more pectin and help jam to set quickly.*

## STORAGE

*Blackberries deteriorate quickly so they are best eaten on the day of purchase or collection, but they will keep in the fridge for a day or so.*

*Blackberries can be frozen to ensure year-round availability and make excellent preserves.*

# blackcurrant

Redcurrants, blackcurrants and white currants are the small, round fruit of the *Ribes* species of low-growing bushes. The blackcurrant is the largest of the currants, juicy and with a slight tart, robust flavour. They are valued for their high vitamin C content and are used to flavour the cordials often given to children. Blackcurrants are best when cooked; they make an ideal sauce to accompany pork, chicken or game, or can be used in jams, jellies, ices and sorbets. Blackcurrants are the basis of the French liqueur crème de cassis, which is used to make kir royale when mixed with sparkling wine.

**Blackcurrants go with — cream, duck, game, mint, pastry, sugar, venison**

## PREPARATION

*To stem blackcurrants, hold them over a dish and place the prongs of a fork at the top of the stem. If you run the prongs down either side of the stem towards the blackcurrants, they will drop off into the dish.*

■ *See also* **berries**

## BLACKCURRANT SAUCE

*In a saucepan, bring 500 ml red wine to the boil and add 50 g sugar. Reduce by half, or until thickened, then add 200 g blackcurrants and 1 tablespoon red wine vinegar. Simmer until blackcurrants are tender and serve over grilled duck breasts. Serves 6.*

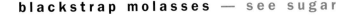

# blackstrap molasses — see sugar

A semi-solid dessert, blancmange is similar to custard but thickened with cornflour or gelatine and set in moulds. In medieval England, blancmange was a savoury dish, a thick gruel made with almonds, milk, rice and chicken or fish—all white or pale ingredients—and hence its French name, blancmange, meaning 'eat white'. Blancmange is often served with a tart sauce or fruit to counterbalance its richness.

## blinis

Small, yeast-raised pancakes originally from Russia and made from buckwheat flour. Traditionally served with caviar, they are also good with salmon roe and herbed cream or smoked salmon and sour cream. A variation on the original recipe uses a mixture of buckwheat and plain flour to give the mixture a lighter texture. *Blin* is Russian for 'pancake'; blini is the plural.

*Blinis can be made in a special blini pan, but any heavy-based frying pan or griddle will do.*

### BLINIS

*Sieve 200 g buckwheat flour and 125 g plain flour into a large glass bowl. Add 2 teaspoons dried yeast and ½ teaspoon salt and mix. Make a well in the centre and pour in 625 ml warm milk. Mix to a batter and beat for a couple of minutes to get rid of any lumps. Cover the bowl and leave to rise for 1–2 hours (the batter should be full of bubbles after this time). Use your hand to beat the bubbles out of the batter. Add 2 tablespoons melted butter and 3 egg yolks and beat them in. In a separate bowl, beat 3 egg whites, fold these into the batter and leave to stand for another 10 minutes. Grease a heavy-based frying pan with butter and fry spoonfuls of the batter until bubbles rise to the top surface and the underneath browns. Flip the blinis over and cook the other side for 1 minute, or until brown. Keep warm in the oven until you are ready to serve them. Makes about 40.*

*Blinis served with sour cream and chives and salmon roe.*

## blintz

Blintzes are thin pancakes, similar to a crêpe, filled with either a sweet or savoury filling. The pancake is folded into a rectangular packet and baked or fried until golden brown. Blintzes are of Eastern European origin and are traditionally eaten at Shavuot, the Jewish celebration held after Passover, when it is customary to eat dairy products. Typically, they are filled with fresh cheese, sprinkled with cinnamon and served with sour cream.

**Also known as — blintze**

*Blintzes filled with fresh cheese*

## blueberry

A dark-blue berry covered with a slightly grey bloom, and a member of the *Vaccinium* species. Blueberries are not blue inside but white or pale green, and have small, soft seeds that are hardly noticeable. The berries are about the size of a pea, but this varies with the variety. Blueberries are sweet and can be eaten raw, with ice cream, or in a fruit salad, but are also excellent when stewed or baked in muffins or puddings.

**Blueberries go with — brown sugar, cream, orange, port**

**See also  berries**

### BUYING

*Choose firm, plump berries without any squashed or leaking fruit—these will be stale and tasteless.*

### STORAGE

*Blueberries react with metal, which causes both the berries and metal to discolour, so don't store them in metal containers and line cooking tins with parchment or clingfilm.*

*Remove crushed or mouldy berries before storing to prevent mould spreading to the other berries and store in the fridge for up to 1 week.*

*Blueberries freeze well, but should be cooked while still frozen to retain their flavour.*

### BLUEBERRY AMARETTI CRUMBLE

*Divide 200 g blueberries between 2 ceramic bowls. Using a food processor, crush 100 g amaretti biscuits and cover the berries with the crumbs. Bake at 180°C for 15–20 minutes. Serve with cream. Serves 2.*

A savoury meat loaf unique to South Africa, bobotie is often described as the best example of Cape Malay cooking. It is made from minced lamb or beef mixed with onion and garlic and spiced with curry powder and turmeric. The meat is blended with bread soaked in milk, flavoured with lemon juice, sultanas and almonds, and baked in a casserole dish. An egg custard topping is added halfway through cooking. Bobotie is traditionally accompanied by rice and chutney.

**b o l l i t o   m i s t o**

A classic of northern Italian cuisine, bollito misto (meaning 'mixed boiled') is a rich stew of meat and vegetables. The types of meat vary regionally, but it is usual to include beef, veal, chicken, tongue, cotechino (sausage), and sometimes pig's trotters or head, or half a calf's head. In restaurants, bollito misto is served ceremoniously on a trolley that is wheeled beside the table. The meat is cut as it is served so it doesn't dry out, and served with a sharp sauce such as salsa verde or a tomato-based salsa rossa.

**B o m b a y   d u c k**

A dried and salted Indian fish, which is often deep-fried or grilled before being eaten as an accompaniment to curry and rice, or added to sambals, curries and fish stocks. Why a duck? Most explanations suggest it's because the fish skims through the water like a duck.

***Also known as — bummalo***

**b o m b e**

A frozen dessert, made by lining a mould with a layer of plain ice cream or sorbet and filling the centre with a softer mixture, often another type of ice cream or a custard or mousse. Sometimes more than two layers are used, and often the ice cream in the centre is mixed with nuts, glacé fruits or liqueurs. Classic bombes include the Chateaubriand—apricot ice cream filled with a vanilla bombe mixture and Kirsch-flavoured apricots, or Sarah Bernhardt—a layer of strawberry ice cream filled with a caramel centre. A bombe Alaska is a baked Alaska made in the shape of a bombe.

Traditionally, bombes were made in copper spherical moulds and were named after the old-fashioned cannon-like bomb. Today, bombe moulds are available in many sizes and shapes. Metal moulds are popular as they conduct the cold well, which helps set the bombe, and they are easy to heat when the bombe is unmoulded. Plastic moulds are suitable, but don't use glass as it may crack when frozen. Avoid antique moulds as they may be lined with lead.

***Also known as — bombe glacée***

## börek

A Middle Eastern pastry, usually eaten in Turkey and the Balkans, börek is made from filo or puff pastry wrapped around sweet or savoury fillings, which typically include feta cheese; spinach; ham or ground, spiced meat; and a sweet version made with honey and nuts and soaked in sugar syrup. The shape, too, varies and can be triangular or circular, when they are known as *ceviz börek*, or cigarette shaped, *sigara börek*. The Tunisian *brik*, or *brik à l'oeuf*, a deep-fried pastry triangle enclosing an egg or egg and minced lamb, is one variation. The börek are usually deep-fried or baked until crisp and golden and are often eaten as an hors d'oeuvre.

Making the pastry for börek is a labour of love and one that requires skill and patience to roll the sheets of dough into paper-thin layers, so they are usually only made for special occasions. Nowadays, commercially made pastry is a convenient and acceptable alternative.

## botargo

Botargo is the salted, pressed and dried roe of the tuna *(pictured)* or grey mullet and is favoured as a delicacy in Italy, France, Greece and Egypt. As an antipasto it is sliced extremely thinly and dressed with olive oil and lemon juice, or it can be grated onto scrambled eggs or shaved into curls and tossed with pasta dressed in olive oil. Botargo commands high prices and is sold pressed in blocks or coated in wax and shrink-wrapped.

*Also known as — batarekh, bottarga, boutargue*

## bouillabaisse

Traditionally, bouillabaisse was made with white fish cooked in a broth of tomatoes, oil, garlic, saffron and herbs, but now it is common to include shellfish as well. Bouillabaisse was once a humble affair, made by French fishermen on their boats as a way of using up the fish that weren't suitable for market.

The soup and the fish can be served separately, the soup followed by the fish, but it is usual to see them eaten together, accompanied by a garlicky sauce called 'rouille' and eaten with crusty bread. A good bouillabaisse includes at least seven types of fish and the debate over which fish to include is an ongoing one. The people of Marseille, the home of the bouillabaisse, consider the strong-tasting rascasse fish to be the quintessential element of bouillabaisse, and because it is a fish not widely available, they believe a true bouillabaisse can only be made in Marseille. This aside, you can achieve excellent results using monkfish, John Dory, sea bass, gurnard or bream, and add colour with lobster, mussels and crab. All ingredients should be really fresh.

Used for flavouring sauces, stews, soups or stocks, a bouquet garni is a bundle of herbs tied together with string. It should be removed at the end of cooking and, to make this easier, tie the end of the string to the handle of the saucepan. If using dried herbs or peppercorns, wrap them in muslin and tie with string.

See also **herbs**

### MAKING A BOUQUET GARNI

*Wrap the green part of a leek around a bay leaf, a sprig of thyme, a sprig of parsley and celery leaves. Tie the bundle with string, leaving it long at one end for easy removal. Vary the herbs to suit the dish.*

**boxty**

Originating in Ireland, boxty is made from grated raw potatoes and mashed cooked potatoes mixed with milk, flour, egg, salt and sugar. There are two versions: boxty cooked on the griddle is a type of potato bread, rolled out and cut into circles; boxty cooked in the pan is more like a potato pancake, dropped directly from the spoon onto the griddle. Boxty is often buttered and served as a side dish, usually with meat or stews, or eaten with an Irish hot breakfast of sausages, bacon, black pudding and eggs.

**bran**

Bran is the coarse outer layer of cereal grains such as wheat, oats and rice that is removed during milling. Bran is widely recognized as an excellent source of fibre. It may be toasted and made into breakfast cereals or, when raw, bran may be used in baked goods such as bread, muffins *(pictured)*, biscuits or cakes, or added to soups and stews. Also a good source of iron, zinc and niacin and contains some B vitamins.

## brandy

Distilled from wine or fermented fruit juice and aged in oak barrels, brandy is a spirit used to flavour desserts, fruit cakes, pâtés, terrines, and to flambé food such as crêpes. Brandy has an alcohol content of 40–50 per cent. Its name comes from the Dutch *brandewijn*, meaning 'burnt wine' ('burning' or boiling wine to distil it). Cognac and Armagnac are brandies distilled from wine; Calvados is a fruit brandy made from apples. Cognac is double-distilled and when ready for bottling, caramel and sugar are added. Armagnac is distilled once, it is a little drier with added sugar.

Labels indicate age. Up to 3 years is a young brandy and 10–12 years is a good brandy. A 'VSOP' (very special old pale) cognac indicates 4–10 years, the 'pale' indicating it has not been heavily coloured with caramel. Brandies labelled as 'Napoleon' have aged 6–20 years.

**Brandy goes with — cream, custard, fruit salad, prune**

*See also* **Calvados, eau de vie, Kirsch**

## brandy snap

Brandy snaps are thin biscuits that are baked until golden brown and, while still warm and pliable, shaped into tubes, cones or baskets. Recipes vary (they don't always contain brandy), but they are usually made from flour, butter, sugar, golden syrup, ginger and lemon juice. When cooled, fill with whipped cream (or try with brandy-flavoured cream) or ice cream. Keep unfilled brandy snaps in an airtight container in the fridge for a few days, but if filled, serve after 1 to 2 hours or the snaps will become soggy.

## brazil nut

Brazil nuts are not actually nuts, but seeds that grow on tropical trees in the thick rainforests of the Amazon. The nuts are cream in colour and encased in a hard, dark-brown shell. About 15–20 of these nuts are enclosed in a hard, round pod, about the size of a coconut. The pod falls to the ground, is collected and taken out of the jungle, and then is usually cracked open by hand. Brazil nuts have rarely been successfully cultivated on plantations—they take about 35 years to mature and only seem to function within their own ecosystem.

The nuts have a sweet, rich flavour and are high in fat and calories. They can be eaten raw, used in pastries or cooked in fruit cakes. Because of their high oil content, the nuts turn rancid quickly: keep unshelled nuts in a cool, dry place for up to 6 months and shelled nuts in an airtight container in the fridge for 3 months. Unshelled nuts are easier to crack if they have been frozen first.

**Also known as — butter nut, cream nut, para nut**

Bread is a staple food made from flour, salt and water. Some breads are leavened, that is, they use a raising agent such as yeast to give them a lighter texture, and others such as flat breads use no leavening. Recently there has been a revival in sourdough bread, leavened using natural wild yeast starters, the original leavening before commercial yeasts were developed. Bread can be finished in many ways: dusted with flour and sprinkled with toppings, nuts and seeds, brushed with an egg wash, salted water or milk, slashed with a razor or snipped with scissors.

## STORAGE

*Most breads will keep for a couple of days and those with fat in them will keep longer. Always cool bread thoroughly before putting it in a plastic bag—the steam will give it a stale texture and cause it to go mouldy quicker. Store bread in a bag or wrapped in a cloth at room temperature—putting it in the fridge will dehydrate it and make it go stale.*

## MAIN INGREDIENTS IN BREAD

| | |
|---|---|
| ***Flour*** | Different flours produce breads with different flavours and textures. When wheat flour is kneaded, the protein develops into gluten, forming the structure of the bread. Non-wheat flours have little or no gluten, resulting in a dense bread. Strong or 'bread' flours are best. |
| ***Salt*** | Controls the rate of fermentation, which strengthens the gluten, as well as adds flavour. If used on its own, salt will kill the yeast, so mix it with flour first. |
| ***Sugar*** | A source of food for yeast. Too much sugar will slow the fermentation process. Sweet dough takes longer to rise. |
| ***Fat*** | Gives bread dough a softer crumb, but has to be used carefully as fats inhibit fermentation. If large amounts of fat are used, they are usually added after the first rising. |
| ***Liquid*** | Activates the yeast. Water is usually used—it strengthens gluten, resulting in a chewy bread and crisp crust. Milk gives a softer crumb and beer gives a malty flavour. |
| ***Yeast*** | The active ingredient in bread. Can be commercially produced or natural wild yeast, as used for sourdough. Kneading distributes the yeast through the dough. Other leavening agents are baking powder or cream of tartar. |

## BREAD SAUCE

*In a saucepan, bring to the boil 500 ml milk and 1 onion studded with 6 cloves. Infuse for 30 minutes. Strain, reheat and add 90 g fresh white breadcrumbs, 2 tablespoons butter and 2 tablespoons cream. Reheat (do not allow to boil or it will separate) and season. Serve with roast turkey, game or poultry. Serves 4.*

### Daily breads

These breads vary worldwide from the rough-textured, unsalted Italian loaf, *pane Toscana*, to factory-produced sliced white bread. Countries with a continuing tradition of baking such as France, where every village has to have a bakery by law, continue to produce fine breads such as baguettes, ficelles and batards at least once a day using good-quality flour and traditional techniques. Bread is bought here on a daily basis and is only expected to last until the end of the day. Breads can be free-formed like bloomers, ciabatta and *pane pugliese,* or baked in tins to give a more even loaf shape, such as milk loaves, granary loaves and split tin loaves. The crumb of the bread can vary from a looser, rougher texture made with brown, rye or wholemeal to the fine pale crumb of a milk loaf.

*Clockwise from top left to centre:*
*granary loaf, bloomer, rye bread, ciabatta, pane pugliese.*

### Flat breads

The most basic of all breads, flat breads are the ancestors of the modern loaf. Flat breads are produced in virtually every cuisine in the world from Mexican tortillas, Middle Eastern pitta and lavash breads, Indian naan to the paper-thin *carta de musica* produced by Sardinian villages. They can be cooked on hearths, griddles, on the sides of ovens and over open fires, can be made from low-gluten grains like buckwheat, corn and barley, which can't be used for ordinary bread, and are the staples of the poorest peoples. Flat breads not only add carbohydrate to a meal but also often act as the dish or cutlery—chapatis are used to pick up food in India, *injera*, a spongy pancake-like bread is used in Ethiopia as both a dish and scoop for eating food, tortillas are used to wrap Mexican food and pitta bread are the universal pocket stuffed with all kinds of filling.

*Clockwise from top left to centre:*
*carta de musica, pitta, naan, lavash, tortilla.*

### Flavoured or enriched breads

Flavoured or enriched breads are usually not an everyday bread, but eaten as part of a celebration or religious meal. Challah, the plaited Jewish bread is eaten on the Sabbath, stollen and panettone are eaten at Christmas in Germany and Italy, and fougasse is made with candied peel and is an Easter bread in the south of France. Rich breads are usually soft in texture, flavoured with spices or with dried and candied fruit, then glazed to a shine. They are the centrepiece rather than a side dish and are often given as gifts. Other rich breads such as raisin breads or *pane con l'uva*, which is made using fresh grapes, are often the legacy of recipes conceived by people without the luxury of sugar. They enriched the daily dough for special occasions with eggs, milk and whatever fruit or nuts were accessible.

*Clockwise from top left to centre:*
*fougasse, panettone, stollen, challah, raisin bread.*

**See also** **bagel, baguette, brioche, ciabatta, focaccia, grissini, panettone, soda bread, sourdough, stollen, yeast**

To make leavened bread you need flour (preferably high gluten 'strong flour'), a liquid and a leavening agent such as yeast. After the dough is made, it is left to rise, preferably at room temperature. Dough will rise quickly if the room is very warm but it won't develop as good a flavour or texture. The dough is then knocked back (deflated) to rid it of any large or irregular air bubbles, then shaped and left to prove until it doubles in size—don't over-prove or your bread will collapse when cooked. Baking gives bread a final rise as the moisture in the dough turns to steam and expands. As soon as the bread gets hot enough the yeast dies and the crust forms. Steam can be sprayed into the oven with a water sprayer during the first few minutes to give a thinner outer crust, and baking bread on unglazed ceramic tiles will give a crisp crust and base.

## MAKING WHITE BREAD

1. Sieve 450 g plain strong flour, 1½ teaspoons salt into a bowl and make a well in the centre.

2. Dissolve 15 g fresh yeast and 1 teaspoon sugar in 15 ml hand-hot water and leave until it sponges (foams).

3. Add 275 ml hand-hot water, starting with half the water, then adding enough to make a moist dough.

4. Knead the dough for about 10 minutes, stretching and folding, until smooth and elastic.

5. The dough will now be smooth and a finger indent will pop out quickly. Leave to rise in a covered, greased bowl.

6. The dough is ready when it has doubled in size. A finger indent will pop out slowly.

7. Knock back the dough by punching gently. Turn out onto a floured surface. Knead out any air pockets for 3–4 minutes.

8. Knead the dough into an oval shape, then roll it into a tight sausage shape.

9. Put seam side down in a lightly oiled tin. Leave to prove until the dough doubles in size.

10. Bake at 220°C for 45 minutes, or until it sounds hollow when tapped on the base.

# bread and butter pudding

As its name suggests, bread and butter pudding is made from slices of buttered bread layered into the base of a dish. The bread is soaked in a mixture of eggs, milk, vanilla and spices and the dish is set in a tray of hot water and baked. The pudding is brushed with warm apricot jam and dusted with icing sugar. For added flavour, sultanas or fruit are often added to the dessert, which can be eaten hot or cold. Bread and butter pudding was traditionally made with bread, but variations can include brioche, croissants or panettone.

Bread pudding is similar to bread and butter pudding, but made with cubes of bread, often day-old bread, and mixed with eggs, sugar, milk and vanilla. The mixture is poured into a baking dish and set in a tray of hot water and baked. The pudding is usually served cold and cut into slices to serve. Bread pudding is a popular dessert in New Orleans, where it may be served with a whisky or rum sauce, flavoured with sliced bananas or chocolate.

# breadfruit

Breadfruit is a fruit, similar to a melon in size and shape, with yellow to green knobbly skin and cream, fibrous flesh. When cooked, it tastes similar to baked bread or potatoes. Breadfruit is never eaten raw and is used in much the same way as potatoes—mashed with milk, boiled, baked or fried as chips. Breadfruit is native to Southeast Asia and the Pacific Islands, where it is an important source of starch and was introduced into the Caribbean by Captain Bligh.

# bresaola

A speciality of northern Italy's Valtellina Valley, bresaola is made from tender cuts of cured, air-dried beef. The beef is very lean and is cured for about 2 or 3 months. Bresaola has a similar, but stronger flavour than prosciutto, and is served in thin slices as an antipasto, often drizzled with olive oil and lemon juice. The beef is sliced just before serving to prevent it from drying and becoming leathery.

# brioche

Brioche is made from a light yeast dough enriched with butter and eggs, which gives the bread a cake-like texture. Brioche dough can be shaped into a loaf, ring, plait or small buns, but the most classic is *brioche à tête*, with its distinctive small knot of dough on the top, resembling the 'head'. *Brioche à tête* is baked in a special fluted mould and is glazed with a gild glaze made from an egg yolk, giving it a dark, shiny finish. Lightly sweetened brioches are often eaten warm for breakfast, but unsweetened versions can be served with soup or used instead of toast.

## SERVING SUGGESTIONS

*Slice the top off, then hollow out a brioche bun. Scramble an egg with a little cream and season, spoon into the bun and top with smoked salmon.*

*Fry 6 sliced mushrooms in butter, add 1 tablespoon cream and some chopped parsley and spoon into a split brioche bun.*

*Fry 2 slices brioche in butter. Serve with a spoonful of fruit compote and a dollop of natural yoghurt.*

## ENGLAND

Like the English language, English food is built upon a strong base comprising regional variations, overlaid with borrowings from its former colonies, current immigrants and close neighbours. As an island nation, it's surprising that shellfish do not play a larger part, though fish (haddock and cod) and England's great gift to fast food, fish and chips, do. The Empire contributed tea, curry and kedgeree, which adds its lustre to a meal for which England is justifiably famous, breakfast, which might also include eggs, bacon, kidneys and toast and marmalade. Other traditional dishes include Lancashire hotpot, roast beef and Yorkshire pudding and cottage pie. Pudding is a great English tradition and includes such classics as spotted dick and Christmas pudding. England has a great tradition of cheesemaking and some of the famous cheeses include Lancashire, Cheshire, Stilton, Wensleydale and Cheddar. English haute cuisine owes much to the French.

*Treacle sponge and custard*

*Fish and chips*

## SCOTLAND

Scotland is most famous for its haggis, which is usually eaten on Burns' night, and Scottish cuisine in general is made up of hearty, wholesome and filling, rather than refined dishes. Oats are used for porridge, and barley (along with mutton and vegetables) for Scotch broth or used to brew Scotland's national drink of whisky. From the land, Scots eat beef, game, fowl and winter vegetables such as neeps and tatties (mashed swedes and potatoes). From the sea, Arbroath smokie (wood-smoked haddock), Lochfyne kippers and salmon are favourites. Local cheeses include Crowdie and Caboc. The Scottish have a love for baking, with some famous examples being shortbread and Dundee cake.

*Scotch broth*

*Dundee cake and tea*

*Welsh cawl*

## WALES

Traditional Welsh food relies on fresh local produce, an example being sweet Welsh lamb or bacon served with potatoes, leeks, cabbage and mutton to make the famous Welsh cawl, a one-pot chunky soup. Baked goods include the famous *bara brith*, meaning 'speckled bread', a rich, fruit bread served sliced and buttered, or Welsh cakes, small flat scones cooked with currants.

■ *See also* **cock-a-leekie, Dundee cake, haggis, Irish food, jellied eels, kedgeree, Lancashire hotpot, ploughman's lunch, shortbread, smoked fish, spotted dick, Yorkshire pudding**

## broccoli

Broccoli (meaning 'little arms' in Italian) is related to cauliflower, cabbage and kohlrabi. There are many varieties of broccoli, but the most common is the calabrese with green, densely packed heads. Other varieties may be purple, lime-green and white. Hybrid varieties such as broccolini are also available *(pictured far left)*.

When buying broccoli look for firm, tightly closed green heads, with no tinges of yellow. Broccoli can be eaten raw, steamed or boiled, and the stalks, which are quite sweet, can be peeled and diced and used in the same way as the florets. Drain well before serving as the florets hold lots of water. Broccoli is an excellent source of Vitamin C and is rich in vitamins A and B.

### ROAST BROCCOLI

*Toss 800 g broccoli florets in 1 tablespoon ground cumin, 1 tablespoon ground coriander, 5 crushed garlic cloves, 2 teaspoons chilli powder and 4 tablespoons oil. Spread out the broccoli on a baking tray and roast at 200°C for 20 minutes, or until cooked through. Serves 4.*

**Broccoli goes with — almond, chilli, coriander, cumin, garlic, ginger, lemon, onion, soy sauce, tomato**

## brown sauce

Brown sauce started life as a competitor for tomato ketchup, which had quickly become a popular and affordable condiment, particularly in Britain. Often known simply as 'sauce', brands such as HP (Houses of Parliament) and Daddies are now very popular.

## brownies

Brownies are a dense, moist chocolate cake and are as much a part of North American cuisine as apple pie and hominy grits. Some brownies are fudgy and soft in the centre and dry and cracked on top, while others may have a more cake-like texture. Sometimes, nuts such as walnuts or pecans may be added to the basic mixture, or it may be flavoured with caramel or rum. Brownies are cut into squares and served with cream or ice cream or eaten with a glass of milk. Blondies are brownies made with white chocolate and vanilla.

### BROWNIES

*In a saucepan, melt 125 g butter with 125 g dark (plain) chocolate. Beat 2 eggs with 285 g caster sugar until mixture is light and fluffy. Fold in the melted chocolate mixture and 125 g sieved plain flour with 4 tablespoons cocoa powder, then pour into a greased and lined 17 cm square tin. Bake at 180°C for 30 minutes. Allow the brownies to cool, then cut into squares. Makes 9 brownies.*

### BASIC BRUSCHETTA

*Cut the bread into thick slices and grill on both sides until brown. Cut 1 garlic clove in half and rub the cut end over one side of the bread. Add one of the toppings below.*

### TOMATO AND BASIL TOPPING

*Finely chop fresh tomatoes and mix with chopped basil. Season, then spoon onto toasted bruschetta and drizzle with extra virgin olive oil. Season and serve immediately.*

### MUSHROOM TOPPING

*Fry sliced mushrooms in olive oil until browned, add 1 chopped garlic clove and some chopped parsley. Season well and spoon onto bruschetta.*

Pronounced 'broos-ketta', and Tuscan in origin, bruschetta is designed to make the most of the new season's olive oil. It's made by rubbing a piece of grilled, crusty bread, *pane casa*, with a clove of garlic and slurping the oil over it. It is then sprinkled with salt. Nowadays, bruschetta is served as a snack or part of an antipasto, often topped with chopped tomato. Bruschetta is derived from the Italian word *bruscare*, meaning to 'roast over coals'.

Bruschetta with tomato and basil topping, and bruschetta with mushroom topping.

 *See also* **crostini**

## Brussels sprouts

A member of the cabbage family, Brussels sprouts grow in long rows on a single stem. Brussels sprouts were first cultivated in the sixteenth century in Flanders, near Brussels.

When buying Brussels sprouts, choose the smaller ones as they are more tender and tastier, and check they have tight heads and that the leaves are bright green with no tinges of yellow. Brussels sprouts can be steamed or boiled, or shredded and used in a stir-fry. To boil them, remove the outer leaves and soak in salted water for a few minutes to remove any bugs. Cooking in lots of boiling water with the lid off helps them to stay green.

**Brussels sprouts go with — almond, bacon, butter, chestnut**

### BRUSSELS SPROUTS STIR-FRY WITH BACON

*Fry 400 g shredded Brussels sprouts in a little oil until tender. Add 4 finely chopped bacon rashers and fry together until crisp. To serve, season with pepper and sprinkle a few chopped almonds over the Brussels sprouts.*
*Serves 4.*

## bubble and squeak

Traditionally, bubble and squeak was made from leftover cabbage and mashed potatoes or other vegetables, fried until crisp and brown. The name is thought to come from the sound the ingredients make as they fry. 'Bubble and squeak' is now loosely used to refer to any leftover meat or vegetables that are fried together.

### BUBBLE AND SQUEAK

*Heat 45 g butter in a frying pan and fry together 300 g mashed potato and 400 g cooked savoy cabbage. Each time a crust forms on the bottom, fold it over into the pan. Cook until brown and crisp, then drain on paper towel. Season well and serve with grilled chops and sausages. Serves 4.*

## bûche de Noël — see yule log

## buckwheat

Buckwheat is cooked and used as a cereal, but is actually the fruit of a plant related to rhubarb and dock. The small triangular seeds of the plant are ground to make a strong-tasting, nutty flour used in pancakes, Russian blinis, Japanese soba noodles, pasta and, in Brittany, to make galettes, a flat bread baked on a griddle. Whole, husked buckwheat (groats) form the basis of the dish kasha, which is used like rice and popular in Russia and Poland. Buckwheat is traditionally served with borscht, and may also be used instead of rice in pilaffs and risottos. The seeds are sold toasted (sometimes called kasha) and untoasted. The flour has no gluten so it must always be mixed with other flours for use in cakes and breads.
**Also known as — beech wheat, kasha, saracen corn, sarrazin**

### KASHA

*Dry-fry 200 g buckwheat seeds until brown and crunchy. Add enough water or stock to cover the seeds and simmer with the lid on until the liquid is absorbed and the seeds are soft. Add 30 g butter and leave for 5 minutes with the lid on. Stir through 2 tablespoons chopped herbs. Serve kasha with meat dishes such as goulash or beef stroganoff. Serves 6.*

*See also* **blinis, noodles**

## buffalo

Buffalo meat is tender and tastes like beef, and is mainly eaten in Southeast Asia, India and Nepal in curries and stews. Buffalo is lower in fat than beef, so it needs to be cooked quickly on a low heat or it will become tough. Buffalo milk is used for drinking or to make cheese or yoghurt. In India, it is used to make *sarati*, a cheese that is matured in earthenware vases and, in Italy, it is used to make sublime *mozzarella di buffala*. In North America, buffalo is known as a bison.

Buffalo wings are deep-fried chicken wings. The recipe was invented in Buffalo, New York, but they are now a popular snack food throughout North America. The chicken wings are brushed with hot chilli sauce and, when cooked, they are often served with a blue cheese dressing. The spicy sauce used to baste the buffalo wings is sold commercially in bottles.

## burghul

Burghul is a processed food made by boiling wheat until soft, drying it, then grinding it. This technique is possibly man's first attempt at processing food. To use burghul, cover with boiling water and allow the liquid to absorb. Burghul has a slightly nutty flavour and is used widely in vegetarian, Greek, Turkish and Middle Eastern cuisines, in tabbouleh, kibbeh, pilaffs, stews or soups. Cracked wheat is sometimes erroneously called burghul or bulgar.

**Also known as — bourgouri, bulgar, burgul, pligouri**

### BURGHUL PILAFF

*In a frying pan, fry 1 chopped onion until soft. Add 6 finely chopped tomatoes and 1 crushed garlic clove. Bring ingredients to the boil, then add 1 drained tin chickpeas and 6 tablespoons burghul (soaked), some chopped coriander and season well. Heat through, then serve the pilaff with a dollop of yoghurt or sour cream. Serves 4.*

## bush tucker

*From left: bunya nuts, wild rosellas, lemon myrtle leaves, lemon aspen fruit (all on paperbark).*

### SERVING SUGGESTIONS

*Lemon myrtle leaves have a distinctive lemon-lime flavour, and 15 times the flavour of a lemon. Add a few fresh leaves to a bottle of vinegar or oil, or grind into a powder and add to shortbread or bread, or mix into hot cooked rice.*

*Add a few strips of paperbark to barbecue coals to give a smoky flavour to meat.*

*Use bunya nuts as you would almonds in puddings and cakes.*

Bush tucker is the native food of Australia, eaten by the indigenous Australians for thousands of years, and includes seasonal fruits, nuts, seeds, vegetables, meat, fish and grubs such as the witchetty grub. Bush tucker was largely ignored by the first European settlers to Australia and it has only been in recent years that bush tucker is beginning to find a place in Australian cuisine.

Bunya nuts are the nut of the native pine tree. The aborigines boiled or baked them in their shells and ate them like chestnuts, but they may also be added to quiches or stews. Wild rosellas have a tart berry flavour and may be used in sauces or pie fillings. Lemon myrtle leaf can be used like kaffir lime leaves. Use to flavour fish or chicken. Lemon aspen fruit has a tart citrus flavour. Use to flavour desserts, or chop and add to pizza toppings. Paperbark is used to wrap fish and meat before cooking. Other bush tucker includes quandongs, a small tart fruit used in desserts and sauces; riberries, small red berries, used like redcurrants; and wild limes.

**Also known as — bush food, native produce**

# butter

A dairy product made by churning cream until it becomes a solid fat. Butter can be made from the milk of a cow, buffalo, yak or ewe. Most butters contain about 80 per cent fat and about 16 per cent water. Normandy, in France, produces some of the finest butters, 'beurre d'Isigny' and 'beurre de Charantes', both of which are recognized and controlled by the French appellation d'origine contrôlée.

Store butter well wrapped in the fridge in the butter keeper or in a sealed container away from vegetables and aromatic foods. Unopened salted butter keeps refrigerated for weeks (salted butter keeps longer than unsalted).

## TYPES OF BUTTER

| | |
|---|---|
| **Salted and unsalted** | Unsalted (sweet) butter is creamy and good for frying and cooking. It is used in baking and in sauces that don't need extra salt. Lightly salted butter can be used as a table butter and for cooking. Salted butter contains more milk solids than unsalted and therefore burns easier (salt was originally added as a preservative). |
| **Whipped** | Contains more air and moisture than regular butter. It spreads better when chilled and is usually used as a table spread. It should not be used for recipes as it gives a false weight and volume reading due to its make up. |
| **Lactic (cultured)** | Found more frequently in Europe, this is made with ripened cream to which active cultures have been added. This produces a pleasingly tangy butter, which has a shorter shelf life than regular butter. |
| **Clarified** | This has a higher burning point than other butters because they don't contain milk solids. Indian ghee (a form of clarified butter but with a higher smoke point) is similar but has a stronger flavour. Concentrated butter has a similar flavour to ghee. It has little moisture and a high butter fat content. Clarified butters can withstand high temperatures and are good for frying. |

### CLARIFIED BUTTER

*To clarify butter, heat a pack of butter until liquid. Leave until the white milk solids settle to the bottom. Use a spoon to skim off any foam, then strain off the golden liquid, leaving the white solids behind.*

**Cooking with butter**

To prevent butter burning when you are cooking with it, turn down the heat or use half oil and half butter in the pan, which allows you to use a higher heat without the butter burning.

Butter can be used to enhance a sauce and make it shiny (*monte au beurre*). To do this, remove the sauce from the heat and stir in a tablespoon of butter, vigorously whisking. To make browned butter (*beurre noisette*), gently heat some butter until it becomes golden and gives off a nutty smell. Use it as it is, or stir in some lemon juice and chopped parsley and serve over fish or vegetables.

# buttermilk

Originally, buttermilk was the by-product of the butter-making process—the liquid left after cream is churned into butter. Today it is made from pasteurized skim milk to which an acid-producing bacteria is added, thickening it and giving it its characteristic tanginess. Buttermilk has less than 1 per cent fat. Purée it with fruit to make a milk shake, use in baking (its acidity reacts with bicarbonate of soda and acts as a raising agent), and as an alternative for oil or cream in salad dressings.

# cabbage

This stalwart vegetable is a member of a family that includes cauliflower, broccoli, Brussels sprouts and many Oriental greens. There are loose-leaved and hearted varieties of cabbages. Loose-leaved cabbages tend to be green or tinged with red, and firm cabbages are red, white or green. Choose compact, heavy cabbages with crisp leaves, free of slime or insect holes. Discard any damaged outer leaves before use. Unless you intend to use them in a day or two, buy whole cabbages as the cut edges of half cabbages give off enzymes that cause them to deteriorate faster. White-hearted cabbages are good raw and shred easily; green wrinkly savoy cabbages can be eaten steamed or boiled as a vegetable.

## COOKING

*The hard white core in the centre of the cabbage can be tough and should be removed before cooking. Cut into quarters, then cut off the base of each quarter to remove the core.*

*Don't cook cabbage for too long or in lots of boiling water as this causes it to lose its colour and nutrients, as well as giving off a sulphurous smell.*

*Adding a bay leaf to the cooking water may help with the smell.*

From left: red cabbage, white cabbage, green cabbage.

*To prevent red cabbage from turning grey, cut it with a stainless steel knife. You can also add a little lemon juice or vinegar to the cooking water, or sprinkle it over the leaves if using raw.*

■ *See also **bubble and squeak, colcannon, coleslaw, kale***

Cabbage can be grated finely and eaten raw in coleslaw or salads; it can be cooked in stir-fries, braised, steamed or added to soups. Cabbage leaves can be used to wrap fillings, or the whole cabbage can be stuffed and baked. Red cabbage, when shredded and cooked with onions, stock, red wine and vinegar, is a classic accompaniment to game and pork dishes. Cabbage is also shredded and salted to make sauerkraut. It should be rinsed and drained well before use to remove any excess salt.

***Cabbage goes with — apple, bacon, garlic, ginger, ham, juniper, mustard, sausage, sesame***

# cactus

Many of this large group of plants are eaten around the world, especially the thick, fleshy slightly tart tasting oval leaf of the Mexican nopal. Remove the spines and eyes and trim around the edges. Rinse off the sticky liquid, cut into strips and boil or steam, or brush with oil and grill until tender. The cooked flesh is added to salads, omelettes or soups. Nopalitos are diced or cut into strips and sold in bottles or cans.

***Also known as — cactus leaves, nopal, prickly pear***

# Caesar salad

There are as many stories of the origin of this modern classic as there are latter day versions. It's generally agreed that ingredients should at least include the following: cos (called Romaine in America) lettuce; coddled egg; anchovy; garlic; Worcestershire sauce; olive oil; Parmesan cheese; and croutons. It is a delicious salad, whether invented by Caesar Cardini in Mexico, or by his brother Alex in the racetrack restaurant in San Diego.

## CAESAR SALAD

*Tear a large cos lettuce into pieces and place it in a large bowl. In a blender, blend 1 egg yolk with 1 garlic clove and 4 anchovy fillets. With the motor running, gradually add 170 ml olive oil, then add 1 tablespoon lemon juice and a dash of Worcestershire sauce. Toss the dressing through the lettuce, then add some chunky croutons and Parmesan shavings. Serves 4.*

# Cajun

A melange of French and southern American cuisine, influenced by the African ingredients used by the local, French-descended Creoles of Louisiana. Cajuns are descended from the French Acadians (hence 'cajun'), driven from Canada when the territory was ceded to the English in the early 1700s. Generally hunters, fishers and trappers, the Acadians settled happily into the Louisiana bayou region.

Cajun cuisine relies heavily on food from the bayous (swampy rivers), such as alligator, rabbit and, most importantly, crayfish, and is heavily spiced. Typical dishes include red beans and rice, gumbo, fish, chicken and shrimp dishes. An important element in Cajun cooking is the roux, a thick paste made of lard and flour cooked until almost burnt, essential in gumbo and other dishes. 'Blackened' and fiery food is thought to be typically Cajun, but while heavily seasoned it is not always fiery. The technique of blackening spiced meat by cooking it over high heat is not truly Cajun, but was popularized by New Orleans chef Paul Prudhomme and has become a distinctive part of today's Cajun cuisine.

*Crawfish étouffée, a thick, spicy stew. Sometimes written as 'A-2-fay', étouffée means 'smothered' and refers to the method of cooking the food in a covered pot in its own juices.*

*Red beans and rice*

*Blackened red fish seasoned with Cajun spice mix*

## CAJUN SPICE MIX

*Combine 2 tablespoons paprika, 1½ tablespoons cayenne, 1 teaspoon garlic powder, ½ teaspoon black pepper, ¼ teaspoon salt, ½ teaspoon dried oregano and ½ teaspoon dried thyme. Rub the spice mixture on either fish, chicken or meat and grill until cooked through.*

■ *See also* **crocodile, gumbo, jambalaya, okra**

A baked food usually (but not always) containing flour, eggs, milk and/or other fats. A cake is usually sweet, but its nature may vary from light and porous sponges to much denser fruit and nut concoctions. Cake has always been seen as somewhat of a treat, especially if it contains other flavourings. The ability to bake cakes was once seen as a necessary skill of housewives who would have one on hand, however plain, at all times. Cakes may be iced or decorated in many different ways, such as elaborate gateaux, Christmas and birthday cakes and simnel cakes, and are universally used as celebration foods.

The word cake is also used to denote something that is shaped into a round with a flat top and bottom. Hence crab cakes, ice cream cakes, hot cakes and rice cakes are all cake shaped but have few of the other attributes.

### see squid — calamari

### Calvados

Calvados is an apple brandy made by distilling cider, and takes its name from Calvados, Normandy, where it is made. Calvados has an *appellation contrôlée*, which requires it to be double-distilled and matured in oak barrels. It is popular in Normandy where it is used in dishes such as *poulet vallée d'Auge*, a chicken and apple dish.

**Calvados goes with — apple, chicken, cream, crêpes, pork**

### calzone

A speciality of Naples and meaning 'trousers' (originally its shape was long and baggy), calzone is a half-moon shaped pizza. The dough is rolled into a thin oval, one half filled, then the dough is folded and sealed. *Calzone pugliese* is filled with onions, tomatoes, capers and anchovies; *Calzone napoletano* is filled with salami or prosciutto, ricotta, mozzarella and Parmesan; *Calzone con prosciutto*, with tomato, mozzarella and prosciutto. Calzone are usually brushed with oil and baked; some are also brushed with tomato sauce or herbs.

### camp coffee

Camp coffee is made from coffee and chicory. It is used as an alternative to coffee to flavour cakes, biscuits and mousses as it produces a better colour and stronger flavour than coffee essence. Camp coffee can be substituted with instant coffee mixed with a little hot water.

# Canadian food

Canada is a vast country divided into ten provinces and two territories, each of which has its own distinct cuisine reflecting the climate, local ingredients and the provenance of its settlers.

Much of the food of the Atlantic provinces comes from the sea. Over the centuries tonnes of fish, mainly cod, have been hauled from the sea by Newfoundlanders, and before them by Basque fishermen, who salted it and sailed it back to Europe as bacalao. Today, a traditional dish still in use is fish and *brewis*, salt cod with soaked hard bread, topped with bits of fried salt pork. Other fare includes thick split pea soup made with salted beef.

The food of Quebec, the French-speaking province, is French-based, but has adapted techniques and ingredients from its new home. Pea soup is traditional, made with dried yellow peas, smoked pork hock or ham

bone and seasonings. Pork also appears in dishes such as *cretons*, a spiced pork rillette-type spread and *tourtière*, a meat pie, often spiced with cinnamon and cloves.

Ontario is the berry centre and these are used in both sweet and savoury dishes. Maple syrup, one of Canada's largest exports, is produced here, and often poured over Canadian bacon.

Traditional British Columbian settlers were hunters and fishers and today the staple diet is still based around game and seafood, especially salmon.

The Prairies produce grains and wheat, including indigenous wild rice, much of which is exported, and food shows influences from Scandinavian, English and Ukrainian communities.

■ *See also* **maple syrup**

*From top: pancakes and Canadian bacon with maple syrup, tourtière pie.*

# candied fruit

To make candied fruit, pieces of fruit are soaked in a heavy sugar syrup. The syrup gradually replaces the water in the fruit, preserving it and making it sweet. Because the process is so time consuming, whole candied fruit can be quite expensive. Candied peel, usually from a fruit such as orange, lemon or citron, is mostly used as an ingredient, often in cakes: as decoration *(pictured below)*; or pieces of orange peel can be dipped in chocolate and eaten as confectionery. Candied peel is sold both as pieces and chopped mixed peel.

Use candied fruit to decorate fruit cakes; mix into dough for breads such as panettone; in biscuits; in desserts such as cassata; or fold into vanilla ice cream or mascarpone and freeze. In Italy, candied fruit may be eaten at the end of a meal, served with a liqueur. Store in an airtight container or the fruit will soften.

***Also known as — crystallized fruit, glacé fruit, preserved fruit***

*Clockwise from back left: orange, mandarin, citron, plum.*

## QUICK CANDIED PEEL

*Remove the zest from 3 oranges, lemons or limes using a canelle knife. If necessary, trim to neaten. Put zest in a saucepan with a little water and bring to the boil. Simmer, then drain the water and repeat the boiling process. Drain, then put 250 g sugar and 60 ml water in the pan and stir until sugar is dissolved. Add the zest and simmer until it looks translucent—don't overcook or it will caramelize. When zest is tender, drain and dry on baking paper.*

A candlenut is a hard, oily, tropical nut. Because of their high oil content, candlenuts were once used to make candles. The nuts are usually crushed and added to soups, or ground and used as a thickening agent in Indonesian and Malaysian cooking, particularly in curries and satays. The raw nut is slightly toxic so it must be cooked before it is safe to eat. Buy candlenuts in Indian and Asian supermarkets and store in the fridge. If candlenuts are unavailable, substitute them with macadamia nuts.

### GRILLED SPICY PRAWNS

*In a blender, process 6 Asian shallots, 3 candlenuts, 6 garlic cloves, 1 cm piece of galangal, 2 red chillies and 1 teaspoon shrimp paste until smooth. Add 80 ml coconut cream, 2 teaspoons palm sugar and 1 tablespoon lime juice. Marinate 500 g peeled prawns in this for 2 hours, then grill or barbecue the prawns until cooked through. Serves 4.*

**cannelloni**

Tubes of pasta, always served stuffed, whose Italian name translates as 'large tubes'. Cannelloni are usually made with rectangles of home-made pasta, which are briefly boiled, then filled and rolled into tubes. The tubes are placed side by side in an ovenproof dish, topped with a sauce and baked in the oven. Today pasta manufacturers have produced a ready-made tube of pasta, which can be filled before cooking using a pastry bag or teaspoon.

*See also* **Italian food, pasta**

### CANNELLONI

*Fry 1 finely chopped onion, 1 finely chopped stick celery and 1 finely chopped carrot together in 1 tablespoon butter. Add 90 g finely chopped pancetta and 440 g minced beef and brown well. Add 200 ml milk and cook for 1 minute, then add 200 ml red wine, 400 g tin tomatoes and 200 ml beef stock. Season well and cook for 2 hours. Pipe or spoon the filling into 8–10 cannelloni tubes and lay in a dish, cover with 6 tablespoons béchamel sauce (page 38) and 4 tablespoons grated cheese. Bake at 180°C for 40 minutes. Serves 4.*

## cannoli

Sicily is famed for its desserts, one of the best known of which is cannoli, deep-fried tubes of pastry. Originally the pastry was wrapped around a bamboo cylinder and deep-fried on the mould, but moulds now are usually metal (or you can use a ready-made cannelloni pasta).

When the pastry is cool, the tubes are filled with sweetened ricotta cheese mixed with cinnamon, candied fruit, pistachios and chocolate. Sometimes cannoli are filled with pastry cream or chocolate cream, or the pastry dough may be sweetened with Marsala.

## canola — see oil

## caper

The small unopened flower bud of a Mediterranean shrub. Once picked, they need to be pickled in brine or cured in salt before they are edible, one of the ways in which they are similar to olives. Capers are tart, piquant, and a wonderful complement to fish like skate with capers and black butter; can be added to tomato sauce for pasta (for puttanesca sauce, add black olives, anchovies and capers to a good tomato sauce, refrigerate and throw over hot spaghetti or linguine); sprinkled on pizzas; or fried (if you like) and used in salads. They should be rinsed, drained and patted dry before use. The caperberry is the pickled fruit of the same shrub, and can be used on antipasto plates, in salads or eaten like olives.

■ *See also* **tapenade, tartare sauce**

*Clockwise from left: capers in brine, caperberries, salted capers.*

## caponata

The recipe for caponata varies, but this popular Sicilian dish usually includes aubergine, celery, capers, tomato, onion and olives. The ingredients are cooked together, left to cool and served as an antipasto or with cold meat or fish. It can also be eaten warm as a pasta sauce or as a topping on bruschetta.

### CAPONATA

*Cut a large aubergine into cubes and fry in olive oil until brown. Drain well. Fry 1 sliced onion until soft, add 2 chopped celery stalks and a tin of chopped tomatoes and simmer for 10 minutes. Add the aubergine, 1 tablespoon capers, 2 tablespoons sliced black olives, 2 tablespoons red wine vinegar and 1 teaspoon sugar. Season well and serve cold. Serves 6.*

## capsicum — see pepper

Carambola is a tropical fruit with waxy golden orange or green skin (depending on variety) and crisp, slightly tart flesh. It has five ridges that run down its length and, when sliced, resembles a five-pointed star. The flavour varies depending on the variety and when it is picked. Some are sweeter than others, but it is difficult to determine the fruit's sweetness by looking at it, though often the fatter fruit are sweetest. Choose shiny, plump yellow fruit without any damage to the ridges. As the fruit ripens, ridges may turn slightly brown, but this is normal. Carambola's decorative shape lends itself to fruit salads, or fry in butter and sugar and add to hot desserts. The sour varieties are often used in pickles and chutneys.
*Also known as — five-corner fruit, star fruit*

**s e e  s u g a r  s y r u p — c a r a m e l**

**c a r b o n a d e  à  l a  f l a m a n d e**

Carbonade à la flamande originated in northern France and Belgium, and is a rich, slow-cooked stew of beef and onions braised in beer. 'Carbonade' comes from the Italian for 'charcoal cooked', although the beef is not grilled but browned in a pan, then transferred into a casserole. The traditional topping for this is pieces of bread spread with mustard. The stew is best served with boiled potatoes or a green salad. The term 'carbonade' is also used for grilled pork loins and southern French beef stews with red wine.

**c a r d o o n**

A popular vegetable in southern Europe, the cardoon is an edible thistle related to the artichoke. Cardoons are cultivated for their fleshy, ribbed stalks, similar in flavour to a combination of celery and artichoke. Like celery, cardoon is often cultivated in the dark (blanched) as this makes the stalks more tender. This is done by either covering the stalks with mounds of dirt, or wrapping cardboard cylinders around the stems.

When cooking cardoons, peel off any tough outer ribs before use. They brown very quickly, so should be cut into pieces with a stainless steel knife and put immediately into water with a squeeze of lemon juice. Cardoons can be braised or baked, but are usually boiled slowly, then baked with butter. They can be topped with Parmesan, béchamel sauce or anchovy butter. In Italy, tender, young cardoons are traditionally eaten raw with bagna caôda, or deep-fried in batter and served as antipasto. They can also be used to top bruschetta or mixed with cheese as a filling for ravioli or tortellini.

# Caribbean food

Caribbean is a term used to cover the West Indies, especially when talking of its food. In that context, it covers the islands between Florida and Trinidad, and includes, among others, Jamaica, Barbados, Cuba, Haiti and Martinique.

## HISTORY
Caribbean cuisine is an eclectic mix of native foods and the ingredients and cooking techniques of waves of Europeans, Africans and Asians who came to trade, colonize and live in what is now one of the world's most multicultural areas. The original inhabitants, the Carib, Arawak and Taino peoples all but disappeared during this process, but they were thought to have cultivated taro root, corn, yams, cassava and pine nuts. Guavas, pineapple, black-eye and lima beans all grew wild.

## INFLUENCES
Columbus introduced sugar cane, which was turned into a potent rum. The French, Dutch, Spanish and English brought coconuts, chickpeas, onions, aubergines, garlic, coriander, oranges, limes, mangoes, rice and coffee. The slave trade also brought new foods from West Africa, including okra, plantains, amaranth, taro, breadfruit and ackee, a vegetable unknown outside the region and usually served with salt fish.

In the nineteenth century, Chinese and Indian immigrants brought their own cuisine, and in islands like Trinidad they use garam masala and ghee. While favourites from rum to banana and coconut pies are universal, the islands do have their own regional cuisines. Cuba and Puerto Rica are very Spanish—the spicy tomato and pepper sauce soffritto, *arroz con pollo* stew and *adobo* seasoning have Spanish roots; Guadeloupe and Martinique are French-owned and use many French seasonings; while Jamaica, as the old

slave-trading centre, is rich in African food, fruit and vegetables. Many dishes use coconut cream.

## FRUIT AND VEGETABLES
The Caribbean abounds in fruit. Mangoes and papaya are used in drinks, desserts and chutneys, while coconuts are used in bread, ice cream, as coconut milk and frying oil. Plantains are eaten hot as chips or in meat pies. Vegetables include yams, pumpkins, okra, sweet potatoes, cassava, chayote and amaranth (also called callaloo), used to make soup. Legumes, especially black beans, are popular and bean dishes are eaten with rice and corn bread.

Desserts make use of Caribbean fruit, sugar and rum in cakes, puddings, flans, soufflés and mousses.

## MEAT AND SEAFOOD
Poultry is marinated with ginger, lime and chillies, then grilled. Curried goat is a Jamaican speciality, while beef and pork are found more on the Spanish islands. Seafood is plentiful, including parrot fish, tuna, grouper, mahi mahi, swordfish, wahoo and snapper, either grilled or served in stews. Spiny lobster, prawns and conches are seen in dishes such as lobster creole or coconut shrimp. Salt codfish is served in salads, fritters or with scrambled eggs and as codfish cakes in Barbados.

Not all Caribbean dishes are spicy, but chillies are used widely. Jerk marinades are made up of onions, thyme, Jamaican pepper (allspice), ginger, Scotch bonnet chillies, black pepper, nutmeg and cinnamon, and jerk pork is a Jamaican legend.

■ *See also* **jerk, plantain**

*From top: chicken pepperpot; Trinidadian callaloo soup; arroz con pollo (chicken and rice) from Cuba, the Dominican Republic and Puerto Rico; stamp and go—Jamaican fried codfish patties; pineapple with rum.*

The long, brown leathery carob pod is the fruit of a tree native to the Mediterranean. The pod contains hard seeds and an edible pulp, which can be eaten fresh, or dried and ground into a powder. Carob is sweet and has a similar flavour to chocolate and because it contains less fat than chocolate, it is often used as an alternative to cocoa and chocolate in cakes, biscuits and puddings (but it is too sweet to act as a substitute for dark or bitter chocolate). As carob has a milder flavour than chocolate and because it contains no cocoa butter, carob is not recommended when you want a really strong chocolate flavour or a smooth glossy finish, such as in mousses or rich chocolate cakes. Carob is sold at health food shops and is available as powder, chocolate bars and drops.

**Also known as — locust bean, St John's bread**

*From left: carob blocks, carob liquid, carob powder, iced carob drink.*

### ICED CAROB

*Dissolve 1 tablespoon carob powder in a highball glass with 200 ml milk. Add a pinch of nutmeg and stir with a cinnamon stick. Serves 1.*

A dish of paper-thin slices of raw beef, carpaccio may be dressed with a mayonnaise sauce or with olive oil and lemon juice. Add the dressing just before serving so that the beef stays red and doesn't oxidize. Carpaccio was created in the 1960s in Venice by Arrigo Cipriani, the owner of Harry's Bar, and was named in honour of the Italian Renaissance painter Vittore Carpaccio, who loved to paint in reds. Now, 'carpaccio' may refer to any meat or fish that is sliced thinly and served raw, such as tuna or salmon.

### CARPACCIO

*Trim a 200 g piece of beef fillet of all fat and sinew and freeze for 30 minutes. Using a sharp knife, slice very thinly, then lay the slices on a platter. Mix 2 teaspoons Dijon mustard, 2 teaspoons lemon juice, 1 teaspoon Worcestershire sauce, 1 tablespoon cream, 2 tablespoons olive oil and 1 tablespoon mayonnaise. Drizzle over the beef just before serving. Serves 2.*

An ancient root vegetable, whose modern cultivars (there are over 100 varieties ranging in colour from yellow to purple) are high in vitamin A, and so versatile as to be used in dishes as varied as cakes and casseroles, raw in salads and as a delicious juice.

New crop or baby carrots are best for eating raw in salads and only need to be cleaned with a stiff brush before use. Remove their fine green tops for longer storage. The larger, older carrots are best peeled and cooked. They can be steamed and served with butter, used in soups, puréed, or added to sweet dishes such as cakes and muffins, and in Indian and Middle Eastern desserts, such as halva. Don't store carrots near apples, pears or potatoes as the ethylene gas produced by these fruit and vegetables causes carrots to turn bitter.

**Carrots go with — apple, chives, cumin, mint, orange, parsley, raisin**

*See also* **vichy carrots**

## carrot cake

In the eighteenth century, root vegetables such as beetroot, parsnip and carrot were sometimes used to give sweetness to cakes and puddings. Of these, only carrot has remained really popular. Carrots add moisture and a pleasant flavour and texture to cakes, without giving the cake a strong 'carroty' flavour. Sometimes, pineapple or walnuts are added to the mixture before it is baked. Carrot cake is usually finished with a cream cheese icing.

## cashew nut

A curious nut that grows on trees native to Brazil. The nuts are encased in a kidney-shaped hard shell and develop inside a fruit called the cashew apple. Each apple only produces one nut, and when the nut is ripe, the nut and shell protrude below the fruit. Removing the cashew nut from the shell is a slow and laborious task as the shells contain a caustic oil known as 'cashew balm', which is highly toxic and can irritate the skin and eyes. The whole nuts are removed from the apples and heated before the nut can be safely extracted.

Cashew nuts, sold shelled, have a rich, buttery flavour. They can be eaten roasted and salted, or added raw to curries or stir-fries. They are high in fat and should be stored in the fridge to prevent them from turning rancid. The tart cashew apple can be eaten raw, and is used to make jams, wine and liqueurs.

### CHICKEN AND CASHEW NUTS

*Heat 2 tablespoons oil in a wok and add 1 diced onion, 4 crushed garlic cloves and 2 chopped red chillies and cook for 30 seconds. Add 1 chopped red pepper and 350 g cubed chicken thighs and toss until cooked through. Add 2 tablespoons oyster sauce, 1 tablespoon soy sauce, 3 chopped spring onions and 75 g toasted cashew nuts and toss together. Serves 4.*

## cassata

An Italian dessert of which there are many versions. The original, *cassata Siciliana,* was traditionally produced by nuns at Easter. It is brick-shaped and comprises an outer layer of cake filled with sweetened ricotta, candied peel and pieces of chocolate and covered with green marzipan. Another version uses layers of vanilla, chocolate, pistachio and strawberry ice cream to line the mould, and is filled with ricotta, cream and candied fruit. The word 'cassata' can now be loosely applied to any dessert made up of at least three layers of differently flavoured ice cream, often filled with chopped nuts and candied fruit, as shown here.

A native of South and Central America, this starchy, tuberous root has thick, bark-like skin and creamy white flesh. It is now grown and eaten as a vegetable in many tropical countries and is a staple in Africa and Central America. There are two varieties, bitter and sweet. Both contain toxic hydrocyanic acid in the roots (the bitter containing most), which is removed by steaming or boiling it thoroughly before use. Tapioca is a refined starch derived from cassava.

Sweet cassava can be cooked, mashed or fried just like a potato and the young, tender leaves can be cooked like spinach. Dried cassava is processed to make a flour used in bread and cakes. In the Caribbean, it's used to make cassareep, a black, syrupy seasoning used in stews. In Africa, it is made into *gari* meal and *foo-foo* porridge. Cassava is also sold frozen.

**Also known as — manioc, yuca**

**See also   African food, Caribbean food, tapioca**

A member of the cabbage family, the cauliflower has a large head of tight flower buds (known as 'curds'). Cauliflowers are usually creamy white, but there are also green and purple varieties, as well as miniature ones. Cauliflower can be eaten raw as crudités or steamed, boiled, stir-fried, pickled or used in soups. Buy cauliflower with firm, creamy white curds with no brown patches or holes. They should smell fresh and have crispy green leaves with no sign of yellowing. Remove the leaves and store in the vegetable crisper in the fridge.

**Cauliflower goes with — bacon, breadcrumbs, cheese, coriander, cumin**

### CAULIFLOWER CHEESE

*Steam a whole head of cauliflower until tender, then cut into quarters and put in a baking dish. Melt 30 g butter in a saucepan, add 30 g flour. Mix and cook until bubbling, then add 300 ml milk off the heat and whisk well. Return to the heat and simmer for 2 minutes. Add 150 g grated cheese to the milk and mix in. Season, then pour the sauce over the cauliflower, sprinkle with a little extra cheese and place under a hot grill until golden and bubbling. Serves 6.*

### COOKING

*Prepare florets or the whole cauliflower by soaking it in salted water to get rid of any bugs.*

*Cook in a non-aluminium saucepan (aluminium reacts with cauliflower and can turn it yellow).*

*Cauliflower can be steamed or boiled, but steaming is better as it keeps the florets intact.*

*If cooking a whole cauliflower, cut a cross in the base of the stalk or cut out the core to help it cook evenly.*

*Cauliflower contains a natural chemical that breaks down into a sulphur compound when cooked. To prevent this, cook until just tender with a bay leaf—the longer it cooks, the stronger the smell will become.*

# caviar

Genuine caviar is the salted roe (eggs) of a number of species of sturgeon fish, the best of which comes from the Caspian Sea, and is mainly farmed by Iran, Russia, and the newer states on the Caspian. The roe is removed from the fish, washed, rubbed through a sieve, mixed with salt and packed into tins. Unfortunately, due to overfishing and degradation of the habitat, the sturgeon has been listed as an endangered species, and caviar from the Caspian has been banned from many countries. Caution is advised when buying 'fresh caviar', which lasts about a week in the fridge. It has a short shelf life of only 2 or 3 weeks if repackaged by the importer so buy it from a shop with a high turnover. Caviar is often pasteurized for warmer climates, but fresh is best.

## HOW TO EAT CAVIAR

*Traditionally, caviar is served in its jar or in a tin set in a shallow bowl filled with crushed ice. If this is not appropriate, then a porcelain or china bowl can be used instead. The tin or jar should be opened just before serving.*

*Caviar is best eaten as a luxury on its own, perhaps accompanied by blinis or toast and crème fraîche, and drunk with iced vodka or champagne. Serve 30 g per person.*

*Caviar is best eaten from a mother-of-pearl spoon as silver will give the caviar a metallic taste and the caviar will discolour the silver. Mother-of-pearl is also less likely to cut through the eggs and break them.*

*Only use lemon juice to flavour your caviar if the caviar is not the best quality. Never eat caviar with minced raw onion.*

*Beluga caviar*

## TYPES OF RUSSIAN CAVIAR

| | |
|---|---|
| **Beluga** | The most expensive caviar and the largest grain size *(pictured above)*. The eggs are grey to black. Alas, due to overfishing, these days this grade is fairly rare. |
| **Osciotre** | Medium grain, golden-brown to brown eggs from albino fish. No different in flavour to black varieties. |
| **Sevruga** | Greyish in colour, milder and less salty than other caviars, this also has the smallest grain and travels best of all. |

# celeriac

A winter vegetable cultivated for its knobbly root. It is a type of celery but, unlike celery, only the root is eaten. To prepare, peel and cut into cubes or strips. The flesh discolours on contact with air, so soak or cook in water with a squeeze of lemon juice. Celeriac can be eaten raw in salads, or used in soups and stews. Cooked and mashed with garlic and potatoes, it is perfect served with game or meat. Choose smoother roots as these will be easier to peel. If sold with its leaves, remove and store the celeriac in the crisper drawer of the fridge for up to 1 week.
**Also known as — celery root, knob celery**

## CELERIAC REMOULADE

*In a bowl, mix 450 g coarsely grated celeriac, 5 tablespoons mayonnaise, 2 tablespoons mustard and 2 tablespoons baby capers. Season; add lemon juice to taste. Serve with bread or as a vegetable with meat dishes. Serves 4.*

Celery is grown for its stalks, roots and seeds. The ancient Greeks, Egyptians and Romans used wild celery for its medicinal properties and used celery leaves, like bay leaves, to crown their victorious athletes. In the sixteenth century, the first cultivated form of celery was developed, and was usually eaten cooked.

Celery grows as a cluster of long ridged stalks, which vary in colour from white to green. Celery stems are often grown under cover to prevent them from becoming too dark and too strong in flavour. Stems are eaten raw in salads; as crudités; cooked and served as a vegetable; braised in tomato or cream; or used as a base flavour in stocks and sauces. Celery leaves are used to add flavour to stocks and soups and the tender inner leaves can be used in salads or eaten with the stalk. Buy celery with crisp, fresh stems and not too big. Celery has a high water content so it should be stored in the crisper drawer of the fridge wrapped in plastic. To revive wilted celery, sprinkle it with water and put in the fridge until it becomes crisp again.

# ceviche

Thinly sliced raw fish left to marinate overnight in lime juice, chilli, onion, coriander and garlic—the acid partially cooks the fish. It is popular in Spanish-speaking South American countries, and is more than likely an adaptation of escabeche, an ancient southern European method of cooking or preserving fish. Traditionally done with firm white fish, today scallops, prawns and even salmon are used. After draining, it is served cold, often as an appetizer, and mixed with tomatoes, peppers, onions and/or avocado, in either a lettuce leaf or an avocado half.

***Also known as — cebiche, seviche***

■ *See also* **escabeche**

# charlotte

A dessert made in a specific mould lined with sponge fingers, cake or bread and filled with mousse, custard, cream or fruit. Apple charlotte, one of the most common variations, is made in a mould lined with buttered bread and filled with apple purée. Charlotte russe is made in a mould lined with sponge fingers and filled with Bavarian cream or mousse and topped with whipped cream.

see steak — **chateaubriand**

see christophine — **chayote**

Cheese is made by coagulating or curdling milk with rennet so that it separates into curds (solids) and whey (liquid). Most cheeses are made by separating the curds from the whey, then processing and maturing the curds to make cheese. However, whey cheeses are made from the whey itself (such as ricotta) and fresh, unripened cheeses do not go through a maturing process.

*Cheese should be cut in such a way that each part of the cheese, from the rind to the heart, can be enjoyed.*

Cheeses vary dramatically and although they are made following the same basic method, the final cheese is governed by the way it has been treated every step of the way. Many French cheeses are governed by *appellation d'origine contrôlée* (AOC), which regulates every process in cheese production—from animal feed to the tools for cutting curds.

## MAKING CHEESE

*All cheese is made from milk, but the type of animal yielding the milk, or the milk itself, can make a difference to the taste and texture of the cheese. The milk may be from a cow, sheep or goat. It may be from a morning or an evening milking, or a combination of both. It may be skimmed or have cream added to it, or it may have come from a particular breed of cow, or from a cow fed on a particular diet. Finally, it may be raw or pasteurized.*

*Rennet and lactic starters are usually added to milk to speed up the coagulating process. Quantities used in individual cheeses may vary and in some AOC regulated cheeses, their use is prohibited.*

*The way in which the curds are cut varies enormously. Soft cheese curds tend to be cut into larger pieces and are allowed to drain naturally. Hard cheeses are cut into small pieces and pressed or heated to extract the maximum whey.*

*The final cheese is pressed, salted and formed into shape, but some cheeses aren't pressed and the amount of salt used varies. Crusts will be formed in different ways and the cheese may be immersed in brine, alcohol or spices.*

## MATURATION

*The maturation period is the point at which cheese gains its character. Some cheeses are left to ripen for a few weeks; others for a year. Cheeses may be inoculated with spores to develop veins on the inside (such as blue-vein cheese) or sprayed with surface bacteria to produce bloomy mould (Camembert and Brie cheeses). Washed-rind cheeses (Livarot) often have their surfaces treated with a 'bacterial broth', which encourages a layer of bacteria to grow on the surface. During the maturation period, the cheese rind is formed either naturally or artificially.*

*A selection of goat's cheeses*

### Appellation d'origine contrôlée

The French *appellation d'origine contrôlée* (AOC) recognizes and controls the production of many foods, including dairy products such as butter and cheese. The AOC is regulated by laws, which ensure that high-quality products are produced following strictly governed methods of production. There are over 30 French cheeses that have been granted AOC status and these include Brie de Meaux, Brie de Melun, Livarot and Roquefort. Italian cheeses such as mozzarella and Parmesan are subject to similar controls in Italy.

## RIPENESS

*Pre-packed (shrink-wrapped) cheese or cheese packed in containers will have a 'best before' or 'use-by' date (expiry date) or 'sell-by' date (pull date). It is assumed that, in the right conditions, the cheese will continue to mature up until the 'use-by' date and from then on it will start to deteriorate. The 'sell-by' date is rather more arbitrary and may mean that the cheese will keep for a few more days or a few more weeks—it just has to have been sold by that date. When buying packaged cheese, check the date to make sure it will be ready on the day you want it. This means that in supermarkets you may have to buy your cheese some days in advance and mature it yourself. Specialized cheese shops will look after the maturing process and will sell you cheese for the day you want to eat it. As a general rule, add at least one week to a sell-by date. Experiment, but you can usually save money and get more mature cheeses by buying special offers after the use-by date has expired.*

## STORAGE

*Cheese is a living substance ('milk's leap to immortality') and should be stored carefully until eaten. It needs humidity, yet it must not get wet. Never freeze cheese, store it in a box (not sealed) in the vegetable crisper.*

*Never store cheese wrapped in clingfilm. If you buy it packed in this, remove it immediately, and wrap it in waxed paper, aluminium foil or in a cloth cheese bag. If the cheese comes properly wrapped by the cheesemaker, use that wrapping.*

*Washed-rind cheeses should be wrapped and kept in cool, damp humid conditions. Blue cheese can be stored at colder temperatures than other cheeses, preferably wrapped in wax paper, and must not touch other foods. Store cut hard cheeses (Cheddar) and grain cheeses (Parmesan) in a cloth cheese bag, or cover the cut surfaces (never the rind) with waxed paper or foil.*

*Store fresh cheese at cooler temperatures (about 4°C), but try to eat these soon after buying them.*

*Unripe*  *Medium*  *Very ripe*

A cheeseboard showing a selection of different styles of cheeses (clockwise from left): goat's cheese, semi-soft cheese, soft-rind cheese, blue cheese, hard cheese.

## SERVING CHEESE

*Always serve cheese at room temperature, so take it from the fridge a minimum of 4 hours before serving.*

*Keep cheeseboards simple and don't clutter with too many accompaniments. Choose a crisp pear, some muscatels, or a slice of candied citron, one good bread and not too many cheeses.*

Different countries categorize their cheese in different ways. French cheeses are categorized according to their method of production, type of rind and who produced them. Italian cheeses are categorized by their milk first, then by consistency and methods of production. Because of the different methods of classification, the cheeses below are classed into families—they taste, behave and look similar and can be used interchangeably in recipes.

## NATURAL RIND

Rinds vary from a young, wrinkled cream colour to a mature, blueish-grey. They are mostly goat's cheeses such as *crottin de chavignol*.

*Goat's cheese (natural rind)*

## DOUBLE AND TRIPLE CREAMS

These have been enriched with cream during their production. Double creams have a fat content of 60 per cent, triple creams have 75 per cent. Cheeses include Petit Suisse, Boursault, Jindi, Brillat-Savarin Blue Castello and Bavarian Blue.

*St Andre (triple cream)*

## HARD CHEESE

These have a thick rind, which may be waxed or wrapped in cloth and a hard, matured pâte. Textures vary greatly. Cheeses include Cheddar, Parmesan, Grana Padano, Emmental, Cantal, Gruyère, Chesire, Manchego, Leicester, Wensleydale, Sapsago and Pecorino.

*Cheddar (hard)*

*Mature Cheddar (hard)*

*Fontina (semi-soft)*

*Top Paddock (washed rind)*

*Cheddar (smoked)*

*Hunter Valley Gold (washed rind)*

*Raclette (semi-soft)*

## SEMI-SOFT CHEESE

These have an elastic, rubbery texture and buttery flavour. Their rind varies in colour from pinkish brown to grey. Some are wax covered. Cheeses include Fontina, Raclette, Edam, Jack and Taleggio.

## WASHED-RIND CHEESE

These are washed with saline or alcohol as they mature. This removes any grey mould and encourages the growth of an orange sticky bacteria that helps mature the pâte from the outside. These cheeses are often smelly and have a strong flavour. They include Epoisses, Livarot, Munster, Maroilles, Limburger and Gubeen.

*Bavarian smoked cheese*

## SMOKED CHEESES

These may include varieties such as Cheddar, which are treated with flavouring. Other cheeses include Applewood and smoked mozzarella.

## GOAT'S AND EWE'S MILK CHEESES

Available in a variety of shapes and sizes such as pyramids, cones and cylinders. The goat or sheep flavour can be mild or pronounced depending on how long they have been aged. These cheeses may be classed under other categories—feta is a fresh cheese and many goat's cheeses have natural rinds. Chèvre is the term for fresh goat's cheese.

*Marinated feta (ewe's cheese)*

*Pouligny St Pierre (goat's cheese)*

*Chèvre frais (fresh goat's cheese)*

*Pepper Cheddar (flavoured)*

*Herb Cheddar (flavoured)*

## FLAVOURED CHEESES

These are cheeses that have their natural flavours enhanced by the addition of a variety of herbs and spices. They include Sage Derby and Pecorino Pepato.

## WHEY CHEESES

Made from the whey left behind when curds are drained. Ricotta is made by heating whey and adding a coagulant to make a cheese that is similar to fresh cheeses like cottage cheese. Gjetost is made by boiling the whey to produce a thick, caramel-like substance.

*Ricotta (whey)*

*St Andre (soft rind)*

*L'edel de Cleron (soft rind)*

## BLUE CHEESES

Characterized by blue or green mould in the pâte. Some have a grey rind. All but a very few naturally blue cheeses, such as 'Cabrales', are internally ripened after they are innoculated with a *Penicillium* spore. They vary from hard to crumbly or soft. Cheeses include Roquefort, Stilton, Gorgonzola, Bresse Bleu and Dolcelatte.

*Gorgonzola (blue)*

*Forme d'Ambert (blue)*

*Brie (soft rind)*

*Camembert (soft rind)*

## SOFT-RIND CHEESE (BLOOMY OR FLOWERY RIND)

These have white mould growth, which may be speckled with red, yellow, pink or grey on their rinds and a creamy smooth pâte that bulges when ripe. Cheeses include Brie, Camembert, Bonchester, Coulommiers and Chaource. Some blue cheeses also fit into this category but are listed under blue cheese.

### THREE-CHEESE MACARONI

*Boil 200 g macaroni until tender and then drain. Melt 20 g butter in a saucepan and stir in 20 g plain flour. Cook for 2 minutes, then gradually add 400 ml milk, stirring until it boils. Simmer for 3 minutes, stirring constantly. Stir in 100 g grated Cheddar and 1 teaspoon Dijon mustard until the cheese has melted. Season well. Add the cheese sauce to the macaroni and stir in 100 g cubed Fontina cheese. Pour into a baking dish. Sprinkle over 2 teaspoons breadcrumbs and 1 tablespoon grated Parmesan and grill until the top browns. Serves 2.*

#### Low-fat cheese

These are traditional-style cheeses that are made to have a lower fat content (not to be confused with cheeses like Parmesan, made with skimmed milk). As fat is important to texture and flavour, low-fat cheeses are often not as rounded as full-fat cheeses.

#### Curd cheese and cream cheese

Any cheese made from fresh, unfermented curds, such as the German Quark or the French fromage frais. Cottage cheese is made from unpressed curds and has a different texture. Quark is made from skim milk and has virtually no taste. Spiesequark is quark with added cream. Quark is often used to make cheesecake in the UK. Fromage frais is made from pasteurized skimmed cow's milk. Mascarpone is a soft fresh cheese made with cream to which citric or tartaric acid is added.

### COOKING

*If using cheese in quiches or other egg mixtures, grate it finely. As cheese melts it gives off oil and finely grated cheese will distribute the oil better throughout the mixture. Similarly, grill cheese under a very hot heat so it melts quickly without oozing too much oil.*

*If cheese becomes too hot, it becomes stringy and separates.*

*When making cheese sauce always add the cheese off the heat and don't reheat it again or the sauce will go stringy.*

*You can substitute cheeses: if you can't get Fontina, use another good melting cheese, like Raclette.*

### ROQUEFORT SOUFFLES

*Melt 30 g butter in a saucepan and stir in 30 g plain flour. Cook for 2 minutes, then gradually add 250 ml milk, stirring until boiled. Simmer for 3 minutes, stirring. Stir in 125 g chopped Roquefort cheese until melted. Whisk in 4 egg yolks, one at a time, beating well after each addition. Season with nutmeg, salt and pepper. Whisk 4 egg whites until medium peaks form. Lightly fold ¼ of the egg whites into the mixture, then fold in the remaining egg whites. Pour into 6 x 200 ml soufflé dishes and bake for 25 minutes at 200°C, or until the soufflés are well risen and golden brown. The centres should be soft and creamy. Serve immediately. Serves 6.*

Cheesecakes are one of the earliest baked desserts and it is thought that the ancient Romans were the first to bake cheese into small cakes. It was the Americans who developed one of the versions popular today—a pastry or biscuit crumb filled with a creamy cheese (usually cream, cottage or ricotta cheese) and egg mixture. The New York cheesecake, one of the most famous versions, is made with cream cheese and cream or sour cream and is the richest, densest version. In Italy, cheesecakes are a popular dessert, and are usually made with sweetened ricotta cheese.

Usually cheesecakes are baked, but sometimes gelatine is added to the mixture and the cheesecake is left to set in the fridge. Before the cheesecake is set, it may be flavoured with cocoa, fruit purée or caramel, or fruit such as pears, apples or berries may be added.

### COOKING

*The different cheeses used in cheesecake recipes have varying moisture and fat contents and are not interchangeable. Using the wrong kind of cheese may result in a cheesecake that separates or sinks.*

*Cool cheesecake in the oven with the door slightly ajar. If cheesecake is cooled too quickly, the top may crack.*

*When cutting cheesecake, dip the knife in hot water, then dry it: it will then be easier to cut it without the cheese sticking to the knife.*

## chef's salad

A chef's salad, as the name suggests, is a creation of the person who made it. Originally the name meant that a chef could experiment with different flavours and combinations and a chef's salad should be a good mix of delicious things. Sadly, chef's salad has also become the name for a rather uninspiring mixed salad—not at all the spirit in which it was intended.

*This chef's salad is made using lettuce, tomato, egg, chicken and cheese.*

## Chelsea bun

A Chelsea bun is a sweet bun made using a rectangle of sweetened yeasted dough that is covered with butter, currants and brown sugar and rolled up. The roll is sliced and the coils are packed flat on a tray. When baked, the bun is glazed with milk and sugar syrup and sprinkled with sugar. These buns date back to the late seventeenth century, where they were first made at the Chelsea Bun House in London.

## chermoula

The recipe for chermoula, a Moroccan marinade for fish, varies from region to region, but usually includes herbs such as parsley, basil or coriander; spices such as cumin, coriander, paprika and cayenne pepper; onions or garlic; lemon and oil. The fish, either whole fillets or pieces, is left to marinate overnight, then may be fried, grilled or baked. Chermoula can also be used as a relish or dressing and may be served with meat, vegetables or fish.

See also **Moroccan food**

### CHERMOULA

*Mix 6 tablespoons olive oil with 2 crushed garlic cloves, a pinch of cayenne, 1 teaspoon paprika, 2 teaspoons cumin, ¼ teaspoon salt, 2 tablespoons lemon juice and 25 g finely chopped coriander leaves. Brush over fish fillets or chicken breasts and leave to marinate for 1–2 hours, or overnight. Makes enough marinade for 4 pieces of fish or chicken.*

## cherries

Cherries are a glossy deep-red stone fruit, related to the plum, peach and apricot. There are over 1,000 varieties, which can be broadly grouped into three types: sweet, sour and hybrids. Sweet cherries can be eaten raw or cooked, and include Napoleon, Bing and Rainier. Sour cherries are usually cooked in pies or added to jams, liqueurs or used as an accompaniment to savoury dishes, and include the Morello and Montmorency. Hybrids such as Duke cherries (called *Royale* in France), can be used for both eating and cooking.

Buy cherries with their stems on and use any without their stems first as they don't last as long. The stems should be soft and pliable: brown, brittle stems indicate the cherries are old. Store sweet cherries in the fridge for up to a week; sour cherries will keep for several weeks. Cherries also make excellent preserves and freeze well. Maraschino cherries are pitted and soaked in a flavoured sugar syrup (originally maraschino liqueur was used), then dyed red or green. They are used to decorate desserts, in fruit salads or as a garnish for cocktails.

## chestnuts

A sweet nut cultivated in Europe, Asia and the United States. Roasted in the shell, chestnuts are a traditional cold weather treat (the shell must be pierced first or it will explode). The kernels can be simmered in stock and served as a vegetable; puréed in soups; used in the stuffing for roast turkey; added to cakes and mousses; sweetened and mixed with cream; or crystallized with sugar (*marrons glacés*). Buy chestnuts with firm, shiny shells and discard any that are wrinkled or dull. Chestnut flour is used extensively in some regions of Italy and France.

### COOKING

*To peel chestnuts, make a slit in each chestnut and put the nuts in a saucepan of boiling water for 5 minutes. Cool slightly and peel off the outer husks. Put the husked chestnuts in cold water and bring the water to the boil. Simmer gently until the inner skin loosens, then drain and rub the chestnuts in a tea towel while still hot to remove the rest of the skin. Take care with this as the chestnuts will be very hot.*

Before intensive farming techniques took over in the 1970s, chicken meat had more flavour and texture, and was considered a luxury. For some time, most chicken meat sold has ranged from tasteless (and possibly dangerous) to just edible. However, more recently, consumer agitation has gradually changed the industry, and more humanely farmed chicken is finding its way onto the market. A chicken that scratches around for its food is a happier, healthier animal than a battery bird, and yields more flavoursome and better textured meat. You can now buy free-range, open-range, corn-fed and organically farmed chickens in most outlets.

## BUYING

*Make sure the chicken looks and smells fresh. The limbs and skin should be undamaged and plump looking. Frozen chicken should not have ice within its packaging as this is a sign it may have defrosted slightly and then refrozen.*

## STORAGE

*Chicken wrapped in plastic should be unwrapped, wiped with paper towel, placed in a shallow dish and covered. If roasting the chicken, leave uncovered for an hour before cooking to dry out the skin (it will crisp better when cooked). If you buy a whole chicken with giblets, remove them before storing.*

*Store on the bottom shelf of the fridge and eat within 3 days.*

*Before cooking, completely defrost frozen chicken in the fridge or a cool place—this can take hours so always check the central cavity for signs of ice. Dry thoroughly and cook as soon as it is defrosted.*

### Roasting

Trim the chicken of any extra fat, truss (tie) its legs together and tuck its wings back under the body. Trussing the chicken helps it to keep its shape and stops its legs springing out. For even roasting, start breast side down, then do each side and finish with it on its back. Baste as often as you can, brushing the bird with the juices. When the chicken is ready, the juices from the cavity will be clear, the flesh just pulling away from the drumstick and the skin crisp and golden. If in any doubt, push a skewer into the thigh—these juices should also be clear. There should be no pinkness when the flesh is carved. Cover with foil to keep warm while making gravy. Roasting times and temperatures vary but generally a chicken to feed four (1.5–2 kg) will take 1 hour in an oven preheated to 200°C.

## JOINTING A CHICKEN

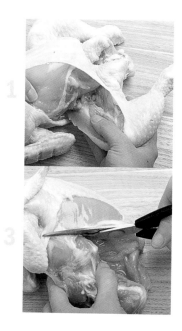

1  Pull the legs from the body and cut at the thigh joints. Ease the oyster from the carcass and leave it attached to the thigh.

2  Cut the legs in half through the thigh and drumstick joint.

3  Cut around the edge of the breast where there is a break in the ribcage and remove the bottom half of the carcass.

4  Cut the breast in half down the centre. Cut diagonally across each breast so some breast meat is attached to each wing.

## TYPES OF CHICKENS

**Chicken**
The most common variety, these are sold drawn, plucked and ready to cook, and may be whole or jointed. Allow 350–400 g per person.

**Poussin**
Baby chickens sold in single or double portion sizes. They benefit from stuffing or marinating and are good grilled.

**Bantam**
Miniature breed of hen. Usually bred for their eggs.

**Boiling fowl**
Older birds that have stopped laying and can be used for slow cooking, stocks and soups.

**Corn, grain or maize fed**
These have been fed a diet of corn and have a yellow skin. Corn-fed does not mean free-range, but some are. This type may be confused with less common breeds of chicken that also have a yellowish skin.

**Free-range**
Free-range can mean a life of complete freedom in a farm yard to statutory amounts of days the birds must roam free, or life in a barn. Laws vary locally.

**Poulet de Bresse**
A particular breed of French chicken with a superior flavour and texture. Sold packaged under its name.

**Cornish hens**
Has a prominent breast and a good covering of meat. Originated in Cornwall but bred mainly in the USA.

*Chicken pieces stuffed with herb butter and whole sage leaves under the skin.*

### Stuffing

To stuff under the skin, gently ease the skin from the chicken breast with your fingers and fill with the stuffing at the neck end only, smooth back the skin and massage the stuffing into place. Cavity stuffing is not recommended unless the stuffing is very well cooked through and this may mean the breast gets too dry. If you do wish to stuff the cavity, dry it well and make sure the chicken is cooked straight away so the stuffing doesn't have time to soak up any raw juices.

*See also* **coq au vin, spatchcock, stock**

## COOKING

*Whole chickens* – These can be roasted, poached, pot-roasted, braised, stuffed or coated with a wet or dry marinade or salt crust. Whole birds can also be spatchcocked, which makes them easier to grill or barbecue.

*Breast meat* – Tends to be dry and is best cooked in a way that will keep it moist such as poaching, grilling with the skin on, or roasting at a high heat. The breast can be slit open and stuffed, rolled around fillings, wrapped in spinach, ham or pastry, or cut into strips and cubes. Breasts on the bone with the skin on retain their moisture better than those without skin. When using boneless breasts, remove any shiny white sinew from the underside.

*Thighs* – Moist, dark meat, perfect in curries, stews and casseroles. Can be marinated and barbecued or grilled. Thighs can be boned out and rolled around fillings or cut into pieces. The skin can be quite fatty so either remove it or trim it very well.

*Legs* – Best roasted, barbecued or grilled. Use in stews and casseroles or as finger food. They are excellent when marinated in robust flavours.

*Wings* – Good for finger food, especially marinated and grilled or dusted with flour and deep-fried. In Chinese cuisine, wings are also boned and stuffed.

*Chicken mince* – Use as you would beef mince, but as chicken flesh is drier with less fat, it benefits from being flavoured well and cooked in a less dry heat.

**chickpea** — see pulses

Not one but a group of leafy vegetables cultivated from European wild chicory, all of which share differing degrees of bitterness. They vary from long-leafed varieties (like frisée) through the various radicchios to the witloof (Belgian) types, tightly curled and usually, like its close relative endive, blanched (grown in the dark) to control the bitterness. Chicory is good in salads and the furled variety can be grilled, braised in stock and caramelized.

Cook chicory in stock until tender, drain well, then barbecue or grill it until browned and caramelized, or fill a cooked pastry case with chicory cooked in stock and drained, sprinkle with blue cheese, drizzle with cream and cook until heated through. All types of chicory can be used as salad leaves but bear in mind their bitterness and use in moderation.

Buy tightly furled pale chicory (green chicory will be bitter) that is undamaged and crisp. Chicory heads are called chicons and they are very sensitive to light, which makes them bitter when exposed to it. Chicory is therefore usually sold wrapped in purple paper. To store, leave them in their paper or put in a brown paper bag.

**Chicory goes with — blue cheese, butter, game, olives, orange, red meat**

### BRAISED CHICORY

*Lay 1 chicon (chicory head) per person in a buttered gratin dish that will hold them snugly. Pour over chicken stock until it comes a quarter of the way up the chicory, season well and add 1 teaspoon brown sugar and a squeeze of orange juice. Cover and bake in a 180°C oven for 20 minutes. Remove the cover and return to the oven for another 15–20 minutes. Drizzle with some cream and sprinkle with chopped parsley.*

### TYPES OF CHICORY

*Chicory*

| | |
|---|---|
| **Chicory** | Also known as Belgian endive, Brussels chicory or witloof, this is a blanched, tightly furled spear-shaped chicon. It is slightly bitter and eaten raw or cooked. |

*Radicchio*

| | |
|---|---|
| **Radicchio** | The Italian name for red chicory. There are several varieties, but two of the most common sold in Italy are *rosso di Verona*, a pink, flower-like chicory that looks similar to a round cabbage and is usually called radicchio in other countries, and *rossa di Treviso*, deep red and creamy streaked and usually called red chicory elsewhere. Red chicory is not as bitter as white, and it adds wonderful colour to salads. Sauté lightly in olive oil and balsamic vinegar. |
| **Frisée** | Loose, open leaves with crisp, almost scratchy leaves. Has a bitter flavour and bulks up salads well. |
| **Escarole** | Escarole has a head of loose or red-tinged leaves. The least bitter tasting type of chicory. |

*Frisée*

*Various methods can be used for measuring the heat in chillies including the Scoville scale, which ranges from grade 0 (sweet pepper) to 300,000 (habanero), or a simple 1–10 used by many supermarkets (and used here). None are completely accurate, as chillies vary quite considerably, even those on the same bush.*

*Ancho chilli*

*Banana chilli*

*Cascabel chilli*

Chillies belong to the *Capsicum* family (the sweeter peppers are not included here) and are native to South and Central America. Chillies were taken by the Spanish and Portuguese to southern Italy, India and Southeast Asia, where they became integrated into local diets. Chillies are not merely hot, each has its own flavour and varies in its degree of 'hotness' and in countries that use a lot of chilli in their cooking, it is important to have the right chilli for each dish. Dried and fresh chillies also taste very different; a smooth, smoky flavouring gained from dried Mexican chillies cannot be achieved with fresh chillies.

## TYPES OF CHILLIES

| | |
|---|---|
| **Anaheim (2)** | Come in green and red and have a mild, sweet flavour. Used to make rellenos and also in soups and stews. |
| **Ancho (3)** | A dried poblano chilli, dark red and mildly sweet. Used widely in Mexican cuisine, often with mulato and pasilla to form the 'Holy Trinity' of chillies used in mole sauces. |
| **Banana (2)** | These are mild and sweet large, long chillies, creamy yellow or orange red in colour. Use split in half and grilled. Also called Hungarian wax peppers. |
| **Caribe (2)** | A medium to mild chilli, pale green or yellow in colour, with a sweet edge. Can be used raw in salads and salsas. |
| **Cascabel (4)** | Small, plum-shaped chilli sold dried. It is named for the rattling sound it makes. Reconstitute and use chopped in salsas, or in soups and stews. |
| **Dutch (6)** | Bright red with a long tapering shape and thick flesh. Use where red chilli is called for. |
| **Fresno (6)** | A small, stubby cone-shaped green or red chilli, which should be hot but is often fairly mild. |
| **Habanero (10)** **Scotch bonnet (10)** | Very similar chillies. Look like a mini pepper and can be green, red or orange. They are very, very hot but with a good, slightly acidic flavour. Use in salsas and marinades. |
| **Jalapeño (5)** | Oval-shaped chilli with thick, juicy flesh and a wheel shape when sliced. Very hot if seeds and septa are used. Ripens to red and when dried is called chipotle. |
| **Pasilla (3–4)** | A dried black chilli often used in mole. |
| **Pepperoncini (4–5)** | From south Italy, sweet and mildly hot, and usually available dried. Crumble into pasta sauces and stews. |
| **Poblano (3)** | Dark green, almost black, long chilli, with thick flesh that ripens to red. Dried versions are mulato and ancho. |
| **Serrano (7)** | A common Mexican chilli, cylindrical in shape, red or green, and often used in salsas or pickled. |
| **Thai (8)** | Also called bird's eye chillies, these are tiny, either red or green, and very hot. Use in Thai curries or sliced raw onto Asian salads. |

*Habanero*

*Pasilla chilli*

*Serrano chilli*

*Thai chilli*

### Capsaicin

Chillies are hot because they contain an irritant alkaloid, a potent chemical that acts directly on the pain receptors in the throat and mouth to produce a burning sensation. The body reacts by secreting endorphins—these are natural painkillers that cause a physical 'high', thought to account for the addictiveness of eating chillies. Capsaicin is primarily found in the ribs (septa) and seeds of the chilli and is released when cut. Capsaicin is not very soluble in water (water does little to extinguish the heat) but is soluble in oil and alcohol (this is why milk, yoghurt and beer are good relief from the heat of curries).

### BUYING

*Buy chillies that are uniform in colour and unbroken or the essential oils will be lost. Fresh chillies will be slightly flexible.*

### COOKING

*When cutting chillies either wear rubber gloves or be very careful— don't put your hands near your face and wash your hands after handling them. Chilli oil remains on your skin for some time. If you do get chilli burn, run your hands under cold water and rub them against a stainless steel surface (the sink) or soak in milk. If you burn your mouth, eat dairy products or starchy foods.*

*Chilli will have different effects and flavours if used raw, roasted or dried. Mexican recipes usually call for the skin to be removed after roasting as it can be bitter. Roasting also gives a smoky flavour to the flesh. Drying chillies intensifies the flavour. These are often roasted before soaking to reconstitute them (be careful not to burn them when you roast them).*

*Cooking a whole chilli in a dish rather than chopping it will contain the heat somewhat. If in doubt about how hot your chilli is, use less than the recipe specifies: you can always add more. If the dish is too hot, add yoghurt, coconut milk or cream.*

### CHILLI CON QUESO

*Seed 1 ancho or pasilla chilli and flatten into one piece. Gently fry on both sides in 1 tablespoon oil, then allow to cool and crispen. Break the chilli into small pieces. Add 250 ml sour cream to the pan and cook for 2 minutes. Add 100 g cubed Cheddar, stir until melted, then add the chilli. Serve with corn chips. Serves 4.*

### CUTTING CHILLIES

1. *Wearing rubber gloves, carefully cut the chillies in half and scrape out any seeds.*

2. *Cut away any septa (fleshy membrane), then chop or slice the chillies.*

### RELLENOS

*Put 6 anaheim, or other large sweet chillies, under the grill and cook, turning, until the skin begins to bubble. Remove skin, cut a slit down one side and remove seeds. Combine 100 g grated Cheddar, 75 g finely chopped red pepper, 2 tablespoons each finely chopped onion and chopped coriander, a pinch of cayenne and ¼ ancho chilli, finely chopped. Stuff the chillies with this mixture, dip in beaten egg, then cornmeal. Tie up with string and chill for 20 minutes. Dip in cornmeal again, then deep-fry for 3–4 minutes. Serves 6.*

■ *See also* **Mexican food, pepper**

# Chinese food

A huge country, with vast geographic and climactic variation and a large population to feed, China has one of the great cuisines of the world, and eating plays a major role in daily life, rituals and festivities. As China has relatively little fertile land, the Chinese utilize everything edible, and this is one of the bases of the genius of Chinese cuisine. Fresh ingredients are all important, and despite regional variations, there is a unity to all Chinese cooking based on a trinity of ginger, spring onions and garlic. Rice was cultivated in China 3,000 years before it spread out of China and Chinese tea has spread around the world, while the regionality of certain ingredients has led to a very varied cuisine. All Chinese cooking strives for a balance between opposites: sweet and sour, hot and cold, plain and spicy—the yin and yang principle from Taoism. Preserving is also an important culinary art in China and along with preserved meat and fish, pickled fruit, vegetables and sauces are used daily by Chinese chefs.

The four pillars of Chinese regional cooking are classic Beijing, spicy Sichuan, delicate Guangzhou and rich Shanghai.

Immigration led to a hybrid western-Chinese food. The first Chinese restaurants abroad were mostly set up by Cantonese immigrants, who, though not usually professional chefs, took the freshness and balance of Cantonese cuisine to produce food that made use of the ingredients that were available to them. Adapted dishes include chow mein, chop suey and sweet and sour pork.

*Fish steamed with ginger and spring onion is cooked all over China. Some versions have chicken stock poured on just before serving.*

*Minced pigeon served in lettuce leaves, sometimes called san choy bau.*

## GUANGZHOU

The food of Guangzhou (Canton) is renowned worldwide as the best regional food in China, and gentle climate and coastal geography provide a base of the freshest and most varied ingredients. Guangzhou abounds in highly trained chefs who insist on the highest quality, freshest vegetables, fruit and seafood, which they transform with ingenuity, simplicity and faithfulness to original flavours. The Cantonese cook simply with ginger and spring onions, but also use a variety of spicy or fragrant condiments, always adhering to the rules for the combination of flavours. Guangzhou, with its long coastline, is famed for its simple seafood dishes, made with seafood picked live from the tank in many restaurants, and pork, the standard meat, marinated, barbecued and glazed. Dim sum takes the bite-sized snack to new culinary heights. Chiu Chow and Hokkien cooking are all important regional elements of Southern cooking, while the southwest of China has the most varied mix of ethnic minorities in China, with goat's cheese and the Muslim influences evident in the use of goat meat and dried beef.

*Congee is a southern Chinese breakfast or supper dish of rice boiled with salt and water. Savoury toppings are sprinkled in.*

## SICHUAN

This fertile bowl in the centre of China is famous for its spicy cuisine. Over 2,000 years ago, Buddhist traders and missionaries brought Indian spices and cooking techniques to Sichuan, leaving a legacy of imaginative vegetarian cooking. Sichuan also has ancient links to the peoples of Thailand and Indochina. Ginger, garlic, vinegar, spring onions and black bean sauce are all important, along with red oil and the various hot bean pastes. Spring onions, garlic, peppercorns, ginger, sesame oil and vinegar are the spicy flavourings used over beans and bean curd, vegetables, mushrooms and bamboo; chilli is widely used, dried whole or ground to powder; and Sichuan pepper adds aroma as well as heat. Neighbouring Hunan is also noted for its chilli cuisine, though not all dishes in either province are spicy, and plates of cold meats are often served.

*Dan dan mian are spicy noodles with chilli and minced pork, sold as street food in Sichuan.*

*Ma po dofu is a classic dish of spicy bean curd made with the red chillies of Sichuan.*

## BEIJING

A rich and fascinating cuisine based on grains—especially wheat—turnips and cabbage. Beijing food is also a fusion of delicacies from the kitchens of the emperors and hearty peasant food, geographically arising in a region of long harsh winters and short scorching summers. Muslim influence can be seen in the use of mutton, and beef and Mongolian hotpot and barbecue are common. Salty soy sauce, spring onions and garlic are important flavours, while Peking duck is perhaps the most emblematic dish. Steamed buns, wheat noodles, pancakes and dumplings are staple foods—rice won't grow in the harsh northern climate.

*In the North, wheat is the staple grain and dumplings are sold on every street. These jiaozi are made with pork and cabbage.*

*Shanghainese red cooking uses Shaoxing wine and light and dark soy sauces of the region. Here the meat is pork.*

## SHANGHAI

The fertile plains of the Yangtze Delta, with Shanghai at its centre, is the home of eastern cuisine. Shanghai has its own characteristic dishes, influenced from all over China through its port. Braising (or red cooking) is a distinctive feature, using soy, Shaoxing wine and sugar with ginger and green onion, often with tangerine peel and fennel as seasoning. The meat thus treated takes on a glazed, reddish-brown colour. Seafood is important, as is the freshwater hairy crab and carp from the local lakes. Shanghai dumplings are a speciality.

# chips

## MAKING PERFECT CHIPS

*Chips need to be blanched at a low temperature to cook the inside, then cooked at a high temperature to brown the outside. To make chips, wash the potatoes and pat dry. Cut into 1 cm wide chips, ensuring they are equal in size so they cook evenly. Rinse or soak in cold water for 10 minutes to wash off the starch. This will stop them sticking and will make the outside crispy. Dry thoroughly or the water will make the oil spit. Cook in batches at 160°C for 4–5 minutes, then remove from the oil; drain. Heat the oil to 190°C and cook again to brown. Drain and sprinkle with salt to soak up excess oil.*

Batons of deep-fried potato. The best potatoes to use are floury or all-purpose varieties such as King Edward, Maris Piper, Sebago, Spunta and Russet (Idaho), as they give a fluffy inside with a golden, crisp outside. Don't stack just-cooked chips, or they'll go soggy. Keep in a warm oven in one layer.

*From left: French fries, chips, shoe-string fries.*

## TYPES OF CHIPS

**Chips** — Roughly finger thick in England and Australia.

**French fries** — In America, chips are known as French fries and French fry is the term used for deep-fat frying. French fries are called *pommes frites* in France. Usually cut into thinner slices, about 5 mm wide, and deep-fried until crisp and brown.

**Shoe-string fries** — Similar to French fries, but these are longer and skinnier.

**Matchstick potatoes** — These are also known as *pommes allumettes*. They are matchstick-thin chips and often used as a garnish.

**Game chips** — Look like crisps, made from thin discs of potato deep-fried in oil until brown and crunchy and served as a garnish for game.

**Oven chips** — Most chips are deep-fried, but these are baked in the oven as a low-fat alternative to deep-fried chips.

*Oven chips*

# chives

Related to the onion and leek, chives are a herb with long, thin hollow leaves that have a mild onion flavour. Chives also produce a delicate lavender flower, which can be eaten but is mainly used for decoration. Chives can be snipped to length with scissors and used to garnish soups and salads. They can be used as decorative ties, and are easier to handle if briefly blanched first. If using in hot dishes, add at the end of cooking to preserve their flavour. Chives are best picked and used when fresh, but can be stored in the vegetable crisper in the fridge for up to 2 days. Garlic chives have flat, dark leaves and a mild garlic taste. Use in stir-fries, minced in stuffings or as a decoration for soups. Bundles can be blanched and dressed with oyster sauce and served as a vegetable.

**Chives go with — butter, cheese, cream, egg, fish**

**Garlic chives are also known as — Chinese chives**

*Flowering chives*

*Chives*

*Garlic chives*

To make chocolate, cocoa beans are roasted, then cracked and husked (winnowed) to expose the nibs, which are ground with water until they become cocoa liquor (mass). Squeeze this mass further and you get cocoa butter and a paste that when dried is cocoa powder. For high-quality chocolate, it is ground again and put in a conching machine with other ingredients for up to 72 hours. This process mixes, stirs, grinds and blends all the ingredients (cocoa liquor, cocoa butter, sugar, lecithin and perhaps vanilla or other flavours). This mixture is then tempered to ensure a smooth consistency. Good-quality chocolate contains at least 50 per cent cocoa liquor, and does not contain vegetable fats.

### Couverture (coating or dipping) chocolate

Has a higher percentage of cocoa butter and is not as stable as dark chocolate, so it needs to be tempered before use. Used mainly by the catering industry as it melts and coats easily, has a glossy finish and an intense chocolate flavour.

### White chocolate

Made from cocoa butter and milk solids, it is not strictly chocolate as it doesn't contain cocoa liquor. Needs to be treated with more care as it will seize more easily than dark chocolate. It is not always interchangeable in recipes.

### Compound (baking) chocolate

Usually contains vegetable fat instead of cocoa butter and doesn't have the same depth of flavour or body as dark chocolate. Because it doesn't need to be tempered to make it stable it is often used for chocolate decorations.

### Dark (plain), semi-sweet and bitter-sweet chocolate

These have vanilla, sugar and cocoa butter added to them. Their sugar content varies slightly, but they are interchangeable in recipes. Good-quality chocolate is glossy, smooth and slightly red in colour. It snaps cleanly, melts easily, has a sweet, fruity smell, and real flavours (vanilla, nutmeg) are used to make it.

### Milk chocolate

Has milk solids added to it. It is sweet and creamy and not as intensely chocolate flavoured as dark chocolate.

## CHOCOLATE MOUSSE

*Chop 110 g dark chocolate and melt, as shown in the steps below. Separate 4 eggs and stir the chocolate into the egg yolks. Whisk the egg whites until stiff peaks form, then fold into the chocolate mixture carefully. Chill overnight. Serves 6.*

**Chocolate goes with — coffee, game, liqueurs, mint, orange, vanilla**

*See also* **carob, cocoa**

## TEMPERING CHOCOLATE

*Cocoa butter is made up of several fats that melt and set at different temperatures. Chocolate is tempered to stabilize these fats—this also gives moulded or dipped chocolate a lovely shiny surface and ensures that it sets properly. The tempering process is done by heating and cooling the chocolate to exact temperatures—a process usually too complicated to do at home. But there is a quick method that helps stabilize the chocolate before use. Grate the chocolate and melt two-thirds of it. When the chocolate is melted, stir in the remaining chocolate in batches until it melts. The chocolate should now be tempered and its temperature about 31–32°C (88–90°F) for dark chocolate and 29–31°C (85–88°F) for milk chocolate.*

*Use melted chocolate to make moulds or leaves by painting the chocolate onto a leaf or into a paper cup. Leave to dry and then peel off.*

## MELTING CHOCOLATE

*When melting chocolate, always use a clean, dry bowl. Water or moisture will make chocolate seize (turn into a thick mass that won't melt) and overheating will make it scorch and taste bitter. If the chocolate does seize, add a few drops of vegetable oil or shortening and stir until smooth.*

1 *Chop the chocolate finely and put it in a heatproof bowl set over a saucepan of barely simmering water.*

2 *Leave the chocolate to soften, then stir until smooth. Don't let water or steam get in the bowl or the chocolate will seize.*

3 *Remove chocolate from the saucepan to cool, or leave in place if you want to keep the chocolate liquid.*

**c h o k o** — **s e e   c h r i s t o p h i n e**

Choux pastry is unlike other pastry in that the dough is cooked twice. Making choux is an exact process; weigh all the ingredients carefully and follow the instructions to the letter. Fill choux buns with cream or crème pâtissière and coat with chocolate to make profiteroles, or make éclair shapes. Choux is best eaten on the day that it is made.

See also **croquembouche, éclair, Paris-Brest**

MAKING CHOUX BUNS

1 Bring 50 g melted butter and 185 ml water to the boil. Remove from the heat and quickly beat in 90 g twice-sifted plain flour.

2 Return to the heat and beat only until the mixture leaves the side of the saucepan. Allow to cool.

3 Gradually add 3 beaten eggs, beating until the mixture is thick and glossy. You may not need all the egg.

4 Pipe the mixture onto baking trays sprinkled with a little water to create steam.

5 Neaten the buns off at the top using a damp finger.

6 Bake for 20–30 minutes at 200°C or until the buns are browned and cooked through.

7 Remove from the oven, make a small hole in the base of each, then return to the oven for 5 minutes to dry out.

8 Cool, then fill through the hole in the base using a piping bag.

# chowder

Originally, a chowder was a thick, chunky soup made with fish or shellfish, but the term is now applied to any type of rich, thick soup, with corn chowder being one of the most typical. Chowder comes from the French word 'chaudière', a cauldron used by fishermen to cook soup in. Today, chowder is popular in North America, where it is often called clam chowder. The New England version uses a milk or cream base; in Manhattan, the preference is for tomato and herbs.

# Christmas cake

Many different cakes are baked around the world to celebrate Christmas from the bûche de Noël of France to Italian panettone, all of which involve the use of a combination of ingredients like dried vine fruit, glacé cherries, nuts, candied peel, spices and alcohol. The English version is a rich, moist fruit cake, often made with brandy or rum, more of which can be poured over prior to serving, after which it is covered with a layer of marzipan, another of fondant and decorated, often with holly and ribbon.

## CHRISTMAS CAKE

*Mix 110 g glacé cherries, 850 g mixed dried fruit and 55 g chopped mixed peel with 200 ml brandy. Leave overnight. Cream 225 g butter with 225 g soft brown sugar until light and fluffy. Add 5 beaten eggs, one at a time, beating after each. Fold in 285 g plain flour, 2 teaspoons mixed spice, then add the fruit, 2 tablespoons black treacle, 1½ tablespoons grated orange zest and 110 g ground almonds. Pour into a double-lined 24 cm round cake tin with a layer of newspaper wrapped around the outside. Bake at 170°C for 2½–3 hours, or until a skewer comes out clean. Cool on a wire rack. Cover with a layer of marzipan, and then sugar paste.*

# Christmas pudding

A boiled or steamed British pudding made from flour, suet, sugar, vine fruit, spices and milk and sometimes breadcrumbs. It is best if the pudding is allowed to mature for at least 2 or 3 days, or up to 6 to 8 weeks. Traditionally, a small coin was inserted into the pudding and was a sign of good fortune for the person who received it in their bowl. Serve with brandy butter or rum sauce.

# christophine

A christophine (or christophene) is a green, pear-shaped fruit of a climbing vine. Its firm, white flesh tastes of a cucumber and apple cross and surrounds a single soft inedible seed. Christophines can be boiled, baked, fried or stuffed. They have a subtle flavour that works well with assertive accompaniments. Quarter, simmer with tomatoes, onions, garlic and herbs, or serve as a dessert, as below. To prepare, peel the skin under running water as it secretes a sticky substance.
***Also known as — chayote, choko, custard marrow, mirliton, pepinello, xuxu***

## CHRISTOPHINES IN RED WINE

*Put 500 ml quality red wine in a saucepan with 150 g sugar and a cinnamon stick and stir until dissolved. Bring to the boil, then add 500 g sliced christophines and simmer until tender. Remove from liquid, then simmer the liquid to reduce it. Serve in the syrup with cream. Serves 4.*

## churrasco

A Brazilian method of barbecuing meat, churrasco is now served in restaurants around the world. Beef, pork, sausages or chicken are placed on large skewers and cooked over coals in a pit, and each diner uses their own churrasco knife to slice off the cooked meat. Today, special barbecues are fitted with an automatic rotisserie to achieve the same effect.

## churros

Especially in Madrid, breakfast consists of an excruciatingly rich, cornflour-thickened hot chocolate with churros dunked in it. The churro is a deep-fried confection made from a light flour and water batter extruded through a ridged mould, giving it its distinctive shape. It is usually sprinkled with icing sugar, sugar or cinnamon. There is a larger form called a *porra*. Churros are also popular in Mexico.

## chutney

Derived from the Indian word '*chatni*', a spicy condiment made with vegetables or fruit cooked in vinegar, sugar and spices. They can be savoury or sweet depending on the ingredients used, which may include apples, sultanas, onions or tomatoes. Serve with hot and cold meat, curries or with bread and cheese. Fresh chutneys, the true chutneys of India, are made just before use and have a clean, fresh flavour.

## ciabatta

The Italian word for 'slipper', ciabatta (cha-baht-tah) is a flattish loaf of bread, shaped vaguely like a shoe or slipper. In Italy, recipes vary regionally. Generally, the bread is formed from a wet dough made with flour, water, milk, yeast, olive oil and *biga*, a starter dough made using a small amount of flour, water and yeast. The *biga* is left to rise overnight, and gives the bread a rich, fresh taste. To make ciabatta, the *biga* is mixed into the dough, then the dough is stretched out to form its shape and left to rise again to produce a light bread with an open, porous texture that is full of *occhi* (eyes). Smaller versions of ciabatta are called ciabatte. These are popular in Italian cafés where they are filled and eaten as sandwiches.

## cider

Cider is made by extracting the juice from a variety of apples, both sweet and sour, which is then naturally fermented in barrels or large tanks. The resulting cider is an effervescent fruity, alcoholic drink that may also be used as a cooking liquor. Cider is used in the cooking of northern France, particularly in Normandy and Brittany, and in southern England, often in recipes for fish, pork, chicken and game. Perry is a fermented drink similar to cider but made with pears. In North America, cider refers to unfermented apple juice.

SERVING SUGGESTIONS

*Add a splash of cider with a dollop of cream to fried pork chops, or to give extra flavour to gravies.*

*Simmer pieces of apple in cider until the apples are tender, then mash them to give an upmarket apple sauce.*

*Bake slices of potato in half chicken stock and half cider until tender and browned on top.*

## cioppino

Cioppino is a version of the Ligurian fish stew *ciuppin*, which originated in the bay area of San Francisco. Like bouillabaisse, it was first made by fishermen from the leftovers after their catch was sold. Cioppino is made with a variety of fish and seafood and any or all of the following ingredients: onion, tomatoes, parsley, garlic, oregano, white wine and stale Italian bread, over which the finished soup is poured.

## citron

A citrus fruit that looks similar to a large knobbly lemon, citrons are grown for their thick peel rather than their flesh, which is quite sour and inedible. Citrons grow mainly in Corsica, as well as in Greece and Italy, and were believed to have been cultivated in Egypt as early as 300 BC.

Citron peel is candied *(pictured)* and used in confectionery, in baking (particularly in fruit cakes or in Italian breads such as panettone and panforte), in cassata, or it may be pressed to extract citron oil, which is used to flavour liqueurs. Citron peel is sold candied in chopped mixed peel, in slices or in pieces.

***Also known as — cedro***

▨ ***See also citrus fruit***

Citrus fruit are native to Asia and grow in tropical to temperate climates. The most important fruit of the citrus species are sweet orange, mandarin, grapefruit, lemon, lime, pummelo, citron and sour lemon. These eight varieties all cross-fertilize to produce other fruit. The pummelo, one of the most ancient of citrus, is the ancestor of the grapefruit. Other lesser-known citrus fruit include citrange, fortunella, kabosu, kalamarsi, lavender gem, limequat and tangelo.

■ *See also* **citron, clementine, grapefruit, kumquat, lemon, lime, mandarin, orange, pummelo, tangerine, ugli fruit**

## clafoutis

A baked pudding made with a layer of cherries, traditionally the first red ones of the season, and also traditionally— but unwisely—with their stones left in, and topped with a pancake batter. The pudding is served warm with cream or ice cream. Clafoutis is a harvest dish from Limousin in France, often baked during cherry season. Sometimes other fruit are used instead, such as apples, apricots or plums.

*Also known as — clafouti*

see shellfish — **clam**

## clementine

A clementine is a cross between a mandarin and a bitter Seville orange. It is thought that they were first cultivated in North Africa by the priest Père Clément. The fruit is small and some varieties are virtually seedless; it has thin, easy-to-peel skin and juicy, sweet flesh with a slight hint of acidity. In the northern hemisphere, clementines are associated with winter and Christmas. They are a popular fruit for bottling in alcohol, candying, or may be used in fruit salads, marmalades and jams.

CLEMENTINES IN BRANDY

*Wash enough small clementines to fill a 2 litre jar. Dissolve 1 kg sugar in 1 litre water, bring to the boil and simmer for 5 minutes. Prick all over the fruit with a needle, then put the fruit in the syrup. Simmer for 1 hour, remove fruit from the syrup and place in the jar. Simmer the syrup until thick, then add 500 ml brandy. Allow to cool, then pour over the fruit. Leave the fruit to infuse for 1 week.*

## club sandwich

The ingredients for a club sandwich may vary but, typically, it is a sandwich made with slices of toast or bread and filled with lettuce, tomatoes, chicken or turkey, bacon and mayonnaise. Originally the sandwich was made with two pieces of toast, but now it is common to see it as a triple-decker made with three. The club sandwich is a North American invention but is now popular all over the world.

## cobbler

Originally a North American dessert, a cobbler is made in a deep dish filled with fruit and topped with dough. The dough is shaped into overlapping circles or squares and, when baked and brown, the topping looks similar to cobblestones. Fruit such as plums, apples and mixed berries are typically used.

Slumps and grunts are similar to cobblers, but are cooked on top of the stove rather than baked. The fruit supposedly 'grunts' as it cooks. A pandowdy is made with sliced fruit, usually apples, mixed with spices, butter, brown sugar or molasses and topped with a pastry crust. Halfway through baking, the crust is broken into pieces and pushed into the fruit to absorb the juices. 'Dowdying' means breaking up the dough.

## cock-a-leekie

A traditional Scottish soup, cock-a-leekie is made from boiling fowl, herbs, leeks and sometimes prunes. Some versions use oatmeal, barley, rice or cream to thicken the soup.
**Also known as — cocky-leeky**

## cocoa

Dutched cocoa powder (back) and ordinary cocoa powder (front).

A by-product of the manufacture of chocolate, made by pressing chocolate liquor, the first stage in turning cocoa beans into chocolate, until it gives up cocoa butter and a paste, which, when dried and powdered, becomes cocoa. Cocoa is used in industry to flavour all manner of biscuits, puddings and sauces. It is also mixed with sugar and boiled with water and/or milk to produce the universally popular night-time drink, cocoa. In the 1800s, Dutch chemist Conrad van Houten perfected a screw press that enabled cocoa to be extracted more efficiently and a process of further treating it to produce a darker, milder cocoa known as 'Dutched' cocoa, which dissolves more easily and is often used for drinking and baking.

If making chocolate cakes or brownies, use cocoa powder instead of flour to dust baking tins and trays. To further enhance the chocolate flavour of baked goods, but without the added fat and sugar of chocolate, use cocoa powder instead.
**Dutched cocoa is also known as — Dutch, Dutch-processed, European-style**

*See also* **chocolate**

Indigenous to India, coastal Southeast Asia and the Caribbean, the coconut is a versatile fruit. Its name is derived from the Spanish and Portuguese word for a grotesque face, because the three small depressions at the base are reminiscent of a grinning monkey. Coconut flesh when immature is soft and jelly-like. It becomes white and harder when mature, and can be eaten fresh or dried. The milk contained within the nut is not the sweet, heavy liquid used in cooking, but a thin, watery milk that makes a refreshing drink. Coconut oil, extracted from the dried flesh, is used in the food manufacturing industry, in Asian cooking and cosmetics and is sold in some countries as 'copha'.

Coconuts are sold fresh: choose ones that are dry, with no 'weeping' in the eyes, heavy and sound full of liquid. The flesh is also sold desiccated or as shreds/flakes (sweeter and more moist than desiccated), frozen or canned. Coconut milk and cream are sold in cans and cartons, in solid blocks or as powder. The milk is often thinner than the cream but this may vary between brands. Light coconut milk has a thinner consistency and is lower in fat.

**Coconut goes with — *chicken, chilli, coriander, lime, pineapple, potato, prawns, rice, sweet potato***

## COCONUT MILK AND CREAM

*Coconut milk can be made by soaking desiccated or grated fresh coconut in the same amount of hot water or milk. Strain through muslin, squeezing the liquid out of the grated coconut. Set aside, then blend. The first lot can be used for coconut cream, subsequent pressings (up to three) can be used as coconut milk.*

## CRACKING OPEN A COCONUT

*1 Push a skewer through two eyes (indentations) and drain the milk. Bake at 200°C (or freeze) for 15–20 minutes to loosen the flesh from the hard shell.*

*2 Hold the coconut in one hand and a hammer in the other. Tap the coconut, turning it slightly after each tap so you are hitting around its equator.*

*3 Continue in this way until the coconut cracks open. This is the best way to crack it and get two equal halves. Prise the meat out of the shells.*

## coeur à la crème

This classic cream dessert means 'heart of cream' in French. To make it, cottage or curd cream cheese is mixed with cream, sugar and egg whites, and the mixture is put into a heart-shaped mould lined with cheesecloth. The mould has small holes in the bottom of it to allow the liquid to drain off, resulting in a firm texture. After draining, the dessert is unmoulded and served with berries or a berry sauce.

# coffee

Raw coffee beans, red in colour, are washed, fermented, husked, dried, roasted and often blended with beans of different origin and variety to add flavour and complexity before being ground, added to water and heated to finally become the drink, coffee. The coffee tree is indigenous to Africa, and coffee was first made as a pleasurable drink in Yemen, from whose port, Mocha, it began its voyage around the world in the fifteenth century. It is still grown in Africa, but also in South and Central America, Indonesia, the Caribbean, New Guinea and Australia. Caffeine, the active ingredient in coffee that gives it its kick, and to which some are allergic, can be removed by soaking the beans in water or with liquid carbon dioxide or organic solvents. For cooking, use very strong coffee, such as espresso, as this will give both colour and flavour.

*Fresh and roasted beans*

## ROASTING AND GRINDING

*This can ruin or enhance the process of turning a bean into a perfect cup of coffee. Coffee roasters—human beings and their machines—must choose exactly the right temperature to roast each bean depending on its origin, variety and end use. Generally, high roast (dark brown) has a richer flavour, while light roast (French roast) has a milder flavour.*

*Coffee is ground according to the method to be used to brew it. Turkish and Greek coffee is ground to a powder; for espresso machines and stove top cafeteras almost as fine; for filter, cafetière (plunger) or drip methods, choose a coarser grind.*

### Making good coffee

Start with a very clean pot (not just rinsed) as coffee leaves a film in the pot, which can turn rancid. Always buy the right grind of coffee for your coffee maker—the wrong grind will make either bitter or weak coffee. Use water that has been heated to 90-95°C (just before it boils). Coffee is best drunk immediately: don't keep it hot on an element for long as it will continue to cook and eventually burn.

## COFFEE GRANITA

*Dissolve 200 g caster sugar in 25 ml water. Bring to the boil, simmer for 3 minutes, then add 1.25 litres strong espresso coffee. Put the liquid in a plastic box and freeze. Using a fork, stir every 2 hours (do this 2 or 3 times) to break up the ice crystals. The granita is ready when almost set but still grainy. Stir a fork through it just before serving. Serves 8.*

**100**

*Espresso*

*Caffe latte*

*Caffe macchiato*

*Cappuccino*

*Café au lait*

*Caffe freddo*

## TYPES OF COFFEE BEANS

| | |
|---|---|
| **Arabica** | These are the finest and most expensive beans. They have less acidity, less caffeine and a rich flavour. |
| **Robusta** | Inferior to Arabica in flavour, but less expensive and with twice as much caffeine. |

## TYPES OF COFFEES

| | |
|---|---|
| **Espresso** | Made from a small quantity of coffee through which water under pressure is forced. This produces a dark, rich coffee topped with an orange-brown *crema* (foam). In the United States an espresso is known as a 'single'. In Australia it is known as a 'short black'. *Caffe ristretto* is strong espresso. *Espresso lungo* is a shot that is pulled with a little more water for a larger espresso. |
| **Caffe corretto** | An espresso that has been 'corrected' with a shot of alcohol such as grappa. |
| **Caffe latte** | An espresso coffee topped up with three times its volume of steam-heated milk. In some countries a latte can have a foam, be served separated into stripes of coffee and milk, or it may be served in a glass or cup. |
| **Caffe macchiato** | An espresso 'stained' with a drop of milk. *Latte macchiato* is a glass of foamed milk with a shot of espresso poured in. |
| **Cappuccino** | An espresso topped up with milk steamed to silky thickness, often served with a dusting of cocoa powder. Cappuccinos are usually drunk before 11 am as it is considered too weak and milky to drink after meals or later in the day. |
| **Caffe americano** | A shot of espresso diluted with hot water. In Australia known as a 'long black', and a 'flat white' if milk is added. |
| **Café au lait** | A coffee made with hot milk rather than water. In France, *café au lait* is typically drunk at breakfast. |
| **Caffe freddo and caffe latte freddo** | Iced coffee, sometimes pre-sweetened and served in a long glass. |
| **Affogato** | A scoop of vanilla ice cream with a shot of grappa or liqueur and an espresso poured over it. |

## STORAGE

*Store coffee in an airtight container, in a cool, dark place. Heat and cold will dry out coffee so the fridge is not a good place to keep it. Don't buy more than a week's supply of coffee at once, especially if ground, as the volatile flavour oils dissipate rapidly.*

## cola nut

Cola nuts are not a real nut, but the seeds of a large tree native to Africa. The nuts yield a red extract containing caffeine, which is used to flavour cola soft drinks *(pictured)*. The nut is also used in alternative medicines. Africans have been eating cola nuts for centuries as the caffeine is thought to stimulate a weak heart, to relieve nausea and reduce fatigue and drowsiness.

*Also known as — cola bean, kola nut*

## colcannon

Irish in origin, colcannon is a dish made with chopped cooked cabbage, finely chopped onions (or spring onions or leeks) and mashed potato mixed with butter and hot milk or cream. The dish may be seasoned with nutmeg, or salt, pepper and parsley. The word is derived from the Gaelic '*cál ceannann*', which means 'white-headed cabbage'. It is traditionally eaten at Halloween.

*Also known as — cally, poundies, stampy*

### COLCANNON

*Steam 500 g curly kale, then chop it finely. Add the kale to 500 g cooked, mashed potatoes and 1 chopped, fried onion. Mix ingredients together and season to taste. Pile the mixture into individual bowls and make a well in the centre. Divide 100 g melted butter among them. Dip each forkful of the colcannon in the butter as you eat it. Serves 4.*

## coleslaw

Coleslaw is a salad made with shredded red or white cabbage mixed with a dressing of mayonnaise, yoghurt or vinaigrette. Other ingredients are usually added to the cabbage and these vary widely, but may include grated carrot, peppers, onion, celery, sliced apples and walnuts. Coleslaw is an adaptation of the Dutch word '*koolsla*', which means 'cabbage salad'. It is often served with chicken or barbecue meats.

*Also known as — slaw*

### COLESLAW

*Toss together 225 g finely shredded white cabbage and 2 grated carrots. Mix in 5 tablespoons mayonnaise with 2 teaspoons French mustard and 2 teaspoons sugar. Season well. Serves 4.*

A compote is a dish of fresh or dried fruit, such as apples, apricots, pears or plums, that has been poached or stewed in sugar syrup, and may be flavoured with spices or liqueur. The fruit, which may be whole or cut in pieces, is cooked slowly so it retains its shape. A compote is served either chilled or warm for breakfast or dessert, sometimes with cream, or sprinkled with cinnamon and sugar. Compote is common to many European cuisines.

See also **dried fruit**

### FRESH FRUIT COMPOTE

*Peel 6 apricots and 6 peaches and cut into slices. Dissolve 185 g sugar in 500 ml water and boil for 1 minute. Add the fruit, 24 pitted cherries and the zest of an orange, cut in strips. Simmer for about 2–3 minutes, or until fruit is tender. Remove fruit and simmer the syrup until it thickens. Add 80 ml dessert wine if you like. Return the fruit to the pan to warm. Serves 6.*

## condiment

From the Latin *condire*, meaning 'to preserve' or 'pickle', but now referring to anything added to or served with a dish to enhance or complement its flavour. Condiments include pickles, chutney, grated Parmesan, mint jelly; in Chinese cuisine, minced ginger, garlic and spring onion with duck; and in Italy, salsa verde served with bollito misto.

*Clockwise from top left: mango chutney, Parmesan, wholegrain mustard, cornichons.*

## consommé

A stock made from meat, fish (often including shin of beef to intensify flavour) poultry or vegetables, which may be clarified and is simmered until reduced and intensified in flavour. Once chilled, when it may set into a soft jelly, it can be eaten, garnished, as a starter or used to enrobe other foods, giving them a glazed appearance.

*Consommé à la julienne is a hot consommé garnished with julienne strips of carrot, turnip, leek and celery.*

*Consommé is sometimes chopped and served cold.*

*Consommé Royale is garnished with poached egg white.*

## cookies

### CHOCOLATE COOKIES

*Chop 150 g chocolate and 100 g hazelnuts. Sift 225 g plain flour, ½ teaspoon bicarbonate of soda and a pinch of salt. Beat 90 g butter and 150 g sugar, then beat in an egg. Fold in the flour, chocolate and nuts. Drop spoonfuls of mixture onto a baking tray. Bake at 190°C for 12–15 minutes. Makes 20.*

Cookie is the term used in North America to refer to what is known elsewhere as a biscuit—a small, sweet slightly raised cake. Derived from the Dutch word *koekje*, meaning 'small cake', cookies are many and varied, from those dropped by the spoonful onto a tray to those shaped by hand or rolled out and cut with a cookie cutter.

## copha — see fat

## coq au vin

This classic French bistro dish consists of chicken cooked in red wine with button onions, mushrooms, bacon, garlic and herbs. The chicken is left to marinate in the wine and herb mixture overnight, then it is slowly simmered to produce a rich, thick sauce and tender chicken. This practice of simmering chicken in wine was to tenderize it because, traditionally, the dish was made with a rooster that was several years old. Typically, a whole rooster was used, but now it is common to used jointed chicken or one type of cut. When served, the dish may be garnished with croutons or parsley. A variation of coq au vin can be cooked with white wine and may be called coq au Riesling, or named according to the wine that is used to cook it in. A common myth is that Julius Caesar invented this dish while fighting the Gauls.

## coquilles Saint Jacques

The recipe for coquilles Saint Jacques varies greatly, but it usually consists of scallops poached in wine, topped with a rich, creamy sauce. The scallops are finished with breadcrumbs or cheese and baked in their shells. Coquilles Saint Jacques is the French for 'Saint James' shells'. The fan-shaped shells were worn as a badge by the pilgrims who made the pilgrimage to Santiago (St James) de Compostela in northwestern Spain in the Middle Ages.

In Europe, the word 'corn' is a general term used to refer to any type of grain, but in America it refers to maize. Now the word 'corn' is usually accepted as meaning maize and other grains are called by their own names. Corn is the major native American cereal grain (wild rice is the other) and was first used by the Incas, Aztecs and Mayas thousand of years ago. Corn is usually yellow but can also be blue, red, white, orange and purple. Blue corn may be ground into flour and used to make corn chips and tortillas.

When buying sweet corn, choose the freshest possible—still in its husk, with a fresh-looking silk and kernels that are not shrivelled or discoloured. Use it as soon as possible, as it loses its sweetness and nutritional benefits quickly. Heat converts the corn's sugar into starch, and about 40 per cent of its sweetness can be lost in 6 hours. Sweet corn should therefore be refrigerated.

## CORN FRITTERS

*Mix 150 g polenta with 40 g plain flour, 1 teaspoon bicarbonate of soda and 500 ml milk. Stir in 300 g corn kernels, 1 tablespoon melted butter and 1 tablespoon finely chopped spring onions. Whisk 2 egg whites until soft peaks form and stir in. Season well. Heat some oil in a frying pan and fry spoonfuls of the mixture. Fry until brown on both sides and cooked through. Serve with roasted tomatoes. Makes about 30 fritters.*

## TYPES OF CORN

**Sweet corn (corn on the cob)**
Also called 'corn on the cob', this is eaten as a vegetable either straight from the cob or the kernels may be sliced off it. It can also be bought frozen, in tins or creamed in tins. Baby cobs are available for stir-fries.

**Dent**
The most widely grown corn, named for the dent in its top. Ground to make maize meal and flour. Hulled grains are used for hominy in the American south; and ground corn (available coarse, medium or finely ground) is used for polenta in Italy, and grits and corn bread in America. Finely ground corn is used for Mexican tortillas and other breads (*masa harina*) and as a staple in Africa (*mealies*) where it is made into a porridge. Corn is also made into cornflakes and other breakfast cereals; the husks are used for cooking tamales (bought dry, then soaked before use); and fermented corn mash can be distilled into moonshine.

**Popping corn**
A small-grained variety of corn (Flint) grown specifically for popping.

## COOKING

*When cooking sweet corn, do not salt the water as it stops the kernels softening as quickly. Cook in slightly sweetened water or add a little milk to retain flavour and softness.*

*To remove the kernels from sweet corn, stand the cob on one end and slice downwards, as close to the cob as possible.*

*To barbecue, strip back the husk and remove the silk, then replace the husk and soak it briefly in water. The husk will burn off as it cooks. This will stop the corn from burning.*

**See also  hominy**

## corn syrup

Corn syrup is a thick, sweet glucose syrup made by processing cornflour with acids or enzymes. Light corn syrup has been clarified to remove colour, and dark corn syrup, which has caramel flavour and colouring added to it, has a deeper colour and tastes similar to molasses. Corn syrup is used widely in America.

## corned beef — see beef

## cornflour

Cornflour is a fine, white powder milled from corn, and used to thicken sauces, custards and in desserts such as blancmange. Cornflour must be slaked into a liquid (first mixed with a small amount of cold water) before it is heated. Cornflour contains no protein (gluten) and, unlike flour, when it is cooked it will turn clear. Cornflour sauces will begin to thin again if cooked for too long. Some types of cornflour are milled from wheat and are labelled as 'wheaten cornflour' to prevent confusion. Pure cornflour has a stronger thickening power and produces a smoother liquid than wheaten cornflour.

*Also known as — cornstarch*

## cornichon — see gherkin

## coronation chicken

A cold buffet dish made with cooked chicken mixed with a mayonnaise flavoured with tomato, onion, curry powder, apricot jam or purée, lemon and cream. Devised by Le Cordon Bleu in 1953 to celebrate the coronation of Queen Elizabeth II.

## cottage pie — see shepherd's pie

## coulibiac

Originally a Russian dish, coulibiac is a pie filled with salmon (or sometimes trout or sturgeon), rice, hard-boiled eggs, mushrooms and cream. The pie is not baked in a tin, but instead the pastry, usually a brioche dough, puff pastry or filo dough, is wrapped around the filling to form a parcel.

*Also known as — koulibiac, kulibiaka, kulibyaka*

Courgettes are baby marrows, usually dark green in colour, but there are also light green and yellow varieties. Young courgettes can be sliced thinly, dressed in oil and lemon juice and eaten raw in salads. Use larger ones in stir-fries, steam or boil them, coat slices in batter and deep-fry, or hollow out, stuff and bake them. If using in fritters or frying, salt them first to degorge them so they soak up less oil. Buy and eat quickly as storage in the fridge makes the texture deteriorate. Courgette flowers are edible too, available in the male (the flower has a stalk) or female (the flower has a baby courgette attached) form. These are usually stuffed before being baked or fried. They are sold at speciality fruit and vegetable shops. Wash before use and make sure there are no insects hidden inside.

**Courgettes go with — aubergine, cream, herbs, oil, Parmesan, peppers, tomato**
**Also known as — zucchini**

*See also* **soufflé**

White courgette

Green courgette

## DEEP-FRIED COURGETTE FLOWERS

*Whisk 2 eggs with 55 g plain flour and some seasoning. To make the stuffing for the courgette flowers, mix 125 g ricotta with 1 tablespoon chopped basil, 2 tablespoons grated Parmesan, 2 tablespoons breadcrumbs and 1 egg yolk. Season well. Stuff the mixture into 10–12 courgette flowers. Add a little cold water to the batter if it needs thinning, then dip each flower and courgette in the batter and deep-fry until golden. Serves 4.*

Courgette flowers

Yellow courgette

A food generally associated with North African cuisine, couscous is usually made from semolina flour, which is laid out on a large round mesh frame, sprinkled with water, and laboriously rolled into tiny balls of grain. Today, couscous is mostly sold pre-prepared and par-steamed using a process invented in Tunisia. Couscous is also the name of the dish that is cooked in a couscoussier. A stew cooks in the lower half while the couscous steams in the perforated upper section.

The preparation of, and accompaniments to, couscous vary widely from Tunisia to Morocco. In Morocco, for example, it is rarely eaten as an evening meal. Couscous makes an appearance in Sicilian cuisine, and is popular in Italy, where it is a traditional accompaniment to Sicilian fish stew. In Egypt, it may be served as a dessert with honey, nuts and dried fruit.

# crab

Crustaceans of which there are between 4,000 and 8,000 species, both saltwater and freshwater. Crabs are hard-shelled, though soft-shelled (just moulted) blue crabs are a delicacy in America, China and Venice. Crab meat is sweet, delicate and versatile and food lovers compare it to lobster. Buy live crabs from reputable sources as they are highly perishable. Never buy a dead uncooked crab. Look for lively crabs that feel heavy for their size. Crabs with worn barnacles and feet will not have just moulted—these crabs will have more meat.

Cooked crabs are also highly perishable, so buy with care. Make sure they smell fresh and are undamaged and their legs and feet are drawn into the body (if they were dead when cooked, their legs will be looser). Crab meat is also available frozen, tinned and in vacuum-sealed plastic bags.

## COOKING

*The most humane way of handling a live crab is to freeze it to make it lose consciousness—this will take about 45 minutes. Drop it into a large pot of boiling, salted water and simmer for 15 minutes per 500 g. Drain and leave to cool. If you are sautéeing crab, kill in the same way but cook for 5 minutes, then drain, cool under running water and cut into pieces.*

**See also  shellfish**

*From left: blue swimmer crab, mud crab.*

## CLEANING AND DRESSING A CRAB

*Dressed crab is presented in the cleaned top shell of the crab. The dark and white meat are served separately, garnished with egg and parsley.*

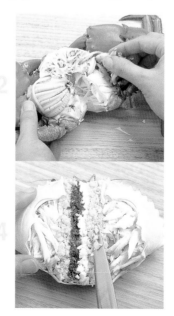

1  Pull the top shell of the crab away from the bottom shell.

2  Remove the feathery gills and stomach sac; snap off the mouth.

3  Pick the meat out of the shells, keeping white and dark separate. Remove and crack the claws; take out any meat.

4  Mix the dark meat with lemon juice and breadcrumbs, spoon down the middle of the shell. Fill the sides with white meat and decorate with chopped egg white, yolk and parsley.

Berries of various varieties native to North America and northern Europe. The American cranberry is larger than the European variety. Cranberries are sometimes called bounceberries and the ripe berries actually do bounce because they contain an air pocket. The berries are harvested by flooding the fields they grow in, then raking the berries off the bushes—the air pocket lets them float.

The berries have a tart, slightly acidic flavour and may be used raw, cooked in desserts, pastries, muffins and cakes, and are a perfect ingredient in jams because of their high pectin content. As a sauce, cranberries are the traditional accompaniment to roast turkey. When cooking, chop slightly to stop them popping and add sugar at the end of cooking to ensure the skin is more tender. Cranberries are high in vitamin C and are used in juices. They are also available dried.

**Also known as — cowberries, lingon berries**
**Cranberries go with — cheese, game, orange, port, turkey**

## COOKING

*The most humane way to deal with a live crayfish is to freeze it to make it lose consciousness—this will take about 1 hour. Drop it into a large pot of boiling, salted water and simmer for 15 minutes per 500 g if large, or 8–10 minutes if they are small.*

*To halve a crayfish, hold the tail firmly in one hand with a tea towel, plunge a large, sharp kitchen knife into the midpoint, where the tail meets the head, and slice quickly down between the eyes. You can ask your fishmonger to do this, but bear in mind that the crayfish will start to ooze black juices about an hour after it has been killed.*

*Crayfish shells make excellent stocks for sauces and soups. Crush the shells, then fry with vegetables, add wine or water and simmer for about 15 minutes. Sieve well.*

*Do not reheat cooked crayfish as the flesh will toughen.*

*Cooked crayfish should have their tails curled tightly against their bodies and smell sweet.*

Any kind of freshwater crustacean, as well as the name often used to refer to the rock or spiny lobster. Crayfish are widely distributed around the world, and include aquatic (river and lake) and semi-aquatic species. In Louisiana, they are known as crawfish. There are about 40 species of crayfish distributed around the world, in North America and Australia, varying in size from 2–60 cm in length. They include the Louisiana crawfish, the French *écrevisse* and the Australian marron, yabby and huge Murray River cray.

*From left: Rock (spiny) lobster, sometimes called a crayfish; yabbies, Australian crayfish.*

Crayfish are extremely popular: in Scandinavia, they are boiled with dill and drunk with ice-cold vodka; in France, they are used to flavour sauces; and in America, especially in Louisiana, whole restaurants are dedicated purely to boiled crawfish.

Crayfish tails yield a reasonable amount of meat and can be used in most recipes requiring prawns. Buy only live crayfish or cooked ones; they should feel heavy and still be fairly lively. If they have not been purged (had their guts cleaned out) before sale, crayfish need to have their guts removed before eating.

If fresh milk is left to stand, a layer of cream will form as the butterfat rises to the surface. The cream can be either skimmed off the top after it is left to rise naturally, or it may be removed by the use of centrifugal force.

Cream varies in its thickness and richness according to how much butterfat it contains—thicker creams have a higher percentage of butterfat. Most cream is pasteurized (this doesn't affect the flavour), but some cream is unpasteurized.

■ *See also* **crème fraîche**

*Reduced-fat cream*

*Pouring cream*

*Whipping cream*

*Double cream*

*Extra-thick cream*

*Clotted cream*

*Chantilly cream*

## TYPES OF CREAMS

| | |
|---|---|
| **Reduced fat** | Has a minimum of 25 per cent fat. Light cream has about 18 per cent fat. |
| **Pouring** | Has a higher butterfat content than English single cream and American light cream (both of which cannot be whipped). The butterfat varies from 35–48 per cent. |
| **Whipping** | Whipping cream must have at least 35 per cent butterfat to trap the air and hold it in place. It whips more slowly than double cream and so incorporates more air. Whipping cream in America may have only 30 per cent cream with added vegetable fat to make it whip. |
| **Double** | Has a minimum butterfat content of 48 per cent. Double cream can be frozen, then defrosted, but will need to be stirred or whipped before use. Known as heavy cream in America and thick cream in Australia, some have gelatine added to them to give them more body. |
| **Extra thick** | This is double cream that has been homogenized and is a spooning consistency. It doesn't need to be whipped. |
| **Clotted, scalded or Devonshire** | The thickest, yellowest cream of all with the highest butterfat content of about 55 per cent. |
| **Chantilly** | Made by whipping cream with sugar to sweeten it. It is named after the French chateau where it was invented. |
| **Frozen** | Sold broken into pieces and can be defrosted in portions. |
| **Longlife** | Needs no refrigeration while on the shelf and is useful to keep in case of emergencies. It is ultra heat treated. |

## WHIPPING CREAM

*Before whipping cream, chill the mixing bowl in the fridge. For maximum volume, use a balloon whisk and beat well. You can use an electric whisk, but be careful you don't overbeat the cream and end up with butter.*

Cream of tartar is a fine white powder made from the crystals that are deposited on the inside of wine barrels. The crystals contain potassium bitartrate, which is purified and ground to form cream of tartar. Cream of tartar is used to stabilize the egg whites beaten into cakes such as angel food and sponge cakes and meringues, and to stop the sugar in candy from crystallizing. Cream of tartar is the acidic ingredient in baking powder, which activates the bicarbonate of soda.

## crème anglaise

A thin custard sauce, served hot or cold. It forms the foundation of Bavarian cream, île flottante and some ice creams. Crème anglaise is traditionally flavoured with a vanilla pod, but also with citrus, chocolate, coffee or liqueur. Unlike flour-thickened sauces, crème anglaise only thickens slightly and it must be cooked with vigilance or it will curdle if it gets too hot. To prevent this, cook it in a heavy-based pan or in a bain-marie, stirring continuously.
**Also known as — creme à la vanilla, English egg custard, sauce anglaise**

CREME ANGLAISE

*Heat 300 ml whole milk with 1 tablespoon caster sugar and 1 split vanilla pod. Bring to the boil, then remove from heat. Beat 2 egg yolks in a bowl; pour on the milk. Discard vanilla pod. Mix well, then strain into the cleaned pan; stir over low heat until mixture thickens enough to coat the back of a spoon. Don't boil or the egg will cook into lumps. Makes about 300 ml.*

## crème brûlée

A thick, rich egg custard usually baked in individual ramekins. Before serving, the top is sprinkled with granulated sugar or brown sugar and heated, often with a blowtorch or under a grill, to form a crisp caramel topping. The dish is thought to have been invented at Trinity College, Cambridge, where it was named 'burnt cream'. The French translation, crème brûlée, is now generally used.

## crème caramel

A smooth, rich egg custard made in individual moulds or ramekins, coated in hot caramel and filled with custard. The custards are baked in a bain-marie, and the secret of their smooth, creamy texture is ensuring that the water in the bain-marie does not bubble, causing the custard to bubble. The custard is cooled, unmoulded onto a plate and the caramel topping runs down the side of the custard.
**Also known as — caramel custard, crème renversée, flan, flan Catalan**

see blackcurrant — crème de cassis

## crème fraîche

Translated from the French, crème fraîche means 'fresh cream', but it is actually cultured cream. It has a slightly nutty, sharp flavour without being too sour, is higher in butterfat than sour cream, so it is creamier. Unlike sour cream, it is ideal in sauces or soups because it can boil without curdling. Used widely in French cooking, its mild acidity complements the sweetness of chocolate and fruit, or serve with green vegetables or in salad dressings. *Crème fraîche d'Isigny* is the only crème fraîche recognized by the *appellation d'origine contrôlée*.

### CREME FRAICHE

*Put 750 ml double cream, 250 ml buttermilk and 2½ tablespoons lemon juice in a saucepan and heat to 30°C. Leave in a warm place for 12–24 hours until it thickens, then refrigerate. Makes approximately 1 litre.*

## crème pâtissière

A creamy, thick custard used for filling cakes and pastries. It is indispensable in chocolate éclairs, profiteroles, cream horns and fruit tarts, and forms the base for some soufflés. It contains cornflour, which helps stop the eggs from curdling.
**Also known as — confectioner's custard, pastry cream**

### COOKING

*If you aren't going to use the crème pâtissière immediately, cover the surface with either a dusting of sugar, a disc of greaseproof paper, or lay a piece of clingfilm flat on the surface to prevent a skin forming on it. If it does form a skin, put it in the blender and blend until smooth.*

*Store crème pâtissière in a piping bag in the fridge until ready to use.*

### MAKING CREME PATISSIERE

*1 In a saucepan, heat 290 ml milk and a split vanilla pod until the milk is hand hot. Remove the vanilla pod.*

*2 Whisk together 2 egg yolks with 55 g caster sugar. Add 20 g plain flour and 20 g cornflour. Pour on the milk and mix well.*

*3 Pour the mixture into the pan and boil, whisking continuously for 2 minutes. Ignore the lumps as they will go as it cooks.*

Creole cuisine is a reflection of the many cultures that left their mark on New Orleans, in particular, the French, Spanish and Africans. Unlike the Cajuns, who developed a more countrified style of cooking, the city-dwelling Creoles based their cooking on the European style, adapting traditional European dishes to suit local produce. The French lobster bisque became the New Orleans crawfish bisque by adding ham and other seasonal ingredients and the Spanish paella evolved into the Creole jambalaya.

Creole is now a more universal term used to define any cuisine that has had a large amount of outside influences. So countries and cuisines that were subjected to foreign imperialism, such as Brazil and Goa, have a modern style of cooking, which could be called Creole.

■ *See also* **Cajun**

*Shrimp Creole*

*In New Orleans, French-style pralines are served with ice cream or coffee.*

## crêpe

Translated from the French, crêpe means 'thin pancake'. Dessert crêpes are made with a sweetened batter and may be wrapped around fillings or soaked in sauces. Crêpes suzette uses crêpes served rolled or folded into quarters in an orange sauce and flambéed in brandy or orange liqueur. Savoury crêpes can be rolled around chicken, vegetables or cheese and baked. Store with a piece of greaseproof paper between each one. Wrap in a tea towel to keep warm, or wrap in foil, then plastic and refrigerate or freeze.

### MAKING CREPES

*1 Sieve 60 g plain flour into a large bowl with a pinch of salt. Make a well in the centre.*

*2 Whisk 3 eggs and 250 ml milk together and slowly add to the well, stirring all the time and gradually drawing in the flour.*

*3 Stir in the remaining milk and 75 g melted butter and pour into a jug. The batter should be the consistency of pouring cream.*

*4 Stand the batter in the fridge for 30 minutes. Heat a crêpe pan and brush it with a little butter. Tip out any excess butter.*

*5 Pour in enough batter to make a thin crêpe, swirling the pan to get an even coverage. Tip out the excess batter.*

*6 When the crêpe starts to lift off the pan and brown underneath, flip it over carefully and cook the other side.*

## cress

Cress are tiny, bright-green sprouts with small, peppery leaves and are used in salads, sandwiches and as a garnish. There are many different varieties, the most widely used of which include the cultivated watercress. Cress is often grown in combination with mustard seed (the mustard seed grows quicker than the cress, and commercially grown punnets tend to contain more mustard than cress).

■ *See also* **watercress**

## crocodile

Crocodiles are farmed for their skins and meat and eaten in Australian, African and Cajun cuisines. Both freshwater and saltwater crocodiles are eaten and the meat is usually taken from the tail or legs. The flesh is pale in colour and has an unusual flavour similar to a combination of fish and chicken. Crocodile is grilled or pan-fried and usually served with a sauce, such as sweet chilli or salsa verde.

## croissant

A rich, buttery yeasted pastry folded into a crescent shape. Like puff pastry, the dough is interleaved with butter. The white flour dough is cut into a triangle and rolled, then bent to form its characteristic half-moon shape. Like most folded dough breads, croissants are cooked on a high heat so the dough puffs and sets before the butter melts. Croissants are usually served with butter and jam, or they may be filled with almond paste and topped with almond flakes. A savoury variation may be filled with ham and cheese. Croissant dough may also be filled with one or two sticks of chocolate and rolled into a rectangle to make *pain au chocolat*. In modern-day France, while the plain croissant still rules the breakfast table, its savoury equivalent is eaten at any time of the day as a snack.

*Clockwise from bottom: plain croissant, chocolate-filled croissant (pain au chocolat), almond croissant.*

## croquembouche

An elaborate pyramid-shaped dessert made with small choux pastry buns. The buns are filled with cream, dipped in warm caramel, then stacked to form a pyramid. A croquembouche mould (a tall cone-shaped metal mould) may be used to hold the buns in place until the caramel sets. The croquembouche is then unmoulded and may be decorated with spun sugar, flowers, sugar-coated almonds or caramel, or as show here, set on a nougatine base. Croquembouche means 'crunch in the mouth' and forms the traditional centrepiece at French weddings and first Holy Communion meals.

■ *See also* **choux**

A popular French café snack, croque-monsieur is a grilled ham and cheese sandwich. The crusts are removed from the bread and the bread may be lightly fried in butter or cooked in a sandwich iron. Sometimes ham is replaced with chicken. If the croque-monsieur is served with a fried egg on top, it is called a croque-madame.

### CROQUE-MONSIEUR

*Butter 8 slices of white bread on one side only and make sandwiches, placing a slice of ham and a slice of Gruyère cheese in each. Press the sandwiches together firmly. Heat 1 tablespoon butter and 1 tablespoon oil in a large frying pan and fry each sandwich on both sides until they turn golden brown and crisp. Makes 4 sandwiches.*

Crostini are thin slices of bread, cut into pieces, brushed with oil or butter, and toasted or baked. The crostini are then topped with various mixtures, such as chicken liver pâté, tapenade, puréed aubergines or chopped mushrooms, and are served hot as an antipasto. Plain crostini may also be used as croutons to be served with soups. Crostini are a speciality of Tuscany.

*See also* **bruschetta**

### CHICKEN LIVER CROSTINI

*Cook 200 g trimmed chicken livers in 1 tablespoon butter until browned. Add 2 chopped garlic cloves, 1 tablespoon chopped sage and 2 tablespoons dry Marsala. Simmer everything together until the liquid evaporates. Process or chop the livers finely with 2 tablespoons double cream. Spread the mixture onto crostini and serve immediately.*

*Crostini toppings from left: tapenade, chicken liver pâté, artichoke hearts.*

Croutons are small cubes of toasted or fried bread, usually served as an accompaniment to soups or as a garnish in salads. Translated from the French, crouton means 'little crust'. A croûte is a disc of fried bread on which a piece of meat or small game bird is served. A croûte may also be a small crescent shape of pastry (fleuron) used as a garnish. A croustade is a hollowed out piece of bread, which is deep-fried or baked and filled with chopped meat, chicken or game.

*Croutons used to garnish soup*

*A croûte*

*A croustade*

## crudités

Crudités are raw or blanched vegetables cut into strips or broken into florets and served as an hors d'oeuvre or snack. Vegetables may include tomatoes, celery, carrots, radishes, broccoli, cauliflower, courgette, asparagus and mangetout. The vegetables are cut into bite-size pieces, crisped in water and usually served on a platter with a dipping sauce such as aïoli, bagna caôda or mayonnaise.

## crumble

### RHUBARB CRUMBLE

*Cut 1 kg rhubarb into 2 cm pieces and put in a saucepan with 150 g sugar. Heat slowly until the sugar dissolves in the juice of the rhubarb, then cover and simmer for 10 minutes, or until tender. Put rhubarb into an ovenproof dish. Rub 100 g butter into 150 g plain flour and stir in 50 g brown sugar. Sprinkle over rhubarb and bake at 200°C for 15 minutes. Serves 4.*

A crumble is a dessert of cooked fruit topped with a crumbly mixture of butter, flour and sugar. The crumble is baked in the oven until the topping is crisp. Sometimes nuts and oats are added to the crumble mixture, or the crumble may be made using biscuit crumbs, muesli or breadcrumbs. Apples, rhubarb and blueberries are popular fruit used in crumbles.

***Also known as — crisp***

## crumpet

A typically British griddle cake, made from a leaven (yeasted) batter with a consistency designed to form many tiny holes on its surface when the crumpet is cooked. These are formed by bubbles rising through the batter as it cooks. Crumpet surfaces are always slightly undercooked as they are always toasted, traditionally on a toasting fork in front of the fire. They are best eaten hot, spread with butter and, most usually, honey or jam. Today, crumpets are sold ready-made in packets, though crumpet rings and flat griddles are also available for cooking your own. Crumpets can also be eaten with savoury toppings such as melted cheese, herb butters and Marmite or Vegemite.

One of the oldest cultivated vegetables, and many would say, the most refreshing. The cucumber today exists in over 100 varieties—including at least one described as 'burpless'—and many shapes. It can be eaten raw; in salads; cooked in a soup; mixed with yoghurt as raita (Indian); used as an accompaniment to curries; or added to yoghurt and garlic to make Greek tsatsiki. Cucumber is the traditional accompaniment to cold salmon, and the main ingredient for a doria garnish for classic fish recipes. Sliced paper thin in white bread sandwiches, the cucumber represents the height of English gentility at afternoon tea.

Many varieties are grown for pickling as dill pickles, gherkins and French cornichons. Choose firm cucumbers with no signs of bruising and store them in the fridge wrapped in plastic to prevent their odour spreading to other foods.

**See also  dill pickles, gherkin**

**Cumberland sauce**

An English favourite, Cumberland sauce is made with redcurrant jelly, port, mustard, orange and lemon zest and juice. The sauce is traditionally served with ham but may be served with any meat. In Edwardian times, Cumberland sauce was typically served with ham, chicken, goose, duck or venison.

**curd**

Made from a mixture of fruit juice (usually citrus), sugar, butter and egg yolks, cooked until thick and used as a spread. Curd also refers to the solid portion of coagulated milk. The curd is separated from the liquid whey and used to make cheese.

see dried fruit — **currants**

**curry**

An English word, derived from the Tamil 'kari' meaning 'spiced sauce', curry travelled home with the returning Raj. Its appearance on menus now refers to a spiced (and usually chilli-hot) dish of meat, vegetables or pulses. From its original association with Indian cuisine, it has spread to Southeast Asian dishes. The sauce of a curry may be made from a commercially produced powder, paste or curry sauce or spices mixed at home. Accompaniments include rice, naan, poppadoms and chutney.

**See also  spice mixes**

### CURRIED LAMB

*Mix 2 teaspoons grated ginger and 1 teaspoon turmeric with 1 kg cubed lamb. Fry 3 sliced onions with 1 cinnamon stick, 8 cloves, 8 cardamoms, 4 crushed garlic cloves, 2 chopped chillies and 1 teaspoon ground coriander. Add the lamb and fry until well browned. Add 400 g chopped tomatoes and 100 ml water and simmer for 1 hour. Stir in 80 ml yoghurt. Serves 4.*

## custard

A custard is a sweetened, milk-based dessert made with flour (usually cornflour) and eggs and flavoured with vanilla. Pouring custard (custard sauce) is a traditional accompaniment to pies and steamed puddings, or custard may form the basis of desserts such as ice creams, soufflés and baked puddings.

Pouring custard is cooked on the stovetop on a low heat. The custard is stirred continuously to prevent lumps from forming but unlike crème anglaise, it is a stable mixture that will not curdle if overheated. Baked custards should be cooked in a bain-marie or water bath so the mixture cooks gently and doesn't bubble. Pouring custard is sold ready-made in cartons, or it may be sold as custard powder: a mixture of cornflour and artificial flavouring first manufactured by Alfred Bird in 1837.

*See also* **crème anglaise, crème pâtissière**

## custard apple

Custard apple is the general name of a group of tropical fruit, which includes cherimoya *(pictured)*, sweet sop (also called sugar apple) and sour sop. Custard apples have thick scaly skin and a soft, smooth custardy flesh, reminiscent in flavour of bananas, pineapples and strawberries. Custard apples are picked before they are fully ripe, so allow 4 or 5 days for firm fruit to ripen, or select mature fruit that are dull brownish green in colour. Cut the fruit open and eat the flesh with a spoon, add to fruit salads, or purée for use in ice creams, sorbets and drinks. Custard apples are available in autumn and winter. Although a member of the same family, the papaw, the fruit of a North American tree, does not have the characteristic knobbly skin of its relatives, but a smooth, yellowish skin and soft, smooth heavily fragrant flesh. Its flavour is similar to pear and banana.

## cuttlefish

A relation of the squid and octopus, which includes specimens ranging in size from 3–50 cm long. Like the squid, cuttlefish contain ink sacs that may be used in cooking. They have 10 large tentacles and an internal shell. To prepare, cut the head and tentacles off, slit down one side to remove the guts and ink sac (keep the sac if you want to use the ink in another recipe). Cut away the hard cuttleshell, cut the tentacles off the head, then discard the head. Cuttlefish can be fried briefly, steamed or barbecued. They are sold fresh, frozen or dried.

CUTTLEFISH IN ITS OWN INK

*Clean 1 kg cuttlefish (keep the ink sacs intact). Cut the body into strips; rinse. Cook 1 finely chopped onion with 2 finely chopped garlic cloves in 2 tablespoons oil. Add the cuttlefish and cook for 5 minutes. Add 2 chopped, peeled tomatoes and 250 ml white wine and simmer for 45 minutes until the sauce thickens. Push the ink through a sieve and stir into the stew. Season well. Serves 4.*

# d

## dacquoise

A classic French patisserie item made from two or three discs of meringue interspersed with whipped cream or butter cream, which is typically flavoured with coffee or mocha. The meringue contains crushed almonds or hazelnuts, and fruit such as raspberries and strawberries may be mixed in with the cream. Dacquoise is also the name given to the meringue discs used to make the cake.

## daikon

A variety of white radish with firm, crisp flesh and a mild flavour, similar to a white turnip. Some varieties have a slight peppery taste, while others are slightly sweeter. Daikon is a popular vegetable in Asia, particularly in Japan where its name means 'large root'. Raw daikon can be diced and added to salads, or used like a potato or turnip and added to soups, stews or stir-fries. In Japan, grated raw daikon is formed into a small pile and is the traditional accompaniment to sashimi or tempura, it may be eaten as pickles, and is used to make the summer version of the pungent Korean condiment kimchi.

Choose firm, smooth and slightly shiny daikon, as this is a good indication that it's fresh. Daikon don't store for long periods as they lose moisture quickly. Remove their green tops and store wrapped in plastic in the vegetable crisper of the fridge. If eating raw, use within 3 to 4 days, or it will last for up to 1 week if you intend to cook it.

**Also known as — Chinese radish, Japanese radish, mooli, Oriental radish**

## damper

A simple bread of flour and water eaten by early Australian settlers and bushmen. The dough may be wrapped around a stick and cooked over the camp-fire coals or cooked in a camp oven. Originally, damper was unleavened, but sometimes salt, a raising agent and milk powder were added, if available. The bread is often spread with golden syrup, known as 'cocky's joy'. Damper is so called because it was said to 'dampen' the appetite.

See also **Australian food**

## damson

Native to Eastern Europe and western Asia, damsons are small dark-purple plums with yellow to green flesh. Because they are sharp and even unpleasantly sour eaten raw, and because they are firm fleshed and transport and store well, they are the cooking plum par excellence for desserts, fools, compotes, chutney and especially jams, conserves and preserves *(pictured)*. Damsons picked in the wild often have a better flavour than commercially grown varieties. Damsons may also be dried or used to make damson cheese, a cooked mixture of damson and sugar, traditionally served with roast lamb. The damson is so named because it was from Damascus in Syria.

See also **plum**

## dandelion

A cultivated version of the wild variety is the dandelion usually seen in supermarkets and used as a salad green. The younger, tender leaves of wild dandelion are edible too, but only if you're sure they haven't been treated with pesticides. Cook the leaves like spinach or use raw in salads and dress with a strong-flavoured oil such as hazelnut or olive oil. 'Dandelion' is derived from the French *dents de lion*, 'lions teeth', referring to its jagged leaves. In France, it's called *pissenlit*, referring to the plant's diuretic qualities.

### SALADE LYONNAISE

*Tear 2 handfuls of dandelion leaves into pieces and place in a large bowl. Fry 4 rashers streaky bacon, cut into pieces, and add to the leaves. Cut 2 slices bread into cubes and fry in the bacon pan to make croutons, then add to the salad. Make a vinaigrette (page 441) and add 1 teaspoon mustard, then toss through the salad. Poach 4 eggs and serve on top. Serves 4.*

## Danish pastries

Made using a yeasted pastry similar to croissants or puff pastry. The dough is rolled and folded several times to produce layers of flaky dough, which are then shaped and filled with either fruit, cream cheese, custard, almond paste or jam. They may be served warm or cold and are often eaten at breakfast. It is thought that they were developed by Viennese bakers, recruited to work in Denmark in the 1860s. The Danes call Danish pastries 'Vienna breads'.

*Also known as — Danish*

## dasheen — see taro

Date palms have been cultivated for their fruit for over 5,000 years. Although now grown commercially in many countries, the date palm is native to the Middle East where its fruit is held in high esteem and the tree honoured with the title of 'tree of life'. The Greek word *daktulos*, meaning 'finger', is thought to be the origin of its name, referring to the shape of the fruit.

Green when unripe, dates turn pale honey to brown when ripened, though colour, texture and flavour vary with variety. Common varieties include medjool, halawy and the highly prized degletnoor. Fresh dates are high in sugar and in the Middle East, they are boiled to a pulp to make *dibbis*, date syrup. Dates can be added to cakes or biscuits, or used in stews, tagines, couscous or pilaffs. Store fresh dates at room temperature, or in an airtight container in the fridge. Store dried dates in an airtight container in a cool, dark place. Choose fresh dates with skin that is translucent when held to the light.

**Dates go with — almond, cream, lamb, poultry, yoghurt**

## POACHED DATES

*Remove the stones from 16 fresh or dried dates. Make a sugar syrup by boiling 250 g sugar in 500 ml water with 2 Earl Grey tea bags, 2 cardamom pods and 1 split vanilla pod. Boil for 5 minutes, then remove the tea bags. Add the dates and poach for 2–3 minutes. Serve hot or cold with cream or mascarpone. Serves 4.*

**d a u b e**

Each region in France has its own version of daube and the ingredients used depend largely on what is available, but generally it is a rich, wine-based beef stew. Traditionally, a daube is cooked in a deep earthenware *daubière* (though any casserole will do), and the meat is simmered for 4–5 hours. Unlike many stews, in which the meat is first browned, the beef is cut into cubes and left to marinate in red wine, garlic and herbs, with orange peel added as an aromatic. Shin of beef or lamb is popular for this dish, or any other cut with connective tissue as this breaks down to give a rich gravy. A pig's trotter or a piece of pork rind may be added as flavouring. Garnishes for a daube include caramelized onions, fried mushrooms, prunes or black olives. To cook *en daube* describes a method of braising meat.

see angel food cake — **devil's food cake**

see angels-on-horseback — **devils-on-horseback**

**dill pickles**

Dill pickles are small cucumbers pickled in brine. The seed of the dill herb is used to flavour the brine and garlic, spices and salt are also added. Dill pickles are popular in North America and in Jewish cuisine.

*See also* **cucumber**

Dim sum literally means 'to touch the heart', and these small dumplings and snacks are a Cantonese culinary form of art. Dim sum is part of the ritual of yum cha, 'to drink tea', a custom that evolved in Chinese teahouses where regular customers would come to drink tea, read the newspapers and talk, while having a few snacks or a bowl of congee. Today, yum cha is taken any time from very early morning to late at night and still revolves around socializing with family or friends or reading papers over a leisurely meal of tea and dim sum. Dim sum restaurants are famous for their noise and bustle, especially in the huge yum cha restaurants of Hong Kong whose highly trained chefs turn out some of the best dim sum in the world. Women push around carts of dim sum fresh from the kitchen, the dumplings stacked in the bamboo steamers they were cooked in, crying out the names of dishes so diners can pick out what they would like. There are thousands of varieties and some of the most famous ones are shown here, but new ones are created all the time.

### CHAR SIU BAU
### (BARBECUE PORK BUNS)
These filling and fluffy steamed buns are well-made and fresh if their tops are slightly open. They are filled with barbecued pork.

### LOH BAAHK GOU
### (TURNIP CAKE)
These are fried out in the restaurant on the trolleys themselves.

### NGAUH YUKH KAUH
### (BEEF BALLS)
Not all dim sum comes in the form of dumplings and these meatballs often also contain pork and are flecked with coriander. A thick soy sauce is poured over them after you order.

### FUHNG JAAU
### (CHICKEN'S FEET)
A great favourite with Chinese children, they are eaten whole, all the flavour is sucked out, then the rest spat out.

### HOM SUI KOK
### (STICKY DUMPLINGS)
These torpedo-shaped sticky dumplings are full of a mixture of pork and shrimp.

## HAR GAU (STEAMED PRAWN DUMPLINGS)

These half-moon shaped dim sum are a classic. The prawn can be seen through the almost translucent rice-flour skin.

## HA CHEUNG FAN (LONG RICE NOODLES FILLED WITH SHRIMP)

These are also a popular *dai pai dong* (street food) snack in Guangzhou and can be filled with any ingredient and eaten with a thick soy sauce.

## PAI GWAT (SPARERIBS)

These tiny plates of spareribs are steamed in a bamboo steamer.

## SIU MAI (PORK AND PRAWN DUMPLINGS)

These steamed cup-shaped dumplings are filled with a mixture of minced pork, prawn and mushrooms.

## DARN TART (EGG TARTS)

Sweet dim sum are also popular, including treats made of beans and lotus. These little tarts are made of egg.

### EATING DIM SUM

*Few dim sum restaurants take reservations and there are often queues at weekends. The dim sum is either ordered or brought around in trolleys and you can lift up the lids of the bamboo baskets to see what's available. The staff usually punch a card on your table so the restaurant can add up your bill at the end. To get your tea refilled, flip the lid backward so it rests on the handle and the waiter will fill it up.*

## dolmades

Stuffed vine leaves of Middle-Eastern origin, particularly popular throughout Greece and Turkey. To make them, vine leaves are blanched, then wrapped around a variety of savoury fillings, usually rice or minced lamb. The little parcels are then braised in stock or tomato juice and served as an appetizer or as part of a meze plate. Dolmades can be eaten hot or cold, but are usually served cold if filled with rice and hot if filled with lamb. Dolmades can be bought ready-made or in tins at delicatessens.

Fresh vine leaves must be blanched in hot water to soften them, but if you buy the vine leaves sold commercially in tins or jars in brine, you only need to rinse them before use to remove the salt.

*Also known as — dolmas, dolmathes*

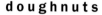 *See also* **Greek food, meze, vine leaves**

## doughnuts

Doughnuts are small rings of lightly sweetened deep-fried yeast dough. They may be sprinkled with icing sugar or sugar or finished with a strawberry, chocolate or butterscotch icing. Some doughnuts are made in twisted, oblong or round shapes and filled with jam. The North American doughnut with a hole in the centre was the original form, and was made by wrapping dough around a stick, which was then immersed in hot oil. The first doughnut cutter was patented in the 1870s by John Blondel.

*Also known as — donuts*

## dragées

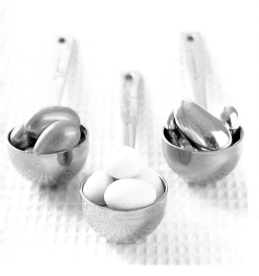

The French name for a hard sugar-coated confectionery, most often an almond, which has been adopted into the English language. Dragées may be white or pastel coloured, and silver ones are used on wedding cakes. In addition to almonds, hazelnuts, pistachios, nougat, chocolate or liqueur may be coated using the same method, known as 'panning'. In Europe, it is traditional for almond dragées to be given as a memento or gift at weddings or religious celebrations, but this custom is now popular in other countries as well. Honey-coated almonds were popular with the ancient Greeks and Romans, and 'dragée' is thought to be derived from the Greek word for sweets. In the seventeenth century, dragées were made using spices such as coriander, indicating an Eastern origin. Today, these are still served at the end of a meal in India.

*See also* **sugared almonds**

Drying fruit, one of the oldest preservation techniques, derives from the discovery that fruit left to dry in the sun were still edible. Drying concentrates the sugar content in fruit, and, although it usually loses its vitamin C in the process, vitamin A and the minerals are still retained. Some fruit are still sun-dried, while others may be dried by mechanical means, and some are coated in sulphur dioxide to prevent them from drying out completely. Dried fruit is high in fibre, is a convenient snack food, and is often used in baking, for compotes or in stuffings for meat.

The three main vine fruit, currants, raisins and sultanas, are all dried grapes. Currants are small black grapes; sultanas are dried, white grapes; and raisins vary according to the variety but are traditionally muscatel grapes. Vine fruit play an essential role in Christmas puddings, in cakes, biscuits, mincemeat, in couscous or stuffings and sauces. Dried peaches and pears make excellent snacks and dried apricots can be chopped and added to muesli, rice dishes and stuffings for chicken and lamb. Dried apricot is also sold rolled into sheets. Dried apples, which retain their Vitamin C when dried, are sold in rings or pieces. Many exotic fruit such as mango and papaya are also dried and these are best eaten as snacks. Prunes are eaten dried as a snack or plump them up by keeping them in brandy or another liquid, then add to stews, cakes or puddings. They go well with pork, lamb, poultry and game.

■ *See also* **date, fig**

*Clockwise from top left: pears, apricots, sultanas, apples, peaches.*

## COMPOTE

*Boil 1 litre water with the zest of 1 lemon, 1 star anise, 1 cinnamon stick and 3 tablespoons sugar. Add 450 g assorted whole dried fruit and simmer until soft. Remove fruit and put in a serving bowl. Boil the syrup until it starts to thicken, then add the juice of 2 oranges and 1 tablespoon orange flower water. Strain over the fruit and leave to cool. Serve with cream. Serves 4.*

see fat — **dripping**

**drop scone**

## DROP SCONE

*Sift 225 g plain flour, ½ teaspoon each of bicarbonate of soda and cream of tartar, ¼ teaspoon sugar and a pinch of salt into a bowl. Mix an egg with 270 ml milk and add the flour, stirring until the batter is smooth and has the consistency of double cream. Rest for 30 minutes. Lightly grease a heavy-based frying pan with butter; fry tablespoons of the batter, turning them once when set. Makes 20–30.*

A flat cake made from a thick batter, dropped onto a hot griddle or frying pan and cooked on both sides. Drop scones are usually served with butter and jam.

**Also known as — griddle cake, pikelet, Scotch pancake, Scottish pancake**

## duchess potatoes

These are potatoes mashed with butter and egg yolks and piped into decorative shapes. The mixture is baked until golden brown, then used as a garnish for roasts or as a decorative border for savoury dishes. Duchess potatoes can also be used as a topping for fish pies or cottage pies. In the 1970s, it was popular for the potato to be piped into a nest shape and filled with peas. The term 'à la duchesse', refers to a dish garnished or served with duchess potatoes.

**Also known as — pommes duchesse**

### DUCHESS POTATOES

*Boil and drain 500 g peeled potatoes. Add 55 g butter and 2 egg yolks to the potatoes and mash the ingredients together. Add enough milk to make a soft potato purée that will hold its shape. Season to taste. Spoon the potato into a piping bag and pipe rosettes of potato onto a lightly buttered tray. Bake at 180°C until browned on top. Serves 4.*

## duck

Any one of over 40 species of web-footed saltwater or freshwater birds that have been domesticated (probably by the Chinese) for over 2,000 years. Their meat is dark, moist and richly flavoured, and because of its high fat content, is often served with fruit to offset its richness. Duck is popular in France, where it may be prepared as duck a l'orange and duck confit, and in China, as Peking duck, a traditional dish that produces a crisp skin and takes many hours to prepare.

### COOKING

*To cook a whole duck, prick the skin all over and rub with salt, then cook on a rack set above a roasting tin to allow the fat to drain. If making gravy with the juices, first skim off the fat. Leave both whole duck and breasts to rest before carving or eating them.*

*When cooking a whole duck, first remove the parson's nose and oil glands that it contains as this will affect the flavour of the dish.*

*To cook duck breast (often called magret), score a lattice into the skin and fat and cook over high heat, skin side down, to crisp and brown the skin and render the fat. Drain off any fat and cook the other side. Duck breasts are usually cooked so they are slightly pink. Alternatively, place breasts or legs and thighs skin side down in a dry heavy pan over a couple of cloves of garlic and a star anise. Cover and cook, on very low heat for 1 hour, then turn and cook for another hour. Deglaze the juices and pour over the duck to serve.*

Breeds of duck vary according to country, although many domesticated ducks are descended from the mallard. In England, Aylesbury and Gressingham ducks are popular; in America, Long Island and Peking ducks; and in France, Nantes, Rouen and Barbary or Muscovy ducks are preferred. The mulard, a cross between a Nantes and a Barbary, is used for foie gras. Wild ducks are also available in some areas, the best are the freshwater varieties. Duck is sold cooked, fresh or frozen. Both domestic and wild ducks are available, but their flavour and texture varies hugely. As a general rule, remember that farmed ducks, unlike chickens, and because of their aquatic habitat, put down fat before they put down flesh. A younger bird of any breed will have more fat, an older bird more flesh—and flavour.

**Duck goes with — cherry, ginger, orange, red wine, star anise**

■ *See also* **foie gras, Peking duck**

Egyptian in origin, dukka is a blend of toasted nuts, seeds and spices. The ingredients, the combination of which vary greatly with each cook, are roasted or grilled, then lightly crushed but not powdered. Dukka is usually eaten with bread dipped in olive oil, or it may be sprinkled over meat and vegetables.

**Also known as — dukkah**

### DUKKA

*Mix 4 tablespoons sesame seeds, 3 tablespoons coriander seeds, 2 tablespoons cumin seeds and 50 g roasted, chopped hazelnuts with salt and pepper. Dry-fry the nuts and spices until aromatic. Remove from the heat and allow to cool. Using either a food processor or a mortar and pestle, grind the ingredients to form a coarse powder.*

### DULCE DE LECHE

*Pierce the top of a tin of condensed milk 2 or 3 times (so the tin won't explode when it is heated). Put the tin in a saucepan of boiling water: the water should reach halfway up the side of the tin. Simmer for about 2½ hours, keeping an eye on the water so it doesn't boil dry. For a more solid dulche de leche, simmer for up to 4 hours. Stir well before eating.*

An Argentinian speciality originally made by caramelizing sugar in milk for many hours. Today, it is often made by boiling a tin of condensed milk to thicken and reduce the milk. When cooled, it can be eaten from the can, used as a dip for fresh fruit and spooned over ice cream or waffles. It is also used as a base in desserts such as banoffee pie or cheesecakes. Dulce de leche literally means 'sweet milk'. It is also used as a flavouring for ice cream.

**Also known as — arequipe, cajas, dulche de leche, manjar**

Generally, small balls of dough cooked in a liquid base, such as a soup or stew, and traditionally served with roast or boiled beef. Dumplings can also be deep-fried, steamed or boiled. Asian dumplings are made with chopped pork or prawns and vegetables wrapped in a thin sheet of dough, then steamed or boiled. Dumplings may also be sweet, simmered in a dessert sauce or fruit juice or the dough used to encase a piece of fruit. Italian gnocchi are also a type of dumpling.

■ *See also* **dim sum**      *Dumplings served in Irish stew.*

# durian

Native to Southeast Asia, the durian is a large fruit covered with an armour of close-set hard spines. Its name is derived from the Malay *duri*, meaning 'thorn'. The fruit has sticky, cream-coloured flesh and is especially noted for the contrast between its putrid odour (described by some as smelling like rotten onions) and its juicy, sweet flesh. Outside of its native home, where it is highly prized and considered to be an aphrodisiac, durian is quite rare and is expensive when available. The fruit is divided into five or six segments, each containing several seeds. The flesh can be eaten with a spoon, used in ice creams or cakes or cooked with Indonesian rice dishes. Roasted or baked, the seeds can be eaten as nuts, and in Indonesia, they may be eaten with rice or mixed with sugar to make sweetmeat.

When buying durian, look for fruit with undamaged skin and a yellowish rind, which is a good indication that it's ripe. At home, insert a knife into the fruit. If the knife comes out sticky, it is ready to eat. Store in the fridge for 2–3 days and wrap the fruit well to prevent its odour contaminating other foods.

# Dutch food

The Netherlands prides itself on its regional specialities, usually simple, wholesome winter dishes. A typical meal consists of potatoes with some meat or stew, boiled vegetables and perhaps gravy. More recently however, the Dutch have absorbed influences from all over the world, especially from their former colonies, and have made many foods their own. Satay sauce is even served with the classic mayonnaise on *patat* (Dutch French fries). The *rijsttafel*, a collection of 'Dutched down' Indonesian dishes served as one meal, bears the same relationship to the original as English curry does to its Indian original.

Some more traditional dishes include *stamppot*, a filling country stew of mashed potato and vegetables, usually served with pork or *rookwurst* (smoked sausage), while *hutspot* is a beef, carrot, onion and potato stew from Leyden, whose origins are traced back to the Spanish occupation in the sixteenth century. There are many vegetable stews, such as *snert,* a green pea soup, often served with *rookwurst* or bacon.

Holland is also an important fishing nation, particularly famous for its mussels and herrings. *Maatjes* are

herrings that have not developed roe. They are cured and eaten raw by picking them up by the tail and sliding them into the mouth. The first catch of the season is called *Hollandse nieuwe* (Dutch new) and is a special treat.

The Dutch eat lots of dairy products and their cheese is famous worldwide. Edam has been a leading export since the Middle Ages, but now Gouda is Holland's most important cheese, sold in huge wheels weighing up to 30 kg.

The Dutch also enjoy cakes and desserts. Small warm pancakes called *poffertjes* are eaten as snacks, while Dutch pancakes are so big they often overhang the plate. *Spekpannekoek* (bacon pancakes) served with syrup are very popular. *Oliebollen* are deep-fried yeasted raisin breads traditionally served on New Year's Eve, while *speculaas* are beautiful biscuits given to children on St Nicholas's Day. The dough is spiced with cinnamon, nutmeg and cloves and then pressed into carved moulds. *Vlaai* are pies from the south filled with fruit. Liquorice, or *drop*, is said to be a Dutch addiction and comes in numerous varieties.

*From top: snert, green pea soup; maatjes salad; speculaas.*

## Eastern European food

Eastern Europe stretches from Germany in the west to Russia in the east; Estonia in the north and Albania in the south. Common characteristics can be found in produce and cooking styles, but such a vast area necessarily exhibits huge diversity in preparing and serving food. With much of its land not particularly fertile, and the climate inhospitable, diet is often influenced by what can be grown. Root vegetables are popular, including beetroot, horseradish and kohlrabi, and in the northern half of Eastern Europe (especially Poland), mushrooms play a prominent part, appearing in soups, stews and pickles. Recurring flavours and ingredients are sour cream, dill, rye breads, apple desserts, buckwheat, and spices such as clove, nutmeg and cinnamon, which made their way into Eastern Europe as they were traded across the world overland to China.

*Cherry strudel*

*Beetroot is the main ingredient of borscht, which may be eaten hot or cold. It is served with sour cream.*

Religion has shaped many of the dishes found in the more Orthodox nations. During periods of semi-fasting, when meat was forbidden, hearty and nutritional alternatives were developed. As many people from Eastern Europe were poor, foods on feast days were particularly looked forward to, with such treats as German stollen at Christmas and Polish *babka* at Easter. Lunch is the main meal of the day when families sit down to three courses. Eastern Europe is well known for combining meat with sour flavours, such as pork with sauerkraut.

With the Baltic Sea to the north, the Black Sea to the south, and endless waterways running through the region, fish, both fresh and saltwater, is traditionally very popular. However, as the rivers become polluted and more frozen fish is imported, traditional dishes are disappearing. Herring is eaten all over, frequently marinated in apples, oil and peppers, eels and carp are also popular and these often appear at Christmas.

*Stuffed cabbage rolls*

Soups are cheap and nutritious and borscht, although mostly associated with Russia, is also a traditional dish in Poland and the Ukraine. The cold table at the beginning of a meal is another established ritual. This course may include cheeses; pickled fish; spicy, garlicky sausages; and caviar. Bread ranges from white through to black rye and yeast-leavened breads.

*Pork stew served with sauerkraut*

Literally meaning 'water of life', eau de vie is the French term given to any strong, colourless brandy distilled from the fermented juice of fruit. Common examples include kirsch made from cherries, and framboise made from raspberries. In cooking, eau de vie is used to add flavour to desserts, pastries, fruit sorbets or compotes, or it can be drunk as an apéritif. However, brandies that are made from vine fruit, such as Cognac and Armagnac, are not generally classed as eau de vie.

## FRUIT IN EAU DE VIE

*Layer 1 punnet each of hulled strawberries, raspberries and blackberries with 2 tablespoons caster sugar in a 1 litre glass jar until ⅔ full. Pour in enough eau de vie to cover the fruit. Put a lid on and store in a cool, dark place for at least 4 weeks. Serve with some of the syrup and whipped cream.*

## Eccles cake

Small flat oval cakes made with currants, chopped peel, brown sugar and spices encased in a flaky pastry. The filling is placed in the centre of the circle of pastry, the edges are gathered up and pressed together, and the cake is turned over and flattened. Three slashes are made across the top of each cake (said to represent the Holy Trinity), then the top is glazed with egg white and caster sugar (Elizabethan frosting) before baking. The cakes originated in Eccles in Manchester and they are traditionally served with afternoon tea. Banbury cakes, from Banbury in Oxfordshire, are similar to Eccles cakes but are oval in shape.

## échalote — see shallot

## éclair

Small finger-shaped lengths of choux pastry, which are baked until brown and hollow. When cooled, the éclairs are split open and filled with Chantilly cream or crème pâtissière and coated with chocolate or coffee icing. Store unfilled éclairs in a cool place for 2 days or freeze for several months (refresh in a hot oven to make the pastry crisp). Filled éclairs should be eaten 2–3 hours after preparation.

*See also* **choux**

## eddo — see taro

A versatile, nutritious high-protein food and indispensable in the kitchen, either cooked on its own or as an ingredient in countless recipes. Eggs are graded into sizes according to the minimum weight of each egg in the carton, ranging from the largest, size 1, weighing greater than 70 g, to the smallest, size 7, weighing less than 45 g. Eggs graded as small weigh about 45 g, medium eggs about 55–60 g, large about 60–65 g, and extra large about 90 g. The standard egg used in recipes is size 3, weighing 60 g. It is important to follow the recommended egg size in recipes as closely as possible, as changing the size may make a difference to the outcome of the recipe. Always bring eggs to room temperature before use. A cold egg will crack when immersed in hot water and cold egg whites won't whisk well.

## EGGS BENEDICT

*Grill 4 bacon rashers until brown and crisp, then set bacon aside and keep warm. Toast the outside of 4 English muffin halves. Poach 4 eggs (see page 132), then place one egg and one bacon rasher on each muffin. Make a foaming hollandaise sauce (see page 186), then pour the sauce over the top of the eggs. Serves 4.*

## STORAGE

*Don't wash eggs unless they are to be used immediately. This washes off the egg's protective film and will cause it to deteriorate more rapidly.*

*Store in the fridge in their carton or in a covered container to prevent moisture loss and the absorption of odours through their porous shells.*

A stale egg will float vertically; a fresh egg will lie horizontally on the bottom of the glass.

### Testing for freshness

Egg shells are designed to let air in so the chick inside can breathe. The small air pocket between the egg membrane and the shell increases in size as the egg ages. This air pocket provides a useful means of testing for egg freshness. To do this, put the egg in a glass of water: if it lies horizontally on the bottom, it is fresh; if it floats vertically, it is stale. Alternatively, when cracked, a fresh egg will have a rounded yolk sitting in a gelatinous white with a thinner bit of white around the edge *(bottom left)*; staler eggs will have a runny white and flatter yolk *(top left)*.

Fresh eggs with good gelatinous whites are best for cooking methods that depend on them staying intact, such as poaching and frying. Eggs that are only 2 or 3 days older have slacker membranes and more air in them and are easier to peel when boiled. They also separate and whisk easily. Eggs older than a week should be used in baking or as an ingredient rather than the main feature.

## COOKING WITH EGGS

*Fried*

*Boiled*

*Poached*

*Scrambled*

| | |
|---|---|
| **Fried** | Bring the eggs to room temperature. Heat the frying pan and add some oil and a knob of butter. Carefully break the eggs into the frying pan and gently fry until the white is set. Spoon some hot oil over the yolks to set them. |
| **Boiled** | Put room temperature eggs in a small saucepan of gently simmering water. Cook for 4–5 minutes for soft-boiled and 9–10 minutes for hard-boiled eggs, depending on the size of the egg. Time them to be sure. Eggs that are overcooked will have a greying around the yolk. Cool hard-boiled eggs quickly under cold running water if you are peeling them to stop this happening. |
| **Poached** | Bring a shallow pan of water to a simmer and carefully crack the eggs into the water, one at a time. Continue to barely simmer until the white has set around the yolk. Lift out and drain on paper towel. Use for eggs Benedict, on salads or vegetables, or in pitta bread pockets. Adding salt, vinegar or lemon juice to eggs will help set the egg white but this will also flavour the eggs. |
| **Scrambled** | Whisk the eggs gently together and season well (add a little cream if you like or some herbs or smoked salmon). Heat some butter in a saucepan and add the eggs. Stir over a gentle heat until softly scrambled. The eggs will continue to cook a little after the saucepan is removed from the heat. Serve on toast or in croissants. |
| **Baked** | Break eggs into buttered ramekins and cook in a bain-marie at 180°C for about 12 minutes, or until set. If preferred, first put some chopped tomato or ham in the bottom of the ramekin before you add the eggs. |
| **Omelette** | Whisk the eggs lightly and season. Heat the frying pan and add a knob of butter. Add the eggs and, as the omelette sets around the edge, pull the edges into the middle, allowing a new area to set. When most of the egg is set, fold one-third into the middle, then the other third on top. Add any filling before you fold the omelette. |

## THOUSAND-YEAR EGGS

*Also called hundred-year eggs, Ming Dynasty eggs or century eggs, these are hen or duck eggs that have been preserved in a paste of lime, salt and ash for 3 or 4 months. After this time, the paste and shell are removed to reveal a firm egg with a grey-green yolk and a pale amber white. The eggs have a smooth, creamy texture and a pungent, cheese-like flavour. Popular in Chinese cuisine, the eggs are usually served at the start of a meal with lime and ginger or soy sauce. They can be purchased at speciality Chinese markets.*

*Soft peaks*

*Stiff peaks*

### Whisking egg whites

Eggs for whisking should be at room temperature as cold egg white will not whisk well. Always use a very clean and dry glass or metal (copper is classic) bowl. Some recipes recommend that you rub lemon juice or vinegar around the bowl. This is to remove any traces of fat as egg whites will not whisk at all if fat is present—this includes any yolk. Whisk the whites gently at first, then more vigorously until you reach the stage you want, ensuring you have beaten all the egg to the same degree. At soft peak, the peaks on the egg white will flop; at stiff peak, only the very tops will flop. Egg whites, when properly whisked, will triple in volume.

## QUAILS EGGS EN CROUSTADE

*Cut 12 circles of bread to fit in a mini tartlet tin. Brush both sides of the bread with 45 g melted butter, then press the pieces into the tin. Bake at 170°C for 15 minutes. Poach 12 quail eggs, put the egg in the croustade and drizzle with hollandaise sauce (see page 186). Serve as canapés. Makes 12.*

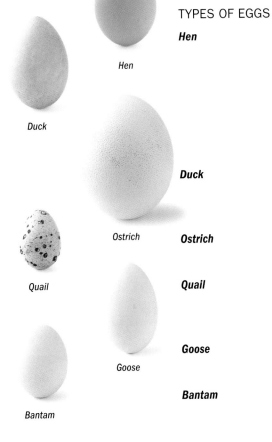

*Hen*

*Duck*

*Ostrich*

*Quail*

*Goose*

*Bantam*

## TYPES OF EGGS

**Hen**
Brown and white eggs are the same: the colour is dependent on the breed of hen and has no bearing on the egg's nutritive value or flavour. Free-range eggs are generally healthier, but the term 'free-range' can vary in each country—check the packaging carefully. Organic and free-range eggs have been produced by the happiest chickens of all.

**Duck**
Chalky white or pale blue with a rich flavour and gelatinous blue-tinted white. Good in custards, mousses and cakes.

**Ostrich**
Very large egg, which can be used as a hen's egg. One ostrich egg is equivalent to about two dozen hen eggs.

**Quail**
Small speckled eggs, usually eaten poached, or soft- or hard-boiled with celery salt. They make perfect canapés or can be added to salads.

**Goose**
Similar to a duck egg but milder in flavour. These are good for baking.

**Bantam**
Similar to but smaller than a hen's egg and can be used in the same way.

## eggah

Of Middle Eastern origin, an eggah is best described as a thick, heavy, omelette, although the eggs are not the main ingredient, but merely act as a binding for the filling, which may include lamb, chicken or vegetables such as courgettes or aubergines. To serve, the eggah is cut into wedges or small pieces, and may be eaten either hot or cold as an hors d'oeuvre, entrée or as a main dish and served with yoghurt and salad.

**Also known as — eggeh, kuku**

## eggnog

Based on egg and cream and laced with a spirit such as brandy, bourbon or whisky, eggnog is a traditional Christmas drink. Serve in glasses and sprinkle with nutmeg.

**Also known as — egg flip**

### EGGNOG

*Beat 6 egg yolks with 200 g icing sugar until creamy, then add 280 ml brandy. Cover and store in a cool place for 2 hours, then add 500 ml double cream. Whisk 6 egg whites until soft peaks form and slowly stir in the egg and cream mixture. Sprinkle with nutmeg. Serves 6.*

## eggplant — see aubergine

## elderberry

The tart red, purple or black fruit of the elder tree. Elderberries can be eaten raw but their slight sourness makes them better suited to cooking in jams, pies or in wine. The creamy white, honey-scented flowers are also edible and can be used to flavour cordials or sorbets, they can be infused in tea, used as decoration in salads or dipped in batter and deep-fried. As they are in season at the same time as the gooseberry, they are often cooked together.

*From left:
dried elderflower, jelly,
elderflower cordial.*

### ELDERFLOWER CORDIAL

*Make a sugar syrup by boiling 2 litres water with 1 kg sugar until the sugar dissolves and the syrup thickens slightly (the syrup will feel greasy when you rub your finger and thumb together). Pour the syrup onto 6 elderflower heads in a glass container and leave to steep overnight. Strain and add lemon juice to taste, and keep bottled in the fridge for a few days. Dilute with water, if necessary.*

In South America, empanadas are small half-moon or square-shaped turnovers made from a pastry crust and filled with either vegetables, fish or meat. Sweet versions may be filled with fruit such as bananas or apples. They may be baked or shallow-fried. Empanaditas are smaller versions, eaten as snacks or appetizers. Empandillas are small semicircular pastries filled with a savoury mixture and deep-fried. In parts of Spain an empanada corresponds in shape to the English pie.

**emu**

A large, flightless bird, native to Australia but now bred in other countries. Emus were once sought for their plumage, hide and decorative egg shells, but are now raised for their lean, tender meat, which is similar in flavour to beef. Cook emu as you would any red meat but, like other lean meats, it should be cooked quickly or first sealed at a high temperature or it will toughen. Emu meat is also cured and dried like prosciutto *(pictured)*. Emu eggs are large, but can be used as hen's eggs.

**epazote**

Important in Mexican cooking, epazote is a wild, often unpleasantly pungent, herb with an acidic, slightly lemon taste. Used sparingly it adds depth to egg dishes, black bean dishes, salsas and tortillas, or is infused to make tea. It is used as a carminative, which means that it reduces the gas associated with eating beans.
*Also known as — Mexican tea, pigweed, wormseed*

**escabeche**

Fried fish is covered with a warm spiced and herbed vinegar marinade to make this Spanish dish. Its origins are ancient, and it exists in various forms around the Mediterranean. It is usually served cold as an appetizer, and can be bought in jars. While this method is normally reserved for pickling fish, chicken and chillies can also be treated in the same way.
*Also known as — caveach, scabetch, scapece*

see snail — **escargot**

## ethylene

Ethylene gas is a naturally occurring plant hormone that is released as fruit and vegetables ripen. The gas is tasteless, colourless and odourless and because it can cause early deterioration of other fruit and vegetables sitting nearby, it is best to store fruit and vegetables separately. High ethylene-producing fruit include the apple, apricot, avocado, banana, cantaloupe, nectarine, papaya, passion fruit, peach, pear, plum and kiwi fruit. Ethylene-sensitive vegetables include artichokes, asparagus, beans, broccoli, Brussels sprouts, cabbage, cauliflower, celery, courgettes, cucumbers, lettuce and potatoes. At home, this natural process can be accelerated to quickly ripen fruit—seal them in a paper bag so the gas cannot escape, or put high ethylene-producing fruit near unripe fruit.

Ethylene gas is also used commercially to ripen fruit such as bananas and tomatoes, which are shipped when hard and unripe to reduce the risk of them being damaged. When unpacked, they are treated with ethylene gas, which accelerates their ripening. The gas is also used on citrus fruit to improve their colour.

## Eton mess

In its simplest form, Eton mess is a dessert made by mashing strawberries with cream. Recipes now usually include crumbled meringues and the strawberries are sometimes flavoured with orange zest or a liqueur such as Cointreau or Grand Marnier.

**Also known as — Clare College mess**

### ETON MESS

*Hull a punnet of strawberries, then cut them into pieces and gently squash the pieces. Crush up 2 ready-made meringues and set aside. Whip 250 ml cream until soft peaks form and fold the strawberries and meringue through the cream. Serve in glass dishes. Serves 4.*

## Eve's pudding

### EVE'S PUDDING

*Stew 500 g peeled and sliced apples with 2 tablespoons sugar and 1 tablespoon water until the apples are soft. Spoon the apples into a soufflé dish. Beat 125 g butter with 125 g sugar until creamy, then add 2 eggs, 125 ml milk and 185 g self-raising flour and fold together. Pour the mixture onto the apples and bake at 180 °C for 40 minutes until the top of the pudding rises and browns. Serves 6.*

Eve's pudding is made of layers of apples and sugar, topped with a light sponge or basic steamed pudding mix. The recipe works well with other fruit such as rhubarb, peaches, blackberries or blackcurrants.

## faggot

Traditional British fare made from minced pork offal, breadcrumbs, onions and spices, which are shaped into small balls or sausage shapes. These are wrapped in pig's caul (a thin, net-like membrane that lines the abdominal cavity), then baked in stock. They are popular in northern England and Wales and in areas of Europe and are a type of sausage that can be easily made at home.

## falafel

### FALAFEL

*Soak 500 g chickpeas in cold water for 8 hours, then process with 1 chopped onion, 2 garlic cloves, 1 teaspoon ground cumin, 1 teaspoon ground coriander, ½ teaspoon baking powder and 4 tablespoons chopped parsley. Season well. Blend the ingredients to form a smooth paste. Deep-fry flattened balls of the mixture until dark brown. Serves 8.*

Small fried balls made with either chickpeas or ground broad beans, and flavoured with spices, onion, garlic and herbs. Recipes vary and many in the Middle East claim falafel as their national dish, especially the Christians of Egypt, for whom it is a lenten dish. The chickpea version is seen in Israel, where it is a popular street food, served in a pitta bread wrapping with hummus, tahini sauce and salad. In Egypt, falafel are made with white broad beans and are known as *ta'amia*.

**Also known as — felafel**

## farci

The word farci, when used in the description of a dish, means to 'stuff' or to 'pad out' (from the Latin, *farcire*). In France, vegetables were, and still are, regularly stuffed with small quantities of meat and other vegetables in order to make a small amount of meat go further. *Chou farci* (stuffed cabbage) is common; the stuffing is pushed between the leaves and the cabbage tied back into its original shape to be cooked. The Provençal dish *farci niçois* (pictured) uses vegetables grown in the area. These are stuffed, then baked and usually served with a tomato sauce.

# fat

Correctly called lipids, fats are organic substances insoluble in water. For cooking purposes, a fat is solid at room temperature; oils are liquid. All fats contain the same amount of calories per gram. Fats are the richest source of energy in food and essential for health. They are used as a cooking medium; they provide an insulating layer for meat and poultry, which keeps the meat tender and moist when cooked; they tenderize baked goods; and add richness, character and flavour to foods.

Fats may be saturated, unsaturated or trans-fatty. They are of either animal or vegetable origin, or they may be a form of shortening, a fatty substance made from vegetable oils to which animal fats are sometimes added. Fats may also be invisible, such as the fats used as texture enhancers in processed foods, or the fats in milk, cheese, yoghurt, avocado, nuts and seeds.

Internationally, the type of fat chosen for use in cooking varies enormously. In some areas of France, goose and duck fat, lard and butter are used; in India, cooks vary in their use of dalda (hydrogenated fat), coconut oil or ghee; in both Italian and Chinese cuisine, vegetable oils and a flavoursome rendered pork fat (lard) are used; in Jewish cooking, chicken fat is used in place of dairy fats such as butter because dairy and meat products cannot be mixed. Store fats well wrapped as they pick up other flavours and smells. Exposure to air causes them to go rancid so ingredients such as nuts (high in fat) need to be kept sealed.

## COOKING

*When heated, fats break down to some extent. The hotter they get, the more they decompose; at smoking point, they give off toxic fumes. For these reasons, throw deep-frying fat away after 2 or 3 uses.*

*Chill soups, stews and stocks overnight to bring any fat to the surface. The fat will solidify and can be lifted off. Alternatively, soak up pools of fat on top of a hot dish by laying paper towel on top.*

*Meat juices left from roasting can be sucked out from under fat using a baster.*

*Clockwise from top left: butter; olive oil; duck fat; lard; margarine; ghee.*

### Saturated fats

Found in dairy products such as butter or ghee; animal fats such as pork, beef and duck fat, lard, suet and dripping (the fat that drips from roasting meat); and some vegetable fats such as copha (from coconuts). Saturated fats are usually solid at room temperature, except in the case of palm and coconut oil.

### Unsaturated fats

Usually from vegetables and may be polyunsaturated and monounsaturated. Unsaturated fats are soft or liquid at room temperature. Polyunsaturated fats are considered to be a healthy type of fat as they are thought to lower bad cholesterol and raise good cholesterol. This group of fats includes polyunsaturated margarines and oils such as corn, safflower, grapeseed and canola (rapeseed). Olive oil is a monounsaturated fat. All vegetable fats are cholesterol free.

### Trans-fatty acids

Although some trans-fatty acids are present in meat and dairy products, most enter the diet as hydrogenated fats (the process that hardens liquid fats into solid blocks) from margarine and vegetable shortening, which are also high in saturated fats as the hydrogenation process converts polyunsaturated fat to saturated fat. Recent research has found that trans-fatty acids raise bad cholesterol and lower the good.

## LARDING AND BARDING

*Both larding and barding techniques are used to add flavour and to ensure tenderness when cooking either very lean or possibly tough meat. To bard a piece of meat, tie a piece of bacon or pork fat around a joint before cooking it. To lard a piece of meat, either use a special larding needle to thread pieces of pork fat through a joint or poke holes in the joint with a sharp knife and force pieces of fat into the holes. The fat will melt into the meat as it cooks.*

See also **butter, oil, suet**

A salad of Syrian origin, fattoush is made with pieces of toasted pitta bread, cucumber, tomatoes, spring onions, pepper, lettuce and herbs. Fattoush means 'moistened bread' and traditionally the bread is added to the bowl first, then moistened with oil and lemon juice before the remaining ingredients are added. It is now fashionable to add the toasted bread just before serving so it remains crisp. The salad may be garnished with sumac and pomegranate seeds.

**Also known as — fatoosh**

## FATTOUSH

*Mix a bunch of chopped parsley, 1 chopped cucumber, 4 chopped tomatoes, 4 chopped spring onions and 2 tablespoons chopped mint. Drizzle with olive oil and toss in 2 crushed garlic cloves. Grill 2 pitta breads, break into small pieces and toss the bread through the salad. Season well. Serves 6.*

■ *See also* **sumac**

Small, egg-shaped fruit with thin green skin and a sweet jelly-like flesh. Native to South America, the feijoa belongs to the same family as guava, with which it is sometimes confused. They have a strong, musky smell and taste of a pineapple and banana mix. Use like most other fruit: peel and eat raw or purée and use to flavour ice cream. As the flesh darkens when cut, sprinkle it with lemon juice. Choose fruit that have a strong fragrance and are slightly tender to the touch.

## BRAISED FENNEL

*Cut 4 baby fennel bulbs into quarters and blanch them in boiling water for 5 minutes. Drain well. Fry the fennel in butter until browned, then add 1 teaspoon brown sugar and caramelize. Add 1 tablespoon white wine vinegar and 150 ml chicken stock. Cover and simmer until the bulbs are tender. Boil until the liquid is reduced and stir in 2 tablespoons double cream. Serves 4.*

Native to the Mediterranean but now widely grown, fennel is cultivated for its aromatic leaves and seeds, similar in flavour to aniseed. The fine feathery leaves can be snipped like dill and used to flavour fish dishes, dressings or sauces. Florence fennel, known as *finocchio* in Italy, is cultivated for its thick stems and bulbous base, both of which may be eaten raw like celery, or the base may braised, sautéed or added to soups.

■ *See also* **spices**

## fiddlehead fern

The young fronds of the oyster/ostrich fern, which grows wild in Europe and America. The young shoots are usually boiled and served with a sauce, added to stir-fries or may be eaten raw in salads. Their flavour is similar to that of asparagus. Fiddlehead ferns are sold fresh or tinned.

## fig

A small, soft, pear-shaped fruit with a sweet pulpy flesh full of tiny edible seeds. The fig probably originated in the Middle East and is one of the most ancient of cultivated plants, playing an important part in ancient mythology. Fig leaves were mentioned in the Bible story of Adam and Eve and they were regarded by the Greeks as a symbol of fertility. Figs were recorded as growing in the Hanging Gardens of Babylon, where they were covered with hot sand to dry and preserve them. High in sugar, figs were originally used as a sweetener for food.

### STORAGE

*Ripe figs deteriorate quickly and are best eaten on the day of purchase. They can be stored wrapped in paper in the fridge for 1 or 2 days. To fully appreciate their flavour, bring to room temperature before serving. Dried figs, if stored in an airtight container, will last indefinitely.*

### BUYING

*If you do buy figs that don't have much flavour, quarter them, then drizzle a little honey over them and flash them under the grill.*

### FIGS WRAPPED IN PROSCIUTTO

*Cut 4 figs into quarters and wrap each quarter in a narrow length of prosciutto. Soak 4 skewers in water, then thread 4 fig quarters onto each skewer. Brush the figs with olive oil and barbecue or grill on both sides until browned. Serve with a cheeseboard or as part of an antipasto platter. Serves 4.*

There are over a hundred varieties of figs, and these vary in colour from pale green and golden yellow to brown, red or purple. Some of the varieties of fig include the Caprifig, Smyrna, San Pedro and Common fig.

Figs are available fresh, dried, in syrup and in olive oil. When buying fresh figs, select firm, unblemished fruit that yield to gentle pressure. Peel the fruit (some thin-skinned varieties may be eaten with their skins on), cut off the stems and eat raw; slice and add to a cheeseboard or fruit salad; or lightly poach them. As an antipasto, figs may be wrapped in a slice of prosciutto or filled with cream cheese. Because they are highly perishable, they are often dried or crystallized/candied. These are much sweeter than fresh, and can be eaten as a snack or added to cakes, puddings or compotes.

Filipino food has Malay origins, but years of trade and colonization, particularly by the Spanish, have blended in the flavours and ingredients of Spain, China and America. The food is not especially spicy, and unusually it often combines two main ingredients, like chicken or pork and seafood. *Adobo,* a vinegar-marinated pork or chicken stew, is perhaps the national dish and a result of the Spanish influence. This is served with rice, which forms the basis of all Filipino meals, sometimes with meat sauce or shrimp paste over the top and just a piece of salt fish. Other dishes include soups such as the tamarind-based *sinigang;* *ginataan,* a coconut milk curry; *lechon,* whole roast suckling pig; and *kare-kare,* an oxtail, tripe and vegetable stew in peanut sauce.

With over 7,000 islands, the Philippines has a lot of shoreline and, not surprisingly, fish and seafood play an important part in the diet. One of the earliest dishes, *kinilaw,* is made by 'cooking' the fish in vinegar or lime juice with onions, red peppers and ginger.

The Chinese influence is seen in the *pancit* (noodle) dishes, and *lumpia,* fresh or fried flour and water rolls filled

with Chinese vegetables and meat. The Americans brought canned food to the islands at the end of World War II, and foods such as corned beef were converted to dishes that now seem uniquely Filipino.

It is in the Muslim islands, where Spanish influence was limited, that the most Malay cooking is now to be found, with the use of coconut milk, cassava, chillies, rice, seafood and lack of pork.

Throughout the day, the Filipinos love to eat snacks, often a sweet bun in the morning, though in the afternoon, the *merienda* (afternoon snack) can be a feast of noodles, *lumpia* and sweet cakes. A favourite street snack is *balut,* a duck egg with the foetus, which is eaten whole.

Food is often washed down with the Filipino beer, San Miguel, and followed perhaps by *halo-halo,* a brightly coloured mix of fruit, such as jackfruit, bananas and kiwi fruit, sweet potato, mung beans, jelly, *ube* (purple yam) crushed ice and milk or ice cream.

*From top: Vinegar-stewed pork adobo; prawn and chicken lumpia; halo-halo, a cooling afternoon refreshment.*

## filo

### COOKING

*Allow frozen filo to thaw in the packet, then take out the sheets and stack them on a cloth. Cover the sheets with a dry cloth and use them one at a time as they dry out quickly when exposed to air.*

*Brush each sheet with a little oil or melted butter to make them crisp when cooked.*

*Filled filo parcels can be frozen and then cooked when frozen.*

A paper-thin pastry made with flour and water. Filo means 'leaf' in Greek, and is used widely in the Middle East, Turkey, Greece and Europe for making a variety of pastries and pies such as spanakopita and baklava, or it may be used to wrap seafood or vegetable fillings. The dough for filo is simple enough to make, but stretching it until it is tissue-thin requires great skill and patience. For this reason, commercially made filo, which is available fresh or frozen, is often used.

**Also known as — brik, fillo, phyllo pastry, yufka**

# f i s h

There are thousands of species of fish, mostly saltwater, but many freshwater. In cooking, it is important to choose the right type of fish to suit the particular recipe or cooking method. The fish below are grouped into families—if a particular fish is unavailable, select another fish from within the same family.

## HERRING FAMILY

These sleek, silver fish vary in size from small anchovies and whitebait (herring fry) to larger herrings. This family also includes sardines, pilchards and sprats. Their fatty flesh goes well with sharp flavours and lots of lemon juice.

## DEEP SEA FISH

These live in the depths of the oceans around New Zealand, the North Atlantic, South Africa and South America. They include hoki, grenadier, orange roughy, redfish and scabbard fish. They tend to have white flesh and can be used interchangeably with many of the cod family. However, due to their bone structure, scabbard fish are usually eaten on the bone.

## EELS

Conger and Moray eels have skin rather than scales and are sea fish. They are usually sold as steaks and have firm flesh. Common eels are migratory. They are spawned in the Sargasso Sea or Coral Sea, then carried by currents to the Pacific and Atlantic Oceans and the Mediterranean Sea. They then live in fresh water and are fished as elvers (babies) or adults. Buy skinned eels as they are only easily skinned as soon as they are killed.

*Whitebait*

*Redfish*

*Conger eel*

*Sardines*

*Ling*

*Flounder*

*Pacific salmon*

## COD FAMILY

Generally found living in deep water and cold northern seas. They include cod, haddock, coley, pollack, whiting and ling. They have flaky white flesh with little fat and are good for pies and soups and are best eaten as cutlets and fillets or salted as bacalao.

## FLAT FISH

These fish have two eyes on top of their head and tend to have firm, white flesh. They include dab, Dover sole, brill, flounder, halibut, lemon sole and turbot. Dabs are smallest, halibut the largest and Dover the most sought after. Best eaten off the bone but easy to fillet.

## SALMON FAMILY

Salmon and sea trout are migrating fish, spending time in both fresh and salt water, but nowadays often farmed. They include Atlantic and Pacific salmon and brown trout, which does not migrate. Wild fish are generally superior in flavour and less fatty than farmed fish. All can be filleted; whole or larger fish are used as cutlets.

## REEF FISH

These are usually colourful fish, often fished from coral reefs. They include barracuda, bourgeois, capitaine, emperor, grouper, parrotfish, pomfret and snapper. They go well with Thai, Moroccan and Indian flavours and are best eaten on the bone or in fillets.

## SURFACE-FEEDING (PELAGIC) FISH

These large shoaling fish vary in size but tend to have a meaty flesh. They include tuna, bluefish, mackerel, horse mackerel, jack, kingfish, mahi mahi, marlin, swordfish and yellowtail. These fish go well with acidic or strong flavours but not butter. All are used for sushi and are excellent for grilling, roasting or barbecuing.

*Parrotfish*

*Kingfish*

*Snapper*

*Rainbow trout*

*Golden trout*

## FRESHWATER FISH

Not as popular as saltwater fish and some types are accused of having a muddy flavour because they feed off the bottom. Trout is the most common and is always available fresh, but others include catfish, freshwater bream, carp, char, perch, pike, sturgeon and tilapia. Regional cuisine from inland areas often includes good recipes for pike, carp and char. Freshwater fish go well with butter sauces or cooked whole in Chinese recipes. Many are now farmed.

*Red mullet*

## INSHORE FISH

These fish live relatively close to the shore and include John Dory, gurnard, monkfish (anglerfish), rascasse, red mullet, sea bass, sea bream and wrasse. They generally have a delicate flavour and are best cooked on the bone as the fillets are usually small due to the amount of waste (bones). The tail of the monkfish is the only part eaten.

## BONELESS FISH

These fish have cartilage rather than bones. They include shark, dogfish, skates and rays. Shark and dogfish are interchangeable in recipes. They are usually eaten as fish and chips. Skates and rays are also interchangeable in recipes: only their wings are eaten.

*Skate wings*

Fish is often thought to be a perfect food: it is low in calories, high in protein and contains omega 3. It is also easy to cook and can be married with lots of different flavours. Fish should be considered seasonal to really get the most out of them, as supplies will vary according to spawning seasons and to fishing patterns. It is wise to buy the best fish that day, whatever it is, rather than an inferior fish just to fit a particular recipe.

Fresh fish should smell like the sea and they should under no circumstances actually smell 'fishy'. They should be firm, have shiny scales and bright, clear eyes. Really fresh fish may have gaping mouths and open gill flaps. Some fish, such as salmon and trout, are covered in a clear slime (old slime is opaque). Oily fish deteriorate faster than white fish so be particularly vigilant when buying them.

## SCALES AND SKIN

Fish skin may be covered in tightly overlapping scales or it may be a rough skin-like covering on fish such as dogfish, skate and sole. Fish with scales need to have them removed as they are hard and unpleasant to eat. Fish with skin are also best with the skin removed as it is very tough.

### Gutting and trimming

Fish need to be gutted fairly quickly as their digestive juices can break down and start to decompose their flesh. Once gutted, use the end of a teaspoon to remove any visible blood lines that run along the length of the spine, then rinse well—leaving blood in the fish may taint the flesh. For the same reason, snip out the gills. If the fins are looking ragged, trim them with scissors. For fish such as salmon, the tail is often mitred (cut into a 'V' shape) to neaten it.

## SCALING, GUTTING AND TRIMMING

**1** Run the back of the knife firmly across the skin against the direction in which the scales lie.

**2** Using a pair of scissors, snip from the vent along to the gills, along the softer belly and remove the guts.

**3** For smaller fish, pull the head downwards and snap the spine, then pull the guts out through the belly.

### Filleting

Fish can be filleted either by the fishmonger or by yourself (you will need a filleting knife that has a sharp flexible blade). Round fish give two fillets, one on each side of the fish. Flat fish give four fillets, two on each side or two large fillets. Depending on the size of the fish, you will need one or more fillets per person, or if very large, then a piece of fillet.

## FILLETING ROUND FISH

**1** Cut through the backbone and down the side of the head.

**2** Lift the fillet by running your knife blade between the flesh and the bones until you reach the tail end.

**3** Turn the fish over and remove the other fillet in the same way.

## FILLETING FLAT FISH

1. Lay the fish dark skin side up. Cut behind the head, then down the centre of the spine.

2. Cut around the edge of each fillet and lift off using the knife to cut between the fillet and the bone.

3. Turn the fish over and remove the other two fillets in the same way.

### Skinning

Depending on the recipe, you may or may not need to skin your fish. If the fish will be covered with a sauce, it will be easier to eat the fish with its skin removed. Remove the skin before cooking, or if cooking a whole fish, carefully peel it off after cooking. Dover sole can have their skins removed whole. To do this, make a small cut at the tail end and loosen a piece of skin, then hold the fish down with one hand and the skin in the other and firmly pull it towards the head—it should peel off.

## SKINNING A FILLET

1. Lay the fillet skin side down on a chopping board, with its tail towards you. Make a small cut through the flesh to the skin.

2. Put the knife blade through the cut against the skin and slide or push the blade away from you. Hold onto the skin firmly.

3. Carry on sliding the blade up to the head. You may need to move the blade from side to side as the fillet gets thicker.

### Boning

Fish can also be boned leaving a whole fish with no bones and a pocket in the flesh, which can be stuffed. Pocket boning is suitable for fish such as trout and mackerel. To pinbone a fish, remove any small bones by running your fingers over the fillet to locate them. Pull them out using your fingers or a pair of tweezers.

## POCKET BONING A WHOLE FISH

1. Slit an ungutted fish along its spine from the head to the tail.

2. Ease the flesh away from the bone on both sides of the fish with a sharp knife.

3. Snip through the spine and pull it out, along with the guts, and rinse well.

## BUYING

*Allow 180-200 g fish fillet per person as a main course and 110 g as a starter. If using whole fish, then buy 'plate' size fish.*

*If buying fish to fillet yourself, then assume you will lose half the weight in bones.*

## COOKING

*Use a slice or tongs to turn fish during cooking and try not to pierce the flesh or the juice will escape.*

*Don't salt skinned fish until just before you cook it as it tends to draw moisture out.*

*Fish cooks much faster than meat, and at a lower temperature, so keep an eye on it as you cook, especially on the barbecue.*

### Cooking

Fish can be eaten raw, cooked in acid or salt, or cooked using heat. The most important thing is to cook fish until it is just done: no more or it will be dry and fall apart. Large fish may benefit from being cooked in a moist heat, such as poaching or steaming, so the outside doesn't dry out before the heat reaches the inside to cook it. Make sure the fish is at room temperature when you cook it or the centre will stay too cold.

A fish is properly cooked when the flesh has turned opaque and may be more flaky in appearance (especially white fish). If the flesh is not visible, it will feel firm and flaky through the skin when you press it. If you are checking a large whole fish, you can also make a slit along the backbone and lift a little of the flesh up to check that it is opaque all the way to the bone. When cooked, the dorsal fin will pull out easily.

*Grilled trout with almonds*

### Grilling and barbecuing

Both these methods are suitable for cooking fish steaks, smaller whole fish and fillets. When grilling fish, make sure the grill is fully preheated to the highest setting—this may take up to 20 minutes. Grill the fish on the top shelf until browned and crisp, then move it down a shelf to finish cooking. Don't turn the heat down or the fish will dry out without cooking through. Don't grill fish thicker than 4-5 cm or it won't cook through. For barbecuing, make sure the flames have died down and the coals are glowing. A fish grill, which holds whole fish in shape and makes them easier to turn, is very useful. Baste fish well when grilling or barbecuing to keep it moist.

### Baking and roasting

Both these methods are suitable for cooking whole fish, steaks and fish fillets. Baking suits whole fish or other cuts that can be cooked in a minimum of liquid. Whole salmon and trout can be flavoured with aromatics, loosely covered with foil and baked. Fish can also be baked *en papillote*—in a paper or foil parcel. Roasting cooks fish at a higher temperature and is particularly good for pieces of fillet such as salmon or whole fish.

### Frying

This method is suitable for small whole fish, fillets and steaks. When shallow-frying, use a little fat in a large open pan. If the pieces of fish are small, they can be tossed quickly in the hot fat; if they are larger, they may need to be browned on each side, then cooked through. When deep-frying, immerse whole or pieces of fish in the hot fat and cook them quickly. Steaks or fillets can be dipped in flour or batter first. Fish can also be deep-fried in a wok and this works well for Asian-style fried fish.

### Poaching

This method is suitable for whole fish and fillets. Poaching is a gentle way of cooking fish by submerging them in a barely bubbling liquid such as court bouillon or milk. Poaching is especially suitable for large whole fish such as salmon as it stops the flesh drying out. Poaching can be done in a fish kettle, in a roasting tin covered with foil or in a large frying pan. Poaching is a good low-fat way of cooking fish. Whole poached fish can have their skin carefully peeled off and then garnished and presented as the centrepiece of a meal.

### Steaming

This method is suitable for cooking fillets, parcels of fish and small whole fish. Steaming cooks the fish in a gentle heat and can also be used for adding aromatic flavours to the fish. Use a bamboo steamer and put the fish on a piece of baking paper or a plate. If you are using flavourings such as herbs, put the herbs in the bottom of the steamer, then put the fish on top of them. When steaming, choose pieces of fish that will hold their shape and will not become too fragile.

### Searing and cooking on a griddle

This method is suitable for cooking fillets with the skin on or whole fish and steaks cut from firm-fleshed fish such as tuna or swordfish. This method cooks the fish on a high heat and gives the fish a crisp skin. Brush the pan or griddle with oil and heat it until very hot. Brush the fish with oil and lay it in the pan or griddle and cook until it loosens from the pan (about 2–3 minutes). If you try to move it earlier, it will stick and rip.

## fish sauce

Popular throughout Southeast Asia, particularly in Thailand and Vietnam, fish sauce is a pungent, salty liquid used as a condiment and a flavouring. The liquid is clear, amber to dark brown in colour, and is used like soy sauce. In Vietnam, fish sauce is served with most meals as a dipping sauce, where it may be flavoured with chillies, peanuts or sugar.

Fish sauce is made from salted and fermented dried fish or shrimp, which are layered into large wooden barrels and allowed to ferment. After about 3 months or so, the liquid is drained off to produce a sauce of high quality, normally reserved for table use. Subsequent drainings yield a fish sauce of lower quality, generally used for cooking. Some bottles of fish sauce, especially those from China and Hong Kong, may be labelled as 'fish gravy'.

***Also known as — nam pla, nuoc mam, nuoc nam, patis***

## flaky pastry

A pastry made with a flour and water dough that has pieces of fat folded into it. The pastry is similar to puff pastry, but folded less often. Flaky pastry (like all layered pastries) is cooked at higher temperatures than normal pastry so the layers rise and the dough cooks before the fat has time to melt and run out. When making flaky pastry, it is important to chill all ingredients or the fat may melt and run out of the pastry. If your kitchen is warm or the pastry gets warm and sticky, chill the pastry for about 20 minutes between each roll and fold. Use flaky pastry for pie or tart cases, as a base for pissaladière or pizza-style toppings. Store in the fridge for 2 days or freeze for up to 3 months.

*Vol-au-vents*

■ *See also* **puff pastry**

### FLAKY PASTRY

*Sift 225 g plain flour into a bowl and rub in 40 g butter. Add enough cold water to make a dough and knead until smooth. Roll into a 15 x 30 cm rectangle and dot the top two-thirds with 40 g lard cut into pieces. Fold one-third of the pastry up onto the larded piece and then the top third down. Chill. Give the pastry a quarter turn, then roll it into another rectangle using short, even strokes so the air between the layers is moved around but not pushed out. Fold, turn and chill. Roll again, then dot 40 g butter over top two-thirds of the pastry; fold, turn and chill. Roll and repeat with another 40 g lard as before, then fold, turn and roll. Wrap in clingfilm and chill for 30 minutes. Without using any fat, repeat the folding and rolling once more, then wrap and store in the fridge until needed. When using the pastry, cut it with a sharp knife and try not to disturb the layers too much. When glazing the pastry, only glaze the top layer; don't dribble it down the sides or the layers will stick together and it won't rise well.*

### CUTTING THE PASTRY

*1 Cut circles from the flaky pastry using a sharp biscuit cutter.*

*2 Knock up the edges using the blade of a knife.*

A flan is an open tart made from either a single crust or sponge shell that holds a sweet or savoury filling. Typically, a flan is round and may be filled with custard and topped with fruit. Flans are often cooked in bottomless, straight-sided metal flan rings (or tart rings) and baked on a baking tray, or in tins that have a removable base. In Spain and France, a flan (especially flan Catalan) refers to an egg custard, similar to a crème caramel.

■ *See also* **pie, tart**

In Britain, a flapjack is a biscuit made with rolled oats, golden syrup and butter. The mixture is pressed into a tin and baked, then cut into squares.

In North America, a flapjack refers to a thick pancake cooked on a griddle. Flapjacks may also be called griddle cakes or hot cakes. The 'flap' refers to the method of flipping the pancake over to cook it. Flapjacks are a popular hot breakfast and are served buttered, stacked in a pile and topped with golden syrup.

*From left: North American flapjacks, British flapjacks.*

A large, flat biscuit made with nuts, honey and sometimes candied fruit. When baked, florentines are coated on one side with chocolate, and fork tines or a pastry comb is run through the soft chocolate to create a wavy pattern. In French cooking, the term *à la florentine* refers to dishes, usually fish or eggs, cooked with spinach and served with a cheese sauce. In Italian cooking, the term *alla fiorentina* denotes that the dish is a speciality of Florence.

### FLORENTINES

*Melt together 55 g butter, 60 g sugar and 2 teaspoons honey, then add 50 g plain flour, 70 g chopped blanched almonds and 70 g chopped candied peel. Mix off the heat. Drop 2 teaspoons of mixture onto a greased baking tray and spread out a little. Bake at 180°C for 10 minutes. Cool for 1 minute, then take off the tray. Melt 200 g chocolate and coat the back of each one. Makes about 10 biscuits.*

# flour

Flour is produced by grinding wheat, cereal grain or vegetables such as dried potatoes, chickpeas or nuts (chestnut). Although all grains can be ground into flour, the term 'flour' usually refers to wheat flour; other flours are denoted by their grain, such as rye or buckwheat.

*From top: stoneground wholewheat flour, semolina flour, plain flour, wholemeal flour.*

## MILLING

*During the milling process, grains are sorted and cleaned, then sheared open by rollers, breaking the outer bran layer to expose the wheatgerm and the endosperm (the inside of the grain that contains the starch and protein). These grains are sieved, the bran and germ are removed and the endosperm is ground to the desired fineness. To make flour whiter, it is stored for a few weeks to oxidize naturally (unbleached flour). Flour may also be bleached industrially. In some countries, it also has nutrients such as niacin, riboflavin, thiamine and iron added to make up for the loss of bran.*

## WHEAT FLOUR

*Wheat crops vary from country to country as the different strains are affected by varying climates. Soft wheat grows in temperate climates and hard wheat grows in climates that have hot summers and cold winters, but low humidity. Flours sold in different countries behave in different ways in recipes—for example, soft wheat flour will absorb less liquid. When using recipes written in a different country to the one you are cooking in, bear this in mind as the liquid quantities may need adjusting.*

## TYPES OF FLOURS

| | |
|---|---|
| **Brown** | Contains the wheat germ but only a little bran. Lighter than wholemeal. |
| **Cake** | A very soft flour made by grinding soft wheat. Its low protein and high starch content produces light, soft cakes with a fine crumb. |
| **Granary** | A mixture of wholemeal, white and rye flours with malted grains. Gives texture and a nutty flavour to bread. |
| **Plain** | A multi-purpose wheat flour made by blending hard and soft flours. It is used for cakes, pastries and bread (but won't give as good a result for bread as strong flour). |
| **Sauce** | A special flour used for making sauces without the addition of fat. It can be whisked into a liquid. |
| **Self-raising** | Has a leavening agent (bicarbonate of soda) and salt added to it and is used where baking powder would have been added to the recipe. To make self-raising flour, add 1½ teaspoons bicarbonate of soda and ½ teaspoon salt to 150 g plain flour. |
| **Semolina** | Ground from durum wheat and available as coarse and fine. Fine semolina flour is known as *semola di grano*, a high-gluten flour used for making pasta and bread. |
| **Strong** | A flour made from hard wheat with a high protein (gluten) content and used for making bread. In some countries, such as France, soft wheat rather than strong flour is used for breadmaking. This gives a characteristic texture and sweetness, but stales quickly. |
| **Wholemeal** | Also known as wholewheat or wheatmeal flour, this is made from the whole wheat grain. The bran makes it slightly heavier and it won't rise as well as plain flour, but is more nutritious. The wheat germ in this flour turns rancid quickly, so store in the fridge. Graham flour is like wholemeal flour but has had the wheat germ removed and flakes of bran added. |

The use of edible flowers in cooking is a tradition that dates back several centuries in Europe. Flowers can be added to food merely as decoration, or to give it texture, flavour and colour. Always confirm the identity of the flower and check it is edible before use. Take care that any flower used as food—wild or cultivated—has not been sprayed with poisonous chemicals.

Some flowers used in cooking are roses, violets, borage, marjoram, lavender, mint, oregano, fennel, marigold and nasturtium. Add marigold and nasturtium to salads, but toss them in after the vinegar dressing or they will turn brown. Use rose petals in jellies, jams or cordials, or use lavender to flavour custards and biscuits. Saffron stamens are used to colour and flavour dishes. Frosted flowers make excellent decorations and can be made by dipping them in beaten egg white, then caster sugar.

■ *See also* **elderberry, saffron**

The precursor to Bavarian cream, flummery is a creamy dessert set with a gelling agent and sometimes lightened with beaten egg whites. In medieval England, it was made by boiling oatmeal, which is then strained to give a thickened jelly-like substance. Later, flummery became a richer dish of cream flavoured with spices and almonds or wine. Today, flummery is usually based on milk or berry fruits and thickened with gelatine or cornflour.

### FLUMMERY

*In a saucepan, crush 600 g ripe raspberries with 250 g caster sugar. Bring to the boil and simmer for 2 minutes. In a bowl, sprinkle 2½ teaspoons gelatine on 4 tablespoons water and leave to sponge. Stir gelatine into the hot raspberries to melt it. Strain the mixture through a fine sieve, pour into 4 glasses and set overnight. Serve with cream. Serves 4.*

An Italian flat bread made from yeasted bread dough. The basic focaccia is made by rolling the dough into a flat rectangular or square shape and dimpling with fingermarks. It is then drizzled with lots of olive oil and salt. Other versions may use a variety of toppings, such as olives, onions or tomatoes. Originally, the bread was cooked over an open fire, which provided the inspiration for its name, derived from the Latin, *focus*, meaning 'fireplace'. Focaccia was eaten in Roman times and is the predecessor of pizza.

There are many kinds of focaccia and each is named according to the region it is eaten in. In Naples, the dough is shaped into a ring and called *tortana*; in Venice, the dough is sweetened and named *fugassa*; while in Tuscany, it is known as *stiacciata*; and in Naples as *pizza*.

## foie gras

Although produced in several countries, foie gras, which means 'fat liver', is a French product, especially from Strasbourg and the Southwest. To make it, geese and ducks are force-fed grain, which encourages their livers to grow abnormally large (a goose liver will weigh 450–650 g; a duck liver, 350–450 g). Once removed, the liver is cleaned, seasoned, spiced and cooked. In the Southwest, it may be marinated in alcohol, brandy or Armagnac. It is sold fresh, preserved, semi-cooked and pasteurized in tins, or preserved (in its own fat) in jars. Foie gras is usually sold in several pieces, while foie gras *entier* is a whole liver. *Bloc de foie gras avec morceaux* is a block of foie gras pieces pressed together and *pâté de foie gras* is puréed liver (minimum 75 per cent foie gras). Fresh foie gras will keep for a week in the fridge, jars of preserved foie gras can keep for years in a cold, dark, dry place. If buying fresh, look for a good pink colour for goose, slightly darker for duck. Foie gras is best eaten on its own, where its texture and flavour can be fully appreciated though it can also be cooked and used in recipes.

## fondue

### CHEESE FONDUE

*Rub the inside of a fondue pot with a cut garlic clove. Pour in 1 bottle dry white wine and bring to the boil. Stir in 500 g each of grated Gruyère and Emmental cheese and 2 tablespoons cornflour. Melt together slowly, stirring constantly. Transfer pot to the fondue burner, add a shot of kirsch and season with nutmeg. Serve with cubes of bread for dipping. Serves 6.*

Most commonly a Swiss or Savoy dish of one or more cheeses melted with dry white wine, and often kirsch, nutmeg or cinnamon. The cheeses are melted in the wine, and the other ingredients stirred in. It is served in a special pot over a gas burner with a fork and cubes of bread for dipping. There is an Italian version, *fonduta*, using Fontina cheese, and a *fondue bourguignonne*, using cubes of beef dipped into hot oil. A sweet version is chocolate fondue, made with chocolate and liqueur with pieces of fruit or pastry for dipping.

## food colourings

Dyes of various colours made synthetically or from natural ingredients. Food colourings are usually denoted by E numbers on packaging. Cochineal red (E120) is made from the fat of a Mexican insect but is now usually made synthetically and is known as ponceau 4R (E124), banned in some countries. Others include tartrazine (E102), a colouring used in soft drinks; chlorophyll (E140), a green food colouring made from plants; and caramel (E150), the brown food colouring made from sugar and used in beer, soft drinks and gravy browning. Food colourings can be bought in small bottles for home use. Some food colourings such as tartrazine are thought to cause allergies and hyperactive behaviour in children.

A classic British dessert made with puréed fruit folded into whipped cream or custard, although some recipes use whipped egg whites to lighten the mixture. Fool is traditionally made from gooseberry, but any fruit such as rhubarb, lime, raspberries or kiwi fruit can be used, as long as the fruit's flavour is detected through the cream. Like other desserts such as flummery, trifle and nonsense, fool may have got its name for being a light, frivolous dessert.

*See also* **flummery, trifle**

### RHUBARB FOOL

*In a saucepan, mix 1 kg chopped rhubarb with 2 tablespoons orange juice and 50 g caster sugar. Cook the rhubarb until it is tender. Purée the rhubarb, then fold in 200 ml ready-made custard and 100 ml whipped cream. Serve cold in pretty glass dishes. Serves 6.*

**f o r c e m e a t**

Originally a stuffing made from minced or chopped meat flavoured with herbs and spices, the term now refers to any type of stuffing based on meat, poultry, fish or vegetables. Forcemeat is also the basis for pies and terrines, it is used to make quenelles or may be rolled into balls as a garnish.

see raspberry — **f r a m b o i s e**

**F r a n g e l i c o**

Frangelico is a hazelnut-flavoured liqueur used to flavour desserts such as cheesecakes and biscuits. It is thought that the liqueur was first made in Italy by a hermit, Frangelico, who distilled wild hazelnuts and other natural flavourings. Today, it is made by infusing hazelnuts in alcohol and water, distilling the liquid and flavouring it with cocoa, coffee, vanilla, rhubarb root and orange flowers.

**f r a n g i p a n e**

### FRANGIPANE TART

*Cream 65 g butter with 65 g caster sugar. Beat in 1 egg, 65 g ground almonds, 3 drops almond essence and 10 g plain flour. Roll out 2 x 375 g blocks puff pastry into two 30 x 16 cm rectangles. Put one on a baking tray, spread frangipane down the centre, brush the rim with beaten egg and lie the other piece on top. Seal edges. Cut slits in the top. Brush with beaten egg. Bake at 220°C for 30 minutes. Serves 8.*

Frangipane is a rich, almond-flavoured paste used in patisserie making and as a filling for croissants, Danish pastries and *gâteau Pithiviers*. Frangipane is also the name of an almond-based crème pâtissière. The name is thought to have been derived from a sixteenth-century nobleman, Marquis Frangipani, who invented a perfume made from bitter almonds, which he used for scenting lady's gloves. The perfume proved to be so popular that the pastry cooks of Paris tried to re-create the scent in their cooking by adding almonds to crème pâtissière.

# French food

*Poule au pot—poached chicken with vegetables.*

No other nation on earth reveres its produce and those who transform it for the table as highly as the French. No other people on earth take as much intense interest, sensually and intellectually, in what goes into their stomachs. The cuisines of France, from haute to bourgeois, may have borrowed from and been influenced by many others—particularly the Italians—but they are, unmistakably, first and foremost French. How important both cooking and produce are to the French may be seen in two institutions. Firstly the Michelin Guide (and its rival the Gault Millau), whose annual bestowal or withdrawal of reputation making and breaking stars is headline news. And secondly, the *appellation d'origine contrôlée* system, which sets the rigorous standards of quality and production for French wine and other regional food products. French gastronomy continues to withstand the onslaught of mediocrity from the supermarket and the fast food chain. And each French village still has, by law, at least one bakery.

*Normandy apple tart*

*French cider*

## ILE-DE-FRANCE, PARIS, BRITTANY AND NORMANDY

Paris is the gastronomic capital city, and home to many of France's great chefs. The baguette originated there, patisserie is at its most refined, and haute cuisine, if not confined to Paris, is at its most vigorous and competitive in the four- and five-star restaurants there. Parisian markets and food shops, like Fauchon, are legendary for their quality. However it is the area around Paris, its 'market garden', that supports this gastronomy. The Ile-de-France produces cheeses like Brie and Coulommiers, Argenteuil is synonymous with asparagus, and carrots from Crècy give their name to carrot soup (*potage Crècy*). Brittany and Normandy are important fishing regions with fish markets, mussel and oyster farms on both coasts. Brittany is known for its seafood and Normandy for its dairy products, apples and Calvados. Brittany is also famous for its crêpes and buckwheat galettes and Normandy for its pré-salé (salt marsh) lamb and Rouen ducks.

*Tarte flambée—the Alsatian version of the pizza.*

## THE NORTH, CHAMPAGNE AND ALSACE-LORRAINE

The area between the Ile-de-France and Belgium is notable for its hearty cooking. *Pommes frites* are eaten with mussels and beer, *flamiche* is a local variety of leek pie and the area produces charcuterie and cheeses such as Maroilles. Champagne is the world capital of sparkling wine and shares many dishes with its neighbours. Bordering on Germany, Alsace-Lorraine is renowned for its charcuterie, used in regional dishes such as quiche Lorraine, *choucroute garnie*, *tarte flambée* and *baeckeoffe*, and its tradition of baking including pretzels, rye

*Sole meunière—whole sole cooked with butter and lemon.*

breads, stollen, kugelhopf and mirabelle plum tarts. Alsation Riesling and Gewurztraminer wines are excellent and distinctive.

## BURGUNDY, LYON AND SAVOIE

One of the most important gastronomic regions of France, Burgundy is known for its wines, beef, *poulet de Bresse* and snails. Regional dishes include *boeuf bourguignonne* and *coq au vin*. Lyon is considered the charcuterie centre of France and products include andouilettes, cervelas and pistachio sausages. Savoie is known for its potatoes and produces some of France's greatest cheeses including Reblochon, Tommes, Beaufort and Vacherin.

*Boulangère potatoes—sliced potatoes cooked in stock.*

## PROVENCE

The food of the South reflects its sunny climate and Mediterranean aspect. Vegetables are plentiful with courgettes, tomatoes, peppers, aubergines and garlic used in dishes such as ratatouille and tians. Meat is made into stews such as daubes and navarins. Fish and shellfish are served simply or in bouillabaisse and *bourride*, a dish that uses aïoli to thicken the final stew. Olives grow abundantly in Provence and both olives and their oil are a mark of the region.

## THE ATLANTIC COAST AND THE LOIRE VALLEY

The coast produces oysters and Bulot mussels, while inland in the fertile Loire Valley, Charentais melons, vegetables, game and wild mushrooms are plentiful. Freshwater fish, such as pike and perch, are taken from the Loire. Typical dishes include *chaudrée* (chowder), stuffed mussels, snails in white wine, duck cooked with grapes and Muscadet, gâteau Pithiviers and tarte tatin. Charcuterie such as rillons, rillettes and andouille are well known, as are the wines of the Loire Valley.

*Bourride—a rich fish soup served with croutons and rouille.*

*Salt pork and lentils*

## LANGUEDOC, THE SOUTHWEST, AUVERGNE AND LIMOUSIN

Close to Spain, Languedoc-Roussillon is home to Roquefort cheese, cassoulet, Bayonne ham and Toulouse sausages. Dishes can be hearty like *garbure*, a cabbage soup, and stuffed lamb. The Southwest is known for duck confit, foie gras, walnuts, black truffles and Armagnac. Dishes like *entrecôte Bordelaise* and *magret de canard* are rich in flavour and go perfectly with Bordeaux red wines.

Auvergne and Limousin are in the centre of France, an area that produces beef, lamb and veal, as well as Puy lentils, Cantal, Saint Nectaire and *Bleu d'Auvergne* cheeses. The cuisine is hearty and includes cheese, pork fat and potatoes. *Truffade*, a potato dish, venison casserole and *potées* (thick soups) are favourites. Auvergne is known for its bottled waters such as Badoit, Vichy and Volvic but mostly for being the home of the Michelin Guide.

*Cassoulet—sausage and duck confit cooked with beans.*

## French onion soup

One of the classics of French cuisine. Onions are cooked until they are tender, then caramelized to give the soup its characteristic deep colour and rich flavour. The soup is served in deep bowls with croûtes topped with grated cheese. The cheese is browned under the grill before serving. In some recipes, the empty bowl is first lined with croûtes and sprinkled with cheese. The soup is poured over the top, the croûtes rise to the surface and are then browned under the grill.

## French toast

French toast is made with slices of bread that are dipped in egg and milk, then fried in butter. The toast can be served as breakfast with maple syrup and bacon, or served as dessert with a fruit compote. Originally, French toast was called 'poor knight's pudding' and was made by soaking slices of toast in wine with sugar and orange juice. In France, French toast is known as *pain perdu*, or 'lost bread', as the bread seemingly disappears when soaked in the egg and milk mixture.

**Also known as — eggy bread**

### FRENCH TOAST

*Mix together 25 ml cream, 2 eggs and 45 g caster sugar. Dip 6 slices bread (either fresh or day-old bread is suitable), one at a time, into the milk and egg mixture ensuring both sides are soaked. Heat a knob of butter in a frying pan. Remove the bread from the mixture, drain off the excess liquid and cook on both sides until golden brown and cooked through.*

## fried rice

Cooked rice stir-fried in oil with other ingredients such as small pieces of meat and vegetables, and seasoned with soy sauce. Meat-based fried rice may include either beef, chicken or prawns and vegetable-based dishes may include bean curd, bean sprouts or spring onions. Sometimes an egg may be added to the rice halfway through cooking time. To make fried rice, leave cooked rice to cool for a few hours before use as this allows the rice grains to separate and prevents them from becoming gluggy when cooked again. If storing cooked rice, keep it chilled, and reheat properly to avoid food poisoning. Fried rice may be served instead of rice with Chinese meals, or it may be served as a dish on its own.

An Italian omelette, which may be thick and cooked slowly (like a Spanish tortilla) or thin and cooked over a high heat, and rolled as a snack. Both sides are cooked, either by flipping in the pan, or heating under the grill. Like an omelette, the eggs may be mixed with various ingredients such as cheese, prosciutto, herbs or vegetables such as artichokes, courgettes or onions. It can be eaten hot or cold, as a snack or as antipasto, and is often used as part of a dish, as in *rolé di vitello.*

■ *See also* **eggah**

FRITTATA

*Fry together 1 sliced onion and 1 crushed garlic clove. Add 2 sliced courgettes and fry until cooked. Beat 5 eggs with 50 g grated Parmesan and season well. Pour the mixture into a hot frying pan and shake everything together. Cook over a very low heat until the base is set, then finish the top under a hot grill. Serves 4.*

## fritto misto

In Italian, fritto misto means 'mixed fry' and refers to an assortment of small pieces of meat, fish, vegetables or cheese dipped in batter and deep-fried, or coated in egg and breadcrumbs and pan-fried. The food is eaten while hot, accompanied by lemon wedges.

Regionally, the ingredients used in a fritto misto vary, but it is usual to see a combination of offal, meat, seafood, vegetables and, in some areas, deep-fried sweet custard and fruit. The Piedmontese and Milanese versions are similar: both include a mix of sweetbreads, calf's liver, brains, vegetables and chicken croquettes, but the Piedmontese version also adds fried apple rings, amaretti and semolina croquettes. The Neapolitan version is known as *frienno magnanno*, which means 'fry and eat'. *Fritto misto di mare*, mixed fried fish *(pictured)*, is common in Italian coastal areas and consists solely of fish and shellfish, which are lightly coated in flour and deep-fried.

## frog's legs

Most commonly associated with France, but also eaten in Asia and North America, frog's legs are considered a delicacy, and are said to resemble the delicate flavour of a young chicken. Only certain species of frogs are eaten, and usually only the back legs. Today, special frogs for eating are usually bred on farms. Frog's legs should be cooked briefly or the flesh will toughen. They may be sautéed lightly in butter and parsley, grilled on skewers or braised in red wine.

## fruits de mer

Translated from the French, fruits de mer means 'fruit of the seas' and the term applies to a combination of seafood including crustaceans and shellfish, often served on ice in either one, two or three tiers.

**157**

## fudge

A semi-soft confectionery made with sugar, butter, cream or milk, and flavoured with nuts, chocolate, vanilla or butterscotch. Fudge is often sold in traditionally dairy producing areas such as Devon in Great Britain and Vermont in North America. Both the flavour and texture of fudge have been adapted into other cookery, such as chocolate fudge cake and fudge icing. A grainier version of fudge, known as 'tablet' is found in Scotland, and in the United States, a similar confectionery is called *penuche*, the Mexican word for 'brown sugar'.

### FUDGE

*Melt 90 g sugar and 500 ml milk in a saucepan and boil for 4 minutes. Add 110 g butter, ¼ teaspoon vanilla extract and 4 tablespoons peanut butter. Beat the mixture with a wooden spoon over moderate heat until it thickens and darkens—this will take about 35–40 minutes. Pour the mixture into a 17 cm square, greased tin. Cut into slices when set.*

## fungi

All mushrooms are fungi, but only some mushrooms are actually called fungi. For example, wood ear or beefsteak.

In Europe, Eastern Europe, China and Russia, hunting for mushrooms and fungi is a national pastime and far more types of fungi are eaten in these countries than can be found or bought elsewhere. Fungi can be bought fresh when it is in season but it is much more likely to be found dried. In this case, it just needs to be soaked in cold water for about 20 minutes, or until it swells up and softens.

White

Wood ear

■ *See also* **mushrooms**

### WARNING

*There are thousands of fungi, but only a few are edible. Never take a risk on eating fungi you have gathered yourself without having them properly identified. Some are lethal, others poisonous and cooking will not make them any less so. If in doubt, do not use.*

### TYPES OF FUNGI

**Bamboo**
Also known as staghorn fungus. A lacy fungus that grows on bamboo. It is quite rare and therefore expensive. It has a musty, earthy taste and is used in Asian soups and stir-fries. Usually bought dried and reconstituted.

**Beefsteak**
A large reddish-brown fungus that grows high up, often in chestnut or oak trees and has a meat-like texture. Cut into slices and fry with butter and herbs.

**Cauliflower**
A frilly fungus that looks like a cauliflower. It should be creamy-white—if it turns yellowish, it's too tough to eat. Bought fresh, preserved in oil or dried. Fry or put in soups or stews. Grows at the base of conifers.

**Orange peel**
Looks like orange peel and grows on bare soil. Toss in butter and use to garnish mushroom dishes.

**White**
A crinkly white fungus found in Chinese cooking. It is used mainly for its texture as it doesn't have much flavour.

**Wood ear**
Also known as black fungus, cloud ear, tree ear, Jews ear. Brown in colour and grows on the trunks of beech, walnut and elder trees. It has a crunchy, gelatinous texture and is shaped like a collection of cups. Mainly bought dried and reconstituted and used in Asian stir-fries and soups.

g

**gado gado**

### GADO GADO

*On a plate, arrange 100 g shredded cabbage, cooked; 200 g green beans, cooked; 250 g carrots cut into batons, cooked; 110 g cauliflower florets, cooked; 1 sliced potato, cooked 100 g cubed bean curd. Top with 2 quartered hard-boiled eggs, ½ sliced cucumber and 100 g bean sprouts. Dress with satay sauce (see page 348) and crispy fried onions. Serves 4.*

A classic and well-loved Indonesian vegetable salad, generally made with carrots, beans, bean sprouts, cabbage, cucumber and bean curd garnished with hard-boiled eggs and served with a spicy peanut sauce. The traditional sauce is called *bumbu*. Gado gado is typically served with *krupuk udang*, which are deep-fried prawn crackers.

**See also   prawn crackers**

**galangal**

A spicy root, similar to ginger in appearance and preparation, used in Southeast Asian cooking, especially in Thailand, Indonesia and Malaysia. There are two types. The most widely known is greater galangal from Indonesia, a knobbly root with creamy white flesh and a delicate peppery ginger flavour. Lesser galangal from south China is smaller and has an orange-red flesh and a pungent and more peppery flavour.

Galangal has a tougher, woodier texture than ginger and needs to be chopped finely before use. Cut into thin slices and add to soup, use in curry pastes or in recipes that call for ginger. Buy galangal with pinker stems as these are fresher than the browner ones. Galangal is also available dried, ground or in brine, in which form it is easier to use, and lasts for months in the fridge.

*Also known as — ground Laos, Siamese ginger, Thai ginger*

**galette**

Galette is the general term for a round flat cake. In parts of France, galettes are savoury and are made with mashed *(pictured)* or finely sliced potatoes. In other areas, they may be made from either puff pastry, shortbread or batter. In Brittany, a galette is a buckwheat or maize crêpe.

# game

Originally meaning any animal hunted, killed and eaten, game today refers to those same animals, even if farmed. This includes pheasant, grouse, wild boar, venison and rabbit. Types of game found worldwide vary. In Europe, there is still a strong hunting tradition for feathered and furred game, but there have been some measures taken to protect certain species and much game is now farm-raised. In Africa, game can also include animals such as zebra, which would not be considered an eating animal in Europe. In China, most animals that can be caught are eaten, including bears.

*Farmed game including, from left: guinea fowl, duck (domesticated), pheasant, squab.*

*Game pies*

## TYPES OF EUROPEAN GAME

**Duck**
Includes teal, mallard and widgeon. It has a strong-tasting flesh, should have the parson's nose removed and be hung for a day. Serve one duck for two people.

**Pheasant**
The most common game bird. Hang for about 3 days to develop flavour. Serve one bird for two people.

**Pigeon and squab**
No hunting season as they are considered vermin by farmers. Hang for 1 day. Serve one bird for two people.

**Snipe and woodcock**
Small birds with long beaks. Hang for 3 days, then roast undrawn with the head on and beaks pushed through their thighs to truss them. Serve two birds per person.

**Partridge**
Usually grey- or red-legged partridge. Best just after the harvest when they have been eating grain. Hang for 3 days. Serve one bird per person.

**Grouse**
Includes red or Scottish grouse, black grouse and capercaillie. Choose young, plump grouse. Serve one young bird per person.

**Guinea fowl**
Farmed since Roman times, guinea fowl are indigenous to Africa where they are still wild. Serve one per two people.

**Hare and rabbit**
Hare and wild rabbit have a stronger flavour than farmed. Hare is hung, but rabbit is eaten straight away.

**Wild boar**
Often farmed but also wild in Europe. Similar to pork flesh but darker and can be cooked in the same way.

**Venison**
Venison is the meat of wild, park or farmed deer. The meat is dark in colour and stronger in flavour than beef.

## PREPARATION

*Hanging tenderizes and encourages a more gamey flavour. Hang game in a cold, well-ventilated place.*

*Before cooking, birds need to be plucked, drawn and hung by the neck; furred game needs to be skinned, paunched (gutted) and hung by the feet, except hare, which is hung before it is paunched in order to collect the blood. Lead shot should be removed where possible.*

*Game is usually a lean meat that benefits from being marinated.*

*Choose young birds for roasting and use slightly older birds for pâtés, casseroles or terrines.*

***See also*** ***duck, goose, guinea fowl, hare, pheasant, pigeon, rabbit, venison***

**gammon** — *see ham*

*Roll ganache into balls, then coat them in grated chocolate or cocoa.*

A mixture of melted chocolate and cream, varying in proportion according to how soft it needs to be. When rolled into balls, ganache can be used to fill truffles, it can be whipped with butter to make butter cream or mousse, used to fill little tartlets, or melted and used as a pouring icing to give a shiny glaze to cakes. Store ganache in the fridge for up to 2 months, or freeze it for up to 6 months. Before use, bring back to room temperature.

## GANACHE

*Finely chop 225 g dark chocolate and melt over a saucepan of barely simmering water, ensuring the bowl doesn't touch the water. Leave the chocolate to soften, then stir until smooth. Bring 175 ml cream just to the boil, then add to the chocolate. Mix until smooth. Use by rolling small amounts into balls to make truffles. Makes about 15 truffles.*

**garlic**

## COOKING

*Raw garlic is more potent than cooked. When garlic is cooked, some of the starch converts to sugar, making the garlic less pungent.*

*Be careful not to overbrown or burn it as it can become very bitter.*

*Chopping or crushing garlic releases the flavours.*

*Crush a whole garlic clove by putting it under the flat blade of a knife and banging the knife with your fist.*

*If the clove has sprouted, cut out the green sprout from the centre.*

*Flavour oil with garlic by frying slices in oil, then discard the slices.*

*Garlic, including garlic oil and fresh garlic (centre).*

*Brush whole garlic bulbs with olive oil and barbecue until soft.*

A strongly flavoured bulbous herb from the same family as the onion and the leek whose folkloric powers are legendary: garlic repels vampires, for example. Each head is made up of a cluster of 10 to 16 cloves, and both head and individual bulbs are covered with a paper-like skin. There are many varieties of garlic, each differing in size, pungency and colour, but the most common are the white-skinned American or Creole garlic; the pink or purple Mexican or Italian garlic; and the larger Tahitian garlic. In dishes such as aïoli, tapenade and pesto, garlic is indispensable, and it adds flavour to a variety of sauces, stews and meats. Don't be tempted to use more than the specified amount, as garlic will overpower the other flavours in the dish.

Garlic is freshest in the summer when the bulbs are firm and the cloves harder to peel. Later in the season, the garlic begins to dry out—it is easier to peel but the flavour is quite intense. Choose fresh, plump-looking garlic with a white skin and fat neck as these have a more delicate flavour; discoloured garlic or bulbs that are sprouting will have a rancid flavour. The green shoots of garlic are also available in some areas. They can be used like chives and snipped onto salads and stir-fries. Garlic can also be eaten as a vegetable, barbecued or roasted whole or as cloves.

## gateau

The French word for cake, although when used in English it usually refers to something elaborate and beautifully decorated—a cake with its best dress on. In some instances, gateau refers to a savoury dish, such as a potato cake. Famous gateaux include Black Forest gateau, *gâteau Saint Honoré*, named after the patron saint of pastry cooks, and *gâteau l'Opera*, named in honour of the Paris opera.

## gazpacho

A Spanish vegetable soup characteristically served chilled. Recipes vary, but it is usually made with puréed tomatoes, peppers, cucumber, onions, olive oil, vinegar and bread. It was originally made by field workers who pounded their bread and oil rations with water and salt and added whatever vegetables were available to the resulting soup. 'Gazpacho' is Arabic in origin and means 'soaked bread'.

## gelatine

A colourless, almost flavourless protein used as a setting agent, mainly for desserts, made commercially from the bones and tendons of cows or pigs. Good-quality gelatine should be clear when dissolved, have no flavour and dissolve easily. Although recipes will give an exact amount of gelatine required, the resulting set will vary according to the brand and what you are setting. If gelatine is boiled or if acidic liquids are added to it, it may lose its setting qualities, and some fruit such as pineapple, papaya and figs contain enzymes that will eat the protein in gelatine and not set. Never freeze products containing gelatine as they may become stringy. Gelatine is sold as granules or as clear sheets (leaves). Generally 3 teaspoons or 6 sheets of gelatine sets 500 ml liquid.

***Also known as — gelatin***

### USING SHEET GELATINE

1 Soak the gelatine sheets in cold water for 1 minute, or until they are floppy.

2 Squeeze out any excess water and then stir the sheets straight into a hot liquid to dissolve them.

### USING POWDERED GELATINE

1 Put 3 tablespoons water into a glass bowl and sprinkle on the gelatine evenly.

2 Leave the gelatine to sponge—it will swell. Add the sponged gelatine to a hot liquid and stir well to dissolve it.

## GENOISE COMMUNE

*Line the base and sides of a moule-à-manqué mould with greaseproof paper. Grease the paper and dust it with flour. Put 4 eggs and 55 g caster sugar in a heatproof bowl and place it over a saucepan of barely simmering water. Whisk together the sugar and eggs until the mixture is white in colour, about four times its original volume and thick enough to hold a trail when it falls from the whisk. Take the bowl off the heat and whisk until the mixture is cold, then fold in 55 g softened butter and sift 125 g plain flour onto the mixture. Using a large metal spoon, quickly fold in the flour, being careful not to lose any air from the mixture. Carefully pour the mixture into the baking tin. Bake for 30–35 minutes, or until the cake feels firm when pressed and has shrunk from the side of the tin. Remove the tin and baking paper and cool on a wire rack. Fill with jam and cream and dust the top with icing sugar.*

A light, airy sponge-like cake that relies on air beaten into the eggs to make it rise. If the eggs are not beaten sufficiently or the flour is folded in too roughly, there will not be enough air in the mixture to make it rise well. There are two types of génoise: *Génoise commune*, which has less butter than flour, and *Génoise fine*, which has equal quantities of butter and flour. Neither is a true sponge as sponge cakes do not contain any fat. Génoise is traditionally made in a *moule-à-manqué* mould, a French cake tin with slightly sloping sides. The cake can be flavoured with chocolate, almonds or liqueurs. Make génoise on the day you want to eat it, or freeze it straight away as it doesn't have enough fat to make it last for more than 2 to 3 days.

Génoise is named after the city of Genoa in Italy and the recipe was adapted by the French. It is not the same as Genoa cake, which is an almond cake. Génoise is used as a cake as well as a sponge base for various gâteaux and desserts.

**Also known as — genoese cake**

## gentleman's relish

Gentleman's relish is a paste made from a mixture of anchovies, butter, herbs and spices used to spread on pieces of buttered toast. The most famous is Patum Peperium, which was invented in 1828 by John Osborn and is sold in a distinctive white pot. It is used for making savouries such as Scotch woodcock and anchovy toasts.

*See also* **Scotch woodcock**

## ANCHOVY BREAD

*Make diagonal cuts along a baguette, cutting only two-thirds of the way through. Spread each cut with some butter and some gentleman's relish, then wrap the loaf tightly in foil. Bake at 200 °C for 10 minutes, or until heated through. Serves 4.*

# German food

There is no one dish that typifies German cuisine, as each of its 16 states has a distinct culinary style. Germany can, however, be roughly divided geographically into northern, central and southern. In the North, the food tends to reflect the influences of the nearby Scandinavian countries and the Baltic sea; in the central region it is richer and heavier; and in the South, it is strongly influenced by neighbouring Italy and Austria.

Germany grows a wide variety of fruit and vegetables and farms all types of meat. The sea and countless rivers ensure an abundance of fish.

Like neighbouring Belgium, Germany is renowned for its excellent beers, with about 5,000 varieties brewed. Its wine-growing regions produce fine wines, most especially the Rieslings of the Rheingau. Schnapps, distilled from fruit such as apples and pears, is widely drunk.

## MEAT AND POULTRY
The pig is an important source of food, of which virtually every part is eaten. The quality and variety of sausages, known as *Wurst*, is famous worldwide and every region has its own distinctive sausage. *Schweinshaxe*, a typical dish, is prepared from a ham hock that is baked until it crisps outside, then served with mashed potatoes and sauerkraut, German cuisine's elevation of the humble cabbage to the heights of gastronomy. Beef is served in dishes such as *Sauerbraten*, marinated in vinegar, sugar and seasonings. Goose and duck are popular, often braised in beer or wine, and stuffed with apples or other fruit. Goose is served widely at Christmas, often with red cabbage.

## SEAFOOD
Southern Germany has countless rivers and lakes providing plentiful fish. Trout, salmon and eel are eaten, carp is one of the most popular river fish, and is

traditionally eaten at Christmas and the New Year. Herrings are eaten pickled, as Bismark herring, and as rollmops.

## COMMON FOODS
Bread is a staple and bakers produce over 200 different breads including rye, wheat, mixed grain, wholemeal and speciality breads, many flavoured with caraway seeds. Among the best known breads are pumpernickel, a heavy rye bread; *Vollkornbrot*, wheat mixed with rye; and *Leinsamenbrot*, linseed mixed with rye. Day-old bread may be used to make a soup of bread and vegetables. Pretzels, made from bread dough, are widely eaten as a snack. Among other wheat products are *Spätzles*, a cross between a dumpling and a noodle.

Potatoes feature prominently in the cuisine, often in specialities such as pancakes and dumplings, but also sliced and fried in butter, sometimes with cumin and onions. Potato pancakes, called *Kartoffelpuffer* in northern Germany, are served with apple sauce.

Apples are widely used in sauces, jellies and cakes, as pie fillings, served with cabbage or made into apple wine. The many coffee *Konditoreien* houses, where streusel cake, apple or plum cake or tortes are served, play an important part in German life. Stollen is traditionally eaten at Christmas and is a heavy sweet dough cake made with marzipan, raisins, candied peel and citrus peel. Spice biscuits, known as *Lebkuchen*, are eaten all over Germany.

■ *See also* **Black Forest gateau, cabbage, German sausage, kugelhopf, lebkuchen, marzipan, Spätzle, stollen**

*From top: Potato cakes (Kartoffelpuffer) with apple sauce, Wurst (sausage) on sauerkraut, Sauerbraten with potato dumplings and red cabbage, plum cake (Pflaumenkuchen), German beer served with pretzels.*

Germany could be considered to be the sausage-eating centre of the world—over 1,500 types of sausages are made there and many sausages eaten throughout the rest of the world are of German origin. Both the frankfurter from Germany and wienerwurst from America claim to be the original hot dog sausage.

*Clockwise from top left: Zungenwurst, Bierwurst, Blutwurst, Cervelat, Landjager.*

## SAUSAGES FOR SLICING AND EATING

**Bierwurst**    Has a coarse texture and flavoured with cardamom or juniper. Once made from ham marinated in beer.

**Blutwurst**    The name for black pudding. Some varieties contain pig's blood, pork, bacon fat, marjoram and allspice. It can be eaten cold or fried.

**Cervelat**    Large sausage with a fine texture. Made from minced pork and beef and sometimes smoked.

**Jagdwurst**    Scalded smoked pork sausage.

**Landjager**    Cured, dried, smoked sausage made mainly from beef, flavoured with cardamom. Pressed into a square shape.

**Leberwurst**    A liver sausage. Mettwurst is a spreadable liver sausage.

**Zungenwurst**    Large smoked sausage made from pork fat, liver, tongue and blood. May be seasoned with nutmeg and paprika.

## SAUSAGES THAT NEED COOKING

**Bockwurst**    Smoked sausage made from pork and veal or beef minced with fat and spices. It looks like a frankfurter and is cooked in the same way.

**Bratwurst**    Grilling or frying sausage with a pale colour and fine texture. Some varieties are smoked.

**Frankfurter**    Cold, smoked sausage originally made from finely ground pork but also made from beef. Poach gently in water.

**Knackwurst**    Sold tied in pairs. May contain a mixture of ground pork and beef, which is seasoned with cumin, garlic and salt. Usually eaten with potato salad.

**Wienerwurst**    Made from pork, beef and veal, smoked, cooked and dried. Sausages are sold linked in chains.

### FRANKFURTER AND POTATO SALAD

*Put 1 kg peeled, chopped, cooked potatoes in a bowl. Fry 4 bacon rashers, chop them and add to bowl. Add 4 tablespoons sour cream, 1 teaspoon wholegrain mustard, 6 tablespoons mayonnaise, 4 chopped, cooked frankfurters and 4 finely chopped spring onions. Mix well. Season with black pepper. Serves 6.*

See also **sausage**

see butter — **ghee**

# gherkin

A small variety of cucumber, which is pickled by soaking it first in brine, then vinegar. Some other types of cucumbers are pickled in the same way, but are not true gherkins. Gherkins are commonly eaten with pâtés, cold meats and ploughman's lunches, as well as being an ingredient in tartare sauce. The French word for gherkin is 'cornichon', and some smaller gherkins are sold under this name.

**Gherkins go with — mature Cheddar**

# ginger

*Fresh ginger*

### GINGERBREAD MEN

*Mix 340 g plain flour with 2 teaspoons ground ginger and 1 teaspoon bicarbonate of soda. Rub in 110 g butter and add 150 g dark brown sugar, 1 beaten egg and 4 tablespoons golden syrup. Mix to a dough. Cover and chill for 30 minutes. Roll out the dough to 5 mm thick, then cut out the men with a cutter. Push currants in the dough for the eyes. Bake at 220°C for about 8–10 minutes. Cool and decorate with glacé icing.*

The knobbly, beige-coloured rhizome of a tropical plant. Ginger is indigenous to Southeast Asia, but is now grown all over the world in tropical climates. It was originally used in Europe in either a powdered, dried, crystallized or preserved form, but as Chinese, Indian, Middle Eastern and Caribbean cooking spread, ginger became increasingly available and can now be bought fresh year-round. Store fresh ginger in the fridge tightly wrapped in clingfilm. Unless very fresh, ginger is usually first peeled, then grated or sliced. If it's fibrous, it may be easier to grate it, preferably with a bamboo or ceramic grater.

**Ginger goes with — coconut milk, coriander, garlic, lemon, lime juice, pear, rhubarb, soy sauce, spring onion**

**See also  spices**

## TYPES OF GINGER

| | |
|---|---|
| **Fresh** | At its best when young and juicy—the root is covered in a tender skin and has a sweet, peppery flavour. As it gets older, the flavour strengthens but the flesh becomes more fibrous. Add to curries or Asian dishes. |
| **Ground (powdered) or dried** | Mainly used in baked goods such as gingerbread, ginger cake and biscuits. |
| **Preserved and crystallized** | Pieces of ginger that have been boiled in sugar syrup to preserve them. Crystallized ginger is then removed from the syrup. Use in baking or drizzle the syrup on ice cream or fruit. |
| **Pickled** | Sliced pieces of young ginger, pickled and often dyed pink. Eaten as a palate cleanser between pieces of sushi. |
| **Mioga** | A close relative of ginger used for its fragrant buds and stems. It is sliced thinly and used to garnish or give flavour to soups, tempura and sashimi. |

*Ground*

*Preserved*

*Pickled*

*Mioga*

# ginseng

An aromatic root found in Asia and North America. In the past, it was thought that its human-like shape was a sign that it was a remedy for ailments afflicting all parts of the body. Ginseng is still widely recognized for its health-giving properties. The Chinese consider it to be 'the root of life' and add it to soups. In Korea it is infused in tea.

*Clockwise from bottom left: ginseng root, ginseng tea and tea granules, ginseng drink.*

Cherries that have been candied to produce a glossy appearance, and often dyed red, green or blue. Undyed, they are a more natural dark-red colour. The cherries are picked just before they are ripe and stored in brine until needed. They are then pitted and candied by boiling them in sugar syrup. Use glacé cherries for baking, in biscuits or Christmas cake, or as a decoration on small cakes.

## gnocchi

Small dumplings made into balls or cylinders, poached in simmering water, then served with a sauce. The original version was made from pieces of boiled semolina pasta dough. A later version was made with potato and is known as *gnocchi di patate*. This type is also made with pumpkin, rice or polenta.

Roman gnocchi are a baked version made of semolina dough but with egg and Parmesan added to them. Gnochetti are small, shell-like pasta shapes with a hollow middle, originally made by pressing the dough around the thumb. *Gnoccho* means 'lump' in Italian, hence *gnocchi* are lumps.

### POTATO GNOCCHI

*Cut 1 kg floury potatoes into quarters and steam until tender. Peel while warm, then mash (don't use a food processor). Mix in 2 egg yolks, 2 tablespoons Parmesan, salt and white pepper to taste, then gradually stir in 125–185 g plain flour. When the mixture gets too dry to use a spoon, use your hands. Once a loose dough forms, transfer to a lightly floured surface and knead gently. Work in enough extra flour to give a soft, pliable dough, which is damp but not sticky. Divide the dough into 6 parts. Working 1 part at a time, roll out to a 1.5 cm thick rope and cut into 1.5 cm lengths. Shape the gnocchi (see photograph). Simmer the gnocchi in batches, about 20 at a time. They are cooked when they rise to the surface. Remove with a slotted spoon and drain. Serve with chopped sage leaves fried in melted butter. Serves 6.*

### SHAPING GNOCCHI

1 *Divide the dough into pieces. Roll the outer surface of each piece over the tines of a fork to form deep ridges.*

## goat

An important source of meat in Africa, the Middle East, the Caribbean, Spain and Italy, goats are also bred for their milk, which is usually made into cheese. In Indian cooking, goat is curried; in Italy, it may be roasted like lamb with garlic and rosemary. Young kid is considered a delicacy in Mediterranean countries. To bring out its rich flavour, goat should be braised or stewed as it can be tough and stringy.
*Also known as — cabrito, capretto, chevron*

## gold leaf

An edible but tasteless thin sheet of pure gold used for decoration on sweetmeats, chocolates and cakes. It can also be used to great effect by floating a sheet on top of a bowl of soup—the steam causes it to puff up into a bubble. Gold has been used as a food decoration for hundreds of years and gingerbread men were once covered in gold leaf. In India, gold has been used since ancient times in sweetmeats or desserts for special occasions.

Gold leaf is sold in specialized cake shops and art shops, and is bought in books of individual leaves. It is very fragile and should be applied from its backing paper or off the blade of a knife. Store in a cool, dry place in an airtight container to prevent the gold from tarnishing. Gold is an authorized food additive, with the number E175.

*Also known as — varak*

## golden syrup — see treacle

## goose

A domesticated wild bird traditionally eaten at Christmas in Northern Europe and to a lesser extent during the rest of the year. The goose is a useful bird—the liver becomes foie gras, preserved goose is a necessary addition to cassoulet, and goose fat is highly prized in France especially. Geese are best roasted. Remove visible fat and prick the skin to allow the fat to run off during cooking. Like all water birds, geese appear large, but yield little meat. Figure on a 6 kg bird to feed eight people.

## gooseberry

A tart berry related to the currant, whose size and colour varies considerably, ranging from green, white, yellow or red, with either smooth or hairy skin. Gooseberries picked when green and immature are very tart, and are the best choice for cooking. The larger, fully ripened variety are better eaten raw as they lose some flavour when cooked. Gooseberries are the perfect accompaniment to oily food, and in England they are traditionally served puréed as a sauce with mackerel. They are also used in pies, puddings, fools and tarts, and their high pectin content makes them an excellent choice for jams and jellies. Gooseberries need to be topped and tailed before they are cooked and generally need a fair amount of sugar to sweeten them. If using them for smooth desserts, sieve when cooked to remove any skin and pips.

*See also fool*

## gougère

A savoury round choux pastry flavoured with cheese—traditionally Gruyère, Comté or Emmental. They can be eaten warm or cold, and in Burgundy small ones are an accompaniment to the tasting of the local wines. Today, gougères can also be circular-shaped choux pastries filled with savoury fillings such as chicken, fish or mushroom, similar to vol-au-vents.

## goulash

A very confusing dish whose only certifiable ingredients are meat cut into cubes, onions and paprika. The confusion arises from the arrival from the New World of the raw material for one of those ingredients, the red pepper for paprika, which replaced ground black pepper. In Hungary, goulash (or *gulyás*) is a soup named after Hungarian herdsmen (known as *gulyáshús*), descended from a stew cooked dry for easy transport. What the world today calls Hungarian goulash, in Hungary is called *pörkölt*, or *paprikás* if it is served with sour cream.

**Also known as — Hungarian goulash**

## gourd

A name applied to a large variety of hard-shelled fruit of mainly Asian and African origins. Gourds are related to pumpkins and squashes, and are as much used for decoration, storage (when dried and emptied) and even music (when dried with the pips left in as shakers) as they are for food. Some edible varieties include the wax, snake and turban gourds.

## graham cracker

Whole-wheat biscuits sweetened with honey, created in the 1830s by the Reverend Sylvester Graham who promoted them as a health food. Graham crackers are rectangular in shape and similar to a digestive biscuit. The crackers may be crushed and used as crust for cheesecake and other dessert bases.

## granita — see ice cream

## granola

Similar to muesli, a breakfast cereal made from a combination of nuts, dried fruit and grains such as oats and wheat. Granola is commercially produced but can also be made at home. It may sometimes be sweetened with honey and toasted or baked. Granola is served with milk and sometimes fruit and yoghurt.

## grape

The history of the evolution of the grape parallels the history of Western civilization, and the Egyptians, Greeks and Romans were all early cultivators of this fruit. They are divided into two main groups: white (sometimes referred to as 'green'), and black (sometimes referred to as 'red'). Dessert grapes (those grown for eating) vary in flavour according to the variety and where they are grown. Muscat grapes have a good flavour but need to be seeded. Thompson seedless, sometimes called 'sultana grapes', are good for cooking when whole grapes are required. Other common varieties include the black and seeded grapes, Cardinal and Muscat; the red seedless grapes, Flame, Delaware and Ruby; and the white seedless grape, Niagara. Black Corinth grapes are tiny grapes with a sweet flavour.

In cooking, grapes can be used in tarts, wine jelly or added to sauces. Cut them into little bunches and serve with cheese, or add to fruit salads.

### STORAGE

*Grapes will ripen quickly at room temperature so are best stored in the fridge. Remove about half an hour before eating as their flavour improves at room temperature, and wash well to remove any insecticide. Don't wash grapes before storing—it's impossible to thoroughly dry between them and trapped water will dilute their flavour and will cause the grapes to deteriorate quickly.*

### SOLE VERONIQUE

*Fry 8 sole fillets in butter until cooked. Set aside and keep warm. Fry 2 chopped shallots in 30 g butter, then add 100 ml white wine and 200 ml fish stock. Reduce the liquid by half. Stir in 200 ml cream, season, then add 200 g peeled, seeded white grapes. Pour the sauce over the fish. Serves 4.*

*See also  **dried fruit, verjuice, vine leaves, wine***

The largest available citrus, a cross between the pummelo and the shaddock, named for the fact that they grow in clusters. First recorded in Barbados, grapefruit now grow all over the world, but particularly in South Africa, South America, the West Indies and Australia.

Of the two major varieties, Duncan (seeded) and Marsh (seedless), the seeded has more flavour. There is also a pink version of each variety. Buy heavy fruit with unblemished skins. Grapefruit are traditionally eaten at breakfast—cut them in half and scoop out the flesh with a spoon or with a special grapefruit knife that has a curved blade to loosen the segments. Grill them with a sprinkling of sugar, add to salads and fruit salads, use for sorbets and granitas or sprinkle segments with Campari. Grapefruit peel can also be candied.

### GRAPEFRUIT AND CAMPARI GRANITA

*Mix 600 ml grapefruit juice with 200 g caster sugar until dissolved. Add 90 ml Campari and a squeeze of orange juice. Pour into a freezerproof container and freeze for 3 hours. Remove from the freezer, stir well, then refreeze. Repeat the freezing and stirring process until you have a rough, icy texture. Serve in glasses. Serves 6.*

**gratin**

The effect of a crisp brown top, which is achieved by placing a dish of vegetables, fish, meat or poultry, with or without a topping of grated cheese and/or breadcrumbs, under a grill or salamander. In common usage, 'au gratin', usually refers to a dish—such as boiled cauliflower—covered with mornay sauce, sprinkled with grated cheese and baked, or sliced potatoes cooked with onions and cream until it is browned and crisp on top.

The word 'gratin' also applies to the dish used for cooking the gratin, either a baking dish or a round or oval dish with flat handles. Gratins are usually served in the dishes in which they are cooked and may be serving sized or individual portions.

### GRATIN DAUPHINOIS

*Finely slice 1 large onion and cook gently in 30 g butter until tender but not browned. Finely slice 800 g all-purpose potatoes. Halve a garlic clove and rub it around the inside of a large ovenproof dish. Layer potato and onion, seasoning as you go. Bring 450 ml cream to the boil and pour over potatoes. Sprinkle with 30 g grated Gruyère cheese and cover with foil. Bake at 180°C for 1 hour, then take off the foil and bake for another 20 minutes. The top should be crisp. Leave to stand for 10 minutes before serving. Serves 6.*

# gravlax

Raw salmon cured with salt, sugar, a spirit such as vodka, peppercorns and flavoured with dill. The salmon is sliced thinly and served on pumpernickel or rye bread as an hors d'oeuvre, usually with a mustard and dill sauce. Gravlax is a speciality of Sweden and it means 'buried salmon', referring to the classic method of burying the salmon in the ground to cure it. It is traditionally served on 30 April in Sweden to celebrate the arrival of spring.

**Also known as — gravadlax, gravlaks**

## GRAVLAX

*Freeze and then defrost 2 x 1 kg salmon fillets to kill any bacteria or nematodes. Remove the small bones using your fingers or tweezers. Dry the fillets with paper towels and lay 1 skin side down on a tray. Combine 3 tablespoons sugar, 1 teaspoon black pepper and 1½ tablespoons salt. Sprinkle the fillet on the tray with 1 tablespoon vodka or brandy, then rub in half the sugar mixture; sprinkle on 1 tablespoon chopped dill. Rub the remaining sugar mixture into the other fillet and lay it flesh side down on top of the first fillet. Cover with clingfilm, put a heavy board on top and weigh down with 3 heavy tins. Put in the fridge for 24 hours, turning it over after 12 hours. Tip off any liquid. Brush off the dill and any seasoning mixture with a stiff pastry brush. Sprinkle with 2 tablespoons dill and press onto the flesh. Shake off any excess. Serve as a whole fillet or pre-slice it thinly on an angle towards the tail. Serve with the mustard sauce. Serves 24.*

## MUSTARD SAUCE

*In a small bowl, whisk together 3 tablespoons Dijon mustard, 3 tablespoons wholegrain mustard, 150 ml oil, 2 teaspoons cider vinegar and 1½ tablespoons chopped dill. Season to taste. Cover and refrigerate until needed. Makes 250 ml.*

# gravy

## GRAVY

*Tip off all the fat in the roasting pan except about 1 tablespoon, then add 1 tablespoon flour to make a roux. Cook until brown, then add enough stock to make a gravy. Stir well, until it comes to the boil, to prevent it from going lumpy. Boiling gravy will make it shiny as it cooks the flour. For extra flavour, add 1 tablespoon redcurrant jelly or port. Serve in a warmed gravy boat.*

Gravy is a sauce made from the juices and residues left in the pan after roasting meat or poultry. The fat is poured off and the pan deglazed with a good stock and/or a suitable wine. This may or may not be thickened with flour. For added flavour, roast the meat on two halves of onion. Today, regrettably, gravy often comes out of a packet. Originally, gravy was a sauce made from broth and a thickening agent such as ground almonds.

The otherwise-varied island and mainland cuisines of Greece share some characteristics. Firstly, a strong foundation in the ingredients used since earliest times: chickpeas, honey, wild greens (*horta*), lemons, olive oil, figs and cheese. Secondly, a greater or lesser adaptation of the influences from 100 years of incorporation into the Byzantine empire, and 400 years under Ottoman (Turkish) occupation. Lastly, strong influences from their close neighbours in Africa and the Middle East can be seen. Other than these strong historical and geographical influences, Greek food is based on fresh produce, treated simply to maximize its flavours.

*Saganaki—pan-fried cheese*

Modern Greeks love to graze on mezes, small snacks, eaten throughout the day: black olives, cubes of feta cheese, spiced sausage, taramosalata and other dips, and stewed octopus, often accompanied by iced ouzo, an anise-flavoured spirit. This habit probably came about because, like the Spanish, the Greeks rarely drink without eating. In recent years, there has also been a steady stream of new Greek wines of exceptional quality to join the beloved or despised retsina, a wine flavoured during fermentation with crystals of pine resin.

Fish is abundant, often simply grilled and served with lemon, or baked with herbs such as fennel, aniseed or coriander. Mussels, crustaceans and octopus are also popular. Sheep and goat are widely farmed as they are well suited to the rocky hillsides. Sheep are kept mainly for their milk, but are also eaten as lamb. The milk is made into feta, Greece's most popular cheese. This salty cheese was traditionally preserved in brine so that it was available even when there was no milk. Feta is indispensable in Greek salad, to fill pies and as a topping.

*Avgolemono soup is a chicken soup thickened with rice and flavoured with a lemon and egg sauce.*

*Fried salt cod served with skordalia*

The Greeks love vegetables, particularly aubergine, which is often stuffed or used in moussaka; courgettes; stuffed artichokes; and vine leaves, filled with rice and known as *dolmades*. Wild greens like chicory and dandelion are an important part of the Greek diet. *Kakavia*, the famous fishermen's soup, is one of the oldest dishes still eaten, and could be the basis of all Mediterranean fish soups.

Dessert is usually fresh fruit. Traditional Greek sweets such as baklava are eaten in the late afternoon or evening, often with a cup of strong coffee. Many sweets are made using Greek yoghurt and honey. Thyme honey is a particular speciality.

*Coffee and ouzo*

*See also*  **baklava, dolmades, meze, moussaka, skordalia, tarama**

**173**

## Greek salad

The salad most often seen outside Greece, and described as 'Greek salad', is *horiatiki*, village or country salad. It is a combination of tomatoes with any number of ingredients from sardines to olives—only sliced onions and feta cheese are obligatory. Add ingredients such as capers, chopped boiled eggs, green pepper, cucumber or fresh or dried oregano. Be sure that all ingredients are fresh and the tomatoes are really ripe.

### GREEK SALAD

*Cut 3 ripe tomatoes into wedges and put them in a large bowl with ½ cucumber and 1 green pepper cut into chunks, and 1 salad onion sliced into thin rings. Season well and pour on 3 tablespoons Greek olive oil. Cut 150 g feta into cubes and scatter over the salad. Add 1 tablespoon chopped flat-leaf parsley, 15 kalamata olives and a few sprigs of oregano. Serves 6.*

## gremolata

A mixture of chopped lemon zest, parsley and sometimes garlic, used in Italian cooking to garnish dishes, most notably the Italian dish osso buco. Gremolata is sprinkled onto the dish just before it finishes cooking to allow it to cook for a couple of minutes. The term *alla gremolata* denotes that this garnish has been used.

**Also known as — gremolada**

  **See also   osso buco**

## grenadine syrup — see pomegranate

## gribiche sauce

A cold sauce made with mashed hard-boiled egg yolks, oil, vinegar, capers, gherkins, tarragon, chervil, parsley and chopped hard-boiled egg whites. The sauce is made like a mayonnaise but uses the cooked egg yolk. Gribiche sauce is classically served with *tête de veau* (calf's head) or fish dishes.

### GRIBICHE SAUCE

*Mash the yolks of 2 hard-boiled eggs (finely chop the egg whites and set aside) and whisk in 250 ml oil, a little at a time. Add 2 tablespoons white wine vinegar, salt and pepper, 2 tablespoons chopped capers, 2 tablespoons each of chopped tarragon, parsley and chervil. Add the chopped egg whites. Serves 4.*

Crisp Italian bread sticks made with flour, water, yeast and often olive oil. The bread sticks were once eaten for breakfast but are now usually served with antipasto or eaten as a snack with a piece of prosciutto wrapped around them. The bread is made either by hand by stretching out the dough to form a long, thin stick, or commercially to form a more uniform shape. Handmade grissini vary in thickness, look somewhat knobbly and are usually the length of their baker's arms.

Grissini originated in Turin but are now produced worldwide. A Piedmontese legend says that they were invented by a Turinese baker, Antonio Brunero, who baked them for the Savoy royal family as a bread to help digestive disturbances. They are so linked to Turin that Napoleon called them *les petits batons de Turin*— the little batons of Turin—and had them transported to his court every day. Turinese grissini are usually very thin, and highly regarded in Italy.

**Also known as — Italian bread sticks**

**g u a c a m o l e**

Guacamole is a Mexican dish made from ripe, mashed avocado, traditionally served as a dip with nachos, as a side dish or a sauce for tacos. The word 'guacamole' is most likely derived from the *Nahuatl* words *ahuacatl*, meaning 'avocado' and *molli*, meaning 'sauce'. Guacamole is best made in a *molcajete*, a mortar and pestle made from basalt rock, which gives a crushed texture without turning the guacamole to a purée.

GUACAMOLE

*Halve 3 large avocados, remove the stones and scrape out flesh with a spoon. In a mortar and pestle, grind 1 small chopped onion, 2 chopped serrano chillies and 2 tablespoons chopped coriander. Add avocado, mash until mixture is slightly rough, then stir in 2 finely chopped tomatoes. Season well. Garnish with chopped onion, tomato and coriander. Serves 4.*

**g u a v a**

A tropical fruit from a tree related to the myrtle family, native to Central America but now grown in most tropical areas. There are many varieties and these vary in size and shape, but generally the fruit is round or oval and has a thin skin and fragrant, slightly acid flesh, which can vary in colour from red to pinkish yellow or cream. Their flavour varies with each variety and may taste of either lemon, strawberry or pineapple. Peel the fruit first, then eat raw or cooked, add to fruit salads or platters or use in fools, juices, jellies and ice creams. The flavour can be quite strong and may overpower more subtle fruit. Make sure the fruit is ripe or it will be very astringent. Ripen at room temperature until soft, then store in the fridge. Guavas are an excellent source of vitamin C. They are also found tinned in syrup.

## GUINEA FOWL IN CREAM SAUCE

*Cut 1 guinea fowl into 4 portions and fry in butter until it is brown all over. Add 2 chopped spring onions and cook until the guinea fowl is cooked through. Add 150 ml single cream and bring to the boil. Stir in 2 tablespoons redcurrant jelly and season well. Serves 2.*

More than 20 species of Guinea fowl are available in their native Africa, many of which have now been domesticated in Europe. Guinea fowl have a relatively dry flesh, which benefits from being cooked either in a liquid, or barded with a piece of fatty bacon. They can be substituted for small chickens in most recipes but have a darker flesh colour. Guinea fowl eggs can also be eaten. Guinea fowl are available from butchers and some supermarkets.

■ *See also* **game**

## gumbo

A speciality of Cajun cuisine, gumbo is a cross between a soup and a stew. Okra, the characteristic ingredient in gumbo, has a sticky, gelatinous texture and is used more as a thickener for the stew than for its flavour. When okra isn't used, the gumbo is thickened with filé powder, and this has become so synonymous with gumbo that it has earned the alternative name of 'gumbo filé'.

The main ingredients for gumbo vary from recipe to recipe but commonly include chicken, ham, andouille (a type of smoked sausage) and seafood, either on their own or in combination, and it is also usual to include a small amount of cooked rice. At the base of the gumbo is a dark roux, a slowly cooked and browned amalgam of flour and lard, which is said to be the heart and soul of the gumbo and gives it its rich flavour and colour. Gumbo, a Bantu word brought with African slaves to America, is a derivation of the African word for 'okra'.

### COOKING

*Filé powder is made from dried sassafras leaves and is used as a thickener in gumbo. Stir filé into the gumbo at the end of cooking or it will go stringy.*

■ *See also* **Cajun, okra, sassafras**

### GUMBO

*In a large pot, mix together 85 ml oil or lard and 75 g plain flour. Cook the mixture over low heat, stirring constantly, until it turns into a rich, dark, mahogany brown roux. Add 1 finely chopped onion and cook until the onion is tender. Add 1.5 litres water and bring to a simmer, stirring to dissolve the roux thoroughly. Cut 4 cleaned crabs into small pieces and add them to the roux mixture, then add 450 g Cajun andouille sausage cut into bite-size pieces, 6 sliced spring onions, 1 coarsely chopped green pepper, 3 tablespoons chopped parsley and ¼ teaspoon powdered chilli. Cook the mixture for 30 minutes, then add 500 g peeled and deveined prawns (see page 317) and 24 shucked oysters and their juices and cook for another 5 minutes. Season well, then stir in ½ teaspoon filé powder, or to taste. Ladle the gumbo into 6 bowls, each containing 2 or 3 tablespoons of cooked rice. Serves 6.*

Scotland's best known and least eaten delicacy, haggis is made from a sheep's heart, liver and lungs (collectively known as the 'pluck'), which are cooked with oatmeal, onion and seasoning, then stuffed into a sheep's stomach and boiled. Of obscure origins, haggis was originally a highland food, a frugal, yet hearty meal made from animal parts that would otherwise be discarded, and would last 1 or 2 weeks before it needed to be eaten. On Burns' Night, January 25, the haggis arrives on a platter preceded by bagpipes, Burns' poem 'To a Haggis' is read, and the haggis is ceremoniously stabbed with a sharp knife. It is accompanied by champit tatties, bashed neeps and a glass of whisky.

*Haggis served with champit tatties (mashed potatoes) and bashed neeps (mashed swedes).*

## COOKING

*Shop-bought haggis is always pre-cooked and only needs to be heated to serve. You can do this in two ways: wrap it in foil, then put into a dish with a little water and bake at 180 °C for 1 hour, or until hot in the centre (insert a skewer into the centre to see if it's hot); or wrap the haggis in foil and poach in simmering water for 45 minutes. Haggis can be microwaved, but it needs to be removed from its skin first so it doesn't explode.*

## HALVAH

*Using a food processor, process 310 g sesame seeds to a smooth paste. Add 4 tablespoons runny honey and 2 teaspoons vanilla extract and process together. Line a 12 cm square tin with baking paper and press the mixture into the tin. Put in the fridge to chill for 1 hour, take out, and slice into 2 cm cubes. This recipe can also be made using a mortar and pestle. Makes 350 g.*

Middle Eastern in origin, halvah is a sweetmeat made with sesame seeds and honey. Some are flavoured with chocolate or vanilla, while others may contain pistachios, walnuts or almonds. Halvah is sold in blocks or slices from some supermarkets or delicatessens. Not to be confused with halvah is *halwa*, an Indian sweet made with grated carrot and white pumpkin or lentils. These are cooked in milk, mixed with nuts, then sweetened and perfumed with cardamom.

***Also known as — halva***

# ham

The salt cured and/or smoked hind leg of a pig (though now ham may also be made from other meats such as mutton or venison and labelled as such). The flavour of the ham is attributed to many factors—the breed or age of the pig, its diet and method of curing. Curing methods may vary, but the process is always based on salt, using either a dry-cure or brine, sometimes with added herbs, spices and treacle or molasses. The hams are often then either smoked or air-dried and possibly aged for months or even years to give each its unique flavour. Hams are eaten raw or cooked according to how much they have been cured. A short curing process followed by smoking does not cure a ham to the same degree as slow curing (dry salting) and air drying over time. Some hams are only available locally while others are produced on a more commercial scale and exported. Ham is sold either by the whole leg (for boiling or baking) or sliced.

*See also* **bacon**

## SMOKED HAMS

These are hams that have been salt-cured, either in dry salt or brine, then smoked. The smoking further cures the hams as well as adding flavour. Generally aromatic woods such as hickory, apple and oak are used, though some Irish hams traditionally use peat and hams from Eastern Europe and Germany (*Knochenschinken*) that have black skins are a product of smoking over piney resinous woods.

Smoked hams are for eating both raw and cooked depending on where they come from. Well-known smoked hams for eating raw include jambon de Bayonne, jambon d'Ardennes and Westphalian ham. Smoked hams for cooking include Kentucky, Smithfield and York hams.

*Smoked ham*

*Smoked ham*

*Prosciutto*

*Danish ham*

## AIR-DRIED HAMS

These are hams that have been salt-cured, usually dry-salted, then hung in cool air to dry. These are traditionally made in mountain areas that have steady breezes and little pollution and in climates that are low in humidity. The most famous dry-cured ham is prosciutto di Parma from the area around Parma in Italy, San Daniele, from the northeast of Italy, is similar, as are many prosciutto produced all over Italy and named after their place of production, such as Tuscany. Jamon Iberico and jamon serrano are Spanish air-dried hams somewhat similar to the Italian ones. Air-dried hams are for eating raw but can be used in cooking.

## QUICK-CURED HAMS

These are quick cured by pumping them with brine and flavourings. Some are ready to eat, others need to be cooked, though as they are often low in salt they can be baked without needing to be soaked first. Danish hams are a by-product of the bacon industry—they are legs off each side of bacon. Often sold tinned so are shaped into round slices.

## BOILED AND BAKED HAMS

These are hams that need to be boiled and/or baked before they are eaten. They can be any type of ham and are traditionally served at Christmas or on special occasions as they are bought whole and serve lots of people.

*Baked ham*

## NON-LEG HAMS

These are not true hams as they are not from the whole leg but are cuts of the leg or other cuts such as the shoulder or loin, cured like hams. Italian *coppa* is a good shoulder ham and *culatella* is made from the rump in the same way as prosciutto. Treat as you would ham.

*Culatella*

*Sweet-cured ham*

## SWEET-CURED HAMS

These include hams such as Bradenham ham, cured with spices and molasses. This gives a sweetness that would be unattainable simply by curing or smoking. These hams may be eaten raw or cooked depending on where they come from.

## GAMMON

Not a true ham, gammon is made from the hind leg of a pig and cured like bacon. Available as a joint or in steaks, smoked or unsmoked. It needs to be cooked before it is eaten. Gammon is a term peculiar to Britain.

*Gammon*

## hamburger

A patty of ground beef, grilled and served between two bread buns, often with a salad such as lettuce, cheese and tomato. Contrary to its name, the hamburger has never contained any ham, but chicken, pork, fish or vegetables may replace the beef.

Thanks to the efficiency of American marketing, the hamburger is now the most prevalent fast food item around the world. It is believed to have originated in the Baltic area as a beef cake and was adopted by the sailors of Hamburg who took it with them to America. It was later referred to as 'Hamburg steak', which was eventually abbreviated to 'hamburger'.

**Also known as — beefburger, burger**

## hare

A similar animal to a rabbit, but larger, with darker flesh and a rich, gamey flavour. Young hares up to a year old are called leverets and these can be roasted, while older meat is usually jugged (simmered in red wine or port and gravy) or stewed. A large hare will feed 6 people. Hares are hung by the feet for 3–8 days without being drawn. The blood is usually collected and used as a thickening agent for the sauce (*au sang*). In North America, rabbit and hare meat may not be differentiated.

## harissa

### HARISSA

*Soak 30 g dried red chillies in hot water until softened. Chop chillies roughly, then grind in a mortar and pestle with 2 garlic cloves, a pinch of salt, 1 teaspoon each of caraway seeds and coriander seeds, ½ teaspoon cumin seeds, 1 tablespoon coriander leaves, 3 tablespoons of the soaking water and 2 tablespoons olive oil. Keep in a sterilized jar and cover with a little oil. Makes 125 ml.*

A North African (most probably Tunisian) condiment of chillies and spices—always caraway seeds—used to flavour stews, as an accompaniment to couscous, and just about anywhere aromatic heat and red colour is required. Harissa can be fiery hot or milder and more aromatic. The harissa bought in tubes is a pale imitation of the real thing, which is remarkably easy to make. Home-made harissa should be stored in the fridge where it will last for up to 2 months—keep the top covered in a thin layer of oil to help preserve it.

Grated cooked potatoes, which are formed into cakes and fried until browned. The word comes from the French *hacher* meaning to 'chop up'. Recipes for hash browns first appeared in the 1900s and were originally called 'hashed brown potatoes'. Hash browns are popular fast food in North America and can be bought frozen in packets. They are generally deep-fried and eaten with breakfast.
**Also known as — home fries, skillet fries**

### HASH BROWNS

*Cook 1 whole waxy potato (leave the skin on) per person by either baking or microwaving. Peel, then coarsely grate into a bowl; season. Melt 1 tablespoon oil and a knob of butter and fry the potato, either all at once or form into small cakes and cook until browned on one side. Turn over by sliding the cake onto a plate, then invert it back into the pan to brown the other side.*

Any one of a number of varieties of round hard-shelled nuts that grow in pairs or groups of three. In England, hazelnut refers to the wild or cultivated version, and cob and filbert are two varieties. In America, the wild nut is a hazel, and the cultivated a filbert. Unlike other oilier nuts, shelled hazelnuts keep well in an airtight container or in the freezer. Hazelnuts tend to be used in sweet dishes but are also used in savoury dishes, such as the Catalan *salsa romesco*.

### COOKING

*To skin hazelnuts, put the nuts in a single layer on a baking tray. Toast either in a 180°C oven for 6–8 minutes or under a preheated grill for about 2 minutes (turn after 1 minute). Watch carefully as nuts burn quickly. When toasted, tip the nuts into a tea towel and rub the husks off.*

The edible young shoots (or hearts) of several types of palm tree. Firm in texture with a mild flavour similar to artichokes, the hearts may be lightly boiled and eaten in salads, eaten raw, battered and deep-fried or added to curries. Hearts of palm are usually sold in tins or jars, but can be bought fresh in countries where the palms are grown. Harvesting the heart is usually lethal to the tree.
**Also known as — palm cabbage, palm heart**

A blend of herbs used widely in southern French cuisine. The herbs may vary, but usually include thyme, lavender, savory and rosemary and sometimes marjoram, basil, sage, fennel or oregano. Usually sold dried, the herbs can be added to meat, creamy pasta dishes, soups and salad dressings.

The leaves, flowers and sometimes stems of a group of aromatic non-woody plants used in cooking. The same and additional plants are also used medicinally. The word is derived from the Latin *herba*, which means 'grass'.

Culinary herbs are used to impart an aromatic quality to food either individually or in a mixture. The flavour comes from the oil stored in the leaves, which is released when the herb is crushed, chopped or heated. Particular herbs suit different styles of cooking and every cuisine has its favourite herbs—the Middle East and Greece favour oregano, mint and dill; Thai cuisine uses coriander and lemon grass; in Italy, basil, parsley and oregano are commonly used; and in France, tarragon, chervil and fennel. The types of herbs used may also vary according to the season. Obviously you can use herbs at any time, but the type of recipe they suit is often applicable for that time of year. Typical summer herbs are basil, dill, mint, oregano and parsley; spring herbs are chives, sorrel and chervil; and typical winter herbs are sage, rosemary and thyme.

*Herb sauce served with poached salmon.*

### Fresh herbs

Most herbs are best when fresh. Buy them cut or grow in pots on the windowsill or in the garden. If fresh herbs are unavailable, use dried, but these are often more concentrated in flavour (unless stale) and you only need to use half or less of the quantity specified for fresh herbs. In some cuisines, dried herbs are preferred: the Greek preference for dried oregano (*rigani*) for example.

### RACK OF LAMB IN A HERB CRUST

*Mix together 1 teaspoon mustard, 1 tablespoon fine breadcrumbs, 2 tablespoons chopped fresh herbs (such as mint, parsley and thyme) and 2 teaspoons butter to form a paste. Season to taste. Press onto the skinned side of a trimmed rack of lamb and roast skin side up at 220 °C for 25 minutes. Serves 2.*

## COOKING

*Chop herbs with scissors, a flat knife or mezzaluna. Chop large bunches of more robust herbs like parsley in the food processor.*

*Fine herbs such as tarragon or chives can be left large, shredded or snipped. Basil should be torn.*

*Coarse herbs such as rosemary and parsley benefit from fine chopping.*

*Flavour vinaigrette or mayonnaise by finely chopping or pounding the herbs in a mortar and pestle, then add the rest of the ingredients.*

*Herbs such as basil, coriander and sage discolour if chopped too early.*

*Whole leaves of mint or basil can be steeped in water to make 'tea'. Crush them gently in your hand first to release the aromatic oils.*

## HERB SAUCE

*Mix together 1 tablespoon finely chopped parsley, 1 tablespoon finely chopped chervil, 1 tablespoon finely shredded basil, finely grated zest of 1 small lemon and 300 g crème fraîche. Season with salt and freshly ground pepper. Serve with poached fish (pictured) or chicken or use as a filling for baked potatoes. Makes 350 ml.*

## ANISE

Liquorice-flavoured leaves used in salads and to flavour fish and vegetables, especially in Eastern European cuisine.

## BALM

Leaves can be used in salads and stuffings and to scent custards. Its strong lemon flavour is lost when dried. It is also used to brew tea and is a good substitute for lemon grass.

***Also known as — lemon balm***

## BASIL

There are several types of basil, all of which have a different flavour. Genoa or sweet basil is the best known, it has a spicy smell and is used extensively in Italian cooking. Opal basil has purple leaves, Greek basil has smaller leaves and a pungent flavour, and Thai or holy basil complements Thai and Southeast Asian dishes. Basil should be torn, not chopped, and added to hot food at the last moment to preserve the flavour. It doesn't dry well.

## BORAGE

Borage flowers are small, bright blue or violet and star-shaped and are used in salads or to garnish drinks—the most famous being Pimms. The youngest, least hairy leaves can be finely chopped and used in salads. They are similar to cucumber in flavour.

## CHERVIL

Delicate, lacy, pale-green leaves that deteriorate quickly and should be added to hot dishes just before serving. Chervil is one of the classic fines herbes. Use in salads or with creamy dishes, it is also a classic ingredient in ravigote sauce and is often used with tarragon to make Béarnaise sauce. Chervil has a subtle parsley flavour with a hint of aniseed. It goes particularly well with fish.

## COMFREY

Comfrey belongs to the same family as borage, to which it is similar in that the smaller leaves can be eaten as a vegetable. These may be dipped in batter and fried. The plant's white, yellow or pinkish bell-shaped flowers can be used for decoration in salads.

## STORAGE

*Herbs that are sold in plastic boxes or cellophane bags keep well in them.*

*Put loose herbs into plastic bags and store in the vegetable crisper of the fridge. Herbs with more robust leaves will keep longer than more fragile ones.*

*Big bunches of mint, parsley and coriander will keep in a jug of water for a few days.*

*Preserve fresh herbs by setting sprigs into ice cubes.*

## CORIANDER

The leaves, stem and root can all be used and each has its own purpose. The roots are used in curry pastes, the stems are used when a strong coriander flavour is needed, and the leaves are added at the end of cooking, both as a flavouring and a garnish. Coriander is used extensively in Asian, South American, Mexican, Middle Eastern and Mediterranean cuisines. It goes very well with chilli, lime juice and meat dishes. Coriander freezes well.

***Also known as — cilantro***

## CURRY LEAF

Dark, shiny green leaves that look like bay leaves but have a distinctive curry flavour. Used widely in southern Indian and Malay cooking. The leaves are added to dishes during cooking or may be used as a garnish.

## MINT

Traditionally used in British cooking to go with lamb as mint sauce and on new potatoes. Mint also goes well in salads and with steamed fish. There are lots of types of mint, including applemint, peppermint and spearmint.

## LAVENDER

It has a strong flavour that needs to be used sparingly. Use dried, chopped flowers in shortbread, cakes, sorbets and custards or add to roasting lamb for extra flavour. Crystallized lavender flowers may be used as decoration on cakes.

## DILL

Dill has feathery leaves that have a strong aniseed flavour. Common to Scandinavian dishes such as gravlax and goes well with fish, chicken, creamy sauces, in salads and as a garnish for vegetables. Chop it and add at the end of cooking.

## PARSLEY

Available as flat-leaf (Italian) or curly-leaf parsley. Flat-leaf parsley tends to be stronger in flavour but the two can be used interchangeably. Parsley can be used as an ingredient as well as a decoration and is used extensively in European cooking.

## LOVAGE

Has a strong celery flavour and grows well as a pot herb. Both the leaves and stem can be used in soups, sauces and to marinate meat and poultry.

## GERANIUM

Geranium leaves come in a range of scents usually denoted by the name of the plant, such as rose geranium. Use to scent custards, sugar and jams or use whole in cakes as a decoration—use the leaves to line the base of a cake tin.

## MARJORAM AND OREGANO

Traditionally used to flavour tomato sauces in Italian and Greek cooking, usually used dried. It can be used in sausages and in stuffings. Both herbs come from the same family, of which there are several varieties. These herbs have a strong flavour and should be used sparingly.

## ROSEMARY

A strong-flavoured herb that needs to be used judiciously. If using rosemary in food, chop very finely; if using as a flavouring, use small sprigs and remove before serving. Goes well with roast lamb and pork and in breads.

## SAGE

Sage leaves are traditionally used with onion to stuff goose and in Italian cuisine to flavour butter served with pasta, as well as in pork, veal and liver dishes. The whole leaves can be deep-fried and used as a garnish. Use sparingly as the flavour can be strong.

## SALAD BURNET

Used in French and Italian cooking, the young leaves can be added to salads, finely chopped in ravigote sauce, soups and casseroles and to flavour vinegar. Similar in taste to cucumber and can be used in iced drinks.

**Also known as — burnet**

## SAVORY

A pungent herb similar in flavour to thyme and mint. It is customarily used in bean dishes but also in pâtés, meat and fish, such as trout. Its name is a German word, meaning 'bean herb'. It dries very well.

## TARRAGON

Tarragon has a hint of aniseed to its flavour and is used in many classic French dishes. It makes good aromatic sauces for poultry and can be used to flavour vinegar. It is important to use French tarragon and not Russian, which has a coarser flavour.

## THYME

There are many varieties and all have small leaves that can be used as a flavouring in casseroles and soups. Thyme gives a rich, aromatic flavour to slow-cooked food and roasts.

## VIETNAMESE MINT

Not a member of the mint family. The leaves are served as a garnish for laksa, beef pho and with spring rolls and dipping sauce. It can be used in salads to give a spicy flavour.

**Also known as — hot mint, laksa leaf**

## OTHER HERBS

**Bergamot** – *Lemon-scented leaves and flowers used in summer drinks, or in teas. Add the young leaves to salads or use in pork dishes.*

**Costmary** – *Also called alecost or bibleleaf, this mildly bitter, minty herb has silver leaves. It was traditionally used to flavour beer, but is now used in soups, sausages or with veal and game.*

**Fenugreek** – *Mildly bitter leaves are used in India as a vegetable or may be used in salads.*

**Hyssop** – *Pungent, bitter minty leaves used to flavour liqueurs such as Benedictine and Chartreuse or may be used in salads, soups, stuffings and stews.*

**Lemon verbena** – *Lemon-scented leaves are used to add flavour to drinks and salads.*

**Melilot** – *Also known as sweet clover, the leaves of this herb are used to flavour Swiss cheeses, such as Gruyère, or may be added to sausages and stuffings.*

**Myrtle** – *The spicy orange-fragrant leaves are used to wrap pork, in lamb dishes or in stuffings.*

**Sweet cicely** – *The large, sweet feathery leaves are used in puddings or raw in salads. The roots can be grated raw as a salad or boiled as a vegetable.*

**Tansy** – *Hot, bitter-tasting herb with fern-like leaves used to flavour sausages, egg and fish dishes.*

■ *See also* **angelica, bay leaf, bouquet garni, chives, fennel, fines herbes, herbes de Provence, sorrel, spices**

## hoisin sauce

### PORK HOISIN

*In a bowl, mix 3 tablespoons hoisin sauce, 1 tablespoon soy sauce, 1½ tablespoons black vinegar and 2 crushed garlic cloves. Add 2 pork chops and marinate for 1 hour. Fry 1 sliced onion until brown, add the drained chops and fry on both sides. Add marinade, 1 tablespoon hoisin sauce and 2 tablespoons water and boil briefly. Garnish with sliced spring onions. Serves 2.*

A spicy reddish-brown sauce made from fermented soy beans, garlic, sugar and spices, used both as a condiment and a flavouring agent in Chinese cooking. It may be used as the sauce for Peking duck (though it is not the authentic sauce), in stir-fries or as a marinade for poultry, or meat, especially *char siu* (barbecued pork) and shellfish. Hoisin sauce is sold in bottles or jars in supermarkets and Asian markets. Store in the fridge after opening.

**Also known as — Peking sauce**

## hollandaise sauce

One of the classic French sauces, hollandaise is made from an emulsion of butter and eggs, either over a double boiler (the classic method) or quickly, in a blender. Hollandaise is best made just before you need it (it can't be reheated), but can be kept warm over a bain-marie. Serve with asparagus or artichokes, on egg dishes and with poultry and seafood. If preferred, flavour with freshly chopped herbs, but add them to the sauce at the end of cooking.

**See also  sauce**

### BLENDER HOLLANDAISE

*Separate 2 eggs and put yolks in a blender. Melt 90 g butter with 1 tablespoon lemon juice until boiling. Switch on the blender and pour the butter and lemon through the top onto the yolks: the mixture will thicken as the hot liquid cooks the yolks. Season. Makes 125 ml. To make a foaming hollandaise, whisk the egg whites until soft peaks form and fold them into the sauce.*

## hominy

Made from the hulled, dried kernels of corn, soaked, then boiled in water and bicarbonate of soda until the hulls can be rubbed off, leaving the soft, white kernel. The kernels are then either boiled and eaten as a starchy food source or dried and ground into grits. Hominy grits, commonly called grits, are popular in southern America where they are boiled until thick and porridge-like and served for breakfast with milk and butter or bacon and eggs. Hominy is sold in tins, in either a cooked or dried form.

A sweet, viscous liquid made by bees from flower nectar. Bees eat the flower nectar, which then passes through their digestive system to be expelled as honey. Honey is mostly made up of sugar and water, but also contains small amounts of pollen, wax and mineral salts. In ancient times, honey was regarded as the food of the gods and a symbol of wealth. Before the introduction of sugar, it was widely used as a food sweetener. Honey is one of our oldest foods, and has been found, still edible although a little hard, in Egyptian tombs.

The colour, flavour and aroma of a honey depends on the type of flower the nectar is taken from. There are many varieties, ranging from pale or even clear, mild honeys such as acacia, clover, orange blossom and alfalfa, to the darker coloured, strongly flavoured honeys such as thyme and heather. In cooking, honey is used in both sweet and savoury dishes, it is commonly used as a spread, as a sweetener for drinks and cereals, in confectionery and in baked goods such as gingerbread. In North Africa, honey is popular in savoury dishes such as couscous, tagine, roast lamb and chicken.

*Clockwise from top left: clover honey, set honey, New Zealand honey, leatherwood honey, honeycomb.*

## TYPES OF HONEYS

**Clear (runny) honey**
Commercial honey is obtained by extracting honey from the honeycomb. The honey is strained, then pasteurized to destroy any fermenting agents. Some honeys are blended, which means the honey is made from several varieties of flower. Blended honeys may often be labelled as such or simply as 'honey'. These are good all-purpose honeys. Flower honeys are made from only one specific flower and this will be indicated on the label. Some labels may also indicate which country the flower is from. These honeys should be reserved for eating.

**Honeycomb**
Chewy, wax structure in which bees store their honey. Both the chewy wax and the honey stored in it are edible. Honey from the honeycomb has not been treated and is appreciated because of its pure, unrefined flavour.

**Set (creamy) honey**
A crystallized honey made by stirring or whipping clear honey. Finely crystallized honey is added to liquid honey to encourage crystallization.

### HONEY CHILLI CHICKEN

*Cut 4 chicken breasts into strips, then stir-fry in 1 tablespoon oil with 1 crushed garlic clove until golden. Remove from pan. Stir-fry 100 g peanuts in 1 tablespoon oil, then fry 4 sliced spring onions, 2 chopped red chillies. Add 2 tablespoons each of soy sauce, clear honey and white wine vinegar. Add chicken, toss together and serve on baby lettuce leaves. Serves 4.*

### COOKING

*Honey is an invert sugar, which means if you add a little to sugar syrup or caramel, it will stop the sugar crystallizing.*

*Good honey should be kept for eating raw and not cooked: when honey is heated, the aroma is lost and the sugar begins to caramelize.*

*Honey does not have any nutritional value over sugar, and in fact contains more calories than sugar per volume. In some instances, honey can replace sugar in recipes but the quantity of honey should be reduced because it is sweeter than sugar.*

*Liquid honey will crystallize after some time. If this happens, stand the jar in hot water until the crystals dissolve and the honey liquifies.*

*To accurately measure spoonfuls of honey, first dip the spoon in hot water, then dip it into the honey—the honey will slide off easily. Reheat the spoon and repeat.*

## hopper

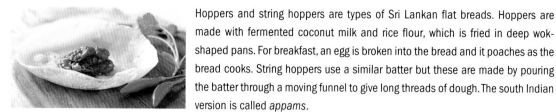

Hoppers and string hoppers are types of Sri Lankan flat breads. Hoppers are made with fermented coconut milk and rice flour, which is fried in deep wok-shaped pans. For breakfast, an egg is broken into the bread and it poaches as the bread cooks. String hoppers use a similar batter but these are made by pouring the batter through a moving funnel to give long threads of dough. The south Indian version is called *appams*.

## hopping John

A dish made of rice, black-eyed beans (also called black-eyed peas) and salt pork, said to have originated with the African slaves who worked on southern American plantations. It is traditionally served on New Year's day and is supposed to bring good luck. Limping Susan is another similar rice dish made with okra, rice and shrimp.

**Also known as — hoppin' John**

HOPPING JOHN

*Soak 300 g black-eyed beans in water overnight, then drain. Dice 4 bacon rashers; fry in a little oil with 1 each finely chopped onion and red pepper until bacon is crisp and vegetables are soft. Add the beans, 100 g long-grain rice and 500 ml water. Cover and simmer for about 20 minutes, or until cooked. Season with salt, pepper and Louisiana hot sauce. Serves 4.*

## horchata

A milky drink of water with ground rice, almonds *(pictured)* or most especially, chufas. Chufa (sometimes called tiger nuts, although they are not a nut at all), are the small, dried chestnut-flavoured tubers of an African plant. Horchata is usually served chilled in summer and sweetened or spiced with cinnamon. The drink is popular in Mexico and Spain, especially in Valencia where chufas are grown. It is increasingly being used as a dairy-free health drink.

## horse

Widely eaten in France, Belgium and Italy, where it is sold by specialist butchers, and often taken from animals bred for the table. The idea of eating horse is, however, repugnant to many Anglo-Saxons. In Italy, it is often fed to invalids, as it is considered more fortifying than other types of meat. In Europe, both horse and donkey meat are made into sausages (this will always be marked on the ingredient list).

A plant cultivated for its pungent, spicy root whose young leaves can also be used in salads. Horseradish root is generally grated—the greatest concentration of flavour is just under the skin—and used as a condiment or in sauces. Folded into cream, horseradish makes a good accompaniment to roast beef, but also goes well with smoked fish and other meats. When not available fresh, it can be bought bottled or dried. Once peeled, it can be stored for a few days in vinegar.

### HORSERADISH CREAM

*Lightly whisk 150 ml double cream. Fold in 2 tablespoons grated fresh or bottled horseradish, 2 teaspoons lemon juice, a pinch of salt and sugar. Don't overwhisk the cream as the acid from the lemon juice and horseradish will act as a thickener—if the cream is heavily whisked from the start, it may split. Makes about 185 ml.*

## hot cross buns

Traditionally eaten on Good Friday, hot cross buns are small yeast buns flavoured with spices and raisins or sultanas. Before baking, a cross is slashed into the top of the bun, which is filled with a flour and water mixture. The custom of eating the buns on Good Friday was popularized in Tudor England when a law was introduced that forbade the sale of the spiced buns except on Good Friday, Christmas and at burials.

## hot dog

A frankfurter served on a split long soft bread roll, typically garnished with mustard but often with pickles, relish, onions or cheese (or a mixture of all of these). Hot dogs are considered an American institution, with hot dog stands commonplace outside sporting events or nightclubs. They are now a popular and convenient fast food around the world.

While the frankfurter has its origins in Eastern and Central Europe, the hot dog shot to prominence at the World Fair in Chicago in 1893. This makes it the first mass-produced industrial fast food: portion controlled, easy to serve, easy to go and easy to eat. Chicago remains the American capital of the hot dog, with over 3,000 hot dog stands, and at least one culinary historian whose academic speciality is—the hot dog.

## hot water pastry

A dense pastry, most often seen enrobing pork pies, the most famous being from Melton Mowbray in England. It is made by adding boiling water and lard to flour and egg and mixing it with a wooden spoon. The pastry is set into a shape while still warm, cooks to a dark crust and has a melting texture when eaten. Hot water pastry was invented to use as a case for transporting cooked meat and game hygienically. The pastry was broken off and discarded when it reached its destination.

## hummus

One of the best known Middle Eastern dishes, hummus is made from puréed chickpeas flavoured with tahini, lemon juice and garlic. Hummus is usually served as a dip with pitta bread but also goes well in wraps (made from pitta or lavash bread), with kebabs or in sandwiches. The ingredients vary only slightly from country to country: the Egyptian version uses a little ground cumin, which is sometimes garnished with sumac or pomegranate seeds.

*Also known as — hoummos, houmus, hummus-bi-tahina*

### HUMMUS

*In a blender or food processor, put a 400 g tin drained chickpeas, 2 tablespoons tahini, 2 tablespoons lemon juice and 1 crushed garlic clove and blend to form a paste. Add enough olive oil or water to give a creamy paste. Season well and add more lemon juice if you like. To serve, spread the hummus on a plate, drizzle with olive oil and dust with paprika.*

## hundreds and thousands

Tiny bright and multi-coloured balls of sugar used as decoration on baked goods such as doughnuts and cakes, on puddings such as trifles, or to decorate children's food. In Australia, hundreds and thousands are used to make fairy bread—sprinkled onto triangles of buttered bread *(pictured)* and served at children's parties.

*Also known as — jimmies, nonpareil, sprinkles*

## hush puppy

Small deep-fried cornmeal and onion dumplings, traditionally served with fried fish, especially catfish. Legends abound as to its exact origins. One story suggests the name evolved from the practice of throwing them to the dogs to quieten them while dinner was being prepared. Another says that hunters threw the fritters to their dogs to quieten them.

*Also known as — corn dodgers*

# i

Ice cream is a general term now applied to many frozen desserts. Ice cream in its original form is a frozen dessert based on milk or cream, sometimes thickened with eggs. Other types of ice cream include semifreddo, parfait, Indian kulfi and Italian gelato, as well as ice creams made with yoghurt or bean curd. Sorbets and granitas are actually based on water ices and generally do not contain dairy products. These are usually made from fruit pulp or juice. Ice creams vary from country to country as does the legislation concerning their commercial production.

## LEMON ICE CREAM

*Blend 250 ml condensed milk with 185 ml lemon juice, 3 tablespoons cream and 2 tablespoons grated lemon rind. Churn in an ice-cream maker or pour into a freezerproof container and freeze. Stir hourly to break up ice crystals (do this 3 times, or until smooth and thick), then freeze overnight. Serves 4.*

## MANGO SORBET

*Purée 700 g mango and pour into a measuring jug. Dissolve 250 g sugar in 250 ml water to make a sugar syrup and add it (calculate half the quantity of purée and use the same quantity of sugar syrup) to the purée with 4 teaspoons lime juice and 150 ml orange juice. Freeze and stir as per recipe above. When the mixture is an icy slush, add 1 loosely beaten egg white to the churn or beat in by hand; freeze. Stir hourly to break up any large crystals, then freeze overnight. Serves 8.*

From left: lemon ice cream, mango sorbet.

### Making ice cream

Ice cream, gelato and sorbet are elegant, simple desserts that can easily be made at home by hand or with an ice-cream maker. Churned ice cream is continuously stirred by a machine as it freezes to give a smooth, creamy texture. Still-frozen ice creams are beaten by hand, in a food processor or with an electric whisk during the freezing process to incorporate any ice crystals. Ice cream is best served at just above melting point for the full flavour to be appreciated.

## STORAGE

*Store home-made ice cream in plastic or metal freezer-proof containers filled almost to the lid, allowing a little room for expansion when the ice cream freezes. Cover the surface of the ice cream with greaseproof paper to stop crystals forming (pictured).*

*Home-made ice creams made with raw eggs should be eaten in 2–3 days. Those without eggs will keep longer but their flavour may change as they age.*

*See also* **parfait, sundae**

191

Ice cream is not a recent invention—the Chinese have been making drinks and desserts chilled with ice for thousands of years. The Arabs learnt to make syrups chilled with snow, called *sharbets*. The Italians, perhaps the supreme ice dessert makers, adopted the technique, which spread throughout Europe. Ices became richer in flavour, often using milk, cream, eggs and blends of fruit and liqueurs. When it reached America, ice cream, in the Old World the province of the rich, was sold by street vendors and in soda fountains as banana splits, sundaes and knickerbocker glory, an elaborate sundae made with ice cream, chocolate syrup, cherries and cream.

## GELATO

An Italian ice cream that can contain cream, eggs, sugar, fruit and water, but which is usually made with milk rather than cream.

## SALEP

A traditional Middle Eastern ice cream made with milk and sugar and the ground root of an orchid known as salep. This gives it a particular texture and flavour that can be described as elastic and slightly metallic. The ice cream may also be flavoured with rose-water or orange flower water.

## SEMIFREDDO

An Italian light ice cream with a smooth, creamy texture that never sets very hard (semifreddo means 'chilled'). It is set in a mould and usually served in slices.

## GRANITA

An Italian water ice with a coarse texture. It is still-frozen (not churned) and the crystals broken up by beating them with a fork. It is traditionally flavoured with lemon or coffee and served in a tall glass.

## SORBET

A water-based ice made without dairy products or egg yolks but containing egg whites. A purely water-based sorbet is a water ice. Sorbet has a fine, grainy texture and is eaten as both a dessert and a palate cleanser between courses. In Italian, its name is *sorbetto*.

## SHERBET

Similar in texture to a sorbet, but it contains some dairy products.

## KULFI

The traditional ice cream of India, made by boiling milk until it reduces and condenses, then flavouring it with pistachios, cardamom and rose-water and set in a special conical mould. To serve, the ice cream is cut into a deep cross. On special occasions, it is decorated with gold or silver leaf.

## SPOOM

A sorbet mixed with Italian meringue, then frozen.

# icing

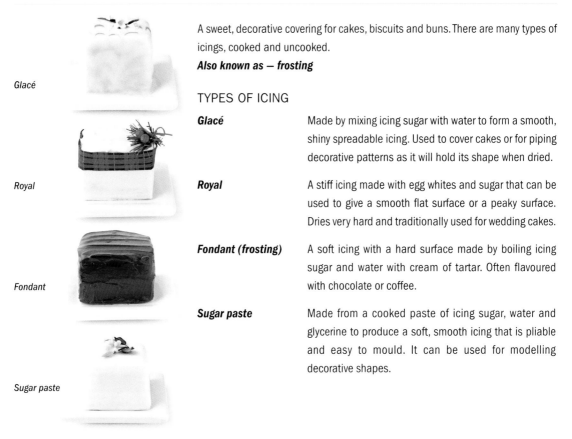

*Glacé*

*Royal*

*Fondant*

*Sugar paste*

A sweet, decorative covering for cakes, biscuits and buns. There are many types of icings, cooked and uncooked.

***Also known as — frosting***

## TYPES OF ICING

| | |
|---|---|
| ***Glacé*** | Made by mixing icing sugar with water to form a smooth, shiny spreadable icing. Used to cover cakes or for piping decorative patterns as it will hold its shape when dried. |
| ***Royal*** | A stiff icing made with egg whites and sugar that can be used to give a smooth flat surface or a peaky surface. Dries very hard and traditionally used for wedding cakes. |
| ***Fondant (frosting)*** | A soft icing with a hard surface made by boiling icing sugar and water with cream of tartar. Often flavoured with chocolate or coffee. |
| ***Sugar paste*** | Made from a cooked paste of icing sugar, water and glycerine to produce a soft, smooth icing that is pliable and easy to mould. It can be used for modelling decorative shapes. |

# île flottante

A light dessert made with poached meringue floating in a rich crème anglaise, usually decorated with crushed praline or drizzled with caramel. Ile flottante consists of one floating 'island' of meringue, while oeufs à la neige, meaning 'eggs in snow', may use several smaller meringues.

***Also known as — floating islands, oeufs à la neige***

# imam bayildi

A classic of Turkish cuisine, made with aubergines hollowed out or slit down one side and cooked, then stuffed with onions, garlic, tomatoes and parsley. Translated from the Turkish, imam bayildi means 'the imam (priest) fainted'—presumably because the dish was so wonderful. Usually served cold, but it can be served warm, either as an entrée or with salad as a light meal.

### IMAM BAYILDI

*Halve 3 aubergines, hollow out the middle, sprinkle with salt and leave to degorge for 30 minutes. Fry 2 chopped onions, 4 garlic cloves and 250 g chopped tomatoes until liquid evaporates, then stir in 6 tablespoons chopped parsley; season. Rinse and dry aubergines; shallow-fry on both sides. Stuff with mixture, put in a baking dish with 150 ml tomato juice and bake at 200 °C for 40 minutes. Serves 6.*

A country using 15 major (and around 1,600 minor) languages and which consisted, until independence, of around 600 semi-independent states— today 17—might be expected to be culinarily complex. One Indian chef has even said 'you can go from one town—or suburb—to another, and the cooking styles are different.' What follows is a review of the major influences and regional variations.

## VEGETARIANISM

Especially in the South and Gujerat, a major influence, due to the dietary practices of several religions including the Hindus and the Jains. Some restaurants have separate eating areas for 'non-vegetarians'. Not all vegetarian diets are the same: some people do not eat garlic or onion, others allow fish, and some restrict the use of various vegetables, depending on their 'positive and negative' energy.

## MOGHUL CUISINE

The Moghul (Mongol) emperors brought with them their own style of cooking, which affirmed their religion, Islam, and its Arabic heritage, and the rich cooking style of their court chefs, trained in Central Asian, Persian and Afghani culinary styles. Moghul influences are most apparent in northern India and in areas where there are a lot of Muslims such as Hyderabad, but many dishes such as *pullaos, biryanis, shahis*, kebabs, kormas and tandoori are eaten widely across India. The use of almonds, saffron and gold and silver leaf reflect the opulence of Moghul cuisine, as do the vast range of sweet dishes, especially those involving cream or rose-water.

## PORTUGUESE INFLUENCES

Goa, under Portuguese influence for 450 years, was used as a base for controlling the spice trade. With the

Portuguese came Christianity and a new style of eating to add to the already established Muslim and Hindu ways. The Portuguese, along with other Europeans, also brought foods from the New World such as potatoes, tomatoes, peppers and chillies. As in Portugal, sausages are called *chouriço*. Vindaloo is not just a curry, but a vinegar-based pork stew, and *quisade de peixe* is a Portuguese-style fish dish with extra spices added to it. Many Goan dishes, like these, combine Indian ingredients with a Western style of cooking.

## BRITISH INFLUENCES

The British influenced Indian cuisine much less than Indian cuisine influenced British food, although the Indian cooks of the British Empire leant towards making cakes, yeasted bread, *cutlis* (cutlets) and 'curries', which were more suited to the British palate. The British also established the tea gardens of India in Assam, Darjeeling and the Nilgiri Hills.

## THE NORTHEAST

Bengal has a diet rich in fish and vegetables. Hilsa (*elish*) is a much feted fish, which is used in a number of recipes, usually married with mustard seeds and mustard oil. *Bhaja*, pieces of vegetable or fish dipped in batter or rubbed in a spice and fried often start a meal, *jhol* (soupy curries) made with fish and vegetables are popular, as are dhals. Bengal has its own spice mix, panch phoran, and a large repertoire of dairy-based sweets such as *rasgollas, gulab jamun* and *sondesh*. The capital of Bengal, Calcutta, has a rich legacy of of foreign influence—it was the capital of British India until 1911. Uttar Pradesh has *kakori* kebabs from

*From top: tandoori chicken served with naan bread; lamb biryani; dosa, a rice and lentil pancake filled with curried potato and served with pickles and chutneys; pork vindaloo.*

Lucknow and *puris*, deep-fried circles of wheat dough, from Benares. The state is also known for the quality and variety of its mangoes.

## THE NORTH

Jammu and Kashmir are the northernmost states in India. Rice is grown on terraces and fruit and vegetables on floating islands in the many lakes. Their cuisine differs from the rest of the country quite considerably. Breads like *kulcha* and *shirmal* are more Middle Eastern than Indian and a spice mix called *ver* is used extensively by both Hindus and Muslims. The Punjab is the home of the tandoor oven and naan breads. Lamb *rogan josh* is a speciality.

## THE NORTHWEST

Rajasthan has a legacy of Moghul food with its *pullaos* (pilaffs), game dishes and *dum* dishes (meat and rice dishes, which are slow cooked in a sealed pot). Gujarat produces sugar cane from which they make jaggery (raw lump sugar) and sugar cane juice, as well as chillies, turmeric, cumin and coriander. Breads like *batloo* are made from millet and dishes such as *kadhi* (yoghurt and potato curry) and vegetable *thalis* (platters) are popular.

## THE CENTRE

Orissa has a diet rich in seafood and lightly spiced dishes, with coconut in many of them. Bhopal in Madhya Pradesh has many Muslim dishes, such as kormas and pilaffs. Maharashtra, and especially its capital Mumbai (Bombay) has an eclectic mix of food, including the Parsi speciality *dhansak*, and sweets like *jelabis* and *kheer*. Seafood is widely eaten, including the prized pomfret. Most widely consumed is probably the *bhel puri*, a snack made from puffed rice, chopped onion and potato, sweet and sour chutneys and *sev* (dried noodles) all tossed together.

## THE SOUTH

Hyderabad is the capital of Andhra Pradesh, a city with a Muslim history set in predominantly Hindu southern India. Its cuisine is rich and varied, combining the cooking of the royal court with the flavours of southern India such as tamarind, curry leaves and chillies. *Khichri*, a mixture of rice and lentils eaten with minced meat (*kheema*), poppadoms and chutney is a breakfast dish and *dopiaza* and pilaffs are popular. Karnataka and Tamil Nadu both have a strong vegetarian bent to their cuisine. Rice is the main staple along with pulses and legumes. Pulses are eaten as dhals and also ground into flours and used to make *sev*, steamed breads such as *idlis*, and pancakes like *dosas*. Kerala, a strip of land on the southwest coast is the spice centre of India. Cardamom, turmeric, vanilla, pepper and ginger grow here.

There are also ancient Chinese influences, for example Chinese-style fishing nets and cleavers are still in use. Food influences from various trading groups who once settled in Cochin include Jews and Syrian Christians. Arab cuisine remnants are also evident. *Appams* (rice pancakes) are common to all groups, beef is eaten by the Syrians (Kerala is the only state that has beef butchers) and fish cooked in coconut milk (*molee*) is popular. Both the coast and waterways of the state provide many different types of fish and shellfish. Tea grows in the hills of Tamil Nadu and Kerala and coffee is grown all over the South.

**See also** *curry, dhal, pilaff, tandoori*

*From top: gulab jamun; bhel puri; a thali with (clockwise from top left) aloo gobi, gulab jamun, rice, raita, mutter paneer and dhal served with a poppadom; Indian sweets including jelabis (top) and three types of barfi, a dairy-based sweet.*

A Southeast Asian nation comprising some 13,000 islands, covering 200,000 square kilometres. With three of the earth's tectonic plates meeting here, volcanic activity produces rich volcanic soil that grows rice, coconut, all manner of fruit, vegetables and spices, supporting 190 million people.

If there was a typical Indonesian meal—and there is much ethnic and religious diversity—it would consist of boiled white rice, dried fish and chilli. Some of Indonesia's diversity arises from the influences of religion: Islam, Buddhism, and Balinese Hinduism. In addition, many of the foods most identified with Indonesia are not strictly Indonesian. Like the noodles seen everywhere, *nasi goreng*, fried rice, is of Chinese origin, and the fried egg that often sits on top of it is from the Dutch, whose colonization lasted 400 years. *Rijsttafel*, a collection of dishes, was adapted—and Europeanized—by the Dutch from the village feast.

*Nasi goreng—Indonesian-style fried rice.*

*Lamb satay served with sambal kacang.*

Important ingredients include the chilli, made into any number of sauces and relishes bearing the collective name of sambal, like *sambal kacang*, a peanut sambal served with satay, grilled chicken or goat on skewers, a ubiquitous street snack. A sambal might also be a 'curry' dish of fish, meat or poultry. *Terassi* (sometimes *trassie*) is a fermented prawn paste, which is crumbled into and cooked with a wide variety of dishes. Common flavourings include chilli, galangal, lemon grass, turmeric, shallots, garlic, candlenuts, coconut milk, tamarind and kaffir lime.

*Fish steamed in banana leaf.*

*Beef rendang, served with boiled rice and sambals.*

White rice, boiled in water or coconut milk, is, for most Indonesians, at the centre of every meal, which ideally consists of many dishes combined to give a balance of flavours, nutritional value and seasonal appeal. Typical dishes are satay, and beef rendang, beef boiled dry in coconut milk and spices, then fried. Soy sauce is widely used as a seasoning and it comes in two varieties, *kecap manis*, which is a sweet version, and *kecap asin*, which is salty.

Fresh fruit is usually the choice of dessert for most Indonesians, although rice cakes with fruit and coconut-based puddings are also popular.

*Jajan pasar—sweets made with ground rice, beans, cassava (manioc) flour and flavoured with pandanus and palm sugar.*

Situated in the Atlantic Ocean and separated from Great Britain by the Irish Sea, Ireland is split into two distinct parts: Northern Ireland, which is part of Great Britain, and the Republic of Ireland situated in the south.

Irish food has been influenced by many peoples, beginning with the Celts and the Vikings. Modern influences include French haute cuisine and the usual modern ethnic mix (such as Chinese and Indian), although Ireland retains its strong foodways, and the Irish are still, even after the tragedy of the nineteenth century potato famine, the highest per capita consumers of potatoes in the European Union.

Historically the diet of most Irish families was based on cereals, milk products, pork and vegetables. The pig is the oldest domestic animal in Ireland and each family used to have its own pig which, once killed, was preserved in salt, and would provide the family with meat for a year. Its blood would also be used to make black pudding.

## CHEESE-MAKING

Cheese-making has developed from individual farmhouses into a thriving international industry. Popular cheeses include Gubbeen from Cork, which has a creamy texture, and Cashel Blue, a rich, creamy blue from Tipperary.

## TRADITIONS

Faith has always played a large part in what Irish people eat and to this day particular dishes are served on certain religious feast days. Goose is served on 29 September, Michaelmas Day, and very few practising Catholics will eat meat on Friday, preferring fish instead. Corned beef and cabbage was traditionally served on Easter Sunday, although today it is more commonly eaten on St Patrick's Day.

All Hallows Eve, better known as Halloween, is one of the most important Irish festivals. It celebrates the end of

the harvest and some of its associated dishes are barm brack, boxty pancakes and colcannon. Barm brack is a fruit cake that often has a wedding ring hidden inside it before it is baked. Whoever finds the ring is supposedly the next person to get married.

Irish coffee, a combination of coffee, Irish whiskey and cream, is sometimes enjoyed after meals.

## VEGETABLES

The vegetable most associated with Ireland is the potato. Once introduced, its popularity amongst farmers spread because it produces high yields from little land. Potato dishes abound, one of the most common being champ, mashed potato combined with spring onions or leeks and served with butter. Each spoonful of potato is dipped in the melting butter before eating.

## MEAT AND SEAFOOD

The most celebrated and argued over Irish dish is Irish stew. The arguments arise over the correct ingredients, although it can be safely said that it should contain mutton, potatoes, onions and seasoning. Additions such as carrots and green vegetables are more controversial.

Although Ireland is surrounded by sea and dotted with countless unpolluted waterways, the Irish were long wary of seafood. However, today, seafood plays a large part in the diet. A diverse range of fish is eaten fresh, dried, salted and smoked. Irish oysters, once considered poor man's food, are now considered more of a delicacy, and are traditionally eaten with soda bread and a pint of Guinness. Mussels, cockles, lobster, crab and prawns also feature widely.

▣ *See also* **boxty, colcannon**

*From top: champ, mashed potato served with butter; barm brack; oysters and Guinness, a beer made from hops and malt; Irish stew; Irish coffee, the perfect end to a meal.*

Fifty years ago, Italy could be divided geographically by its cooking. The North ate butter, polenta, risotto and stewed meats; the Centre enjoyed fresh pasta and lard; while the South cooked with olive oil, dried pasta, chillies and tomatoes. Today these distinctions have blurred, proof being that in recent years *piatti tipici* (regional cooking), especially using local produce such as beans, chestnuts, grains and wild salad leaves, and *cucina povera* (the cuisine of poorer southern Italy) have increased in popularity all across Italy. Outside of Italy, what is thought of as typically Italian, from pizza to pasta with tomatoes, basil and garlic, is actually the food of the South, a style of cooking spread throughout the world by Italian emigration. These days, Italy is also home to the Slow Food Movement, which champions the cause of regional food and tradition in the face of fast food and mass production.

*Tortelli di zucca—pasta filled with pumpkin and served with sage butter.*

*Brasato al Barolo—beef cooked in red wine.*

## THE NORTHWEST

Piedmont and Valle d'Aosta form the gastronomic centre of this region. Most of Italy's rice is grown on the fertile plains, while some of the best wines, such as Barolo, are produced here. The city of Turin is famous for grissini, Alba for white truffles and the alpine areas of Valle d'Aosta for Fontina and Robiola cheeses. Regional specialities include: *bagna caôda*, vegetables with a dip of olive oil; *bollito misto*, a rich stew of boiled meats; and *brasato al Barolo*. The plains of Lombardy are good dairy country and produce such superb cheeses as Gorgonzola, Taleggio and Grana Padano. Lombardy dishes include *tortelli di zucca*, *risotto alla milanese* and veal osso buco. The region of Liguria is known for its olive oil and use of herbs, most notably basil, which is used in pesto, a sauce eaten with pasta, gnocchi and in minestrone.

*Canederli—bread dumplings served in a broth.*

*Risi e bisi—rice and peas.*

## THE NORTHEAST

Trentino-Alto Adige and Friuli-Venezia Giulia border Austria and Slovenia and have strong Germanic and Central European influences, producing speck, San Daniele ham and white polenta, along with *knödel*, *gulasch* (similar to Hungarian goulash), sauerkraut and veal stews. The cuisine of Venice, part of the fertile region of Veneto, absorbed culinary ideas from the Arabs and Turks who were once part of its community, but its cuisine is essentially simple, with polenta, bean soups and risottos. Vegetables are plentiful, as is seafood, the speciality being *moleche* (small soft-shelled crabs). Some of Italy's best-known desserts are also from Veneto: Treviso claims tiramisu and *pandoro* is from Verona. Dishes include *pasta e fagioli* (bean and pasta soup), *risi e bisi* and *fegato alla Veneziana* (liver).

*Pandoro—a yeasted cake baked in a star-shaped mould.*

**199**

*Zampone—stuffed pig's trotters.*

*Papa al pomodoro—a thick tomato and bread soup.*

*Parmigiana di melanzane—layers of tomato, aubergine and Parmesan.*

*Baked sardines stuffed with lemon, breadcrumbs and parsley.*

## THE CENTRE

Emilia-Romagna, one of the great gastronomic regions of Italy, is home to *prosciutto di parma*, mortadella, balsamic vinegar, *Parmigiano Reggiano* and the fresh egg pasta used for tagliatelle, lasagne and stuffed pastas like tortellini. *Ragù bolognese*, usually served with tagliatelle and *zampone* are specialities of the area. Le Marche is renowned for its seafood and rich *vincisgrassi* lasagne. Tuscany is famous for its wine and olive oil and the city of Siena is the origin of medieval cakes such as *panforte* and *pan pepato*. In Florence, huge steaks are grilled *alla fiorentina*, and soups such as *ribollita*, made with cabbage and beans, are widely eaten. Umbrian cuisine is rich and varied, and includes the black and white truffles of the region, game, lentils from Castelluccio and olive oil. Umbria is renowned for its charcuterie and the town of Norcia gives its name to *norcino*—'pork butcher'. Specialities include *salsiccia con lenticchie* (sausages with lentils), olive tapenade, grains like farro and spit-cooked meats.

*Abbachio arrosto— roast baby lamb.*

## THE SOUTH

Roman cuisine is based on pasta, beans, offal and dishes like *abbachio arrosto* (roast baby lamb) and *saltimbocca,* thin layers of veal and prosciutto. *Spaghetti alla carbonara* and *all'amatriciana* are its most popular pasta dishes. Neapolitan cuisine dominates the area of Campania and produce includes fresh buffalo mozzarella, ricotta and lemons. Southern cuisine was heavily influenced by tomatoes, peppers and chillies from the New World and famous dishes include pizza, *calzone*, pasta with garlic and oil, *spaghetti alla puttanesca*, *crespelle* (crêpes) and cannelloni. Calabria is famous for its seafood, though its fishing industry is, unfortunately, dwindling, especially with declining stocks of tuna and swordfish. Citrus groves, olives and figs grow well here and the aubergine is the most important vegetable. Dishes include *parmigiana di melanzane* (baked aubergine with Parmesan), baked vegetables and grilled lamb.

## THE ISLANDS

Sicily's cuisine is influenced by the Greeks, Romans, Spanish and the Arabs. Rice dishes and couscous (*cucusu*) are legacies of the Arabs. Fish is important in the island's diet, and there are ancient tuna markets at Catania and Palermo. Well-known dishes include *caponata* (fried aubergines, onions and tomatoes), *arancini* (stuffed rice balls), stuffed sardines and desserts such as lemon granita and cassata.

Sardinians have a reputation for disliking the sea and not eating fish, despite being an island people. The cuisine is based on meat, cheese, bread and herbs. Sardinian dishes include *culingiones* (cheese ravioli), fried cheese pastries with honey, crispy flat bread called *carta de musica* and *aragosta* (spiny lobster).

# j

## jaboticaba

A native Brazilian fruit, similar to a large, black grape in appearance, taste and texture. The most unusual thing about the fruit is that it grows in large clusters directly from both the branches and trunk of the tree. The fruit has thick, tough, tannic skin and juicy white flesh with one to four seeds. Eat the fruit whole—it is aromatic with a very sweet grape-like flavour—add it to fruit salads or make it into jellies and jams (if making jam, remove the skin from at least half the fruit first to reduce the tannin content). In Brazil, jaboticaba is also used for wine-making. If stored covered in the fridge, the fruit will keep for about 2 weeks.

**Also known as — Brazilian tree grapes**

## jackfruit

Native to Malaysia and India, jackfruit is one of the world's largest fruit, some weighing up to 40 kg. It's covered with green, knobbly skin, which turns yellow or brown as it ripens, and has a juicy, sweet flesh. When unripe, both seeds and the flesh are eaten as a vegetable, usually cooked in curries or made into chutney. Ripe fruit may be eaten on its own or added to fruit salads. Its ripeness is easily detected by a strong and unpleasant odour (although the flesh inside smells sweet). Jackfruit is sold fresh and in tins.

### SWEET JACKFRUIT ROLLS

*Lay 1 piece jackfruit (cut it to about 1 x 4 cm in size) and 1 slice of banana (roughly the same size) on a spring roll wrapper. Sprinkle with caster sugar and a few drops of lime juice, then roll up like a spring roll. Heat some flavourless oil in a frying pan and fry the rolls on all sides until golden brown and cooked. Serve as a snack. Each serves 1 person.*

## jaffle

An Australian version of the toasted sandwich, which may be filled with anything from cheese and tomato to egg and bacon. It was traditionally toasted in a long-handled cast-iron jaffle iron, usually over a campfire, but today an electric jaffle iron may be used instead.

see sugar — **jaggery**

201

# jalousie

A long rectangular flaky pastry filled with apples, apricot jam or marzipan. Translated from the French for 'shutters', it gets its name from its appearance—the top of the pastry is slashed across its width to resemble shutters on a window.

# jam

Jam is made by boiling fruit with sugar, and is set by pectin, which will either be present in the fruit or added. Jams are used as spreads, as an ingredient in tarts, steamed puddings or as filling in cakes. In Eastern Europe, tea is sweetened with jam.

*From left: raspberry jam, cape gooseberry jam, apricot jam, pear jam.*

## PLUM JAM

*Remove the stones from 1 kg under-ripe plums and coarsely chop the flesh. Put in a plastic or glass bowl with 1 kg sugar and leave overnight (this will bring out the juice and start to dissolve the sugar). Put in a large saucepan and cook over low heat until sugar dissolves, then boil the jam rapidly until it reaches setting point—start testing after 8 minutes. Bottle in sterilized jars (see page 296). Put the warm jam into warm jars and put on the lid—this will form a vacuum as it cools. Label the jams when cold. Makes 2 x 500 ml jars.*

## COOKING

*Sugar not only sweetens jam but it also works with pectin as a setting agent, and inhibits the growth of microorganisms. Jams must contain over 55 per cent sugar to inhibit the growth of microorganisms, so the amount of sugar needed to preserve the fruit will depend on its natural sweetness. Follow the recipe carefully as using too much sugar will cause the jam to crystallize; too little sugar won't allow the jam to set.*

*When using jam sugar, warm the sugar in a low oven so it dissolves quickly when added to the fruit. This will ensure the fruit doesn't overcook, or boil and caramelize.*

*To test if your jam is cooked, lift up the wooden spoon and see if the jam falls off it in drips or sheets. When it falls in sheets, drip a little onto a chilled plate and push your finger through it: if it wrinkles up as you push, it's ready.*

▮ *See also* **loquat**

### Making jam

Choose firm, just-ripe fruit for making jam, as overripe fruit lack the pectin needed for setting. Jams containing fruit that have a low pectin content, such as blackberries, cherries, figs and nectarines, will need extra pectin. Use either a commercial setting agent or add pectin-rich fruit such as apples or citrus fruit. The acidity of the fruit acts as both a preservative and a setting agent. Fruit that have low acid levels, such as apricots, figs, kiwi fruit, pears and strawberries, can be supplemented with lemon juice or by adding fruit that are high in acid, such as blackberries, blackcurrants, cherries, citrus or green apples.

## Jamaica flower

Not to be confused with the ornamental hibiscus plant that grows in tropical areas worldwide, Jamaica flower (*Hibiscus sabdaraffia*) is a tropical plant grown for its enlarged, fleshy, deep-red sepals. The sepals are edible, slightly tart in flavour and may be bought fresh, dried or frozen. When dried, they may be infused in teas; used fresh, they may be cooked into jams or a sauce similar to cranberry. In the West Indies and the Caribbean, the flower is used to make wine. It also adds colour and flavour when mixed with rum and spices to make drinks, a favourite at Christmas time when the flower is available fresh. In Mexico, the Jamaica flower is used to make a drink *(pictured)* by infusing the flower in boiling water, then adding sugar.

**Also known as — flor de Jamaica, Jamaica sorrel, rosella, roselle**

## jambalaya

A New Orleans dish of Spanish origin, and a speciality of Cajun cuisine, jambalaya is based on long-grain rice, green peppers, celery and onion and mixed with ingredients such as chicken, sausage, prawns, ham or even alligator. A red jambalaya uses tomatoes and tomato sauce; a brown one uses chicken or beef stock. The origin of its name is thought to be a jumbling together of *jamón*, Spanish for ham, and the rice dish, paella.

## Jansson's temptation

### JANSSON'S TEMPTATION

*Soak 45 g drained anchovy fillets in milk for 5 minutes to lessen their saltiness. Cook 1 finely sliced onion in a knob of butter until golden. Cut 5 peeled potatoes into matchsticks and season well. Put half the potatoes in a buttered baking dish, sprinkle on the drained anchovies and onion and top with remaining potato. Pour over 500 ml cream and bake at 200 °C for 55 minutes, or until cooked. Serves 6.*

A gratin of grated potato, anchovies, butter, onions and cream, Jansson's temptation is supposedly served at the end of a party to make the guests stay longer. This dish is a version of the anchovy gratins that were popular in Sweden during the nineteenth century. The debate of how it acquired its interesting name is ongoing—some say the dish was thought to have tempted a religious fanatic who had vowed to give up all earthly pleasures, while other theories suggest it came from the Swedish opera singer Pelle Janzon or from the title of a 1928 film.

*Cold soba noodle salad with sesame seed dipping sauce.*

A nation made up of over 1,000 small islands, with the four major ones being Hokkaido in the north, Honshu, the largest, and Shikoku and Kyushu in the south. Much of Japan is mountainous, and subsequently there is little land left for agriculture, so the early Japanese relied instead on the coastal waters to supply fish and seafood. As a result, the Japanese diet, even today, strongly reflects that of the early Japanese, a diet based on rice, fish, seaweed and vegetables.

## INFLUENCES

Historically, Japan was isolated from the West for many years, only occasionally opening its doors to foreign ideas and foods. The Chinese, who entered Japan for a brief period between the sixth and ninth centuries, had considerable influence on many aspects of Japanese life. They introduced Buddhism, and with it, respect for nature and vegetarianism, and foods such as soya beans and tea. From soya beans, the Japanese made bean curd, miso, and soy sauce. Later, in the sixteenth century, Japan established a relationship with Portuguese traders. The Portuguese introduced the technique of deep-frying foods in batter, which the Japanese refined to create *tempura*.

After the Meiji Restoration of 1868, Japan increasingly began to adopt Western practices. Meats such as beef, pork and chicken began to appear in their largely vegetable-based diet. Today, red meat, although extremely expensive, is popular, and is seen in dishes such as *shabu shabu* and *sukiyaki*, one-pot dishes made from a combination of beef and vegetables. Pork appears in dishes such as *tonkatsu*, fried breaded pork, or *katsudon* (also called *katsudon donburi*), a pork cutlet on rice.

*Katsudon*

*Temaki-zushi—hand-rolled sushi.*

## CHARACTERISTICS

The most distinguishing features of Japanese cuisine are freshness, insistence on seasonal produce and aesthetics. Dishes are designed around the flavour of the principal ingredient, and so are only lightly seasoned. Rarely are heavy sauces used. The meal designed to accompany the tea ceremony, *kaiseki ryori*, best illustrates the artistic sensibility of Japanese cuisine. In a *kaiseki* meal, the seasonality and the beauty of the presentation of the food and its containers are all carefully considered. At a more basic level, sashimi is also testament to this philosophy. The sashimi is artfully arranged on the plate with only a few simple garnishes, often with pickled ginger and a dipping sauce. Each fish will be prepared and cut differently, according to its size, shape and texture. Some sashimi restaurants specialize in fugu, a highly poisonous fish, which is considered a great delicacy but can only be prepared by highly specialized and licensed chefs.

*Bento box, a partitioned food box, often used as a lunchbox or on picnics. Disposable versions are sold at train stations.*

Flavourings are minimal and usually consist of one or more of the following: soy sauce (*shoyu*), widely used as a condiment and an ingredient in many dishes; *dashi*, a fish stock made from kelp and dried bonito flakes, used as the basis for soup and also as a stock; sugar (*sato*), added to dishes such as *sukiyaki* and omelettes; rice wine (*sake*); salt (*shio*); vinegar (*su*) and miso, a thick paste made from fermented beans and used in miso soup, which is eaten at almost every meal.

*Tempura*

Very few Japanese homes have an oven, so most cooking is done on a stove, under the grill or at the table in an electric frying pan. All styles of cooking seek to retain as much of the natural flavour of the food as possible. The five basic methods of cooking are: deep-fried (*agemono*), steamed (*mushimono*), one-pot (*nabemono*), simmered (*nimono*) and grilled (*yakimono*).

*Natto and rice served with miso soup.*

Short-grain white rice is widely eaten and cooking it to perfection requires dedication, although nowadays, most families use an electric rice cooker. The rice is often cooked in the morning, kept warm in the cooker and used throughout the day. While rice is often eaten on its own, it may be served for breakfast with miso soup and *natto* (fermented beans), or used to make dishes such as sushi. Most sushi are enlivened with wasabi, a hot green paste made from the root of a plant.

Noodle dishes are numerous and restaurants all over Japan specialize in these. The two main types are *soba*, made from buckwheat and *udon*, made from wheat. *Ramen* are Chinese-style wheat noodles served in a bowl of stock with slices of roast pork or beef. The noodles are picked up with chopsticks and the broth is slurped out of the bowl. Slurping is quite acceptable—it's a sign of a good appetite, eating with pleasure, and helps to cool the piping hot noodles.

Eating out is popular in Japan and most socializing is done outside the home in the small *izakayas* or *robatayaki* that serve beer and snack foods. These range from *yakitori*, grilled chicken; *gyoza*, dumplings; or *okonomiyaki*, a large pancake made with eggs and cabbage and typically filled with pork, beef or prawns.

Although beer is widely drunk throughout Japan, the traditional rice wine, sake, is popular too, served warm in winter and chilled in summer. Green tea is often drunk before, during and after a meal.

▦ *See also* **miso, sake, sashimi, shabu shabu, sukiyaki, sushi, tempura, teppanyaki, teriyaki, wasabi, yakitori**

*Miso ramen soup*

## jellied eels

Eels skinned and cooked in stock and vinegar, which solidifies around them when cooled. Jellied eels were traditionally a favourite of London's East Enders, sold from street stalls in small china bowls and sprinkled with chilli vinegar, or in 'pie and mash' shops, where they are often served with steak and kidney pie and mashed potatoes and 'liquor', a type of gravy made with parsley.

## jelly

Jellies can be made with either a sweet or savoury liquid and are set, usually in a mould, with a setting agent such as gelatine, agar-agar, pectin, carageen moss or isinglass (a form of setting agent made from the swimming bladders of fish). Jellies aren't always made from clear liquids but can be made with flavoured milk, yoghurts and creams as well as wine, champagne and coffee.

Some jellies are made by boiling fruit juice and allowing it to set using its natural pectin (these jellies won't melt at room temperature); others are made with fruit juice using a setting agent such as gelatine (these may melt quickly at room temperature); they may be made with commercially prepared cubes or crystals that are stirred into boiling water and then set in the fridge; or obtained by boiling meat or fish bones and tissue (rich in gelatinous substances), and used as a garnish, like aspic, or served on their own like consommé.

***Also known as — jello***

*Fruit juice jellies*

### FRUIT JUICE JELLY

*Pour 250 ml of any sweetened fruit juice (except pineapple) into a saucepan (add 1–2 tablespoons of liqueur if you like). Sprinkle over 4½ teaspoons gelatine powder and leave to sponge (see page 162). If using leaf gelatine, soak 9 sheets in cold water until floppy. Heat the juice gently, then stir in gelatine until completely dissolved. Add another 500 ml juice, then pour into jelly moulds. Allow to set in the fridge (some fruit juices take longer to set than others and jellies that have alcohol in them take longer to set than those that don't). To turn out the jellies, wrap the mould in a hot cloth and then gently turn them out onto a plate. Serves 6.*

**See also** *agar-agar, aspic, gelatine*

## jelly roll — see swiss roll

The edible parts of some varieties of jellyfish are highly prized in Asian cuisines, but only after they have been salted with bicarbonate of soda and left to dry. Jellyfish is sold either dried, when it needs to be soaked, blanched and shredded, or ready to use in a vacuum pack. Semi-translucent in colour and with a delicate flavour, the appreciation for jellyfish lies mostly in its crunchy, chewy texture.

### JELLYFISH SALAD

*Put a 150 g packet of shredded jellyfish in a colander and allow to drain.*
*Put the jellyfish into a large bowl and add ¼ shredded iceburg lettuce,*
*½ cucumber, peeled and julienned, and 2 teaspoons toasted sesame seeds.*
*Mix 1 tablespoon light soy sauce, 2 tablespoons rice vinegar, 1 teaspoon*
*sesame oil and 1 tablespoon sugar. Pour over salad and toss well. Serves 4.*

## jerk

A Jamaican seasoning used for flavouring grilled meat such as pork and chicken, which is usually barbecued or cooked over an open fire. The seasoning is a variable blend but often contains chillies, allspice, thyme, cinnamon, ginger, cloves, onion and garlic. It is either rubbed on dry or made into a marinade.

## jerky

A strip of tough meat, most often beef or game, that has been dried in the sun or cured by smoking. Jerky, usually eaten in small strips, is chewy but quite flavoursome. It can also be softened by soaking it in water and adding it to stews.
*Also known as — biltong, charqui, chipped beef, jerked beef*

## Jerusalem artichoke

Neither from Jerusalem nor an artichoke, this winter root is a native of Peru and a relative of the sunflower (in Spanish, '*girasol*', mispronounced in English as 'Jerusalem'). They have a mildly sweet, smoky flavour. Finely slice and add raw to salads, boil or roast like potatoes or use to make wonderful velvety soups and mashes. When cut, drop into water with a squeeze of lemon juice to stop them going brown. Jerusalem artichokes have a reputation for causing flatulence. This can be countered with a pinch of asafoetida.

### ROASTED JERUSALEM ARTICHOKES

*Scrub 750 g Jerusalem artichokes, then toss them in 2 tablespoons olive oil with plenty of seasoning. Put them on a baking tray and roast at 200 °C for about 40 minutes, or until tender in the centre, then drizzle with a little hazelnut or walnut oil. Serve as a vegetable or for a salad, toss with rocket leaves and fried cubes of bacon. Serves 4.*

# Jewish food

Jewish cuisine has, over the centuries, been influenced by many cultures and cuisines and is, consequently, complex. It can, however, be sorted into two main branches. Ashkenazi (Eastern European, including Poland, Germany and Russia) and Sephardi (Middle Eastern, Asian and Mediterranean). The Ashkenazi cuisine evolved amongst predominantly Christian cold weather climes and uses chicken fat, potatoes, winter vegetables and freshwater fish, whereas the Sephardi cuisine developed in warmer climes, Moorish Spain, North Africa, India and Christian Italy and uses peppers, aubergines, tomatoes, rice, olive oil and saltwater fish.

*Gefilte fish—cold poached fish balls.*

## INFLUENCES

However, for all observant Jews, the preparation, serving and eating of food is governed by a dietary law called Kashrut, which results in food that is said to be kosher. The practical aspects of Kashrut law have kept Jewish cuisine separate and somewhat old-fashioned in style. Jews could not traditionally eat in non-Jewish homes and so kept a close-knit community, largely unaware of new trends and ideas, until the Reform movement in Germany and North America in the nineteenth century declared that Jews could still be Jews without practising Kashrut.

*Challah— plaited bread.*

*Stuffed roast chicken*

## JEWISH FEASTS

Traditionally, Jewish food is linked to festivals and the Sabbath. The rest of the week, much plainer food is eaten in preparation for the feasts themselves, which must be made from the best food available. Sabbath starts 18 minutes before sunset on Friday and lasts until after sunset on Saturday when stars are visible in the sky. A Sabbath dinner is a family occasion, with all dishes commonly served at once in a buffet style. These may include savoury pastries like *knishes*, *challah* (bread), *gefilte* fish, chopped liver, a roast chicken or lamb, soup and a dessert such as almond cake. Ashkenazi menus are standard for the Sabbath but Sephardi dishes vary from family to family and community to community.

Cholent (Sabbath stew) is served for Saturday lunch as it can be prepared the day before—no work, including cooking and baking, is allowed on the Sabbath. The evening meal is usually made up of cold dishes to observe this law.

Traditional dishes for the Jewish New Year (Rosh Hashanah) for Ashkenazi Jews include *challah*; slices of apple dipped in honey; and carrots, taken to represent gold coins, and made into *tzimmes*. Sephardi Jews eat different round-shaped food like sesame rings, meatballs and chickpeas to symbolize hope for a full year ahead.

*Tzimmes—honeyed carrots.*

*Cholent—a meat casserole, often cooked with potatoes, barley and beans.*

*Chicken soup with matzo balls*

Pomegranates are eaten as they are represented in the Torah and are said to have 613 seeds, the same number as the commandments. Nothing bitter or sharp like lemon juice is eaten and no black is eaten including aubergines, chocolate, black olives and tea—green or mint tea is drunk instead.

Yom Kippur is a day of fasting. The meal before the fast is made up of bland food that will not induce thirst. The Ashkenazim eat chicken soup with matzo balls or *kreplach* (ravioli) filled with chicken, and the Sephardim, chicken soup and boiled chicken with rice. Fasts are broken with a cold drink such as almond milk, lemonade or juices and little savoury and sweet pastries like *börek*, which are dairy-based. This can also be followed by another meal usually based on chicken, which is made the day before and reheated.

*Almond cake with orange syrup*

Hanukah is the festival in which candles are lit one by one over 8 days to symbolize the miracle of the holy oil that lasted for 8 days rather than the expected 1 day. The food reflects this in its use of oil by frying potato *latkes*, fritters and chicken. The only religious feast at which heavy drinking is encouraged is Purim, where it is seen as a way of showing elation. The symbolic foods are representative of the demise of the Jewess, Queen Esther and Haman (who had imposed a sentence of death for all Jews)—deep-fried pastries, made in the shape of his ears and *hamantashen*, in the shape of his hat.

During passover, all leaven foods (*hametz*) are forbidden, as well as all foods containing wheat, barley, rye, oats and spelt. Ashkenazim also forbid foods such as rice and lentils as they also have the capacity to ferment and leaven. The house and all its contents are cleaned, sometimes the walls are whitewashed in order to clean out any *hametz* food. The most important meal is Seder, in which the dishes served tell the story of the Israelites' escape from Israel. Ritual foods include bitter herbs, matzo, and parsley dipped in salt water, each of which have a story to tell.

## DIETARY LAWS

*The basis of Kashrut was revealed to Moses by God as part of the commandments, which make up the Torah. Kashrut laws deal with what is kosher or 'fit' to eat and what is terefah, or forbidden.*

*All fruit and vegetables are permitted, animals that chew the cud and have cloven hooves are clean, but those with cloven hooves that do not chew the cud, such as pigs, horses and rabbits, are not. Beasts of prey are not allowed, game cannot be eaten as it is not ritually slaughtered, and nor can animals that die of natural causes. Fish have to have both scales and fins and therefore shellfish and crustaceans are forbidden.*

*Blood is forbidden and must be drained from meat during shehitah (ritual slaughter). Meat then has to be soaked in cold water and salted before being washed three times.*

*The sentence, 'Thou shalt not seethe the kid in its mothers milk' is interpreted as requiring the complete separation of milk and meat. They are never eaten in the same meal, cannot be cooked, stored or washed up together. Observant households have two entirely separate sets of utensils, crockery and linen.*

*Milk cannot be drunk until several hours have passed after eating meat, but meat can be eaten after milk is drunk if the mouth is rinsed and bread eaten in between. Pareve, or neutral foods like vegetables, grain, fruit, eggs and fish, can be eaten with both milk and meat.*

*Hamantashen—three-cornered pastries filled with poppy seeds, made in the shape of Haman's hat.*

## jicama

A bulb-like root vegetable, similar in appearance to a very large turnip, with thin, beige leathery skin and sweetish, crisp white flesh. A native to Mexico, jicama is also eaten extensively in Southeast Asian cuisine. To use it, peel the skin including the fibrous flesh directly under it, then slice and use raw in salads, add to stews, or cut into cubes and use in stir-fries as a substitute for water chestnuts, which it resembles in flavour. Jicamas are a good source of starch and, like potatoes, if stored in the fridge for too long will convert their starch to sugar. Buy firm, heavy roots with smooth skins that are relatively free of blemishes.

***Also known as — jicana, Mexican potato, Mexican turnip, yam bean***

## jujube

Olive-sized, red leathery-skinned berries, with soft sweet flesh surrounding a hard stone. The fruit is used in China, where it is called a Chinese date, in both savoury and sweet dishes where it is considered medicinal. In the Mediterranean it is often candied or preserved in honey; in Bolivia, it is made into a drink called *chicha*. The berries are often available dried *(pictured)* and need to be soaked before use. It is thought by many to be the 'lotus' mentioned by Homer in the Odyssey.

## junket

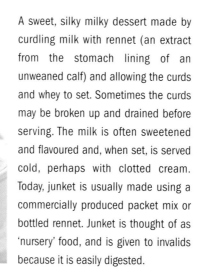

A sweet, silky milky dessert made by curdling milk with rennet (an extract from the stomach lining of an unweaned calf) and allowing the curds and whey to set. Sometimes the curds may be broken up and drained before serving. The milk is often sweetened and flavoured and, when set, is served cold, perhaps with clotted cream. Today, junket is usually made using a commercially produced packet mix or bottled rennet. Junket is thought of as 'nursery' food, and is given to invalids because it is easily digested.

### JUNKET

*Warm 550 ml full cream milk to hand hot, then add 2 junket tablets and 2 teaspoons caster sugar. Pour the mixture into a dish and refrigerate until set. Cover the surface with a layer of whipped cream and sprinkle with ground cinnamon or nutmeg. Serves 4.*

## jus

French for 'juice', it can be the juice of fruit, vegetables or meat. The term *au jus* usually refers to a dish of meat served in its own juice, made from a roast's 'gravy'—the meat juices mixed with water and stock. Jus or *jus viande* is known as 'God's gravy', that is, a naturally occurring gravy and not one that has to be made. *Jus lié* is a thickened jus and is more like what the English call gravy.

# k

## kaffir lime

Small, fragrant citrus fruit widely used in Thai and Southeast Asian cuisine. The fruit have a distinctive knobbly, dark-green skin and uniquely double-shaped, glossy leaves. Finely shredded or grated, both the leaves and zest are added to soups, curries and chilli dishes to give them a wonderful tangy flavour. To chop fresh kaffir lime leaves, stack two or three leaves in a pile. Roll leaves from tip to stem into a tight bundle, then slice finely. Discard the tough central stem. Whole leaves can be simmered in dishes but remove them before serving as they are tough. The juice and flesh are not used as they are bitter.

Kaffir limes and leaves are available fresh or dried from Asian food stores or supermarkets. If unavailable, use lime zest and young lime leaves. Because of the racist connotations of the word 'kaffir', they are increasingly likely to be found as 'makrut' limes.

## Kahlúa

A richly flavoured Mexican liqueur, made from coffee, cane spirit and vanilla. In cooking, Kahlúa can be used in cakes, cheesecakes, tiramisu and brownies. Add a shot to coffee; make a Sombrero—the classic cocktail drink of Kahlúa and milk; or pour over gelato and top with an espresso to make the Italian dessert, *affogato*.

## kale

A relative of the cabbage, with a similar but stronger flavour and, depending on the variety, dark-green or purple, smooth or curly leaves. As it grows happily in colder climates, kale has long been a popular winter vegetable in northern European countries, and is eaten widely in the southern United States as 'collard greens'. Use as you would cabbage or stir into soups and stews.

**Also known as — borecole, cole, curly kale**

## kangaroo

Low in fat and cholesterol, kangaroo meat has a dense texture and gamey flavour. It can be used in much the same way as beef—grilled, barbecued, fried as a roast or in casseroles. Kangaroo meat is usually sold vacuum-packed, and because the meat oxidizes and turns brown when unwrapped, it needs to be cooked immediately. Lightly brush with oil before cooking to help prevent oxidization. Kangaroo can also be bought smoked and can be eaten like Parma ham.

# kebab

Popular throughout the Middle East, kebabs are usually small chunks of marinated lamb, beef, veal or fish, or minced lamb and beef, threaded onto skewers and cooked, often over coals. Kebabs also appear in the cuisine of other countries, for example, tikka in India. The meat may be served on or off the skewer, often with a salad, or commonly as a street food sold wrapped in flat bread.

***Also known as — doner kebab, shashlik, shish kebab, souvlakia, yeeros***

*From left: kofta, chicken doner kebab, shish kebab, hummus and tabbouleh.*

*See also* **churrasco, kofta**

## TYPES OF KEBABS

| | |
|---|---|
| ***Shish kebab*** | Chunks of meat cooked on a skewer. The name comes from the Turkish *sis* meaning 'skewer' or 'sword' and *kebab* meaning 'roast meat'. |
| ***Doner kebab*** ***(kebab, brochette)*** | A stack of seasoned meat cooked on a vertical spit and sliced off as needed. Often served wrapped in a flat bread with salad and with sauces such as chilli or garlic. |
| ***Kofta (kofte)*** | Finely ground and seasoned minced meat, usually lamb, formed into a tube or balls around a skewer. |

# kecap manis

Indonesian in origin, a thick, sweet dark soy sauce used as a condiment, a dipping sauce, an ingredient, as a marinade or for basting food. There are many varieties and these range from sweet and medium sweet to the salty *kecap asin*. Buy from supermarkets or Asian food stores and store in the fridge once opened.

***Also known as — ketjap manis***

# kedgeree

## KEDGEREE

*Cook 150 g long-grain rice and drain. Melt 50 g butter in a large frying pan and add the rice, 300 g cooked, skinned and boned smoked haddock fillet, 3 quartered hard-boiled eggs, a pinch of good-quality curry powder and 4 tablespoons cream. Season well with salt, pepper and cayenne pepper. Stir ingredients together until hot, then serve garnished with extra egg quarters. Serves 4.*

A popular English dish made of smoked fish, boiled eggs, curry powder and cream mixed into rice. The dish evolved from the Indian breakfast dish *khichri* made with boiled rice, lentils and spices. Kedgeree is best made using smoked haddock though any white or smoked fish will do, and some recipes use salmon. Kedgeree is traditionally served for breakfast but it does make an enjoyable light lunch or supper.

Fermented milk, similar in flavour to drinking yoghurt, with a varying alcohol content (about 1 per cent), depending on how long it is left to ferment. Originally made from camel's milk in Russia and the Caucasus, kefir is now usually made from sheep or cow's milk. Long respected for its health benefits and contributions to longevity, it was originally used to treat stomach and intestinal diseases. It is now manufactured commercially and can be bought from health food stores.

Originally a Chinese fermented fish sauce, with its name probably coming from the Malay *kecap*, meaning soy sauce. Today, ketchup (catsup) is a vinegar-based relish flavoured with anything from anchovies to mushrooms. At the end of the nineteenth century, Henry Heinz first bottled tomato ketchup. A little added to tomato soups and sauces takes the acid edge off fresh tomatoes.

There are many versions of this popular Syrian, Lebanese and Iraqi dish, but essentially kibbeh are made from minced meat (lamb, beef or veal) and burghul pounded or mixed together to form a thick paste. The paste is then treated in different ways: *kibbeh naye* is eaten raw, the paste is shaped into rolls or served on a dish to be scooped up with lettuce leaves; *kibbeh bil sanieh* is made by spreading a tray with a layer of minced meat sandwiched between two layers of kibbeh and baking it; stuffed kibbeh are long hollow tubes shaped around the finger, filled with minced meat and then fried. Kibbeh can also be made with a ground rice or potato base.

Kibbeh can be eaten on their own, or they may be cooked in a yoghurt sauce, steamed or eaten like dumplings in soups. The ability to make good kibbeh is held in high esteem: women born with long fingers are considered blessed for they will be able to make long, slender kibbeh.

*Also known as — kibbe, koubba*

A fiery condiment eaten by Koreans with practically every meal. Kimchi is made by fermenting Chinese cabbage in brine with cucumber, onion, garlic, ginger and chillies. Sometimes daikon is used instead of or with the cabbage. Its strong smell and flavour take some getting used to. Kimchi is traditionally prepared during the autumn to last through the winter months. When fermentation is complete, the kimchi is buried in the ground in jars and dug up when needed. There are innumerable recipes for kimchi and each family has its own. Some kimchis are unfermented (summer kimchis) and some may use dried shrimp or fish.

*Also known as — kimchee*

■ *See also* **Korean food**

*Cabbage kimchi*

see smoked fish — **kipper**

## kirsch

A clear brandy distilled from fermented black cherries. The brandy has a bitter almond flavour and is used in gateaux and desserts like Black Forest gateau and cherries jubilee, as well as to flavour cheese fondues. Cherries jubilee is made using pitted cherries, sugar and kirsch, and is flambéed with kirsch before serving.

*Also known as — kirschwasser*
*Kirsch goes with — almond flavours, cherry, orange*

## kiwano

Bright yellow in colour and covered in short, fat spikes, the kiwano is a most intriguing fruit. Inside, the flesh is watery, lime green and filled with large seeds. The flesh is similar in texture to its relative, the cucumber, and its flavour is likened to that of a banana and a cucumber. The fruit's many seeds make it difficult to eat from the hand, so it's usually sliced, cut into cubes or stirred into salsas. The name kiwano is not the fruit's real name, but a registered trademark.

*Also known as — horned melon*

## kiwi fruit

Kiwi fruit have a brown hairy skin enclosing a lime-green or gold flesh with tiny black seeds that grow around a paler core. Both the core and seeds are edible. Originally the kiwi fruit was called a Chinese gooseberry, but it was renamed as it was first grown commercially in New Zealand. When ripe, kiwi fruit are sweet with an acidic tang to them.

Generally, kiwis are best eaten uncooked; the easiest way to eat them (and maybe the best) is to cut the fruit in half and scoop the flesh out of the skin with a spoon, or you can peel and cut into cubes or slices. They can also be eaten with savoury dishes, chopped up in salsas, but during the 1980s and early 90s they were heavily used as a garnish on just about anything. Kiwis contain an enzyme that tenderizes meat (add a slice of kiwi fruit to your stew or casserole), but this same enzyme also inhibits the setting qualities of gelatine so the fruit are not recommended in jams and jellies.

## knish

A Jewish pastry eaten as a snack, especially in New York. The dough is wrapped around a variety of fillings, traditionally potato, onion and buckwheat groats, or they may be filled with cream cheese, chicken liver, meat or rice, and then baked. Doughs vary from country to country. In America, they tend to be potato or egg doughs; in France, where they take the Russian name *pirozhki*, they use yeasted dough or puff pastry. Buy knishes from delicatessens, knish specialists and bakeries.

Fingers, cylinders or balls of finely minced meat (usually lamb) mixed with flavourings and spices. The meat may be threaded onto skewers and grilled or simmered in sauces. Each country has its own favourite spices and these may be cinnamon, allspice, cumin or coriander. There are lots of kofta from all over the Middle East and India and some have colourful names like the Turkish *kadin budu* (lady's thighs).

**Also known as — kofte**

**See also  kebab**

KOFTA

*Mix together 1 kg finely chopped lamb, 2 finely chopped onions, 6 tablespoons chopped parsley, 1 teaspoon cinnamon and a pinch of cayenne pepper and salt. Process in a food processor to a paste. Form into walnut-sized balls and fry on both sides until well-browned. Serve as a snack or simmer in a tomato sauce (see page 302) and serve with rice. Serves 4.*

The bulbous stalk and the leaves of this cabbage family member are edible. The stalk is somewhat like a turnip, and can be eaten in the same way, either grated or sliced raw, added to stir-fries or stews, mashed or cooked in chunks and tossed in butter. The flesh is crisp and mild in flavour. Kohlrabi is more popular in Asia and continental Europe, particularly Germany, than Britain and the United States.

**Also known as — knol-khol**

Similar in appearance to vermicelli, konafa is a pastry used to make Middle Eastern sweet pastries. It is made by pouring a flour and water batter through a sieve onto a hotplate. The strands are swept off when set, but not cooked through. The pastry is then coated in melted butter and wrapped around a filling of walnut or pistachio and baked, or stuffed with cream or soft cheese. The uncooked pastry can be bought at Greek and Turkish shops and bakeries.

**Also known as — kadayif, kataifi, kunata, qata'if**

215

## Korean food

Populated since 3,000 BC, the Korean peninsula has been invaded repeatedly since then by the Mongolians, Chinese, and most notoriously, the Japanese, who retained it as a protectorate until 1945. Today, Korea is divided into North and South, with North Korea bordering China. Both Japan and China have had an influence on its cuisine.

Koreans believe in the harmony of the Five Flavours—hot, bitter, sweet, sour and salty—and this is reflected in flavourings like chilli, spring onions, ginger, vinegar, soya bean paste and sesame oil. Colour is also important, and cooks attempt to incorporate the Five Colours—red, green, yellow, white and black—in each meal.

Rice and *kimchi*, the fiery fermented cabbage condiment, are served at practically every meal, including breakfast. Noodles are common, with *chapchae*, a popular dish of stir-fried

vermicelli, meat, vegetables, sesame oil and soy sauce.

Fish, seafood and seaweed are eaten widely. Beef is the most popular meat, then pork. Beef *bulgogi*, slices of marinated beef fillet cooked on barbecue grills, is a popular dish.

Soya bean products, bean curd and bean pastes are much used, often spiced with chilli. Spice pastes (*changs* or *jangs*) are built from a base of fermented soya beans. *Dejan* paste, fermented soya bean paste, and *gochu jang*, a hot, fermented chilli paste, are much like Japanese versions.

As few Koreans have ovens, much cooking is done over a flame in a clay stewing pot called a *tukbaege*.

■ *See also* **kimchi**

*From top: bulgogi, barbecued beef fillet; kimchi, fermented turnips and cabbage; chapchae, a stir-fried dish of vermicilli, meat and vegetables.*

## kumquat

Although it resembles a small orange, the kumquat (cumquat) is in a family of its own, mainly because, unlike citrus fruit, it can be eaten whole—pith, rind and pips included. Indigenous to southeastern China, the name comes from the Chinese, meaning 'golden orange'. Their bittersweetness adds tang to fruit salads (try one before you slice them all—you may want to simmer them in a sugar syrup first), preserve in brandy or other spirits, or use in marmalades. In China, they are more often used in savoury dishes, especially poultry.

### KUMQUATS IN SYRUP

*In a saucepan, heat 200 g caster sugar with 200 ml water until sugar dissolves. Cut 125 g kumquats in half, then simmer in water until tender. Add to syrup and simmer for 5 minutes. Spread 15 g flaked almonds on a baking tray and grill for 3 minutes, or until browned. When cooled, add to the syrup. Use over ice cream or as a topping for sponge cakes and puddings.*

## kuzu

Both the stem and leaves of the kuzu plant are edible, but the vine is mainly grown for its tubers, which are ground to make a grey starch powder called kuzu. Similar in texture and function to cornflour, kuzu is used mainly in Chinese and Japanese cuisine as a thickener in soups, sauces and glazes and for dusting food before it is fried.

*Also known as — kudzu*

Labna is made by draining yoghurt through muslin to produce a soft, creamy cheese that is rolled into balls, coated with paprika or herbs and served as part of a meze; preserved in jars of olive oil (the oil may be flavoured with garlic, chillies, peppercorns, mint and bay leaves); or mixed with oil and eaten as a spread. Labna may also be served as a sweet, sprinkled with honey and cinnamon. In the Middle East, labna is eaten for breakfast with olives and bread.

**Also known as — labne, labneh**

## LABNA

*Line a sieve with muslin and pour in 1.5 litres full-fat natural yoghurt mixed with 1 crushed garlic clove and 2 teaspoons salt. Place sieve over a bowl and drain overnight, or until it forms a soft cheese. Using wet hands, roll the cheese into little balls, then roll in a mixture of chopped mint and parsley. Chill on a tray in the fridge. Store for 2–3 days in the fridge. Serves 6.*

## PRAWN LAKSA

*Heat 1 tablespoon oil in a wok, add 2–3 tablespoons ready-made laksa paste and cook over medium heat, stirring, for 2–3 minutes. Stir in 540 ml coconut milk and 750 ml chicken stock, bring to the boil and simmer for 5 minutes. Add 600 g peeled prawns, bring to the boil, then reduce heat and simmer for 5 minutes, or until the prawns are cooked. Cook 250 g rice vermicelli for 3 minutes. Drain and divide among 4 deep serving bowls. Divide 100 g bean curd puffs, ½ sliced cucumber and 100 g bean sprouts between the bowls and ladle in the hot soup. Garnish with sambal oelek (chilli paste) and Vietnamese mint and serve with lime wedges. Serves 4.*

A spicy noodle soup, popular in Malaysia, Singapore and the Philippines, laksa is a blend of Chinese (the noodles), Indian (the curry) and Malaysian (the coconut) cuisines. More meal than soup, it can be eaten at any time of the day, including breakfast. There are many versions including spicy laksa lemak and the more sour Penang laksa, but the base is usually flavoured with coconut, shrimp paste, lemon grass, garlic, lime and palm sugar. It contains laksa noodles (rounded rice noodles), rice vermicelli and either prawns, seafood or chicken. Other versions vary regionally—the soup may be quite thin, it may be flavoured with tamarind, or the type of noodle may vary. Laksa can be made using a ready-made laksa paste, sold in supermarkets and Asian markets.

# lamb

Meat from a young sheep, usually up to 1 year old, depending on local definitions. The meat from older sheep, either hogget (up to 20 months) or mutton (30–40 months) is darker in colour and stronger in flavour. Lamb is a festival food and has strong associations with springtime, as well as many religious feast days in the Christian, Jewish and Muslim calendars. Lambs are raised in most parts of the world where there are grasslands, from Mongolia to Patagonia, and their meat (and milk) is widely utilized. Very young milk-fed (sucking) lambs are a speciality in Italy, France, Spain, Portugal and the Middle East and pré-salé lambs (those that feed on the salt marshes) are also reared in parts of France and Wales.

## COOKING

*Because lamb is a fatty meat, it is traditionally served with acidic accompaniments, such as mint sauce and redcurrant jelly, to cut through the fat, or strong herbs such as rosemary. In some cuisines, fruit and sweet root vegetables are used to complement the lamb's fattiness. Lamb is particularly good in tagines, navarins and hotpots.*

*Crown roast of lamb*

## BUYING

*Lamb is often hung and aged for a week to give it a better flavour and more tender texture; however, milk-fed lamb is never hung.*

*Young lamb has a pinker flesh than older lamb or mutton, though what the lamb has been fed on can also affect the colour of the meat. Milk-fed lamb is very pale.*

*Lamb should have a healthy pink colour with waxy, dry, firm white fat.*

*Make sure that you buy the correct cut of lamb for your recipe, as cheaper cuts tend to be for longer, slower cooking and will not benefit from being grilled or pan-fried.*

## STORAGE

*Cover pieces of lamb and store them in the fridge until ready to use. This will stop the surface of the meat from oxidizing and turning brown.*

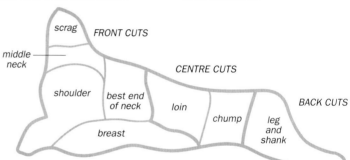

## CUTS OF LAMB

**Fronts cuts (forequarter)**

These range from the fatty neck or scrag end to the tender meat of the racks. Cuts include the breast, scrag end and middle neck, the shoulder (bone in or bone out), and the rack (sometimes called the 'best end of neck'), which can be bought in one piece, cut into chops and cutlets, or two racks can be joined to make a crown roast, or if inward facing, a guard of honour. The fattier cuts are good for slow cooking and casseroles and the racks and shoulder are good for roasting, grilling and pan-frying.

**Centre cuts**

Cuts include the saddle (both loins and often the tail and kidneys), the loins (on the bone), chump chops and noisettes. These cuts are good for roasting or, when off the bone, for frying and grilling.

**Back cuts (hindquarter)**

The leg (gigot) as a whole is good for roasting, and the shank or knuckle end is good for slow cooking. Leg chops are cut from the top of the leg.

### Roasting

For roasting, choose joints such as saddle, rack (joined cutlets), crown roast (what the French call *carre d'agneau*), guard of honour, loin, shoulder or leg. A loin (six to seven chops) will feed three people and a chop loin (four to five chops) will feed two people.

Roast lamb is best cooked on the bone at 200°C and will need to cook for about 20 minutes per 500 g, with 15 minutes standing time, for pink lamb. For well-cooked lamb, it will need 25 minutes per 500 g with an extra 25 minutes cooking. If the skin and fat are not browned or crisp enough, grill them for a few seconds. A light covering of fat will baste the meat as it cooks, but remember to serve on hot plates as lamb fat congeals fast.

### Slow cooking

Cuts such as scrag end, middle neck, shoulder, leg and shanks can all be slow cooked, though generally lamb is very tender. Shanks benefit from braising as they are leaner and tougher, but when casseroling fattier cuts, trim them as much as possible or let the finished dish go cold so you can lift off any fat before reheating it.

Many traditional British dishes such as Lancashire hotpot and Irish stew use cutlets and chops while French recipes use both these and cubed shoulder and leg to make navarins, daubes and casseroles. Indian and Arabic dishes also use cubed shoulder and leg in curries and spiced stews such as korma, and Moroccan and Middle Eastern cuisines use it in tagines. As for roasting, always serve lamb on a hot plate to stop the fat congealing.

### BRAISED LAMB SHANKS

*Soak 150 g haricot beans for 8 hours, drain, then boil them for 40 minutes in plenty of water. Fry 1 finely chopped onion and 2 crushed garlic cloves in 2 tablespoons olive oil. Add 6 lamb shanks and fry them until browned all over, then add 2 chopped carrots, 1 chopped celery stalk and a bay leaf. Pour in 250 ml dry red wine and 250 ml brown stock and bring to the boil. Drain the beans and add them to the lamb, cover and cook over low heat for 1½ hours. When the meat is tender, take off the lid, add 250 g cherry tomatoes and cook for 5 minutes, or until they break down. Stir in 2 tablespoons parsley, remove the bay leaf and serve with crusty bread. Serves 6.*

### Festive lamb

Many cuisines use whole lamb as a centrepiece for feast days and special occasions, such as the muslim festival of *Eid-el-Kurban*, where a whole lamb is roasted. Usually the whole lamb is spit-roasted. Lamb is also used to welcome spring in Europe—spring lamb tends to have a better flavour than those born in the autumn as their diet is richer in young grass and flowers. New season lamb is generally considered to be better quality than older lamb, and frozen cuts from the other side of the world may be preferable to older lamb in its own country. Lamb mince is also used extensively in some cuisines in dishes such as shepherd's pie and moussaka as it is fattier and stays more moist than beef mince when cooked.

## Lancashire hotpot

A casserole made from lamb middle neck chops and kidneys (the kidneys are sometimes still attached to the chops), which are layered with onions, potatoes and carrots, topped with a layer of overlapping potato slices, then baked. Hotpots vary regionally and the Lancashire version is somewhat like an Irish stew.

### LANCASHIRE HOTPOT

*In a buttered casserole dish, layer 1 kg sliced potatoes, 1 kg lamb neck chops, 2 sliced onions and 2 sliced carrots—start and finish with a potato layer and season each layer. Sprinkle the top with 1 teaspoon chopped thyme. Add 600 ml lamb or beef stock and dot top with 20 g butter. Bake, covered, at 180 °C for 2 hours; take off lid and bake for 30 minutes. Serves 4.*

## langues de chat

French for 'cat's tongues', because they are long, flat biscuits with rounded ends. The batter is piped into finger-like shapes onto baking trays or cooked in a *langues de chat plaque*—a special tray with shallow indentations in it. They may be used as accompaniments for ice cream, sorbet and dessert wines or sandwiched together with icing or cream. Langues de chat are sometimes referred to as 'lady fingers', but these are usually fatter and more spongy.

▧ *See also* **sponge fingers**

## lasagne

One of the world's favourite pastas, lasagne is actually the name of the pasta shape, the classic whole dish being *lasagne al forno*. A dough, made using flour and eggs, is rolled into thin sheets, which are blanched, layered with various fillings, then baked. In Italy, each area has its own lasagne dough and its preferred filling. The dough may be coloured with spinach, when it is known as *lasagne verdi*; a softer dough may be made using water instead of eggs; or the sheets may have curly edges, which are designed to give a lighter result by trapping air throughout the dish. Lasagne pasta can be bought ready-made in either fresh or dried form.

There are many variations of lasagne: *lasagne al forno*, prepared using layers of egg or spinach lasagne, meat ragù and béchamel; *vincisgrassi*, a dish from the Marche, made using a rich ragù of offal, porcini and pancetta, layered with béchamel and strips of lasagne; and a sweet version often baked at Christmas time, *lasagne da fornel*, made with apples, figs, raisins, walnuts and poppy seeds.

*Also known as — lasagna*

### ROSE-WATER LASSI

*Blend 350 ml yoghurt, 1 tablespoon rose-water, 3 tablespoons double cream and 4 tablespoons sugar. Add 8 ice cubes; blend until frothy— the ice won't all break up. Serves 2.*

### MANGO LASSI

*Blend 350 ml yoghurt, the flesh of a mango and 3 tablespoons double cream. Add 8 ice cubes and blend until frothy. Serves 2.*

A refreshing yoghurt drink popular in India and the Middle East. Yoghurt is blended with ice cubes or water and served lightly salted or sweetened. Lassi is often flavoured with mango or rose-water, or with herbs such as cumin, coriander or mint. Lassi is the ideal drink to have with curries as the fat in the yoghurt helps dissolve the fiery hot capsaicin found in chillies. When making lassi, use creamy, full-fat yoghurt as the ice will dilute its flavour.

*From left: mango lassi; rose-water lassi.*

## latkes

One of the most celebrated Jewish dishes, deep-fried crispy cakes of grated potato and eggs mixed with onion and crushed matzo. Although similar to Rösti, they are often eaten alone as a snack. Latkes may also be made from cheese, vegetables or slices of apple dipped in batter and deep-fried. Latkes are specifically associated with the festival of Hanukah, which is celebrated by eating food cooked in oil.

■ *See also* **Jewish food**

## lebkuchen

A German speciality, particularly in Nuremburg, lebkuchen are cake-like biscuits made with honey and spices. The biscuits are similar to gingerbread and may be shaped in many ways or embossed with patterns. They are usually glazed with a clear or white icing, and may also be dipped in chocolate or may have pieces of citron or lemon in them. Lebkuchen are particularly associated with Christmas and their German name means 'cake of life'.

# leek

A mild-flavoured member of the onion family. The thick white stem of cultivated leeks are blanched by piling up dirt around them as they grow. Smaller leeks are best as the green tops are still tender. Some recipes ask for just the white part, but most of the leek can be used if it is young and the green leaves are not too tough. Leeks are particularly good in creamy sauces and soups, most famously vichyssoise. Like onions, they need to be cooked for a reasonable amount of time or they will be crunchy rather than tender and sweet; if overcooked, they will go slimy. Leeks can be boiled, steamed or braised in butter and cooked. Whole cooked leeks can be wrapped in pieces of ham or covered in a béchamel sauce and grilled. The leek is the national emblem of Wales.

■ *See also* **cock-a-leekie, vichyssoise**

## PREPARATION

*Leeks often contain earth and dirt between their layers and need to be washed thoroughly. Trim the roots, remove any coarse outer leaves, then wash in a colander under running water. If using whole leeks, carefully separate out the leaves to rinse—making a cut halfway through to open the leaves. Wash the leek leaf end down so the dirt runs out.*

## FLAMICHE

*Line a 24 cm loose-based fluted tart tin with 350 g shortcrust pastry (see page 367), reserving enough pastry to make a lid, then chill. Blanch 500 g finely sliced leeks in boiling water for 10 minutes, then drain. Cook the leeks in 50 g butter for 5 minutes, then add 180 g Maroille or other soft cheese and stir. Take off the heat and add 1 egg, 1 egg yolk and 60 ml double cream; season well. Spread filling onto the tart and roll out the rest of the pastry to make the lid, cover the tart and trim, then press the edges together. Cut a 1 cm hole in the top of the pastry to let out the steam. Bake at 180°C for 40 minutes, or until golden. Serve warm. Serves 6.*

## LEEKS A LA GRECQUE

*In a large frying pan, simmer together 250 ml water, 60 ml olive oil, 30 ml white wine, 1 tablespoon tomato paste, ¼ teaspoon sugar, 1 crushed garlic clove, a sprig of thyme, 1 bay leaf, 4 peppercorns and 4 crushed coriander seeds for 5 minutes. Add 12 thin leeks and cook until tender in the middle. Remove leeks, add a squeeze of lemon juice and 100 ml water and boil until the liquid forms a sauce. Stir in 1 tablespoon chopped parsley, then return to the pan. Cool before serving. Serves 6.*

# legumes

There are thousands of plants whose seed pods split open down both seams when ripe, and it is these seed pods that are known as legumes. Some of the most common include beans, peas, soya beans *(pictured)* and lentils, as well as vetches, alfalfa, tamarind, carob and peanuts *(pictured)*. Legumes provide much of the world's staple protein and they play an important role in vegetarian diets. When dried, the seeds of legumes are referred to as pulses.

Rarely eaten on their own, lemons are an indispensable ingredient in the kitchen, useful for their aromatic qualities and their sharp, acidic flavour. Lemon juice can be used instead of vinegar in sauces; for seasoning vinaigrettes and mayonnaise; and as an instant dressing for fish and shellfish. It can also be squeezed over certain fruit and vegetables, such as apple and celeriac, to prevent them from discolouring. Lemon zest is used to add flavour, for example in gremolata, or shredded and used as a classic garnish. Lemon wedges can be used to squeeze over many different dishes to enliven them as it acts as a flavour enhancer. Lemon is also a classic flavour for sweet dishes such as soufflés and ice creams.

## STORAGE

*Store lemons in the vegetable crisper in the fridge where they will keep for several weeks, or in a fruit bowl for a shorter time. Check them often—if one starts to spoil, the rest will quickly follow.*

## COOKING

*For zesting, buy unwaxed varieties or scrub the skins with warm water before you use them. The zest contains the flavour-imparting oil of the fruit.*

*The best way to remove zest is with a zester, which strips it off, leaving the bitter pith behind. You can pare zest with a potato peeler, then cut it into fine strips. To grate zest, first cover the grater surface with a sheet of greaseproof paper, as pictured—the zest will stick to the paper rather than the grater.*

*When juicing lemons, warm them for a couple of seconds in a microwave, as this helps the juices run.*

Shop-bought lemons have been picked while still green to prolong their shelf life and they may also be waxed to stop them drying out. Choose your lemons with care and pick ones that are firm, fragrant and heavy—this is a good indication that they are juicy. Different varieties have different degrees of acidity so taste the juice to make sure you will get the right effect—a *tarte au citron* made with sweeter lemons will be very different from one made with sour acidic lemons. The thickness of the fruit's skin is important too—thicker skins are better for making candied peel and thinner ones for slicing and using cooked in dishes. The acidity in lemons is also helpful in setting jams and jellies.

**Lemon goes with — avocado, chicken, lamb, oysters, seafood, veal**

*See also* **candied fruit, citron, lime, preserved lemons**

With a subtle lemon flavour and fragrance, lemon grass adds a refreshing taste to many Thai and other Southeast Asian dishes. Lemon grass grows all over Southeast Asia, where, in some tropical climates, lemons won't grow. Strip off any tough outer layers and use whole in soups by lightly bruising the stems (remove before serving); finely chop and use in curry pastes; thinly slice the paler lower part of the stem and add to salads; or use whole as skewers for cooking meat, prawns and chicken. Although a classic in Southeast Asian cooking, lemon grass is now used more widely, often instead of lemon zest to make desserts such as lemon grass brûlée.

Wrap in plastic and store in the fridge for 1–2 weeks. Lemon grass can also be bought dried in sticks or in powdered form, when it is called sereh powder. If lemon grass is unavailable, use grated lemon zest instead.

**Lemon grass goes with — chicken, chilli, coconut, ginger, pork, seafood**

# lentils

## PREPARATION

*Contrary to popular belief, lentils don't need to be soaked before they are cooked; soaking may cause some varieties to break up. First, pick over lentils to remove any discoloured ones or pieces of grit, then rinse and discard any lentils that float (these may have been partially eaten by bugs).*

Tiny, flat, lens-shaped pulses that grow in pods. Originating in Southeast Asia, lentils are now grow worldwide in warm countries, and vary in colour and size. The most common lentils are green, brown and red. Some of the rarer varieties are named after the area they are grown in, such as *lenticchie di Castelluccio,* Puglian lentils from Alta Mura in Italy, and *lentilles vertes du Puy* from France.

Lentils have a high food value (they are high in protein, fibre and B vitamins) and are considered adequate protein to replace meat. Lentils must be cooked and can be puréed and used in soups and curries or added to stews and salads. But choose your lentils accordingly: some lentils, such as the red and brown ones, will cook to a mush and are good for purées; others, like Puy lentils, will hold their shape no matter how much you cook them.

## SAUSAGES AND LENTILS

*Fry 4 chopped bacon rashers and 8 large pork sausages until brown. Add 200 g Puy lentils, 1 chopped garlic clove and a sprig of thyme, then pour over 400 ml beef consommé or 400 ml beef stock. Cook at a simmer for about 30–40 minutes, or until the lentils are tender. Stir in 1 tablespoon redcurrant jelly and 1 tablespoon cream and serve. Season with black pepper. Serves 4.*

## TYPES OF LENTILS

**Red**
Also called Egyptian lentils, these break down when cooked and can be used for making soups and purées. They are often used in Indian dishes such as dhals.

**Green and brown**
Largest of the lentils, they keep their shape when cooked. Good in casseroles, soups and dishes where you want texture. Green and brown vary in size and colour and aren't always easy to differentiate from each other—treat in the same way.

**Puy**
Tiny, speckled grey-green lentils that are grown organically and contain more minerals than other varieties. *Lentilles vertes du Puy* are governed by the French *appellation d'origine contrôlée* (AOC) and must be from that area. The same type of lentils are grown elsewhere—these are sold simply as Puy lentils.

**Castelluccio**
From Umbria in Italy, these are small, brownish-green lentils. They cook quickly (about 30 minutes) and retain their shape when cooked. Often served with game.

Lettuces vary greatly in colour and texture: from light green to deep red, from those with loose, floppy leaves to those with crisp leaves and firm stems. Lettuce is mainly used fresh in salads or sandwiches but can also be cooked. In France, lettuce is cooked with baby onions and peas in stock and in China, lettuce is a common cooked vegetable. In a green salad, lettuces are generally interchangeable, but when adding other ingredients, pick a leaf type that will suit them—floppy leaves won't go well with heavy ingredients like potatoes, and crisp firm leaves need a fairly robust dressing. Always dress lettuce just before you serve it.

*Clockwise from bottom left: little gem, lollo rosso, lollo biondo, iceberg lettuce, cos lettuce.*

## TYPES OF LETTUCES

**Round or cabbage**
These are round and vary in crispness. The main types are butterhead and crisphead. Butterhead or butter lettuces are either green or red and have soft, floppy leaves. They include Bibb, Boston, Batavia, Continuity and Webb's Wonder. Good in salads and sandwiches. Crispheads have crispy, juicy leaves that last well and include icebergs, which have crisp, pale-green, tightly wrapped leaves. Good in salads or use the small, firm leaves as wraps or cups to hold other ingredients.

**Leaf or loose-leaved**
These include *lollo rosso* (red leaves), *lollo biondo* (frilly, green leaves) and oakleaf (*feuille de chêne*) and are good as the backbone to salads. Use the red-leaved lettuces in moderation as they can be slightly bitter.

**Long-leaved**
This group includes cos (romaine) lettuce, which has long, crisp leaves and nutty flavour. The smaller variety is little gem. Goes well in salads that have hot ingredients or dressings, as the firm leaves won't wilt easily.

**Celtuce**
Has long stalks like celery and leaves at the top. Not a common variety except in the United States. Can be eaten as salad leaves or cook the stalks like celery.

■ *See also* **chicory, mesclun, salad leaves**

### PREPARATION

*Lettuce leaves need to be washed thoroughly and dried very well before use. Either dry them in tea towels or paper towels or use a salad spinner, as any moisture left on the leaves will dilute the dressing.*

*Don't leave lettuce to soak for any length of time as the leaves will absorb water and lose their flavour.*

### COOKED LETTUCE

*Soak 12 whole small dried Chinese mushrooms in hot water for 30 minutes, or until they are soft. Meanwhile, heat 1 tablespoon oil in a wok, then add 1 tablespoon Shaoxing wine, 1 teaspoon sesame oil and 1 large shredded leafy lettuce. Stir-fry quickly until wilted, then put the lettuce onto a plate. Remove mushrooms from the water, pat dry, then add them to the wok and briefly stir-fry. Dress with oyster sauce, then tip the mushrooms over the lettuce. Serves 4.*

# lime

Any of a number of varieties of small green-skinned citrus fruit native to the tropics, where they are widely used in cooking. Limes are only green because they are picked unripe, but if left to ripen they turn yellow. The West Indian or key lime, rather than the Tahitian or Palestine lime, is considered the 'true' lime. They are related to the lemon, but have a distinctive taste. Limes can be used like lemons but as the juice is more acidic, usually less is needed. Both lime juice and the zest add a piquant flavour to sweet dishes such as ice cream and sorbets, as well as curries, stews and in fish dishes. In South America, lime juice is used to 'cook' raw fish in the dish ceviche, and in India and North Africa. Types of pickled limes are served with meat and fish dishes. Like lemons, warm limes in a microwave for 2 to 3 seconds before squeezing them to make the juice flow.

*Lime goes with — fish, pickle, pork, salad*

▣ *See also* **candied fruit, lemon**

### LIME PICKLES

*Fry 10 ripe Indian limes in hot oil for 2 minutes without browning. Cut each lime into 8 wedges and chop wedges. Discard any seeds. Heat 100 ml oil; add 1 teaspoon ground fenugreek, ¾ teaspoon ground turmeric, 3 teaspoons chilli powder, 1 teaspoon asafoetida and 1 tablespoon salt. Add limes, stir, then spoon into a 750 ml sterilized jar. Add a thin layer of the oil to the surface. Leave for 1 month before eating.*

# liqueur

An alcoholic syrup distilled from wine or brandy and flavoured with fruit, herbs or spices. Liqueurs can be used to flavour a range of sweet and savoury dishes, such as kirsch in cherry dishes; Calvados in Normandy-style chicken or pork dishes; or they can be drunk with coffee after a meal.

▣ *See also* **amaretto, brandy, Calvados, Frangelico, Kahlúa, kirsch**

From left: Cointreau, Kahlúa, amaretto, advocaat, Galliano, limoncello.

# liquorice

Although commonly associated with the chewy, jet-black aniseed-flavoured confectionery, liquorice (licorice) is also the name of a small plant whose long roots are cut into strips and dried *(pictured left, also in powdered form)*. The confectionery is made from an extract from the root, which is mixed with sugar and gelatine. It is also used to make tea, to flavour liqueurs such as Sambucca, and occasionally in cooking. It is also available in powdered form.

Generally, large crustaceans found in cold waters. True lobsters have eight legs and two large front pincers, which distinguish them from rock lobsters, or crayfish, which have no pincers and are found in warmer waters. Other crustaceans sometimes called 'lobsters' are the foot or slipper lobster (*cigale* in French), the smaller Norwegian lobster, and the Australian Moreton Bay bug, sometimes called a bay lobster. Of the true lobsters, the American (and Canadian) tend to be larger than the European. Lobsters are often dark blue or almost black in colour when alive and turn red when cooked. As lobsters grow bigger, their claws grow larger in relation to their body and they can reach considerable sizes. Lobster flesh is firm, delicate and slightly sweet. The classic dishes for lobster include lobster bisque, lobster Newburg, lobster thermidor and lobster à l'américaine.

### Cooking live lobster

The best way to kill a lobster—combining humanity and gastronomy—is to first put it in the freezer for an hour or so to slow it down, then plunge it in boiling water. If you put a live lobster straight into boiling water, it is liable to shed its legs. If the recipe calls for live lobster to be split in two, it can still be killed by this method first, then removed from the boiling water when it is dead, drained and split as the recipe directs.

## BUYING LIVE LOBSTERS

*When buying a live lobster, make sure it's lively and has its tail tucked under its body. The shell should be hard—a soft shell indicates it has just moulted and is not in peak condition (during this time, the lobster hides and does not come out to eat until its shell calcifies and toughens). The shell should have no holes and the lobster should have all its limbs.*

*When picking up a lobster, first make sure its claws are taped together, then pick it up just behind the head using your finger and thumb. Don't grasp it around its middle as it might close up on you suddenly.*

*Despite popular opinion, male and female lobsters don't vary much in flavour, but male claws may have more meat.*

*Don't buy dead uncooked lobster as there is no way of telling what condition it is in and the meat deteriorates very quickly.*

## LOBSTER WITH HERB BUTTER

*Remove the flesh from 2 lobster tails. Cut the flesh of each tail into 3 or 4 pieces. Dry-fry 100 g pistachio nuts until they start to brown. Process with 100 g butter and 2 tablespoons chopped basil. Season. Heat half the herb butter and sauté the lobster pieces. Gradually stir in the rest of the butter. Add 125 ml brandy, flame, then stir in 2 tablespoons cream. Fill the lobster shells with the mixture and serve at once. Serves 4.*

▧ **See also crayfish**

## BUYING COOKED LOBSTER

*Cooked lobsters should be sweet and fresh smelling. Their tail should be tightly curled (this indicates it was alive when it was cooked) and spring back when you stretch it out. Discoloured meat can indicate that the lobster has been dead for too long. The meat from a cooked lobster tail can be removed in the same way as the raw tail shown below. The claws will need to be cracked to extract the meat.*

## COOKING LOBSTERS

**Boiling**
Boil lobsters in salted water for 5 minutes per 250 g, drain and, if serving cold, plunge into iced water. If serving the lobster whole, pierce a hole in its head and each claw to drain it more thoroughly.

**Grilling**
Brush the lobster with butter or oil and flavourings and grill under a medium heat until it cooks through. Crack the claws so the heat can penetrate.

**Barbecue or griddle**
Brush the lobster with butter or oil and flavourings, place shell side down on the barbecue or griddle and cook until the flesh becomes opaque. Crack the claws so the heat can penetrate.

**Pan-fry**
Remove the flesh from the tail when raw and pan-fry as a whole piece or medallions. Pan-fry the claws intact and then remove the meat.

**Soups**
Use the lobster shells to make a stock for a soup. Fry the shells, crush or break them up, then add to the stock. Strain the stock before adding to the soup.

## LOBSTER SALAD

*Put an 800 g lobster in the freezer for 2 hours. Boil a large pan of water, drop in the lobster; return to the boil. Cook for 25 minutes, drain and cool. Remove the cooked meat from the shell. Cut into chunks and put in a large bowl. Blanch 100 g sugar snap peas, add to the lobster with 1 mango cut into chunks, 2 sliced spring onions, 1 sliced orange pepper and ¼ cucumber cut into batons. Mix together the juice of 2 limes, 1 tablespoon fish sauce, 2 tablespoons olive oil, 1 teaspoon each sesame oil and dark soy sauce, 1 chopped red chilli and a pinch of sugar. Toss through the lobster mixture. Serves 4.*

## REMOVING THE MEAT FROM A LOBSTER TAIL

1 *Remove the head by twisting or cutting it off.*

2 *Cut down the centre of the underside of the tail with a pair of scissors.*

3 *Peel open the tail and carefully pull out the flesh in one piece.*

A berry first raised in the garden of Judge Logan in California. It is thought to be a hybrid of the raspberry and the blackberry. Resembling both of these fruits in flavour, loganberries can be used as you would raspberries and are delicious both raw or cooked. Like most berries, loganberries are available in summer. Store in the vegetable crisper in the fridge and wash just before use.

*See also* **berries**

A native of China, but now grown in many parts of Southeast Asia, longan fruit range in size from olives to small plums. Longans are covered with a smooth, leathery skin that changes colour from orange to brown when ripe. Inside, the flesh is translucent, similar in both flavour and texture to its closest relative, the lychee. Longans are also noted for their fragrance, which is likened to that of a gardenia. Peel the fruit and eat fresh, add to fruit salads, use to garnish ice creams, or in sauces. Longans can also be used instead of grapes in any recipe. Longans are in season in summer, when you should look for heavy, uncracked fruit. They last for 2 to 3 weeks in the fridge, but can also be frozen in their skins (defrost just before use and use slightly frozen or the flesh will become flabby). Longans are also available in cans or dried.

*Also known as — dragon's eye, lungan*

Small fruit with pale-orange waxy skins, often spotted with brown, and native to China and Japan. Loquats are known for their delicate nature—they are soft and bruise easily—so are not widely grown commercially. The flesh is juicy and quite tart and contains between one and three large brown seeds. Choose tender fruit, even if they have a bruise or two, as these will have a better flavour. Eat raw, add to fruit salads or use to make jams and jellies. Add a splash of lemon juice to bring out the flavour.

*Also known as — Japanese medlar, Japanese plum*

### LOQUAT JAM

*Top and tail 450 g loquats, then cut them in half and pull out the stone, scraping away any white 'skin' left behind. Chop the fruit coarsely, put in a saucepan with 250 ml water and boil until tender. Add 375 g sugar and bring back to the boil. Continue boiling until a drop of jam will set on a plate. Pour the jam into sterilized jars (see page 296) and seal. Makes 350 ml.*

## LOTUS ROOT AND VEGETABLE STIR-FRY

*Thinly slice 1 peeled lotus root and 2 courgettes. Heat a little oil in a frying pan, then briefly fry 2 crushed garlic cloves and 1 tablespoon grated ginger. Add the lotus root and courgettes and stir-fry for 2 minutes, then add 1 chopped carrot, 1 chopped red pepper and 12 mangetout, cut in half, and fry for a further 2 minutes. Add 2 tablespoons oyster sauce, 1 tablespoon soy sauce and 1 teaspoon sesame oil and toss together. Add some snowpea sprouts and toss everything together until the snowpeas are wilted. Serve the vegetables with noodles or rice. Serves 4.*

An aquatic member of the water lily family, with beautiful white and pink flowers. In cooking, it is the root that is most commonly used. When sliced horizontally, it displays a floral-like pattern of holes. This decorativeness along with its crisp, delicately flavoured flesh is much appreciated in Chinese and Japanese cuisine. First peel the root, then slice it before eating it raw or cooked. Add it to salads or stir-fries, or cut into chunks, stuff it, or serve it as a vegetable. Store in water with a squeeze of lemon juice to prevent it from turning brown. The seeds are also edible, eaten out of the hand or used in Chinese desserts and soups, and the leaves are used to wrap food such as whole fish for cooking. Lotus root can be bought fresh, dried, frozen and in tins.

## lychee

The lychee has been cultivated in its native China for thousands of years, but it is now also grown in Southeast Asia and India. About the size of a small plum, the lychee fruit has a knobbly, rust-coloured leathery skin, which encases a sweet and fragrant creamy flesh around a hard, non-clinging stone.

Lychees are important in Chinese cuisine as they are said to promote fertility and good luck. They appear in dishes such as chicken cooked with lychees, as well as desserts and sweets. Eat fresh or add to fruit salads and ice creams, purée or poach in a light syrup. Because fruit with green skins won't ripen once picked, you must buy lychees at their peak—when their skin is red. As the fruit ages, its skin becomes more brittle and brown. Lychees are also available canned and dried. When dried, the fruit acquire a nutty, raisin-like taste, perfect for snacking.

*Also known as — litchi*

## LYCHEE SORBET

*Peel and stone 1 kg lychees, then purée until smooth. Mix in 60 ml lime juice and 150 g caster sugar. Churn in an ice-cream maker or pour into a freezerproof container and freeze. Stir hourly as it freezes to break up any ice crystals (do this 3 or 4 times, or until the sorbet reaches a smooth and thick consistency), then freeze overnight. Serves 6.*

## m

### macadamia nut

Native to Australia, macadamia nuts are now also grown in Hawaii, Central and South America and the Caribbean. The sweet, buttery nut is encased in a hard and extremely difficult to open shell. Macadamia nuts are used in baking, in stir-fries, crushed and used to coat chicken or fish before frying, or as a dessert nut with fruit and cheese. They make a good substitute for candlenuts in Asian cooking or pine nuts in pesto. The oil, which is extracted from the nut, is excellent in salad dressings, but loses its flavour when heated. Once shelled, store the nuts in a sealed container in the fridge as their high fat content makes them turn rancid fairly quickly. For the same reason, only buy shelled nuts that have been vacuum-packed. Macadamias are also sold roasted.

**Also known as — bobble nut, Queensland nut**

### macaroon

Made from sugar, egg whites and ground almonds, macaroons are small flat, round biscuits that are light and crisp on the outside and soft, moist and slightly chewy on the inside. They are typically made with almond, but variations include those flavoured with chocolate, coffee, other nuts or coconut. Macaroons may be served with dessert wine, crushed for use in desserts such as trifles, or served with syllabub. Although popular in France, the recipe is thought to have Italian origins, where macaroons have been documented as early as the eighth century.

*See also* **amaretti, ratafia**

### MACAROONS

*Line a baking tray with rice paper. Mix 110 g ground almonds with 170 g caster sugar and 1 teaspoon plain flour. Stir in 2 unbeaten egg whites, 2–3 drops almond essence and ½ teaspoon vanilla essence. Beat well. Spoon heaped teaspoons onto a tray, allowing room for spreading, and bake at 180°C for 20 minutes. Cool completely on the tray before removing. The rice paper will tear off as you remove the biscuits, but is edible. Makes 24.*

# Madeira

A Portuguese fortified wine from the island of the same name. Originally made as a wine, it was discovered that its flavour benefited from prolonged exposure to heat after barrels full were shipped across the world. From then on, the wine was sent backwards and forwards across the world as ship's ballast until a system was invented to treat the wine in *estufas* (hot stores) at temperatures up to 45°C (113°F) for up to 6 months. In cooking, Madeira is used in soups, in sauces for meat and ham and as the traditional accompaniment to Madeira cake (so named because it is often served with a glass of Madeira) and to add flavour to aspic preparations. When cooking with Madeira, it is important to use the type specified in the recipe or to choose one that is similar in flavour.

### CHICKEN IN MADEIRA

*Brown 200 g halved button mushrooms in 1½ tablespoons each of butter and oil. Set aside. Cook 3 finely chopped shallots until soft. Add 45 ml Sercial Madeira and 300 ml chicken stock; simmer for 10 minutes. Make 3 diagonal slashes on the top of 4 boned and skinned chicken breasts and poach, covered, for 12 minutes. Remove the chicken and keep warm. Boil sauce until thickened, strain, then return to pan. Stir in 1 tablespoon butter, 1 teaspoon tomato paste and season. Add mushrooms, then spoon over chicken to serve. Serves 4.*

### TYPES OF MADEIRAS

| | |
|---|---|
| **Sercial** | The driest, it is pale gold in colour. Often drunk as an apéritif. In cooking, it is used as a flavouring, particularly for savoury dishes. |
| **Verdelho** | Medium-sweet and slightly darker than Sercial. Sometimes served as a wine to go with the soup course or as an after-dinner drink, usually with Madeira cake. |
| **Bual** | Elegant, medium-sweet blend, used to flavour desserts and cakes and as an after-dinner drink. |
| **Malmsey** | The richest and darkest variety with fruity, liqueur-like qualities. Used to flavour desserts and as an after-dinner drink with fruit, nuts and cakes (such as Madeira cake) or biscuits. |

## madeleine

Petite, sponge-like cakes baked in ribbed, scallop-shaped cake moulds. They vary in size and are usually flavoured with lemon or vanilla. The madeleine was immortalized by the French novelist Marcel Proust for whom the taste of one dunked in tea unlocked the flood of memories that led to his three-volume work of genius, *Remembrance of Things Past*. It is thought that they may have been named after Madeleine Palmier, a French pastry cook in Commercy during the nineteenth century, a place with which they are still associated.

Malaysia is a prosperous and geographically diverse Southeast Asian nation divided into eastern and western parts. East Malaysia is made up of part of the island of Borneo and is separated from the west by the South China Sea. Western, or peninsular Malaysia is bordered by Thailand in the north and Singapore in the south. Before separation in 1965, the British colony of Malaya included the Republic of Singapore (and the Sultanate of Brunei). Given this shared history, and the same cultural mix of Malay, Indian and Chinese (although Singapore is predominantly Chinese), both cuisines feature these influences, often blended. Also influential are the three major religions: Hinduism, Islam and Buddhism.

Arab traders sailing their dhows through the Malacca Straits were among the first to arrive on the peninsula, bringing with them onions, almonds, pistachios and kebabs. The Indians introduced breads, curry spices and rice pilaus, and the Chinese, the wok and ingredients such as soy sauce, noodles and bean sprouts. These Chinese and Indian influences were stronger than in other parts of Southeast Asia because of the mass movement of labour under British colonization. In northwestern Malaysia, cross-border Thai influences are evident in such dishes as northern *assam laksa*, which is similar to Thai *tom yam* soup.

*Fish head curry*

*Penang laksa*

Rice is common to all three cuisines, although it is often cooked differently, eaten as an accompaniment to fish, shellfish, meat and vegetables, with sambals and curries. *Lontong* are compressed rice cakes eaten with dishes such as satay. In Malaysia, satay, cubes of meat threaded on skewers and served with a peanut dipping sauce, also has coconut milk added to it. Coconut milk features strongly in the cooking, as does lime and tamarind, although tastes vary regionally.

Given the strong Indian influence, curries are popular and are made with seafood, lamb, mutton, beef or goat. Fish head curry demonstrates the fusion of Indian and Chinese cuisines. Since fish heads were considered delicacies in China, originally this dish appealed to the Chinese in Singapore. Today it is quite common in both countries, and the curry base is made with both Indian and Malaysian spices. Salads such as *rojak*, made from fruit and vegetables, are a popular snack in between meals.

Nonya cooking is a blend of Chinese techniques and Malaysian ingredients, which evolved from the marriage of Chinese men to Malaysian women (known as 'nonyas'). Chillies, shrimp paste and coconut milk are popular as in Malaysian cooking, and noodles and hot and sour flavours are also a common influence. *Laksa*, a soupy noodle dish richly flavoured with coconut, is a typical nonya dish and there are many types, with either chicken, fish or vegetables. Fried, flat rice noodles, *kway teow*, are a popular street food. Nonya meals usually have several accompaniments, for example hot sambals and crunchy side dishes such as *ikan bilis*, which are fried dried anchovies with onion, chillies and peanuts.

*Ikan bilis*

*Kway teow goreng—stir-fried noodles with beef.*

See also **candlenuts, laksa, satay**

# malt

Any grain can be malted, but the term 'malting' usually applies to barley. The grain is encouraged to sprout, this converts its starch to maltose and dextrins, then the grains are dried and the sprout is rubbed off, leaving behind sweet-tasting grains. The colour and flavour of the malt is determined by the amount of heat the grains are given and ranges from pale malt to black malts, which have a burnt taste and are used for making stout.

Malt is mainly used in the brewing and whisky-making industry, in baking or as a flavouring for cereals. When used for making bread, the malt helps give the bread a good flavour and texture (a large quantity of malt produces a sweet, brown sticky loaf). Malt is also available as malt extract, a thick, brown liquid, and dried ground malt powder, which can be added to milk to make malted drinks like Horlicks. Malt vinegar is a dark-brown vinegar generally used for pickling or on fish and chips.

*Clockwise from front left: malt powder, malt extract, malted milk drink, malt vinegar.*

# mandarin

Mandarins are citrus fruit that resemble small, slightly flattened oranges and are members of the same family as tangerines and satsumas. Mandarins have loose, easy-to-peel skins and sweet flesh. There are many varieties and these include Ellendale and Murcott. Mandarins were originally called mandarin oranges and the tree is native to China.

Choose fruit that are heavy for their size as these will be the juiciest. Use as you would oranges—eat fresh, add to fruit salads, sauces, use the small segments to decorate cakes, or squeeze as a good alternative to orange juice. In Chinese cooking, the peel is dried and used both for its fragrance and flavour. Mandarins will keep in the fridge for 1 to 2 weeks.

*See also* **tangerine**

# mangetout — see pea

# mango

Mangoes are a fruit native to India, but now grown in many tropical climates worldwide. The fruit ranges in colour from green to golden yellow and orange-red, and its flesh is a juicy, deep orange surrounding a large, flat, inedible stone. Mangoes are best eaten out of hand, but they also make excellent ice creams, sorbets and sauces; are good in drinks like smoothies; go well with seafood or in salads; make good pickles and chutneys; and act as tenderizers when added to curries. In Asian cooking, green mango is used in pickles, raw in salads or as a vegetable. You can determine if the mango is ripe, not by its colour, which can vary, but by both its smell and feel—a ripe mango has a wonderful aroma and will yield when gently pressed. Store unripe mangoes at room temperature, then put them in the fridge when ripened.

The best way to eat a mango is to cut it into a 'hedgehog'—slice off the two cheeks of an unpeeled mango close to the seed and, without cutting the skin, score the flesh in a hatched pattern. Push the skin inside out so the cubes of flesh pop out.

Contrary to its name, the mangosteen doesn't resemble or taste like the mango; rather, it is deep purple and round, similar in size to a mandarin. It comes from a native Asian tree that takes from 10 to 15 years to bear fruit. The highly prized fruit has a thick skin that is hard and inedible and which, when cut open, reveals a soft, white flesh divided into segments, some of which contain seeds. The taste is delicate, reminiscent of pineapple. To open, cut it in half through the skin only and lightly twist the halves apart. Eat the white flesh in segments like an orange, add to fruit salads or use in sorbets. Look for mangosteens during spring and summer. Colour is a good indication of ripeness—pale-green fruit are immature and turn dark purple or red-purple when ripe. The fruit will keep for a few days without refrigeration but will keep for longer if wrapped and stored in the fridge.

The kokum, a relative of the mangosteen, is used dried in southern Indian cooking as a souring agent like tamarind. Kokum butter is also extracted from the seeds and can be used for cooking.

**m a p l e   s u g a r**

Maple syrup and sugar are made from the sap of certain species of maple trees found only in Canada and parts of North America. A hole is cut into the trunk of the tree, the sap runs down a metal spigot, and is caught in buckets or collection tubes below. Maple sap is watery, almost flavourless, and needs to be reduced to roughly a quarter of its volume to produce maple syrup, and further reduced to produce maple sugar. Large quantities of sap are needed to produce only a small amount of maple syrup, one of the main reasons that the syrup is so expensive.

## COOKING

*Bottles labelled as maple-flavoured syrup do not have the same flavour as 100 per cent pure maple syrup.*

*In recipes, 100 per cent pure maple syrup can be substituted for granulated sugar. For each 225 g granulated sugar, use 375 ml maple syrup. The syrup has a higher moisture content than sugar, so decrease the amount of liquid called for in the recipe by 30–60 ml for every 225 ml maple syrup used. You may also want to decrease the oven temperature by 15°C as pure maple syrup tends to caramelize and burn on the top and edges sooner than a mixture that uses granulated sugar.*

Maple syrup can be used as a sweetener like honey as well as a pouring syrup. It goes well with waffles *(pictured)* and pancakes, can be used as a glaze for ham, or in desserts and baking. A traditional breakfast in America consists of hot cakes (pancakes) and sausage or bacon drizzled with maple syrup. Pure maple syrup is expensive and its price tag is a good indication that what you are buying is 100 per cent pure. Less expensive versions may be synthetically reproduced or the syrup may be mixed with corn syrup.

*See also  **Canadian food***

## marmalade

Generally speaking, a jam made using citrus fruits, although long before marmalades were synonymous with citrus, the word was used to refer to any thick jam made from quinces or other fruit such as plums, damsons and strawberries. In fact, the word marmalade (French *marmelade*) is derived from the Portuguese word for quince, *marmelo*. The word marmalade is still loosely used for other preserves or jams, for example onion marmalade.

When making marmalade, make sure any wax is first scrubbed off the fruit. Marmalade sets well as there is a lot of pectin in citrus fruit. It is very important to cook the fruit until tender before adding the sugar, as sugar inhibits the cooking process and the fruit will not soften.

**Marmalade goes with — brioche, duck, quail, toast**

■ *See also* **jam**

*From left: orange poppy seed, grapefruit and lemon, Seville orange.*

## marmite

A French cooking pot with a lid, usually made of earthenware, used for casseroles, pot-au-feu and stews, also known as marmites. A type of beef stew is known as *petite marmite* and a type of seafood stew as *marmite dieppoise*. Also a branded yeast extract in Britain.

■ *See also* **yeast extract**

## marrow

From the same family as the squash, pumpkin, gourd, christophine, melon and cucumber. Marrows are best eaten young as their flavour deteriorates and becomes more watery as they get bigger. Marrows are best stuffed, either halved lengthways or cut into rings with stuffing in the middle. Use stuffings that will absorb water without going soggy, such as rice or couscous. A whole marrow needs to be baked for about 2 to 3 hours, depending on its size.

■ *See also* **squash**

### STUFFED MARROW

*Cut a marrow into thick rings, scoop out any seeds; blanch for 5 minutes. Fry 1 chopped onion with 250 g minced lamb, add 75 g cooked rice, 1 chopped tomato, 2 tablespoons chopped parsley and ½ teaspoon cinnamon; season. Fill the rings and put on a baking tray, drizzle with olive oil, cover and bake, covered, at 180°C for 30 minutes. Serve with yoghurt. Serves 6.*

## marrowbone

The long hollow limb bones that contain a soft, fatty tissue called marrow. Marrow is traditionally used to flavour bordelaise sauce, is contained in veal shanks used for osso buco, is added to risotto Milanese, or is simply eaten on toast. It can be roasted in the bone or taken out and poached. The marrow is extracted using a special spoon or, less delicately, sucked out of the cut marrowbones. Marrow can also be melted like butter and used to cook vegetables and meats.

A fortified wine from Sicily, made by mixing grape juice with white wine, which is then left to mature in casks. Marsala has a sweet, smoky flavour that ranges from dry to sweet. Some may be flavoured with almond, cream or egg. Dry Marsala is best for cooking and appears in many sauces for Italian dishes such as saltimbocca and chicken cacciatora. Sweet Marsala is best known for its use in the classic Italian dessert zabaglione and it is the traditional accompaniment to slices of cake.

### VEAL MARSALA

*Coat 4 veal escalopes with seasoned flour. Heat 1 tablespoon butter and 1 tablespoon oil and fry the veal until golden brown on both sides. Add 200 ml dry Marsala to the pan, remove the veal and keep warm, then deglaze. Reduce the sauce over high heat until halved, then whisk in 1 tablespoon butter. Pour over the veal and serve. Serves 4.*

## marshmallow

A soft, fluffy confectionery originally made from an extract of marshmallow roots, but today more typically made by boiling sugar, gum arabic and water, then stirring in beaten egg whites to make a sweet spongy mixture, or setting whipped sugar syrup with gelatine.

Marshmallows are also used as an ingredient and sold in different sizes. Mini marshmallows can be added to cake, cookie and ice-cream mixtures. In America, they may be used to top dishes of sweet potato. Large marshmallows are traditionally toasted over the fire on the end of a stick or added to hot chocolate drinks. Spreadable marshmallow can be bought in jars and is used as a topping or icing for cakes or eaten on slices of bread.

## marzipan

A paste of ground almonds and sugar. The German type is made by combining the ingredients and cooking them (that from Lübek being the most famous); the French type is made by adding almonds to boiled sugar syrup. Marzipan is sold in block form for use in baking or sold made into varying miniature shapes of fruit, animals or vegetables. It is also used as a tart filling, to stuff dates and sweetmeats, or can be rolled out into thin sheets to decorate and cover fruit cakes and cassata.

Though marzipan is often said to have been named after the Latin *marci panis* (Mark's bread), it is more likely to have come from the Middle East, where it was originally made from sugar, ground almonds and rose-water. It was regarded as a choice delicacy and sometimes covered with gold leaf. For a long time only apothecaries were allowed to produce and sell marzipan and it was not until the eighteenth century that confectioners took over its production.

see Mexican food — masa harina

# mastic

A resin collected from bushes related to the pistachio on the Greek Island of Chios. It has an earthy, aromatic flavour and is used for flavouring Turkish delight, ice cream and in a Greek liqueur called *mastika*. It is also used in Egyptian and Moroccan cuisine. It was probably the original chewing gum, and the source of the verb 'masticate'.

# matzo

Unleavened Jewish flat bread traditionally eaten during Passover. While usually made with only flour and water, some add flavourings such as onion. Matzo (matzoh) can be ground into a meal, which is used as an ingredient in a variety of foods such as matzo balls and pancakes. It is used to thicken soups and as a substitute for leavened breadcrumbs to coat food during Passover.

# mayonnaise

Strictly speaking, an emulsion of egg yolks, olive oil and vinegar or lemon juice. It can be used in a multitude of ways: to accompany seafood, as a dressing for vegetables, or mixed with garlic to make aïoli. Commercially made mayonnaises have a 'softer' texture than homemade as they have water added—add 1 teaspoon water to each 300 ml mayonnaise made to achieve the same effect. Store homemade mayonnaise covered in the fridge for up to 4 days.

## MAKING MAYONNAISE

## COOKING

*Mayonnaise can be made with a hand whisk, an electric whisk or in a blender. Whatever you use, the most important rule is to add the oil very slowly, drop by drop to begin with, ending in a steady stream. If you pour in the oil too quickly, the mayonnaise will curdle.*

*If it does curdle, it may be possible to save it by adding 1–2 teaspoons hot water. If it still won't emulsify, start again with a new egg yolk and add the curdled mixture very slowly.*

*Use a good-quality extra virgin olive oil. For a light-flavoured mayonnaise use vegetable oil, or use equal quantities of each.*

1 *Start with all ingredients at room temperature. Put 2 egg yolks in a deep bowl and season well. Measure 300 ml oil into a jug.*

2 *Add a drop of oil onto the eggs and blend. Repeat, then continue to add the oil, drop by drop, until an emulsion is formed.*

3 *As the mixture thickens and becomes pale and glossy, add the oil faster and faster, in a steady stream.*

4 *When most of the oil has been added, add 1–2 tablespoons of vinegar or lemon juice. Whisk in the remaining oil and season.*

## MEAT LOAF

*Mix 1 kg pork and veal mince with 120 g fresh breadcrumbs, 1 finely chopped onion, 150 g chopped bacon, 2 crushed garlic cloves, 200 g grated courgette, 250 ml evaporated milk, a pinch of nutmeg and cayenne. Season. Press into a loaf tin; bake at 180°C for 1 hour. Heat 250 ml orange juice with 2 teaspoons lemon juice and reduce by half. Spoon over loaf. Serves 6.*

Minced or chopped lamb, beef, pork or veal mixed with herbs, seasonings and other flavourings, bound with egg or flour, moulded into a loaf tin and baked. Meat loaf was originally invented as a means of making meat stretch further. Once cooked, meat loaf is unmoulded and sliced and can be served hot or cold accompanied by sauces and relishes.

## medlar

Related to the quince but grown in much cooler climates, medlar are small apple-sized fruit with light tan skin. The fruit is easily recognized by the five large seeds that stick out of its base. Because the fruit are quite sharp in flavour, they are usually eaten when overripe, when they are known as 'bletted', or they can be used to make delicious jellies, jams *(pictured)* and ice creams. The fruit is commonly found in old kitchen gardens or growing wild.

## Melba toast

Very thin, dry triangles of toast for accompanying soups, pâtés and salads. The bread for Melba toast can be cooked either in the oven or under a grill but the colour should be as even as possible. Because the edges of the toast curl slightly, Melba toast also makes a good base for hors d'oeuvres. Like the dish peach Melba, Melba toast is named after the Australian opera singer, Dame Nellie Melba.

**Also known as — toast Melba**

### MELBA TOAST

*Remove the crusts from thinly sliced fresh white bread. Roll out thinly with a rolling pin and slice in half horizontally, cut into triangles. Space on a baking tray and bake at 200°C for 15 minutes, or until golden. Alternatively, toast the unrolled bread, cut it in half horizontally, then cut into triangles and bake until the raw side browns. Allow to cool totally before storing in an airtight container.*

# melon

Like other members of their family—cucumbers, squashes and courgettes—melons grow along the ground. Varieties abound, so there's usually one in season. Watermelons, however, are not true melons, they just share the same name. A melon should give slightly at the base (the opposite end to the stalk) when it is ripe and have a good 'melony' smell.

**Melon goes with — ham, fig, fortified wine, mint, prawns, smoked chicken**

■ *See also* **watermelon**

## STORAGE

*If storing cut melon in the fridge, wrap it well or its strong smell may flavour other foods in the fridge. Flavour is best at room temperature, so allow 30 minutes before serving.*

*Clockwise from bottom left: netted; watermelon; white honeydew; watermelon; yellow honeydew, whole and cut.*

## TYPES OF MELONS

**Cantaloupe**  Small round melons with segmented skin. Ogen, Galia and Chanterais are varieties.

**Gallia**  Spherical with a netted pattern on its skin. As it ripens, its skin turns from dark green to golden.

**Honeydew**  Smooth yellow or white skin and a pale yellowy-green flesh. Best eaten when really ripe.

**Netted (musk)**  Lovely musky smell when ripe. The skin has an irregular netted pattern of sections of green or gold, with either bright-orange or pale-green flesh. Also known as rock melon and commercially as cantaloupe in America.

**Ogen**  First cultivated in Israel, this small melon has green skin and pale-green, sweet flesh.

**Piel de Sapo**  A Spanish variety similar to honeydew. For the best flavour it should be eaten when very ripe.

**Watermelon**  These have bright-red flesh and black seeds, although there are now some seedless varieties. The seeds are edible and have a slightly nutty flavour. Try half-freezing wedges for a refreshing end to a meal in summer.

# melting moments

Small, crisp, round biscuits made from butter, sugar, egg, vanilla essence and flour. Before cooking, they are rolled in crushed cornflakes or rolled oats. Fresh from the oven, they are soft and pliable, but become brittle after a few minutes. As their name suggests they melt in your mouth when eaten (*pictured on the left*). An Australian version (*pictured on the right*) of the same name is more like a very crumbly shortbread, often sandwiched together with a cream filling such as passion fruit—these definitely melt in your mouth.

Made from stiffly whisked egg whites and sugar, and used both cooked and uncooked in many desserts. There are three types: Swiss, cooked (meringue *cuite*) and Italian. For good results, ensure the egg whites are at room temperature and are free of any yolk, and the mixing bowl is clean and dry.

*See also* **baked Alaska, île flottante, pavlova**

## TYPES OF MERINGUES

| | |
|---|---|
| ***Swiss*** | A softer meringue used for meringues, as well as desserts such as île flottante, baked Alaska and pavlova. |
| ***Cooked*** | Made by whisking egg whites and icing sugar over simmering water. The mixture is thicker than Swiss meringue and holds its shape well. |
| ***Italian*** | Made by boiling sugar and water, then whisking this into stiffly beaten egg whites. Use to decorate or to add lightness to mousses. |

## MAKING A MERINGUE BASE WITH SWISS MERINGUE

1 *Whisk 2 room-temperature egg whites in a clean glass or metal bowl until very stiff.*

2 *Gradually whisk in 60 g caster sugar, then fold in an extra 60 g caster sugar.*

3 *Spread onto a baking tray and bake at 150°C for 1 hour. Turn oven off and leave inside to cool.*

Originally a mixture of the leaves and shoots of young plants as a salad, today a Provençal mixture of salad leaves and herbs. A typical mesclun may include rocket and dandelion leaves, curly endive and chervil. It is seasoned with a vinaigrette of olive oil, fines herbes and garlic. The aim of a mesclun salad is to provide a contrast of both flavour and textures by combining mild and bitter tastes and soft and crunchy textures. Only young leaves should be used. In Provence, mesclun is served with small baked goat's milk cheeses, pieces of bacon, croutons, or chicken livers fried in butter.

The word 'mesclun' is derived from the Nice dialect *mesclumo*, meaning 'mixture'. A similar mixture in Rome is called *mescladisse*.

*See also* **dandelion, lettuce, rocket, salad leaves**

*Seafood escabeche*

*Mexican rice*

The tomato, the chilli, the pepper, the avocado, maize, chocolate—all of these foods and more came to the world via Mexico after the Spanish conquest.

Mexico is a large country (over three times the size of France) bordered in the north by the United States of America, and to the south by Guatemala and Belize. It comprises tropical and subtropical coastal areas, temperate plateaus and high, cold mountains. As these mountains were impassable for centuries, travel between valleys was impossible, leading to wide regional and local differences. The pre-Hispanic cultures of Mexico included the Olmec, Maya and Aztec, all of whom have had a strong influence on Mexican cuisine today, as have such Spanish imports as rice, olives, sugar, wheat and flour for bread, spices including cinnamon and nutmeg, and meat such as beef or pork.

The thousands of kilometres of coast around Mexico supply the country with a vast amount of fish and shellfish, which are eaten fresh and dried. These areas also provide rich soil for growing coconuts, sugar cane, avocados, mangoes and bananas. The mountain slopes and plateaus are ideal for the cultivation of maize, beans and chillies, and in higher areas, coffee, wheat and oats.

## STAPLES

Mexican food is not necessarily mouth-blisteringly hot. Although a wide variety of chillies are used, both fresh and dried, to add colour as well as flavour, they vary greatly in strength and flavour: some are aromatic rather than spicy, others give a little kick to the food, while some are definitely fiery. Some chillies, such as chipotles and jalapeños are smoked before cooking. When added to a dish they add subtle, smoky flavours.

*Coloradito—red Oaxacan mole made with chicken.*

Salsa, a cooked or uncooked sauce or dip, and guacamole are used in a wide variety of dishes—to spice up refried beans, as a filling for tacos or as a garnish.

*Mole* (pronounced mole-ay) is a spicy Mexican sauce that varies in its heat. Although there are many types, one of the most famous is *mole poblano*. It is an extremely rich dish containing several different types of chillies, spices and nuts, flavoured with a hint of bitter chocolate and is most traditionally served with turkey. *Coloradito* is a red Oaxacan *mole* and is one of the seven *moles* of the state of Oaxaca. The different *moles* are distinguished by the colour of chillies used, which, in this case, are deep reddish brown. In the case of the green *moles*, dishes are coloured by distinctive herbs.

## TORTILLAS

Tortillas, originally made from maize, but today often from wheat flour, are the mainstay of Mexican cooking. Corn tortillas are made from *masa harina*, a maize flour, water and salt. Flour tortillas are made from plain flour with lard and baking powder added, but these are more expensive to buy. They are used more for large

*A popular Mexican dessert, caramel custard flan.*

*burras* (burritos), which are tortillas filled with savoury fillings. To make tortillas, a dough is made and then shaped into flat discs, traditionally by slapping the dough from hand to hand, but today the use of a tortilla press is more common. The dough is pressed between two pieces of metal or plastic, then peeled off and cooked on a *comal*, which is a round, cast-iron baking tray placed directly over the fire, or nowadays, on the griddle. Making tortillas is a time-consuming process and they are now readily available at the supermarket. *Totopos* or *tostaditas* are small pieces of tortilla crisps used for scooping up salsa or guacamole. They are made by toasting pieces of tortilla.

Another staple of Mexican food is beans (*frijoles*) and these include black, red and white beans, pintos and pinquitos. They are eaten as part of the main meal or as an accompaniment, particularly with breakfast eggs (*heuvos rancheros*). Refried beans are cooked beans that are recooked in lard and mashed once cooked.

*Burras, made with flour tortillas.*

*Tostaditas with guacamole*

## MEALS AND SNACKS

Meal times are not set, but the main meal is often eaten in the middle of the day. Two types of soups are eaten, the first a traditional 'wet' soup, served at the beginning of a meal. The second is a 'dry soup', actually a rice or pasta dish. For a complete Mexican meal, these 'soups' would be followed by a meat or fish dish accompanied by tortillas, beans, and then fruit or dessert, such as a custard flan, with coffee. Meat is generally cooked for a long time, then shredded and used as a filling. A popular seafood dish is *escabeche,* which is poached or fried fish covered with a spicy marinade and refrigerated for at least 24 hours. A slice of *membrillo* (quince paste) is served either by itself or with a fresh cheese as a typical dessert.

*Huevos rancheros—'ranch' eggs.*

*Antojitos* are little snacks similar to Spanish tapas but bought instead from street stalls, and are enjoyed at all times of the day. Examples are *empanaditas*, which are small pastry turnovers; *tamales*, which are corn dumplings filled with savoury or sweet mixtures before being steamed; roast corn; and boiled peanuts.

The word 'chocolate' was derived by the Spanish from the Maya language. Both the Maya and the Aztecs enjoyed it frothed into a drink, often mixed with chilli, vanilla and sometimes honey. In Mexico, chocolate is still more popular as a drink than as confectionery. Tequila, invented by the Spaniards, is the best known of *mezcal* drinks, a variety of alcoholic drinks distilled from the agave plant.

*Membrillo—quince paste.*

**See also   escabeche, chillies, guacamole, tortilla**

# meze

Meaning 'little morsels', meze (or mezze) include virtually anything that can be served in a small portion and eaten by hand. The tradition of meze is popular throughout Greece, Lebanon, Turkey, the Balkans, Egypt, Morocco and North Africa, and although some dishes are common to all, each has its own specialities. Meze are traditionally served in bars—they were probably once served as free bar snacks—a large selection is ordered and these are shared among several people. Some meze are simple like cubes of cheese, olives and slices of meat, or snacks of nuts and pumpkin seeds; others are made up as dishes and portioned out, such as salads, dips, tabbouleh and kebabs.

**Also known as — mezedes, mezze**

## DOLMA

Dolma are stuffed vegetables, filled with meat or vegetables such as aubergines, peppers, tomatoes and courgettes, often mixed with a grain such as burghul wheat. Dolma may also include stuffed leaves such as vine leaves (dolmades) and cabbage leaves. Generally meat-filled dolma are served hot and vegetable ones cold.

## MEATBALLS

Meatballs and kofta are made with minced lamb flavoured with herbs, raisins or pine nuts. They may be served plain or in a tomato or yoghurt sauce. Meatballs are not always round; they may also be shaped as fingers or ovals.

## BEANS

There are many types of bean dishes served as meze—some may be mashed, others left whole. Different beans are used in different areas but are often interchangeable in recipes. Beans cooked with onion and tomato and flavoured with garlic are common and these can be eaten warm or cold.

*Stuffed peppers*

*Dolmades*

*Broad (fava) beans in tomato sauce*

*Black olives (left) and chilli olives (right)*

*Meatballs with yoghurt*

*Olives stuffed with pimiento*

*Chicken and lamb kebabs*

*Labna rolled in herbs*

*Olives*

## CHEESE

In its simplest form, cubes of cheese such as feta are served on their own with a little oil. Slices of cheese such as haloumi and kasseri can be fried and served with bread while still soft. Fresh cheeses such as labna are made by draining yoghurt until it is firm enough to shape into balls.

## KEBABS

Small chunks of marinated lamb, beef, veal, chicken or fish threaded onto skewers and cooked, often over coals.

## OLIVES

Olives are the simplest form of meze. They may be black or green, pitted or unpitted and flavoured variously with garlic, chilli or herbs.

## BOREK

These little pies and pastries can be made from a variety of fillings such as minced lamb, fish, cheese or spinach, which are enclosed in pastry or bread dough, or baked as whole dishes and cut into small pieces. Some of the more common shapes include cigars, squares and triangles. Börek-like pastries are also known as *sanbusak*, *pasteles*, *briouats* and *brik*, depending on which country they come from.

*Börek*

## FISH

Small fish like sardines, anchovies and garfish are often chargrilled or grilled and served with lemon wedges. The grilled fish may then be marinated in herbs, oil and vinegar and eaten cold.

*Grilled sardines*

## SALADS

Tabbouleh, a mixture of burghul wheat and herbs, is traditionally scooped up with small lettuce leaves. Horiatiki, a Greek salad that can vary in make up, usually contains cucumber, tomato, olives, onion and feta. Aubergine salads also vary; some are fried and layered with yoghurt, others are flavoured with tomato and onion.

*Horiatiki*

*Tabbouleh*

*Dips, clockwise from top: baba ghanoush, taramosalata, hummus, cacik.*

*Marinated mushrooms (top) and artichoke hearts*

*Marinated octopus*

## MARINATED VEGETABLES

Vegetables such as mushrooms and artichoke hearts can be marinated to give them extra flavour. The vegetables are simmered in oil and flavourings such as garlic, lemon and herbs and then left to cool in their cooking liquid.

## DIPS

Common meze dishes, these dips are sometimes called 'cream salads'. Hummus is made with chickpeas and flavoured with tahini; baba ghanoush with puréed roasted aubergine; taramosalata with smoked cod's roe and oil; and cacik from diced cucumber, yoghurt and garlic. All are served with bread for dipping.

## MARINATED SEAFOOD

Both octopus and squid benefit from being marinated or pickled as this tenderizes the flesh. Some are marinated in vinegar, others dressed with oil and lemon juice and herbs.

**245**

Middle Eastern cuisine is a loose term that covers many countries, races, religions and cultures, its most unifying feature being the common use of Arabic. The cuisines of the Middle East (taken here to be Egypt, Lebanon, Algeria, Syria, Iran, Turkey, Iraq, Saudi Arabia, Yemen, Sudan, Tunisia, Morocco, Oman, The United Arab Emirates and Israel) are closely linked, and the same types of dishes appear throughout the region, spread by the movement of people and Islam, so that many areas now claim the same dish as their own—*kibbeh* is the national dish of Syria, Lebanon and Iraq, and falafel is common in both Israel and Egypt. Middle Eastern cuisine is based on tradition, it does not tend to have new or modern versions and relies on recipes that have been cooked in the same way for centuries, with slight regional or personal variations. Some dishes are simple and others elaborate, such as *kibbeh*, *börek* and pastry-making, all of which require time, patience and skill. This is a cuisine handed down and practised by women in its home cooking form and by men in its professional form.

*Brik a l'oeuf—parcels of filo pastry usually filled with a whole egg.*

*Vegetables filled with meat and rice, then baked.*

*Shish kebabs served with braised beans and onion salad.*

Many would say that the most refined cuisine of the Middle East is Persian (Iranian), which uses such ingredients as sour cherries, pomegranates, long-grain rice, nuts, spices and aromatics to produce a fine, perfumed cuisine.

However, the true 'Arab' style cooking is based in countries such as Lebanon, Syria, Jordan and countries that were part of the old Ottoman Empire. It is based on burghul wheat and rice, dishes such as kebabs, salads, stuffed vegetables, tabbouleh and roast meats. Originally this cuisine was that of the Bedouin and other nomadic people and included foods like dates, milk, rice and meat such as sheep and goat.

North African and Moroccan cuisines make much use of couscous, from the indigenous Berber dish, and incorporated European influences from Iberia, Sicily and France. In Tunisia, fiery harissa, a paste made from chillies and spices, is common, as is *brik*, a thin, crisp, pastry case with filling inside. In Morocco, they enjoy *bisteeya*, a savoury pie, and various tagines (stews).

*Whole barbecued fish*

In the Middle East, ovens are still not common in many houses, so dishes such as pilaffs and bean dishes are slow cooked on a small stove. Legs of lamb, stews and casseroles may be baked in a local baker's oven, or meats may be grilled over charcoal. The art of cooking food on a skewer is attributed to the Turks who supposedly invented it on the battlefield. Kebabs now appear throughout Middle Eastern cuisine and are popular as street food and in restaurants.

## SPICES

As transport throughout the Middle East improved, ingredients from China, India and northern Africa were introduced. Pepper, ginger, cinnamon, cloves, nutmeg, coriander and cumin were incorporated into the cuisine, rice from India became a staple and sugar came into common usage. *Mahlab* (cherry kernels), mastic (resin), musk (from musk deers), orange flower water, rose buds, *sahlab* (powdered orchid bulb), sumac (a sourish red seed), *dibbis* (date syrup), *ras el hanout* (Moroccan spice mix), *tabil* (Tunisian spice mix) and *noumi basra* (dried limes) are all aromatic ingredients of various parts of the Middle East.

*Middle Eastern breads*

## MEAT AND OTHER DISHES

Meat is used economically, except on feast days when a whole spit-roast lamb may be cooked. Lamb is the meat of choice, often grilled (*meshwi*) as pieces, served whole or cut up for kebabs. Mince is made into meatballs such as *kibbeh*, lady's thighs or kofta. Generally pork is forbidden, as communities tend to be Muslim or Jewish and pork is considered unclean. Though all religions tend to eat the same sort of food, it would be unthinkable for Jews to mix meat with a dairy product such as yoghurt, whereas for Arabs it is one of their most common combinations. Where it is available, fish is eaten widely, marinated in spice mixtures such as chermoula, grilled over charcoal or cooked with tomatoes, parsley and onions and served hot or cold. Poultry such as chicken, duck and game birds are eaten on feast days. Salads may be raw or cooked, dressed with olive oil and lemon juice or vinegar, and can be as simple as grated carrot flavoured with spices or the more complicated lentil or rice salads. Soups are often hearty enough to be a full meal in themselves. Staple foods include bread, rice and noodles and common ingredients include yoghurt, tomatoes, aubergines, lemons, garlic, parsley and mint. Pastries are sweet and savoury but desserts such as *komposto* (fruit compote) and *muhllabia* (a cornflour-based cream dessert) are usually eaten with coffee rather than at the end of a meal.

*Middle Eastern sweets served with mint tea.*

*Meze, including hummus, dolmades, stuffed cabbage and börek.*

## MEZE AND SNACKS

Hospitality is a way of life in the Middle East, food is always available and it would be unthinkable not to offer food to a visitor at any time of the day or night.

Meze and snacks are an important part of the cuisine as leisure time is spent sipping coffee and mint tea, and drinking and eating snacks is very much enjoyed. Finger foods such as chickpeas, pumpkin seeds, pastries, dolmades and slices of smoked meat are laid out to nibble on as well as dips such as tahini, hummus and baba ghanoush, labna, tabbouleh, olives, pastries and falafel. Lebanon has a reputation for the best meze.

■ *See also* **mastic, meze, Moroccan food, sumac, tagine**

# milk

Milk comes from cows, sheep and goats, its by-products include cheese, butter, cream, buttermilk, whey, yoghurt and sour cream. One of the most versatile ingredients, milk can be used in beverages, puddings, soups, sauces and ice cream. Different types of milk are identified either by labelling on the carton or, in some countries, by the colour of their lid. Milk in different countries is treated differently and some milk may have vitamins, extra calcium or iron added to it.

*From left: powdered milk, pasteurized milk, condensed milk, skim milk.*

## TYPES OF MILK

**Raw**
Untreated milk, straight from the cow, which is perfectly safe if from a well-tended herd, and certainly more flavoursome. It is illegal in some countries.

**Pasteurized**
Most milk sold is pasteurized, a process that destroys any harmful bacteria and improves the milk's keeping quality. Two types of pasteurized milk are whole milk, which has a visible cream line, and homogenized, which has the fat broken up into small particles.

**Skimmed**
Pasteurized milk with virtually all the fat removed, leaving 0.1–0.3 per cent fat. Semi-skimmed has 1.5–1.8 per cent fat. This process also removes the majority of the fat-soluble vitamins A and D. It is not suitable for children under 5 years.

**UHT and sterilized**
'Long-life' or ultra-heat treated (UHT) milk is heated at very high temperatures for 1 to 2 seconds. Sterilized milk is heated for 20 to 30 minutes but at a slightly lower temperature. This causes the milk sugars to caramelize a little, giving it a slightly caramel taste.

**Evaporated**
This is made by heating milk so that most of its water evaporates.

**Condensed**
Sticky, rich and creamy, made like evaporated milk but has sugar added to it, which also helps to preserve it.

**Powdered or dried**
Made from skimmed milk. The water is evaporated to produce a powder. It is reconstituted by adding water.

## LACTOSE INTOLERANCE

*Some people suffer from lactose intolerance, which is caused by a deficiency in the digestive enzyme lactase. These people are unable to break down lactose for assimilation in the intestine, creating symptoms such as abdominal pain and diarrhoea. Milk in these cases can often be substituted with rice or soya milk.*

## STORAGE

*Milk should be stored in the fridge where it will last 3 to 4 days.*

*Spoiled milk is not 'sour milk', recipes that require sour milk usually refer to buttermilk. Add a splash of lemon juice to instantly 'sour' milk for cooking.*

*When cooking with milk do not use unhomogenized milk as this froths and boils over more easily.*

*Milk protein coagulates and burns easily when heated so use a heavy-based pan over medium heat and stir the milk to stop it catching on the bottom.*

*Milk protein flocculates (separates) when it is heated, causing a skin to form on hot milk. The only way to stop this is by stirring continuously.*

*See also* **buttermilk**

# millefeuille

Classically made with sheets of puff pastry rolled thin and then pricked to prevent the pastry 'puffing up' but retaining a very flaky texture. It is then separated by layers of cream, fruit such as strawberries, jam or fruit purée, and usually served in individual slices although sometimes it is found as one large dessert. Translated from the French, millefeuille means 'a thousand leaves', referring to the multitude of fine layers of pastry.

*Also known as — Napoléon*

# millet

A grass seed used as a cereal in many African and Asian countries as it can grow in areas of extreme aridity and heat. Millet can be boiled in water, milk or stock, is a good accompaniment to spicy casseroles and is used to thicken soups. The flour is used for flat breads and griddle cakes, but as it lacks gluten it is not suited to many types of baking. Millet can also be fermented and made into a crude beer, or malted and made into a more sophisticated brew.

# mince

Mince (or ground beef) is generally derived from cuts of beef such as stewing, chuck or skirt as it needs to contain a certain amount of fat. Some hamburger mince is made from minced steak but the lack of fat will cause it to break up more easily. Generally, the paler and more streaky the colour, the more fat it contains. Mince can also be made from lamb, pork, chicken and veal.

# mincemeat

## MINCEMEAT

*Mix together 40 g chopped raisins, 30 g sultanas, 40 g mixed peel, 2 tablespoons currants, 1 small grated apple, ½ teaspoon each of grated orange zest, grated lemon zest and mixed spice, a pinch of nutmeg, 60 g brown sugar, 25 g melted butter and 1 tablespoon each of brandy and chopped blanched almonds. Makes enough for 24 tarts. Will store for up to 3 months in an airtight jar.*

A mixture of dried fruits such as raisins, sultanas and candied peel, nuts, grated apple, spices, lemon rind, brandy or rum. It is usually made with a fat such as beef suet or butter to help give it keeping qualities—the fat melts around the fruit to form a protective coating. Mincemeat is used as a filling for cakes, puddings and most famously, in mince pies. Mince pies originally contained chopped meat but because meat was expensive it was bulked out with dried fruits and eventually the meat component disappeared, leaving only the suet and other ingredients.

## minestrone

Italian for vegetable soup. Each region has its own recipe for minestrone, but most use onions, tomatoes, courgettes, beans and celery. The vegetables are cooked for 2 to 3 hours so their flavour is completely amalgamated. In some recipes, grated Parmesan or spoonfuls of pesto are added at the end of cooking. In the South of Italy, the soup is thickened with pasta; in the North, rice is used. Although the soup can be served as a starter, minestrone is so thick and filling that a bowl can constitute a meal in itself.

## mint sauce

An English sauce, traditionally served with roast lamb. It is made by steeping chopped mint leaves in boiling water, sugar and vinegar. Variations include mint jelly and mint gravy.

### MINT SAUCE

*In a small dish, mix together 4 tablespoons chopped mint leaves and 1 teaspoon sugar. Add 2 tablespoons boiling water: this sets the colour. Add 2 teaspoons sugar and 3 tablespoons wine vinegar, a pinch of salt and mix together. Leave to stand for about 1 hour to allow the flavours to develop before serving. Makes 125 ml.*

## mirin

A sweet spirit-based rice liquid used predominantly in Japanese cooking in basting sauces and marinades, in salad dressings and stir-fries. Its high sugar content adds a sheen to the food. Mirin, when mixed with soy sauce, forms the basis of yakitori and teriyaki marinades. The real thing, *hon mirin (pictured)*, contains 14 per cent alcohol, and is far superior to the low-alcohol imitation mirin. It is exclusively used in cooking, and not as a beverage.

Some recipes suggest that if mirin is not available, that you can replace it with either sweet sherry or dry sherry (add a little extra sugar if using dry sherry), but this will alter the flavour.

■ *See also* **sake**

One of the most important ingredients in Japanese cooking, miso is a paste of fermented soya beans with other flavourings. It is made by boiling soya beans, which are then ground to a paste with wheat and barley or rice. The mixture is injected with a yeast mould and left to mature. Miso is used as a condiment and a flavouring and there are over 50 different types, each with a distinctive flavour and colour, and each suited to a particular type of recipe. Colours range from light brown to a dark brown, but generally the lighter the colour the milder the flavour. Buy miso in tubs or plastic packs. It will keep in the fridge for several months.

### MISO SOUP

*Bring 5 cups dashi to the boil. First mix 3 tablespoons shinshu-miso with 3 tablespoons hot dashi, then add to the rest of the dashi. Bring to a simmer but do not boil. Add 250 g diced bean curd and simmer for 5 minutes. Serve in 4 bowls garnished with diagonal slices of 4 spring onions. Serves 4.*

### TYPES OF MISO

**Hatcho-miso** — Very dark, strongly flavoured, salty miso predominantly used in soups. It is made only from soya beans. A similar miso is called *akadashi-miso*.

**Inaka-miso** — Sometimes called red miso, this has barley mould added and is red in colour. Used in soups and stews and can be either sweet or salty.

**Shinshu-miso** — One of the most commonly found outside of Asia. It is smooth, yellow and salty and can be used in most recipes.

**Shiro-miso** — Its sweet taste is good for dressings. Mild in flavour, low in salt, it can also be used in soups.

**see sugar — molasses**

**monstera**

The fruit of the *Monstera deliciosa*, a tropical tree, each one about 30 cm long and resembling an elongated pine cone. The fruit is covered in a thick, green skin patterned with individual hexagonal scales. As they ripen, these scales 'pop' and separate from the body of the fruit and fall off. When it begins to break apart, it is ripe enough to eat. Inside, the ripe, pulpy flesh has overtones of banana, pineapple and mango flavours, which is why it is sometimes called fruit salad fruit. The texture resembles firm custard and is eaten in segments. The fruit contains a non-toxic oxalic acid, which may irritate the mouth and throat, especially if it is underripe.

*Also known as — ceriman, Mexican breadfruit*

**see lobster — Moreton Bay bug**

## mornay sauce

A white béchamel sauce to which grated cheese, usually Parmesan and a Swiss cheese, is added. Other ingredients such as egg yolks, mustard, cream or stock may also be added. Food served with mornay sauce is usually coated in the sauce, sprinkled with additional grated cheese and/or breadcrumbs, then grilled. This sauce is served with fish, shellfish such as oysters *(pictured)*, eggs, vegetables and chicken.

## Moroccan food

A North African kingdom bordered by the Mediterranean to the north, the Atlantic to the west and the Sahara to the south. Invaders and traders have all left their legacies and the flavours of Morocco are a fusion of African, Arabian and European, as well as indigenous Berber dishes. The Arabs invaded in the seventh century and converted many to Islam, still the dominant religion, which dictates much of what can and cannot be eaten. They introduced dates, milk, grains and bread, and when the Moors returned from Spain they brought across olives, fruit, nuts and herbs.

Meals are eaten sitting at a low table where platters of food are shared and eaten using the right hand to scoop up the food. Bread (*kisra*) is used to soak up the juices. A daily meal usually consists of one main dish, but *diffa*, or feasts, are a more elaborate affair, with as many as 20 dishes. Spices play an important role and include chilli, cumin, paprika, ginger, saffron, coriander, cayenne and cinnamon. *Ras el hanout* (literally top of the shop) is a mixture of anything from 10 to 100 spices, and can include anything from dried rose buds to Spanish fly. Preserved lemons

are widely used to flavour dishes and can be bought ready-made.

Tagines are rich, slow-cooked stews of vegetables and meat. Many Moroccan dishes, including tagines, are flavoured with both sweet and sour ingredients, an influence from the Arabs who added honey, sugar and fruit to dishes. Couscous is the national dish (of Berber origin) and is served every day, as well as at the end of a feast to ensure that no guests leave hungry.

*Harira* is a rich, red and spicy soup made from meat, rice, chickpeas and fresh herbs. *Bisteeya* is a pie with several layers of pastry (*warga*) and three distinct layers of filling: the first usually stewed pigeon, the second eggs and the third sweetened almonds. It is sprinkled with cinnamon and icing sugar and served as a first course.

Mint tea, made from spearmint, is served in a glass throughout the day and is heavily sweetened. Almond milk is served as an alternative or as a complement to mint tea.

■ *See also*  **couscous, spice mixes, tagine**

*From top: tagine, harira soup, bisteeya.*

## moussaka

Although best known in Greece, moussaka is a favourite dish throughout the Middle East. At its most basic, it is made from layers of minced lamb, slices of aubergine and tomato. Greek versions finish with a layer of béchamel sauce or beaten egg on top; and some Turkish versions use courgette instead of aubergine. Once it is layered up, it is baked in the oven and served cut into squares.

*Also known as — mousaka, musaka, musakka, musaqqa'a*

## mousse

From the French term meaning 'froth' or 'foam', a mousse is a light, soft and airy dish, which can be either sweet or savoury. Cold dessert mousses are usually based on a flavouring such as a fruit purée or chocolate to which cream and eggs or egg whites are added. Some are set with gelatine and set in moulds; others are frozen before serving. Savoury mousses may be made from fish, shellfish, meat, cheese or vegetables such as avocado.

*See also* **chocolate, raspberry**

### BERRY MOUSSE

*Heat 300 g mixed blackberries and blueberries with 200 g sugar until the sugar dissolves. Push berries through a sieve and allow to cool. Dissolve 4 teaspoons gelatine in 4 tablespoons water. Whisk 4 egg whites to soft peaks. Mix into the berries with the gelatine, then fold in 150 ml whipped cream. Spoon into 4 dishes, cover and chill overnight, or until set. Serves 4.*

## MSG

MSG is the abbreviated term for monosodium glutamate, a flavour enhancer first extracted from plants in which it naturally occurred (such as seaweed and sugar beet) in the early 1900s. It has no flavour of its own and is a white powder. As an additive it has the number 621. Ingredients containing MSG naturally do not have to be labelled. Though MSG is often thought to cause allergic reactions, the body synthesizes it in the same way as it copes with naturally occurring MSG.

## muesli

A combination of raw or toasted cereals, such as oats, wheat, millet and barley mixed with dried fruit and nuts. When combined with milk, yoghurt or fruit juice, muesli makes a nutritious breakfast cereal. Muesli was developed by a Swiss nutritionist Dr Bircher-Benner in the early 1900s. The name comes from the Swiss-German dialect word for 'mixture'.

## muffins

There are two muffins: the English and American. An English muffin is a round, bread-like cake made from yeast and strong flour, milk, some semolina and salt. To eat, the muffins are split open, toasted, then spread with butter and jam. Muffins are frequently used as the basis for breakfast dishes such as eggs Benedict. An American muffin is made with a sweet cake-like mixture, which often contains fruit and nuts and other flavourings, such as chocolate. They are cooked in muffin tins and baked in the oven. Muffin tins come in a variety of sizes from mini through to jumbo.

### APPLE CINNAMON MUFFINS

*Sift together 375 g self-raising flour, 3½ tablespoons caster sugar, 3 teaspoons cinnamon and a pinch of nutmeg. Melt 155 g butter with 3 tablespoons honey and pour over the flour. Add 2 beaten eggs and 3 green apples, peeled and finely diced. Stir until just combined. Spoon into 12 muffin tins, sprinkle tops with cinnamon and caster sugar. Bake at 200°C for 20 minutes.*

*From left: American apple cinnamon muffins, English muffins.*

**253**

# mulberry

These are soft, purple berries, similar to blackberries in size and shape. In some countries, there are also red and white varieties. Although sold commercially, most are collected from suburban trees—lay a sheet below the tree to catch the fruit as they fall or pick them. Until ripe, the fruit are very sour and even ripe fruit have a sweet-sour flavour. Mulberries are soft, so wash carefully and eat soon after picking. Use like blackberries—serve with cream or ice cream or use in jams, sorbets, summer pudding or to make mulberry wine.

# mulled wine

## MULLED WINE

*Stud 2 oranges with 10 cloves each. Put into a saucepan with 2 teaspoons nutmeg, 90 g sugar and 2 cinnamon sticks. Add 500 ml water, boil, then simmer 20 minutes until liquid is halved. Strain and cool. Add a bottle of good red wine and heat until almost boiling, then turn off heat. Do not boil or the alcohol will evaporate. Serve in heatproof glasses. Makes 1 litre.*

A popular winter drink, especially in the northern hemisphere, made on a base of red wine and flavoured with spices such as cinnamon, cloves and orange zest, and sometimes brandy. The wine is heated and served warm. As *gluhwein*, it is served in European ski resorts.

# mulligatawny soup

A spicy soup, mulligatawny is based on the Tamil soup, *rasam*, and was adapted by the Colonial British in India. Mulligatawny soup may be made as either a thin broth or a thick purée and may contain any number of ingredients. Mrs Beeton's version is a mixture of chicken, curry powder, onion and good strong stock. Like *rasam*, it is often served over rice. The word is derived from a Tamil word, *milagu-thannir*, meaning 'pepper water'.

# mung beans

Small, olive-green beans sold dried as pulses or after the seed has sprouted as mung bean sprouts *(pictured)*. As a pulse, mung beans may be cooked in soups and casseroles or in purées. The Chinese use the sprouts in sweet cakes or ferment them to make sauces. In Southeast Asia, mung beans are ground to make a flour used for sweets and doughs. The starch is used for making fine thread noodles.

*Also known as — green gram, green lentil*

Some of the most exciting food known to humanity is found in dark, damp habitats, on forest floors, living off live, decaying and dead organic matter. Mushrooms are the fruit of the fungus that grows above ground. There are countless varieties of edible mushrooms, some cultivated, others gathered from the wild. Wild mushrooms are generally in season during autumn, with the exception of morels, which are picked in spring, and cultivated mushrooms are available year round.

The flavour of some mushrooms intensifies when dried, so mushrooms such as Chinese shiitake and Italian porcini are often bought dried, then reconstituted. Soak in warm water for 30 minutes, or simmer with a little sugar for 15 minutes. Cut off the stalk and chop the caps. The soaking water will be flavourful, so strain it and add to stock or a sauce. Dried mushrooms reconstitute up to six or eight times their original weight. Canned mushrooms should be drained and rinsed before use.

**Mushrooms go with — butter, échalote, egg, game, garlic, pork, risotto**

## STORAGE

*Store mushrooms in the fridge in a paper bag to allow them to breathe. Don't leave them in plastic as this makes them sweat.*

*Mushrooms do not keep for long. Wild mushrooms are best eaten on the day they are picked and will last no longer than a day in the fridge; cultivated mushrooms will last up to 3 days.*

| Button | Open cup | Flat |

**Cultivated mushrooms**

Cultivated mushrooms are available in varying stages of development. The smallest, button mushrooms, have a mild flavour and keep their pale colour when cooked. Use raw in salads or cook in white sauces. Closed cup mushrooms are good for slicing and adding to stir-fries. They turn darker when cooked and will taint the colour of a white sauce. Add a few drops of lemon juice, wine vinegar or white wine to prevent this happening. The larger, open cup mushrooms are more flavoursome and are ideal for stews and casseroles. Flat (open or field) mushrooms have a good earthy flavour and a meaty texture and are delicious grilled or stuffed. They make a good, dark-coloured mushroom soup, but if cooked with white meat like chicken they may turn the dish grey.

Chestnut (crimini) and portobello mushrooms are relatives of the button mushroom. They have a creamy brown cap, buff-coloured stalks and a more pronounced flavour than button mushrooms. They are a good all-round mushroom.

## MIXED MUSHROOM STIR-FRY

*Trim and clean 500 g mixed mushrooms, slicing any larger ones. Melt 25 g butter in a frying pan and add 1 tablespoon olive oil. Add 1 finely chopped chilli, 1 finely chopped shallot and 1 garlic clove and fry briefly. Add mushrooms and toss over high heat until cooked through and beginning to brown (if you are using shimeji or enoki mushrooms, put them in at the end). Add 1 tablespoon chopped coriander, 1 tablespoon soy sauce, season well and drizzle with sesame oil. Serve tossed through noodles or pasta or on bruschetta. Makes enough for 12 bruschetta or 4 entrée noodle or pasta serves.*

## PREPARATION

*Cultivated mushrooms don't need to be washed before use—simply wipe over them with paper towel. To prepare wild mushrooms, wipe them with a damp cloth or paper towel. Remove the gritty base of the stem and brush the caps with a soft brush to remove earth or grit. If necessary, quickly run them under cold water, then pat dry with a paper towel.*

*Mixed mushroom stir-fry using enoki, oyster, swiss brown, shiitake and shimeji mushrooms.*

**WARNING**

*Some innocuous-looking mushrooms are highly poisonous. Never eat a mushroom unless you are certain that it is edible, especially if picking them in the wild. Always ask a professional to identify any suspect mushrooms before eating.*

*Cep (porcini)*

*Chanterelle*

*Enoki*

*Horn of plenty*

*Oyster*

*Shiitake*

*Shimeji*

*Straw*

See also **fungi**

## TYPES OF MUSHROOMS

**Blewitts and wood blewitts**
Also known as blue legs, these two slightly different species have a light blue-lilac stem, cap and gills, although sometimes these are very pale blue, almost greyish white. They respond well to frying or stewing.

**Cep (porcini)**
Also known as penny bun, these have a brown cap and thick white stem. They have a rich, sweet and nutty flavour and are sold fresh and dried (usually called porcini). Good in risottos and stews or raw in salads.

**Chanterelle**
Also known as girolles, these are golden yellow with a concave cap. The underside has blunt, gill-like waves and folds. A good all-round mushroom.

**Enoki**
Also known as enokitake, these grow and are bought in clumps. They have tiny cream caps on slender stalks and a delicate flavour and crisp texture. The base can be sliced off or they can be cooked in clumps.

**Horn of plenty**
Also known as black trumpet and *trompette des morts*, these saggy, leather-like mushrooms have a strong, earthy taste. Slit down the side to clean them. Fry in butter and garlic or good in cream sauces with chicken.

**Morel**
Short, stubby mushrooms, resembling a domed sponge. Usually found dried. They are good with chicken or veal and make an excellent creamy mushroom sauce.

**Oyster**
Wild mushroom, now cultivated widely. Tear large mushrooms into long pieces along the lines of the gills. Add to stir-fries or fry quickly and add to leafy salads.

**Pied de mouton**
Also known as hedgehog fungus, this wild mushroom is also commercially available. Identifiable by the clusters of spines underneath its cap. Scrape away the gills before cooking. Use in soups, risottos, pasta sauces.

**Shaggy ink cap**
Also known as lawyer's wig, these are tall and bell-shaped and go soggy as they get older. Choose firm mushrooms, discard the stalks, peel the caps, then fry in butter.

**Shiitake**
Dark-brown caps, available fresh and dried. Dried are best with crazed top. Fresh are best when very smelly. Cut a cross in the top of the cap of large mushrooms to allow them to cook through the thickest part.

**Shimeji**
Also known as beech, these are small oyster mushrooms with long stalks. When cooked they retain a slightly crunchy texture and are good in mushroom mixtures.

**Straw**
These are grown on beds of straw. They are small and globe-shaped with an internal stem. They are usually found canned.

From left: common mussels, New Zealand green-lipped mussels.

Bivalve molluscs that grow in clusters around sandbanks, rocks and other objects in the sea. They hold onto the rocks with their byssus (beard), a mass of long silky threads found at the opening of their shell. There are many varieties found worldwide, including common varieties such as the green-lipped mussel from New Zealand, the common mussel and the European mussel. The flesh of female mussels is orange while that of the male is a pale whitish colour. Small mussels are more tender and have a better flavour than larger ones.

Mussels are farmed extensively and these are safer to eat than wild ones as mussels are filter-feeders and many harbour toxins.

Mussels can be stuffed, baked or grilled or, when removed from their shells, they can be added to soups, salads, paellas, omelettes and stews. An easy way to eat mussels is to use an empty mussel shell like a pair of pinchers to remove each mussel from its shell. Store mussels in the fridge in a wet hessian bag or on a damp cloth as keeping them in cold water will only drown them.

■ **See also  shellfish**

## BUYING

*In general allow 500 g–600 g per person (a lot of the weight is the shell) for a main course and serve with bread or French fries. Always buy mussels from a reputable source.*

## PREPARATION

*Fresh mussels must be bought alive, as any that are dead may be toxic. The shells should be uncracked and closed, or should close when tapped on the bench. If they remain open, they are dead and should be discarded. On cooking, any mussels that don't open should also be discarded.*

## PREPARING MUSSELS

*1  Scrub mussels thoroughly under cold running water to remove any dirt or slime.*

*2  If the hairy beard is attached, pull it off, then rinse again. Discard any with open or cracked shells.*

## MOULES A LA MARINIERE

*Heat 2 tablespoons oil in a large saucepan. Add 3 finely chopped shallots and sauté until softened. Add 180 ml dry white wine and bring to the boil. Add 20 mussels and cover. Cook over high heat for 3–5 minutes until the mussels open, shaking the pan frequently. With a slotted spoon, transfer mussels to warmed serving bowls. Strain sauce into a clean pan. Return to the boil and add 2 tablespoons chopped parsley, season, then pour sauce over the mussels. Serves 4.*

# mustard

A condiment made from the ground seeds of the mustard plant. There are many species, but it is usually the black (the hottest and most pungent), brown and white seeds (sometimes called yellow) that are commonly used. Prepared mustard is made by macerating the seeds in liquid, such as water, vinegar or wine, then grinding them to a fine paste. Some mustards are flavoured with other ingredients such as herbs, honey, chilli or garlic. The pungency, colour, flavour and texture of the mustard will depend on the type of seeds used and the style of mustard.

Whole mustard seeds are used to flavour marinades and sauces and in a whole host of Asian recipes. They are widely used in pickling. In Indian cooking they are fried in oil until they pop. Mustard oil is also popular. Mustard powder is simply ground mustard seeds and can be added to salad dressings, mayonnaise and sauces. It helps the emulsification of sauces such as mayonnaise and vinaigrette. The powder can be mixed with water and used in the same way as prepared mustard. Prepared mustard should be stored in the fridge as it loses its flavour at room temperature. Store mustard seeds and powder in a cool, dry place.

*Clockwise from bottom left to centre: smooth mustard, mustard oil, mustard powder, yellow and brown mustard seeds, wholegrain mustard.*

| Dijon | American | German wholegrain | Hot English |

## TYPES OF MUSTARD

**French**
Most famous include Dijon, Bordeaux and Meaux. Dijon is a strong, smooth, pale-yellow to light-brown mustard. The seeds are blended with white wine or verjuice (the juice of unripe vine grapes). Meaux is a milder mustard of unmilled crushed seeds.

**American**
Mild mustard, sometimes flavoured with sugar, vinegar or white wine, served with hot dogs and hamburgers.

**German**
Typically dark, medium to hot, usually eaten with German sausages or cold meats.

**English**
Made from brown and white seeds, smooth and very hot. Use with roast beef and ham, with hard cheeses such as Cheddar, or as a condiment with ham, sausages, herring or mackerel. Often prepared from mustard powder.

## SERVING SUGGESTIONS

*Rub a little mustard onto ham before baking it, or onto a chicken before roasting.*

*Add some to a white sauce or soup to add extra flavour.*

*Combine some mustard with a little oil, chilli and soy sauce for a quick meat marinade.*

*Mix some with softened butter, add some chopped fresh herbs and use on top of beef or pork steaks.*

*Cook some cocktail sausages, then add 1 tablespoon wholegrain mustard and 1 tablespoon honey and toss everything together.*

# mutton

Traditionally, lamb that was over 1 year old was called mutton, but it now varies from 1–2½ years. Mutton has a stronger flavour than lamb, is less tender and has darker flesh. It is widely used in North African and Middle Eastern cooking, is good in curries and the fat is used in the Scottish dish, haggis. To cook, trim the meat of any fat and serve with robust, starchy accompaniments. Mutton, like lamb, has 'hard fat', which solidifies once the meat has been cut, so serve on hot plates to prevent this.

# n

## navarin

A ragout of mutton or lamb with potatoes and vegetables. Navarin is a hearty stew made with potatoes and onions in winter; in spring, *navarin printanier* is served using carrots, turnips, beans and peas. Although it is often said that the name comes from *navet*, the French for turnip, the original main accompaniment, its origin is obscure.

## navet

In France, navet is the word for any type of turnip, but it is the specific name for small, immature turnips, available in spring and summer. These are white, tinged with red and more delicate in flavour than winter turnips. Navets generally don't need to be peeled before cooking. If the leaves are perky and bright green, they are also edible—sauté them in a little butter with garlic and black pepper.

## nectar

A thick, sweetened juice made from fruit, although some may have water added. Nectars are most commonly made from peaches, apricots, pears, blackcurrants, guavas or sour cherries. Nectar also refers to the sugary liquid produced by flowers and collected by bees. The bees ingest the nectar, which is then chemically transformed and regurgitated as honey.

## nectarine

A smooth-skinned stone fruit similar to, but distinctively different in flavour to, its relative the peach. How the nectarine originated is a mystery: peach trees sometimes bear nectarines, and vice versa. The modern fruit is mainly cultivated in California, where over 150 varieties grow. Their colour ranges from silvery white or yellowy orange to pinkish red. The white-fleshed varieties are considered the best and are usually the most expensive. Nectarines can be used in recipes instead of peaches, although are best eaten fresh out of hand.

### AMARETTI-STUFFED NECTARINES

*Put 100 g amaretti biscuits in a plastic bag and crush with a rolling pin. Put in a bowl with 4 tablespoons mascarpone. Cut 4 firm, ripe nectarines in half, remove the stones and put in an ovenproof dish. Pile the biscuits into the nectarine cavities. Sprinkle with 1 tablespoon brown sugar and bake at 180°C for 8–10 minutes. Serve with mascarpone. Serves 4.*

## nettle

Despite its reputation as a stinging weed, the nettle is edible. The stings are caused by little hairs on the leaves, which lose their irritating properties when cooked. It's rare to buy nettles commercially, so if picking them from the wild, ensure they aren't from areas that have been sprayed with pesticides. Wear gloves and choose plants with small leaves and soft stems. Prepare in the same way as spinach and use in soups, braise with onions or use to stuff ravioli.

## New Zealand food

New Zealand is an island group to the southeast of Australia, bordered by the South Pacific Ocean and the Tasman Sea. The Maoris, who arrived by canoe from Polynesia in the ninth century, were the first inhabitants and they found a rich source of food on the land and in the sea. They also brought foods such as taro and kumera, a type of sweet potato. Cooking was done in a large pit, called a *hangi*, which was lined with hot stones and covered with vegetation. This method of cooking is still used today, mainly for ceremonial occasions and as a tourist attraction. The original settlers were of English, Irish and Scottish stock so traditional foods of those countries were produced.

Today, New Zealand is a farming and fishing country. Sheep and dairy-related products dominated local food consumption and trade export in the twentieth century. Lamb, beef, chicken, duck, venison and the Maori delicacy, mutton bird, are all readily available. Seafood is plentiful including blue cod, snapper, hoki, orange roughy, toheroa (a type of clam), salmon, whitebait, which are often made into whitebait fritters, green-lipped mussels, bluff oysters and crayfish.

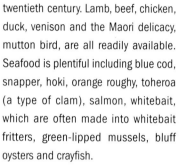

Common fruit include the kiwi fruit and tamarillo, which were found to grow well in New Zealand and exported worldwide, as well as apples. Pavlova, a much-loved meringue dessert that New Zealand claims as its own, as does Australia, is popular.

■ *See also* **kiwi fruit, pavlova, sweet potato**

*From top: New Zealand dairy products, green-lipped mussels with garlic and herb butter.*

## niçoise salad

A speciality of southern France, which typically may include quartered tomatoes, black olives, tuna tinned in oil, anchovies, boiled potatoes, boiled egg quarters, sliced green pepper, raw onion, and broad or green beans dressed with *pissala*, anchovies pounded with oil. The debate as to what exactly is typical is an ongoing one—purists would say that niçoise is an uncooked salad, except for the hard-boiled egg.

The term *à la niçoise* refers to dishes that are typical of Nice and the surrounding region. This type of cooking includes both hot and cold dishes and these usually contain tomatoes, black olives, anchovies and garlic.

*Also known as — salade niçoise*

A type of pasta made from flour, water and sometimes egg, the word noodle can be used to describe hundreds of different types used in cuisines around the world. Noodles are important to Asian cuisine, especially to China and Japan, and long egg noodles are eaten with stews in Eastern Europe. In Asia, noodles may be served at main meals along with other dishes or eaten as a snack, especially served in soupy broths. Short lengths of noodle may be cooked in soup or the pasta may be filled to make wontons (this was probably the original form that noodles took).

In Asia, noodles are not only a staple but a symbol of longevity. Chinese e-fu noodles are eaten on special occasions such as birthdays and at New Year. Chinese noodles, unlike pasta and Japanese noodles, are very long and are never cut—this would only bring bad luck. There is also some symbolism attached to the noodle in Japan, especially soba, which are eaten on New Year's Eve and special

## SLURPING

*In Asia, noodles are eaten by sucking the noodle up, as noisily as possible, between the lips. The slurping oxygenates the hot soup liquid and so cools it. Soup stocks are always served boiling and need to be cooled in this manner as you eat them, although it could be said that the slurp is also an exuberant sign of enjoyment.*

## COOKING

*Some noodles need to be softened in boiling water; others are cooked in water or fried, so always refer to the instructions on the packet. Cook noodles in plenty of boiling water and drain well.*

*If cooking small or individual portions of fresh noodles, put them in a sieve and dunk them in a saucepan of boiling water. This is a good method for quick-cooking noodles, such as egg noodles or rice noodles, and keeps them separated for individual servings.*

*Cold noodles can be tossed in a little oil to keep them from sticking and then reheated in boiling water.*

occasions. Japanese noodles are not made from rice, as it is too precious a commodity. Instead they are made from buckwheat and/or wheat.

Choose noodles that are appropriate to the recipe if they are not specified exactly. Thin, delicate rice vermicelli will soak up Vietnamese flavours well but thick egg noodles won't. Noodles for use in soups must be robust enough to pick up without breaking and falling back into the soup. Noodles can now be bought pre-cooked to various stages.

## PORK NOODLE SOUP

*Cook 200 g dried egg noodles and drain well. Heat 1.5 litres chicken stock in a saucepan with 8 thin slices ginger and 4 sliced spring onions. Bring to the boil, then add 200 g chopped bok choy. Divide the noodles among 4 large bowls, pour in the stock and then top each bowl with a drizzle of soy sauce, a drizzle of hoisin and a few slices of sliced Chinese barbecued pork. Garnish with a few coriander leaves. Serves 4.*

**See also  Chinese food, Japanese food**

Noodles are eaten by many of the world's cultures and they can be made from many different ingredients, from rice and wheat to vegetable starches.

## ARROWROOT NOODLES

Sold in bundles, these need to be softened in hot water before use and are used in soups and desserts.

*Arrowroot noodles*

## RESHTEH

Middle Eastern egg noodle, hand cut into either ribbons or fine noodles like vermicelli. Eaten daily and also on special occasions such as New Year. Like Asian noodles, they have a significance because of their shape and length. *Sha'riyya* is the name given to a vermicelli noodle eaten in North Africa.

*Reshteh*

## SWEET POTATO NOODLES

Korean *dang myan* are thin, wiry grey noodles when raw and need to be soaked to soften them. They have a fairly chewy texture when cooked and are used for *chapchae*. A version is also eaten in some areas of China.

*Sweet potato noodles*

*Shiratake noodles*

*European noodles*

*Bean thread noodles*

## BEAN THREAD NOODLES

Also known as cellophane, glass or jelly noodles, these are translucent, vary in thickness and are popular in China and Vietnam. They are usually made from mung bean starch and become transparent when cooked. Use in the same way as rice stick noodles although when cooked their texture is never as soft as rice noodles.

## EUROPEAN NOODLES

These vary in shape and size and are eaten with stews, in soups and with meat dishes. Spätzle are made by pressing noodle mixture through a sieve or scraping the dough into boiling water. Egg noodles are available dried and some may be coloured with spinach. Short soup noodles are also available dried for use in Jewish dishes such as chicken noodle soup.

## SHIRATAKE

Also known as devil's tongue noodles, these are thin strands of jelly-like konnyaku, made from the tuber of an Asian plant, and widely used in sukiyaki. Not considered true noodles by the Japanese, they are usually sold packaged in liquid—they don't need to be cooked, just drop into hot liquid. Shiratake means 'white waterfall'.

## BUCKWHEAT NOODLES

These include Japanese soba noodles, which are sold fresh and dried and are made from buckwheat or a mixture of buckwheat and wheat flour. They are eaten cold or in soups. *Chasoba* are made from buckwheat and green tea. Buckwheat noodles are also eaten cold in soups in Korea where they are called *naeng myun*.

*Buckwheat noodles*

## EGG NOODLES

In China, these are sold fresh and dried in skeins and clusters and called *dan mian*. They are made from wheat flour and duck or hen eggs and used in soups and stir-fries. *E-fu* noodles are pressed into a cake and need to be boiled to soften. Hokkien noodles are precooked and just need to be heated. In Japan, egg noodles such as ramen are used in soups. Yakisoba noodles can be stir-fried with vegetables and meat. In Thailand and Malaysia, egg noodles are *mee*, in the Philippines, *pancit mami* and in Vietnam, *mi*.

*Egg noodles*

*Egg noodles*

## WHEAT FLOUR NOODLES

Chinese wheat noodles, *mian*, can be dried in flat, long thin strands, wrapped in skeins or fresh, as in wheat Shanghai noodles. They are used in soups and stir-fries. Japanese wheat noodles include udon, which are round or square plump noodles used in soups or eaten cold with a dipping sauce. Somen are very thin and often served chilled. Both are sold fresh and dried. *Hiyamugi* are thin noodles eaten cold with a dipping sauce. Wheat noodles in the Philippines are called *miswa*, in Korea, *gooksu* and in Thailand and Malaysia, *mee*.

*Wheat flour noodles*

*Rice noodles*

*Bean curd noodles*

## RICE NOODLES

Dried noodles such as rice stick and vermicelli are made from rice powder and are popular in China and Vietnam. These are softened in hot water, then used in soups, stir-fries or deep-fried until crispy. Thicker rice sticks are used in Thailand for *pad Thai*. Fresh rice noodles may be shaped in sheets, ribbons or long, round strands, such as laksa noodles. Fresh noodles are best eaten the day they are made. Steam to make them more pliable before use. Folded noodles are rolled around other ingredients or cut into ribbons.

*Harusame*

## HARUSAME

Harusame, meaning 'spring rain', are noodles made from potato and corn starches and sometimes mung bean or soy bean starch and are not considered true noodles by the Japanese. They are often used for sukiyaki and shabu shabu. Sold dried in small packets, these are also called salad noodles.

## BEAN CURD NOODLES

Also called soya noodles, these are made from pressed bean curd cut into ribbons. They are thin and brown and are usually used in cold dishes. These are eaten in China and also Japan. Bean curd noodles are available both plain and with flavourings such as soy sauce added.

# nougat

A sweetmeat made from sugar, honey and nuts, generally made by beating a paste of sugar, glucose syrup and honey to which egg whites and gelatine are added. Chopped nuts such as almonds, pistachios, walnuts and hazelnuts are mixed in and then the paste is spread into wooden frames to set. Nougat can be soft or hard and chewy depending on the preparation: white nougat is made with egg whites and is softer than brown nougat, which is made from caramelized sugar syrup and honey.

Nougat is a speciality of southeastern France, especially the region of Montélimar, and is one of the traditional '13 Christmas desserts' given there at Christmas. *Torrone* is the Italian version, usually packed with whole almonds, and in Spain, many different versions of *turrón* are eaten at Christmas and Easter. Nougat is an ancient food; its origins can be traced back to early Arab sweetmeats.

# nougatine — see praline

# nuts

Usually a fruit with an outer shell that encases an edible kernel, also called a nut. Their shells vary from very hard to brittle or soft. Nutritionally, nuts and seeds are high in fat and calories, but as they are of plant origin they contain no cholesterol. All nuts provide dietary fibre, with the amount in brazil nuts being particularly high. Some nuts are not true nuts—the peanut is a legume; the chufa, a tuber.

Nuts are great for eating fresh, chopped and sprinkled on breakfast cereal and in a wide variety of sweet and savoury dishes. The flavour of some nuts is improved when they are toasted, particularly pine nuts. In some countries like France, Italy, Turkey and China where nut trees are prolific they are also ground to make nut flours, pressed to extract their oils and incorporated in various savoury dishes.

## BUYING

*It is preferable to buy nuts with their shells on, particularly if they are to be stored, as the shell protects the nuts from turning rancid.*

*Buy nuts that feel heavy for their weight and avoid those that rattle. This usually means that the nut inside has dried up and shrunk.*

*Buy nuts in sealed bags or airtight containers rather than loose, and buy from a supplier that has a rapid turnover to ensure their freshness.*

## STORAGE

*Store nuts in their shells in an airtight container away from heat, sunlight and moisture. Store unopened packets of shelled nuts in an airtight container at room temperature. Once opened, transfer the nuts to an airtight container and keep in a cool, dark place.*

*For longer-term storage, keep nuts in the fridge for about 4 months or freeze them for 6 months.*

*Clockwise from bottom left to centre: flaked almonds; almonds; almonds in shells; macadamia nuts; pecan nuts in shells; pecan nuts; pistachio nuts; hazelnuts; hazelnuts in shells.*

## COOKING

*To remove the skin of shelled nuts, blanch (almonds and pistachios) or roast (hazelnuts) before rubbing the skins off.*

*Nuts are more easily chopped if they are warm and moist. If very hard, soak in boiling water for 2–3 minutes.*

*Cracking open walnuts*

▥ **See also  almond, brazil nut, candlenut, cashew nut, chestnuts, hazelnut, macadamia nut, pecan nut, pine nut, pistachio nut, walnut**

A nutritional cereal grain that grows in cool, wet climates and provides food for both humans and animals. Oats are rich in soluble fibre and they contain more protein and fat than other cereals. In cooking, oats are most commonly eaten at breakfast time as porridge, in muesli and granola mixtures, or they may be added to muffins, cookies, crêpes, cakes and bread. Oats are also used in beers and other beverages. Particularly in Scottish cooking, they are used frequently in stuffings, to thicken soups and stews, in Athol Brose, a traditional Scottish dish of oats and honey, in oatcakes and in haggis.

*From left: Duchy oaten biscuits, oat flour, groats.*

*Groats*

*Oat flakes*

*Oat flour*

*Oat bran*

## TYPES OF OATS

| | |
|---|---|
| **Oatmeal** | Cut or ground grain separated into sizes by sieving. Available in various grades such as pinhead, rough, medium rough, medium fine and superfine. |
| **Groats** | Crushed dehusked oats. |
| **Oat (porridge, rolled) flakes** | Pinhead oatmeal that has been steamed and flattened with large rollers. Cooked in two to three times its volume of liquid for 25–30 minutes. Quick-cook rolled oats are oats that have been finely cut, then steamed and rolled into thinner flakes. Their nutritional content is the same as rolled oats, but they cook in about 5 minutes. |
| **Oat flour** | Flour ground from oats. It does not contain gluten and needs to be combined with a wheat flour for use in baked goods that rise, such as breads. |
| **Oat bran** | The outer casing of the oat made up of both germ and bran. These are removed when oat flour is made. Oat bran is high in soluble fibre and can be mixed with rolled oats in porridge or added to flour used in baked goods. |

### ATHOL BROSE

*Whip 250 ml double cream until it reaches soft peaks, then stir in 50 ml whisky, 3 tablespoons honey and 45 g toasted pinhead oatmeal. Divide among 4 small bowls or glasses and serve straight away. Serves 4.*

### STORAGE

*Oats and oat products are high in oils, so become rancid quickly. Store in a cool place for up to 3 weeks. Rolled oats that have been toasted last longer and can be stored for up to 9 months.*

# octopus

A relation of the squid and cuttlefish found in warm seas worldwide. The octopus has eight tentacles and its curved and parrot-like mouth is found underneath its body along with an ink sac, which squirts out indelible black ink when the octopus is threatened. While the ink sac should be removed before cooking, the ink can be used in cooking and makes great pasta and a dramatic black risotto. Larger octopus tend to be tough—tenderize before cooking by pounding with a wooden mallet, blanching or freezing. Small or baby octopus are more tender and need neither beating nor blanching before cooking. Octopus can be grilled, poached, sautéed, fried or steamed. Cooking it slowly over low heat makes the flesh more tender. Larger octopus should be simmered gently for about 60 to 90 minutes. Baby octopus are perfect for barbecuing. Fresh octopus will last for 1 to 2 days in the fridge and for about 3 months in the freezer.

## OCTOPUS SALAD

*Clean 600 g baby octopus, then boil for 10 minutes or until tender. Drain. Mix 4 tablespoons lemon juice, 100 ml olive oil, 1 crushed garlic clove, 2 tablespoons chopped parsley and 1 chopped red chilli in a large bowl. Add the octopus, toss well and leave to marinate for 2 hours. Season to taste. Serve with a mixed leaf salad. Serves 4.*

*See also* **squid**

## PREPARING OCTOPUS

**1** Cut between the head and tentacles, just below the eyes. Remove the beak by pushing it out through the centre of the tentacles.

**2** Cut the eyes from the head by slicing off a small round.

**3** Remove the intestines by pushing them out of the head.

**4** To tenderize, pound the octopus with a wooden mallet for 2–3 minutes, or blanch it in boiling water.

## oeufs à la neige — see île flottante

## oeufs en gelée

Poached eggs served in aspic, usually as a starter or as part of a buffet. To make them, a flavoured jelly (often made using veal stock) is poured into the base of a ramekin, a few herbs are added and a poached egg is placed on top. More jelly is poured on top, decorated with herbs and left to set. The herbs from the base of the ramekin become the decoration when unmoulded. Aspic is best when fat-free—use spotlessly clean utensils, and avoid touching the eggs.

The edible non-muscular parts of slaughtered animals. The name comes from 'off-fall', that which falls off the butchered carcass. Much prized in French, Italian and many Asian cuisines, and feared by others, North American and Australian included.

Types are usually divided into red offal and white offal. Red offal includes heart, tongue, lungs, spleen and kidneys. White offal includes the brains, teats, marrow, testicles, feet, head, tripe, caul and sweetbreads. Most offal is rich in iron, particularly kidneys and liver. It's also rich in vitamin A and folic acid. When buying offal, ensure it is very fresh as it will keep only 1 to 2 days in the fridge. Offal can be frozen but this adversely affects the flavour, texture and appearance.

Some offal, such as heart and tongue, needs long, slow cooking to produce the best results, whereas others such as liver, kidneys and brains should be cooked quickly.

**Also known as — variety meats**

■ *See also* **haggis, marrowbone, tongue, tripe**

## KIDNEYS WITH ROSEMARY

*Strip the leaves from long, sturdy rosemary stalks and skewer through 8 butterflied kidneys. Combine a little olive oil and balsamic vinegar and brush over the kidneys. Season with salt and pepper. Grill for 2–3 minutes each side. Serves 4.*

*Clockwise from bottom left: veal sweetbreads, calf's liver, lamb's kidneys, veal kidneys, calf tongue, ox tongue, lamb's brains.*

## TYPES OF OFFAL

| | |
|---|---|
| **Brains** | Sold as a 'set'. They should be greyish pink, plump and free of spots. Sheep and lamb's brains are the most tender. Brains need to be soaked in cold salted water to remove any blood, then blanched. Best fried in butter. |
| **Kidneys** | Ox and calf's kidneys are multi-lobed; those from the pig and sheep have a single bean-shaped lobe. Buy plump, firm, shiny kidneys that don't smell of ammonia. Remove the membrane and core, then cook quickly and serve while still pink, or cook for a long time, as for a pie filling. |
| **Heart** | Should be bright red and firm. Calf, lamb and chicken hearts are the most popular. Ox heart is tougher and needs to be cooked for several hours. |
| **Tongue** | Buy tongue that has no spots on it. Calf's tongue is the most tender; ox tongue takes longer to cook. Remove skin after cooking and serve hot or cold. |
| **Sweetbread** | Culinary term for the thymus gland of calves, lambs and pigs. Has a delicate flavour and needs to be blanched and cooled to make it firmer and easier to handle. Remove the membrane and grill, sauté, poach or fry. |
| **Tripe** | The stomach of cud-chewing animals such as cows and sheep. Cream in colour and usually sold blanched and bleached. Common varieties are blanket, book and honeycomb. Soak for 10 minutes; then poach, or fry for 10 minutes, or braise for 3 to 4 hours. |
| **Liver** | Calf's liver has the most delicate flavour. It should have a glossy sheen. Remove the membrane or it will shrink when cooked, causing the meat to curl up. Cook liver quickly so it browns on the outside and stays pink in the middle. |
| **Caul (crepinette)** | Fat that surrounds the intestines, used for basting by wrapping it around meat and poultry while it cooks. |

Fats that remain liquid at ambient temperatures. They can be extracted from seeds, nuts and fruit by crushing and pressing, or by using heat or chemicals. Cold-pressed oils and extra virgin olive oil tend to have the best flavour as the more refined oils lose their natural characteristics. Oils can be divided into three categories depending on which fatty acids they contain: saturated, monounsaturated or polyunsaturated. All vegetable oils are cholesterol-free as they are derived from plants.

*All oils contain the same number of calories (45 per teaspoon). Oils marked light refer to the flavour; not the calories.*

*Light and heat cause oils to lose colour and flavour. Store in a cool, dry and dark place. If kept in the fridge, some oils will solidify.*

*Different oils are suitable for different uses. The flavour of good-quality oils is destroyed by heat and they are much better used cold.*

*Oils break down and lose their stability when heated to smoking point—a danger sign is a blue haze coming off the surface of the oil. Each time an oil is used its smoking point is lowered.*

From left: extra virgin olive oil, rapeseed oil (back), sesame seed oil, grapeseed oil, walnut oil.

### Deep-frying

Deep-frying seals the outer surface of food so the exterior is golden and crisp while the interior cooks in the heat of its own steam. Use a deep-fat fryer or a deep heavy saucepan. Fill the saucepan one-third full and heat the oil—never leave the saucepan unattended. Dry the food thoroughly to prevent the oil from 'spitting', and cook the food in batches to maintain the oil temperature.

Certain recipes require the oil to be at a certain temperature. Test the oil with a thermometer or drop a cube of white bread into the hot oil and time how long it takes to turn brown. At 160°C, the bread will take 30 seconds to brown, at 170°C it will take 20 seconds, at 180°C it will take 15 seconds and at 190°C it will take 10 seconds.

*Oil for frying can be re-used once or twice if it is filtered after use and used for the same thing each time (oil used for frying fish will take on a 'fishy' flavour).*

*Oil for deep-frying and frying should have a high smoking point and be flavourless or at least unobtrusive. These include peanut and olive oil.*

*Salad dressings should be made from appropriately flavoured oils as they are an intrinsic part of the recipe—strong extra virgin olive oils, while they may be good quality, can overwhelm a delicate salad.*

*Oils like walnut, pumpkin seed and pistachio are not suitable for frying but can be used as a seasoning on dishes like steamed fish, risottos and mashes.*

### OLIVE OIL

*Virgin olive oil is made by crushing the flesh of olives and 'cold pressing' it to extract the oil. The various grades of olive oils are supervised by the EU in Europe, and the IOOC in the USA. Their names, which appear on the label, are: 'extra virgin', meaning an olive oil of outstanding flavour and aroma with a maximum acidity of 1 per cent; 'virgin', with an acidity no higher than 1.5 per cent; and 'olive oil' (in America and Australia, 'pure olive oil'), a refined oil made by hot pressing—often the 'cake' of cold-pressed olives is hot pressed, then refined to produce this. 'Light' or 'extra light' denotes a refined oil with a little less extra virgin olive oil added, and has nothing to do with the fat content. The colour of olive oil is governed by the type of olive used and does not indicate quality. Olive oil is best stored in dark-coloured glass bottles or in tins.*

■ *See also* **fat**

*Grapeseed*

*Hazelnut*

*Macadamia*

*Peanut*

*Vegetable*

## TYPES OF OILS

| | |
|---|---|
| **Almond** | Light-coloured oil with a neutral flavour. Use for baking as it will not add flavour. |
| **Coconut** | Contains 90 per cent saturated fat, but is good for frying as it contains natural lecithin, which makes it non-stick. |
| **Corn** | Deep gold coloured with a pronounced flavour, which makes it unpleasant when cold but useful for all other methods of cooking. Its smoking point is 210°C. |
| **Grapeseed** | No real flavour, pale in colour with a high smoking point of 230°C, so it is very good for deep-frying. |
| **Hazelnut** | Monounsaturated oil with a delicate flavour. Use cold as a dressing or seasoning. Hazelnut oil goes well with raspberry vinegar. Must be stored in a cool, dark place. |
| **Macadamia** | Pale, delicate oil, ideal for salad dressings. |
| **Olive** | Virgin and extra virgin have a strong flavour and are best used for dressings. Refined olive oils are best for cooking. |
| **Palm** | Called dende oil in Africa, where the oil palm is native. Palm oil is red. Commercially it is used as an ingredient in ice creams and margarines. |
| **Peanut (groundnut)** | Refined peanut oil has no peanut flavour but cold-pressed varieties do. Can tolerate high heat so is ideal for deep-frying. Good in salad dressings and mayonnaise. |
| **Pine nut** | A light-brown oil, excellent in vinaigrettes and as a dipping oil for vegetables such as artichokes. It is very expensive. |
| **Pistachio** | Bright-green oil used mainly for dressings. |
| **Poppy seed** | Flavourless oil, used mainly in baking. |
| **Rapeseed (canola, colza)** | Common oil with a bland flavour, useful for frying and baking. Lower in saturated fats than other oils. |
| **Sesame seed** | Available as a light-yellow oil with a medium flavour or a dark-brown oil with a strong flavour. Use sparingly as the flavour is strong. Good for stir-fries. |
| **Soya bean** | Good all-purpose oil with a neutral flavour, often used in blends. Its smoking point is 210°C; it keeps very well. |
| **Sunflower** | A good all-purpose oil, which is high in polyunsaturated fat and has a neutral flavour and light texture. Has a smoking point of 200°C. |
| **Vegetable** | A blended oil, which may contain a number of different oils such as cottonseed. |
| **Walnut** | A polyunsaturated oil with a good walnut flavour. Use cold as a dressing. It goes well with cider vinegar. |

*Olive*

*Rapeseed*

*Walnut*

# okra

A slender, five-sided pod that contains numerous white seeds. When young, okra is eaten as a vegetable; the older pods are usually dried, then powdered and used as a flavouring. When cooked, okra releases a sticky, gelatinous substance, which serves to thicken stews and soups such as the Cajun and Creole dish, gumbo. Okra is also used extensively in India, the Caribbean, Southeast Asia and the Middle East. It can also be eaten raw in salads or blanched, then dressed in a vinaigrette.

Buy pods that are tender and healthy green in colour. They should snap rather than bend and should be no more than 10 cm long. If too ripe, the pod will feel very sticky. To prepare, gently scrub with paper towel or a vegetable brush. Rinse and drain, then slice off the top and tail. If using as a thickener, blanch whole first, then slice and add to the dish about 10 minutes before the end of cooking. In some recipes, the pod is used whole, thus preventing the release of the sticky substances within.

**Okra goes with — aubergine, onion, pepper, tomato**
**Also known as — bhindi, gumbo, ladies' fingers**

# olive

The fruit of the olive tree, an ancient tree whose origins lie in the eastern Mediterranean, most likely Phoenicia (present day Lebanon), and which was first cultivated some 3,000 years ago for fruit and oil, eaten and burnt in lamps. Today, olives are still grown around the Mediterranean and, increasingly, in North and South America and Australia.

Unless left in the sun to ripen and cure naturally, olives must be treated to rid them of their bitterness. There are hundreds of varieties of olives grown around the world, often, confusingly, with different regional names for the same variety.

To marinate olives, fill jars with olives, chopped garlic, chillies and thyme sprigs, then fill with olive oil. Store in the fridge.

## CURING OLIVES

*Green olives are cured by repeated soaking and rinsing in water over many months; immersing in brine for up to 6 months; cracking the pit and immersing in brine for 1 month; or chemically by immersing in lye (caustic soda). Black olives, which are riper and less bitter, can be cured in the same way; left in the sun to dry cure; dry-cured in salt; or partially dried and stored in oil.*

## CURING OLIVES

From left: stuffed, Ligurian, Spanish Sevillana

**Green olives**

Young olives picked green and cured. Herbs, spices, and flavourings such as fennel and chilli can be added to the curing liquid to add flavour. Green olives are also stuffed, most notably with anchovies, almonds or pimientos. Varieties include Ligurian, Picholine, Cerignola, Sevillana and Toscana.

**Black olives**

Olives picked half ripe (purple) or fully ripe (black) and cured. Very black-looking pitted olives in brine are green olives cured in lye and artificially blackened, either with bubbled oxygen or ferrous glucamate. Varieties include kalamata, Gaeta, Nyons and Niçoise.

From left: dried salted, kalamata, Gaeta

There are many versions, perhaps the most typical being a savoury French omelette made from lightly beaten eggs, cooked in a frying pan until just firm. Some omelettes are folded around fillings like cheese, ham, tomatoes or mushrooms; others have flavourings like herbs, cooked spinach or bacon mixed in with the raw eggs. Sweet omelettes are usually filled with poached fruits or jam, sprinkled with sugar and then glazed in the oven or under the grill.

*See also* **eggah, frittata, tortilla**

## SPRING ONION AND DOLCELATTE OMELETTE

*Lightly beat 8 eggs, then add 1 tablespoon milk and season. Heat 25 g butter in a nonstick frying pan. Add half the eggs and stir with a fork, drawing edges to the centre as soon as they begin to set. Add 2 chopped spring onions and 60 g cubed dolcelatte cheese. Fold into thirds. Repeat with remaining mixture. Serves 2.*

One of the most important ingredients in the kitchen, onions are used in just about every nation's cuisine, adding a depth of flavour to dishes, although they are a delicious vegetable in their own right. Onions grow as single bulbs (globe) or in clumps (aggregate), though most onions sold in the West are single bulbs. They are sold as either dry onions or green onions. Dry onions are left in the ground to mature where they develop a papery brown skin; green (spring or salad) onions are pulled out while young and the bulb is still small. Onions are also sold dried, as flakes, in a powder-like onion salt or as fried flakes.

*See also* **shallot, spring onions**

## TYPES OF ONIONS

**Yellow** — The most common, and available year round. Varieties include a sweet onion called vidalia, Spanish onions, pickling onions and cipolline, small flat onions.

**White** — Generally mild and slightly sweet. Can be used for cooking or salads. Pearl onions are small white onions, which are ideal for pickling but can also be added whole to stews and casseroles.

**Red** — Delicious in salads, adding both flavour and colour. Good for barbecues and grilling. When cooked, red onions have less flavour than other varieties, although they can be slightly sweeter.

### STORAGE

*Store in a cool, dark place, but not in the fridge as their strong odour will permeate into other foods. If stored correctly, they (except red and spring onions) will keep for up to 2 months.*

### COOKING

*Slicing onions causes the cell walls to rupture, releasing the sulphurous contents. When mixed with air, these turn into allyl sulphate, which irritates the eyes.*

*To remove the smell of onions from your hands, rub them with lemon juice or vinegar.*

*If frying onions, don't chop them in the food processor as they release too much liquid and will steam rather than fry. To bring out their sweet flavour, sweat them gently over low heat without letting them brown.*

# orange

Any one of a number of varieties of a citrus fruit, native to Southeast Asia, now widely cultivated, especially in temperate climes. There are both bitter and sweet varieties, as well as many hybrids such as ortaniques. Sweet oranges are eaten fresh, used in sorbets and granitas, squeezed for their juice, or their aromatic rind can be used in baking or added to meat and fish stews and soups. Bitter oranges are usually cooked and used in marmalades or dishes such as duck à l'orange, used for their oils or to make orange flower water, made from a distillation of the blossoms. Buy oranges that feel heavy and have tight skin and store at room temperature for a day or so, then store in the fridge after this time.

## COOKING

*If using the zest in cooking, scrub, wash and dry the orange first. Grate the zest, but make sure you don't remove the bitter white pith, or use a zester to scrape down the side of the orange. Use a pastry brush to brush all the loose bits from inside and outside of the grater.*

*If using the zest in a sweet dish, rub a sugar cube over the orange before grating it to extract the oils.*

*Use a sharp knife or vegetable peeler to slice off pieces of orange zest, then cut it into fine strips and use these as decoration. Blanch the strips to make them more tender, if you prefer.*

## CARROT AND ORANGE SALAD

**Combine 2 grated carrots with the segments of 2 oranges. Mix in ½ sliced red onion, 90 g pitted black olives and 2 tablespoons chopped fresh coriander. Combine 2 tablespoons orange juice with 3 tablespoons olive oil, add to the salad and mix well. Serves 6.**

## SEGMENTING ORANGES

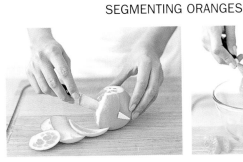

1  *Cut a thin slice from each end of the orange. Slice off skin and pith following the curve of the fruit.*

2  *Slice down the side of each segment to free it from its membrane.*

## TYPES OF ORANGES

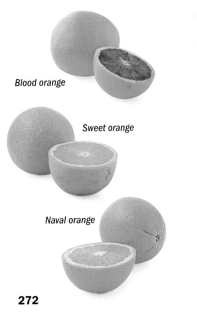

Blood orange

Sweet orange

Naval orange

**Blood**  These have lots of red pigment in the flesh and skin, which gives the appearance of blood. They are rich, sweet and aromatic, but their season is short.

**Sweet**  Including Valencia, these have smoother, firmer skin than the navel and more seeds. Ideal for juicing.

**Navel**  Characterized by a navel-like depression at its base. It has a slightly pebbly skin and bright-orange colour and is nearly always seedless. Ideal for desserts or eating fresh.

**Bitter**  Including Seville, these are ideal for marmalade and jellies. They have a thick rind, tough membrane and lots of seeds. The aromatic oils extracted from the skin are used to make Grand Marnier, Cointreau and Curaçao.

The fastest-growing food segment in Europe and America. Organic food is cultivated and processed without the use of any chemicals, including fertilizers, pesticides (in some cases, permission may be sought to use botanical pesticides under restricted conditions), artificial colourings, flavourings and additives. The primary strategy of organic farmers is to prevent disease by building healthy soils as healthy plants are better able to resist disease and insects.

Theoretically organic food should taste better as it has not been artificially encouraged to grow faster or bigger. This is not always the case, nor is it the point for many who seek out organic food. The major advantage for them is sustainability: farming and manufacturing practices that do not permanently and irreversibly harm the environment. Organic food is more expensive than non-organic because it must meet strict regulations, so generally, organic farming is more management and labour intensive and the farms tend to be smaller.

### IS IT ORGANIC?

*It isn't possible to tell by looking at a product if it is organic or not. Most products rely on registered logos, symbols and trademarks but these are not always reliable or honest. It is best to check if the food in question is certified by one of the many certifying bodies that oversee farming, manufacture and even the retailing of organic foods.*

### OSSO BUCO

*Roll 12 pieces veal shank in seasoned flour. Heat 2 tablespoons olive oil in a casserole dish, add veal and brown. Add 1 chopped garlic clove, 250 ml white wine, 1 bay leaf and a pinch of allspice. Add the veal shanks and cook for 45 minutes. Remove shanks, add 2 teaspoons grated lemon zest and 4 tablespoons chopped parsley. Season; pour over veal. Serves 4.*

A classic Italian veal stew originally from Milan, and traditionally made from the hind leg of a milk-fed calf chopped into rounds and braised in white wine, olive oil, onions, garlic and lemon rind. Tomatoes, which are used in most recipes today, are not traditional to *osso buco alla milanese* but are used elsewhere. Osso buco is served with *risotto alla milanese* and traditional recipes sprinkle gremolata over to serve. Its name derives from the literal translation of the Italian 'bone with a hole', marrowbone.

The ostrich is a large flightless bird from Africa. The ostrich is farmed in many countries for its feathers, skin and meat. Its meat is becoming increasingly popular and is sometimes compared to lean beef. Ostrich can be used instead of beef or veal in many recipes and is particularly good for stir-frying. In South Africa it is dried and used to make biltong. The large ostrich eggs can also be used.

## oyster

Bivalve molluscs that grow, wild or farmed, on coastlines around the world. Of particular interest are: the European oyster (known as a 'native' in Britain), which has a round flat shell; the Portuguese, an oyster with a concave whitish-brown shell, now thought to be the same as the Pacific oyster; the greyish shelled American oyster; and the Sydney rock oyster.

Oysters are often named for their place of origin—Breton, Colchester and Sydney. The old rule of eating them only when there is an 'r' in the month applies only to the European oyster in Northern Europe. These spawn inside the shell, which makes the flesh, full of baby shells, very gritty. Oyster farming is a highly skilled occupation and today, when most oysters are cultivated, oyster lovers rely heavily on the oyster farmer for both flavour and safety. Ideally, an oyster should be bought live, with the shell closed. In this state, it should be heavy and full of water. If buying an open oyster, prick the cilla (little hairs around the edge of the flesh): it should retract if the oyster is alive. Look for plump, glossy oysters that smell fresh. Unopened, oysters can be kept in the fridge for up to 1 week. If opened, store in their liquid and eat within 24 hours.

*Pacific oyster*

*Sydney rock oyster*

### COOKING

*Though oysters are most often served raw, they can also be cooked. Shuck and add to stews or soups, leave in the shell and top with creamy sauces, or grill or steam dressed with Asian flavours. Shucked oysters can also be deep-fried, shallow-fried and poached and are traditionally used in steak pies or to stuff carpetbag steaks. Be careful when combining oysters with spirits as they may cause the oyster flesh to harden inside the gut, causing discomfort.*

*Top the oysters with a mixture of chopped shallots, chilli, rocket and a little white wine vinegar and olive oil.*

### SHUCKING OYSTERS

*When shucking (opening) oysters, use a proper oyster knife, as an ordinary knife may break or slip and cut you. Use a knife with a stainless steel blade to avoid transferring the taste of metal to the oysters.*

1 *Hold the oyster in a cloth, rounded side down. Insert a knife between the two shells, near the hinge.*

2 *Twist the knife to separate the shells. Sever the muscle that connects the oyster to the shell.*

3 *Slide the knife blade underneath the oyster to detach it from the shell.*

## oyster sauce

Widely used in Chinese cooking, oyster sauce is a thick, richly flavoured brown sauce made of dried oysters, brine and soy sauce. Oyster sauce imparts colour and a rich, salty flavour to stir-fries and braised dishes without overpowering their natural flavours. It is sold in bottles and once opened should be refrigerated. It is also used as a table condiment. When buying oyster sauce, check the ingredients list to ensure it contains 'premium oyster extract' rather than an imitation.

# p

An ancient dish based on rice, which was brought to Spain from Asia by the Arabs, and cooked in a pan also called a paella (sometimes paellera), a word of Roman origin. The ingredients, strictly adhered to only in and around Valencia (where the definitive paella is made), include chicken, rabbit or pork, lima and butter beans, snails, tomatoes, paprika and saffron. Today, with seafood replacing most of the meat (except chicken) it has become the emblematic Spanish dish. Traditionally cooked outdoors, over a wood fire, by men.

## palm sugar

A dark, unrefined sugar obtained from the sap of palmyra or sugar palm trees. The sap is collected from the trees, boiled until it turns into a thick, dark syrup, then poured into moulds where it dries to form dense, heavy cakes. Palm sugar is widely used in Southeast Asian dishes, not only in sweet dishes but to balance the flavours in savoury dishes. It can also be used as a sugar alternative. The easiest way to use it is to shave the sugar off the cake with a sharp knife. Buy in blocks or in jars from Asian shops. If unavailable, any full-flavoured brown sugar can be used as a substitute.

**Also known as — gula jawa, gula melaka**

### STICKY BLACK RICE

*Soak 200 g black glutinous rice in cold water for 6 hours, or overnight. Rinse the rice, then put in a pan with 100 g palm sugar, 800 ml water and 400 ml coconut milk. Bring to the boil, then simmer for 1½–2 hours, or until soft. Stir in the juice of 1 lime and pour over 2 tablespoons coconut cream. Serves 6.*

## palmiers

A sweet, crispy pastry made by sprinkling puff pastry with sugar, which is then folded, cut into slices and rolled out. These expand into heart shapes as they cook and the pastry bakes until golden brown and caramelized. Palmiers may be served with tea or coffee or as a basis for a dessert with whipped cream and strawberries, or with ice cream or sorbet.

**Also known as — palm leaves**

275

# pan bagnat

A Provençal sandwich, which is a speciality of Nice, originally made by tossing pieces of stale bread into a niçoise salad to soak up the juices and flavours. Today the technique for making it is reversed: a cut is made into a loaf or bread roll, some of the bread is removed, the cut slices are rubbed with garlic and the hole is filled with salad. Pan bagnat makes an ideal picnic food—in the same way you can fill a whole French loaf, seal it in foil and then slice on arrival.

**Also known as — pan bagna**

### PAN BAGNAT

*Take 1 large flattish roll, slice in half, without separating the halves, and remove some of the dough. Rub the inside with half a garlic clove and drizzle with a little olive oil. Fill with slices of tomato, black olives, cucumber, hard-boiled egg and anchovies or tuna. Drizzle with a little oil and season well. Close the roll and leave in a cool dark place under a weight for a while to allow the flavours to mingle.*

# pancake

A pancake can be one of many things. Some are large and crêpe-like, made from a thin batter of water, flour and eggs, and often served sprinkled with lemon juice and sugar or folded or rolled around a filling of ice cream, fruit or a savoury mixture. Others are more like drop scones, made from a thick batter and served in a stack with maple syrup. Pancakes are traditionally served on Shrove Tuesday to celebrate renewal, family life and hopes for future good fortune and happiness.

# pancetta

Italian cured belly pork, a similar cut to streaky bacon, but cured with salt and spices. Pancetta can be bought pre-sliced or diced from supermarkets, or it can be cut as needed if bought from the delicatessen. Pancetta is made either as *pancetta stesa*, which is the whole piece of meat, or *pancetta arrotolata*, which is rolled and occasionally smoked with pepper and cloves.

■ *See also* **bacon**

### PANCETTA AND CABBAGE SOUP

*Heat 50 g butter in a frying pan, then fry 1 finely chopped onion, 1 crushed garlic clove, 2 tablespoons chopped parsley and 200 g cubed pancetta until soft and gold in colour. Add 2 sliced celery stalks, 2 sliced carrots, 1 teaspoon tomato purée and a 400 g tin chopped tomatoes. Stir ingredients together, then add 2 litres chicken stock and bring to the boil. Simmer for 1¾ hours, then add 150 g soup pasta and cook for 5 minutes. Add ½ shredded savoy cabbage and 200 g peas and cook for another 2 minutes. Taste for seasoning. To serve, sprinkle grated Parmesan over the soup. Serves 6.*

## PANCOTTO

*Fry 2 finely chopped onions in a little olive oil for 5 minutes. Add 2 crushed garlic cloves, 12 ripe, peeled, chopped tomatoes, a sprig of basil and 800 ml chicken stock. Bring to the boil, then simmer for 15–20 minutes. Season, then stir in 200 g cubed, day-old Italian bread, crusts removed. Add 500 ml water, cover and sit for 30 minutes. Whisk to break up bread pieces. Serves 4.*

Translated from the Italian meaning 'cooked bread', pancotto is a rustic soup whose ingredients vary regionally but always includes bread. In northern Italy, the soup includes butter and onions; herbs are added in areas where they are abundant; and in the South, tomatoes are added. The Tuscan version is called *pappa al pomodoro*.

Long, flat, emerald-green pandanus leaves are used for their colour and fragrance and as a food container—which also imparts flavour—in Southeast Asian cooking, particularly in Indonesia and Malaysia. The leaves are crushed and added to dishes such as rice or curries during cooking or tied in a knot so they fit easily into the pot, then removed before the dish is served. Another way to impart the appealing fragrance is to wrap the leaves around pieces of meat or fish whilst marinating or grilling. For colouring (Malaysian and Indonesian sweets for example), the leaves are boiled and the colour extracted. Pandanus leaves are sold in bundles and are available both dried and frozen. Dried ones lack the intensity of flavour and the frozen leaf is much less fragranced.

Pandanus leaf essence, called *bai toey* in Indonesia, is a brilliantly coloured fragrant flavouring used in cakes and sweet dishes. Vanilla extract is an acceptable substitute in sweet dishes.

***Also known as — kewra, pandan, screwpine***

A speciality bread-like cake from Milan, originally known as *panettone di Milano*, now eaten all over Italy during Christmas and Easter. Easily recognized by its tall, large cylindrical shape (panettone means 'big bread'), it is made from a raised dough enriched with egg yolks, which also gives it a soft yellow colour, and contains raisins, candied orange and lemon peel. Panettone can be made in individual portions or in one large cake and some may be coated with or contain chocolate. Panettone can be eaten for breakfast with coffee or it may be served as a dessert with liqueur wine.

**277**

## panforte

Siena's best-known export, panforte is a rich Italian flat bread or cake whose name translates as 'hard bread'. Traditionally panforte is made with candied pumpkin (although today, the pumpkin is usually replaced with candied citrus peel), nuts, honey and spices such as coriander seeds, cloves, cinnamon and nutmeg. Its origins can be traced back to the twelfth or thirteenth century. Panforte can be made at home but is also produced commercially worldwide.

**Also known as — Siena cake**

## panna cotta

An Italian cream dessert made using cream, sugar and milk and set with gelatine. Some versions are delicately flavoured with vanilla or almond, coffee or grappa, others use spices such as cinnamon and nutmeg. Translated, panna cotta means 'cooked cream', although the cream is only brought to the boil to dissolve the sugar and bring out the flavours. The dessert is set in moulds or ramekins and turned out before serving.

**Also known as — crema cotta**

## panzanella

### PANZANELLA

*Tear 2 thick crustless slices of day-old country bread into pieces. Put in a bowl and sprinkle with a little water. Mix in 4 cubed ripe tomatoes, ½ cubed cucumber, 1 sliced green pepper, 1 sliced red onion, and a handful of torn basil leaves. Mix 100 ml olive oil with 2 tablespoons red wine vinegar; season; pour over salad. Sit for 30 minutes. Serves 6.*

A Tuscan summer salad made with day-old bread to which tomatoes, red onions, cucumber and basil leaves are added. Panzanella comes in many guises with some recipes adding anchovies, tuna, hard-boiled eggs and capers. Traditional recipes soak the bread in water for a few minutes, then squeeze the water out before adding the rest of the ingredients; some modern versions soak the bread in a tomato-based dressing made from a mixture of tomato juice and olive oil.

**papaw** — see custard apple

## papaya

A large tropical fruit whose ripe flesh can be juicy, creamy orange, red or yellow. In the centre is a mass of large peppery black seeds, which are edible and sometimes crushed and used as a spice. Papayas, particularly unripe ones, contain an odourless, whitish liquid from which papain is extracted. Papain is an enzyme that breaks down protein and is used to tenderize meat. It also prevents gelatine from setting, so papaya is not a good option for desserts such as jellies. Chopped papaya can also cause fruit in a fruit salad to soften if left for a while, so add it just before serving. Sprinkle papaya with a little lime juice to bring out the flavour. A relative of the papaya is babaco, a five-sided seedless fruit, with golden aromatic flesh. Although papayas are sometimes called papaws, these are actually a member of the custard apple family.

**Also known as — pawpaw**

*Green (unripe) papayas are cooked as a vegetable or used raw in salads, especially in Thai cuisine.*

## parfait

An iced dessert made from fresh cream, which makes it very smooth. The base of a parfait is an egg custard to which cream and flavourings such as coffee (its traditional flavour), alcohol, fruit or chocolate are added. The mixture is poured into a loaf tin or the traditional parfait tin, which is cylindrical in shape with a rounded end. When frozen, the parfait is turned out and sliced. An American parfait is similar to an ice-cream sundae.

### PARFAIT

*Beat 4 egg yolks with an electric whisk in a bain-marie until light and thick. Mix 1 tablespoon instant espresso with 150 g sugar and 190 ml water and dissolve thoroughly over low heat. Pour into egg yolks, whisking well. Whisk over heat until mixture thickens. Beat off the heat until cold, then fold in 250 ml whipped cream. Freeze overnight. Serves 4.*

## Paris-Brest

A large, ring-shaped choux pastry cake, split and filled with praline-flavoured cream, sprinkled with flaked almonds and dusted with icing sugar. It was developed by a French pastry chef during a cycle race that travels between Paris and Brest. He designed the cake to resemble a bicycle wheel.

## parkin

Yorkshire, Lancashire and Scotland all lay claim to the parkin, a crumbly, oaty, gingerbread cake, sweetened with golden syrup or black treacle. It was traditionally made for Guy Fawkes night when it was shaped like gingerbread men.

# parsnip

A Mediterranean native, the parsnip is a root vegetable with a nutty, sweet flavour belonging to the same family as the turnip and celery. It has creamy yellow flesh and can be served roasted, mashed or added to casseroles and soups. Parsnips are an autumn/winter vegetable and they become sweeter after the first frosts as the cold causes them to convert their starch into sugar. When buying parsnips, choose firm, smooth vegetables. Leave the skin on for cooking, then peel once cooked. If peeled before cooking, store in water with a squeeze of lemon or vinegar (acidulated water) as their flesh darkens on contact with the air. Particularly large or old parsnips may need their core removed before cooking as they can be hard, flavourless and very fibrous. Parsnips will keep in the fridge for about 4 weeks.

*Parsnip goes with — Parmesan, potato, roast meat, swede*

## CURRIED PARSNIP SOUP

*Heat 2 tablespoons olive oil in a large saucepan. Add 2 large, peeled and chopped parsnips and 1 chopped onion. Cook over a medium heat for 5 minutes. Add 2 teaspoons good quality curry paste, such as Madras, and cook, stirring, for 1 minute. Add vegetable stock or water to cover. Cover with a lid, bring to the boil, then simmer for about 20 minutes until the parsnips are tender. Cool slightly, then blend in a food processor until smooth. Return to the pan, stir in 500 ml water and 3 tablespoons double cream or fromage frais. Check seasoning and serve with crusty bread. Serves 4.*

# passato

Passato commonly refers to puréed, sieved tomatoes, which are used in pasta sauces, as pizza toppings, in casseroles and soups. Passato can be bought in cartons and bottles. The word is also used to refer to anything that is puréed, a creamed soup or a soup of puréed vegetables.

# passion fruit

A tropical fruit, originally from Central America, so named because of the composition of the flower parts, which were used to illustrate the Crucifixion by Jesuit missionaries. Hence passion flower, and fruit.

The most common variety are purple-skinned but some are yellow or orange. The pulp is sweet but tart, juicy, very fragrant and refreshing. The seeds are edible and crunchy, but if only the pulp is wanted, push the flesh through a sieve. Passion fruit can be eaten out of hand, just slice it in half and scoop out the flesh; squeeze the pulp over pavlova, fruit salads or ice creams; or use it in cocktails, mousses, custards or drinks. It is hard to tell if a passion fruit is ripe—purple varieties may be ripe either when the skin is still smooth or when it starts to wrinkle (not withered). The lighter yellow varieties are ripe when smooth and have a little 'give'. Unripe passion fruit are very tart. Passion fruit pulp is available tinned or frozen.

*Passion fruit goes with — cream, fruit*
*Also known as — curuba, grenadilla*

## COOKING

*Always cook pasta in lots of salted, boiling water (about 1 litre per 100 g pasta). Keep the water at a rolling boil and stir the pasta only once or twice to stop it clumping together. Adding a little oil to the water may prevent the pasta from sticking together, but this will make it slippery and harder for the sauce to stick.*

*Cook pasta until it is al dente (to the tooth)—the pasta should retain a little bite. Taste the pasta until it is right, following the cooking instructions on the packet as a guide. When the pasta is cooked, add cold water to the saucepan to stop it cooking, then drain—do not rinse it.*

*Drained pasta should still have a little water clinging to it to stop it sticking.*

Pasta may have originated in ancient Greece but references to it appear in the Roman world and in ancient Persia. The first Italian reference is from twelfth century Sicily, which had been occupied by both Greeks and Arabs. Pasta-making flourished in Italy; there are now over 200 pasta shapes and each may have a different regional name. Pasta in the South tends to be made of hard durum wheat flour and water, in central Italy with soft flour and eggs, but in the North, risotto is usually eaten instead of pasta.

## TYPES OF PASTA

| | |
|---|---|
| **Dried pasta** | Basic dried pasta made with durum wheat semolina and water, which is passed through a die to make shaped pastas or long pasta such as spaghetti. Some pastas are produced with a rough or ridged (*rigate*) surface, which helps sauces stick to them. Mostly industrially produced. |
| **Fresh pasta** | Made either with a soft wheat or durum wheat semolina and water. This is a speciality of southern Italy, where it is usually made into shapes like *orecchiette* and *strozzapreti* (priest strangler). It is often hand-made. |
| **Dried egg pasta** | Made with durum wheat semolina and eggs. Shaped into filled pasta such as ravioli or ribbon shapes, which are dried as nests to stop them breaking. |
| **Fresh egg pasta** | Made with eggs and 00 (*doppio zero*) or *grano tenero* (tender) flour—Italian plain flours made with soft wheat. This pasta is traditional to Emilia-Romagna and used to make ribbons, sheets, shaped or filled pastas. |

## BASIC EGG PASTA DOUGH

*Pile 500 g 00 flour into a mound on the bench top. Make a well in the centre and add 4 eggs, whisk these into the flour using a fork and add enough iced water to make a smooth dough. Knead the dough for 8 minutes, then rest for 30 minutes. Roll out the dough in portions using either a pasta machine or a rolling pin, folding it in half and rerolling it 6 times, then roll it to the thickness you need. Cut into desired widths. Makes 700 g pasta.*

Different pasta shapes are appropriate for different sauces and it is important to choose the right shape to suit the sauce. Long pastas aren't suited to chunky sauces as the chunks end up at the bottom of the bowl and won't stick to the pasta, and filled pasta should be eaten with simple sauces that won't overshadow their own flavour. Pasta is traditionally eaten as a first course or in soup and is dressed with less sauce in Italy than is expected in other countries.

## CANNELLONI

Cannelloni was originally made with sheets of pasta but is now made commercially into large short tubes, which can be stuffed using a spoon or piping bag. Made from egg pasta.

## BUCKWHEAT PASTA

Made with buckwheat and 00 flour from the Valtellina valley in Lombardy. It is cut into flat noodles and is cooked with potato cubes, beans or cabbage and cheese to make pizzoccheri.

## LONG THIN PASTAS

Long thin pastas such as bavettini, linguine, spaghetti, tagliarini, vermicelli and bucatini go well with simple sauces such as garlic and oil, which stick to their long lengths without falling off, or with shellfish like clams—the clams can be easily picked out to remove the flesh from the shells. Usually bought as durum wheat or dried egg pasta, though some fresh spaghetti-type pastas are available. Long pasta does not need to be broken before cooking but can be folded into the pan—it will soften as it hits the boiling water.

*Cannelloni*

*Buckwheat trenette*

*Spaghettir*

*Linguine*

*Lasagne*

*Spinach ravioli*

*Lasagne*

*Tortellini*

*Ravioli*

## SHEETS OF PASTA

Lasagne is the name of sheets of pasta that are baked in dishes such as *lasagne al forno*. Some sheets are flat; others have a ridged or curled edge, which helps give lightness to the pasta layer. Sheets of pasta are also rolled up to make cannelloni. Lasagne is usually made from egg pasta and may be coloured with spinach (*lasagne verde*).

## FILLED PASTA

This group includes ravioli, raviolini and agnolotti (stuffed squares of pasta); tortelloni and tortellini (stuffed squares or rounds of pasta); capelletti (stuffed hat-like shapes of pasta); and agnolini (similar in shape to capelletti). The fillings for these pastas vary regionally. In Piedmont they use spinach, Parmesan and cooked sausage, in Mantua tortellini are filled with pumpkin and nutmeg, and in Emilia-Romagna, capelletti are filled with meat or ham.

## SOUP PASTAS

These are called pastina and include imaginatively shaped pastas such as stelline (stars), alfabeto, ditalini (little tubes), orzo (barley), semi di melon (melon seeds) and anellini (little rings). Pastina are usually small, about the size of the pieces of vegetable in the soup, and are added at the end of the cooking time. Pastina are sold dried and are made from durum wheat.

## PASTA SHAPES

Usually made from durum wheat, these vary hugely. They include spiral shapes like fusilli, shell shapes like conchiglie, as well as rotelle (wheels), lumache (snails), orecchiette (ears), farfalle (butterflies), casareccie (small twists) and ditali (thimbles). They go well with thick, chunky meat or tomato sauces, which get caught in their shape.

## COLOURED PASTAS

Made with added natural colours to give them different flavours and visual appeal. Cuttlefish or squid ink is often used to make black pasta (*nero*) and spinach for green (*verdi*). Red pasta (tomato), pink pasta (beetroot) and brown pasta (chocolate or mushroom) are also available.

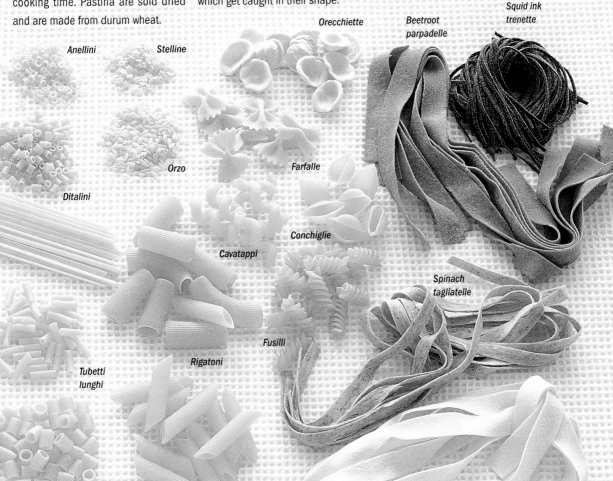

Anellini

Stelline

Orzo

Ditalini

Orecchiette

Farfalle

Conchiglie

Cavatappi

Fusilli

Rigatoni

Tubetti lunghi

Tubetti

Penne rigate

Beetroot parpadelle

Squid ink trenette

Spinach tagliatelle

Parpadelle

## TUBE-SHAPED PASTAS

Short tubes such as maccheroni, rigatoni, penne and tubetti, and long tubes such as candele, maccaronelli, ziti and zitoni are eaten with meat ragùs and tomato sauces. The tubes catch the sauce in their holes. Long pasta, such as ziti, are also used to line dishes and make timballo and pasticcio. These pastas tend to be dried and are made from durum wheat.

## PASTA RIBBONS

Long flat pastas such as tagliatelle, fettucine, mafaldine, tagliarini and parpadelle go well with creamy sauces such as mushroom, prosciutto or seafood as the finer textured sauces stick better to their lengths. Flat pasta is usually available both fresh and dried. Fresh ribbons are made from egg pasta; dried pasta are made from durum wheat, with or without egg.

## SALSA AL POMODORO

*Cook 2 finely chopped garlic cloves in olive oil over low heat for 1 minute. Add 8 firm, ripe tomatoes (seeds removed, chopped), and 1 teaspoon sugar. Simmer until thickened, about 30–40 minutes, stirring frequently, then add 3 tablespoons chopped basil; season. Cook 250 g rigatoni and serve with the tomato sauce. Serves 2.*

## AGLIO E OLIO E PEPERONCINO

*Cook 3 crushed garlic cloves in 4 tablespoons olive oil over low heat for 2 minutes. Add 1 finely chopped seeded red chilli and cook for a further 3 minutes. Cook 250 g spaghetti and drain, then add to the pan, tossing it around to soak up the oil and flavourings. Serve sprinkled with chopped fresh parsley. Serves 2.*

## SPAGHETTI E NOCI

*Put 250 g walnuts in a bowl and cover with boiling water. Drain, then place in a 200°C oven for 8 minutes. Allow the walnuts to cool, then chop finely and mix with 2 tablespoons finely chopped parsley, 2 finely chopped garlic cloves and 250 ml olive oil. Cook 500 g spaghetti. Drain the pasta, then toss through the walnut sauce. Sprinkle with extra parsley. Serves 4.*

## SPAGHETTI ALLA CARBONARA

*Beat 5 eggs with 100 ml double cream and a pinch of salt. Fry 200 g diced pancetta in olive oil for 5 minutes. Cook 500 g spaghetti, drain and add to the pan, stirring well. Remove from heat and stir in the egg mixture and 25 g grated Parmesan—the eggs will coagulate on contact with the hot pasta. Season with pepper and sprinkle with extra grated Parmesan. Serves 4.*

## BUCATINI ALLA AMATRICIANA

*Fry 200 g cubed guanciale or pancetta in 1 tablespoon olive oil until crisp, then add 1 chopped onion and cook until the onion is soft and translucent. Chop 6 ripe tomatoes and 1 chilli and add to the frying pan. Season to taste and simmer for 20 minutes. Cook 250 g bucatini, drain and serve with the sauce. Serves 2.*

## LINGUINE CON VONGOLE

*Fry 2 crushed garlic cloves and a pinch of dried crushed chillies in 4 tablespoons olive oil. Cook for 1 minute over low heat. Add 500 g cleaned clams (see page 365) and 150 ml dry white wine. Bring to the boil and cook until the wine has evaporated, stirring occasionally. Cover and cook for 3 minutes until clams open; discard any closed ones. Cook 500 g linguine, drain and serve with the clams and 3 tablespoons chopped parsley. Serves 4.*

## pasticcio

A generic term in the Italian kitchen referring to a pie made up of various layers. It can be made with a pastry crust or without, but these days it always tends to contain pasta, usually lasagne, tagliatelle or macaroni. Recipes vary regionally, most are savoury, but it is sometimes prepared as a sweet dish.

The dish's origins date back to the Renaissance when it was made using meat such as hare, partridge or fish, encased in a sweet pastry. The preparation is time-consuming, so pasticcio is often a special occasion dish. During carnival week in Romagna, *pasticcio di maccheroni* is served with preparations starting up to 3 days before the event. The dish starts with a tin that is lined bottom and sides with sweet pastry, then filled with layers of Parmesan, breadcrumbs, macaroni mixed with a prosciutto sauce and a sweetbread mixture. A sweet pastry lid is then added and the dish is sealed and baked.

## pastitsio

A well-known Greek dish made using layers of cooked pasta and meat, usually beef or lamb, grated cheese, tomato and topped with a layer of creamy béchamel sauce. The dish is baked until golden brown, then cut into squares and served either warm or cold. It is obviously related in some way to pasticcio, above.

## pastrami

A cut from the underside or brisket of beef from which the fat is removed, after which it is dry-cured in a mixture of sugar, spices and garlic for about 7 days, then smoked. For serving, the meat is thinly sliced and served hot or cold. Pastrami is perhaps best known for its popularity in New York Jewish cuisine where it appears most famously as pastrami on rye *(pictured)*, and often served with sliced gherkins. Pastrami is a Yiddish derivation from the Romanian verb, *pastra*, meaning 'to preserve'.

# pâté

A savoury dish made from a variety of meats, such as pork, veal, game and their livers, combined with fat and seasonings. The ingredients are either finely minced or coarsely chopped, then placed in moulds to set. Pâtés may be cooked *en croûte*, wrapped in a pastry crust, or *en terrine*, cooked in a dish without any crust. Pâtés are usually served as a hot or cold hors d'oeuvre, either cut into slices or spooned out of the dish, and because of their high fat content, are served with unbuttered bread or toast. A pâté's flavour will improve if left for at least 24 hours before serving. They are often pressed after cooking to solidify the mixture.

■ *See also* **terrine**

## CHICKEN LIVER PATE

*Melt 25 g butter in a saucepan, then sauté 1 small chopped onion and 1 crushed garlic clove for 5 minutes, or until the onion is softened. Wash 250 g chicken livers, then cut away any greyish stains. Add to the saucepan and cook for 2 minutes until the livers are golden brown on both sides, but still soft in the middle. Add 1 tablespoon brandy and cook for 1 minute. Purée the livers in a food processor, then push them through a sieve to remove any sinews. Melt a further 25 g butter, stir into the pâté and season well. Spoon the mixture into 1 dish or 4 small individual ramekins and chill in the fridge. If not serving for more than 24 hours, cover the top with a thin layer of melted butter. Serve with toast. Pâté will keep for several weeks in the fridge. Serves 4.*

*Pâté en croûte*

*Terrine de maison*

*Pâté de campagne*

## TYPES OF PATES

| | |
|---|---|
| **Pâté en croûte** | A cooked pâté of meat, game or fish served surrounded with a pastry crust. Often baked in a terrine tin and served either hot or cold. |
| **Terrine de maison** | A speciality pâté of a particular restaurant or charcuterie. The ingredients may change daily—this depends on what the butcher or chef has to hand. |
| **Pâté de campagne** | Traditionally contained only pork meat, but now often contains a selection of meats such as pork fat, lean pork, pig's liver, veal, chicken livers and smoked beef tongue or baked ham, often with a bacon jacket. The pâté is coarsely textured and often flavoured with Cognac. Commonly served in thick slices, accompanied by gherkins and crusty bread. |
| **Chicken liver pâté** | One of the most common pâtés. It has a silky smooth texture and is often flavoured with brandy. |
| **Pâté de fois gras** | One of the most sought-after pâtés, made from the enlarged livers of geese or ducks. The livers are often marinated and then baked in a terrine at a low temperature. |

Patisserie refers to three different things: the art of pastry making, the shop where the baked goods are made and sold and, more commonly, the general name given to sweet baked goods such as cakes, pastries and biscuits, candied fruit and chocolates. Much of the charm of patisserie lies in their elaborate construction and the beautiful decorations that sometimes adorn the pastries—often this is as important as their taste. Antoine Carême, probably the best-known French pastry chef of the nineteenth century, was well known for his architectural patisserie creations and worked for the courts of Vienna, England, Russia and France. Patisserie today still has something of an architectural quality, especially in creations such as *gâteau Saint Honoré* and millefeuille.

*Rum babas*

■ *See also* **choux, crème pâtissière, gateau, millefeuille, petits fours**

## PATISSERIE

*Some of the most well-known patisseries include the following:*

**Macaroons** – *Light, chewy biscuits flavoured with almond.*

**Rum baba** – *Rum-soaked yeasted cakes, often garnished with cream and fruit.*

**Opéra** – *An almond cake filled with coffee butter cream and ganache and covered with chocolate.*

**Succès** – *Varies, but often made from layers of sponge and meringue spread with praline-flavoured butter.*

**Pêches** – *Resembling little peaches, and made from two hollowed out brioche, filled with cream and decorated with angelica.*

*From left: éclairs, apple tarts, strawberry tartlets, mini Danish pastries.*

Patisserie can be made from choux, puff, sweet or shortcrust pastry. Choux pastry is often piped into shapes, which then puff up on baking to form crisp, hollow shells. These may be filled with flavoured creams. Puff, shortcrust and sweet pastry are similarly used to make shells, which hold fruit or cream fillings, or as layered pastries, which contain their fillings. The icings are usually made from a base of sugar paste flavoured with lemon juice or other flavouring.

### RASPBERRY TARTS

*Mix 200 g flour, 100 g ground almonds, 30 g caster sugar, rub in 150 g butter, then add 1 egg. Mix to a dough. Chill for 1 hour. Roll out pastry and line 12 mini tartlet tins. Prick base and blind bake at 200°C for 10 minutes (see page 419). Cool, then fill with a layer of mascarpone, then raspberries tossed in sugar. Glaze with warm redcurrant jelly. Makes 12.*

# pavlova

Named for the Russian ballerina Anna Pavlova, and made with a meringue base, slightly indented in the middle. After cooking, the pavlova is filled with whipped cream and fruit such as kiwi fruit, strawberries, passion fruit and mangoes. The inside of a pavlova has a gooey, marshmallowy texture. It's important to cook pavlova for the right amount of time—if syrupy droplets appear on the outside of the meringue, it is overcooked; if liquid oozes out, it is undercooked. Both Australia and New Zealand lay claim to its invention.

## FRUIT PAVLOVA

*Mark a 20 cm circle on a baking-paper lined tray. Beat 4 egg whites to soft peaks. Beat in 250 g caster sugar, then 1 teaspoon cornflour and 1 teaspoon vinegar. Beat until stiff and shiny. Mound into the marked circle, and make a dip in the centre. Cook at 150°C for 1½ hours. Turn off oven and leave the pavlova inside to completely cool. Top with cream and fruit. Serves 6.*

# pea

Small, round, juicy seeds encased in a green pod. The three main varieties are the garden pea, the field or grey pea (these are dried and not eaten fresh) and the wild Mediterranean pea. Peas should be cooked quickly in boiling water or a little butter. They are usually served hot as a vegetable or added to soups and risottos. Both pease pudding, made from split peas boiled in a pudding cloth, and mushy (mashed) peas are eaten in the North of England.

**Peas go with — baby onions, bacon, duck, ham, mashed potato, risotto**

## BUYING

*Peas should be bought at their optimum time—if harvested too late, they become dry and less sweet as their sugar converts into starch. Look for bright, shiny, green pods that feel firm and taut. Peas can also be purchased frozen, tinned, bottled and dried. In some cases, frozen peas are actually fresher than freshly podded peas because fresh peas deteriorate so quickly. The frozen pea manufacturers pick and pack the peas at their optimum freshness.*

## TYPES OF GARDEN PEAS

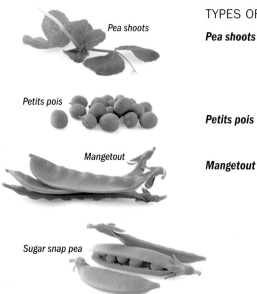

*Pea shoots*

*Petits pois*

*Mangetout*

*Sugar snap pea*

**Pea shoots (pea leaf)** These are the tender leaves of the garden pea that have been prevented from flowering or shooting to encourage the growth of the small leaves. Good in stir-fries. They don't stay fresh for more than 2 days.

**Petits pois** Not a different variety but peas that have been harvested young. The peas are shelled before cooking.

**Mangetout** A variety of garden pea, eaten pod and all (top and tail before eating). There are two types, those with a flat, thin pod (called mangetout or, in some countries, snow peas) and those with a more rounded pod (sugar snap or snap peas). Mangetout are eaten raw in salads or used in stir-fries. Sugar snap peas are more developed than mangetout. Use whole, in stir-fries or noodle dishes.

A fragrant, juicy stone fruit with rosy-pink, downy skin, white or yellow flesh, either slipstone (flesh separating easily from the stone) or clingstone (flesh clinging to the stone). Amongst the many varieties, white-fleshed peaches are considered to be the best eating. The peach is a native of China.

The edible skin of the peach is slightly fuzzy. The woody stone contains a kernel, which, although edible, contains a toxic substance called hydrocyanic acid, so their consumption should be limited. Peaches spoil quickly so only buy as needed. They should last 3 to 4 days at room temperature, unless already very ripe. If stored in the fridge, remove before eating as they are less flavoursome when chilled. The flesh can turn brown on contact with air, so prepare as needed or sprinkle the flesh with a little lemon juice. Eat out of hand, use in jams, sorbets and tarts, as a purée or to make peach Melba, the dish invented by Escoffier to honour the Australian soprano, Dame Nellie Melba.

**Peaches go with — chicken, cream, fruit salad, pork, seafood**

*Yellow peaches*

*White peaches*

Not in fact a nut, the peanut is a member of the legume family, like peas. Its 'nut' is encased in pale-brown brittle pods. Peanuts are an important ingredient in the cooking of Southeast Asia, where they are used in sauces, salads and the well-known dish, satay, and in Africa, where they are a staple and used in stews. Peanut oil is extracted from the nut.

Peanuts can be bought shelled or unshelled, raw, roasted, salted or boiled. Once opened, store in an airtight container in the fridge and use within 3 months. Raw peanuts deteriorate more quickly than roasted ones. Some people are allergic to peanuts, and for them, eating just one peanut can be fatal.

**Also known as — groundnut**

### PEANUT BRITTLE

*Put 1 kg sugar in a heavy-based saucepan with 4 tablespoons water and 1 teaspoon lemon juice. Heat over low heat until the sugar melts. Simmer slowly until the hard crack stage is reached, 150°C (300°F) on a sugar thermometer. Stir in 600 g roasted peanuts, then pour into a greased 23 x 33 cm shallow tin. After 10 minutes, mark out squares with a sharp knife. Cut or crack into pieces when cooled.*

■ *See also* **gado gado, oil, satay**

### PEANUT BUTTER

*A spread made from ground, roasted peanuts and oil, sold in smooth or crunchy form. Some brands contain sugar and additives. It is mainly used as a spread on toast and bread, but the crunchy variety can be used In Indonesian cooking, especially satay sauce. Peanut butter and jelly (jam) sandwiches are popular in the United States. Commercially made peanut butter can be stored in the cupboard but home-made peanut butter should be stored in the fridge.*

A tear-drop or round-shaped fruit with juicy white flesh, the pear is one of the most widely eaten fruits, after apples. Most varieties eaten today are the results of crosses developed in the seventeenth and eighteenth century in Europe and America as growers tried to develop a variety that was free of the tiny, hard grains within its cells that made pears gritty.

## POACHED PEARS

*In a saucepan (big enough to take 4 upright pears plus stalks), dissolve 300 g sugar in 750 ml water over low heat. Bring to the boil, add 50 ml lemon juice, ½ cinnamon stick, 4 cloves and 1 vanilla pod. Peel 4 pears, keeping their stalks attached. Place upright in the saucepan. Cover and poach very gently until tender, about 30–45 minutes. Remove pears and simmer the syrup until slightly thickened. Spoon a little over the pears and serve warm or chilled with whipped cream or mascarpone. Serves 4.*

*Beurre bosc*

*Conference*

*Red William*

*Packham's triumph*

*Winter nelis*

*Corella*

## TYPES OF PEARS

| | |
|---|---|
| **Beurre** | Soft, juicy pears. Includes beurre bosc and beurre d'Anjou. |
| **William (Bartlett)** | Golden yellow skin, smooth white flesh. Some varieties are red. Highly aromatic, slightly musky pear. Good dessert and cooking pear. |
| **Conference** | Easily recognized by its long thin shape and russet skin. It is sweet, juicy and refreshing. A good all-purpose pear. |
| **Packham's triumph** | Large pear with a small neck and green-yellow skin. Slow to ripen but very soft, smooth flesh. Good dessert pear. |
| **Comice** | Large round pear with a short neck. Its skin turns pinkish or brown when ripe. Considered to be one of the finest pears in the world, it is exceptionally juicy. Often the variety served for dessert with cheese. |
| **Rocha** | Medium-sized pear with a short brownish neck. Its yellow skin is dotted with brown and green, and its flesh is soft and buttery when ripe. |
| **Winter nelis** | Small with a rough skin and spicy, juicy flesh. |
| **Corella** | Small with a pretty green skin and pink blush; very white juicy flesh. |

## STORAGE

*Pears do not ripen well on the tree so they are picked when underripe— store in a cool place for ripening. Pears pass through their period of perfect ripeness in a matter of hours and spoil quickly.*

Choose smooth, firm but not hard pears. Cut just before eating, or sprinkle with lemon juice to stop flesh oxidizing. Although perfect for eating out of hand, pears also cook well, usually by poaching. If poaching or adding to compotes, choose pears that are slightly underripe. Some pears are grown to make perry, the pear equivalent of cider. Pears can be used to make fruit salads, sorbets, ice creams, pies and chutneys. They are also good in savoury dishes with sweet onions, radicchio, chicory and watercress. Pear Belle-Hélène is a famous pear dessert in which pears are served with ice cream and chocolate sauce.

*Pears go with — cheese, chocolate, ginger, prosciutto, red wine, vanilla*

## pecan nut

The fruit of a large hickory tree, a relative of the walnut and a native of North America. The pecan has a high oil content and because of this, shelled pecans go rancid quite quickly. Unshelled pecans will keep for about 3 months. When buying pecans, look for nuts that do not rattle. Pecans are traditionally used in pecan pie and ice cream and in turkey stuffings in America. They can also be used in any recipe that uses walnuts.

## Peking duck

One of the best-known Chinese dishes, the characteristic crunchy, deep-brown skin of Peking duck is produced by blanching and drying the skin before glazing it and roasting the duck hanging in an oven. The duck is carved by the chef, ensuring each piece of flesh has a bit of crispy skin attached. Peking duck is traditionally served by rolling up the skin and meat in a Mandarin pancake with a special sauce and spring onion shreds.
**Also known as — Beijing duck**

## peperonata

An Italian mixture of sweet peppers, tomatoes, onions and garlic stewed gently in olive oil. It is either served cold as part of antipasto or warm as an accompaniment to meat and fish.

### PEPERONATA

*Heat 5 tablespoons olive oil in a large frying pan. Add 1 large, thinly sliced onion, cover the pan and fry gently for 15 minutes until lightly golden. Add 2 crushed garlic cloves and fry for a further 5 minutes. Add 2 sliced large red peppers and 1 sliced large yellow pepper and fry for 5 minutes, stirring frequently. Add 6 firm, ripe, seeded and chopped tomatoes and simmer for about 20 minutes. Season well and serve warm or cold. Serves 4.*

## pepino

A tropical fruit native to Peru, golden yellow in colour, mildly fragrant when ripe and usually streaked with purple. The fruit has a mild cucumber or melon flavour and can be used in fruit salads (it benefits from a sprinkling of citrus juice), prepared and eaten like a melon or puréed and used to make ice creams and sorbets. Underripe fruit will ripen at room temperature after a few days.
**Also known as — melon pear, tree melon**

# pepper

The fruit of a tropical plant (*Capsicum annuum*) deliberately misnamed pepper (*pimiento* in Spanish) by Columbus in order to sell its close relation—the chilli (*Capsicum frutescens*)—as an alternative to the spice pepper that was, at the time, much sought after. Although peppers are a fruit, they are treated more as a vegetable or salad ingredient. Peppers vary in appearance but they are all basically smooth, shiny and hollow, containing thin white membranes and seeds. Most sweet (bell) peppers are green at first, they then turn red, yellow or orange or even purple-black, depending on the variety. Other types include wax peppers, which are yellow or white; cherry peppers, which are small, round peppers; and anaheim and poblano peppers (ancho when dried), which are usually classed as chillies although they are actually sweet peppers.

*Clockwise from left: green and red Hungarian peppers; yellow, blonde (white) and green sweet peppers; red mini sweet peppers.*

Peppers can be prepared in many ways. Simply cut into slices, chunks or quarters, and eat raw in salads; stuff or fry; skinned peppers can be sliced and added to salads, or drizzle with olive oil for the antipasto table. Eat raw peppers as crudités or use in soups, stews and stir-fries. Peppers feature in ratatouille, peperonata and gazpacho. Buy peppers that are firm, glossy and plump. Those with a thick flesh are juiciest and red peppers are generally sweeter than green ones. Avoid any that have bruises, soft spots or blemishes. Store in a bowl like fruit and they will sweeten as they ripen. Pimiento are ready-prepared red peppers.

**Peppers go with — garlic, olives, onion, tomato**
**Also known as — bell pepper, capsicum, pimiento, sweet pepper**

## COOKING

*When stuffing whole peppers, cut a slice off the top and remove the seeds and white veins. Blanch each pepper for 2 minutes. Fill the pepper with the stuffing, replace the top slice and bake.*

*Roasting or grilling peppers makes them sweeter and also gives them a smoky flavour if you use a char-grill or barbecue. To remove the skin of peppers, put whole or halved peppers under the grill until the skin blackens and blisters. Turn the pepper so that all sides are blackened. Alternatively, roast them whole at 180°C for 15–20 minutes. Allow to cool, then peel away the skin. Peeled, seeded peppers can be kept covered in oil in the fridge for 1 week.*

*To make pepper sauces, grill and remove the skins (as explained above), then purée or push the flesh through a sieve.*

*Roasted and peeled peppers*

## STUFFED PEPPERS

*Fry 2 chopped onions in 4 tablespoons olive oil until soft. Stir in 3 crushed garlic cloves, 1 teaspoon each of cinnamon and paprika and 2 tablespoons currants. Cook for 1 minute. Cook 125 g mixed wild rice and long-grain rice. Stir this into the onion mixture and season. Slice the tops off 4 medium red peppers, discard the seeds and fill with the stuffing. Replace the tops, stand in a baking dish and drizzle with olive oil. Cover with foil and bake at 200°C for 1 hour. Serves 4.*

■ *See also* **chillies**

True pepper (vine pepper) is black, green or white and comes from the same plant but picked at various stages of ripeness. Red pepper, Sichuan pepper, cayenne pepper and other peppers are not true peppers but were so called because pepper was an expensive commodity. Pepper contains piperine, which is an alkaloid, and it is this that gives pepper its distinctive flavour. Pepper is sold whole, cracked, and coarsely or finely ground. Freezing makes the flavour of pepper more pronounced.

■ *See also* **Sichuan pepper**

## STORAGE

*Freshly ground black pepper is more pungent than pre-ground, which loses its flavour quickly and should not be stored longer than 4 months. Whole peppercorns will last about 1 year in a cool, dark place.*

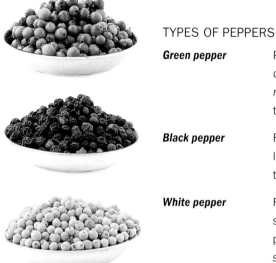

## TYPES OF PEPPERS

| | |
|---|---|
| **Green pepper** | Picked when unripe and usually preserved by artificial drying or by bottling in brine, vinegar or water. *Poivre rose* are green peppercorns that have just begun to turn reddish. |
| **Black pepper** | From berries that are red, but not completely ripe. When left to dry, they shrivel and take on a dark colour. This is the most pungent and flavourful of peppers. |
| **White pepper** | From ripe, red berries that are soaked in salt water until soft, then the white seed is removed and dried. White pepper is less aromatic than black but hotter and sharper, so use sparingly. Useful for seasoning white sauces. |

## persimmon

Similar in appearance to a tomato, but with an orangey-red skin and lush and tangy, sweet and fragrant flesh, which has a slightly viscous texture. Varieties include Fuyu and Hachiya. Unripe persimmons are astringent and inedible. Eat as a dessert in fruit salads, in baking or in preserves.

**Also known as — kaki, Sharon fruit**

## pesto

Originating in Genoa, pesto is an uncooked sauce of basil, pine nuts, garlic, olive oil and either Parmesan or pecorino sardo cheese, with basil being the prominent flavour. Pesto is usually served as a pasta sauce, but it also works well with chicken and fish. Traditionally it is made in a mortar and pestle but can also be made in a food processor—turn the machine off and on as you make it so the blade does not heat up and spoil the basil leaves. Use a sweet rather than peppery olive oil such as a Ligurian olive oil, so that it doesn't overpower the flavour.

### PESTO

*Put 2 crushed garlic cloves in a mortar and pestle, add a pinch of salt and 50 g pine nuts. Pound to a paste. Gradually add 50 g basil leaves and pound the leaves against the side of the bowl. Stir in 75 g grated Parmesan, then gradually add 150 ml olive oil. Use immediately or store covered in the fridge for 1 week. If storing, cover the pesto surface with a thin layer of olive oil. Makes 250 ml.*

## petits fours

Delicate little biscuits, cakes and confectionery, usually served at the end of a meal or at cocktail parties. Translated from the French, meaning 'small oven', possibly because they were put in the oven after the large cakes had been cooked. Petits fours are often miniature versions of larger pastries such as éclairs, choux buns or iced cakes, or small biscuits such as langues de chat and tuiles and served with coffee, ice cream, sorbet and dessert wines. Savoury versions are called *amuse gueule*.

## pheasant

A medium-sized game bird with brightly coloured plumage, available wild and farmed. Pheasants are often sold by the 'brace', which means both a cock and a hen. In the United Kingdom, wild pheasant are at their best in November and December. These should hang for 3 to 14 days, which tenderizes the flesh and enhances the flavour. Farmed pheasant is not hung.

Pheasant flesh can be quite dry so it is usually stuffed or barded (wrapped in a layer of fat) to keep the flesh moist. The younger birds are better for roasting; older birds are best in casseroles or for making terrines or pâté. Serve one bird between two with breast meat and leg meat for each person. Almost any chicken recipe can be adapted to use pheasant. Pheasant is available from specialist poultry shops.

**Pheasant goes with — apple, fruit jelly, red wine**

*Roasted pheasant with garlic*

## Philippines — see Filipino food

## pho

The name for a Vietnamese noodle soup. The noodles in the soup, called banh pho, are white rice stick noodles and these are either first cooked in boiling water or added directly to the boiling soup stock. Street vendors are a common sight in Vietnam selling bowls of freshly prepared soup. A boiling broth is poured over the noodles and slices of raw beef, then herbs such as Vietnamese mint and coriander, bean sprouts and chilli are added to taste by each customer.

**Also known as — Hanoi soup**

### BEEF PHO

*Cook 200 g banh pho rice noodles in boiling water following packet instructions. Drain; refresh under cold water. Boil 1.8 litres quality beef stock, add 2 tablespoons fish sauce; season. Divide noodles among 4 bowls and top with 200 g very thinly sliced raw beef fillet. Pour over broth, then scatter with some bean sprouts, sliced red chilli, Vietnamese mint and a squeeze of lemon juice. Serves 4.*

A cherry-sized, yellowy-orange fruit unusually hidden inside an inedible paper-thin membrane, which is closed at one end, resembling a Chinese lantern. The fruit is full of small edible seeds and has a sweet and pleasantly acidic flavour that leaves a slightly bitter aftertaste. To use in cooking, peel back the membrane and twist the base of the fruit to release it. Physalis also make great cake decorations and petits fours. Because of its high pectin content, physalis makes very good jams.

**Also known as — alkekengi, cape gooseberry, golden berry, ground cherry, poha**

### TOFFEE PHYSALIS

*Carefully fold back the paper membranes of each of 200 g physalis and twist them together. Put 250 g sugar in a heavy-based saucepan and melt over low heat, tipping the pan backwards and forwards until you have a golden caramel. Remove from the heat. Dip each physalis in the caramel and sit them on baking paper to set.*

A highly seasoned hot or mild pickled vegetable relish. English piccalilli is a mustard pickle—the vegetables used vary and may contain cauliflower florets, sliced gherkins, peppers, onions, courgettes and beans, which are preserved in a spicy mustard and vinegar sauce. Piccalilli is often served with cheese but it also goes well with cold meat, particularly roast pork and ham. American piccalilli uses green tomatoes, onions and sweet pickles in spices and vinegar.

Pickles are vegetables or fruits, such as cabbage, onions and mango, preserved in brine or vinegar. Pickles were originally invented as a way of preserving food so there was a ready supply of vegetables all year round. Today, they are a popular accompaniment to many dishes and a delicious addition to sandwiches. Pickles can be sweet or sour or flavoured with garlic, herbs and spices.

The Western pickle is a milder version of the Indian achar, which more often than not contains chilli, while the Western pickle need not. The word 'pickle' comes from the old German word, *pekel*.

**Pickles go with — cheese, cold meat, curry, hors d'oeuvres**

### STORAGE

*Pickles need varying times to mature; some are ready in a day, while others take 6 months. Store in a cool, dry place as sunlight can cause alcoholic fermentation.*

*See also* **dill pickles, piccalilli, pickling**

*Branston pickles*

*Cucumber and mint pickles*

*Piccalilli*

*Dill pickles*

*Whisky and walnut pickles*

*Tomato and vegetable pickles*

*Slice 2 red and 2 yellow peppers into thin rings and put in a bowl. Add 900 g thinly sliced onions and 300 g quartered shallots. Sprinkle over 4 tablespoons salt. Mix well and leave to stand for 2 hours. Drain off any liquid, rinse under cold water and drain. Put 1 litre cider vinegar in a non-corrosive saucepan and add 100 g sugar, 2 teaspoons salt, 2 tablespoons dried mint, 2 tablespoons dried paprika, 1 tablespoon dill seeds, then add the vegetables. Bring to the boil, reduce heat and simmer for 5 minutes. Pack vegetables into prepared jars and pour in the vinegar, ensuring the vegetables are completely covered. Poke the contents with a wooden skewer to remove any air bubbles and seal. The pickles can be eaten after 1 week, although they will improve with age and will last up to 6 months if stored in a cool dry place. Makes 1.5 litres.*

Pickling has been used for thousands of years as a way of preserving food, particularly fruits, vegetables, meat and fish. Food is simmered in brine or vinegar or a mixture of the two, which prevents the growth of microorganisms. Occasionally lemon and lime juices are used for pickling. Methods of making pickles vary but there are a few important rules. The food to be pickled must be as firm and fresh as possible and the pickling medium must be sufficiently concentrated to ensure that the pickle keeps. The balance between sourness, saltiness and sweetness is crucial. Air should be kept out of the pickle jar as it causes discolouration and encourages mould to grow. This can be prevented by filling jars to the brim and dislodging bubbles before covering. Traditional British pickling spices include allspice, bay leaves, cardamom, cinnamon, cloves, coriander, mustard seeds, ginger and peppercorns.

## COOKING

*It is important to follow a few hygiene and safety rules when making pickles:*

*Wash hands with soap, before and during preparation.*

*Always keep utensils and kitchen surfaces clean.*

*Sterilize the jars for storing pickles before filling them and ensure the lids are non-corrosive.*

*Check stored pickles at regular intervals and discard any that have an unpleasant smell or any that are beginning to deteriorate.*

### Sterilizing the jars

Always use sterilized containers with the correct lid or seal. The jars can be sterilized in an oven or in boiling water. To sterilize jars in the oven, preheat the oven to 160°C. Place clean, dry jars and lids on a tray and heat in the oven for 10 minutes. Allow to cool slightly, then fill with the warm pickles and put the lid on. As the pickles cool, they will form a vacuum, which will help preserve them.

To sterilize in boiling water, put a wire rack in the bottom of a saucepan. Place washed jars on the rack and cover completely with boiling water. Bring to the boil and boil rapidly for 10 minutes. Lids and rubber seals should be added for a few seconds. Lift the jars out and drain upside down. Place on a tray and dry in a cool oven.

*See also* **dill pickles, piccalilli, pickle**

## pie

In its simplest form, a mixture of ingredients encased in pastry, usually enclosed with a pastry lid. Pies can be sweet or savoury, filled with meat, fish, fruit or vegetables. Some have both a pastry case and lid; deep-dish pies have a lid but no pastry case. The lid may be made of pastry or even of mashed potato, such as shepherd's pie, or of meringue, such as lemon meringue pie. Pies vary in size and shape and the crust can be made from any type of pastry.

## pigeon

A bird eaten wild and farmed, although farmed pigeon is hard to find in the United Kingdom. Wild pigeon is leaner, darker and stronger tasting than the farmed bird. A wild pigeon should be hung for 1 to 2 days to improve its flavour and texture. The flavour of a farmed pigeon can be improved, once it has been killed, by allowing the blood to spread internally and darken the flesh. Squab are young pigeons. If storing, remove any packaging, wrap in greaseproof paper and store in the fridge. Wash and pat dry before cooking.

Pigeon can be boned and stuffed before baking. It is advisable to cover the breast with bacon to prevent it drying out. Older pigeons are best cooked with liquid, especially wine, in a casserole, stewed or baked in a pie.

**Pigeon goes with — garlic, juniper berries, mushroom, peas, red wine**

### ROAST SQUAB

*Mix 16 chopped dates with 2 cubed apples, ½ teaspoon each allspice and cinnamon, 100 g softened butter and 4 tablespoons Cognac. Stuff into 2 squab, truss the legs and season. Roast with breast side resting on 2 thickly sliced onions with 250 ml apple juice, 2 tablespoons Cognac and 60 g butter. Cook at 180°C for 40 minutes, basting every 10 minutes. Serve with the pan juices. Serves 4.*

## pikelet

Pikelets are yeasted pancakes with a holey surface, somewhere between a crumpet and a drop scone. The batter is thinner than that used for crumpets; they are slightly crispy and have a free-form shape. Pikelets are usually served warm with sweet accompaniments such as honey and jam, although they can be topped with grated cheese and grilled. In Australia the word pikelet refers to what are known as drop scones in the United Kingdom.

■ *See also  crumpet, drop scone*

## pilaff

### TOMATO AND HERB PILAFF

*Fry 200 g chopped onion and 1 crushed garlic clove in olive oil. Add 1 kg skinned, chopped and seeded ripe tomatoes and fry together. Add 200 ml water and simmer for 30 minutes. Add 500 g basmati rice and enough water to cover the rice. Simmer, covered, until rice is cooked, then stir in 2 tablespoons chopped parsley and season well. Serves 8.*

See also **burghul**

Pilaff is a Middle Eastern dish of cooked rice, the important part being that each grain of rice remains separate. There are many variations of pilaff—the Russians eat *plov*, the Turks eat *pilav*, and the Indians, *pullao*. In Spain, the pilaff, introduced by the Arabs, has been transformed into the paella. Middle Eastern cuisine contains many such dishes. They can be cooked on the stove, boiled, then steamed or baked in the oven and may be flavoured with meat or vegetables. Though associated with rice, pilaff can also be made with other grains such as burghul, as it is in Syria.

**Also known as — pilau, pulao, pullao**

### ONION AND PEA PULLAO

*Fry 1 tablespoon grated ginger, 1 cinnamon stick and 2 crushed garlic cloves in olive oil. Add 500 g basmati rice and enough water to cover the rice; simmer covered until the rice is almost cooked. Add 110 g green peas and cook until the rice is cooked; season. Fry 1 thinly sliced onion until brown and crisp, and add to the pullao. Serves 4.*

## pine nut

The small edible seeds that grow at the base of the cone of various varieties of pine tree. Those taken from the northern hemisphere genus *pinus* are more in demand, and not just because they are more difficult to cultivate. American nuts are also very good, but Chinese are the most prolific. The 'nut' is enclosed in a hard shell, which is always removed before going to market. Pine nuts have quite a soapy texture with a slight 'piney' taste. They may be eaten raw but the flavour is enhanced when roasted or fried. Because the nuts are high in oil, they burn quickly when heated. For the same reason, they also go rancid quickly so buy in small quantities.

Pine nuts are used in stuffings, salads, cakes, pastries, biscuits and, most notably, in the Italian sauce, pesto. They are widely used in the cooking of India, southern France and the Middle East. Pine nut flour is used in confectionery and the oil is good in salad dressings. Store in an airtight container in a cool, dark place or freeze for up to 6 months.

**Also known as — Indian nut, pignola, pine kernel**

Derived from the Spanish word *pina* meaning 'pine cone', the pineapple is a tropical fruit native to South America. The pineapple plant bears over one hundred purple flowers in a spiral shape and it is these unfertilized flowers that fuse together to form a single fruit. The pineapple is actually a composite of several individual fruits, called eyes.

Pineapples have a juicy, sweet—but sometimes slightly tart—fragrant flavour. They are best eaten fresh; simply slice down the side of the fruit to remove its hard skin, then cut into chunks or slices, use in fruit salads or grill and serve with gammon. Choose pineapples that are heavy for their size and slightly aromatic. A good test for ripeness is to pull out a leaf from the crown—if it comes away easily, it is ripe.

**Pineapple goes with — cheese, chicken, ham**

### COOKING

*Pineapple contains bromelin, an enzyme that breaks down protein (similar to the papain in papaya). This means that meat that is marinated in fresh pineapple juice will fall apart if left for too long. Also, if pineapple is added to gelatine, such as in jellies, the bromelin will prevent the gelatine from setting. Bromelin is destroyed by heating, so cooked or tinned pineapple or pasteurized pineapple juice can be added to gelatine with no detrimental effects.*

### PIPERADE

*Cook 2 sliced red peppers, 1 sliced green pepper, 10 peeled, seeded tomatoes, 1 thinly sliced onion and 1 crushed garlic clove in olive oil. Cook, uncovered, on low heat for 30 minutes. Beat 8 eggs, season; add 2 tablespoons chopped parsley. Stir into vegetables until eggs are scrambled but still soft. Fry 4 slices ham in 25 g butter. Serve piperade with the ham and toast. Serves 4.*

Piperade is a Basque dish, made up of a combination of sautéed onions, tomatoes, peppers and garlic cooked in goose fat or olive oil. Chopped herbs and beaten eggs are then added and the mixture is scrambled. It is traditionally served with fried or grilled ham and triangles of fried bread.

The name of a very hot, small chilli pepper and also a dish of meat or fish served with a hot chilli sauce. The sauce is usually a preparation of simmered chillies and peppers, sieved and served with meat such as chicken *(pictured)* or prawns. Piri piri is of Portuguese African origin, whereas those spellings with an 'l' (pili-pili) are more likely to be French. Piri piri is sold as a sauce, whole chillies and as a powder.

**Also known as — peri-peri, pilli-pilli**

## pirozhki

The diminutive for *pirog*, Russian for pie, these semicircular pastries are made from various pastries or yeasted doughs. They are either baked or deep-fried and fillings include rice, fish, game, poultry, vegetables or cream. Pirozhki are served as an accompaniment to soup, especially borscht, with sour cream, or as a snack or hot starter. In Poland they are known as pierogi. Pirog are larger pies of varying shapes and can be served as a main meal.

**Also known as — *pierogi, piroshki***

## pissaladière

A speciality of Nice in southern France and similar to an Italian pizza, a pissaladière is an open tart made with either a bread dough or pastry base topped with onions and garnished in a chequerboard pattern with anchovy fillets and black olives. Traditionally, the top was spread with *pissala* (from which the dish takes its name), a paste of anchovy purée, herbs and olive oil, and then baked. Some versions include tomatoes. Pissaladière can be served hot or cold as a light lunch.

## pistachio nut

A nut enclosed in the soft fruit of a native Asian tree. The fruit grow in clusters, encasing a beige, brittle, half-open shell, which holds the nut. Most are green but some varieties are yellow or ivory. They can be eaten from the shell, added to sweet and savoury dishes, or, in patisserie, added in slices to show off their green colour. They are used to flavour ice cream and used in cassata. Add to salads, stuffings, pâtés or cereals. The nuts can be bought shelled or unshelled, and, for a short time in autumn, fresh.

**Also known as — *green almond***

*From left: fresh pistachio nuts; unshelled pistachio nuts; shelled pistachio nuts.*

## PISTOU

*Put 6 garlic cloves, 80 g basil leaves and 100 g grated Parmesan in a mortar and pestle (or use a food processor). Pound ingredients together to form a paste. Add 200 ml olive oil, pouring the oil in a steady stream, and mix in thoroughly. If using a processor, keep the motor running as you add the oil. Add salt to taste. Makes about 400 ml.*

A paste or dip made from basil, olive oil, Parmesan (or Gruyère) and garlic. Although its ingredients are similar to a pesto, it is not served with pasta or meat but as a garnish for soup. Pistou is also the name of the Provençal soup, similar to minestrone, made from beans, potatoes, tomatoes, garlic and vermicelli. The pistou paste is stirred into the soup just before serving—pistou should only be heated gently, otherwise it may become bitter.

## pitahaya

The fruit of a Central and South American cactus, it has a scaly reddish-pink skin, the flesh is densely packed and bright pink and is embedded with lots of tiny, edible black seeds. Although the fruit has a rather mild, bland flavour, it is enhanced by sprinkling it with lime juice or sugar. It can be eaten out of hand, puréed in drinks or added to fruit salads. There is also a variety that has yellow flesh.

**Also known as — dragon fruit, dragon's eye**

## pithiviers

A large puff pastry tart from the French town of the same name made from two layers of puff pastry encasing a layer of frangipane (almond cream). The edges are sealed and scalloped and the top is scored with either diamond or rosette patterns. Once baked, the tart is dusted with icing sugar then returned to the oven for a couple of minutes to glaze the top. Traditionally it is served at Twelfth Night when a bean or small pottery token is buried in the filling and the tart is crowned with a gold paper crown. Pithiviers can also have savoury fillings.

*See also* **frangipane**

see bread — **pitta bread**

**301**

# pizza

The Neapolitan version of the many flat breads baked in Italy since pre-Roman times. Originally in Italy, pizza was *pizza bianca* (white) and the topping was garlic, lard, salt and anchovies. The arrival of the tomato from South America gave rise to pizzas topped with tomato, such as the marinara. In 1889, a pizza-maker called Raffaele Esposito created the Margherita (tomato, basil and mozzarella) in honour of Queen Margherita who was visiting Naples. With the royal seal of approval, pizza went from strength to strength and the *Associazione Vera Pizza Napoletana* (still going strong) was set up to make sure the standards for pizza size, toppings and cooking temperature were maintained. The true Neapolitan pizza has a thin crust and is baked on the floor of a wood-fired oven for 1 to 2 minutes at a very high temperature. Pizza spread across Italy and the rest of the world as Neapolitans emigrated, and captured the heart and stomach of America at the start of the twentieth century. The deep-pan pizza was invented in Chicago and has a thicker, more doughy base and more topping on it.

## TOMATO SAUCE

*Remove the cores from 240 g ripe San Marzano or plum tomatoes, then chop them finely by hand or in a food processor. Add 6 finely chopped basil leaves, 4 crushed garlic cloves, 2 tablespoons passata and 1 tablespoon olive oil. Mix well and leave to stand for 30 minutes to allow the flavours to infuse. Season with salt and pepper. Makes enough sauce for 2 large pizzas.*

## PIZZA BASE

1 *Mix 2 teaspoons dried yeast with 1 tablespoon sugar and 90 ml warm water and leave until the mixture bubbles.*

2 *Sift 450 g plain flour into a bowl with a pinch salt, add the yeast and 125 ml water and mix to a soft dough.*

3 *Knead the dough until smooth and springy—at least 5 minutes. Put in a bowl, cover and leave to rise until doubled in size.*

4 *Punch the air out of the dough with your fist and divide it into two equal pieces.*

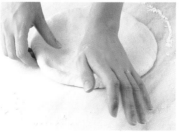

5 *Flatten each piece of dough into a circle, then, working from the centre out, make the circle bigger using the heel of your hand.*

6 *Leave a slightly raised rim around the edge and place it on an oiled tray dusted with cornmeal. Add the topping.*

### MARGHERITA

Spread the prepared pizza base with a layer of tomato sauce (see page 302), leaving a gap around the edge. Scatter 60 g chopped mozzarella and some basil leaves over the pizza. Drizzle with some olive oil and bake at the highest temperature your oven will reach for 12 minutes, or until the crust is browned and the centre is bubbling. Drizzle with a little more oil and serve.

### QUATTRO STAGIONI

Prepare the pizza base as for Margherita pizza, above. Scatter 60 g chopped mozzarella over the pizza. Visually divide the pizza into quarters. Put 30 g sliced prosciutto on one quarter, 4 quartered artichoke hearts on another, 4 sliced mushrooms on the next and 1 sliced tomato on the last quarter. Bake for 12 minutes, as described in the Margherita recipe.

### ROMANA

Prepare the pizza base as for Margherita pizza, above. Scatter 60 g chopped mozzarella, a pinch of dried oregano and 6 chopped anchovy fillets over the pizza. Drizzle with some oil and bake at the highest temperature your oven will reach for 12 minutes, or until the crust is browned and the centre is bubbling. Drizzle with a little more oil and serve.

### PIZZA BIANCO

Spread the prepared pizza base (see page 302) with 100 g chopped mozzarella, 3 sliced garlic cloves, 2 teaspoons chopped rosemary and drizzle with olive oil. Season, then sprinkle with 55 g grated Parmesan. Bake at the highest temperature your oven will reach for 12 minutes, or until the crust is browned and the centre is bubbling. Drizzle with a little oil.

### MARINARA

Prepare the pizza base as for Margherita pizza, above. Sprinkle on a pinch of dried oregano and 3 chopped garlic cloves and drizzle with olive oil. Bake at the highest temperature your oven will reach for 12 minutes, or until the crust is browned and the centre is bubbling. Drizzle with a little more oil and serve.

### SPINACHI

Spread the prepared pizza base (see page 302) with 1 kg chopped, cooked spinach, then drizzle the base with olive oil and season well. Scatter 150 g chopped mozzarella and 15 small black olives over the pizza. Bake at the highest temperature your oven will reach for 12 minutes, or until the crust is browned and the centre is bubbling. Drizzle with a little more olive oil and serve.

## pizzaiola

A sauce of skinned, seeded and chopped tomatoes, garlic, herbs such as parsley, oregano, thyme, basil and/or bay leaf, and lots of black pepper. The word is also used to describe any dish in which this sauce appears, such as steak or chicken. Pizzaiola comes from Naples and is so called because of its resemblance to the tomato topping found on pizzas.

### BISTECCA ALLA PIZZAIOLA

*Lightly cook 3 crushed garlic cloves in 3 tablespoons olive oil. Add 550 g peeled and chopped tomatoes and cook until mixture is quite thick. Add 2 tablespoons chopped basil and season well. Serve over grilled or barbecued rump steak. Makes about 350 ml.*

## plantain

It looks like a plumper, longer banana, but it's only ever eaten cooked, at all stages of ripeness. As a plantain ripens, it becomes sweeter and its skin colour changes from greeny-yellow through yellow to black. Brownish-black skin does not affect the quality of the flesh. It is used in both sweet and savoury dishes, and can be boiled or baked in the same way as potatoes—split the skin down the middle and bake for about 45 minutes; peeled and added to curries; or cut into thin slices and deep-fried in oil as chips *(pictured)*.

## ploughman's lunch

An example of manufactured authenticity, the ploughman's lunch originated in pubs (public houses) in the United Kingdom, not in the fields, and was based on the idea of what a field worker may have had for his lunch. It usually consists of a chunk of bread or a bread roll served with a piece of Cheddar or Stilton cheese, a pickled onion, pickle and a tomato—a quick meal for hungry drinkers rather than that of a ploughman.

Any one of over 2,000 varieties of a fruit, which is native to both Europe and America. Varieties include the greengage, damson and mirabelle. Plums can be either clingstone or freestone, pale yellow or dark purple, tart or sweet. They can be eaten fresh, used in savoury dishes, preserved or made into jams. Look for pleasantly scented, healthy fruit that yield slightly when pressed, with a whitish bloom on the skin. Prunes are dried plums.

*Clockwise from bottom left: President, Ruby blood, Black Amber, Radiance.*

■ *See also* **damson**

A sort of a porridge usually made from cornmeal and eaten extensively in northern Italy, either just cooked and soft or spread into trays, cooled and cut into squares that can be baked or fried. Traditionally, it is poured onto a wooden board and set in the middle of the table to be served with accompaniments such as meat, mushroom or vegetable ragùs.

The name polenta is now also used to describe the cornmeal itself. Polenta comes in different grades, which are matched to the dish they are being served with—coarser versions go with richer, heartier accompaniments. There is also a whiter version, *polenta bianca*, which is eaten in the Veneto.

## POLENTA PASTICCIO

*Cook 2 garlic cloves, 800 g tinned tomatoes and 1 tablespoon thyme until thick. Season. To cook the polenta, fill a large saucepan with 1.8 litres cold water, then add 250 g polenta and ½ teaspoon salt. Bring to the boil. Whisk or stir the mixture over low heat for 40 minutes, or until cooked. Pour ½ the quantity of polenta into a baking dish, pour ½ the tomato sauce over the polenta, then dot with 100 g cubed Taleggio cheese. Top with the rest of the polenta and finish with the tomato sauce, 100 g cubed Taleggio and 100 g mascarpone. Bake at 180°C for 30 minutes. Serves 6.*

Depending on the coarseness of the grain, polenta takes up to 40 minutes to cook. It is poured into boiling water and stirred constantly, not only to give it lots of air and thus, a lighter texture, but to prevent it from sticking to the pan. Make sure it is firm enough for a spoon to stand up in it and serve straight away or it will set. Generally, use 300 g polenta per litre of water. Polenta can be flavoured with cheese, chilli or herbs and needs to be well seasoned.

Polenta can also be used to make a type of gnocchi called *gnocchi alla Romana*, it can be cooked and layered up in pasticcio or can be added to cakes and biscuits to give them texture.

## BUYING

*Easy-cook polenta has been precooked, dried and milled again. It takes much of the effort out of making polenta and reduces cooking time. The results are satisfactory but not as good as using unprocessed polenta. It is best mixed with butter and cheese or set, cut into pieces and grilled.*

*Polenta can also be bought in precooked tube shapes. This polenta is ideal for frying, grilling or baking. Simply slice off a piece and reheat it as needed.*

*Choose a grade of polenta that will match the dish that you intend to serve it with.*

# Polish food

Poland is a central European country covered in thick forests, fields of corn and crisscrossed with rivers. Its cuisine is based on a tradition of peasant cooking, using ingredients dictated, as ever, by soil—rich and dark—and climate—cold and harsh. Other influences are the produce of the forest, and the neighbouring countries such as Russia and the Ukraine. For centuries Poland has had its shape changed and been divided by various invaders, and traces of this history have been left on the table. The cold climate necessitated hearty, warm and filling food. Hospitality is of great importance to the Poles and no excuse is needed to stop for a cup of tea (with a spoonful of jam) or coffee or a glass of vodka.

*Bigos, meaning 'hunter's stew', is considered to be Poland's national dish.*

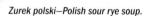

*Zurek polski—Polish sour rye soup.*

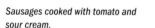

*Sausages cooked with tomato and sour cream.*

Mushrooms form the basis of many traditional Polish dishes, and the forests supply them in abundance. Morels, ceps and milk caps are particularly sought after. They are used in a multitude of dishes including *zrazy*, which is meat rolls with mushroom stuffing, or in *pierogi*, semicircular dumplings filled with anything from potato to a mixture of mushroom and sauerkraut, and served with sour cream. The rich soil grows a host of grains, including barley, maize, wheat, oats and millet. Buckwheat is used as a flour to make blinis or the grains are cooked to make *kasha*, and barley is used to make hearty, warming soups. Polish rye bread is dark and moist, and breadcrumbs are used extensively in cooking, giving rise to the French description, *à la polonaise*.

*Herrings with smetana served with pickled beetroot.*

*Stuffed cabbage leaves*

Cabbage grows abundantly and is eaten all year round, either fresh or pickled as sauerkraut. Although each housewife will have her own recipe, *bigos* is from sauerkraut cooked with meat, pork and bacon and sometimes with dried mushrooms. Cucumbers, potatoes and beetroot also grow abundantly. As with most Eastern European cuisine, dill is widely used to flavour soups, salad dressings and potato dishes, and sour cream and curd cheese are common ingredients, used in foods such as pancakes and potato cakes.

The pig provides meat in all forms, from sausages and bacon to dishes made from the snout and trotters. Piquant sausages in numerous shapes and forms are a distinctive feature of Polish cooking.

*Pancakes filled with curd cheese and sour cream.*

■ *See also* **pirozhki, smetana**

Polynesia is the name given to a group of islands covering a vast area of the South Pacific—some 20 million square kilometres—the best known of which are Western Samoa, Tonga, Cook Islands, Tahiti and Hawaii, and whose peoples include the New Zealand Maoris.

Polynesia was first settled 2,000 to 3,000 years ago, by whom is still in dispute. Today, the islands' cuisines are diverse, fusion cuisines created by successive immigrations from China, Korea, Puerto Rico, the Philippines and Europe, resulting in each island group having its own style.

Fish is the staple food and is served in a multitude of ways, cooked or raw, in soy sauce or coconut milk, or marinated in lime juice, such as *kokoda* and Hawaiian *poke*, cubes of raw fish dressed simply with salt and seaweed or with chilli and soy. Staple plant foods are taro and sweet potato. Taro may be used to make *poi*, a sour, fermented paste made from the boiled and mashed corms of the taro. *Poi mochi* are deep-fried dough-like balls made from *poi* mixed with coconut milk.

Another popular tuber is *ti* (also known as *auti* and *ki*) the leaves of which are eaten as a herb. *Ti* leaves are

used to wrap meat, which is then steamed. Fruit and nuts are eaten in abundance, in particular, coconut. Two more incongruous but popular foods are spam and corned beef, introduced to the islands during the Second World War. Part of their appeal is that both keep well without refrigeration. Spam is used in sushi (*musubi*), tempura, wontons and for teriyaki.

Perhaps the most interesting cuisine is to be found on the island of Hawaii, which, before the arrival of the first humans around the third century AD, was devoid of any land food. As well as taro and sweet potato, they brought pigs and dogs (both were eaten), sugar and other edible plants. What developed over the next 700 years can only be described as a Creole cuisine, layered by the later arrival of the Chinese, Koreans, Japanese and Filipinos. Today, that has translated into a style known as 'local food', a curious European-Asian mixture of rice, meat and pasta only to be found in Hawaii.

■ *See also* **taro**

*From top: Laulau, salt pork and fish wrapped in taro leaves; kokoda, raw fish, onions and tomatoes in lime juice and coconut milk; poi mochi.*

# pomegranate

A round fruit the size of a large apple, the pomegranate has thick, tough, reddish skin enclosing hundreds of edible seeds, each encased in a juicy, translucent-red pulp. To use, cut the fruit in half with a very sharp knife and scoop out the tangy-sweet seeds, separate them from the white pith, and eat them fresh, add to salads, use as a garnish on sweet and savoury dishes, or press to extract the juice. Sprinkle the seeds over lemon granita and splash with gin for a refreshing dessert. Pomegranates are very important in Persian cuisine. Originally, pomegranates were the main flavouring ingredient in grenadine syrup, which is used in cocktails, ice creams and sorbets. Choose pomegranates that are heavy for their size with smooth skin that gives slightly when pressed. Pomegranates are usually available in autumn.

*Also known as — Chinese apple*

## poor boy

Popular in New Orleans, a poor boy is a sandwich made from a small loaf of French bread, which is split lengthways and filled with ingredients such as fried oysters, sliced meats, cheese, shrimps, tomatoes and lettuce, usually with a dressing of gravy. The classic is roast beef poor boy *(pictured)*, made with thin slices of leftover roast beef, lettuce, gravy and mayonnaise. The poor boy is so called because it was once considered inexpensive, yet filling, food. ***Also known as — hero sandwich, po' boy, submarine***

## popover

### POPOVERS

*Beat 2 eggs with 310 ml milk, then stir in 140 g plain flour and ½ teaspoon salt. Add 1 tablespoon warm melted butter and beat lightly to form a batter. Pour into 12 greased muffin tins and bake in a preheated 225 °C oven for 15 minutes. Reduce to 180 °C and bake for 20 minutes, or until golden brown and crisp on top. Makes 12.*

Made from a batter of eggs, milk, flour and butter, similar to that used for Yorkshire puddings, popovers are crisp and golden brown on top and moist and light on the inside. Baked in individual muffin or deep popover tins, they get their name from their tendency to swell over the sides of the tin when cooking. Popovers are often served with butter and jam or as a savoury with a salad.

## poppy seeds

Poppy seeds come from the opium poppy but once mature they lose their narcotic properties. The seeds vary in size, shape and colour. The blue-grey seed is the most common, and is sprinkled on top of breads and biscuits or used in cakes. The white-grey Indian poppy seed is used for thickening sauces and curries. They are often dry-fried before use in cooking. When roasted, the seeds take on a slight nutty flavour. The seeds are also used for their oil.

## porcini — see mushrooms

## BUYING

*Pork should have firm white fat and pale pink flesh. Avoid any pork that looks wet or has waxy-looking fat.*

*The quality of pork varies greatly—animals that are reared organically or in a non-intensive manner tend to have better quality meat. Traditional breeds often have better flavoured meat than modern breeds, which are bred more for their leanness than flavour. Look for meat from such breeds as Tamworth, Welsh Saddleback and Gloucester Old Spot.*

*Pork is usually bought fresh after it has been hung for 2 to 3 days, but it is better hung for about 7 to 10 days so flavour can develop. Generally only the best cuts are aged.*

One of the oldest and most important meats worldwide, except in areas where Jewish or Muslim communities predominate. Pigs were domesticated in China about 5,000 years ago, and in Europe every family that could afford to had at least one pig. They were (and still are in southern Europe) traditionally killed in November, when their offal was eaten fresh and most of the rest of the animal was cured, turned into sausages or preserved to be eaten throughout the rest of the year—nothing was wasted. Pigs that are to be eaten as fresh pork, called porkers, are less than 6 months old and their meat varies in colour from pale pink to white, depending on their breed. Pork is eaten as joints, smaller cuts or as a whole sucking pig. It appears in most world cuisines, is very adaptable and carries flavours well.

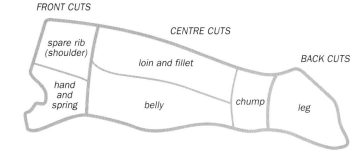

FRONT CUTS
CENTRE CUTS
spare rib (shoulder)
loin and fillet
BACK CUTS
hand and spring
belly
chump
leg

## CUTS OF PORK

**Front cuts**    Cuts from the front of the pig tend to be inexpensive and are good for braising and casseroling as they have a high gelatinous content. They include the hand and spring, spare rib, which can be cut into shoulder chops or spare rib chops.

**Centre cuts**    The cuts from the underside or belly of the pig have an equal proportion of fat and meat and can be braised, roasted and casseroled. The pork from the belly makes good fatty mince for pâtés and terrines. The top cuts include the loin and fillet. These can be cooked as whole pieces, on or off the bone, or cut into loin and chump chops or noisettes.

**Back cuts**    The leg is sold either as a whole joint or cut into the knuckle and leg fillet. Both cuts are good for roasting.

## COOKING

*Nearly all cuts of pork are tender and can be grilled or roasted.*

*Pork from Western countries no longer needs to be well cooked as the threat of tapeworm has been eradicated. Pork from other countries may contain trichonella but this is killed off at the relatively low temperature of 58°C. If in doubt, cook your pork thoroughly.*

*Cooking pork at lower temperatures will keep the meat moist and prevent it from becoming tough.*

*Add a pig's trotter or piece of pork rind to stews and casseroles to give them a rich flavour and a gelatinous sauce. Remove the pork before serving the dish.*

*Dry out pork rind thoroughly if you want really crunchy crackling.*

### Roasting

The loin and leg of pork are the best for roasting. A whole loin should feed four people and a leg will feed a large gathering. If cooking a joint on the bone, ask your butcher to chine it (detach the backbone) for you, as this will make it easier to carve. Part of the attraction of roast pork is the crackling and this can be roasted either on the pork or separately, which will make sure it is really crisp.

Roast pork at 180°C for 25–30 minutes per 500 g. Take the skin off, leaving about 1 cm fat on it, score the skin with a stanley knife, rub it with salt and roast next to the pork. If your joint is particularly lean, rest the fat on top and remove it for the last 20 minutes to crisp it—doing this will help baste the meat as it cooks. Pork fat can be used to roast potatoes and the meat juices make good gravy. As well as this version of roast pork there is porchetta, a whole roast pig from Italy, and *char siu*, the Chinese version of roast pork.

*Scoring crackling for roasting*

### Slow cooking

Though pork is a tender meat, it cooks particularly well slowly, especially when cuts with plenty of connective tissue, such as neck, are used, giving the dish a smooth, velvety texture from the gelatinous parts. All cuts of pork can be braised, casseroled or pot-roasted. Most cuisines of the world have some slow-cooked pork recipes—the Chinese have especially good methods of cooking belly pork with soy and star anise until it is very tender, the French use it in cassoulet, the Americans use it in Boston baked beans, and in the Philippines, pork is cooked in vinegar to make *adobo*. Slow cook pork for several hours in plenty of liquid to keep it tender and moist.

*Chinese hoisin and five-spice roast pork*

### OTHER PARTS OF THE PIG

*It is said that any part of a pig except the squeak can be eaten. Pork fat is very useful, rendered down as lard or as sheets of fat for barding around lean cuts of meat. Pig cheeks are excellent slow cooked as are trotters, which can be boned and stuffed like sausages. Pig's head is made into brawn and the ears may be eaten whole or shredded. The heart, kidneys and liver can be used as for other animals though their strong flavour is best in pâtés and terrines. Pig's caul (fat) is used to wrap meat while it cooks.*

### PORK WITH APPLES

*Remove the skin, leaving a 1 cm layer of fat on it, from a 1.8 kg pork joint. Score the skin well, then tie it back on the joint and rub with salt. Season and put bone side down in a roasting tin with a few garlic cloves and some pearl onions. Roast at 180°C for 25–30 minutes per 500 g, or until cooked through. Rest for 15 minutes before carving. If necessary, remove the crackling and crisp it under the grill. Peel and slice 4 eating apples and sauté them in 60 g butter, add 2 teaspoons brown sugar and caramelize them over high heat. Add 1 tablespoon Calvados and cook for 1 minute. Serve apples with the pork, roast onions, garlic and a gravy made with the meat juices (see page 172). Serves 8.*

Made from rolled oats cooked in milk or water, porridge is a warm, filling breakfast dish, particularly popular in colder climates. Some recipes use additional hot milk or cream when serving, some add sugar or golden syrup. In Scotland, porridge is eaten with salt, a tradition possibly dating from the dish's predecessor, pottage, a savoury dish of boiled cereals or meat. Today, branded porridges are almost instant foods and do not need long, slow cooking.

## PORRIDGE

*Bring 1 litre milk to the boil, sprinkle in 100 g medium oatmeal, stirring all the time. Simmer for 30 minutes, stirring often to stop it sticking, until the porridge is cooked and creamy. Serve with salt or extra milk and brown sugar. Serves 2.*

*From left: white, ruby, tawny.*

A fortified wine from the Douro valley in northern Portugal. Originally a red wine with brandy added to make it keep better while transported. Now brandy is added when the wine is half fermented, which stops the fermentation instantly. Its sweetness will depend on when the brandy is added as more or less sugar will have fermented. It is then matured, and blended. Most port will not continue to mature once bottled. Vintage ports, however, are aged in the bottle rather than in wooden casks. Port is served as an after-dinner drink and can be used in sauces and for macerating fruit.

## TYPES OF PORTS

| | |
|---|---|
| **Vintage** | Most expensive port made from a single harvest and aged in the bottle rather than in wooden casks. Vintage port is available at 5 years old but should really be kept until it is at least 25 to 50 years old. Older ports develop a complex flavour they don't have when young. |
| **Late-bottled vintage** | Made from grapes very nearly up to vintage standards. They are kept for 4 to 6 years in a cask. Ready when bottled, they will continue to mature if kept. |
| **Ruby** | A blend of young fruity wines, very red in colour and the cheapest port. On average are aged for only 3 years. |
| **Tawny** | Have a more complex flavour as they are aged longer than ruby port but are lighter in colour. The best tawnies are aged in casks for between 10 and 40 years. |
| **White** | Made from white grapes. Can be served chilled as an apéritif. Like red port, can range in flavour according to sugar content. |
| **Colheita** | Made from the same wines as tawny port but from a single year's grape harvest and aged for 7 years. |
| **Riserva** | Classic-style port made with blended older wines and aged for 7 years. |

## FRANCATELLI SAUCE

*Simmer together 2 tablespoons port, 250 g redcurrant jelly, 1 cinnamon stick and the zest of 1 lemon for about 5 minutes. Stir to dissolve the jelly. Strain into a jug or store in a sealed jar for later use. Serve over venison steaks, lamb or chicken. Makes 250 ml.*

# Portuguese food

Caldo verde (green soup)—a soup made with cabbage and potatoes, and sometimes one or two slices of sausage.

Portugal is bordered by Spain in the east and north and by the Atlantic Ocean along the whole of its western coast. Its topography is varied and the contrast between food eaten on the coast and inland is marked. In contrast to many countries where the cuisine has been influenced by invaders and colonizers, the Portuguese were great explorers, bringing back spices and foods from the East Indies, Far East and the New World. African and Moorish influences are in evidence with the use of spices such as piri piri, a fiery hot chilli from Africa, used with shellfish, as well as in poultry dishes and stews. Spices such as curry, cinnamon and nutmeg, and herbs such as coriander, mint and bay leaves are widely used.

Although both Portuguese and Spanish cooking make good use of ingredients like rice, cabbage, potato, pork, cod and other seafood, Portuguese cuisine has its own regional touches. For example, soups such as *caldo verde*, originally from the northern province of Minho, are now eaten throughout Portugal. This emerald-green soup is made with shredded cabbage and potatoes and spiced with one or two slices of cured pork sausage (*chouriço*). Other soups include *açordas*, made from stale bread soaked in oil and flavoured with garlic and herbs, usually garnished with seafood, chicken, pork or vegetables.

Grilled sardines with peppers and onions

Caldeirada—a fish and seafood stew.

The coastal areas offer a wealth of seafood. *Bacalhau*, salt cod, is a favourite and can be prepared in a myriad of ways, many of them very regional—fried as croquettes and topped with eggs, or poached with mussels and cooked in wine and tomato sauce. *Caldeirada*, a fish and shellfish stew, is served in nearly every coastal city and village. Sardines are usually barbecued, as are sole, red mullet, swordfish, Conger eels, squid, crabs, mussels and clams. In spite of the abundance of seafood, meat is popular too, with dishes such as steaks cooked in port; mutton; goat stews and roast kid; duck; lamb; and sucking pigs common on Portuguese menus.

Cod fritters

Portuguese tarts

The Portuguese are well known for their sweet desserts and pastries, often based on a rich egg custard. In the eighteenth century, these pastries were a speciality of the convents, such as the convent at Aveiro, the birthplace of *ovos moles*, a sweet paste made with egg yolk and sugar, eaten sparingly on its own or with sponge cake or filled into rice paper shaped into forms such as fish, shells and snails, its sweetness often offset by a glass of port. Other regional specialities include honey cake from Madeira and marzipan cake from Algarve.

Native to South America, the potato is now a staple in the global diet. Potatoes are cheap, hardy and easy to grow, and are high in starch, protein and vitamins. Almost all nationalities have a traditional dish based on potatoes, such as gratin dauphinois, Rösti and Irish stew. There are thousands of varieties of potatoes, but only a hundred or so are grown for commercial use. Potatoes can be divided into new crop (early) potatoes and old (main crop) potatoes and their texture can be floury or waxy. Some potatoes are good all-round types, others are more suitable for specific recipes. Potatoes are never eaten raw but must be cooked first as they contain 20 per cent indigestible starch, which, when cooked, converts into sugar.

**Potatoes go with — bacon, egg, mayonnaise, roast meat, sausage**

## NEW POTATOES

*Originally, new potatoes referred to early varieties of potatoes such as Jersey Royals and Duke of York. Today, the term may also be used to refer to a baby potato of any variety. Early variety potatoes have a better flavour than baby potatoes, as these have not yet developed a full flavour.*

## STORAGE

*Store potatoes in paper bags to allow moisture to escape and to keep light out. Keep in a cool and dry, dark, well-ventilated place to prevent them from sprouting. If exposed to light, potatoes turn green—these will be bitter and indigestible and can be poisonous.*

*Ready-washed potatoes have a shorter storage life as the washing process removes their protective coating of earth. Older potatoes keep for 2 weeks or so, but new potatoes are best eaten soon after purchase, so buy in smaller quantities.*

*If stored in the fridge, potatoes become sweeter than if stored at room temperature.*

Russet (Idaho)

King Edward

Pink Fir Apple

Desiree

Bintje

Pontiac

Pink Eye

## TYPES OF POTATOES

| | |
|---|---|
| **Floury** | These have a low moisture and sugar content and are high in starch. They are good for baking, roasting, mashing and chips, gnocchi and in bread, but disintegrate when boiled. They include Russet (Idaho), Pentland Squire and King Edward. |
| **Waxy** | These have a high moisture content and are low in starch. They hold their shape when boiled or roasted but don't mash well. Use in salads or stews. These include Roseval, Charlotte, Pink Fir Apple, Kipfler and Cara. |
| **Salad** | These are waxy, have a distinct flavour and are not usually peeled. Boil or roast. These include Kipfler, Pink Fir Apple, Jersey Royal and La Ratte. |
| **All-purpose** | Use in recipes that don't specify the type of potato needed. These include Desiree, Nicola, Maris Piper, Romano, Wilja, Bintje, Spunta, Pontiac and Pink Eye. |

## PREPARATION

*Scrub well to remove dirt and cut off any green parts and any 'eyes'.*

*It is the thin layer immediately underneath the skin that is the most nutritious, so potatoes should be eaten with their skin on, where possible.*

## COOKING POTATOES

**Baked**
Scrub and dry 4 large floury potatoes. Prick all over with a fork or skewer and put in a 220°C oven for 1 to 1½ hours or until cooked through. To give a firmer skin, rub oil and salt into the skins before you bake them or wrap in foil.

**Roast**
Peel 1 kg floury potatoes and cut into quarters. Parboil for 5 minutes, drain in a wire sieve, shaking them around to rough up the surfaces. Put into a roasting tin that has been preheated with 4 tablespoons hot oil or dripping, stir to coat, then roast at 180°C for 50 minutes. Turn once or twice as they cook.

**Boiled**
Peel 1 kg waxy potatoes and put in a pan of lightly salted cold water with a sprig of mint. Bring to the boil; simmer for 15 to 20 minutes, or until tender. Don't boil too hard or they'll break up. Drain, discard the mint and toss in butter.

**Mashed**
Peel and chop 4 large floury potatoes. Put in cold water and bring to the boil. Boil until tender, drain well and put back in the pan over low heat with 2 tablespoons hot milk, 1 tablespoon butter and plenty of seasoning. Mash with a masher (or use a potato ricer, a mouli or a wire sieve, but don't use a food processor or the mash will go gluey), then beat with a wooden spoon until fluffy.

**Croquettes**
Make one quantity of mashed potato and leave it to cool. Break off portions of potato, roll into a log shape, then dip in flour, egg and breadcrumbs and chill for 1 hour. Deep-fry the croquettes at 180°C for 5 minutes.

**Hasselback**
Peel and cut 1 kg potatoes in half horizontally. Sit each one flat and make parallel cuts along its length, almost down to the bottom. Brush with melted butter and sprinkle with 1 tablespoon combined grated Parmesan and breadcrumbs, then bake at 180°C for 50 minutes.

### SPICY POTATO SALAD

*Put 650 g new potatoes in boiling salted water. Cook for 10 minutes, or until tender, drain and cut each potato in half. Mix 4 tablespoons olive oil, 1 teaspoon grated lime rind, 1½ tablespoons lime juice, 1 small red chilli, seeded and finely chopped, and 2 tablespoons chopped coriander. Season, pour over hot potatoes and cool slightly. Serve warm or cold. Serves 4.*

**See also** Anna potatoes, chips, colcannon, hash browns, potato crisps

Thin slices of potato fried in oil until crisp. Commercially produced potato crisps are sometimes made with processed potatoes to keep a uniform shape. Some potato crisps may be salted or flavoured with spices such as salt and vinegar or cheese and onion. To make chips successfully at home you will need a mandolin or slicing attachment on a food processor, though a large, sharp knife will also do. **Also known as — crisps, potato chips**

POTATO CRISPS

*Peel 6 large, all-purpose potatoes. Wash and pat dry. Slice the potatoes very thinly using a mandolin or knife. Deep-fry in batches at 180°C for 3–4 minutes, or until golden and crisp. Drain on paper towels and season with salt. Serves 4.*

A traditional French dish meaning 'pot on the fire', of boiled meat and vegetables. Different cuts of meat are used such as shin, belly, oxtail and marrowbone with vegetables such as leeks, carrots, turnips, onions, celery, parsnips and potatoes. Herbs and seasoning are added and the dish is left to cook for several hours. The broth is served separately, the marrowbone is served on toast, followed by the meat and vegetables served with beetroot, horseradish, mustards and pickles. Any leftover meat can be eaten in salads.

The process of sealing meat such as poultry or game in a pot, under a layer of clarified butter or molten fat to preserve it. Potted meats were popular in the seventeenth and eighteenth centuries as this ensured that the meat would last for up to 1 month. The meat is cooked with seasonings, reduced to a paste, placed in the container and covered with fat. It is usually served spread on bread or toast. Potted meat will keep for several weeks in the fridge. Commercially made potted meat may contain preservatives. Potted fish such as char and shellfish such as shrimps are also very popular.

315

## pound cake

A cake made with equal weights of flour, butter, eggs and sugar. Traditionally it was a pound of each, so made a very big cake. Its French equivalent is called *quatre quarts* meaning 'four quarters', that is, one of each ingredient. Originating in the eighteenth century, today the pound cake has many variations, some adding lemon, brandy or spices, some separating the eggs and whisking the whites to add air to the cake, others contain no fat. Pound cakes are usually baked in a loaf tin.

**Also known as — Madeira cake**

### POUND CAKE

*Cream together 240 g butter and 240 g caster sugar, then beat until fluffy. Beat in 4 egg yolks, then 240 g plain flour. Whisk 4 egg whites and fold them into the mixture. Pour into a lined 21 x 11 cm loaf tin and bake at 180 °C for 50-60 minutes.*

## praline

Traditionally made with almonds, a praline can be any nut coated in caramelized sugar and left to harden. Once hardened, the mixture can be eaten as is, or pulverized and added to other dishes such as ice cream, cakes and patisserie or used as a filling or coating for chocolates. Praline is also the name of a type of chocolate. Nougatine is similar to praline, made from a caramel mixed with almonds or hazelnuts.

### PRALINE ICE CREAM

*Whisk until pale 4 egg yolks with 2 tablespoons caster sugar, then fold in 300 ml lightly whipped double cream and crushed praline (see steps below). Whisk 4 egg whites until stiff peaks form, then fold into mixture. Put in a container and freeze, stirring hourly, until hard (about 6–8 hours). Serves 4.*

### MAKING PRALINE

1 *Put 200 g blanched almonds in a hot frying pan and dry-fry until well browned. Set aside.*

2 *Melt 200 g sugar in a saucepan over medium heat until golden. Take off the heat and immediately stir in the almonds.*

3 *Spoon onto a greased baking sheet and leave to harden. Break into pieces and crush in a food processor.*

Crustaceans found all over the world living in fresh, briny and saltwater of varying temperatures called prawns in most English-speaking countries, but shrimps in North and South America. Prawns vary in size from 2.5 cm to 30 cm long, have two long antennae and five pairs of legs. Their flesh is translucent and can be coloured pink, yellow, grey, brown, red or dark red, depending on the species. They become opaque and turn pink once cooked. Prawns can be steamed, boiled, fried, grilled or baked. They can be made into mousses, sauces and stuffings and can be served as salads and hors d'oeuvres. Whichever way they are cooked, they should not be overcooked or they will become tough and rubbery; 2 to 3 minutes is sufficient to cook average-sized prawns. If adding cooked prawns to a dish, add them at the last minute.

**Prawns go with — chilli, garlic, lemon, mayonnaise, mango**

## BUYING

*Prawns perish easily, so they are often frozen on board the ships from which they are fished. They can be bought shell on or shelled, head on or off, cooked or uncooked. They can also be smoked, dried or canned.*

*Avoid frozen prawns covered in frost or with freezer burn. Choose fresh prawns with a pleasant smell, and firm shells. Avoid any that smell of ammonia or with dark discolouration around the head or legs—this means they are starting to deteriorate.*

*500 g of shell-on prawns will yield about 250 g of shelled weight.*

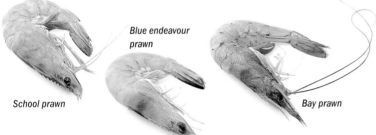

Blue endeavour prawn

School prawn

Bay prawn

## PREPARING PREWNS

1. Pull off the head by holding the body and tugging gently at the head.

2. Peel off the shell and legs from around the body, then (if removing) gently pull on the tail to remove it in one piece.

3. Using a sharp knife, score down the back and remove the thin digestive tract.

## PRAWN COCKTAIL

*Mix together 6 tablespoons mayonnaise, 3 teaspoons tomato ketchup, 2 teaspoons lemon juice and a few drops of Tabasco sauce. Arrange a handful of salad leaves in 4 serving glasses and top with 6–8 cleaned and cooked prawns. Spoon over a little sauce and serve with a pinch of cayenne pepper sprinkled on top and with lemon wedges. Serves 4.*

**See also  shrimp**

## prawn crackers

Deep-fried crisps made from a batter of dried prawn and flavoured rice flour or tapioca flour, which, when deep-fried, puff up into light and crunchy foam-like crackers. Prawn crackers are commonly served as an accompaniment to Southeast Asian meals and with drinks. Chinese prawn crackers come in an assortment of vivid colours. In Indonesia and Malaysia they are called *krupuk udang* and in Vietnam they are called *bahn phong*.

## preserved lemons

A Middle Eastern ingredient made by steeping lemons in salt and lemon juice, and leaving them to mature for at least a month before use. Once preserved, the whole lemons are eaten, including the pith and skin, which becomes soft and moist. These aromatic lemons are used widely in North African cooking in soups, stews and Moroccan tagines, or are used to season salads and steamed potatoes and couscous. They greatly enhance stuffings and are delicious with chicken. Rinse before use and use whole or chopped, with or without the peel. Preserved lemons can last over a year without being refrigerated.

## preserves

Fruit and vegetables preserved in a bottle or container or made into jams and jellies. Preserves can be made at home or industrially. They are often made when there is a glut of fruit or vegetables to ensure supply through unseasonal months. When fruits are preserved they are sorted, tailed, seeded, washed, peeled and sometimes blanched. They are then placed in glass bottles or jars with their own juice or a sugar syrup and cooked, which prevents the growth of microorganisms. Store in a cool, dry place.

***Also known as — conserve***

### PRESERVED PLUMS

*Cover 2.5 kg plums with boiling water for 30 seconds, drain and peel. Halve the fruit and remove the stones, then pack tightly into 5 clean 500 ml jars. Dissolve 500 g sugar in 1 litre boiling water and pour into the jars. Close the lids tightly and put the jars on top of a tea towel in a large saucepan. Pour on warm water, bring slowly to a simmer, then simmer for 15 minutes. Remove and cool.*

Originally a hard, chewy, salty snack to be eaten with beer, the pretzel originated in Germany and Austria and is now popular in New York. The dough is shaped into its characteristic loose knot shape and poached in boiling water before it is sprinkled with salt and baked. Pretzels are also similarly shaped (or sticks or rings) crisp snacks or even sweet biscuits, or may refer to other shaped snacks made with pretzel dough.

### prickly pear

Neither pear nor fig (they are also known as Indian figs), but the fruit of a cactus, which is native to parts of America but are now found in the Mediterranean, India and Australia. The skin ranges from green, yellow and orange to dark red and is dotted with several sharp spikes. Care should be taken when handling the fruits and the spikes can be removed by gently rubbing with a thick, rough cloth. The flesh is soft and spongy and smells like watermelon. It is full of crisp edible seeds, although they are not to everyone's liking. Prickly pears yield slightly to gentle pressure when ripe. They can be eaten out of hand, sprinkled with lemon or lime juice. They can also be cooked, but should be pushed through a sieve to remove the seeds, which harden on heating. Use in sorbets and ice creams or try in salads to add a little sweetness. The leaves (nopales) can be eaten as a vegetable.

**Also known as — barbary pear, cactus pear, Indian fig, Indian pear**

### see choux — profiterole

### prosciutto

Italian for ham, which is generally taken to mean cured ham, such as Parma ham and San Daniele. In Italy, cooked ham is known as *prosciutto cotto*, and raw ham is *prosciutto crudo*.

### see dried fruit — prune

### pudding

The name given to numerous dishes, both sweet or savoury, which are cooked or presented in a pudding basin or other type of mould, or pudding cloth. Pudding also refers to the general term for dishes eaten at the end of a meal, which can be hot, cold, steamed, boiled or baked. Savoury puddings include steak and kidney pudding with its filling encased in a suet crust; or pease pudding, split peas boiled in a pudding cloth. Sweet versions include suet pudding filled with apple *(pictured)*.

## puff pastry

A delicate, crisp pastry made up of many, many layers, the making of which is a lengthy procedure. Only some of the butter is incorporated into the basic dough, the remainder is wrapped in the dough, which is then rolled and folded so that the butter becomes trapped between the layers, causing it to puff up as the layers separate. The pastry is then rolled and folded in three several times to create over 700 layers. It is important to keep the pastry rectangular as you make it and roll it out—every layer must be exactly the same or it will rise unevenly. It is used for tarts and tartlets, vol au vents and millefeuille.

### MAKING PUFF PASTRY

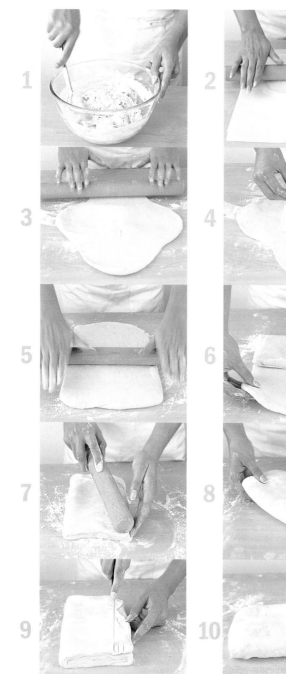

1  Mix 500 g flour, 250 ml cold water, 75 g melted butter and 2 teaspoons salt to a rough dough and chill for 30 minutes.

2  Put 300 g butter between two sheets of greaseproof paper and flatten with a rolling pin.

3  Roll out the dough on a floured surface to form a cross shape.

4  Put the butter in the centre and fold in the sides. The butter and dough should be the same consistency.

5  Roll out the dough to a 20 x 45 cm rectangle.

6  Fold the bottom third of the dough up towards the middle, then bring the top third of the dough over the folded thirds.

7  Turn the dough through a quarter turn, gently seal the edges and roll out to a 20 x 45 cm rectangle.

8  Fold in thirds again, keeping the edges straight, then chill.

9  Repeat the rolling, folding and chilling a total of 6 times. Mark the side of the dough each time so you remember how many you have done.

10 After the final roll and fold, leave it folded. It is now ready.

The edible seeds of any legume, although the term usually refers only to the dried seeds. Pulses are an important protein source and staple food in many countries, especially in countries like India, where a large part of the population is vegetarian. In India, pulses are further split into 'gram', which are whole seeds and 'dal', split, skinned seeds.

*From left: green and orange lentils, broad beans, black-eyed beans, red kidney beans, yellow and green split peas, white split urd, black whole urd.*

## TYPES OF PULSES

**Lentils**
Usually sold split, these lentils include brown, green and red varieties.

**Beans**
Adzuki beans are sweet and are ground to make flour or used in desserts in Japan. Haricot beans, including flageolet, cannellini and navy beans, are used widely in Europe and America where they are known as white beans. Butter or lima beans are large white beans, which break down to a purée when cooked. Red and black kidney beans and black turtle beans are a staple of South and Central America and are used in soups and stews or refried as a paste. Borlotti and pinto beans have speckled skins. Pintos are used in Central and South America and borlotti in Italy. Black-eyed beans, an ingredient of hopping John, are eaten in southern America but are native to Africa. Broad beans or fava beans are large brownish beans with a thick skin; they are used to make falafel. Ful medames are a staple of Egypt and are also known as Egyptian brown beans. Chickpeas (garbanzos) are not peas but beans and are eaten all over Europe, India and the Middle East. They are used to make hummus.

**Peas**
Peas are generally sold split and skinned. There are two main types, yellow and green, and these both turn to purée when cooked. Pigeon peas, a staple in India, are used in the Caribbean to make rice and peas. Split peas are yellow and sometimes sold as lentils.

**Urd (black gram)**
Urd are a type of pulse, similar to mung beans, which are black or green when whole and white when split and skinned. They are often soaked, ground to a paste and used in batters and breads such as dosa.

### STORAGE

*Pulses do not keep indefinitely—they get harder as they get older and do not cook as well.*

### PREPARATION

*To quick-soak beans, put them in cold water with a pinch of bicarbonate of soda, then simmer for 5 minutes, leave to cool, then rinse and cook as for the recipe, or boil for 2–3 minutes, then soak in the same water for 1 hour.*

*Peas and lentils don't need to be soaked before they are cooked. Beans are usually soaked overnight to soften them but this is not strictly necessary—soaking may also start the germination or fermentation process if it gets too warm.*

*Kidney beans must be boiled for 15 minutes and then rinsed before cooking to get rid of the toxins on their skins. Soya beans must be properly cooked to inactivate their anti-nutrients and to make them digestible.*

*See also **beans, lentils, pea, soya bean***

**321**

## pummelo

One of the largest of the citrus family, and related to the grapefruit. Ranging in size from a cantaloupe to a basketball, the fruit's flavour varies too. Some are sweet, others slightly acidic, some full of seeds and others seedless. Before eating, peel off the thick skin and pith and remove all the membrane from each segment. Use in salads, with poultry or as a substitute for grapefruit. Use the rind to make jam.
**Also known as — pomelo, shaddock**

## pumpernickel

A wholegrain rye bread from Westphalia, Germany. It is dark brown and has a slightly sticky texture. Commercially made pumpernickel is often baked in a low oven, resulting in a moist, dense bread. It is usually sold and eaten in thin slices, often with cheese, smoked sausages or gravlax.
**Also known as — black bread**

## pumpkin

Queensland blue pumpkin (back), orange minikin (front).

A member of the gourd family classified as a winter squash, often with orange skin and flesh as used in Halloween lanterns. Their flesh has a pronounced sweet flavour and is used in both sweet and savoury dishes. Pumpkins can be boiled, steamed, roasted or mashed. In some countries, all squashes are referred to as pumpkins; in others, only large round segmented ones *(pictured)*.

If boiling pumpkin, remove the skin and seeds. If roasting larger pieces, the skin can be left intact for cooking. The seeds of pumpkins are dried and used in both sweet and savoury food. They are delicious toasted and sprinkled on salads and soups, or they can be eaten out of hand. The roasted seeds are also used to make a thick, dark brown oil with a strong flavour and aroma, used as a salad dressing and seasoning. Choose pumpkins that are heavy for their size and have unblemished skins. Store whole at room temperature for around 1 month. Wrap cut pumpkin in clingfilm and store in the fridge.
**Pumpkin goes with — cinnamon, coconut, nutmeg, roast meat**

### COOKING

*When making pumpkin purée or mash, steam or roast it to give a better flavour as boiling it tends to make the flesh a little watery.*

▥ **See also squash**

From left: pumpkin seeds, pumpkin bread, pumpkin oil, shelled pumpkin seeds.

### THAI PUMPKIN AND COCONUT SOUP

*Heat 2 tablespoons olive oil in a large saucepan and gently fry 1 finely chopped onion for 5 minutes. Add 1 tablespoon red curry paste and 1 tablespoon tomato purée and fry for 30 seconds. Add 450 g cubed pumpkin flesh and fry for 5 minutes. Add 400 ml coconut milk and 500 ml vegetable stock. Cover and simmer for 15 minutes. Remove lid and simmer for a further 5 minutes. Cool slightly, then purée in a food processor until smooth. Return to a clean saucepan and reheat. Stir in 3 tablespoons chopped coriander and garnish with sliced red chilli. Serves 4.*

A small European game bird, prized both for its meat and eggs. Quail are native to many countries including America, Europe and most of Asia. Most quail used in cooking are farmed. Quail have delicate flesh that can dry out during cooking, so to keep the meat moist, cover the breasts with fat (bard) or pieces of bacon and roast, grill or casserole. They perish rapidly, so store for no longer than 2 to 3 days. Serve two per person.

**Quail goes with — bacon, cherry, lemon, prunes, red wine, thyme**

### STUFFED QUAIL

*Put 40 g wild rice in 300 ml chicken stock; cook for 30 minutes, or until tender; drain. Sauté 2 tablespoons chopped onions in a little olive oil for 5 minutes. Mix with 35 g each of finely chopped dried apricots and prunes and 1 tablespoon chopped mixed parsley and chervil; season. Season inside 4 boned quails, fill loosely with stuffing and fasten with cocktail sticks. Heat 80 ml oil in a frying pan; brown quails all over. Transfer to a roasting tin; roast at 200°C for 15–20 minutes. Serves 4.*

### BONING QUAIL

*Quail is a small bird so use a small sharp knife and your fingertips to bone it out. This method leaves the whole bird intact with leg bones still in, ready for stuffing and roasting.*

1 *To remove the wishbone, pull back the skin from the neck cavity, cut around the wishbone and cut away at the base.*

2 *Pull the thigh bones from their sockets. Cut down the back and start to cut the flesh from the carcass.*

3 *Insert a knife between the rib cage and the flesh. Scrape all around to free carcass from the flesh, then pull the carcass out.*

## queen of puddings

A traditional British pudding made with cake or breadcrumbs topped with egg custard, a layer of jam, finished with meringue and browned in the oven. The pudding dates from the seventeenth century.

### QUEEN OF PUDDINGS

*Mix 3 teaspoons lemon zest with 100 g breadcrumbs in a 1 litre ovenproof dish. Heat 200 ml milk and 300 ml single cream, then add to 3 eggs yolks, 25 g caster sugar and 1 teaspoon vanilla essence and mix. Pour the mixture over the breadcrumbs and set aside for 30 minutes. Bake at 160 °C for 45–60 minutes. Spread 3 tablespoons jam over the custard. Whisk 3 egg whites with 50 g caster sugar, then fold in another 50 g caster sugar. Spoon over the jam and bake for 15–20 minutes until lightly golden. Serves 6.*

## quenelles

Originally small balls of minced or chopped fish, meat or poultry shaped into a small oval using two spoons and then poached. They were then used to decorate dishes such as clear soup or served as a main course with a sauce. Today, the term more widely refers to the shape, and quenelles can be made of anything from fish to thickened cream, mousse or sorbet.

### PIKE QUENELLES

*Purée 500 g pike or salmon fillets in a food processor with ¼ teaspoon salt. Sieve then add 2 egg whites and mix. Gradually fold in 300 ml double cream and 1 teaspoon cayenne pepper. Season with ground white pepper. Shape the mixture into quenelles (see steps below) and chill for 20 minutes. Poach quenelles in vegetable or chicken stock for 5–10 minutes, remove with a slotted spoon, and allow to drain well. Lay the quenelles in a gratin dish, pour over 200 ml double cream and grill briefly. Serves 4.*

### SHAPING QUENELLES

1. *Take 1 heaped spoonful of mixture. Take a second empty spoon and dip it in water.*

2. *Holding the bowl ends of the spoon opposite each other, round off the sides of the quenelle with the second spoon.*

3. *Gently push the quenelle off the spoon, keeping all three sides intact.*

A savoury dish originating in the Alsace Lorraine region of France. The classic is quiche Lorraine, an open tart with a pastry base filled with eggs, cream and bacon and served hot or cold, but variations today can include almost anything, including onion, cheese, fish and herbs. It was originally made with a bread dough base. Due to its tradition of containing very little meat, it was said in the 1970s that 'real men don't eat quiche'. The secret to a well-cooked quiche is crisp pastry, baked blind so that the filling does not make it soggy, and a creamy, just-set filling.

## SALMON AND SPINACH QUICHE

*Line a 22 cm flan tin with shortcrust pastry (see page 367). Chill for 20 minutes, then bake blind for 12 minutes (see page 419). Put 200 g spinach in a saucepan with 1 tablespoon water. Cook until wilted. Place in a sieve and squeeze out the water. Chop and mix with 180 g canned salmon and 3 beaten eggs. Beat in 300 ml cream, season with salt and pepper and a pinch of nutmeg. Pour into the flan case and bake for 10 minutes at 200 °C. Reduce heat to 180 °C and bake for a further 20 minutes until set. Serves 6.*

## COOKING

*A preheated baking tray placed under your quiche tin will help crisp the bottom crust. Metal tins are best for making quiche as ceramic quiche plates do not conduct heat as well and the pastry will not crisp up properly.*

*Lightly buttering the quiche tin will make the pastry easy to lift out.*

*Blind baking the pastry until it is very dry will help stop it going soggy when you add a liquid filling. Brush the pastry while it is still hot with a beaten egg first. This will fill in any holes that may leak during cooking.*

*The easiest way to fill a quiche is to put the case on the oven shelf and then pour in the mixture.*

## QUICHE LORRAINE

*Line a 22 cm flan tin with shortcrust pastry (see page 367) and blind bake (see page 419). Fry 4 chopped bacon rashers until crisp and scatter over the pastry. Beat together 3 eggs, 300 ml cream, 50 ml milk, a pinch of nutmeg, then season. Pour into the flan tin and bake at 200 °C for 10 minutes. Reduce heat to 180 °C and bake for a further 20 minutes until set. Serves 6.*

## quince

A fragrant relative of the apple, held sacred by the ancient Greeks as the fruit of Aphrodite, goddess of love. Golden when ripe, and often coated in a soft grey down, their flesh is firm, dryish and rarely softens sufficiently to eat raw. Quinces can be baked, stewed or poached, all of which make the flesh meltingly soft, enhance the delicate flavour and can turn the flesh a golden pink. When buying quinces choose the smoother, larger varieties as these are easier to prepare and less wasteful. Quinces contain large amounts of pectin so are particularly good for making jams and preserves. Quinces will keep for several months in the fridge.

### POACHED QUINCES ON BRIOCHE

*Peel 2 large quinces, core and cut into quarters. In a saucepan, put 350 ml water, 350 g caster sugar, 1 vanilla pod, 1 cinnamon stick and 1 cardamom pod and bring to the boil. When the sugar has dissolved add the quinces, cover and simmer for 2–3 hours, or until very tender. Drain and simmer the cooking liquid to a syrup, then strain. Toast 8 slices brioche, butter lightly, sprinkle with cinnamon and sugar and top with poached quince. Drizzle some syrup over the top and serve hot or cold. Serves 8.*

Before cooking, peel and core the quince and remove the seeds. They go brown instantly when cut, so rub the cut surface with lemon juice as you cut them up. Quinces are popular in the cuisine of many countries. In Spain, they are made into a thick paste, *membrillo*; in France, into a clear jelly, *cotignac*; and in Italy, a paste called *cotognata*. In the meat and fruit combinations of Middle Eastern cuisine, quinces are used in stews, tagines and stuffings.

**Quince goes with —  chicken, cream, ginger, mascarpone, pigeon, star anise**

## quinoa

Pronounced *keen wa*, a tiny seed used as a cereal for over 5,000 years, and regarded as a sacred food by the Incas who called it 'the mother seed'. The plant produces masses of small seeds, usually pink or white, but some varieties may be orange, red, purple or black. Quinoa provides one of the best sources of vegetable protein and provides an essential amino acid balance. Quinoa can be substituted for most cereals and is a good replacement for rice. It has a very delicate flavour, comparable to couscous. Cook it like rice or add to soups or stews. The seeds can be made into flour and the spinach-like leaves of the plant are also edible.

### COOKING

*Quinoa takes about 15 minutes to cook. Add 200 g to 500 ml water, bring to the boil, then reduce to simmer. Serves 4 as an accompaniment.*

## rabbit

A native of North Africa and the Iberian Peninsula, particularly Spain, the rabbit is now eaten around the world, both as rabbit, and its larger darker fleshed—and always wild—cousin, the hare. Rabbit was originally an expensive meat, and still is in places without feral populations. Now, most rabbit is farmed, and has a milder flavour than wild rabbit. Most recipes for rabbit and hare call for it to be stewed, as the meat tends to be dry. Rabbits should be eaten young when their flesh is still pale and tender; older animals need to be marinated to help tenderize them. Rabbit can be treated like chicken and recipes are often similar. When roasting rabbit, the meat should be barded with fat or bacon to keep it moist. Buy rabbit as joints or whole and ready skinned and gutted. Whole rabbits should come with their kidneys (to indicate freshness) and do not need to be hung.

**Rabbit goes with — cream, garlic, herbs, mushroom, tomato**

see chicory — **radicchio**

## radish

A peppery root vegetable related to the mustard plant, whose many varieties are grouped under red, black or white (daikon) radishes. Red are the mildest and are crisp and juicy, usually eaten raw in salads. Black radishes have a stronger flavour, and are often peeled before use to reduce their pungency. Add to stir-fries and soups. Buy smooth, firm radishes that are not too large as they may be tough. Store without leaves as these accelerate moisture loss.

■ *See also* ***daikon***

## ragout

A thick stew of meat, game, poultry, fish or vegetables cooked in a stock with a little wine. The word is derived from the French *ragoûter*, which means 'to stimulate the appetite'. Not to be confused with *ragù*, the Italian name for what in English is called Bolognese sauce.

see dried fruit — **raisin**

## rambutan

The most distinguishing feature of the rambutan, a native of Malaysia but grown widely in Southeast Asia, is its long, dense red tendrils. The fruit, about 5 cm in diameter, is named from the Malay for 'hair of the head'. Related to the lychee and the longan, it has a juicy whitish pulp, which is mildly sweet to refreshingly acidic, depending on the variety, surrounding a single inedible seed. Rambutans are mostly eaten fresh or added to fruit salads, but can also be served in a syrup or cooked and served with meat or vegetables. To prepare, cut in half, just through the skin, then twist in half. Choose brightly coloured fruit with fleshy tendrils. Remove the flesh and halve to remove the seed. Store for only a short time in a plastic bag in the fridge—they are best eaten as soon as possible after buying as they perish easily.

*Also known as — hairy lychee*

See also **longan, lychee**

## raspberry

A relation of the blackberry, the loganberry and the boysenberry, the raspberry is made up of numerous smaller fruits called 'drupelets', clustered around a central receptacle. Each drupelet contains a small seed. Most raspberries are red, although there are yellow, orange, amber, white and black varieties. Although a more delicate fruit than strawberries, they can be used in much the same way and are interchangeable in most recipes. Raspberries do not ripen once picked, so they should always be bought when fully ripe. Buy them on the day they are to be eaten, and avoid washing them, or wash them just before eating, and handle them as little as possible.

### WHITE CHOCOLATE AND RASPBERRY MOUSSE

*Melt 150 g white chocolate in a microwave or in a heatproof bowl over a pan of simmering water. Cool slightly, then stir in 150 ml cream (at room temperature). Separate 4 eggs and stir the yolks into the chocolate. Whisk the whites until they just hold their shape, then fold into the mixture. Fold in 250 g crushed raspberries, then divide among 4 serving dishes. Chill for at least 4 hours. Serves 4.*

See also **berries**

### RASPBERRY DRESSING

*Push 100 g raspberries through a plastic sieve to remove the seeds (you will need about 2 tablespoons purée). Whisk in 2 tablespoons lemon juice and 5 tablespoons olive oil. Season with salt and pepper. Drizzle over salad leaves. Makes 180 ml.*

A sweet, brandy-based liqueur flavoured with fruit or almonds and popular in Victorian times. Ratafia liqueur and ratafia essence, both derived from apricot, peaches and plum kernels, are used to flavour desserts and pastries. Today, ratafia is commonly associated with ratafia biscuits, small crunchy biscuits flavoured with bitter almond and similar to a macaroon. They are eaten with liqueurs and used as the basis for desserts like trifle.

■ *See also* **amaretti, macaroon**

### RATAFIA TRIFLES

*Put 5 ratafia biscuits in each base of 4 individual glass dishes. Drizzle 1 tablespoon ratafia liqueur or sherry into each dish. Mix together 125 g chopped strawberries and 125 g chopped raspberries and divide among the 4 dishes. Pour over 500 ml ready-made custard and leave to set in the fridge. Decorate with cream and raspberries. Serves 4.*

A typical Provençal vegetable dish made from aubergines, peppers, tomatoes, onions and courgettes simmered in olive oil. Water should never be added to a ratatouille. It is served hot or cold as an accompaniment to chicken, roasts, scrambled eggs and omelettes or as a vegetarian main course.

### RATATOUILLE

*Fry 1 thinly sliced onion in 3 tablespoons olive oil for 10 minutes. Add 2 crushed garlic cloves, 200 g peeled, chopped tomatoes and a bouquet garni. Simmer, uncovered, for 30 minutes. Heat 2 tablespoons oil, add 1 sliced aubergine, 3 sliced courgettes and 2 sliced red peppers. Cook gently, uncovered, for 20 minutes, then add to tomatoes; season well. Cover and cook for 45 minutes until vegetables are very soft. Serves 6.*

An Italian dish made of small squares of pasta enclosing a variety of fillings. These are cooked in boiling water and served with a sauce or with butter or olive oil and seasoning. Fillings for ravioli vary, from the simplest of spinach and ricotta to fillings of veal, sweetbread, lamb's brains, pork, Parmesan and breadcrumbs. The common ingredients in ravioli seem to be Parmesan for flavour, and egg as a binding agent. Round or semicircular ravioli are called agnolotti.

■ *See also* **pasta**

## redcurrants

Small summer berries used in both savoury and sweet dishes, which, although tart, can be eaten raw, but are best when mixed with other fruit. They are more commonly cooked in jams, jellies and sauces. Redcurrants are a traditional ingredient in summer pudding. They are often sold still attached to the stalk, and the easiest way to remove this is to slide the tines of a fork down either side of the stalk, popping off the berries on either side.

*Redcurrants go with — goose, lamb, pear, plum, raspberries*

## reindeer

Eaten by the people of Sweden, Finland and Russia, where the reindeer lives in the wild. It has a slightly gamey taste, and can be cooked in a multitude of ways, making a good stew or soup, and is delicious smoked. As reindeer has quite a pronounced flavour, it needs little extra seasoning and is most commonly spiced with black pepper, allspice and bay leaves. The tongue may be made into pâté or smoked.

## rhubarb

Botanically classified as a vegetable, it is now generally thought to be a fruit, and this is how it is usually eaten. Rhubarb is usually sold with its leaves on, and although this helps prevent the stalks from wilting, the leaves should be removed before cooking as they contain poisonous oxalic acid. The edible part of rhubarb is the crisp, pink or red stalk. These can be cut into 2 cm pieces and stewed or used in pies, crumbles, ice creams and jams. Any tough stalks should be peeled first to remove the tough fibres. 'Forced' rhubarb is grown in long tubes that force the stalks to grow up towards the light. This type is usually found at the beginning of the season and takes only about 5 minutes to cook.

*Rhubarb goes with — custard, duck, ginger, orange, pork*

▦ *See also* **crumble, fool**

### RHUBARB TARTS

*Chop 6 rhubarb stalks into lengths, toss in 75 g caster sugar, then put in a saucepan with 1 tablespoon orange juice. Cook gently with the lid on until just soft, then allow to cool. Fill 8 individual pre-baked pastry cases with mascarpone and lay some rhubarb on top of each, then drizzle them with a little of the cooking juice. Makes 8.*

A staple grain eaten daily by over 300 billion people. Rice comes in many colours (black, white, brown, red), sizes (short-grain, long-grain, round), consistencies (sticky, glutinous), and forms (whole, milled, popped, flaked and ground). Most rice eaten is white rice, that is with the husk removed and milled, because it stores better and is more highly esteemed. It is sold under its culinary use (pudding rice), according to its method of processing (easy-cook), according to its grain shape (long-grain), its country or place of origin (Dhera Dun) or its degree of stickiness (glutinous). Rice varies in cooking time, so refer to the packet instructions.

■ *See also* **risotto, wild rice**

## TYPES OF RICE

Short-grain rice

Long-grain rice

Easy-cook brown rice

Sushi rice (glutinous)

Black glutinous rice

Basmati rice

Jasmine rice

Camargue

Short-grain brown rice

Calasparra (paella)

**Short-grain**
Often sold as round or pudding rice. When cooked, the grains swell without disintegrating and its high starch content makes it sticky and good for puddings, moulds and stuffings. The rices used for making risotto are short-grained.

**Long-grain**
This may also be sold as Texmati, Calrose and Patna. It is an absorbent, fine long-grained rice mainly used for savoury dishes. Good all-purpose rice.

**Easy-cook**
This rice may be either white or brown, short or long grained. The rice is parboiled before milling and it is a non-sticky all-purpose rice.

**Glutinous**
Also called sticky rice or sold as Japanese sushi rice, Korean rice or black sweet rice and may be either white or black. It is a sticky, short-grained rice used in Asian cooking. Its name is purely a description of its texture as rice does not contain gluten. Once cooked, the grains stick together, making it suitable for using in sushi or for eating with chopsticks. Use for sweet and savoury dishes.

**Basmati**
Often sold as Punni, Dehra Dun, Jeera-Sali or Delhi. It is a long-grained rice used predominantly in Indian cooking. It has a light, dry texture, is lightly perfumed and the grains are very fluffy when cooked.

**Jasmine**
Often sold as Thai fragrant rice. It is a fragrant rice, usually long-grained. Serve with Indian and Thai food.

**Camargue red**
Also sold as Griotto rice. It has a distinctive nutty flavour and chewy texture. It is good with duck and game. The rice is grown in the Camargue region of southern France.

**Brown**
The whole grain with just the hull removed. It is the most nutritious rice and has a pronounced nutty flavour. It takes longer to cook than most other varieties of rice.

**Paella**
Varieties of short-grained Spanish rice include bahia, Calasparra, sequia and the firm-grained bomba.

*Clockwise from top left: fresh noodles, sake, Chinese rice wine (Shaoxing), rice sticks, rice crackers and cakes sitting on rice paper wrappers, dried noodles.*

## RICE PRODUCTS

| | |
|---|---|
| ***Noodles*** | Both fresh and dried and in varying widths from thin vermicelli to sheets of rice noodle. |
| ***Rice paper wrappers*** | From Vietnam, these are dipped in water to soften them and served soft or deep-fried wrapped around a filling. |
| ***Mochi cakes*** | Blocks of pounded cooked glutinous rice, which are rehydrated and then grilled or added to dishes. Available in different shapes in Asian countries. |
| ***Ground rice*** | Used as a flour substitute or to dust foods before frying. Adds texture to biscuits and batters when used with flour. |
| ***Flaked rice*** | Processed white or brown rice that is rolled to produce light flakes of rice. Used in desserts or added to muesli. |
| ***Rice crackers (cakes)*** | A low-kilojoule snack food made of puffed rice. |
| ***Rice wine/spirits*** | Includes Chinese Shaoxing, for drinking and cooking, Japanese sake for drinking and mirin for cooking. |
| ***Rice vinegars*** | Red, black and white, these are available in different grades and are used in dressings, marinades and dips. |

## COOKING

*Rice can be cooked in many ways, including the absorption method, boiling the rice in water, cooking it in a microwave, in a rice cooker or in the oven. Rice can also be steamed, first by boiling it, then finishing it in a steamer.*

*There is some dispute about how much water is needed to cook rice. The easiest method is to put the rice in the saucepan, then add water so it comes up to one joint of your finger above the rice (see steps below). Rice such as that for sushi and risotto need different amounts.*

*Rice doesn't necessarily need to be soaked, especially in the West. Asian cooks often both wash their rice and soak it to shorten the cooking time.*

*If reheating cooked rice, make sure all the rice is piping hot to destroy any bacteria that may be present.*

### RICE PAPER

*Rice paper is not actually made from rice but from the pith of a small tree. The thin, edible paper is used to line baking trays or the base of sticky baked goods, such as macaroons.*

## COOKING RICE BY THE ABSORPTION METHOD

1 *Put 200 g rice in a saucepan, stick your finger into the rice, then add enough water so it comes up to the first finger joint.*

2 *Cover pan with a tight-fitting lid and bring to the boil. Reduce heat to low and cook until little steam holes appear in the rice.*

3 *Remove the lid to allow the steam to escape. Fluff up the grains with a fork and transfer to a serving dish.*

Similar in appearance to a pâté, made by cooking meat, usually pork slowly in lard, then pounding it into a smooth paste. This paste is potted into small dishes and served cold as an hors d'oeuvre, accompanied by toast or bread. Pork rillettes, a delicacy from Anjou and Tours, are characterized by their fine, smooth texture; rillettes from other regions such as Le Mans and La Sarthe usually contain larger pieces of meat. Rillettes can also be made from goose, rabbit, poultry and fish.

## risotto

### RISOTTO ALLA MILANESE

*Soak a pinch of saffron threads in 200 ml white wine for 10 minutes. Put 1.5 litres chicken stock in a saucepan and bring to a low simmer (keep it at a low simmer). Heat 100 g butter and 75 g beef marrow (optional) in a large high-sided frying pan, then add 1 chopped onion and 1 crushed garlic clove and sauté for 5 minutes. Add 350 g risotto rice and stir well to coat the rice in the butter. Add the saffron mixture to the rice and stir until all the liquid has been absorbed. Add a ladleful of stock and stir well. Once the stock is absorbed, add another ladleful and stir. Continue adding the stock in this way for at least 20 minutes, stirring constantly until the rice is al dente. Season with salt and pepper. Remove from the heat and stir in 3 tablespoons freshly grated Parmesan and a knob of butter (optional). Leave, covered, for 3 minutes. Serve the risotto with extra Parmesan. Serves 8 as an accompaniment and 4 as a main course.*

An Italian method of cooking rice primarily made by stirring stock and often wine into rice that has been sautéed in butter and/or olive oil and sometimes onion. The stock is added slowly, and the rice must be stirred continually as it cooks, resulting in a soft, creamy mass of rice. Some risottos are cooked without stirring, or even baked. They can be flavoured with anything from saffron, mushrooms and asparagus to seafood and poultry.

Risotto originated in the rice-growing areas of northern Italy. The consistency of risotto is regional—some areas prefer it almost soup-like (Venice); others slightly thicker (Milan). It is important to use the right type of rice for risotto. These rices are high in starch, which gives the risotto its classic creaminess, and can absorb large quantities of liquid without breaking up.

### GRADES OF RISOTTO RICE

| | |
|---|---|
| **Riso comune** | The lowest quality, it has a small, round grain, which is very starchy. A good pudding rice. Cook for 12–13 minutes. Varieties include balilla, originario and selenio. |
| **Riso semifino** | Has a larger grain than riso comune and needs to be cooked for 14–15 minutes. This rice is very good for suppli, arancini and in timballo. Varieties include Italico, Piemonte, Padano and vialone nano. |
| **Riso fino** | A very starchy rice with a large grain size. It makes good risotto and cooks in 16–20 minutes. Varieties include Europa, RB, riva Smeraldo and ariete. |
| **Riso superfino** | The best of the risotto rices with large grains, which takes 18–20 minutes to cook. Varieties include arborio, the largest grain, and the best, carnaroli. |

## rissole

A ball or disc-shaped mixture of chopped meat, seasoned and bound with egg, often rolled in breadcrumbs and fried until golden, then served with or without a sauce. In France, a rissole is either a sweet or savoury filled pastry that is baked or fried. Often made with puff pastry, although brioche can be used. They are usually turnover shaped and are served as an appetizer, main course or dessert, depending on the filling.

## roast

### CUTS FOR ROASTING

**Beef** – Best cuts are fillet, eye fillet, sirloin, rump and rib.

**Veal** – Best cuts are leg, loin, rack, shoulder and fillet.

**Pork** – Best cuts are leg, loin, fillet and shoulder.

**Lamb** – Best cuts are leg, shoulder, loin, rack and crown roast.

Food cooked in an oven or on a spit, either in its own juices or with added fat, is said to be roasted. It usually refers to meat but fish and vegetables can also be roasted. Usually the more tender cuts of meat are roasted. To prevent meat from drying out during cooking, it can be basted, either by spooning meat juices over the meat or by barding the meat, that is, laying strips of bacon or pork fat over it. This should not be done with the tender cuts, as the flavour of the bacon or pork may overwhelm. Once cooked, leave meat to 'rest', covered and in a warm place, for about 15 minutes. This allows the juices to be absorbed back into the meat, and makes it easier to carve. Meat will continue cooking when it is resting so calculate this into your cooking time. It will also continue cooking when carved if you serve it on a hot plate.

The shape of a joint affects how evenly it will cook: a leg of pork or lamb will never cook as evenly as a rib roast or fillet. Stuffing a joint will also affect its cooking time—the meat needs to be cooked for longer. Meat can be roasted on or off the bone; boned joints do not roast any better than those on the bone and joints roasted on the bone can be taken off the bone before carving.

■ *See also* **beef, chicken, lamb, pork**

### COOKING

*Most joints (on the bone) can be cooked at 180°C, though tender prime cuts (rib and fillet of beef and rack of lamb) may be cooked at 210°C. For rare beef, cook for 15–20 minutes per 500 g; add 5 minutes for medium beef. For pork or veal, cook 25–30 minutes per 500 g. For pink lamb, cook 15–20 minutes per 500 g; add 5 minutes for medium lamb. For off the bone, extend the cooking time by 5 minutes per 500 g. Cook chicken for 20 minutes per 450 g plus 20 minutes at 190°C. Chicken can be cooked at any temperature between 190°C and 220°C, depending on how brown you want it.*

### CARVING A LEG OF LAMB

1 *Hold the bone with a napkin and start carving, parallel to the bone, cutting away from you.*

2 *When you reach the bone, turn the joint and carve the other side in the same way.*

3 *Carve the remaining meat on the shank, starting at the point where you are holding the shank.*

Biscuits made from irregularly shaped mounds of dough studded with raisins or currants, so called not (hopefully) because of their texture, but because of their resemblance to a rock. They can be eaten warm or cold, with or without butter.

### ROCK CAKES

*Preheat oven to 200°C. Sift 250 g flour into a bowl and rub in 90 g butter with your fingertips until the mixture resembles coarse breadcrumbs. Add 125 g caster sugar, ½ teaspoon mixed spice, 4 tablespoons currants and 50 g sultanas. Lightly beat 1 egg and stir it into the dry ingredients. Mix into a dough. Grease a baking tray and drop 3 tablespoons of dough on it for each cake. Bake for 10–15 minutes until golden brown. Makes 8.*

## rocket

### ROCKET AND PARMESAN SALAD

*Put 2 bunches of washed and dried rocket in a serving dish. Mix 4 tablespoons olive oil with 1 tablespoon balsamic vinegar. Pour dressing over the rocket and mix well. Use a vegetable peeler to shave off pieces from a block of Parmesan. Scatter over the rocket, sprinkle with a little coarse salt and pepper. Serves 4.*

A slightly bitter salad leaf with a nutty, peppery flavour. Younger leaves are milder than the mature, which can get quite hot. Rocket is used predominantly as a salad ingredient, and is one of the traditional ingredients of Provençal mesclun salad; it can be used as a pizza topping, added to soups and purées or served wilted as a vegetable. Rocket is sold in small bunches and is best used on the day of purchase as it wilts quickly but will keep in the fridge wrapped in plastic for up to 2 days.

**Also known as — arugula**

## roe

The eggs or spawn of a female fish, also called hard roe. Soft roe is the sperm (or milt) of a male fish. Caviar, the most sought after roe, is from the sturgeon. Lesser but still delicious roe can come from salmon, trout, herring, flying fish and lumpfish. Taramosalata is ideally made with the roe of the grey mullet, as is botargo, which is salted, pressed and dried roe. Roe is eaten fried in Europe, and in Japan it is used for sushi.

■ *See also* **botargo, caviar, tarama**

*Golden tobiko or flying fish roe (yellow roe); orange tobiko or flying fish roe (small orange roe), salmon roe (large orange roe).*

# rollmop herring

A Scandinavian speciality, rollmop herrings are boned unsalted herring fillets marinated in spiced vinegar. The vinegar is flavoured with juniper berries, black peppercorns and cloves. The fillets are wrapped around chopped onions and gherkins and secured with a small cocktail stick. They are then left to marinate for about 6 days before serving cold as an hors d'oeuvre. Rollmop herrings are also sold ready-made in jars.

***Also known as — rollmops***

# romesco sauce

A classic sauce from Tarragona in Catalonia, Spain, authentically containing romesco peppers. Today, there are many versions, but in Tarragona, it typically is made with tomatoes, garlic, romesco peppers, parsley, hazelnuts, almonds, chilli and fried bread. The vegetables can be grilled or baked before they are puréed.

### ROMESCO SAUCE

*Roast 2 halved tomatoes, 2 romesco peppers (or ancho peppers) and 4 garlic cloves at 200°C for 20 minutes. Fry 4 tablespoons breadcrumbs with 100 g hazelnuts and 50 g almonds. Put them in a mortar and pestle or food processor. Crush to form a paste, adding the tomato and garlic as you go, then add ¼ teaspoon chilli powder, 1 tablespoon red wine vinegar, 1 tablespoon olive oil and season. Serve with grilled fish. Makes 400 ml.*

# rose

Rose petals are used for flavouring and decorating cakes and confectionery, they can be boiled in water or sugar syrup to flavour food, or crystallized and used as decoration. All rose petals are edible as long as they haven't been sprayed with any chemicals. Rose-water, made from a distillation of petals, is used in the Middle East and India to flavour dishes such as Turkish delight, baklava and lassi. It gives a sweet fragrance to curries and rice dishes when sprinkled over the finished dish. The thicker, sticky sugar syrup is used in Middle Eastern sweets and pastries.

### ROSE SUGAR SYRUP

*Put 500 g caster sugar in a heavy-based saucepan. Add 250 ml water and 2 teaspoons lemon juice. Bring to the boil, stirring frequently. When the sugar has all dissolved, reduce the heat and simmer for about 10 minutes, or until the mixture is syrupy. Do not stir while the liquid is simmering. Stir in 1 tablespoon rose-water, then remove from the heat and cool. Makes 500 ml.*

Swiss-style fried potatoes. The potatoes are grated, formed into a cake and fried until golden and crisp. Sometimes, Rösti are flavoured with bacon and onions. For serving it is cut into large wedges, and usually eaten for breakfast with sausages and eggs or as an accompaniment to meat.

■ *See also* **boxty, hash browns**

### ROSTI

*Boil 1.5 kg potatoes of equal size for 10 minutes. Drain well, then grate when cool and season. Fry 100 g cubed bacon in 10 g butter. Add potatoes and form into a thick cake. Fry until golden, loosening the bottom. Carefully tip the Rösti onto a plate, cooked side up, add 15 g butter to the pan, then return the Rösti to the pan and cook the other side. Cook until golden. Serves 6.*

## rough puff pastry

Rough puff pastry is the simplest of the layered flaky pastries. It produces crisp, tender layers of pastry, but these layers will not necessarily rise evenly or particularly high. Ideal for sausage rolls and turnovers. Cook at 220°C or as indicated in the recipe.

### MAKING ROUGH PUFF PASTRY

1 *Sift 225 g flour and a pinch of salt into a bowl. Add 180 g chilled diced butter. Stir to coat the butter in flour.*

2 *Add enough ice-cold water to make a dough. Gather the mixture into a ball and put on a floured work surface.*

3 *With floured hands, form the mixture into a rectangular block. Roll out the pastry to form a rectangle 1 cm thick.*

4 *Fold up the bottom third of the pastry and the top third down and seal the edges lightly with a rolling pin.*

5 *Turn dough through 90 degrees, then roll it again to form a rectangle about 5 mm thick. Fold as before.*

6 *Repeat twice more, then put in a plastic bag; chill for 30 minutes. To use, roll out and cut to the desired shape.*

## roulade

A roulade can be made from soufflé-like cake mixtures, which are soft and fudgy, or from those similar to a sponge cake or genoise, that is baked in a swiss roll tin, spread with a filling and rolled up. Roulades can also be savoury rolls of meat, such as beef filled with mushrooms, or cheese, rolled and secured with string or a toothpick before being cooked.

## rum

A spirit distilled from the by-products of the sugar cane industry, including molasses. It is drunk as an alcoholic beverage and used as a flavouring. Rum can be either white or dark. White rum is pure cane spirit whereas dark rum is more flavourful and contains large amounts of fruity esters. Bacardi rum originated in Cuba but is now made in Brazil. Puerto Rico, Jamaica and Martinique are the biggest producers of rum. Rum sauce is usually either a sweet white sauce flavoured with rum, served in Britain with Christmas pudding and mince pies, or a dark rum sauce served over ice cream, cakes or sticky date pudding *(pictured)*.

**Dark rum goes with — banana, pineapple, roast meat, sweet potato**

### CARAMEL RUM SAUCE

*Put 225 g caster sugar and 150 ml water in a saucepan and stir until sugar is dissolved. Bring to the boil and continue to boil until golden brown. Take off the heat and add 200 ml double cream. Re-dissolve any lumps, then add 45 g butter and 2 tablespoons dark rum. Stir until smooth. Serve on puddings or ice cream. Makes about 350 ml.*

## rumaki

A hot dish served as an hors d'oeuvre made by wrapping a strip of bacon around a slice of water chestnut and a small piece of chicken liver, which has been marinated in soy sauce, ginger and garlic. These are held together with a cocktail stick, then grilled until the bacon is crisp.

Whether under tsar, commissar or modern-day capitalist mafia, there has always been one diet for the Russian poor and another for the rich. After the break-up of the USSR in 1991, 21 republics covering over 17 million square kilometres, stretching from the Baltic Sea in the west to the Pacific Ocean in the east, re-formed as the Russian Federation or, simply, Russia.

The cuisines of such a vast country (or political entity) have been affected by neighbours like Mongolia and Siberia, regional characteristics, religion, invasion, fashion—and poverty.

## HOME COOKING

Cabbages and root vegetables dominate peasant Russian cooking, but due to the climate, fresh vegetables are only available for a few months each year. White cabbage is preserved for eating over winter, as are mushrooms. Vegetables are made into hearty soups with cheap cuts of beef.

A well-known soup, *solyanka,* which translates as 'confused', was made at large village festivals where everybody would bring a different ingredient to add to the pot. Larger joints of meat, those suited to the oven, are generally the preferred cut. Beef stroganoff, Russia's best-known meat dish, is, paradoxically, made of strips of beef.

*Pirogi* (pies) are pastries of varying sizes. They can be open, closed, large, small, round, square, baked or fried and use countless fillings. It is important that a Russian housewife be able to cook *pirogi. Kulibiaka* is a particularly large *pirog,* traditionally filled with fish and rice.

*Pelmeni* are similar in appearance to ravioli and were introduced to Russia in the late eighteenth century from Siberia. They are made from noodle dough, filled with minced meat, boiled and served with melted butter poured over them.

A salad in Russia is very different to a salad in the West. Known as *vinegret,* although today often served without vinegar, it is usually made of cubed beetroot, pickled cucumbers, diced onion, salt and sunflower or olive oil.

Caviar, one of the world's most luxurious foods, comes from the roe of sturgeon that live (today precariously) in the Caspian Sea and the Volga Basin. Vodka, one of Russia's valuable exports, can be distilled from rye, potatoes and corn but the best is made from wheat.

## SPECIAL OCCASIONS

Easter is the high point of the Russian calendar. During Lent, Orthodox Russians are forbidden to eat meat, fish that bleed, eggs, butter and milk, and so at Easter, ceremonial feasts, comprising all these forbidden foods are enjoyed, along with *kulich,* a sweet Easter bread and *pashka*, a cream or cottage cheese dessert studded with candied fruit or raisins.

For other special occasions Russian housewives lay on a spread called a *zakuski.* Similar to hors d'oeuvres, it is made up of hearty, slightly sour dishes intended to arouse the appetite for the dishes that follow. Portions are small, but the variety is plentiful and colour and shape of the food is as important as the range and taste. *Zakuski* includes fish and meat dishes, salads, vegetables, eggs, mushrooms, pickles, seasoning and breads.

## THE FRENCH CONNECTION

French chefs, including Antonin Carême who cooked for Tsar Alexander I (it is thought he renamed his *Charlotte à la Parisienne* 'Charlotte russe' in honour of the mother country), worked in Russia in the nineteenth century, giving rise to many French-Russian dishes.

■ *See also* **blinis, caviar**

*From top: kulich and pashka, vodka and caviar, chicken kiev, fish solyanka, kislyie shchi (sauerkraut soup).*

# Russian salad

More French than Russian, this salad, conceived by the French chefs employed in the houses of the nobility at the time of the tsars, consists of diced vegetables bound together with mayonnaise and garnished. It can be simple or elaborate, especially when garnished with truffles, lobster or langoustines. Curiously, it is a standard item in the Spanish tapas repertoire.

■ *See also* **mayonnaise**

### RUSSIAN SALAD

*Boil 500 g small new potatoes until tender. Cook 2 carrots, 100 g peas and 125 g French beans. Drain, then dice vegetables. Combine all the vegetables, season and bind with 4 tablespoons mayonnaise. Garnish with sliced hard-boiled egg, sliced beetroot and sliced gherkins. Serves 6.*

## rutabaga — see swede

## rye

A strongly flavoured cereal grain, similar to wheat, which, because it will grow in cold conditions, is widely used in Northern and Eastern European and Russian cooking. When milled, rye grains produce a dark flour, which is used to make black breads like pumpernickel. These breads are denser than those made with wheat because rye flour has a low gluten content, and for this reason rye flour is often mixed with wheat flour. Rye flour is also used in crêpes and muffins. Whole rye grains are nutritious and can be cooked like other cereal grains. They should be soaked overnight, then boiled until tender. Rye flakes can be added to muesli or made into porridge. Rye is also used to make whisky, beer and bourbon.

■ *See also* **pumpernickel**

*Rye flakes and rye flour (above), rye (below).*

### PAIN DE SEIGLE

*Mix 2 teaspoons dried yeast or 15 g fresh yeast with 125 g plain flour and 150 ml hand-hot water, then leave for 2 hours. Sift 75 g strong white flour (white bread flour) and 300 g rye flour into a bowl with 2 tablespoons salt. Make a well in the centre, pour in the yeast mixture and 250 ml water and mix to form a soft dough. Knead on a floured work surface until elastic, then put in a bowl, cover and leave to rise until doubled in size. Knock back the dough, then rise again for 15 minutes. Divide into two and form into long loaves. Slash the tops and put on a baking tray. Cover and prove until doubled in size. Bake at 200°C for 30–40 minutes.*

# S

## sabayon

The French version of the Italian zabaglione, made from a mixture of egg yolks, sugar and an alcohol such as white wine or rum. The mixture is beaten in a double boiler over simmering water until thickened. It is served warm or cold as a sauce to accompany desserts; or spooned over fruits and briefly grilled. Sabayon is also a savoury sauce made by whisking egg yolks, fish stock (*fumet*), butter and cream.

## sablé

A classic French biscuit, delicate and crumbly with a sandy texture, made from a buttery dough formed into a roll, then chilled and thinly sliced into rounds and baked. Sablés can be flavoured with ground nuts, such as almonds or hazelnuts; lemon or orange rind; or sprinkled with cinnamon and sugar. They can be presented dipped in chocolate or sandwiched with jam and sprinkled with icing sugar.

***Also known as — sand biscuits***

## Sachertorte

A Viennese gateau, created by chef Franz Sacher in the nineteenth century. Sachertorte ('Sacher's cake') is a rich chocolate cake covered with a chocolate glaze. The cake batter is a mixture of creamed butter, sugar and egg with melted chocolate, beaten egg white and flour folded through before baking. It is usually sliced into three layers, with each layer spread with apricot jam. The cake is iced with a smooth chocolate icing, which is poured over it, and traditionally the word 'Sacher' is piped in chocolate across the top of the cake. It is still served in Vienna's Hotel Sacher, accompanied by whipped cream.

## saffron

The orange-red stigma of one species of the crocus plant, and the most expensive spice in the world. Each flower consists of three stigmas, which are hand-picked, then dried—a labour-intensive process. Its flavour is pungent and aromatic, and its colour intense, so only a little is used. It gives flavour and colour to such dishes as bouillabaisse, paella, risotto and pilaff, as well as saffron cake and buns. Saffron is sold in both powdered and thread form (the whole stigma). Beware—there is no such thing as cheap saffron. The best comes from Spain, Iran and Kashmir.

### COOKING

*Saffron threads are usually soaked in warm water, stock or milk for a few minutes to infuse. The mixture is then either strained or added, with the threads, to the dish. The threads can also be added at the end of cooking.*

## sago

Sago is a starch extracted from various Southeast Asian palms, processed into a flour or granulated into little balls called pearl sago. Pearl sago is commonly made into milky baked or steamed puddings in the West. In Southeast Asia, sago is used both as a flour and in pearl form to make desserts such as the Malay dessert, *gula melaka*, a mixture of sago, palm sugar and coconut milk.
**Also known as — pearl sago**

### SAGO PUDDING

*Put 125 ml golden syrup, 75 g sago, 400 ml milk and 350 ml cream in a saucepan and bring to the boil, stirring. Simmer for 10 minutes, then allow to cool. Stir in 2 eggs, 1 teaspoon vanilla essence, 1 teaspoon grated lemon rind and 2 teaspoons lemon juice. Transfer mixture to an ovenproof dish and bake at 170 °C for 1 hour. Serves 6.*

## sake

An alcoholic Japanese drink made from fermented rice with an alcohol content of 15–17 per cent. Sake is drunk either hot or cold or used in cooking, particularly in sauces and marinades. Expensive sake is often served cold but can be warmed; cheaper sake is served hot to make it taste better.

There are four types of sake, of varying quality and flavours. *Ginjoshu* represents the peak of the sake brewer's art, and is made from the highest-quality milled large-grain rice. It has a fruity aroma and a complex and delicate flavour. *Junmaishu* is a pure sake made from rice and water with no added alcohol, flavourings or sugar and has a full-bodied flavour. *Honjozoshu* is made with rice, water and a small amount of added distilled alcohol. It is mild, but with a rich traditional flavour, and is good served warm. *Nigorizake* is a cloudy (partially filtered) sake, and may even be unpasteurized so that it is 'alive'.

*Namazake* is a term that refers to all unpasteurized sake and can include any of the above types. If stored in a dark, cool place, sake will keep for 6–12 months. It is not necessary to store in the fridge unless it has not been pasteurized (*namazake*).

A wide variety of lettuces and herbs with different coloured and flavoured leaves are the main constituents of salad. Leaves can be used for looks, flavour, or both. For example, red leaves have a bitter flavour, and like peppery green rocket, need to be offset by more delicate flavours. To make a mixed salad, you need a good combination of textures and flavours. Lamb's lettuce (corn salad or mache), is slightly nutty in flavour. Purslane has a slightly sour, peppery taste. Young beet leaves (buy attached to the root) have a good green colour and earthy flavour and mizuna has dark green, feathery and glossy leaves. Mustard leaves are pungent, and crisp lettuce leaves like cos add crunch. Both the flower and the peppery leaf of the nasturtium can be used in salad, as well as herbs such as mint, chervil and basil.

*See also* **chicory, cress, dandelion, lettuce, mesclun, rocket, sorrel**

## see sausage — salami

## salsa

On the one hand, 'salsa' is simply Italian and Spanish for sauce. But in more recent times, it has acquired a second meaning, from South and Central American cuisines, as something between a sauce and a salad, always made of chopped vegetables. Italian salsa verde, an accompaniment to bollito misto, is made with parsley, capers, anchovies, garlic, oil and vinegar. The Mexican version, salsa cruda, is made from chopped green tomatoes, chilli, onion and coriander. Mexican salsas are available fresh and in jars and tins from supermarkets. Ranging from mild to hot and spicy, they can be served as part of a dish, an accompaniment or a dip, especially for corn chips.

### CORN AND CHILLI SALSA

*Lightly brush 4 cobs of corn with vegetable oil and sprinkle with salt and pepper. Place cobs under a hot grill and cook for 5–7 minutes, or until roasted, turning the cobs so they cook all over. Cool, then slice the corn from the cobs and place in a large bowl with 1 small, finely chopped red onion, 1 chopped red pepper, 1 seeded chopped chilli, 2 tablespoons chopped coriander and toss in 60 ml lime juice. Serves 4.*

### SALSA VERDE

*Finely chop 6 spring onions, 1 small onion, 2 garlic cloves, 2 small seeded green chillies, 1 tomatillo and 40 g coriander leaves. Put in a bowl and toss with 4 tablespoons olive oil and the grated rind and juice of 1 lemon. Season well. Serve as a dip, with roast meats or grilled fish. Makes about 375 ml.*

## salsify

A root vegetable shaped like a long carrot, which has a brown skin and creamy flesh. Salsify has a waxy texture and is often served hot with butter, cold with a vinaigrette or used in soups and stews. To use, scrub the root clean, then boil or steam whole until tender. The skins can then be rubbed off and the flesh cut as required. When peeled, keep in water with a squeeze of lemon juice to stop it oxidizing.
**Also known as — oyster plant, vegetable oyster**

## salt

Common table salt, sodium chloride, is essential for the functioning of our bodies. Traditionally used to preserve foods such as fish, cheese, olives and meat, salt is also used extensively in food processing, food preservation and as a flavour enhancer. Salt is mined from seams of rock salt trapped underground or obtained through evaporation of sea water.

*From left: Maldon sea salt, Ile de Ré sea salt, rock salt, seasoned salt, table salt.*

### COOKING

*Salt draws moisture from food. Aubergine slices, for example, are salted to draw out their bitter juices. This is called 'degorging'.*

*When cooking meat and fish, add salt just before or after cooking—salt will draw out the meat juices if left to sit.*

*Use salt with care: it is difficult to disguise oversalted food. One trick, for example if cooking a casserole, is to add more potato—this will help dilute the saltiness.*

### TYPES OF SALT

| | |
|---|---|
| **Rock (halite)** | Unrefined salt from natural deposits found in ancient mines in places like Cheshire (England), Germany and Austria. It has large crystals and is used for grinding. |
| **Table** | Rock salt produced by evaporating salt water under vacuum pressure to produce a fine grain. Iodized salt is table salt with added iodine. |
| **Sea** | Produced by the evaporation of sea water. The crystals are large, about 5 mm, and often flaky. Also called bay salt. Maldon salt (from Essex), Guérande and Ile de Ré (from France) and salt from Trapani in Sicily are all renowned. Grind or sprinkle on food. |
| **Seasoned** | Flavouring agents such as celery, garlic and dried herbs are added to salt to enhance the flavour. |

## salt cod

To make salt cod, whole gutted fish or fillets are coated with a coarse salt, which dries and preserves it. This technique, in use since medieval times, is common to Northern Europe, especially Norway and Iceland, and to Newfoundland. The cod is then exported to Britain, Southern Europe, Africa, the Mediterranean and the Caribbean. Soak the cod in several changes of water for 24–36 hours to reconstitute and de-salt it, then poach to cook. Buy centre cuts of fillet, which are fatter and more meaty.

***Also known as — bacalao, bacalhau, baccala, morue***

A classic Italian veal dish: thin slices of veal (escalopes) are fried with thin slices of Parma ham and fresh sage. In some recipes, the veal is rolled with the ham and sage in the centre and secured with a toothpick; in others it is left flat. It is then dusted with flour and pan-fried with wine or dry Marsala and sometimes cream. Translated from the Italian, saltimbocca means 'to jump (or leap) in the mouth'.

### SALTIMBOCCA

*Put 8 beaten out veal escalopes on a board. Arrange a thin slice of Parma ham and a sage leaf on top of each; secure with a toothpick. Lightly coat each escalope with seasoned flour. Fry in 1 tablespoon hot butter for 3–4 minutes, turning once. Add 250 ml white wine or dry Marsala and cook for 1–2 minutes. Serve with sage side uppermost and pour over the juices. Serves 4.*

Derived from the Latin words *sal petrae* meaning 'salt of stone', saltpetre is potassium nitrate, used in cooking and industrial meat-curing processes to preserve food and to give a good colour to cured meats such as bacon (without it, the cured meat becomes an unappetizing grey colour). Saltpetre is also a constituent of gunpowder. Today, saltpetre has largely been replaced by nitrate for preserving food.

***Also known as — nitrate of potash, prague powder, sal prunella, saltpeter***

A condiment or side dish used in Malaysian, Indonesian and Singaporean cuisines to accompany a meal, adding a fiery sharpness to food. Sambals are served in small amounts with vegetables, meat, fish and chicken dishes or added to rice as a quick meal. There are many variations, both cooked and uncooked, but they usually include chillies and shrimp paste. Home-made or sold in jars, sambals can be kept indefinitely once opened if stored in the fridge. Common sambals include sambal trassi, made from shrimp paste, red or green chillies, sugar and lime juice; sambal oelek, from red chillies, vinegar and sugar; and sambal lado, from anchovies, green chillies and shallots. A sambal is also a curry made with a fried sambal base.

*Sambal trassi*      *Sambal oelek*     *Sambal lado*

A deep-fried Indian pastry filled with spicy meat or with vegetables such as lentils, potatoes, peas and herbs, usually accompanied by a spicy chutney. Samosas may be triangular, circular or cone shaped. The pastry is traditionally made from fine wheat flour, ghee and sour milk or yoghurt. Sweet versions may be filled with nuts, dried fruit and spices. They are eaten as snacks, or before a meal.

***Also known as — samoosas, samousa, singhara***

## samphire

Two quite different plants, both of which can be pickled. The Mediterranean variety, rock samphire, is a small shrub with long, thin fleshy leaves, which grows along the coast on rocks and cliffsides. It has an unpleasant odour that disappears once it is pickled. Known to the Greeks and Romans, it is now added to salads, or eaten as an accompaniment to cold tables. Marsh samphire, which also grows by the sea, is a bright-green plant with thin spiky succulent stems, a mildly salty flavour and a crisp juicy texture. It can be steamed or boiled and served with butter or hollandaise sauce, often as an accompaniment to fish *(pictured)*, or eaten raw in salads. It may also be lightly pickled in vinegar. The name 'samphire' comes from a garbling of the French *herbe de Saint-Pierre,* St Peter's herb, because the name Peter comes from the Greek word for rock. It can be found in fishmongers. One of its other names, glasswort, comes from the fact that its ash was used in glassmaking.

***Marsh samphire is also known as — glasswort, salicorne, sea asparagus***
***Rock samphire is also known as — criste marine, sea samphire, true samphire***

## sandwich

Two slices of bread enclosing a filling of anything and sometimes everything, especially in America. Curiously, two of the most famous sandwiches break the two slice rule. The American club sandwich, with three slices of bread—two layers— and another with only one, the Danish open sandwich, or *smørrebrød*. The sandwich takes its name from the Earl of Sandwich who, during a long gambling session, asked for constant supplies of cold beef between two slices of bread.

## sapodilla

A tropical fruit with rough, brown skin enclosing a creamy yellow pulp with a honey sweet flavour. Make sure the fruit is soft and thoroughly ripe as unripe flesh can be quite bitter. Ripen at room temperature, then store in the fridge. The tree is also a source of chicle, a latex originally used as a chewing gum base.

***Also known as — chiku, naseberry, sapotilla, sopota***

## sapote

A name attached to a number of different tropical fruit native to South America. The black sapote is a Mexican native and a relation to the persimmon. It is an olive-green skinned fruit with richly flavoured dark chocolate brown flesh. It makes delicious ice cream, mousses, cakes, and benefits from the addition of vanilla, rum or lemon juice. The mamey sapote, native to Central America but grown extensively in the West Indies, is an oval-shaped fruit with thick rough brown skin, and aromatic reddish-orange or pink flesh with four large seeds. It can be eaten out of hand or used for ice creams or preserves. The white sapote is plum-shaped and green skinned, turning yellowish when ripe. The yellow flesh has a creamy custard-like texture with a pear flavour.

***Black sapote is also known as — black persimmon, chocolate pudding fruit***
***Mamey sapote is also known as — chicomamey, mamey***
***White sapote is also known as — zapota blanco***

*Mamey sapote*

*White sapote*

A bitter flavouring extracted from the dried root of a number of prickly vines native to Central and South America and the Caribbean. Sarsaparilla (sarsparilla) is used to flavour carbonated drinks and has been used for centuries by herbalists to treat a wide range of ailments, often in the form of tablets or in tea. Today, the flavour is reproduced artificially, although some carbonated drinks made using old-fashioned methods are available. Sold in health food shops in tablet or tea form.

## s a s h i m i

The Japanese method of slicing raw fish, shellfish and crustaceans for the table. It's a general principle of Japanese cuisine that all seafood must be fresh enough to eat raw: sashimi is the proof of the principle. The preparation of sashimi is the reserve of highly skilled chefs with remarkable knives—whose care alone is a matter for intense study. The only exceptions to sliced sashimi are oysters, and the exception to raw is octopus (although squid is eaten raw). Sashimi is usually served with wasabi and a dipping sauce, often with pickled ginger or finely grated daikon or shredded cucumber, and is prepared according to appearance, taste, texture, size and colour. Tuna (*maguro*) is probably the most popular fish used for sashimi, but yellow tail (*hamachi*), mackerel (*saba*), sea bream (*tai*), squid (*ika*), octopus (*tako*), prawns (*ebi*) and salmon (*sake*) are all used. If buying fish for sashimi, find a supplier who sells to sushi restaurants and buy only sashimi-grade fish. Fresh fish is often frozen for 24 hours to kill any parasites and this can be done on the fishing boats. Chicken, beef, whale and horse meat are also served as sashimi, usually vinegared, and called *namasu*. Strictly speaking, sashimi is a type of *namasu*.

## TYPES OF SASHIMI CUTS

There are several cutting methods used for sashimi, depending on the texture of the fish being used.

| | |
|---|---|
| *Ito zukuri* | Very thin strips are cut, usually piled into little mounds. This cut is used for squid and cuttlefish. |
| *Hira zukuri* | The thick fillets are cut across the grain in rectangular slices, which vary in thickness according to the firmness of the fish. This cut is used for tuna or salmon. |
| *Usu zukuri* | The fillet is cut into thin strips at a diagonal, used for firm fish. This cut is used for mackerel or sea bream. |
| *Kaku zukuri* | The fillet is cut into cubes. This cut is used for soft or very firm fish such as skip jack tuna. |

PONZU SAUCE

*Mix together 35 ml rice vinegar, 150 ml soy sauce, 60 ml strained lemon juice, 25 ml mirin and 100 ml dashi. Leave the sauce overnight in the fridge before use. Makes 300 ml.*

■ *See also* **daikon, sushi, wasabi**

## sassafras

A North American native tree whose virtues were much lauded by the Indians and early Spanish colonists. Sassafras leaves are dried and used to make sassafras tea and filé powder (*pictured*), a flavouring and thickening agent in the Creole stew of gumbo. The fragrant lemon-scented oil extracted from the bark of the root is used in the cosmetic industry for its perfume but is also used to flavour soft drinks, root beer, ice cream and confectionery, and is used in the health food industry.

## satay

A speciality of Southeast Asia, especially Malaysia, Thailand and Indonesia, made from small strips or cubes of meat, usually pork, beef, chicken or seafood, threaded onto wooden skewers. The threaded skewers are marinated for a time before being grilled, traditionally over a charcoal fire. Satays are usually served as an appetizer, often with a dipping sauce based on peanuts. In Malaysia, the peanut sauce is flavoured with coconut milk and in Indonesia, it is based on kecap manis, a sweet soy sauce. Probably originally of Middle Eastern origin, it spread throughout Southeast Asia from Java where Arab traders introduced it.

**Also known as — saté**

### PREPARATION

*The bamboo skewers need to be soaked for at least 1 hour before threading with the meat. This helps stop the skewers from burning during cooking.*

### CHICKEN SATAY

*Cut 500 g chicken into strips, thread onto 8 skewers and place in a dish in a single layer. Combine 2 tablespoons soy sauce, 1 tablespoon each lime juice and vegetable oil, 2 teaspoons palm or brown sugar, 2 teaspoons sesame oil, 1 teaspoon each ground turmeric and coriander and ½ teaspoon chilli powder. Pour over skewers and marinate for at least 1 hour, turning once or twice. Char-grill over high heat until cooked. Serve with satay sauce.*

### SATAY SAUCE

*Heat 1 tablespoon peanut oil in a frying pan and add 1 tablespoon red curry paste. Cook over low heat for 3 minutes. Stir in 200 ml coconut milk, add 1 tablespoon soy sauce, 1 tablespoon lemon juice, 300 g crunchy peanut butter and 2 tablespoons brown sugar and stir until smooth. Simmer for 5 minutes. Cool before using.*

**satsuma** — see mandarin

348

A spoonable concoction that may be added to, poured over, cooked with or form the base of other foods. There are hot sauces based on roux mixtures such as white sauce and velouté; cold sauces made up of a mixture of ingredients such as salsa verde and pesto; emulsions such as mayonnaise; and sauces such as ketchup to be splashed on food. Sauces made at home or in kitchens are often called 'composed' sauces. Sauces can be categorized into families as they usually have a base, or 'mother', sauce from which other sauces, called 'daughter' sauces, are made. These sauces are the backbone of French *haute cuisine* but many of them, such as white sauce and mayonnaise, are now an integral part of many Western recipes.

## ROUX-BASED SAUCES

White sauce, made by thickening milk with flour and butter, is used as a sauce on vegetables, gratins and to bind vegetables and meat together in pies. Daughter sauces of white sauce include:

| | |
|---|---|
| **Béchamel** | A white sauce with onion and bay leaves. |
| **Mornay** | A white sauce with grated cheese such as Gruyère, Cheddar or Parmesan. |
| **Parsley** | A white sauce enriched with chopped fresh parsley. |
| **Soubise** | A white sauce enriched with onions. |
| **Green** | A white sauce enriched with herbs or watercress. |
| **Cardinal** | Meaning 'red', a white sauce enriched with lobster butter. |

## SOUBISE

*Sweat 200 g very finely chopped onions in 30 g butter until soft and translucent but not brown. Scald 250 ml milk with 1 sliced onion, 3 peppercorns and a bay leaf and leave to infuse. Melt 1 tablespoon butter, then add 1 tablespoon plain flour and cook for 1 minute over low heat until foaming. Strain in the hot milk off the heat, whisking thoroughly, then bring to the boil, whisking constantly until thick. Season with salt and pepper and simmer for 2 minutes. Mix this with the onion and 3 tablespoons cream. Serve with cooked meats. Makes 300 ml.*

## EMULSIONS

Mayonnaise, made by whisking egg yolks and olive oil together to form an emulsion, is used to dress cold food or as a binding agent in salads such as potato salad. Daughter sauces of mayonnaise include:

| | |
|---|---|
| **Aïoli** | A garlic mayonnaise. |
| **Remoulade** | A mayonnaise with added mustard, chopped capers, cornichons, anchovies or anchovy essence and herbs. |
| **Tartare** | A mayonnaise with chopped capers, gherkins and parsley. |
| **Sauce verte** | A mayonnaise with added herbs. |

## REMOULADE

*Add 1 tablespoon drained and rinsed chopped capers, 1 tablespoon chopped cornichons, 2 chopped anchovy fillets and 2 teaspoons Dijon mustard to 300 ml mayonnaise (see page 238). Stir in 2 teaspoons chopped chervil and 1 teaspoon chopped tarragon; season well. Use with grated or chopped vegetables such as celeriac, carrots or potatoes. Serves 4.*

## STOCK SAUCES

Stock sauces can be made from either a white or brown stock. White stock added to a blond (pale brown) roux gives a velouté or blond sauce; brown stock added to a brown roux gives an espagnole or brown sauce. Daughter sauces include:

| | |
|---|---|
| **Mushroom** | A velouté with added sliced mushrooms. |
| **Suprême** | A velouté with added chicken stock and cream. |
| **Aurore** | A velouté with added tomato purée. |
| **Madeira** | An espagnole with added stock and Madeira. |
| **Poivrade (pepper)** | An espagnole with added crushed peppercorns. |
| **Bordelaise** | An espagnole with red wine. |

## ESPAGNOLE SAUCE

*Fry 1 chopped carrot, 1 chopped onion, 1 chopped celery stalk in 2 tablespoons butter until soft. Add 1 tablespoon flour and cook until brown. Whisk in 400 ml brown stock, 1 teaspoon tomato purée and add a bouquet garni. Bring to the boil and simmer, covered, for 30 minutes, skimming off any scum, then add another 200 ml brown stock. Strain. To make this into a demi-glace, add an equal quantity of brown stock and boil, skimming regularly, until reduced by half. Strain. Makes 400 ml.*

## HOLLANDAISE AND BEARNAISE SAUCES

Hollandaise and Béarnaise sauces are both hot emulsions made with egg yolks and butter. Hollandaise is made by adding melted or clarified butter to whisked egg yolks over heat; Béarnaise is made by adding butter to egg yolks whisked with an acid reduction over heat. Daughter sauces include:

| | |
|---|---|
| **Mousseline** | A hollandaise with added whipped cream. |
| **Moutarde** | A hollandaise with added mustard. |
| **Maltaise** | A hollandaise flavoured with blood oranges. |
| **Choron** | A Béarnaise with added tomato purée. |
| **Foyot** | A Béarnaise with added *glace de viande* (a reduction of clarified meat stock). |

## MOUSSELINE

*Make up a quantity of hollandaise sauce (see page 186); season with 1 teaspoon sugar and grated zest of 1 orange. Fold in 60 ml whipped cream and use to coat a dish of fresh or grilled fruit such as figs. Grill until browned. Serves 4.*

*See also* **Béarnaise sauce, béchamel sauce, hollandaise sauce, mayonnaise, mornay sauce, velouté sauce**

**sauerkraut** — s e e   c a b b a g e

Generally, tube-shaped casings stuffed with chopped meat and other flavourings. However, a much wider range of products can be grouped under the term 'sausage'. Sausages can be made from meat, fish or vegetables; they can be fresh, cooked or cured and fermented (salami); and they don't necessarily have to be stuffed into casings. They range in size and shape—from the traditional tube to round, looped, flat or even square. Fresh sausages tend to be made into links, as are some cured and cooked sausages; some, however, are sold as spirals or lengths. Cured and cooked sausages can also be bought sliced.

### Dried or cured sausages

These are made with raw meat, salt and saltpetre and are usually flavoured with spices such as black pepper, chilli or paprika. The meat mixture is stuffed into casings and then hung to dry, either in cool or hot air, until they have reduced their weight by about half. During this drying time the inside of the sausage goes through lactic fermentation. This increases its acidity and, along with the reduced moisture and high salt content, preserves the sausage. Some cured sausages are also smoked, further enhancing their preservation properties. Cured sausages may have a white yeast bloom on their surface, but this is harmless.

*Clockwise from top left:*
*francfort, chorizo, dried beef, kranksy, cacciatore, pepperoni, kabanosy.*

### Fresh sausages

Sausages tend to be eaten fresh in cold climates or in countries where the air is too moist to successfully dry and cure them. Fresh sausages can be made from any meat, though pork and beef are the most common. Bread and cereal may also be added to fresh sausages as a filler, the amounts of which vary greatly, but generally the more expensive sausages tend to have more meat in them. Fresh sausages are usually flavoured with salt, pepper and mace along with herbs and spices according to their variety. Fresh sausages should be cooked slowly so they don't burst because their insides expand faster than their casings.

*Clockwise from bottom left:*
*curry sausage, tomato and herb sausages, pork and apple sausages, chicken sausages, Nuremberg (a German grilling sausage).*

### Cooked sausages

Sausages may be cooked or partially cooked—these are either recooked before serving or sliced and eaten cold. Cooked sausages are common to Germany: brühwurst is a partially cooked sausage and kochwurst is fully cooked. Cooked sausages range from small, thin ones such as frankfurters to Italy's largest sausage, mortadella. Cooked sausages also include all the pudding-type sausages such as blood sausages like black pudding, morcilla and blutwurst and others like boudin blanc and rotwurst.

*Clockwise from bottom left:*
*white (boudin blanc), mortadella, morcilla, black pudding, blutwurst, white chipolata.*

The sausage is one of the most enduring and varied foods. The book of Apicius, the oldest known cookbook, published around 40 AD, mentions 'forcemeat... seasoned with lovage, pepper, cumin and laser root'. Today, the sausage stars in Germany in over 1,000 guises; in America as the hot dog; and in England as 'bangers and mash'—sausages and mashed potato.

## SPANISH AND PORTUGUESE SAUSAGES

Chorizo (chouriço in Portugal) is flavoured with paprika and sold either fresh or as a hard cured sausage to be eaten cold. Morcilla is a northern Spanish blood sausage, and butifarra, butifurro and butifarron are a family of Catalan sausages, some blood, some pork. Sobrassada is a spreadable, spicy pork sausage from Majorca.

*Spanish chorizo*

*Portuguese chouriço*

*Morcilla*

*Kielbasa*

## BRITISH SAUSAGES

Fresh sausages, generally made from pork, but also beef, lamb, venison, chicken and turkey. Some well-known sausages are Cumberland, sold as a spiral or in long lengths; Lincolnshire, flavoured with sage and thyme; and black pudding, made with blood. Fresh sausages (bangers), tend to be quite thick, and small, thin sausages are known as chipolatas. Commercial British sausages may have rusk or cereal filler added and can be moist as crushed ice is used during manufacture to keep the meat cool.

*London pork sausages*

*Pork sausages*

*Black pudding*

*Chipolatas*

*Pure beef sausages*

## POLISH SAUSAGES

Poland has a wide variety of sausages, cooked, fresh and cured. Polish sausages tend to be made from pork, though beef may be added, and flavoured with pepper, garlic and caraway. Kabanosy (kabanos) are long, thin smoked pork sausages, which are hard in texture; kielbasa (kielbasy or kolbassy), a smoked pork and beef sausage, is sold in links and can be cooked or uncooked. It is used in bigos (hunter's stew). Krakowska is a slicing sausage made from pork and beef and flavoured with pimiento.

*Kabanosy*

*Chinese yun cheong (brown) sausages*

*Chinese lap cheong (red) sausages*

## CHINESE SAUSAGES

Chinese sausages are thin, coarsely textured, yet tend to be sweeter and more fragrant than Western ones, often flavoured with rice wine, soy sauce and paprika. Brown sausages are made from pork liver and red ones from pork meat. They should always be cooked, either stir-fried or steamed over rice.

## AMERICAN SAUSAGES

Many of America's range of sausages arrived with immigrants from Germany, Poland and Italy. Common sausages include wieners (hot dogs), based on German frankfurters; and Bologna or baloney (bolony), based on mortadella, a precooked Italian sausage. Sausages also vary regionally. Pennsylvania has lightly smoked sausages, the Midwest has German-style sausages such as Bratwurst, and dry-smoked 'summer' sausages appear with regional variations across the country.

*Weisswurst*

*Dry-smoked German-style sausage*

*Frankfurters*

*Cervelat*

*Mettwurst*

## GERMAN SAUSAGES

Germany has more types of sausage than anywhere else in the world. Brühwurst are half-cooked sausages, which need to be cooked before eating, and include wieners, frankfurters, bockwurst, knackwurst and bierwurst. Rohwurst are cured sausages, used for slicing or spreading, and include cervelat and mettwurst. Kochwurst are cooked sausages, such as leberwurst and rotwurst. Weisswurst and bratwurst are white sausages often made from veal and these are used for frying or for poaching.

*Lyonnaise*

*Saucisson sec (cured and dried)*

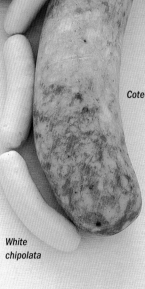

*White chipolata*

*Cotechino*

## FRENCH SAUSAGES

French charcuterie includes fresh, smoked and cured sausages. A small sausage is a saucisse; a large sausage, a saucisson, whether fresh or cured. Well-known sausages include Toulouse, made from fresh pork; Lyon, an air-dried sausage; and andouillette, also from Lyon, made from tripe, chitterlings and mesentery (stomach lining). Merguez, originally from North Africa, are made from beef flavoured with harissa. France also produces lots of boiling sausages, like saucisse de Morteau.

*Merguez*

*Milanese*

*Cacciatore*

## ITALIAN SAUSAGES

Italy's most popular sausage is salami, which varies regionally in size, shape and flavour. Sausages labelled as casalinga and nostrano usually mean they are home-made. Milanese are mild salami with a fairly fine texture; fiocchiona are flavoured with fennel; and Napoletano with black and red pepper. Cooked sausages include mortadella, a large sausage spotted with fat. Raw sausages, called salsiccia, include luganega and cotechino, used for simmering in liquid or for bollito misto.

*See also* **German sausage**

### Skinless sausages

Made by rolling or pressing sausage mixtures into shape. Examples include: chevapcici, a sausage from the Balkans made from beef or pork flavoured with garlic and formed into short squarish fingers; square Lorne sausages from Scotland; and the meatless Glamorgan sausages made with cheese and leeks and bound together with egg white.

### Sausage casings

The casing for sausages can be natural—sheep intestines for standard size, or pig for larger—or manufactured from collagen extracted from the hide of cattle. Sausages from manufactured casings need to be pricked, those from natural casings don't need to be. Good-quality sausages are still made in natural casings and these are easier to cook with as they don't burst as easily. You can tell if the sausage casing is natural by looking at the knots—these will stay tightly twisted if they are natural, and will often unwind if artificial. Other parts of animals such as caul or mesentery are also used to wrap sausages such as andouillettes. Sausages can be made at home using skin bought from the butcher—these are generally salted but may be packed in brine. The casings need to be soaked and then rinsed with lots of cold water. The skins can then be stuffed using a piping bag and twisted into links.

## CHICKEN SAUSAGES

*Soak 75 g fresh white breadcrumbs in 100 ml double cream. Soak 2 metres pork intestine in cold water. Mix together 200 g minced pork belly, 200 g minced chicken and 1 very finely chopped onion. Add the breadcrumbs, 2 eggs, ½ teaspoon mace, ½ teaspoon allspice, 2 tablespoons finely chopped parsley and season. Fry a little of the mixture, taste it for seasoning and adjust if necessary. Drain the intestine and tie a knot in one end, then feed the mixture into the other end through a funnel, making sure you don't fill the casing too full. Tie the intestine at the other end and twist into links. Poach in simmering water for 20 minutes, then drain and cool. Serve fried with apple sauce. Serves 6.*

*Bangers with mustard and tomato ketchup.*

## SPICY CHICKPEAS AND CHORIZO

*Fry 4 chorizo sausages cut into cubes with 1 chopped red chilli and 1 sliced onion. Add 400 g tin drained, rinsed chickpeas and 400 g tin chopped tomatoes. Simmer for 5 minutes; season with salt, pepper, Tabasco and lemon juice. Stir in 1 tablespoon chopped parsley. Serve with a dollop of yoghurt. Serves 4.*

A rich, sweet yeast cake, similar to a baba but made without raisins, and baked in either a large shallow ring mould or in small individual moulds. After baking, the cake is soaked in a sugar syrup usually flavoured with rum. To serve, the centre is filled with chantilly cream (sweetened whipped cream) or pastry cream, and may be topped with fresh fruit, angelica or glacé cherries. The cake was named in honour of Brillat-Savarin, the eighteenth-century food writer and philosopher.

**s c a l l o p**

Named for their fan-shaped shells, scallops are a bivalve mollusc found throughout the Atlantic, Mediterranean and Pacific oceans. There are over 300 species, varying in size from the large Atlantic deep-sea scallops, the great scallop to the smaller bay and queen (queenie) scallops. The enclosed scallop, including the orange or pinky red roe (the coral or tongue), is edible.

Scallop flesh should be pale beige to light pink, moist and glossy with a fresh sea smell. Scallops are sold either still enclosed in their shells or removed from the shell (shucked). Because they deteriorate rapidly once out of the water, they are usually sold shucked and should be refrigerated quickly and used within 1 day. They can also be bought frozen. Scallops only require quick cooking, and are usually simply grilled, poached or sautéed. Add them to soups and stews but at the last minute to avoid toughening their tender flesh. They can also be eaten raw with a little lemon juice or sliced as sashimi.

**Also known as — coquilles Saint Jacques, scollop**

▓ **See also  coquilles Saint Jacques, shellfish**

## SCALLOPS WITH AVOCADO SALSA

*Steam 12 large cleaned scallops for 1 minute, reserve 4 and finely chop the rest. Chop an avocado into dice and mix with ½ chopped green pepper, ½ finely chopped onion, 1 chopped, skinned and seeded tomato, then add the chopped scallop. Stir in 2 tablespoons lime juice and 1½ tablespoons olive oil and season well. Divide the mixture among 4 clean scallop shells and put one of the reserved scallops on top of each. Top with a sprig of coriander and squeeze over a little lime juice. Serves 4.*

## PREPARING SCALLOPS

1  *Clean the closed shell by scrubbing it. For easy shucking, put under a grill for 1 minute to warm, or steam for 30 seconds.*

2  *Hold the scallop in a tea towel and, with a sharp knife, carefully prise open the shell. Lift off the top shell.*

3  *Loosen the scallop from the shell. Pull off and discard the scallop's outer grey fringe and outer membrane.*

*A range of crispbreads from Sweden.*

*Salt cod from Norway.*

Scandinavia encompasses Norway, Sweden, Denmark and Finland. Although these countries are all independent, at different stages alliances were formed between themselves and neighbouring countries, so there is crossover in the kitchen. Common to all four are herrings, cheeses, berries, pork and reindeer.

## SWEDEN

The Swedes like to preserve their traditions. Their cuisine varies regionally, but always includes herrings, eaten in a multitude of ways, both sweet and pickled. The smorgasbord, a Swedish tradition, is world famous and literally means 'bread and butter table'. The table is laden with lots of different dishes and these are eaten in the order of a meal. Due to the abundant nature of the dishes, smorgasbord are usually served in restaurants. Crisp breads were first made by the Swedes and many different varieties are available, also biscuits spiced with ginger, cinnamon and cardamom are popular.

*Smoked herring from Denmark.*

## DENMARK

Denmark's cuisine has a robust simplicity to it; fish and shellfish are abundant and dairy farming is widely practised. Denmark also produces a lot of bacon and pork is a popular meat. *Smørrebrød*, open sandwiches available in hundreds of varieties, are eaten throughout the day. Smoked herring, often known as a *bornholmere*, is very popular. World-renowned Danish pastries are based on *wienerbrød*, the original version.

## NORWAY

Regional foods vary little in Norway. Western and southern Norway border with the North Sea providing plentiful supplies of fish. Salmon, cod (known as *lutefisk*), mackerel and herring are all popular, as are Norway lobsters, known elsewhere as Dublin Bay prawns. Other popular foods include game, reindeer and wild berries and there is a strong dairy culture. The national dishes of Norway are *farikal*, mutton and cabbage stew, and *loker*, a type of rissole. Aquavit, a fiery potato or grain spirit, is the national drink. A particular type, called Linie, is sent around the world whilst it distills. Potatoes also feature heavily in Norwegian cuisine as do grain and flat breads.

*Cardamom tea loaf from Finland.*

## FINLAND

Between the thirteenth and nineteenth centuries, Finland was ruled by both Russia and Sweden and their influence is still evident in dishes today. Everyday foods include herring, salmon, game, wild mushrooms and berries, and dill, caraway and cardamom are used. Specialities include fish roe from a variety of fish and dishes, such as filled pastries, of Russian origin. A well-known dish is *kalakukko*, which is layers of fish and meat baked inside bread and sweet dishes such as *muurinpohjaletut*, a type of pancake and cardamom tea loaf.

An escalope (a thin slice of meat cut from the top of the leg or fillet), usually veal or pork, beaten out until thin, dipped in egg and breadcrumbs, then pan-fried. The most famous is the Viennese breadcrumb-coated Wiener schnitzel. Variations include the Parisian schnitzel, where the veal is first dipped in flour and egg and Naturschnitzel, where the veal is dipped in flour, then fried. Schnitzel is usually served with potatoes and a wedge of lemon but sometimes with a mushroom and cream sauce or sour cream.

## scone

Originating in Scotland, the scone is a flat cake, soft and light on the inside and golden and crisp on the outside. Scones are at their best when served fresh and warm from the oven, most famously with butter or jam and cream. Originally scones were made from oat flour, oatmeal or barley meal, but today the basic scone is usually made with flour (wholemeal or plain), a raising agent and an acid ingredient such as soured milk or buttermilk. Butter, sugar and dried fruits may also be added to enrich the dough. Scone doughs can be cut into individual rounds or into one large flat dough and marked into wedges before baking.

### MAKING SCONES

1 Sift 250 g self-raising flour, ¼ teaspoon bicarbonate of soda and a pinch of salt into a bowl.

2 Rub in 50 g chopped butter with your fingertips until the mixture is crumbly.

3 Make a well in the centre, then add 150 ml milk or buttermilk.

4 Cut the liquid into the flour using a knife and mix to form a soft rough dough.

5 Turn the dough out onto a floured surface and pat to an even 2 cm thick round.

6 Cut 4 cm rounds. Put on a baking tray; bake at 180°C for 10–12 minutes, or until well risen.

## Scotch egg

A peeled hard-boiled egg encased in sausage meat, coated in flour, egg and rolled in breadcrumbs, then deep-fried in oil. To serve, the Scotch egg is usually cut in half or quarters to show the enclosed egg. They are served hot or cold as a starter or appetizer, and, uncut, make excellent picnic fare as they travel well. Scotch eggs are, obviously enough, a Scottish invention dating from the nineteenth century.

## Scotch woodcock

A scrambled egg dish served on toast flavoured with anchovies or anchovy paste. The egg is softly scrambled with the addition of cream. It was a great favourite in Victorian times and was served as a first course.

### SCOTCH WOODCOCK

*Toast 4 slices of bread. Mash 30 g anchovies with 30 g butter. Spread onto the toast, then put the toast on 4 plates. Whisk together 4 egg yolks, 200 ml cream, 1 tablespoon finely chopped parsley and a pinch of cayenne. Pour the egg mixture into a buttered pan and stir gently over low heat until the mixture is creamy and just set. Spoon over the toast and serve. Serves 4.*

## scrapple

A Pennsylvania Dutch dish made from boiled and finely chopped pork scraps and offal. The meat is combined with cornmeal, buckwheat flour, broth and seasonings, often sage. It is mixed to a 'mush' and pressed into a loaf pan, cooked and cooled before being sliced. The slices are fried in butter and served hot for breakfast or lunch with apple slices and brown sugar. Scrapple is standard fare served at road-side diners in Pennsylvania.

***Also known as — Philadelphia scrapple***

A worm-like sea creature prized for its texture, which, like bean curd, absorbs the flavour of the ingredients it is cooked with. To prepare it, the sea cucumber is boiled, then mixed with ashes and left to dry in the sun. To use it in cooking, the flesh is boiled for 4 hours. As the sea cucumber swells as it rehydrates, the Chinese believe that if you eat it, your personal happiness and fortune will swell. In Japan, the sea cucumber is eaten raw, thinly sliced, with vinegar, soy sauce or mustard. Sea cucumber is nearly always bought dried from Asian speciality shops. With a protein content of over 75 per cent it is considered highly nutritious.

***Also known as — balatin, bêche-de-mer, iriko, sea rat, sea slug, trepang***

**s e e  s h e l l f i s h  —  s e a  u r c h i n**

**s e a w e e d**

Any edible sea plant belonging to the algae family. The many varieties can be divided into four main groups: brown (kelp, arame, hijiki, kombu, wakame); green (sea lettuce, sea grapes); red (nori, dulse, carrageen, agar-agar); and blue-green (spirulina). Rich in iodine, seaweeds are widely used in Asian cuisine, especially in Japan in soups, sushi and as a seasoning. Many seaweeds are dried and compressed into sheets, or processed into a powder, which is used as a seasoning.

**See also  agar-agar**

## TYPES OF SEAWEEDS

*Hijiki*

*Kombu*

*Nori sheets and flakes*

*Wakame*

***Dulse***

Reddish-purple with fan-shaped fronds, common around the Mediterranean and Ireland. It has a pungent, briny flavour and is tough and rubbery. Used to flavour soups, stews and condiments and eaten raw in salads.

***Hijiki***

Short, thin sticks of seaweed usually sold dried. Soak before use—it will swell to three times its size. Eat raw in salads, boil and serve with rice or in soups. It is often sautéed then simmered in soy sauce and sugar.

***Kombu***

Also known as kelp and tangle kelp, kombu is a large, flat, olive-green seaweed. Used to flavour Japanese dashi, a salty stock, or cooked as a vegetable with fish. Sold dried. Often coated with a white salty mould—this gives it flavour and should not be washed off—wipe over with a damp cloth and cut into pieces.

***Nori (laver)***

Sold dried in paper-thin sheets, coloured from purple to green, or in flakes. Used for wrapping sushi, shredded into soups or crumbled onto rice. Sheets need to be crisped over a flame or under the grill before use.

***Wakame***

Dark green or brown, used in soups and to flavour salads and vegetables with a vinegar dressing. Usually sold dried in pieces or flakes—soak for 2 hours before use.

**359**

## seitan

A gluten derived from washing the starch from wheat, used as a high-protein meat replacement in vegetarian dishes such as stir-fries and stews. The gluten can be flavoured variously, but when it is simmered in a broth of soy sauce, tamari, ginger, garlic and seaweed, it is called seitan. The texture is firm, spongy and chewy. Ready-to-eat seitan is sold in foil packets or vacuum-packed in health food stores or Asian markets.

## semifreddo

Literally Italian for 'half-cold', usually a parfait-style ice cream made without churning, though can mean any chilled or partly frozen dessert, possibly containing ice cream, sponge cake, cream and fruit.

## semolina — see wheat

## sesame seed

A tropical or subtropical plant that produces seed pods that, when dried, burst open and then are shaken to encourage the release of hundreds of tiny seeds. Sesame seeds are usually cream in colour, but may also be yellow, reddish or black, depending on the variety. The seeds can be used raw, but when toasted, take on a nutty, slightly sweet flavour. Sesame seeds are used in cooking throughout the world—scattered over burger buns, on bread, and as garnishes for salads. In the Middle East, they are used in halvah, are crushed to make tahini or ground with chickpeas to produce hummus. In Japan, sesame seeds form the basis of seasonings such as gomasio.

Because of their high oil content, the seeds become rancid quickly. Purchase in small amounts or store in the fridge for up to 3 months. Sesame seeds may also be frozen.

### SESAME OIL

*Sesame oil is made from crushed seeds and ranges in colour from amber-yellow to darker brown. It has a very strong flavour and aroma. The lighter coloured oil is used as a salad dressing and for frying in the Middle East; the darker coloured oil, made from toasted sesame seeds, is stronger in flavour and is ideal to use in small amounts as a flavouring, condiment and seasoning to Asian foods. Sesame oil can be used for frying as it has a high smoking point (420°C), however the roasted oil burns very quickly.*

*Clockwise from top left: toasted sesame seeds, roasted sesame oil, gomasio (made from sea salt and lightly toasted sesame seeds), white and black sesame seeds, sesame seed biscuits.*

### SESAME PRAWN TOAST

*Process or finely chop 100 g raw prawns with 1 teaspoon each of soy sauce, lemon juice and grated ginger, ½ teaspoon cornflour, 1 chopped spring onion and 1 tablespoon egg white. Season well. Spread onto 4 crustless pieces of white bread, then press sesame seeds onto the top of each piece. Cut into quarters and deep-fry in hot oil for 30 seconds. Makes 16 pieces.*

*See also* **halvah, hummus, tahini**

A Japanese one-pot (*nabemono*) meat and vegetable dish. The ingredients are cooked at the table in a pot of boiling stock or broth. The beef is thinly sliced and the vegetables are cut into bite-sized pieces. Each diner cooks their own food by dipping the beef into the hot broth—the name of the dish is onomatopoeic for the swishing noise made as the meat is moved around the boiling broth. Once cooked, the ingredients are dipped into side dishes of sauces, usually soy sauce and lemon juice, and a sesame seed sauce.

## shallot

### COOKING

*To skin shallots, blanch them in boiling water for 1 minute, then peel.*

*If leaving shallots whole, then only trim the root or they will fall apart.*

*When browning shallots, make sure they are well browned all over as the colour will wash off if they are added to a liquid such as stock.*

A close relative of the onion, but with a milder, delicate flavour, shallots grow in clusters and are joined with a common root end. There are several varieties including the grey or common shallot, which has grey skin and a purple head; the Jersey shallot, a round bulb with pink skin; the French shallot (*cuisse de poulet*), also called banana shallot, which has golden copper-coloured skin and an elongated bulb; and Asian or Thai shallots, which are a lighter pink.

Shallots feature in delicate sauces such as beurre blanc, they can be used as a garnish, thinly sliced and eaten raw in salads, or peeled and cooked whole as a vegetable. In France, shallots are used in sauces as the flesh dissolves well when cooked; in Asia, they are made into pickles. Store in a cool, well-ventilated place for up to 1 month. In some countries, spring onions are erroneously called shallots.

***Also known as — échalote***

French shallot          Asian shallot

### CARAMELIZED SHALLOT TART

*Melt 60 g butter and 2 tablespoons brown sugar in a large frying pan. Add 500 g peeled small shallots. Cook and stir for 20 minutes over low heat, then add 2 tablespoons balsamic vinegar and cook for 10 minutes until the shallots are soft and caramelized. Transfer shallots and syrup to an 18 cm metal pie dish. Roll 300 g shortcrust pastry (see page 367) to 5 mm thick. Trim to a 21 cm circle. Position over the shallots, tucking in the edges around the shallots. Bake at 200 °C for 20 minutes, or until golden. Cool for 20 minutes, then place on a serving dish and turn. Serve warm. Serves 6.*

# shellfish

Any aquatic animal covered by a shell. This includes those with one shell (univalve) or two shells (bivalve), crustaceans, sea urchins and a cephalopod called a pearly nautilus (which has an external shell). In practice, the term is used to refer to other varieties of seafood as well.

## SCALLOPS

Scallops do not have a foot but instead have a strong adductor muscle with which they open and close their shells and propel themselves through the water. There are many varieties and their shells vary in size and roundness. The white adductor muscle, roe, testis and mantle are all edible, but usually just the muscle and roe are eaten.

## COCKLES

There are many different bivalves named cockle but only a few are true cockles. Cockles are found worldwide. Varieties include the common cockle, which can be up to 6 cm wide with a cream, yellow or brown shell, the red-fleshed spiny (or bloody) cockle, the prickly cockle, the Iceland cockle, the large Atlantic cockle and basket cockles. Dog cockles have a striated shell but are not true cockles. Cockles can be eaten raw or cooked and must be bought live.

## CONCHS AND WHELKS

Found in the West Indies, Florida and South America, conchs are single-shelled molluscs, sometimes up to 30 cm long. The flesh often needs to be tenderized by beating or marinating it in an acid such as lime juice. Conchs can be cooked or eaten raw in ceviche or salads. Whelks, similar in appearance but smaller than conchs, are found in Europe, the West Atlantic, California and Canada. Only the large adductor muscle ('foot') is eaten. In France, a type of whelk called murex is found on seafood platters.

*Scallops*

*Cockles*

*Conch meat*

*Pacific oysters*

*Angassi oyster*

*Sydney rock oysters*

*Sea urchins*

*Sydney rock oysters*

## OYSTERS

A bivalve more cultivated than taken from the wild, of which there are many different varieties around the world, all of which vary in size, taste and texture, depending on where they are grown. Oysters are often eaten raw from their shells, but can be cooked.

*Pacific oysters*

## SEA URCHIN

Hidden inside the spiny sea urchin are five orange roe (corals). Cut the top off and scoop out the corals and eat raw or cook with pasta or eggs. Sea urchins are popular in Sicily, Brittany and Ireland but are also found in Europe and America. The purple or green urchins are considered better than the whiter, short-spined ones.

## ABALONE

Also known as ormer or ear shell, these are found in the waters around Japan, Australia, New Zealand, California, the Mediterranean and off the European Atlantic coast, and highly prized in Chinese and Japanese cuisine. The foot or adductor muscle is eaten. Varieties include red, black-footed pauer and pinto abalone. Abalone is sold fresh, dried and frozen. Are now also farmed.

*Black-lipped abalone*

## PERIWINKLES (WINKLES)

Small, blackish-brown single-shelled mollusc found on both sides of the Atlantic, particularly along rocky coasts. Rinse well in several changes of water, then boil in salted water. Extract the flesh with a pin. Use only winkles with a tightly closed operculum.

*Winkles*

## CLAMS

Bivalve molluscs, which can be classed as either soft- or hard-shelled. Hard-shelled clams come in different sizes and colours and can be typically clam shaped or like long razor shapes. Types include quahog (also called littleneck), palourde, pipis, tuatua, toheroa, prarie and warty venus. All are good raw or cooked. Razor-shelled clams are best steamed open.

Soft-shelled clams are found in the North Atlantic, and have soft, brittle shells that gape open as their syphons stick out. Geoduck clams have long syphons and are cooked in clam bakes or chowders. Steamer clams are also a variety of soft-shelled clam. Clams must be bought live, then shucked and cleaned before use.

*Pipis*

*Clams*

*Prawns*

*Rock lobster*

*Dublin Bay prawns*

*Black mussels*

## CRUSTACEANS

This category includes all creatures that have a hinged carapace (a hard upper shell), such as crabs, lobsters, prawns and crayfish. Crustaceans are at their best when eaten in their local area. With the exception of prawns, they should be cooked when alive or bought already cooked.

*Blue swimmer crab*

*New Zealand green-lipped mussels*

## MUSSELS

Bivalve molluscs found worldwide. Now mostly farmed, which are safest to eat. Wild mussels should be treated carefully as they filter and harbour any toxins in the water. Common varieties include the blue mussel and green-lipped mussel from New Zealand. Mussels are the national dish of Belgium but also feature in French, Italian and Middle Eastern cuisine.

**363**

Shellfish need considerable care and attention. Their flesh is delicate and deteriorates rapidly, so they should be bought on the day they are to be eaten. They should be collected from clean fresh water or purified water, as they are notoriously good at collecting and storing bacteria and other toxins, so only buy them or collect from reliable sources. Bivalves have a tendency to be sandy or gritty and can be put in a bucket of sea water or heavily salted water for a couple of hours so they expel their grit. Bivalves can be shucked or steamed open. Univalves can be cooked before removing the meat or have the meat removed when raw.

**See also abalone, crab, crayfish, lobster, mussels, oyster, prawn**

## BUYING

*Shellfish should be bought live or frozen but not dead unless they are prawns, which are not generally sold live. Shellfish should look healthy and smell of the sea; any unpleasant or fishy smell usually means their flesh has started to deteriorate. Check each bivalve before cooking and eating it. Cooked shellfish such as crab and lobster should smell sweet and look fresh. Lobster tails should be tightly curled. Live crab and lobster should be lively and feel heavy.*

## IS THE BIVALVE DEAD OR ALIVE?

*1* *Tip the shells into a sink and sort through them—they should all be closed.*

*2* *If any shells are open, tap them on the sink. If they stay open, throw them away—they are dead.*

## COOKING

*Shellfish only need the minimum amount of cooking time or the flesh will toughen.*

*If cooking them in a liquid, such as stock or wine, remove them and pour the liquid through a sieve lined with muslin to get rid of any grit that was in the shells.*

*Eat crustaceans when warm rather than very hot or chilled as they will have a better flavour.*

*Steaming is a simple way of opening bivalves and can be a prelude to most recipes. Once the shellfish are steamed, they can be added to a base mixture with their sieved liquid and briefly heated through.*

*Grilling and steaming helps open shells easily. If you want to remove the meat and cook it raw, steam or grill for a few seconds until the shells just start to open.*

## MANHATTAN CLAM CHOWDER

*Scrub 1 kg large clams and discard any dead ones. Put 1 cm water in a pan and boil, add the clams and cook for 3 minutes or until they all open—discard any closed ones. Take out the clam meat and strain the liquid. Fry 100 g chopped bacon, 1 chopped onion and 2 chopped celery stalks, add 1 diced potato, 1 chopped leek and a bay leaf, then add the clam liquid, 400 g tin chopped tomatoes and 1 litre fish stock. Simmer until the potato is cooked, season well and stir in the clams. Serves 4.*

## MUSSELS WITH LEMON GRASS

*In a large saucepan, put 2 chopped spring onions, 2 tablespoons grated ginger, 1 finely chopped red chilli, 2 chopped lemon grass stems and 100 ml coconut milk. Bring to the boil, simmer for 2 minutes, then add 1 kg cleaned mussels. Put the lid on and cook until all mussels have opened; about 4 minutes. Remove mussels with a slotted spoon and reduce the liquid by half. Season and pour back over mussels, leaving any grit behind in the pan. Sprinkle with fresh coriander leaves. Serves 6.*

## OPENING A SEA URCHIN

1 *Using scissors or a coupe-oursin, cut a round piece out of the top of the shell (opposite end to mouth).*

2 *Lift off the piece of shell as if you were opening an egg. Drain off any juices.*

3 *Carefully scoop out the roes.*

## PREPARING HARD-SHELLED CLAMS

1 *Check to make sure all the clams are alive. Leave them in cold salted water for a couple of hours to expel any grit.*

2 *Drain the clams and put them in a large frying pan or steamer tray. Heat until they just start to open, then remove from heat.*

3 *Pull off the top shell and lift out the meat, collecting any juices in a bowl. Strain the juices through a piece of muslin before using.*

## STORAGE

*Keep live shellfish covered in a damp cloth in the salad compartment of the fridge or in a cool place for 1–2 days. Don't store them in water unless it is clean sea water or they will drown.*

## PREPARATION

*As shellfish tend to be scavengers, make sure that you always remove the dark intestinal tracts from prawns and lobsters and the stomach sacs from lobsters and crabs. Scrub any dirty shells and remove any barnacles. If boiling crabs and lobsters to eat cold, make holes in the claws so they drain well, otherwise the water gets trapped in the shell.*

*It is easier to take the flesh out of single-shelled molluscs, such as this whelk, after they have been cooked.*

## shepherd's pie

A pie traditionally made with the minced or diced leftovers from the Sunday lamb roast, mixed with vegetables and topped with mashed potato. A similar dish is cottage pie, made using minced cooked beef instead of lamb.

### SHEPHERD'S PIE

*Fry 1 chopped onion, carrot and celery stalk in 1 tablespoon oil. Add 500 g diced cooked lamb, 1 tablespoon tomato paste, 2 teaspoons Worcestershire sauce and 250 ml beef stock; season. Simmer for 20 minutes. Spoon into an ovenproof dish. Mash 500 g boiled potatoes with 50 ml milk and 50 g butter. Season, then spread over meat. Bake at 200°C for 30 minutes. Serves 4.*

## sherbet — see ice cream

## sherry

*From left: medium amontillado, fino muy seco, golden oloroso, medium dry amontillado.*

A fortified wine first made in, and named after, the Jerez de la Frontera ('jerez' means sherry) region of southern Spain, now made in other parts of the world. Sherries differ in colour and flavour. Dry sherries are used in savoury sauces and chicken dishes; sweet sherries in cold desserts such as trifles. Manzanillas, dry and delicate, and finos, dry and light, are best drunk chilled; amontillados are darker and sweeter with a nutty flavour; and oloroso is mostly used as a base for sweet sherries, blended as 'cream' sherry for the English market.

## shortbread

### PETTICOAT TAILS

*Beat 110 g butter and 55 g caster sugar until creamy. Sift 110 g plain flour and 55 g rice flour into the butter mixture and mix to a smooth dough. Line a baking tray with baking paper. Press the dough into a 15 cm baking ring, then crimp the edges. Chill for 20 minutes. Prick with a fork and lightly mark wedges with a knife. Sprinkle with extra caster sugar. Bake at 160°C for 40 minutes, or until golden. Cool before cutting into wedges.*

A rich biscuit made with butter, sugar and flour—the high butter content giving it its characteristic crumbly texture. The flour may be plain wheat flour or wholemeal flour with a little rice flour or cornflour. The Scottish version may also use oatmeal. Associated with Christmas and Scottish New Year (Hogmanay), shortbread was traditionally baked in a frilly edged round wooden mould, turned out and cut into wedges known as petticoat tails. It may also be made into a large free-form circle with fluted edges or shaped into rounds or squares.
**Also known as — Scottish shortbread**

## SHORTCAKE

*Cream 90 g butter with 60 g sugar until light and creamy. Add 1 egg and mix well. Sift in 140 g flour, 2 teaspoons baking powder and a pinch of salt, then add 80 ml milk. Fold well. Put the mixture in a 20 cm greased cake tin and bake at 180°C for 20 minutes. Cool slightly, then split and fill with cream and strawberries. Dust with icing sugar to serve.*

An American speciality dating back to the 1850s, made with a rich scone dough, which is cooked as a round, then split in half. The centre is filled with sliced or chopped fruit, usually strawberries, sometimes peaches, and whipped cream. It may be cooked as small individual rounds or as one large cake, filled, then cut into wedges to serve. The cake is sweet and crumbly and should be served warm. There are also savoury variations such as those filled with creamed chicken.

## shortcrust pastry

A pastry made using flour, fat and water, which may be enriched with egg yolks. Lard and butter can be combined to give a well-flavoured short pastry, the lard giving texture and the butter flavour. Solid margarines can also be used. Egg is sometimes added in place of some or all of the liquid to enrich and produce a softer, less crisp pastry. Use just enough liquid to hold the pastry together—if it is too wet it will toughen and be inclined to shrink on baking; if too dry, it will be crumbly.

**Also known as — pâte brisée**

### MAKING SHORTCRUST PASTRY

**1** Sift 170 g plain flour and a pinch of salt into a bowl. Add 55 g cold butter and 30 g cold lard, cut into cubes.

**2** Rub the fat into the flour with your fingertips until the mixture is crumb-like.

**3** Add 2–3 tablespoons cold water and use a knife to mix to a soft, but not sticky, dough.

**4** Turn onto the work surface and knead once or twice until you have a smooth dough. Wrap in clingfilm and refrigerate.

**5** Roll out the pastry and fit into a 20 cm tart tin.

**6** Roll the rolling pin across the top of the tin to cut off any excess pastry.

## shortening

The fat or oil used in baking and pastry making to make them 'short'—that is with a soft, crumbly texture. Baked goods such as shortbread and shortcrust pastry all use a high ratio of fat to flour to produce their characteristic soft, crumbly texture.

*Clockwise from top left: butter, margarine, processed lard, lard.*

## shrimp

### CHINESE SHRIMP WITH CABBAGE

*Soak 30 g dried shrimps in boiling water for 15 minutes. Heat 1 tablespoon oil in a preheated wok, add 400 g Chinese cabbage cut into strips and toss for 2 minutes, or until wilted. Add the soaked prawns, 1 tablespoon soy sauce, 2 teaspoons sugar and 1 tablespoon rice vinegar and cook for another minute. Sprinkle with 2 teaspoons sesame oil and serve. Serves 4 .*

**See also** *shrimp paste*

Shrimps are small crustaceans similar to prawns but members of a different family, except in North America, where both prawns and shrimps are encompassed under the general term of 'shrimp'. There are hundreds of species, which thrive in both warm and cold water. In Europe the most common is the brown shrimp. The colour of raw shrimps varies greatly but most will assume a pale to bright pink or brown colour on cooking. Shrimps are used in seafood cocktails, canapés, potted shrimp, and open sandwiches. They may be dried and used in Asian cooking. Shrimps are usually sold frozen or in tins. If buying fresh, they should have a firm shell and flesh and a fresh, slightly sea smell. Store in the fridge for up to 2 days or freeze.

**Also known as — brown shrimp, crevitte gris**

## shrimp paste

Partially fermented shrimps that are ground, salted and dried before being either compressed into blocks and further left to dry in the sun, or bottled as it is. This type is manufactured mostly in Malaysia and Indonesia; the Chinese version is softer and more sauce-like.

Shrimp paste has a strong, salty flavour and is used—sparingly—as a flavouring in Southeast Asian and Chinese foods such as soups, sauces and rice dishes, or it may be mixed with chillies and shallots to make a flavouring. Shrimp paste from Malaysia, called blachan, should be fried first in a little oil to bring out the flavour.

Shrimp paste has a very pungent odour and, when opened, should be wrapped in plastic or stored in an airtight container. If stored in the fridge, shrimp paste should keep indefinitely.

**Also known as — bagoong, blacan, blacang, blachan, kapi, trassi**

# Sichuan pepper

A Chinese spice native to the province of Sichuan, made from the red berries of the prickly ash tree and sold whole or ground. Although not related to the peppercorn, the Sichuan berry resembles the black peppercorn in appearance but has enclosed seeds. The flavour and fragrance has a distinctive woody-spicy smell and a strong, hot, numbing aftertaste. Sichuan pepper is widely used in Chinese everyday cooking (often in very large amounts). The peppercorns are sometimes crushed and dry-fried to bring out the flavours. Sichuan pepper is also one of the spices used in Chinese five-spice powder. The Japanese pepper *sansho*, a close relation, is mostly bought ground and used with grilled eel and chicken, and in the seven spice mixture *shichimi togarashi*.

*Also known as — anise pepper, Chinese aromatic pepper, Chinese pepper, Szechuan pepper, xanthoxylum*

See also  **peppercorn**

see Swiss chard — **silver beet**

# silver leaf

A precious metal, which is edible when beaten into paper-thin sheets. Although it has no aroma or taste, silver leaf is used to decorate desserts, cakes, rice dishes, sweetmeats and dishes for special occasions, particularly in India. Because the leaf is very fragile, it tears easily when handled or may tarnish if in contact with the oils in your hands—remove the sheet with a pair of tweezers or use a soft brush to tamp the leaf into position. Silver leaf is purchased in small packets interleaved with parchment paper or sold in powdered form. It will keep indefinitely in a cool, dry place. It is assigned additive number E175. Silver balls are small sugar balls about 2 mm in diameter and used to decorate cakes and confectionery.

*Also known as — varak, varaq, vark, varq*

See also  **gold leaf**

# skordalia

Traditionally a Greek garlic sauce served cold with grilled or fried vegetables (especially aubergine), meat, poultry and fish, such as salt cod fritters with boiled eggs and in soups. It is also used as a dip for raw vegetables and bread. Today skordalia may be thickened with either puréed or mashed potatoes, as well as the original breadcrumbs, or almonds, pine nuts or walnuts. Classically made in a mortar and pestle, the oil is added drop by drop until a thick mayonnaise-like consistency is reached.

*Also known as — skorthalia*

### SKORDALIA

*Mix 250 g mashed potato with 2–3 crushed garlic cloves and 1 slice day-old bread, which has been first soaked in cold water and squeezed dry. Using electric beaters or a mortar and pestle, beat in 185 ml olive oil, allowing the oil to slowly drizzle into the mashed potato, then add 2 tablespoons white wine vinegar and 1 tablespoon lemon juice and season well. Serves 8.*

### sloe

A small black plum, the only one native to Britain, from the blackthorn bush, a thorny shrub common throughout Europe. About 1 cm in diameter, it has yellow-green flesh and a central stone. An extremely tart fruit, it is never eaten raw, but is used to make jams, jellies, sloe wine, brandy and sloe gin, a liqueur made by steeping and crushing sloes in gin.

#### SLOE GIN

*Prick 450 g washed sloes with a pin. Put them in a large bowl with 1 litre gin and 110 g caster sugar. Add 5–6 drops almond essence and leave to steep for 3 months in a cool place. Strain and bottle in sterilized bottles. Makes about 1.25 litres.*

### sloppy joe

A toasted hamburger bun filled with a cooked mixture of minced beef, onions, celery and peppers and a spicy tomato sauce flavoured with chilli, Tabasco and Worcestershire sauces. Its origins are unclear but it is thought to be so named because of the tendency of the sauce to drip, making it very sloppy eating indeed. Sloppy joe is a classic dish of road-side diners in America.

### smetana

A dairy cream soured by bacterial fermentation, used in Eastern European cooking. Smetana has a mildly tangy flavour, milder than that of sour cream, and is served with savoury dishes such as fish, borscht and as a sauce for sauerkraut and cabbage rolls. Like sour cream, it must not be boiled or it will curdle. The smetana found outside of its native Russia is a low-fat dairy cream, similar to thick buttermilk. It can be used in cheesecakes or recipes that ask for sour cream.

#### CROATIAN POTATO SOUP

*Fry 50 g chopped bacon and 1 chopped onion in 50 g butter. Add 1 tablespoon sweet paprika, a pinch of dried marjoram and 1 tablespoon plain flour. Mix well. Add 700 g chopped potatoes and 1 litre chicken stock. Bring to the boil and cook until tender. Purée with 200 ml stock, season and stir in 200 g smetana and 2 tablespoons chopped parsley. Serves 4.*

The technique of smoking meat and fish to help preserve them has been in use, along with salting and drying, since prehistoric times. The fish is usually first salted or immersed in brine, then exposed to smoke, usually from hardwoods such as oak, beech or hickory, which not only preserves, but adds flavour. An aromatic wood such as juniper or rosemary may be added towards the end of the process. Fish may be cold-smoked or hot-smoked. Fish smoked at home must be hot-smoked or cured to preserve it. Smoked fish are popular in Europe and are also smoked in Africa, sometimes until they turn black, on a wire mesh over a charcoal fire. In Japan, fish such as mackerel and tuna are steamed, smoked and then dried.

## SMOKED FOODS

*Although smoking is usually associated with fish or meat such as ham and bacon, poultry and game, other smoked foods include eel, sausages, cheese, nuts, hard-boiled eggs, oysters and mussels.*

## SMOKING FISH

*Heat a heavy-based frying pan or wok until very hot, sprinkle with 3–4 tablespoons sawdust (use fruitwood or hardwood but not resinous wood) and cover quickly with a sheet of foil pierced with lots of holes. Put an oiled cake rack on top, lay the fish on the rack, cover, and smoke for 20 minutes per 2.5 cm thickness of fish. Press the fish—when it feels flaky under the skin, it is ready.*

Whole smoked trout

## SMOKING FISH

**Cold-smoked**
The fish is smoked at around 24°C. Cold-smoking is used to flavour already cured fish and while it partially dries the fish, it does not cook it—cold-smoked fish can look shiny and translucent. Examples of cold-smoked fish eaten raw include salmon, haddock, kippers and trout.

**Hot-smoked**
The fish is first cold-smoked, then the temperature is raised to around 82°C. Hot-smoking involves cooking the fish until the flesh is opaque and cooked through. The fish is allowed to cool for 24 hours, then may be eaten cold. Examples of hot-smoked fish include mackerel and herring.

## CULLEN SKINK

*Cook 1 chopped onion in 30 g butter, add 2 chopped bacon rashers, 1 sliced celery stalk and 200 g chopped potato and fry until lightly browned. Add 250 ml milk and 300 ml fish stock and cook until the vegetables are soft. Add 250 g smoked haddock cut into cubes and 2 tablespoons double cream and simmer for 2 minutes. Season and stir in 1 tablespoon chopped parsley. Serves 4.*

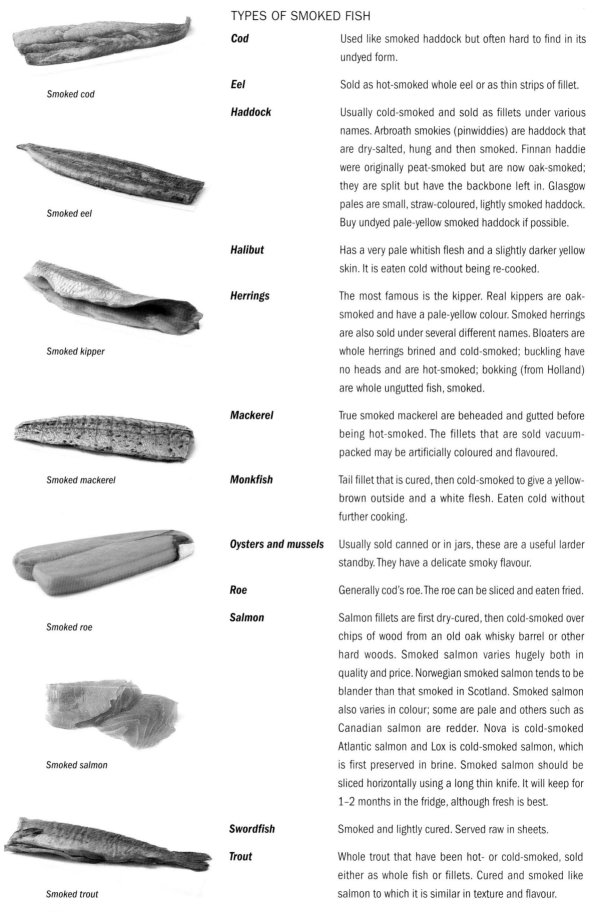

*Smoked cod*

*Smoked eel*

*Smoked kipper*

*Smoked mackerel*

*Smoked roe*

*Smoked salmon*

*Smoked trout*

## TYPES OF SMOKED FISH

| | |
|---|---|
| **Cod** | Used like smoked haddock but often hard to find in its undyed form. |
| **Eel** | Sold as hot-smoked whole eel or as thin strips of fillet. |
| **Haddock** | Usually cold-smoked and sold as fillets under various names. Arbroath smokies (pinwiddies) are haddock that are dry-salted, hung and then smoked. Finnan haddie were originally peat-smoked but are now oak-smoked; they are split but have the backbone left in. Glasgow pales are small, straw-coloured, lightly smoked haddock. Buy undyed pale-yellow smoked haddock if possible. |
| **Halibut** | Has a very pale whitish flesh and a slightly darker yellow skin. It is eaten cold without being re-cooked. |
| **Herrings** | The most famous is the kipper. Real kippers are oak-smoked and have a pale-yellow colour. Smoked herrings are also sold under several different names. Bloaters are whole herrings brined and cold-smoked; buckling have no heads and are hot-smoked; bokking (from Holland) are whole ungutted fish, smoked. |
| **Mackerel** | True smoked mackerel are beheaded and gutted before being hot-smoked. The fillets that are sold vacuum-packed may be artificially coloured and flavoured. |
| **Monkfish** | Tail fillet that is cured, then cold-smoked to give a yellow-brown outside and a white flesh. Eaten cold without further cooking. |
| **Oysters and mussels** | Usually sold canned or in jars, these are a useful larder standby. They have a delicate smoky flavour. |
| **Roe** | Generally cod's roe. The roe can be sliced and eaten fried. |
| **Salmon** | Salmon fillets are first dry-cured, then cold-smoked over chips of wood from an old oak whisky barrel or other hard woods. Smoked salmon varies hugely both in quality and price. Norwegian smoked salmon tends to be blander than that smoked in Scotland. Smoked salmon also varies in colour; some are pale and others such as Canadian salmon are redder. Nova is cold-smoked Atlantic salmon and Lox is cold-smoked salmon, which is first preserved in brine. Smoked salmon should be sliced horizontally using a long thin knife. It will keep for 1–2 months in the fridge, although fresh is best. |
| **Swordfish** | Smoked and lightly cured. Served raw in sheets. |
| **Trout** | Whole trout that have been hot- or cold-smoked, sold either as whole fish or fillets. Cured and smoked like salmon to which it is similar in texture and flavour. |

A thick drink made by blending fresh fruit or fruit juices such as bananas, berries or orange juice, with milk, ice cream or yoghurt. Smoothies are often made using low-fat dairy products such as low-fat frozen yoghurt, or soya or skim milk. They are touted as being a nutritious breakfast substitute or sport's drink and some may be supplemented with honey, wheat germ or bran.

***Also known as — smoothee***

### BANANA SMOOTHIE

*For each person put 1 large chopped banana, 2 tablespoons natural yoghurt and 250 ml milk in a blender. Blend until smooth, sweeten with honey, if desired, then pour into tall glasses. Sprinkle with nutmeg.*

Originating in Sweden and translated as 'bread and butter table', smorgasbord is a buffet meal consisting of many small dishes, both hot and cold. A full buffet may include herrings followed by a second course of small plates of fish, eggs, salads, meats, pâtés and sausages with gherkins, pickles and red beet. Warm dishes of meatballs and fish make up the third course and cheeses, fruit, dessert and cakes complete the meal. It is customary to serve oneself only small portions of food at a time, returning to the table many times.

There are many edible varieties of snails, most commonly associated with France, but they are also found, cultivated and eaten in Britain, Yugoslavia, Algeria, Spain, Turkey, China, Indonesia and Africa. Snail flesh has a firm texture but a delicate, sweet flavour. The best eating varieties are the popular, but increasingly rare, large Burgundy (Roman) snail and the smaller but sweeter *petit gris* (the common garden snail), now more widely used.

After collection, live snails are starved for a week or so to rid them of any toxins, or fed on a diet of lettuce or herbs. They are removed from their shells, cleaned, then boiled. Classically, snails are served in garlic butter; simmered in olive oil and flavoured with tomatoes and herbs; or served with a white wine sauce. Snails may be served in a dish called an *escargotière*, which is divided into sections to hold each snail. Special forks are used to remove the snail from its shell. Preparing live snails for cooking is quite complex, so those that are ready-cleaned or canned are a good alternative. Imported varieties are sold frozen, cooked or canned.

***Also known as — escargot***

## soda bread

An Irish 'quick' bread made from white or wholemeal flour. The raising agent is bicarbonate of soda and soured milk or buttermilk instead of yeast.
**Also known as — Irish soda bread**

### SODA BREAD

*Sift together 500 g wholemeal flour, 250 g plain white flour, 1 teaspoon bicarbonate of soda and ½ teaspoon salt. Make a well in the centre and add 250 ml buttermilk. Mix quickly and thoroughly with a knife (the bicarbonate of soda will activate as soon as the liquid is added). If necessary, add a little more liquid to make a soft dough. Turn out the dough onto a lightly floured board and knead lightly into a smooth ball, about 4 cm thick. Cut a cross in the top of the dough. Put on a lightly floured baking tray and bake at 200°C for 45 minutes, or until the bread sounds hollow when tapped on the base. Leave to cool on a wire rack.*

## soffritto

Of Italian and Spanish origin, soffritto (or sofrito) may contain any or all of: finely chopped pancetta, ham or pork, garlic, onion, carrot, celery, tomatoes or peppers, slowly cooked in oil. This forms a base for stews, soups and sauces. Soffritto is also used in Central and South American and Caribbean cooking.

## sorbet — see ice cream

## sorghum

A cereal grain, similar to millet, cultivated in semi-arid and tropical regions, particularly Africa and India where it is an important staple. The white seeded variety may be cooked like rice, used to thicken soups or ground to a flour to make porridge or flat unleavened breads. The red-seeded variety is more bitter and used to brew beer. Sweet sorghum is used to produce a molasses-like syrup.

## sorrel

A leafy green plant that grows wild in northern Asia and Europe. There are many species including common sorrel and round-leaved (French) sorrel, the mildest in flavour. Sorrel has large, spinach-like leaves that have a lemony, acidic, slightly bitter taste, due to the presence of oxalic acid. Sorrel can be used in a mixed green salad or cooked like spinach. Sorrel is also made into soups, purées and sauces or used as a flavouring herb in omelettes.
**Sorrel goes with — chicken, fish, veal**
**Also known as — dock sorrel, garden sorrel, sour dock, sour grass**

A light and fluffy dish made with either a sweet or savoury base into which beaten egg whites are gently folded. A savoury soufflé is usually based on a panade of butter, flour and water, which may be enriched with egg yolks and flavours such as cheese, vegetables, herbs, ham or fish. It may also be made from a vegetable purée with the egg whites folded in. A sweet soufflé is based on a custard-type base or fruit purée and may include liqueur, melted chocolate, nuts and fruit.

A soufflé is held up by the beaten egg whites and hot air. As it cooks, the air within it expands and pushes the mixture outwards, sometimes as much as doubling its height. The height of soufflés can be encouraged by adding a paper collar to the dish, though if the dish is full anyway the soufflé will automatically rise above the rim. It is important that the egg whites are not too soft or the soufflé will not rise; and not too stiff or they will not mix into the base well and the cooked soufflé will contains blobs of white egg. Technically, soufflés are always hot, although ice or cold mousses are sometimes referred to as being a soufflé glacé.

## COOKING

*Before cooking the soufflé, run your thumb or a knife around the inside rim of the dish, between the dish and the mixture. This ridge helps the soufflé to rise evenly.*

*Brush the inside of a soufflé dish with butter, then coat it with ingredients such as caster sugar, breadcrumbs, grated Parmesan or ground nuts. This rough coating helps the soufflé to rise as it sticks to the side of the dish.*

*Once the soufflé is poured into the dish, it should be baked immediately in a preheated oven on a preheated baking tray so that the egg white will puff and set on cooking. Once cooked, serve the soufflé straight away before it collapses.*

See also **cheese**

## COURGETTE SOUFFLE

*Preheat oven to 180°C. Prepare the soufflé dish following the steps below. Cut 350 g unpeeled courgettes into chunks. Steam until just tender, then process with 125 ml milk until smooth. Melt 30 g butter in a saucepan, stir in 30 g flour, stirring constantly for 2 minutes until it boils and thickens. Remove from heat and stir in the courgette mixture. Return to heat and simmer uncovered for 3 minutes, stirring occasionally. Pour the sauce into a large bowl and stir in 75 g grated Gruyère cheese and 4 egg yolks and season well. In a clean, dry metal bowl, whisk 4 egg whites until soft peaks form. Fold in ¼ of the egg white to soften the mixture, then gently fold in the remaining egg white. Pour into the prepared dish. Place on a baking tray and bake for 45 minutes, or until well risen. Serves 4.*

## PREPARING A COLLARED SOUFFLE DISH

1  *Brush the inside of the soufflé dish with melted butter, then coat it evenly with dry breadcrumbs.*

2  *Cut a sheet of baking paper longer than the perimeter of the dish; fold the paper to form a double layer.*

3  *Place the paper strip around the outside of the dish so that it projects 5 cm above the rim, then secure with string.*

## soul food

A term referring to traditional African-American, Jamaican and Caribbean food, usually associated with the southern states of North America. The term became popular in the 1960s to celebrate the culture and traditions of the cuisine. Dishes that define 'soul food' include collard greens and callaloo, ham hocks, black-eyed peas, fried chitterlings (pig's intestine) and hog maws (pig's stomach), corn breads, hominy grits and hush puppies.

*Ham hock served with collard greens.*

## soup

Any dish based on a liquid. Historically, soups were either thick and a meal in themselves, or thin and broth-like and used medicinally. Today, soups in the Western world can be clear like consommés and broths, velvety smooth like veloutés and bisques, or chunky and thick like chowders and minestrones. They can be served as starters or as a main meal, depending on their heartiness. In Asia, noodle soups tend to be considered more of a meal or snack, while others such as miso or some Chinese soups are served more as drinks to accompany a meal. These are light and clear and are sometimes drunk for their health-giving properties.

*Also known as — potage, soupe*

### TYPES OF SOUPS

*Bisque*
*Bisque* — A thick soup or purée made with shellfish and cream. The intense flavour comes from adding the shells during the cooking process. Popular bisques include crab bisque and lobster bisque.

*Asian broth*
*Bouillons and broths* — Semi-clear broths obtained from boiling vegetables, meat, seafood or other flavourings, which are then used as a stock for soups or clarified to become a consommé. Asian noodle soups are also based on broths as are Chinese tonic soups and steamed soups.

*Velouté*
*Chowder* — These are thick chunky soups usually based on seafood, especially clams, and mostly containing milk or cream.

*Cream and velouté* — These soups may not include cream but have a creamy consistency. Cream soups are thickened with flour and velouté soups are enriched with egg yolks and cream.

*Potage*
*Potage* — A vegetable broth with added chopped vegetables, such as minestrone.

*Puréed* — A thick soup made with puréed vegetables and/or grains and pulses. The vegetables are cooked in stock or water, then puréed until smooth.

*See also* **consommé**

376

Traditionally made by allowing fresh cream to sour naturally, but today cultured sour cream is made using pasteurized single or double cream that is soured by adding a lactic-acid producing bacteria. This results in a thick, smooth and slightly acidic cream. To add shelf life, it is often stabilized with additives such as gelatine. Sour cream is a traditional ingredient in Eastern European and Russian cooking, adding richness to goulashes and soups, but its use is now more widespread— as a topping for baked potatoes, in soups, dips, sauces and baked goods like cheesecake.

**Also known as — soured cream**

See also **smetana**

### COOKING

*Make a sour cream by adding a few drops of lemon juice or vinegar to pasteurized cream. The flavour will only be similar to sour cream as the sourness will be due to citric or acetic acid, not lactic acid.*

*Add sour cream to hot food just before serving. The dish can be gently reheated but if allowed to boil, the sour cream may curdle.*

# sourdough

Made with a fermented starter (*poolish* or *biga* or *levain*) as leavener, rather than manufactured yeast. The starter can be a paste of flour and water, which is left to ferment for several days, allowing it to absorb the naturally occurring yeasts from the air, or it can be a ferment of potato or fruit. The fermentation process produces the distinctive sour taste that is characteristic of these breads. The starter is then mixed with more liquid and flour and left to 'sponge'. It is traditional to save a quarter of the starter dough to mix in with the next batch. In France, some starter doughs have been kept alive for over a hundred years, passed down through the generations. As the starter ages, it picks up the yeasts and develops its own characteristics and flavours.

### SOURDOUGH BREAD

*Add 1 tablespoon sea salt and 2 tablespoons oil to the sponge (see steps below). Mix in 100 g rye flour and 360 g plain flour and enough unbleached white bread flour (about 230 g) to make a soft, non-sticky dough. Turn out onto a floured surface and knead for 10 minutes until elastic. Cut away ¼ of the dough to use as the next starter dough (store covered in the fridge). Form into 2 round or oval loaves, then place on a floured baking tray. Sprinkle the bread surface with a little extra rye flour. Cover loosely and leave to rise in a warm place until doubled in size. Bake in a preheated 200°C oven for about 1 hour, or until the base sounds hollow when tapped. Makes 2.*

### MAKING THE STARTER AND SPONGE

**1** *To make the starter, mix 230 g rye flour and 280 ml lukewarm water to a stiff dough. Cover with a damp cloth.*

**2** *Set aside at room temperature for 4 days, re-dampening the cloth every day. The mixture will be grey and foamy.*

**3** *To make the sponge, stir 280 ml lukewarm water and 280 g rye flour into the starter. Cover and leave for 18 hours.*

South America comprises 13 different countries. Each has developed its own cuisine, partly defined by a pre-existing indigenous cuisine, partly by the Spanish and, in the case of Brazil, the Portuguese, who conquered them in the early sixteenth century, as well as by the African slaves brought in to work the land. Before conquest, the land had been farmed by the highly developed Indian civilizations of the Aztec, Maya and Inca peoples, who developed many food crops still eaten today. Native foods include corn, beans, squash, tomatoes, potatoes, peppers and chillies, vanilla, pineapples, avocados and cocoa.

### NORTH

Comprising Colombia, Venezuela, Guyana, Suriname and French Guiana, the northernmost part of South America includes coastlines on both the Pacific and Caribbean and several mountain ranges including the Andes. Food varies regionally and the cuisines include cassava, coconuts, annatto, bananas and coconuts. *Ajiaco* (stew) made from meat or seafood is common, maize is widely used except in Colombia where rice is the staple. Spanish influences include the use of Old World ingredients such as capers and spices like cumin.

### EAST

Brazil, which has the largest landmass in South America, differs from the rest of the continent in climate, people, language (it was conquered by the Portuguese), history and food. The Portuguese brought with them their own cuisine, and the African slaves introduced staples of West Africa such as *dende* (palm oil), okra and coconut milk—these were added to the native cuisine. Brazil grows many varieties of tropical fruits, as well as brazil nuts, cashews and coffee. The national dish is *feijoada completa*, a black bean and meat stew, usually served with *farofa* (toasted cassava meal).

### WEST

Made up of Ecuador and Peru on the west coast and land-locked Bolivia to the east of Peru. Before the conquest, all these countries were part of the original Inca empire, and their cuisine today is *Criolla* (Creole), a combination of native Indian and Spanish. Guinea pig is widely eaten, and most dishes of the Andes contain *aji* (a term for chilli). Popular dishes are *tamales* (corn dumplings) and *ceviche*, made with scallops. Bolivia is also famous for its potatoes, especially freeze-dried *chuno*.

### SOUTH

Made up of Argentina, Chile, Uruguay and Paraguay. Argentina has rich grassland plains, which are used for growing wheat and corn and for grazing cattle and sheep. Beef, the food most representative of Argentina, is often grilled on an open fire. In Uruguay, sheep are more commonly grazed and eaten. *Empanadas* and *matambre*, an elaborate dish of stuffed, rolled beef, are popular dishes in both countries. Spanish influences include *dulce de leche* and cream pastries. Wine is produced in the north of Argentina.

Chile is a country of extremes: the northern third is pure desert, the bottom third has cold, storm-swept mountains, the area in between is fertile land where grapes, fruit and vegetables grow well. The diet includes seafood, often made into *chupe* (a stew), squash and beans. The national dish is *porotos granados*, a dish of beans, corn and squash, most likely of Indian origin. Corn is used abundantly (both ripe and unripe), as is pork. Chilli, coriander, garlic and paprika are common flavourings. Chile is also world renowned for its wine.

■ *See also* **ceviche, churrasco, dulce de leche, empanadas**

*From top: tamales, which may be wrapped in corn husk, as here, or in banana leaves; feijoada; chargrilled steak; seafood chupe.*

An emblematic southern American dish, made using pieces of chicken coated in flour, then fried until crisp. The flour is usually seasoned with salt and pepper but some versions add garlic, cinnamon, paprika or rosemary. Most often served with mashed potatoes and a creamy gravy.

## soy sauce

An essential condiment and ingredient in the kitchens of Japan, China and Southeast Asia. Produced for thousands of years, soy (or soya) sauce is a naturally brewed salty liquid made from fermented soya beans mixed with wheat, water and salt (a good sauce will contain only these ingredients). The mixture is injected with yeasts and bacteria and left to ferment for 3 months, before it is filtered to extract the sauce. Some soy sauces are made synthetically from hydrolysed plant protein blended with caramel colouring and corn syrup—these are inferior in flavour. Soy sauce is used to colour and flavour marinades, dips, sauces and many Asian dishes, often combined with garlic, onions, fresh ginger and oil.

### COOKING

*For best results, use Japanese soy sauce when cooking Japanese recipes and, likewise, Chinese soy sauce for Chinese recipes. The different sauces vary considerably in saltiness and flavour.*

### TYPES OF SOY SAUCES

*Dark soy sauce*

*Shoyu*

*Kecap manis*

*Tamari*

**Dark soy sauce** — Less salty, thicker and darker than light soy because it has fermented for longer and is usually mixed with caramel or molasses. Good in stews or meat dishes where you want to add richness of colour and flavour. Some dark soy sauces are flavoured with mushrooms.

**Light soy sauce** — Also called soy sauce, this has a light, delicate flavour, but is saltier than dark soy. Used in soups; with seafood and white meat dishes; as a dipping sauce; or in dishes where you don't want to darken the colour of the food. It may be labelled as 'superior soy sauce'.

**Kecap manis** — A thick, sweetened soy sauce made from black soya beans, used in Indonesian cooking.

**Shoyu** — A Japanese soy sauce, naturally brewed and left to mature for up to 2 years. It is slightly sweeter, less salty and lighter in both colour and flavour than Chinese soy sauce. Some brands are reduced in salt.

**Tamari** — Naturally brewed thick, Japanese soy sauce made with soya beans and rice. Although thought to be wheat-free, tamari may contain from 5 to 20 per cent wheat.

■ *See also* **kecap manis, miso**

**379**

## soya bean

The most nutritious and versatile of all beans, they have been cultivated in their native China for thousands of years. Soya beans (or soybeans) contain a higher proportion of protein than any other legume, even higher than that of red meat, making them an important part of vegetarian diets and in Japanese, Chinese and Southeast Asian cooking where little meat is used. Soya beans may be red, green, yellow, black or brown. The beans are eaten fresh or dried but are also used as a source of oil, milk, curd, pastes, sauces and flavourings. They may also be cracked, sprouted and even roasted and ground as a coffee substitute.

*See also* **bean curd, bean pastes and sauces, miso, soy sauce, sprouts, tempe, TVP**

### PREPARATION

*Dried soya beans contain a trypsin inhibitor, which must be destroyed by soaking and cooking them for a long time before they are digestible. Soak dried beans for at least 6–8 hours before use. Yellow beans need longer soaking than black. Discard the soaking water before cooking.*

### COOKING

*Soya beans have little flavour and a slightly oily texture and benefit from being cooked with strong flavours such as chilli, garlic and soy sauce.*

*As with other pulses, they can also be puréed, added to casseroles or used in soups and salads. Fresh soya bean pods can be rubbed with salt, then boiled. These are eaten as a snack with beer in China and Japan.*

Clockwise from top left: shelled soya beans, fermented soya bean paste, dried soya beans, soya bean pods, soya bean sprouts.

### SOYA BEAN PRODUCTS

*Soya milk*

**Soya milk**
Made from yellow soya beans that have been soaked, then ground with water, boiled and filtered. It contains half the fat (some of which is polyunsaturated) but only one fifth the calcium of cow's milk. It is a good milk substitute for people with lactose intolerance. Full-fat and reduced-fat, flavoured and powdered versions are now widely sold. Soya milk can be used as a milk substitute in ice creams, sauces and soups.

*Soya bean oil*

**Soya bean oil**
Used as cooking oil and in the manufacture of margarine and shortening. It is low in saturated fats and has a high smoking point, so is a good frying oil.

*Soya flour*

**Soya flour**
Finely ground flour used to thicken sauces and added to cakes, biscuits and muffins as a flavour enhancer as it is high in fat. Sometimes used in bread-making as a bread improver. It contains no gluten but is high in protein.

**Soya bean paste**
Made from fermented yellow, brown, black or red beans and used as a flavouring in Asian cooking.

**Soya bean sprouts**
The most nutritious of all sprouts. The beans are soaked for 10 hours and take 3 to 4 days to fully germinate. Use raw, steamed or in stir-fries.

*Soya bean paste*

A classic Italian ragù, based on minced beef or veal cooked with chicken livers and a soffritto of pancetta, onion, garlic, celery, carrot, tomato paste, seasoned with lemon zest and nutmeg, cooked in stock and red wine for at least 2 hours. Sometimes cream is added. In Bologna, this sauce is never served with spaghetti, but most often with tagliatelle or in lasagne. The authentic recipe is codified at the chamber of commerce in Bologna, although many people use their own version.

*Also known as — spaghetti Bolognaise*

### spam

The trade name for a tinned meat loaf made from ground pork and ham flavoured with salt, sugar and spicy seasonings. The name is derived from the words 'spiced pork and ham'. Spam originated in the United States and was first imported in vast amounts by Great Britain during World War II. Spam may be served hot or cold or sliced and fried in a batter. It is also popular in many other countries, especially Hawaii and the Pacific Islands where such dishes as spam and eggs, spam and rice, spam wonton, spam tempura and spam sushi are served.

### spanakopita

A Greek and Middle Eastern pie made with cooked spinach and feta enclosed in layers of filo pastry. It may include other cheeses such as kefalotiri, Parmesan, cottage cheese and Cheddar, and onions, eggs, herbs and seasonings.

#### SPANAKOPITA

*Chop, wash and place 1 kg wet spinach leaves in a saucepan with 50 g butter. Cover and steam for 2–3 minutes. Drain well, then stir in 125 g mashed feta, ½ teaspoon nutmeg; season. Melt 90 g butter and brush over 5 sheets filo pastry. Line the base and sides of a deep, buttered baking dish with the sheets, spread with spinach filling, then top with 5 more buttered filo sheets and trim to fit. Lightly cut diagonally across top of the pie. Bake at 160°C for 45 minutes. If necessary, increase heat to 220°C during the last 10 minutes to brown the pastry. Serves 4.*

# Spanish food

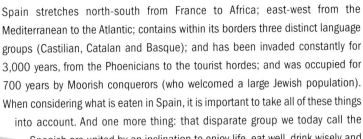

Spain stretches north-south from France to Africa; east-west from the Mediterranean to the Atlantic; contains within its borders three distinct language groups (Castilian, Catalan and Basque); and has been invaded constantly for 3,000 years, from the Phoenicians to the tourist hordes; and was occupied for 700 years by Moorish conquerors (who welcomed a large Jewish population). When considering what is eaten in Spain, it is important to take all of these things into account. And one more thing: that disparate group we today call the Spanish are united by an inclination to enjoy life, eat well, drink wisely and sleep little.

At the end of the working day, from around 7 pm until 10 pm, Spaniards, in company with family and friends, go out to eat little snacks known as tapas, together with glasses of wine, beer or sherry in bars called *tascas*. Tapas can range from a simple bowl of olives to more elaborate dishes of garlic prawns, or meatballs. Dinner is consequently eaten very late, especially in summer.

*Fabada asturiana—a hearty dish of morcilla and chorizo sausages, pork and dried fava beans.*

*Bacalao a la vizcaina—dried salt cod with red peppers, onions and garlic.*

Much of what is seen as traditional in Spanish cooking, by way of ingredients and the type of food that is eaten, was introduced by the Moors, who brought with them, among other things, oranges, rice, saffron, and spices such as cinnamon, nutmeg, sesame and aniseed. Saffron gives many of Spain's traditional dishes their distinctive flavour and orange colour.

*Chorizo—a pork and paprika sausage.*

With so much of the land bordered by the sea, and a history of seafaring, fish and seafood are plentiful. The Andalucians have perfected the art of frying fish in olive oil. Bacalao, dried salt cod, was brought back from the North Sea by medieval Basque whale fishermen, and is enjoyed today in such recipes as the Basque *pil pil*. Fruit and vegetables grow abundantly, and Spain is the second-largest producer of olive oil in the world, and a leading supplier of table olives.

On feast days, whole sucking pigs and lambs are spit-roasted. Spanish cured hams are sought-after delicacies, some, including Jabugo, from native Iberian pigs fed predominantly on acorns. Chorizo sausage, eaten fresh or dried, is the most well known of Spain's *embutidos—small goods.

Gazpacho is a traditional cold soup from Andalusia. In the northern province of Asturias, you find *fabada asturiana* made with sausages, pork and fava (broad) beans. *Cocido* is a slow-cooked one-pot stew of chickpeas, meat and vegetables, the speciality of Madrid. Chickpeas (*garbanzos*) are an essential ingredient in many of the more robust country dishes. Eggs are used in a variety of dishes including soups, desserts and the ubiquitous tortilla. Paella is only one of well over a hundred rice dishes that include *arroz a la banda* and *arroz negro*. Fruit and some of the world's finest goat, sheep and cow cheeses, including Cabrales and Manchego, end a meal, rather than a dessert, which is reserved for festival days. All this marvellous food is accompanied by Spanish wines, from such major wine-growing provinces as the Rioja, Catalonia and Navarra.

*Seafood paella*

■ **See also  churros, gazpacho, paella, saffron, tapas, tortilla, zarzuela**

## GRILLED SPATCHCOCK

*Prepare 4 x 450 g spatchcocks following the steps below. In a bowl, mash together 120 g butter, 4 tablespoons finely chopped parsley and 2 crushed garlic cloves. Season. Divide the mixture among the spatchcocks, and push it under the skin of each breast. Brush each with a mixture of lemon juice, a pinch of cayenne, salt and pepper, then set aside for 1 hour. Brush with olive oil and then cook breast side up under a preheated grill until golden brown. Turn over and cook for a further 7 minutes, or until juices run clear. Brush frequently with the pan juices. Serves 4.*

A word used to describe the method of preparing a chicken by either cutting it in half along each side of the backbone, or splitting it along the breastbone. The chicken can then be opened out and flattened, seasoned and grilled. The word is thought to have derived from 'to dispatch cock' meaning that the chicken was killed, then split so it could be cooked in a hurry. The spatchcock can be skewered to keep it flat, then brushed with oil and grilled. It may be marinated or stuffed under the flesh, usually with butter and herbs or cheese.

## SPATCHCOCKING A POUSSIN

**1** Split a 450 g poussin down either side of the backbone using poultry shears or a pair of scissors.

**2** Open out, pressing down hard on the breastbone to flatten it out completely.

# Spätzle

A speciality of Alsace and southern Germany, Spätzles are a cross between a noodle and a dumpling, and are made from flour, eggs and water or milk. Spätzles vary in size and shape and may be made either by forcing the dough through a sieve or colander with large holes or using a knife to slice the dough into roughly shaped strips, which are dropped directly into boiling liquid to cook. Once cooked and drained, the Spätzles may be tossed in butter, served with buttered breadcrumbs or used as an accompaniment to casseroles and stews.

## SPATZLES

*Sift 500 g flour into a bowl. Add 5 lightly beaten eggs, 450 ml water and 1 teaspoon salt. Beat to a smooth batter. Use a small spoon, piping bag or colander to drop small amounts of the mixture into boiling water. Poach until they rise to the surface. Drain and serve at once. Serves 4.*

An established mixture of spices, usually dried or powdered, used specifically for certain cooking or peculiar to the local region or country. In some instances, spice mixes can refer to a paste such as tandoori or masala. Although each spice mixture is usually made in a certain way, the amount and type of spice used can vary, depending on local preferences, the spices available to hand, or the desires of an individual cook. Buy good-quality spice mixes—those that contain whole spices should be in good condition and not just a way of using up broken spices; powdered mixes should be freshly ground, if possible. Today, many cooks bottle and brand their own spice mixes.

*Baharat*

*Bebere*

*Chaat masala*

*Garam masala*

*La Kama*

*Masala (goda)*

## SPICE MIXES

| | |
|---|---|
| **Baharat** | A mixture of black pepper, cassia, cloves, cumin, nutmeg, paprika, cardamom and coriander with loomi (dried Omani limes). Used in the Gulf States to spice meats and vegetables. |
| **Bebere** | A complex Ethiopian blend of spices of which chillies, ginger and cloves form the basis. |
| **Chaat masala** | An Indian mix that includes cumin, salt, fennel seed, amchur, garam masala, asafoetida and chilli. Used in Indian dishes to season potato and vegetables. |
| **Chinese five-spice** | Of Chinese origin, consisting of equal parts of Sichuan pepper, cassia or cinnamon, fennel seed, star anise and cloves. Used in stir-fries and pork and beef dishes. |
| **Curry powder** | Ready-made curry spice mixes can include up to nine ingredients, usually coriander, poppy seeds, cumin seeds, mustard seeds, dried chillies, turmeric, fenugreek, black pepper and ginger. The South Indian version is called kari. The spices used vary regionally and vary from country to country. Versions include Madras, rendang, Ceylon, tandoori and vindaloo. |
| **Garam masala** | An Indian mix, meaning 'hot mixture'. The spices may include coriander seeds, chilli, black pepper, cinnamon sticks, fennel seeds, cardamom seeds and cumin seeds, which are added to a dish at the end of cooking. Can also be purchased ready-made. |
| **La Kama** | A Moroccan mixture of five spices—cinnamon, pepper, ginger, turmeric and nutmeg, used to flavour stews, soups and lamb dishes. |
| **Masala** | An Indian spice mixture of which there are many regional specialities and spice combinations—garam masala, chaat masala and goda masala *(pictured)* are common, but every family has their own version. Masala may be dry or wet, strong, mild or aromatic in flavour. In northern India, masala is generally made with dry spices, freshly roasted and ground. In southern India, the spices are usually ground when green with liquid such as coconut milk, lime or vinegar. |

*Mixed spice*

*Panch phoran*

*Pickling spices*

*Quatre épices*

*Seven-spice powder*

**Mixed spice**

A mixture of cinnamon, allspice, cloves, coriander, mace and nutmeg. Often added to sweet puddings, desserts, mince pies, yeasted buns and biscuits.

**Panch phoran**

An aromatic Indian blend of equal quantities of seeds: cumin, fennel, fenugreek, brown mustard and nigella. May be used whole or ground and has a bittersweet flavour. Usually added to hot oil to bring out the flavour before adding to lentils, pulses and vegetables.

**Pickling spices**

A mixture of spices used in chutneys, pickles and vinegar. The quantities and number of ingredients vary depending on the recipe but usually consists of allspice, bay leaves, cardamom, chilli, cinnamon, cloves, coriander, mustard seeds and peppercorns. The spices are tied into a muslin bag so it can be removed at the end of cooking.

**Quatre épices**

The French word meaning 'four spices', although it may consist of more. The main ingredients are black pepper, nutmeg, ginger and cloves and possibly cayenne and cinnamon. The spices are tied in muslin, then either removed or left in the dish. They are often added to casseroles as a flavour enhancer.

**Ras el hanout**

Meaning 'top of the shop', a Moroccan spice mixture that can include many ingredients, sometimes up to 50 to 100. Typically it includes aniseed, allspice, cloves, cayenne pepper, cinnamon, cardamom, cumin, dried rose buds or petals, galangal, ginger, mace, nutmeg, orris root and various peppers. Some versions may include green Spanish fly, believed to be an aphrodisiac. It is used to flavour rice and couscous, meat and game dishes.

**Seven-spice powder (shichimi togarashi)**

A Japanese mixture of seven ground spices, seeds and flavourings, which varies from city to city. It may consist of, for example, two hot and five aromatic flavours—red pepper, sansho pepper, sesame seeds, flax seeds, poppy seeds, ground nori (seaweed) and dried tangerine or orange peel. Used as a seasoning in noodles and on cooked and grilled meats and fish.

## STORAGE

*Most spices are available whole, ground and powdered. Ground spices lose their flavour and aroma quickly so buy in small quantities and store in an airtight container in a cool, dark place for up to 6 months only. Where possible, buy spices whole and grind as needed using a spice grinder or mortar and pestle. Similarly, spice mixes will only keep for a short time and as the individual components may have different rates of staling, this may upset the balance of flavour.*

**See also** *chermoula, dukka, spices, tandoori, zahtar, zhug*

## ALLSPICE

Dried berries of the *Pimenta dioica* tree indigenous to the West Indies, where it is used for 'jerk seasoning'. Used whole or ground. The taste is a combination of nutmeg, cinnamon, cloves and black pepper. Used to flavour curries, relishes, preserves and marinades, and to give a mild spiciness to cakes and biscuits. Grind berries prior to use. Not to be confused with mixed spice.

*Also known as — Jamaica pepper, pimento*

## ASAFOETIDA

The creamy sap from the root of a giant plant from the fennel family that dries to a hard resin. Used in powder form as a flavour enhancer in Middle Eastern and Indian cooking, in curries, fish and vegetable stews and pickles. Use in very small quantities as it has a strong sulphurous odour and taste. An effective anti-flatulent. Store in an airtight container for up to 1 year.

*Also known as — devil's dung, giant fennel, heeng, hing, stinking gum*

## CARDAMOM

Of the many varieties, the green cardamom from South India and Sri Lanka is superior. Use the whole pod or the seeds whole or ground to flavour both sweet and savoury Indian food from curries and rice dishes to sweet milk desserts. The seeds have a sweet, mild flavour. Also flavours tea, coffee, cakes and breads.

*Also known as — cardamon, cardamum*

## CASSIA

Dried bark used as small pieces or ground. It has a similar taste to cinnamon but has less flavour and is harder and coarser. Used in curries, rice and vegetable dishes. An ingredient of Chinese five-spice powder. Also has buds that are sold dried with the stalk attached, used in pickles and 'paan', a betal leaf parcel filled with nuts, seeds and spices.

*Also known as — Chinese cinnamon*

*Spices are aromatic seasonings obtained from tropical plants and trees. They include the seed pods, seeds, stems, bark, roots, buds, berries and fruits. Spices enhance the flavour of both sweet and savoury foods and drinks. They should be used sparingly so as not to dominate or overpower the other flavours of the dish.*

## ANISE

Liquorice-like flavoured seeds from the bush of the hemlock family. Used in the Mediterranean, where it is a native, anise has a sweet flavour used in both sweet and savoury cooking—in cakes, breads and confectionery, as well as with seafood and meat. Used to flavour Pernod and ouzo. Buy the seeds whole as the powder quickly loses its flavour.

*Also known as — aniseed, sweet cumin*

## CARAWAY SEED

Native to Europe and western Asia. Related to anise, it has an aromatic, pungent flavour. Popular in German and Austrian cooking, as well as Tunisia, where it is essential in harissa. The elongated seeds are used in breads, especially rye breads, seed cakes, cheeses and savoury dishes such as goulashes and cabbage dishes. Used to flavour the liqueurs Kummel and Akvavit. Available as seeds or ground.

## CAYENNE PEPPER

A powder made from ground dried red chilli peppers, native to South America. It is very pungent and should be used sparingly. Used in curry powder, chilli sauce and Tabasco sauce. Common in Indian and Latin American cuisines.

## CELERY SEED

The seed of a wild celery called lovage. They have a slightly bitter, strong concentrated celery taste. Use whole or crushed to flavour soups, in stuffings, sauces, stews and pickles.

## CINNAMON

A member of the laurel family native to Sri Lanka. The inner bark is dried and sold as quills or sticks. Used whole to flavour milk puddings, curries, pullao rice, in pickles and mulled wine. Ground or powdered cinnamon is used in baking and desserts and is sometimes added to savoury dishes such as curries and stews.

## CLOVE

The dried aromatic unopened flower buds of an evergreen tree native to the Moluccas (Indonesia). Cloves are used whole to flavour stews, game dishes and to decorate whole ham. Also added to blended spice mixtures. The bud head is ground and used in sweet and savoury dishes, spiced wines, and liqueurs. Available whole and ground.

## CORIANDER

Native to southern Europe and the Mediterranean, the dried seeds are left whole or ground. Crushed, they form a basis for curry pastes and powder. The whole seeds are enhanced if they are lightly dry-roasted before crushing. Used in curries.

## CUMIN

A herb indigenous to the East Mediterranean. The fruits of the seeds are used whole and ground in many cuisines, particularly North Africa, India, Mexico and Japan. It has a hot pungent taste. Light dry-roasting of the seeds releases their aroma. Used in couscous, rice, kebabs, stews, curries and yoghurt.

## DILL SEED

Native to western Asia and today grown worldwide, especially in Europe and North America. The leaves are used dried and the seeds whole or ground. Used to flavour dill pickles, meat and egg dishes, breads and in soups, salads and sauces.

**Also known as — dill weed**

## FENNEL SEED

Originally from southern Europe but grown worldwide. The seeds have a slightly liquorice or aniseed taste, used whole or ground. Use in stuffing, salads, fish and seafood dishes. Also added to curries, pickles and chutneys in Indian cuisine. Often offered after an Indian meal as a palate cleanser.

## FENUGREEK

Pods containing seeds of a native plant from western Asia. The flavour of the dried seeds is enhanced by lightly roasting before using as seeds or grinding to a powder. The flavour is mild and aromatic. Fenugreek is a popular flavour in Indian cooking.

## JUNIPER BERRY

Hard blue to purple in colour when ripened. Used to flavour gin, game, pork and pâtés. Popular in German cuisine in sauerkraut and preserves. The flavour is slightly pine scented. Crush lightly before use.

## MACE

The outer lace-like covering of nutmeg. It has a similar but more delicate flavour. Sold as fragments known as blades. May also be ground into a powder. Used to flavour delicate dishes, such as soups, sauces and milk puddings. Traditionally used in English potted meats.

## NIGELLA

Seeds have a slight peppery taste. Used in Indian and Middle Eastern cooking, especially with vegetable and fish dishes. It is also sprinkled on salads and breads. The aromatic flavour is enhanced if the seeds are heated.

**Also known as — black cumin, black onion seed, kalonji**

## NUTMEG

Nutmeg is the hard kernel or nut of an evergreen plant native to the Moluccas (Indonesia). The best flavour, described as warm and spicy, is from the whole nutmeg, freshly grated just prior to use. Also available powdered. Used to enhance the flavour of savoury dishes but particularly good with milk-based desserts and sauces.

## PAPRIKA

The national spice of Hungary, famous for its goulash flavoured with paprika. The sweet red peppers were originally from South America. Paprika varies in flavour from hot to mild (also called sweet) depending on the type of pepper used and whether the seeds have been added.

## STAR ANISE

A native Chinese tree, related to the magnolia, that has a star-shaped fruit that contains a seed. Similar to anise but stronger and more liquorice-like in flavour. Star anise is an ingredient of five-spice powder, it is used in Arabic and Asian cooking, especially Chinese cuisine with pork and duck. Use whole or powdered.

**Also known as — badian**

## TURMERIC

A relative of ginger, turmeric is from the underground root of a tropical plant. It has a musky, faintly peppery aroma and flavour and is used in curry powders, rice, lentil and potato dishes and commercially to colour drinks, butter, cheese and mustards. It is sometimes called 'poor man's saffron'—its vivid yellow resembles that of the expensive spice—the two are not interchangeable.

## SPICE TRADE

*3,000 years ago, Arabs brought spices overland via the Spice Routes. During the Middle Ages, the British, Portuguese and Dutch trading companies brought spices to Europe by sea. The demand was so great that spices were valued higher than gold and the trade was responsible for changing forever the way food was prepared in Europe. New World spices were first brought to Europe by Columbus in the fifteenth century.*

## OTHER SPICES

**Ajowan** – *Also known as ajwain, bishops weed and omum, ajowan is a small seed of a native Indian plant with a strong, thyme-like flavour. Used in Indian vegetarian cuisine, often to flavour root vegetables, green beans and flour-based dishes such as breads. Also used in Middle Eastern cooking.*

**Amchur** – *Also known as amchoor, made from dried green mangoes ground to a fine powder. Use like tamarind to sour curries and also to season fish.*

**Grains of paradise** – *Native to West Africa and also known as Guinea pepper and malegueta pepper. The seeds are often used as a substitute for pepper.*

**Kokam** – *The dried outer skin of a fruit. Used like tamarind, especially in Kerala, India. Pieces are added to curries to give an acidic flavour.*

▌ *See also* **annatto, chillies, ginger, mustard, pepper, saffron, Sichuan pepper, spice mixes, sumac, tamarind, vanilla**

Originally native to Iran, spinach is a green leafy plant with slender stems. The young leaves (ponsse) are used in salads; the older ones are cooked. Use within 1 to 2 days and store with the roots attached in the fridge in a plastic bag. It contains iron and vitamins A and C, but also oxalic acid, which is responsible for the slightly bitter taste and which acts as an inhibitor to the body's ability to absorb calcium and iron. This knowledge has somewhat diminished its famous 'Popeye' reputation.

New Zealand spinach (or Warrigal greens), though not botanically related, is an Australian and New Zealand native, fleshy leaved variety with tough leaves that looks and tastes similar. It now also grows in France where it is called 'tetragon'. Basella or Ceylon spinach, grown in Asia and Latin America, is similar in flavour to spinach. Swiss chard, known as spinach in Australia, has large, thick leaves that are crinkled with pronounced white veins and thick white stems. It is actually a form of beet leaf.

## COOKING

*Cook spinach in the minimum of water—the water that is left on the leaves after washing is often enough.*

*Steam or cook in a covered pan.*

*Spinach that is to be added to dishes needs to be squeezed dry. This is best done by pressing it between two plates.*

### SAG ALOO

*Cook 600 g trimmed spinach leaves until tender. Drain and chop finely. Cut 800 g potatoes into 2 cm cubes. Melt 50 g butter and add the potatoes, 2 sliced onions, 2 teaspoons each of crushed coriander seeds and grated ginger, 2 crushed garlic cloves, 1 teaspoon paprika, 2 cardamom pods and 2 chopped green chillies. Fry until the potatoes are browned. Stir in the spinach, then add 250 ml water. Cover and cook until potatoes are tender. Remove the lid to allow any moisture to evaporate. Serves 6.*

## sponge fingers

As their name suggests, these are finger-like strips of sponge cake. To make them, the mixture is piped in thin lines about 10 cm long and sprinkled with crystallized sugar. The cooked fingers are light and crisp and used to accompany desserts such as mousses, fruit desserts and ice creams, as a border for cold charlottes or as a base for trifles and tiramisu. They can also be bought ready-made from supermarkets.

**Also known as — ladyfingers, savoiardi, savoy biscuits**

*See also* **langues de chat**

## spotted dick

A traditional British pudding made with a sweet suet pastry, which is rolled out and filled (spotted) with raisins, currants and sugar, then rolled into a log. A similar pudding, spotted dog, has raisins mixed into the pastry. Because the differences between the two are minimal, the two names are often used interchangeably. Both puddings were, traditionally, steamed either in a basin or in a cloth, but today may well be baked. A 'nursery food' favourite with many Englishmen of all ages.

## spring greens

The outer leaves and inner cones of brassicas, especially cabbages, harvested while still young and before a heart forms. They are usually lightly boiled and tossed in butter and served with roast meats. Varieties include collards, sugar loaf cabbage and curly kale.

## spring onion

An immature onion that, if left in the ground, would grow to full size. Depending on when it is picked, it has a small, white bulb of varying size and long green tops. There is also a variety called a Welsh onion with a papery brown skin. Spring onions have a mild, delicate flavour and both the green tops and the white bulb can be sliced and added to salads or omelettes, tossed into stir-fries or shredded finely and used as a garnish on fish or in noodle dishes. Spring onions are normally sold in bunches—look for ones that have firm white bases and undamaged green tops. The thinner onions will have a milder flavour. Store wrapped in plastic in the fridge.

**Also known as — salad onion, scallion, shallot**

See also   onion, shallot

### SPRING ONION PANCAKES

*Sift 310 g flour into a bowl and add 250 ml boiling water and 1 tablespoon oil. Stir, knead to a smooth dough and leave to stand for 30 minutes. Roll the dough into a sausage and divide into 12. Roll each to form a 20 cm pancake and divide 8 finely sliced spring onions, 80 g lard and 1 tablespoon sea salt among them. Fold sides into the centre and roll out again to 5 mm thick circles. Fry for 3 minutes on each side until golden and crispy. Makes 12.*

### RICE PAPER ROLLS

*Soak 6 large rice paper rounds in warm water until softened. Line each with a lettuce leaf, then place 1 spring onion down the centre of each. Divide 1 shredded cooked chicken breast, 1 small grated carrot, 20 g bean sprouts, 12 mint leaves and 12 Thai basil leaves among them. Fold in one end, leaving the green part of the spring onion sticking out at the other end, and roll up. Serve with a dipping sauce of 4 tablespoons lime juice, ½ tablespoon fish sauce and 3 teaspoons sweet chilli sauce. Makes 6.*

So popular in the West, it's sometimes hard to remember that the spring roll is Chinese. A thin pancake is wrapped around a filling of shredded vegetables such as bean sprouts, carrot and Chinese cabbage, sometimes with shredded meat or chicken, then deep-fried until crisp and golden. The pancake batter may be based on water and flour or egg. Spring rolls are traditionally served on the first day of the Chinese New Year, which also coincides with the beginning of spring.

**Also known as — egg roll, pancake roll**

# sprouts

Germinated from many varieties of seeds, peas, grains and beans, sprouts are an excellent source of vitamin C, contain many B vitamins, are high in fibre and protein and contain enzymes that aid digestion and metabolism. Although most sprouts can be easily grown at home, some of the more common varieties such as alfalfa, cress and mung bean sprouts are sold already sprouted in containers. Other sprouts include sunflower, sesame, pumpkin, poppy, clover, fenugreek, linseed, mustard, radish, adzuki beans, chickpeas, lentils, green peas, wheat, rye and soya beans. Sprouts are usually eaten raw in salads or sandwiches, briefly stir-fried (boiling them drastically reduces their vitamin content), steamed or sautéed.

*See also  **alfalfa, bean sprouts, cress, mung beans, soya bean***

## STORAGE

*Sprouts deteriorate quickly and begin to lose their vitamin C after they reach their peak. Store in their containers in the crisper drawer of the fridge for up to 3 days. They will also keep well in a bowl of cold water in the fridge.*

Sprouts, clockwise from top left: snow pea, adzuki bean, mung bean, soya bean, alfalfa.

Mixed sprout salad made using snow pea sprouts, mung bean sprouts and soya bean sprouts.

## MIXED SPROUT SALAD

*Put 600 g mixed sprouts (straggly ends picked off) in a large bowl, add 4 fried, chopped streaky bacon rashers, 2 cooked skinless chicken breasts cut into cubes and 4 finely chopped spring onions. Crush or chop 2 garlic cloves and whisk together with 100 ml extra virgin olive oil, 1½ tablespoons lemon juice and 2 tablespoons chopped parsley. Toss through the sprouts. Season well. Serves 4.*

## squash

Any one of the many vegetables belonging to the marrow family, which also includes melons, marrows, gourds, gherkins and cucumbers. They come in a wide variety of colours, sizes and shapes. Squashes are divided into winter and summer types. Generally, winter ones have hard skin and flesh and the summer ones have a softer skin and more watery flesh. Squashes are often stuffed and baked or roasted, puréed, braised, boiled, steamed or fried in batter or breadcrumbs. Add them to soups and casseroles or gratins.

### ROASTED SQUASH

*Cut a butternut squash in half and scoop out the seeds. Cut each half into wedges, 2 cm thick. Brush the wedges with olive oil and season well, then lay skin side down in a roasting tin. Bake at 230 °C for 15 minutes. Sprinkle with sea salt flakes, turn and bake for a further 15 minutes, or until tender to the point of a knife. Serves 4.*

*Clockwise from top left: butternut, spaghetti squash, sweet dumpling, pattypans, golden nugget.*

### SQUASH GRATIN

*Slice 750 g peeled winter squash, such as turban, and 250 g floury potatoes. Layer in a baking dish with a finely sliced onion; season well. Mix 100 g grated Gruyère, 2 eggs and 250 ml milk and pour over the squash. Cover and bake at 180 °C for 40 minutes. Uncover, sprinkle with 2 tablespoons grated Parmesan and grill until golden and bubbling. Serves 6.*

### SOME COMMON TYPES OF SQUASHES

| | |
|---|---|
| **Pattypan** | A saucer-shaped squash, yellow or green in colour with white flesh. Usually picked when young and very small, it does not need to be peeled and cooks quickly. |
| **Sweet dumpling** | Dark green with deep ridges and yellow markings and a hard skin. The flesh is yellow-orange in colour. |
| **Spaghetti** | Has a hard yellow skin and a flesh that is made up of fibres. Steam or bake, then gently pull out the fibres—these resemble spaghetti. |
| **Butternut** | Buff coloured, hard skin and firm, orange flesh. Generally these are sweet in flavour. Use in soups and mashes. |
| **Golden nugget** | Small squash that look like baby Halloween pumpkins. They have a hard skin and can be baked whole or in halves. Best cooked with their skins on. |
| **Turban** | A large squash with a crown at the top and a hard, dark skin that can be dark green or orange. It has a dry, sweet orange flesh with a nutty flavour. |
| **Hubbard** | Has a hard, coarse skin that may be ridged and varies in colour from green to bluish green to red. The flesh is pale orange. |
| **Kabocha** | Dark green with paler markings and like a flattened ball in shape. Has yellow flesh and a hard skin and bakes well. |

*See also* **pumpkin**

A group of cephalopods, of which there are over 300 species. These range greatly in length from a few centimetres up to 18 m. The edible part of the squid is its tentacles and its long body, which can be sliced, then battered and deep-fried, stewed or left whole and stuffed. Squid are popular in Mediterranean cuisines, in Southeast Asia and China. In Japanese cooking they are used as sashimi and sushi. Like cuttlefish, squid have an ink sac. The black ink is used to give a dramatic colour and flavour to pasta dishes. Cooking time should be short or the flesh toughens; or long, so that it becomes tender again. Sold fresh or frozen but also tinned or dried.

**Also known as — calamari, calamaro, inkfish**

## SALT AND PEPPER SQUID

*Cut 450 g cleaned squid into rings, leaving the tentacles as 1 piece. Put 6 tablespoons cornflour, 2 teaspoons salt and 1 teaspoon ground Sichuan pepper in a bowl and toss in the squid. Deep-fry for 1 minute at 190°C, or until browned. Drain well and serve with soy or sweet chilli sauce. Serves 4.*

## PREPARING SQUID

1 *Firmly pull the head and innards from the body—keep the ink sac, if required. Wash the body well.*

2 *Cut the head off just below the eyes, leaving the tentacles intact. Discard the head.*

3 *Pull the transparent quill out of the body and rinse out the tube. Peel off the outer membrane.*

see carambola — **star fruit**

# steak and kidney pie

A traditional British dish made from cubed beef, ox kidneys and onions, sometimes with added potatoes, oysters and mushrooms, slowly simmered in stock. Often the meat has been marinated in red wine before cooking. The pie is finished in a pie dish with a puff, flaky or shortcrust pastry topping and baked until golden. Steak and kidney pudding is made in a pudding basin, lined with suet pastry into which the raw ingredients are added and a suet pastry lid placed on top to seal. It is then boiled or steamed for 2 to 3 hours.

# steaks

A cut of meat, usually beef, but it can also refer to lamb, veal and fish. Cuts of steak vary from country to country, depending on the way the carcass is jointed. The most tender meat comes from the least exercised parts of the animal—from the hind quarter to the loin. Tenderness and optimum taste of the steak depend on age and breed, feed (grain or pasture), how the animal is handled during slaughtering and whether it has been aged or hung to make it more tender. In Britain, steak is usually named by the joint from which it is cut; in the United States, steaks are larger; French and Italian cuts also vary. The main steak cuts are from the fillet, also called tenderloin or undercut, which is tender rather than flavourful; sirloin, which has a superb flavour; and rump, for many, the best flavour of all.

*From top: blue, rare, medium, well-done.*

## BUYING

*Choose steaks with a bright red colour, flecked through with tiny streaks of white intramuscular fat. The flesh should be firm and upstanding, and the selvage fat (on the edge of the steak) should be crisp and waxy, flaking on the outside, but firm enough so that it would carve easily into pieces.*

## COOKING

*These cooking times apply to a steak that is about 2.5 cm thick (its weight is irrelevant to the cooking time), has been brought to room temperature before cooking and is pan-fried in a heavy-based pan. If you want to grill your steaks, they will take about a minute longer.*

*For a blue steak, cook for 1–2 minutes per side. The steak will feel fleshy and soft when pressed. For a rare steak, cook for 2–3 minutes per side. The steak will spring back a little when pressed. For a medium steak, cook for 3–4 minutes per side. The steak will spring back when pressed. For well-done, cook for 4–5 minutes per side. The steak will feel very firm when pressed.*

## TYPES OF STEAK

**Châteaubriand** — A thick steak cut from the centre of the fillet. Serves two people.

**Tournedos** — The tender 'eye' or centre of the fillet steak cut into small rounds.

**Mignon** — A small round steak cut from the thin end of the fillet, sometimes called filet mignon.

**Entrecôte** — Cut from between the ribs. It is boneless and thin with a marbling of fat. It is also known as rib steak and in America is served as Delmonico or Spencer steak, which is the eye of the rib.

**Sirloin** — A boneless steak from the sirloin, which can be cut short or long. In America, this is not always boneless, depending on which part of the sirloin it is cut from. In Australia, a boneless sirloin with the fat removed is a New York steak.

**Porterhouse** — A steak from the sirloin and the tenderloin separated by a bone. Often cut very thick (5 cm) and served for two people.

**T-bone** — Cut across the sirloin and includes a piece of fillet.

**Club steak (USA)** — A cut from the thin end of the loin, which includes no fillet.

**New York (USA)** — A strip of steak cut from the loin when the fillet has been removed.

**Rump** — A large steak from the top of the rump.

**Minute** — A thin steak (sometimes called a frying steak) that has been tenderized so it cooks quickly—in a minute.

*Sirloin*

*T-bone*

*Rump*

*Filet mignon*

Table-top cooking is popular in much of Asia, and the steamboat, usually called a hotpot in northern and eastern China and Korea, is a cooking vessel that is placed at the table and filled with hot stock. It has a circular chimney in the centre, which sits over a heat source, surrounded by a stock-filled 'moat'. Bite-sized pieces of vegetables and meat are placed on a fork, chopsticks or in small wire baskets and cooked in the hot stock. Side dishes of dipping sauces accompany the food.

*Also known as — Mongolian hotpot*

## steamed pudding

Both sweet and savoury, and cooked in a pudding basin by boiling or steaming. The savoury versions include steak and kidney pudding. The sweet versions include all varieties and flavours of cake-like mixtures from steamed puddings to dried fruit puddings such as Christmas pudding. Some puddings are sponge mixtures; others have suet crusts like Sussex pond pudding.

*See also* **spotted dick, steak and kidney pie**

### COOKING

*When cooking steamed pudding, check the water level a few times during cooking to ensure it stays at its original level. If necessary, top up with boiling water to keep the water simmering.*

*A pleat across the centre allows the pudding batter to expand.*

### JAM SPONGE PUDDING

*Place a large saucepan of water, half filled, on to boil. Place a trivet or small saucer in the bottom. Grease, then line the base of a pudding basin with a circle of baking paper. Put 3 tablespoons blackcurrant jam into the base of the basin. Sift 175 g self-raising flour into a large bowl. Add 125 g softened butter, 150 g caster sugar, 3 eggs and 2 tablespoons treacle. Mix until smooth. Pour into the basin and smooth the surface. Cover the bowl with a sheet of baking paper, then foil. Make a pleat across the centre. Tie with string under the rim and make a string handle across the top. Lower into the boiling water and cover the saucepan. Simmer for 1¾ hours. Turn out and serve hot with custard. Serves 8.*

An essential cooking ingredient produced by cooking meat, poultry, vegetables or fish in water with additional flavourings, and then straining it to give a clear liquid. So basic is stock to cooking, the French call it *fond*, meaning base.

Stock can be made from raw or cooked meat and poultry, but fish stock should be made from raw non-oily fish. The quality of stock depends on the type of bones that you use—marrow bones, pig's trotters and chicken wings will help give a jellied stock (when cold) as they contain collagen. Vegetables should be aromatics: leek, onion, carrot, celery, as should herbs (bay leaves, thyme and parsley) and spices such as whole black peppercorns (ground pepper would not give a clear stock). Vegetables that give off starch, such as potatoes, are never used—they would make the stock go cloudy. Stock is not generally made from pork as it is too strong.

Brown stock is made by browning beef or veal bones for varying lengths of time—but do not burn the bones or you will get a bitter flavour. White stock is made with uncooked bones or poultry.

Never boil a stock, it must be simmered for a long time (shorter for fish)—boiled stock is cloudy and greasy as the fat is incorporated into the liquid. Scum that rises to the surface should be skimmed. To precipitate scum (fat and impurities) cold water is added at regular intervals (*depouiller*). Once made, a stock can be reduced (by boiling) to a glace for freezing. Reconstitute glace with water to use it. Store stock in the fridge for up to 3 days, after that freeze for up to 6 months.

## COOKING

*Do not add salt to stock. As the liquid reduces, the salt will concentrate and the glace will be too salty to use.*

*For a really clear stock, strain it through muslin.*

## BROWN STOCK

1 Roast 1.5 kg beef or veal bones in a single layer in a large roasting tin at 220°C for 20 minutes.

2 Add 1 quartered onion, 2 chopped carrots, 1 chopped leek and 1 chopped celery stalk and roast for 20 minutes.

3 Transfer to a stockpot with 10 peppercorns and a bouquet garni; cover with 4 litres cold water. Bring to the boil.

4 When the stock boils, turn it down to a simmer and skim off the scum.

5 Skim regularly—adding a little cold water to the pot (depouiller) will help any impurities rise up—then remove the scum.

6 After 6–8 hours, strain the stock and leave it to cool in the fridge. Lift off any fat that congeals on the top.

## CHICKEN (WHITE) STOCK

1 Put 1 kg chicken carcasses into a stockpot with a bouquet garni, 1 quartered onion, 1 chopped carrot and 10 peppercorns.

2 Add 4 litres cold water and bring to the boil. When the stock boils, turn it down to a simmer and skim off the scum.

3 Skim regularly—adding a little cold water to the pot (depouiller) will help any impurities rise up— then remove the scum.

4 Strain the stock, remove any fat by dragging a sheet of paper towel over the stock's surface.

5 If not using immediately, cool in the fridge. When cool, lift off any congealed fat.

6 To store stock, reduce it to a concentrated glace, then put in ice cube trays and freeze.

## FISH STOCK

1 Put 2 kg fish bones and heads, a bouquet garni, 1 chopped onion and 10 peppercorns in the pot.

2 Add 2.5 litres cold water, bring to the boil and simmer for 20–30 minutes. Skim off any scum.

3 Strain the stock, then cool in the fridge. When cool, lift off any congealed fat.

## VEGETABLE STOCK

1 Put 500 g mixed chopped carrots, celery, onions and leeks in a stockpot with a bouquet garni and 10 peppercorns.

2 Add 2.5 litres cold water and bring to the boil. Skim off any scum.

3 Simmer the stock for 1–2 hours, pressing the solids to extract all the flavour, then strain and cool in the fridge.

## stoemp

A Belgian dish of boiled potatoes, mashed and seasoned with nutmeg, butter, salt and pepper, then mixed with vegetables such as leeks, carrots, spinach or endive. Stoemp is usually served with bacon or sausages.

## stollen

A sweet yeasted bread, eaten at Christmas time (and sometimes called Christstollen), originally from the German city of Dresden. The dough is enriched with egg, sugar, butter, dried fruits and almonds and sometimes marzipan is placed along the centre, before it is folded into an oval and baked. The shape is said to represent the baby Jesus wrapped in swaddling cloths, although the word supposedly comes from the Old German word for 'post'. Before serving, the stollen is drenched in icing sugar.

**Also known as — Christstollen**

## stout

A strong, dark malted beer with a bitter-sweet flavour made with roasted barley. Of British origin, although the most famous example of the style is Irish Guinness, first brewed in Dublin in 1759. It is the heaviest, darkest and most full-bodied of all the beers, has a high alcohol content and is often added to beef stews.

## stracciatella

A soup made from a paste of eggs and cheese dropped into a hot chicken or beef broth, stracciatella is a speciality of Rome. In Italian, the word means 'little rags', referring to the rag-like strands that form as the paste cooks. Stracciatella also refers to a chocolate chip ice cream.

**Also known as — minestra mille fanti, stracciatella alla romana**

### STRACCIATELLA ALLA ROMANA

*Boil 2 litres beef or chicken stock in a saucepan. Beat 3 eggs with 25 g grated Parmesan, 1½ tablespoons fresh breadcrumbs, 2 tablespoons finely chopped parsley and season with pepper. Lower the stock temperature to a simmer. Dribble the egg mixture into the stock. When the egg is set, stir in 25 g more grated Parmesan and serve straight away. Serves 4.*

The luscious red conical fruit of a low spreading plant. Native to both Europe and America, strawberries are now cultivated in temperate zones around the world and are in season from late spring to early summer. The fruit is unique in that the seeds grow around the outside of the fruit rather than inside it. Their name comes from the fact that they were originally grown on straw. Wild strawberries, such as alpine strawberries, may be completely white, and wood strawberries are often smaller but more flavoursome than their cultivated counterparts. Use in desserts, fruit salads, as fruit soup and preserves, purée as a sauce (coulis) or in milk shakes. Whole or sliced, they can be sweetened with sugar, which helps to maintain their bright red colour.

**Strawberries go with — balsamic vinegar, Cointreau, cream, lemon juice, sugar**

### FROZEN STRAWBERRY PRESERVE

*Hull, purée and strain 1 kg strawberries, then stir in 300 g sugar. Place in 4 freezerproof containers and freeze until firm. When needed, defrost a portion slowly in the fridge. Serve as a preserve with scones or toast. Keep refrigerated and use within 2 days. Makes 1.3 kg.*

*Californian strawberry*

*English strawberry*

*Wild strawberry*

### BUYING

*The biggest and reddest strawberries aren't always the tastiest; in fact, those that are smaller or have paler tips are often the sweetest. Instead, choose strawberries that are plump, glossy, unbruised and firm. Check the bottom of the container for mould.*

### STORAGE

*Store strawberries in the fridge in their container for 2–3 days. Bring to room temperature to serve.*

### PREPARATION

*Wash just before eating. To 'hull' a strawberry means to remove the leafy top and stalk—pinch it off with your fingers.*

### STRAWBERRIES ROMANOFF

*Hull and coarsely chop 375 g strawberries (set aside 2 whole strawberries). Place the chopped strawberries in a bowl with ¼ cup caster sugar and 3 tablespoons liqueur such as Cointreau or kirsch. Cover and refrigerate overnight. Beat 300 ml thickened cream and stir in half the strawberries. Place remaining strawberries in the base of 4 glasses, divide the strawberry and cream mixture on top and decorate with half a strawberry. Serves 4.*

# streusel

A crumbly topping sprinkled over the top of baked goods such as cakes, tarts *(pictured)* and muffins. It is made by rubbing butter into a mixture of sugar, spices and flour or breadcrumbs. The word comes from the German word for 'sprinkle'. Streusel cake, popular in central and northern Europe, is a yeast cake topped with a crumble topping of sugar, cinnamon or mixed spice.

# strudel

### APPLE STRUDEL

*Put 250 g plain flour in a bowl. Mix together 150 ml warm water, 1 teaspoon vinegar, 1 egg yolk and 1 tablespoon oil, then add to the flour. Mix to a smooth paste, knead until elastic, then cover and stand for 1 hour. Roll and stretch dough to a large rectangle (see steps). Peel, core and dice 1 kg apples and sprinkle with 3 tablespoons sugar. Brush the pastry with 75 g melted butter, scatter on 100 g chopped walnuts and 100 g lightly browned breadcrumbs. Spread over the apple, sprinkle with 200 g raisins, 125 g caster sugar and 1 teaspoon cinnamon. Roll up and firmly tuck in ends. Brush with butter and cook at 200 ºC for 40 minutes. Sprinkle with icing sugar. Serves 6.*

Inspired by the Turkish baklava, strudel is made using layers of wafer-thin pastry wrapped around a sweet filling. The Austrians embraced the art of strudel-making, and it is with Austria that it is most commonly associated. The classic strudel fillings are apple and raisin or cherries and cream cheese. Savoury strudels can be filled with minced or chopped meat, bacon and onions or cabbage. You can make the pastry yourself or ready-made filo dough is an acceptable substitute.

### ROLLING THE STRUDEL DOUGH

*1 Place the dough on a large floured cloth over a large bench top and start to roll out.*

*2 Keep rolling until you have formed a 30 cm rectangle.*

*3 Stretch out the dough by draping it over the back of your hands.*

*4 Work the dough with your knuckles to stretch it thinly and evenly.*

A speciality of the American South, made with lima beans and corn kernels, sometimes cooked in cream, though there are many variations. The name comes from Narragansett or Algonquin Indian words 'misickquatash' and 'sukquttahash'. Versions of succotash were adapted by the Pilgrim Fathers, but today it is more seen in southern cooking where it is often served at Thanksgiving.

### SUCCOTASH

*Soak 100 g lima beans overnight. Drain, then cover the beans in water and cook until tender (this will take about 1 hour). Boil 250 ml cream until reduced by half. Combine beans, cream, 250 g fresh corn kernels and simmer for 10 minutes. Add 20 g butter, 1 teaspoon chopped thyme, salt and pepper. Serve with poultry or pork. Serves 4.*

An unweaned baby pig, killed between 3 and 6 weeks. Sucking pig is used in many cuisines, including Portuguese, Spanish and Chinese, often as a festive meat, and usually roasted. The meat is particularly tender and pale, and the delicate skin is scored to make crackling. The cavity may be stuffed, but often is left plain as the flesh is so flavoursome. Sometimes sucking pigs are erroneously referred to as 'suckling pig', but it is the young pig who sucks and the mother who suckles.

**Also known as — suckling pig**

The firm white fat surrounding the kidneys of beef and mutton or lamb. Suet has excellent cooking properties: it is stiff and melts slowly, and is used extensively in British cooking to make pastry, suet puddings and mincemeat. It is used to a lesser extent today, though in the past it was the preferred fat for pastries as it gave them a good 'short' texture. Today it can be bought commercially packaged, usually granulated and coated with flour. Some butchers will supply fresh suet, which can be grated either by hand or in the food processor. Suet puddings are traditionally cooked in a pudding basin or formed into a cylindrical shape wrapped in a cloth and steamed or baked in foil.

*Commercially prepared suet (back) and fresh suet, whole and grated (front).*

# sugar

A pure carbohydrate used as a sweetener around the world. Today, it is mostly produced from sugar cane, then sugar beet (which tastes no different), and other sources such as honey, sorghum, palm trees and maple trees.

## GRANULATED SUGAR

A bleached sugar, refined from sugar cane or sugar beet, with medium-sized crystals. The most common, all-purpose sugar. The crystals do not dissolve as easily as caster sugar so it is not suitable for all kinds of baking. It is good for syrup and caramel, producing a good clear syrup if dissolved slowly. Less-refined golden-coloured versions are also available. Preserving sugar is a very coarse granulated sugar. The large crystals give off little scum.

**Also known as — white sugar**

## SUGAR CRYSTALS

Large crystals often used in coffee or as decoration. Some sugar crystals are grown on sticks and used as coffee stirrers. They may be white, dyed pale brown or multi-coloured.

## VANILLA SUGAR

Caster sugar with added vanilla extract used in baking and for desserts. Make your own by burying a vanilla pod in an airtight jar filled with caster sugar. The flavour from the pod gradually infuses into the sugar.

*Sugar crystal sticks*

*Vanilla sugar*

*Sugar crystals*

*Granulated sugar*

*Commercial vanilla sugar*

*Barbados sugar*

*Light soft brown sugar*

*Icing sugar*

## BROWN SUGAR

Originally a partly refined sugar flavoured with the molasses that it was made from. Now also made by adding molasses to white sugar. Types include Barbados (muscovado) sugar, a light or dark, moist strongly flavoured sugar; light soft brown sugar, with a light fine grain and a caramel sugar flavour; and dark soft brown sugar, which is moist and has a molasses flavour.

*Dark soft brown sugar*

## ICING SUGAR

Made by grinding granulated sugar to a fine powder, which dissolves instantly. Mixed with water, it forms a glacé icing used to ice cakes, it sweetens whipped cream and is dusted over baked cakes as decoration. Often contains an anti-caking agent to stop lumping.

**Also known as — confectioners' sugar, powdered sugar**

## CANE SUGAR SYRUPS

The by-products of sugar refining. Treacle has a strong flavour, and adds richness and colour to baked goods. It may be light or dark in colour (when it is sometimes called blackstrap molasses). Golden syrup is an invert sugar syrup (it won't crystallize) with a honey-like texture. It has its own distinctive flavour and can be used in baking or as a pouring syrup.

## CUBE SUGAR

Made from crystallized sugar, shaped into small cubes to portion it out. It can be rubbed over citrus skins to extract the flavoursome oils and then used in cooking. Brown and raw cube sugar are also available.

*Also known as — loaf sugar, lump sugar*

## MAPLE SUGAR AND SYRUP

Maple syrup reduced and refined to produce a sticky, moist sugar, which does not form individual crystals. Maple sugar was once the preferred product, but when cane sugars became cheaper, preferences switched to maple syrup.

Treacle

Golden syrup

Raw sugar cubes

White sugar cubes

Maple syrup

Raw sugar

Demerara sugar

Caster sugar

Palm sugar

## DEMERARA SUGAR

Large golden crystals that have been crystallized from partly refined sugar, or in the case of London demerara, by adding molasses to refined sugar. Used for sweetening coffee or for adding a caramelized flavour to meat dishes such as baked hams.

## CASTER SUGAR

A fine, white sugar with very small crystals that dissolve easily. Used in meringues, cakes and desserts where it is necessary to dissolve the sugar before baking. As it dissolves quickly, it is good for sprinkling over fruit or desserts. Less-refined versions with a golden colour are also available.

*Also known as — castor sugar, superfine sugar*

## RAW SUGAR

Crude, unrefined sugars often sold in lumps. Jaggery (gur) is an Indian unrefined cane sugar or date palm sugar, and piloncillo is a sugar from Mexico, which is made into little cork shapes. Palm sugar is not made from cane but the sap of a palm and is used in Southeast Asian dishes.

Sugar cane *(pictured left)* was first cultivated in India over 2,000 years ago. In the seventh century, the Persians set up sugar refineries, and it is from their word for it, 'sakar', that we get the English name. Sugar, like spices, reached the Western world via the Arab trade routes, and when it first appeared, was considered an exotic and prohibitively expensive commodity, often called 'white gold'. Until the eighteenth century when sugar cane from the West Indies became more plentiful and less expensive, food was sweetened with honey, fruit syrups and maple syrup.

Sugar is made by extracting crystals from sugar cane juice. The crystals obtained after the first extraction are golden brown and contain some molasses. Refined white sugar is often made from sugar crystals that have been chemically treated and bleached, though some brands, like Billingtons, are unrefined.

*Clockwise from top left to centre: boiled sweets, marshmallows and butterscotch, fudge, candy floss, toffee, nougat, spun sugar, hard caramel, pulled sugar sweets, barley sugar.*

### Sugar syrup

Sugar syrups are solutions of sugar dissolved in water. The lightest (thinnest) syrup uses 500 ml water to 250 g sugar; 250 ml water to 250 g sugar for a medium syrup; and 225 ml water to 250 g sugar for a heavy syrup. Different concentrations dictate the application of the syrup—it can be used as a basic syrup to poach fruits (light) or used to make confectionery and caramels (heavy).

For the home cook, a sugar thermometer is helpful in determining the exact temperature and stages of the boiled syrup. Chefs and confectioners use a more precise measure called a 'hydrometer', which measures the density of the syrup at a specific temperature.

### TESTING SUGAR SYRUP

1 To test for soft ball, drop some syrup into a glass of cold water—it should form a soft ball.

2 To test for soft crack, drop some syrup into cold water, then pull it to see if it forms threads.

■ *See also* **palm sugar, sweeteners**

## SUGAR SYRUP

*Put sugar and water into a saucepan and dissolve sugar over low heat. Wash down the sides of the pan with a wet brush to dissolve any crystals. To make the syrup stronger, bring the mixture to the boil and keep boiling until you reach the following stages:*

**Thread** – *(106–113°C) At this point, the syrup will form threads when dropped from a spoon into water. Use as a poaching syrup.*

**Soft ball** – *(112–116°C) A blob of syrup dropped in water will form a very soft ball. Use for Italian meringue, fondant and fudge.*

**Hard ball** – *(121–130°C) A hard blob will form. Use for toffee, hard caramels and marshmallow.*

**Soft crack** – *(132–143°C) The ball of sugar will stretch to form threads. Use for butterscotch and nougat.*

**Hard crack** – *(149–154°C) The ball can be stretched and snapped. Use for barley sugar and glazed fruits.*

**Caramel** – *(160–177°C) The sugar syrup starts to change colour, getting darker as it cooks. Stop it cooking by putting the base of the pan into cold water. Re-melt as necessary. Use for praline, spun sugar and caramel sauces.*

## sugared almonds

Whole almonds coated with a fine layer of sugar. They are an example of a dragée, a French name for a type of confectionery, and are usually either white or pastel coloured. Some may be coated with silver and gold leaf. Sugared almonds are a symbol of good fortune for the French, Greeks and Italians and are offered at christenings and weddings. They are flavoured with rose-water in Iran and Afghanistan and given at New Year in the hope of a 'sweet' year ahead.

■ *See also* **dragées**

## sukiyaki

A one-pot Japanese beef dish originating in the nineteenth century when beef was introduced to the Japanese diet by Westerners. Thin slices of marbled beef are cooked in a shallow pan along with various vegetables including *negi* (spring onion), bean curd and shirataki noodles, flavoured with a stock of soy sauce, mirin or sake and sugar. Other ingredients, such as shiitake mushrooms and chrysanthemum leaves, are added and the ingredients are brought to a boil. When cooked, the diners pick out pieces of food from the pot and dip them in a lightly beaten egg. Many Japanese restaurants specialize in this style of cooking.

■ *See also* **shabu shabu**

## see dried fruit — sultanas

## sumac

A spice used extensively in Lebanese and Turkish cooking. The reddish-purple berry has a fruity but mildly astringent lemony flavour. The seeds are dried, then crushed or powdered. Sumac is used in many dishes to add flavour and colour to meat, especially kebabs, fish, pilaffs and vegetables. Sumac berries are also used in North African, Indian and Asian cuisines.

### MARINATED SARDINES

*Mix 1 crushed garlic clove with ½ teaspoon salt and 2 teaspoons ras el hanout. Add enough oil to make a paste and rub into 18 sardine fillets. Fry in oil until browned; remove from pan. Cook 1 chopped onion with 3 chopped tomatoes, 2 teaspoons sumac and 1 chopped chilli for 5 minutes. Add 185 ml water and cook a further 5 minutes. Add 4 tablespoons lemon juice and season. Pour over the sardines and cool to room temperature. Serves 6.*

## summer pudding

A dessert that utilizes fresh berries, seasonal in summer, enclosed in a pudding basin lined with a bread casing. Redcurrants and raspberries are commonly used but other seasonal fruits including gooseberries, blackcurrants, strawberries and blackberries can be included.

### SUMMER PUDDING

*Put 500 g raspberries and 250 g each redcurrants and blackcurrants with 400 g caster sugar and 3 tablespoons water in a large saucepan. Gently cook for 2–3 minutes. Dip triangles of crustless bread in the juice and use them to line the base and side of a 2 litre pudding basin, leaving no gaps. Spoon in the fruit and cover with a bread layer. Cover and place a weighted plate on top. Refrigerate overnight. Turn out to serve. Serves 8.*

## sundae

Originally a dessert made with syrup, ice cream and fruit, topped with whipped cream, nuts and a cherry. The term now covers an array of elaborate ice cream desserts—almost anything topped with whipped cream and a cherry. Famous sundaes include the banana split and knickerbocker glory, a British adaptation of the New York knickerbocker sundae. This starts with chocolate syrup, then vanilla ice cream, crushed raspberries, more ice cream, crushed pineapple, yet more ice cream, then whipped cream and a cherry.

## sun-dried tomatoes

Originally an Italian method for drying tomatoes in the sun to preserve them. Many varieties of tomatoes can be sun-dried. The basic method is to cut them in half, sprinkle with salt and leave in the sun. The salt dehydrates the tomato and concentrates the flavour. Because the tomatoes are very salty, they are usually soaked in water to leech out the salt and then eaten as part of an antipasto. Sun-dried tomatoes are also commercially available in jars. These are soaked in a solution of vinegar and water, they are then drained, dried and covered in olive oil, often with other flavours such as chilli and herbs. Sun-blushed or semi-dried tomatoes are partially dried in a dehydrator. They need to be immersed in oil to preserve for any length of time.

**Sun-dried tomatoes go with — antipasto, pasta**

*Sun-dried tomatoes*

*Sun-blushed (semi-dried) tomatoes*

The seeds of the sunflower, the largest member of the daisy family, a North American native now grown around the world. Today, Argentina and North America are the largest producers of the large yellow flower, which yields several hundred black seeds. These seeds are a major source of oil production as sunflower oil or sunoil and in the manufacture of margarine. The oil is 52 per cent polyunsaturated, 34 per cent monounsaturated, and is being bred to lift the level of monounsaturates. The seeds are delicious raw, roasted or salted, and are added to baked items.

*Sunflower seeds*

*Polished sunflower seeds*

*Shelled sunflower seeds*

# suppli

A speciality of Rome, suppli are best made from leftover risotto, bound with eggs, butter and Parmesan, and usually filled with cheese or meat. One of the classics, *suppli al telefono*, is filled with a mixture of mozzarella, prosciutto or mortadella, then formed into orange-sized balls and deep-fried. When the hot suppli is pulled apart, the mozzarella stretches into long strands like telephone wires. Other suppli may be filled with mixtures like chopped ham and cheese or with a ragù of minced meats or chicken livers and fungi.

# surf 'n' turf

Any dish consisting of both seafood (surf) and meat (turf). The seafood, often prawns or lobster, is served with meat, usually a steak. Surf 'n' turf is an American invention and is mostly served in restaurants. A popular Australian variation is the carpetbag steak, a steak stuffed with oysters, then grilled.

## STEAK WITH LOBSTER TAILS

*Fry 4 filet mignon steaks for 2 minutes on each side (rare) and keep warm. Fry 2 lobster tails until they turn red and the flesh inside is cooked. Cut down each side of the underneath of the tail and peel back the shell. Remove the tail meat in one piece. Slice into medallions, then return to the frying pan for 30 seconds. Add 1 tablespoon brandy, cook for 30 seconds, then add 125 ml cream. Place a steak on each plate and top with some lobster. Spoon some sauce over the top. Serves 4.*

## sushi

A favourite dish right across Japan and now the rest of the world consisting of various ingredients served with sushi rice (rice prepared with sweetened vinegar). The rice encloses or sits under fillings such as seafood, vegetables (mostly cooked), omelette, bean curd, or pickles. Sushi rolls (*maki-zushi*) are wrapped in thin sheets of lightly toasted seaweed (nori).

Sushi takes on many shapes and forms. *Nigiri-zushi*, from Edo (now Tokyo) consists of a pillow of rice smeared with wasabi, usually topped with a slice of raw fish or other seafood, sometimes wrapped with a thin strip of nori. From Kyoto comes *maki-zushi*, of which there are countless variations, at their simplest made using a square of nori, spread with rice and topped with a filling such as fish, cucumber or pickles. Using a bamboo mat (*maki-su*), the rice is rolled up into a cylinder and sliced into little rolls. This type of sushi can also be rolled by hand into a cone shape when it is usually called *temaki*.

*Salmon nigiri-zushi (back) and tuna nigiri-zushi (front).*

### SUSHI RICE

*Wash 750 g sushi (short-grain) rice until the water runs clear. Leave the rice to dry for 1 hour. Put the rice and an equal volume of cold water into a rice cooker or deep pot with a 5 cm piece of kombu. If using a pot, bring the rice to the boil, then cover. Boil for 2 minutes, then simmer for 20 minutes, by which time the rice should be cooked and all the water absorbed (the absorbency of the rice will vary from brand to brand and according to how old it is). Cool the rice in a special wooden tub or non-metallic bowl, tossing it with a rice paddle and fanning it. Add 150 ml sushi-su (sushi vinegar) as you cool the rice, just enough to make the rice grains stick together slightly.*

### CHIRASHI-ZUSHI

*Meaning 'scattered sushi', this is the easiest sushi to make. Cooked rice is placed in the bottom of a bowl. Pieces of raw or cooked fish, vegetables and omelette are scattered over the top. It is usually accompanied by pickled ginger, wasabi and soy sauce.*

### MAKING MAKI-ZUSHI

*1* *Lay a sheet of toasted nori on a sushi mat and cover with a layer of rice, 1 cm thick. Leave a small gap at each end of the nori.*

*2* *Place the filling down the centre of the rice, then roll up from the edges nearest you, using the mat to guide you.*

*3* *Tidy up any ends and then, using a sharp knife dipped in vinegared water, cut the roll into equal-sized pieces.*

## BEAN CURD STUFFED WITH RICE

An *inari-zushi* (a sushi packed into a deep-fried bean curd pouch), filled with rice, sometimes flavoured with pickled ginger or sesame seeds. The bean curd pouches (*aburage*) are slightly sweet, and can be bought ready-made.

## SALMON, CUCUMBER AND PICKLE

A *maki-zushi*, these thin rolls are filled with fish such as salmon *(sake)*, yellowtail *(hamachi)*, or vegetables such as cucumber or pickles.

## EEL AND PRAWN

Often used in *nigiri-zushi*, freshwater eel *(unagi)* is cooked before it is used as sushi. The eel is basted with sugar and mirin, then grilled. *Anago* is saltwater or conger eel. Similarly, prawns are also cooked. The prawn is cooked on a skewer to keep it straight, then butterflied.

## INSIDE-OUT ROLLS

These are made with the rice on the outside and the nori sheet and filling on the inside. The rice may be coated with flying fish roe.

## LARGE ROLLS

These are called *futomaki-zushi* and can be made using anything, but are usually vegetarian. They typically use spinach, egg, cucumber, mushrooms, bamboo shoots and lotus root.

## CALIFORNIA ROLL

A thick *futomaki-zushi* roll made with crab or fish, avocado and cucumber. These are sometimes made 'inside-out', that is, the seaweed on the inside and the rice on the outside. The rice may be coated with flying fish roe.

## OCTOPUS AND SQUID

Often used for *maki-zushi*, octopus *(tako)* is always first lightly cooked. Only the tentacles are used. Squid *(ika)* is used raw but only the body is used.

## SEA URCHIN

The roe of the sea urchin are often used in *gunkan maki* (battleship sushi), where the sides of the seaweed are higher than the rice so as to form a little wall to hold in the soft sea urchin.

## OSHI-ZUSHI

Meaning 'pressed sushi', this is made using a special box. The rice is pressed into the box, then topped with fish. It is then removed from the mould and cut into slices to serve.

## FISH ROE

Like sea urchins, fish eggs used in sushi are generally soft and are made into *gunkan maki*. The most common is the large orange salmon roe *(ikura)* and the smaller, red flying fish roe *(tobiko)*, often served as part of *maki-zushi*. Salted cod roe *(tarako)* is also popular.

## TUNA

*Maguro* is the flesh from the side of the blue fin tuna, while *toro* is the fattier flesh from the belly. Served in rolls or as *nigiri-zushi*.

## OMELETTE

A *nigiri-zushi* topped with an omelette *(tomago)* and held in place with a strip of nori. The omelette, usually slightly sweetened, is cooked in a square or rectangular frying pan. The omelette is built up in thin layers and is traditionally eaten at the end of the sushi meal.

## Sussex pond pudding

An old English pudding whose name is derived from the high butter content of the pudding that melts out, pond-like, from the suet crust when it is cut. To make it, a pudding basin is lined with a suet crust. A butter and sugar mixture is placed in the centre along with a lemon that has been pricked all over to extract its juices. The pudding is cooked for several hours then cut into wedges and served with a little of the cooked lemon and juices.

See also **suet**

## swede

Not a true root, but a vegetable with a swollen base at the stem, the swede is a close relation of the turnip, but different in flavour and texture. The most marketed swede has dense yellow flesh with a strong flavour. Older specimens have more flavour, are better for mashing, and also hold their shape when added to stews and pies. In Scotland, swedes (neeps) are mashed (or bashed) as a traditional accompaniment to the haggis. In North America, they are known as rutabaga.

### CLAPSHOT

*Peel and cut 500 g swedes and 500 g potatoes into even-sized pieces. Put 1 finely chopped onion, swedes and potatoes in a saucepan and cover with boiling water. Cook until tender, then drain and mash with 1 tablespoon each chopped chives, butter and milk. Season well. Serves 4.*

## sweet potato

The tuberous roots of a tropical vine, which, although also native to Central and South America like the potato, are not true potatoes. Today, they are an important crop in southern America, South America, Asia, Japan, the Mediterranean, Hawaii, Australia and New Zealand, where one variety, orange in colour, is known as kumera, close to the original Peruvian name of *kumar*. There are several varieties of sweet potato, and their flesh, which may be white, orange or yellow, ranges from mealy to moist and watery, and their skins may be white, yellow, red, purple or brown. Orange-fleshed sweet potatoes are softer when cooked.

Sweet potatoes can be cooked as you would a potato—roasted, boiled, mashed or fried, but their soft, slightly sweet flesh makes them an ideal ingredient in cakes or sweet dishes, in breads, soups and casseroles. Sprinkle sweet potatoes with brown sugar and butter and roast them. Sweet potatoes don't store for as long as potatoes but will last for 1 week if kept in a cool, dry place.

See also **potato, taro, yam**

Substances used to sweeten foods without using sugar or any of its derivatives. Some are natural, such as glycyrrhizin in liquorice or stevia, a substance obtained from a South American shrub; others, such as saccharin, aspartame, acesulfame-k (Sunett) and sucralose (Splenda) are artificial. Artificial sweeteners are much sweeter than sugar and contain far less calories per weight. Sweeteners available on the market are licensed by the government of each country and may vary from place to place.

A sweet delicacy, which can be any one of several types of confectionery, baked goods or sweets. These vary from cuisine to cuisine; marzipan fruit, fruit pastes such as cotignac (quince paste), marron glacés, nougat and candied fruits are all sweetmeats, as are fruit jams that are eaten by the spoonful in the Middle East.

# Swiss food

Landlocked within Europe, Switzerland is bordered by France to the west, Austria to the east, Germany to the north and Italy to the south. While these countries have had a distinctive influence on Swiss cooking, and each language group—French, German, Italian and Romansch—has their own culinary allegiances, Switzerland also has its own distinctive cuisine.

Switzerland's alpine meadows are ideal grazing land for cattle, which produce two of Switzerland's 'national treasures': cheese and chocolate. Switzerland produces over 150 different cheeses, including Emmental, Gruyère, Vacherin and Walliser. The importance of cheese to the Swiss led to the creation of such dishes as fondue and Raclette, which is traditionally prepared by holding a half-round of cheese before an open fire. As the cheese begins to melt, it is scraped off (*racler* means 'to scrape') and eaten with potatoes and pickled vegetables. Modern Swiss use an electric raclette grill. Fondues vary around the country, but the best known are from Neuchâtel and Geneva. As an extension of their dairy industry, the Swiss make superb milk chocolate, with Lindt being one of the better-known brands.

An important feature of Swiss cuisine is its charcuterie, which includes smoked sausages, salted meats and bacon. Air-dried beef, *Bündnerfleisch*, is eaten as a snack, served in thin slices. One of the true delicacies of Swiss cooking is the Berner platter, named after the capital city, consisting of green beans, boiled bacon, smoked sausage and ham. Potatoes are used in dishes like *papet vaudoir*, made from leeks and potatoes, and *Rösti*, shredded fried potatoes. Fish is plentiful from the many alpine rivers and lakes.

The Swiss sweet tooth is satisfied by sweet cakes and delicacies of all kinds, like *Leckerli*, spiced honey cakes topped with icing sugar, *Gugelhopf*, a type of sponge cake with a hollow centre, and *Schaffhausen*, cream-filled cakes.

But the world really knows Swiss chefs through their long and distinguished careers in the hospitality industry. It has been said that Switzerland solved its unemployment problem by training large numbers of excellent chefs and hotel managers, and exporting them.

■ *See also* **fondue, Rösti**

*From top: Raclette, fried perch fillets, Swiss milk chocolate.*

# Swiss chard

A relation of the sugar beet mostly grown and eaten around the southern Mediterranean. Swiss chard has fleshy stalks and large leaves, both of which can be prepared as for spinach. The leaves may be eaten raw in salads or cooked and the stalks served in a sauce, added to soups or sautéed. Ruby chard has a red stalk and can be cooked in the same way. Store covered and unwashed in the fridge for up to 4 days. Swiss chard is sold under the name of 'spinach' in Australia.

*Also known as — chard, leaf beet, seakale beet, silver beet, spinach beet, white beet*

# swiss roll

A thin sponge cake rolled while hot in baking paper or a tea towel and set aside until cooled. It is then unrolled and filled with a moist filling, often jam, but may also have whipped cream or buttercream. The filling can be flavoured with melted chocolate, chopped fruit, nuts, citrus or essences. The filled cake is then re-rolled and cut into thick slices to serve.

*Also known as — jelly roll*

■ *See also  roulade*

# syllabub

In one early form, syllabub (sillabub) is a seventeenth century rural British dessert made by whisking together fresh milk and cider or ale with sugar and nutmeg, then leaving it to form curds and an alcoholic whey. Sometimes, cream was poured over it. Nowadays, it is a light-textured lemony dessert made from lemon zest and juice with white wine and sherry. This is folded through lightly whipped cream and sometimes whipped egg whites. It is usually served in small glasses, which are well chilled, and accompanied by a sweet biscuit.

### SYLLABUB

*Put the grated zest and juice of 2 lemons, 125 ml dry white wine and 60 ml dry sherry in a bowl with 125 g caster sugar; leave for 1 hour. Whisk in 250 ml cold double cream in a thin stream until mixture is light and fluffy. Spoon into wine glasses and decorate with julienned lemon zest. Serves 4.*

## Tabasco sauce

The trade name of a fiery sauce first produced in southern Louisiana by Edmund McIlhenny in 1868. Still made there today, its essential ingredients, chillies, salt and vinegar, remain unchanged. Used in small amounts as a condiment and flavour enhancer, particularly in Creole, Tex-Mex and Mexican cooking, and in the cocktail, Bloody Mary. Green Tabasco is milder in flavour, and Habanero the hottest.

## tabbouleh

A Middle Eastern salad of fine burghul mixed with tomatoes, onions, mint and parsley. Olive oil and lemon juice add moisture and flavour. Tabbouleh is typically served with baby cos lettuce leaves used to scoop it up with or as a salad accompaniment to meat dishes. The 'greenness' varies as some recipes use larger amounts of herbs.

*Also known as — tabbuli, tabouleh*

### TABBOULEH

*Soak 175 g burghul in hot water for 20 minutes, or until soft. Drain and squeeze out any excess water using your hands. Mix burghul with 6 finely chopped spring onions, 2 skinned and chopped ripe tomatoes, 6 tablespoons each finely chopped mint and parsley. Stir through the juice of 2 lemons, 60 ml olive oil, then season well. Serves 6.*

## tagine

A North African dish, whose name inadequately translates as 'stew', particularly popular in Moroccan cooking. The same name is given to the conical earthenware cooking pot in which it is traditionally prepared. The stew is usually made with meat, generally lamb or chicken, but also fish. It is characterized by its sweet and savoury mix of flavours, often due to the presence of fruit—prunes and quinces or preserved lemons—honey or orange-flower water. Serve with couscous or rice.

*Also known as — tajine*

413

## tahini

A thick oily paste extracted from husked white sesame seeds, whose name comes from the Arab word *tahana*, meaning to 'grind' or 'crush'. The seeds are husked by crushing and soaking them, they are then dried and lightly roasted before being ground to produce a thick paste or cream. In the Middle East and Greece, tahini appears in the dips often served as part of a meze—mixed with ground chickpeas to make hummus or with puréed aubergine to make baba ghanoush. When blended with garlic and lemon, tahini can be used as a dressing over roast vegetables or as an ingredient in the sweetmeat, halvah. Tahini can be made at home by grinding the seeds in a mortar and pestle or blender until smooth, or is commercially available as both a dark and light paste—the latter of which is usually of the better quality.

***Also known as — sesame seed butter, sesame seed paste, taheena, tahina***

 *See also* **Middle Eastern food**

## tamarillo

An egg-shaped South American fruit with glossy, tough purple-red or orange skin. The flesh is somewhat tart and contains small, black seeds, much like the tomato to which it is related. Tamarillos are usually poached whole in a sugar syrup, made into jam, added fresh to fruit salads, grilled with sugar or cut lengthways and baked with meats, especially lamb. Choose firm, brightly coloured fruit. If using the red fruit, peel off the skin after poaching.

***Also known as — tomarillo, tree tomato***

### POACHED TAMARILLOS

*Make a cut down the centre of each of 8 tamarillos, almost to the stem. In a deep saucepan, bring to the boil 600 ml water, 100 ml juice from an orange, 150 g sugar and a cinnamon stick. Turn down to a simmer, add tamarillos and poach for 15 minutes, turning them halfway. Remove fruit and reduce syrup by half. Serve warm or cold with the syrup. Serves 4.*

## tamarind

The tropical tamarind tree is prized for its pods, each containing a sticky, fleshy sweet-sour pulp wrapped around small hard seeds. The pulp is used in Indian curries and chutneys, or in sauces such as Worcestershire sauce. It may be sweetened into syrups and sweetmeats. Tamarind is sold in ready-made concentrated paste in jars, or in blocks or cakes that still contain the seeds. Cut off a little, mix with hot water and press through a sieve to extract the pulp. Store the paste or blocks in the fridge where they will last up to a year.

***Also known as — Indian date***

A method of cooking meat, chicken, fish or bread in a clay oven, which originated in the Middle East, and is now often featured in Indian restaurants around the world, made popular by the Punjabi cuisine. Tandoori meats and fish are characterized by their reddish-orange colour, the result of using red-coloured commercial tandoori powder (usually called tandoori masala). This spicy, aromatic mixture is added to yoghurt, ginger, garlic, turmeric and chilli to make a paste, which is rubbed over the meat, left to marinate, then cooked in the intense heat of the tandoor oven. Tandoori masala consists of cumin, coriander, cinnamon, cloves, chilli, ginger, turmeric, mace, salt and colouring, though recipes do vary.

## TANDOORI CHICKEN

*In a blender, put 300 g plain yoghurt, 1 small chopped onion, 2 crushed garlic cloves, 1 chilli, 2 tablespoons grated ginger, 3 teaspoons tandoori paste and 1 teaspoon turmeric. Blend to form a paste, then add a few drops of red food colouring. Pour into a bowl and stir in some seasoning and the juice of 1 lemon. Add 4 chicken legs and 4 chicken thighs, coat in the marinade, cover and refrigerate overnight. Drain the chicken and cook on a rack set over a baking tray for 25–30 minutes at 250°C, or as hot as your oven will go. Sprinkle with lemon juice just before serving. Serves 4.*

## TANDOOR OVEN

*A tandoor (tandur) is an unglazed earthen or clay oven used throughout the MIddle East and India for cooking breads and meats. The oven is shaped like a large jar with a top opening, with another opening near the base for adding the charcoal. Flat breads, called rotis, are cooked against the vertical walls until they puff up. Meat and kebabs are cooked within the oven, usually on skewers. Tandoori cooking is a dry form of cooking.*

A naturally occurring hybrid of the mandarin. Much confusion exists between the mandarin and the tangerine. The tangerine is darker in colour than a mandarin, but is also loose-skinned, its segments are easily separated and the flesh is exceptionally sweet. Tangerine varieties include satsumas and murcott (honey tangerine). Tangerine segments can be used as you would oranges and the zest can be grated and used as you would orange zest. Dried tangerine peel is used whole in strips or ground in Chinese, French, Italian and Vietnamese cooking.

■ *See also **mandarin***

# tapas

A word of obscure origin describing a set of small dishes; a way of eating; and a way of life, all arising from the Spanish habit of eating the evening meal very late, and a predisposition towards eating while drinking. Whole streets in Spanish cities are dedicated to *tapeando*, or 'tapasing', which is to stroll with friends and family from bar to bar, nibbling at little plates of delicacies while drinking chilled dry sherry, or tiny glasses of beer. The object of tapas is to whet the appetite, not satiate it: the main meal is yet to come. So popular has the idea of tapas become, it has spilled over from the pre-dinner snacks to become, especially in large cities, lunch. Regional specialities abound.

## BANDERILLAS

A speciality of northern Spain, these are tiny pieces of food skewered onto toothpicks and named after the darts used in bullfighting. Banderillas are often simple but piquant mouthfuls of food such as pieces of cornichon, marinated anchovies and olives, or a slightly more complicated version using prawns, some ham and a piece of egg in a garlicky dressing.

## GAMBAS AL AJILLO

Whole shelled prawns heated in small clay pots (*cazuelitas*) with oil, garlic and chilli until sizzling.

## CALAMARES ALA ROMANA

Rings of squid tubes dipped in batter and then deep-fried and served with lemon wedges. Squid also appears as a stew in its own ink, grilled or marinated and as a cold salad.

## ALBONDIGAS

Bite-sized fried meatballs served in a variety of sauces. *Albóndigas caseras* is served in a sauce of tomato, onion and peppers; *albóndigas en salsa de almendra* (meatballs in almond sauce) is served in a sauce thickened with ground almonds.

## CROQUETAS

Croquettes coated in crumbs and fried until golden and crunchy. Egg croquetas (*croquetas de huevo*) are popular, as are prawn, pimiento or ham fillings.

## TORTILLA

The simple and delicious thick omelette of potato, onion and often garlic, which is found everywhere, and by whose standard you can often judge the quality of all the tapas in a bar.

## EMPANADAS/EMPANADILLAS

Large and small pies made with a type of puff pastry based on lard. These pies come with a huge range of fillings, ranging from pork to seafood and egg and vegetables. Served either as a slice or as individual servings, which look like turnovers.

## CHORIZO

Pieces of grilled chorizo sausage are known as *chorizo ala plancha*. These are a common tapas, as are pieces of chorizo in a spicy tomato sauce, chorizo kebabs and slices of chorizo on pieces of bread. In some bars, slices of blood sausage (morcilla) are grilled.

## SALADS

Small portions of salad are also popular and these range from simple tomato and pepper salads to marinated vegetables or seafood, such as sardines, and bean mixtures. Russian salad and potato salads are also common.

## RINONES AL JEREZ

Calf's kidneys sautéed with garlic and onions. A rich sauce is then made with sherry and parsley.

## OLIVES

Served in different guises in every tapas bar. Spanish olives are varied, and Sevillanas, Manzanillas and Gordals are served marinated in different ways. Other olives are stuffed, or stuffed and crumbed, then deep-fried.

## PATATAS BRAVAS

Pieces of potato that have been sautéed, deep-fried or baked, then tossed in a garlicky chilli tomato sauce.

## tapenade

A Provençal paste of black or green olives, anchovies and capers pounded in a mortar and pestle and seasoned with olive oil and lemon juice. The name comes from *tapeno*, the Provençal word for 'capers'. Tapenade is served with crudités; with bread and freshly chopped tomatoes; as a dip for raw vegetables; or with grilled fish or meats. Tapenade is also sold ready-made in jars.

### TAPENADE

*Using a food processor or mortar and pestle, process 110 g pitted black olives, 60 g capers, 3 anchovy fillets and 2 chopped garlic cloves. Slowly pour in 100 ml olive oil. Season with lemon juice and pepper to taste. Store in an airtight container, covering the top with a thin layer of oil. Serves 4.*

## tapioca

A starch extracted from the cassava plant. The tubers are pulped and dehydrated and the dried starch, the tapioca, is formed into whitish beads of various sizes called 'pearl tapioca'. It is also made into flour, flakes and granulated to make 'instant tapioca'. Tapioca can be used as a thickener in soups and desserts and pearl tapioca is used in milk puddings or baked egg custard puddings.

## tarama

Salted, dried roe, traditionally from the grey mullet, but now usually from cod or carp. Tarama is probably best known as the main ingredient of taramosalata, a creamy dip, popular in Greek and Turkish meze. The strongly flavoured tarama is pounded with bread, oil, lemon juice and sometimes onion, parsley or dill. Tarama is sold as whole roes from fishmongers. Taramosalata can be purchased ready-made and is usually dyed pink.

*From front: tarama, taramosalata (recipe), taramosalata made with bread and dill.*

### TARAMOSALATA

*Soak 1 slice crustless white bread in water, then squeeze dry. Put in a bowl with 250 g fresh smoked fish roe (remove the membrane). Beat with electric beaters, then beat in 150–180 ml olive oil, drop by drop, until smooth and thick. Add juice from ½ lemon and pepper to taste. If preferred, thin with a little cold water. Serve with pitta bread. Serves 6.*

## tarator

A Middle Eastern fish sauce that can be made in two ways. One, expensive, uses pine nuts, bread, garlic, lemon juice and fish stock. The other, cheaper and more popular, uses tahini in place of the pine nuts. Both are served with cold fish. In Bulgaria, tarator is a cold soup of yoghurt, cucumber, walnuts and garlic.

The general name for a family of tropical tubers, and a staple in Asia, the Pacific Islands and West Indies. Brown skinned, their flesh ranges from white and pink to purple. Taro cannot be eaten raw as it contains indigestible substances, but these are neutralized after cooking. Like potato, taro can be boiled, steamed or used in soups and stews, but add at the end as they fall apart easily. Taro starch used in Asian cooking is similar to arrowroot. Some types of taro produce smaller corms called dasheen as well as the smaller cormel, eddo.

A shallow open pastry case, baked with a sweet or savoury filling. The pastry is rolled and lined into the base and sides of the tin. Use a metal tin rather than a ceramic one, as tin heats quickly and helps the pastry to cook. The tin may have straight or fluted sides, with a removable base, it may be round, rectangular or square in shape.

There are three methods for cooking a tart. The filling may be spread onto the uncooked pastry and baked. In this instance, it is best to sit the tart on a hot, preheated tray to help the pastry base to cook. The pastry can also be blind baked, particularly if the filling is heavy, as with egg-based vegetable fillings such as onion tart (*tarte à l'oignon*). The third method is to completely pre-bake the pastry in the tin. The pastry is blind baked and the filling is added when cold, as for fresh fruit flans and jam tarts.

### BAKING BLIND

*Baking pastry blind ensures that the pastry base is cooked through and will not be soggy when the filling is baked in it. Prick the pastry lightly to help it cook evenly.*

1  Line the tin with the pastry. Crumple a piece of greaseproof paper and line the pastry.

2  Fill the base with baking beads, dried beans or rice, spreading them in an even layer. Bake the tart as instructed in the recipe.

3  Carefully lift out the paper and hot beans and briefly re-bake the still-raw tart base.

4  Use the tart base as is, or brush with beaten egg to seal any holes.

## tartare sauce

A piquant mayonnaise-based sauce containing chopped hard-boiled egg, onion, chopped gherkins (often cornichons), capers and herbs and usually served with fried fish and vegetables. Tartare is a French word that dates back to the thirteenth century and refers to a Mongolian tribe, the Tatars, whose ferocity translates in the kitchen to piquancy, and is also used for the chopped raw steak dish, steak tartare. The sauce may be home-made or sold commercially.

### TARTARE SAUCE

*Pour 250 ml mayonnaise into a bowl (make your own mayonnaise referring to page 238 or use a thick, good-quality ready-made mayonnaise). Stir in 2 tablespoons capers, 2 tablespoons finely chopped parsley, 2 finely chopped small cornichons, 1 finely chopped shallot and 1 finely chopped egg. Season with salt and pepper. Makes 350 ml.*

## tarte Tatin

A French upside-down apple tart of recent invention named after the two French sisters who first served it in their restaurant. The French give it the name of *la tarte des demoiselles Tatin*, meaning 'the tart of the two unmarried women named Tatin'. The sliced apples are caramelized in sugar and butter in a shallow baking dish. A pastry case completely covers the top, it is baked, then turned upside down to show the apple and juices. Tarte Tatin is now also made with pears, pineapple, mango or even vegetables such as shallots.

### TARTE TATIN

*Put 70 g butter and 185 g sugar in a 25 cm frying pan with an ovenproof handle (or a tarte Tatin tin). Heat until melted together. Tightly arrange 800 g peeled and quartered Granny Smith apples in the frying pan, making sure there are no gaps. Cook over medium heat for 35–40 minutes, or until the apple is soft, the caramel is lightly browned and any excess liquid has evaporated. Roll out 350 g shortcrust pastry (see page 367) to 3 mm thick. Lay the pastry over the apples and press around the edge. Trim the edge of the pastry and then fold the edge back on itself. Bake at 180°C for 25–30 minutes, or until the pastry is golden. Remove from the oven and leave to rest for 1 minute before turning out. Serves 6.*

### COOKING

*Tarte Tatin can be made in any metal pan, but there are special tins for it, similar to a frying pan but without a handle. If you don't have one, any frying pan or crêpe pan with a heatproof handle will do. Ceramic dishes do not make good tarte Tatin dishes as the heat conduction is often not high enough to make the caramel darken.*

■ *See also* **tart**

The leaves of a number of members of the camellia family. When dried, (sometimes fermented first) and steeped in hot water, they make a drink also called tea. Tea was first cultivated by the Chinese 4,000 years ago, and known as *cha*, but since its introduction to Europe in the sixteenth century, it has become the drink that unites East and West, as popular in Birmingham as in Beijing. There is one distinction. In the West, tea is drunk with milk or lemon and often sugar. In the East, it is undiluted. Today, the major producers of tea are India, China, Sri Lanka, Kenya and Japan.

Tea is still picked by hand, with only the top two leaves and bud being used. It takes 2 kg leaves to produce 450 g black tea. Although teas are made from the same leaves from the same plant, they vary greatly in aroma, taste, flavour and colour, depending on climate, the height at which the tea is grown, soil, processing and blending methods. Tea is also used in cooking.

## COOKING

*Tea can be used to soak dried fruit prior to cooking but it must be strong or will not add much flavour.*

*Tea leaves can be used to smoke food and flavour it as it cooks. A good recipe should specify the type of tea to be used.*

*Cold brewed tea (let the leaves brew in cold water overnight) can be made into iced tea or used as a base for a delicate sorbet. Green tea is a popular ice-cream flavour in Japan.*

*Black*

*Blended*

*Brick*

*Green*

*Oolong*

*Flower*

## TYPES OF TEAS

**Black**

An aromatic, fermented tea from India, Sri Lanka, Africa and China. The leaves are wilted and bruised, then allowed to ferment and oxidize in the air before they are dried. The leaves produce an amber tea. Black teas include Sri Lankan (Ceylon), Assam and Darjeeling, as well as Pu'er and Keemun (sold as Prince of Wales blend).

**Blended**

Blends of tea usually formulated to be drunk at different times of day. Most of the tea drunk in the West is blended and blends can contain up to 35 different teas, some for colour others for flavour. English Breakfast is a strong blend designed to start the day and afternoon teas are lighter and more delicate in flavour.

**Brick**

Black or green tea, steamed and pressed into blocks for easy transportation and broken off as needed for brewing.

**Green**

An unfermented tea grown in China, Taiwan and Japan. Leaves are dried immediately after picking, thus stopping oxidization. The tea is greenish-yellow in colour, has a distinctive fragrance, a subtle flavour and is drunk without milk. Well-known Chinese green teas include Gunpowder and Long Jing (Dragon Well).

**Oolong**

A semi-fermented tea with large leaves, combining the flavours of both black and green teas, drunk without milk. Oolong teas come from China and Taiwan (Formosa Oolong). Iron Goddess is a strong-flavoured example.

**Flower**

Not strictly teas. Some flower teas may not even contain tea; others may be a mix of petals and tea. Common flowers used are rose, jasmine and chrysanthemum. Teas like Earl Grey and Lapsang Souchong have flavour added directly to the tea leaves.

### Tea manufacture

The top leaves and bud are picked by hand every 2 weeks during the picking season. To make black tea and oolong, these leaves are spread on drying racks and left to wither. The leaves are then broken down mechanically, they are either rolled to produce large leaf pieces (orthodox) or chopped into smaller pieces (unorthodox). The tea is left to oxidize or ferment (oolong for a shorter time) before being fired or dried. Green teas are not fermented but are parched or dried immediately.

*Orange pekoe*

*Dust*

*Broken orange pekoe*

### Grading tea

Indian tea is graded by passing it through a series of sieves to determine its size. Orthodox grades are termed flowery pekoe through to orange pekoe and broken orange pekoe to fannings and dust. Unorthodox teas have a similar grading system. The size of the tea bears no relation to the flavour but does bear a relation to the brewing time. Quick-brew tea bags are filled with dust, whereas longer brewing pot tea can be various sizes.

Chinese black tea is graded by name—Pouchong, Souchong and Congou are grades not types. Green teas are graded by leaf size, with pinhead the highest grade where the leaf is rolled tightly.

*Chinese tea set*

*Japanese green tea*

### MAKING TEA

*For black tea put 1 teaspoon tea or 1 tea bag per person into a warmed pot. Pour on just boiled water, which has only been boiled once, and leave to brew. Brew Indian black tea for 3–5 minutes, depending on the leaf size, brew Assam for 5 minutes, Kenyan tea for 2–3 minutes and Chinese black tea for 5–7 minutes.*

*In Japan, green tea is made with cooler water than for black tea— pour boiling water into the pot, leave it uncovered for 2 minutes, and then add the leaves to the pot.*

*In China, black and oolong teas are washed in boiling water before being brewed in small teapots; green teas are brewed in the glass they are served in. Black and oolong teas are served in small cups without milk, and green tea in glasses.*

*The debate over adding milk first or last is ongoing. Milk added first will disperse throughout the tea better but there is no real merit to either method. Good-quality tea is better drunk without milk or lemon and should be appreciated for its own flavour.*

### STORAGE

*Tea leaves should be stored in an airtight container and consumed within a few months of purchasing. As the tea ages it loses its aroma and flavour.*

■ *See also* **tisane**

### Japanese teas

Japan produces mainly green tea, which is also used in the Japanese tea ceremony, an elaboration of the Chinese ceremony, which has both social and religious (Buddhist) significance. The top Japanese grade is *gyokuro*, young shoots picked in April and May; the middle grade is *sencha*; everyday tea is *bancha*. *Genmaicha* is green tea mixed with puffed brown rice; *tencha* is usually dried flat leaf green tea and this is powdered to make *matcha*, used in the tea ceremony. The powdered tea is whisked into the water to make a froth on top.

# teff

A tiny cereal grain native to northern Africa. In Ethiopia, it is a staple food and is classically ground into flour and used to prepare a spongy, slightly sour flat bread called injera *(pictured)*. Teff is now cultivated in the United States and is finding a niche in the health food market as both a nutritious flour and grain, high in iron, fibre and minerals.

# tempe

A vegetable protein food made from soya beans, which are cooked, inoculated with a starter culture of mould, then left to ferment. Unlike bean curd, the beans in tempe are still visible, giving it a nutty aroma and flavour. Tempe is eaten cooked, sautéed or deep-fried, in stews or a salad. It is sold in blocks in sealed packets, often marinated in spices. Keep sealed and refrigerated to prevent mould forming.

# tempura

A Japanese dish of Portuguese origin (dating from the sixteenth century) consisting of bite-sized pieces of vegetable or seafood, such as prawns or white fish, coated in a light batter and deep-fried until crisp and puffed. The batter is a paste made from a fine flour, water and sometimes egg. Kakiage, which is slightly different to tempura, is made with two or three ingredients, which are chopped small, mixed into the batter and fried in portions.

Tempura is served with a dipping sauce of dashi or bonito flakes, soy sauce and mirin. Both the flour and the dipping sauce are sold in Japanese food stores and large supermarkets. One of Japan's most widely recognized dishes.

See also **Japanese food**

## COOKING

*The secret of crisp tempura is to have the food and batter as cold as possible prior to cooking and to keep the oil maintained at 180°C. The batter is made with ice-cold water and only just whisked enough to incorporate flavours. The lumps are not beaten out.*

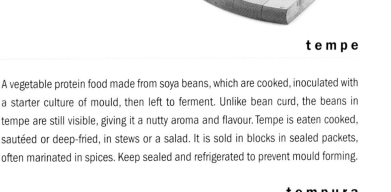

## PRAWN TEMPURA

*Combine 100 g tempura flour with 160 ml ice-cold water. Heat a large deep-fryer with vegetable oil to 180°C. Peel and devein 12 large raw prawns, leaving the tails intact. Dip 3–4 prawns into the batter and cook in batches until crisp and golden. Drain on paper towels. To make a dipping sauce for the tempura, put 250 ml water, 50 ml each mirin and soy sauce and 10 g bonito flakes in a saucepan. Bring to the boil, then strain and cool. Serve with a small pile of grated daikon (squeeze it dry after grating) and pickled ginger. Serves 4.*

## teppanyaki

A Japanese restaurant dish of meat or vegetables grilled on a griddle called a *teppan*. Patrons select their own cuts of meat, usually steak, but also chicken, pork, seafood or vegetables, and watch as the chef cooks the food on the *teppan*, which is set into the middle of the dining table. The food is served as soon as it is cooked. Restaurants specializing in teppanyaki are also popular outside of Japan, where it is not unusual for the chef to put on an entertaining display of juggling knives and spatulas as he cooks.

## teriyaki

A Japanese method of cooking that involves basting food with a mixture of soy sauce and mirin as it grills. The word comes from teri, meaning 'shine' or 'gloss', and yaki, to 'grill'. The dish is made with pieces of meat, poultry or fish, which are marinated, then cooked under a grill or pan-fried. Teriyaki is also the name of the sauce used as both a marinade and dipping sauce and can be bought ready-made.

### TUNA TERIYAKI

*Mix 125 ml soy sauce, 75 ml mirin, 75 ml sake and 1 teaspoon sugar with 1 tablespoon grated ginger. Marinate 8 pieces of tuna for at least 1 hour in this mixture. Drain the tuna and grill on both sides, basting with the marinade. Remove the tuna. Boil up the remaining marinade until shiny and thick, strain, then pour some on the tuna and some on the side. Serves 4.*

## terrine

Either coarsely chopped or finely processed meat, poultry, game, fish and/or vegetables, cooked in a deep, straight-sided container (also called a terrine). This is lined with thinly sliced pork fat or bacon to keep the mixture moist, covered with a tight-fitting lid and baked in the oven, often in a bain-marie. Fat is essential to the texture of a terrine and enables it to be sliced without it crumbling. Terrines are cooled, pressed to make them more solid, then unmoulded and served in slices, usually as a first course.

A creamy pasta dish named after a famous nineteenth century Italian Opera singer, Luisa Tetrazzini. It was originally made in her honour in San Francisco, where it is best known. It consists of strips of chicken or turkey cooked in a casserole or baking dish with a velouté sauce and spaghetti.

■ *See also* **velouté sauce**

### CHICKEN TETRAZZINI

*Cook 155 g spaghetti, then put it in a buttered casserole or baking dish. Combine 2 cooked and diced chicken breasts with 625 g hot velouté sauce (see page 438) and 60 ml dry sherry. Pour over the hot spaghetti. Mix together 15 g buttered breadcrumbs and 25 g grated Parmesan, then scatter over the top. Grill the top until lightly browned. Serves 4.*

# Tex-Mex

A hybrid of Mexican cuisine, which arose in the southwestern region of southern America, particularly Texas, Arizona and New Mexico. From the middle of the sixteenth century, the conquering Spanish explorers, wealthy settlers and missionaries imported their favourite foods from Mexico. Later, indigenous people from all over Mexico also brought their own styles of cooking and regional dishes. All these cuisines, ingredients and cooking styles were gradually melded together to give rise to a new hybrid style of cooking. Many dishes were born out of the necessity of invention—if corn husks were not available to make tamales, then a tamale mixture was simply baked as a pie instead. American-style cheese was used instead of *queso fresco*, and spicy tomato sauces were used somewhat indiscriminately with every dish rather than the varied fresh salsas. Dishes traditional to the South were also subjected to Mexicanization; beef stew became dishes such as chilli con carne with the addition of beans, spices and chillies. Chillies became a common seasoning and the use of salsas became widespread.

*Chilli con carne served with sour cream, cheese and flour tortillas.*

*Tacos*

The term Tex-Mex came into general use in the 1940s and the cuisine has spread in popularity throughout America and overseas. Most of what passes for Mexican food overseas is, in reality, Tex-Mex. Chillies form the base of many dishes. Tex-Mex also includes corn breads, enchilladas, tacos, tamales, nachos and tortillas.

■ *See also* **Mexican food, tortilla**

*Chicken enchilladas*

# Thai food

A Southeast Asian country bordered to the north by Myanmar; to the east by Laos and Cambodia, and to the south by Malaysia. Thailand is unique out of the nations in the area for never having been colonized by a European country.

Important influences in Thai cuisine include the traditional country and city cooking styles; the monarchy, which encouraged a strong tradition of court food; the funeral books of wealthy Thai women, in which were recorded all the feasts they had planned and executed; visiting European traders such as the Portuguese, who introduced chilli and other New World vegetables, as well as pastry-making, and finally, neighbouring countries, such as China, Myanmar, Cambodia and Malaysia.

## FLAVOURS

This attractive cuisine is characterized by four flavour elements: hot, sour, sweet and salty. Major ingredients include fresh coriander, galangal (Siamese ginger), kaffir (makrut) lime leaves, lemon grass and fish sauce, palm sugar, Thai basil and chillies.

Thai food combines rapidly cooked fresh ingredients with abundant use of herbs and spices—the pungent taste of lemon grass, the creamy richness of coconut milk and the occasional fiery kick of chillies all contribute to the overall flavour. Unlike Western food, a wide variety of flavours in one mouthful is desirable.

Fish sauce (nam pla) is an important ingredient in sauces, dips and main dishes. Toasted peanuts and dried shrimp are favourite toppings. Nam prik, a hot sauce, is widely used to flavour rice or as a dip.

## THE THAI TABLE

A traditional Thai meal will usually consist of one savoury dish per person plus rice; the more people at the table, the more dishes—there must be a balance of taste and texture between all

these. There will usually be at least a soup, curry, a stir-fry or vegetable dish and a salad.

Rice is immensely important to the Thai people, as a crop and a staple. A proper meal is inconceivable without it. Rice is also used to make a wide variety of noodles, like *kwai teow*, fresh flat noodles. *Mee* are wheat noodles. *Pad Thai* is considered to be the national dish and is a substantial one-pot meal with a mix of crunchy peanuts, bean sprouts and soft noodles.

Thai curries, called *gaeng*, are generally thinner than Indian curries and often contain coconut milk. However, southern Thailand is noted for its thicker, creamier curries, like *gaeng Massaman* (a Muslim beef curry). These are influenced by Malaysian cooking just across the border. Pastes form their base and the most common curries are red (*gaeng ped*) and green (*gaeng gwiow wan*), based on red and green chillies. Other curries are jungle curry (*gaeng ba gai*), which does not contain coconut milk, and yellow curry (*gaeng leuang*), a very hot curry from the South.

*Yam* dishes are similar to salads but can include cooked vegetables. Often they are strongly flavoured, with acid and hot chilli being balanced by sweetness and saltiness. There are wet and dry *yams* and hot and sour soups are called *tom yam*. Larb dishes are part stir-fry, part salad and are composed of chopped meat mixed with onions, fresh mint, coriander and basil.

A Thai meal is usually finished with a plate of fresh, seasonal fruit like mango or pineapple. Desserts, such as *gluay buat chii* (banana stewed in coconut meal) or *kanom nam tan* (sticky pudding) are eaten between meals, a sort of a sweet sustenance.

*From top: prawn tom yam soup, chicken green curry, pad Thai, sticky rice and mango.*

# Thousand Island dressing

A pink mayonnaise-based salad dressing consisting of mayonnaise with chilli sauce and finely chopped ingredients such as tomatoes, chillies, hard-boiled eggs, green peppers, green olives and onions. The name is thought to have come from the Thousand Islands region on the Saint Lawrence River, between the United States and Canada. Today, the dressing is widely available commercially and is smooth in texture.

## tiffin

Lunch or a light meal, usually eaten in the middle of the day or the afternoon. Tiffin was invented by the British in India in the nineteenth century. They had previously eaten a heavy lunch, but in the Indian climate changed to eating a light lunch and a main meal in the evening. The idea was adopted by the Indian people, and dishes now served for tiffin include curries, rice, bread and dhal. Tiffin boxes are stackable enamel, tin or aluminium boxes that are packed at home, then delivered to city office workers and school children.

## timbale

### VEGETABLE TIMBALES

*Steam 350 g carrots until soft. Steam 350 g watercress until wilted, then squeeze out any liquid. Purée each vegetable, adding 80 ml cream and 3 egg yolks to each; season. Divide the carrot purée among 4 greased timbale moulds. Spoon the watercress purée on top. Put in a bain-marie and bake at 160°C for 1¼ hours. Turn out to serve. Serves 4.*

A word meaning 'kettledrum', which describes the shape of the mould in which mainly savoury but sometimes sweet fillings are baked. These are often encased in pastry or pasta. Timbales can be served as a starter, as an accompaniment or as a dessert, if sweet. They may be made of finely minced meat, fish, vegetables or fruits. The mixture is baked, then unmoulded.

## timballo

Similar to the timbale but more robust, a timballo is a dish based on rice or pasta, which is cooked in a mould or shaped into a pie. The filling usually includes cooked pasta shapes combined with minced meats, chicken livers or a vegetable and cheese mixture bound together with a Bolognese or tomato sauce. A timpana is a baked moulded pie, lined and covered with puff pastry.

## tiramisu

Italian for 'pick me up', tiramisu is a rich dessert, originally from Venice, but now popular worldwide. Tiramisu is made with sponge fingers soaked in coffee and an alcohol such as Marsala and layered with mascarpone.

*Also known as — tirami su*

### TIRAMISU

*Beat together 500 g mascarpone, 2 egg yolks, 2 tablespoons coffee liqueur and 100 g icing sugar. Fold through 2 beaten egg whites. In a large rectangular dish, combine 375 ml very strong black coffee and 2 tablespoons coffee liqueur or rum. Briefly dip 20 sponge fingers in the mixture, then layer the fingers and mascarpone mixture into the dish, finishing with the mascarpone. Sprinkle with grated dark chocolate. Serves 6.*

## tisane

A herbal infusion drunk as a refreshment or for its medicinal and rejuvenating qualities. Tisanes are made by steeping herbs such as camomile, lemon balm, hyssop, tansy and mint in boiling water.

*Also known as — herbal tea*

■ *See also  tea*

## toad in the hole

A British dish of cooked sausages encased in a batter and baked until the batter is puffed and golden. The batter is similar to a Yorkshire pudding mixture. The original version dates back to the eighteenth century when various cuts of meat were used, such as steak and kidney, leftover cooked meats or even good-quality cuts of beef.

## toffee

A hard, chewy or brittle sweet made by boiling sugar, butter and water (or cream) to 113–130°C until the mixture thickens and will set hard. Nuts, cream, treacle and chocolate can also be added. In America, toffee is softer and called taffy.

*Also known as — stickjaw, taffee, taffy, toughie, tuffy*

## tofu — see bean curd

## tomatillo

A relative of the tomato that is used as a vegetable, either raw or cooked. The fruit may be green, yellow or purple. Used in Mexican cuisine in salsa verde and is essential in a proper guacamole. Like physalis, it has a papery calyx.

*Also known as — Mexican husk tomato, tomate verde*

Although botanically a fruit, the tomato, another gift of inestimable value to the world's cuisines—especially Italian—from South America, is used mainly as a vegetable. So thoroughly has the tomato been assimilated that it's difficult to imagine life in the Western world (no tomato sauce or pizza!) before it arrived in Naples in the sixteenth century. First, it was thought of as a medicinal plant, and it took a generation before it began to appear on the table. Today, tomatoes are grown worldwide, America and Italy being the largest producers for canning, sauces, pastes and purées. There are over 1,000 varieties, in numerous sizes, shapes and colours. Most varieties are red, although others are yellow or pink. Unripe green tomatoes are used in pickles and chutneys.

The best flavoured are those that are vine-ripened. For immediate use, tomatoes should be firm and bright coloured, with no wrinkles and a strong tomato smell. Buy only in small quantities (unless making sauce), or buy some greener than others. For salads and pasta sauces, buy only the reddest, ripest tomatoes. Remember—uniformity of shape or colour has no relation to flavour, only to marketing.

**Tomatoes go with — aubergine, basil, cheese, olive oil, onion, salt**

## COOKING

*Concassée are peeled, seeded and chopped tomatoes. Cut a cross in the base of the tomato, dip briefly in boiling water, refresh in cold water and slip off the skin. Cut in half, squeeze out the seeds with your hand or scoop out with a spoon; dice.*

## STORAGE

*Pale red tomatoes can be left to ripen naturally on your kitchen windowsill. Tomatoes will not ripen if left in the fridge.*

## TOMATO SALAD

*Slice 6 large ripe tomatoes. Arrange the tomatoes on a plate and scatter over 1 finely chopped shallot and 2 tablespoons chopped chives. Drizzle with extra virgin olive oil and top with torn basil leaves. If your tomatoes are not highly flavoured, add a few drops of balsamic vinegar to the olive oil. Serves 4.*

## TYPES OF TOMATOES

*Cherry*

Come in various sizes but essentially are a tiny variety of tomato. Some are red, others are yellow and some are pear-shaped and yellow. Good for salads or use whole or halved in stews and pasta sauces.

*Plum (egg, Roma)*

Commercially used for canning and drying. They have few seeds and a dry flesh, which makes them ideal in sauces and purées. A good variety is San Marzano.

*Beef steak*

These are larger tomatoes, either smooth and rounded or more irregular and ridged. Can be used for stuffing or in salads. Marmande are a good variety.

*Round*

The most common tomato, commercially bred to be round and red. Can be bought vine-ripened or on the vine or in different varieties like the striped tigerella, yellow or orange coloured. An all-purpose tomato.

*Cherry*

*Plum*

*Beef steak*

*Round*

■ *See also* **sun-dried tomatoes**

## tongue

Calf, sheep and ox tongue can be bought fresh or salted and smoked, though in most countries, ox tongue is most commonly eaten. Tongue needs to be cooked for a long time in order to make it tender—poaching or braising are the best methods. If salted, soak the tongue overnight in several changes of water before cooking it. Remove the thick skin after cooking. Cooked tongue is popular in several different countries: in Britain it tends to be pressed and eaten cold *(pictured)*, either with salads or as a sandwich filling; and in France and Italy it is preferred hot, either served with a piquant sauce or as part of a dish such as bollito misto. Fish, bird and game tongues are also eaten, often as a delicacy.

■ *See also* **offal**

## tortilla

In Mexico, a thin unleavened bread made from maize flour *(masa harina)* or wheat flour, shaped by hand or in a tortilla press and cooked on a griddle. Tortillas can be eaten plain or wrapped around fillings. They form the base for burritos, enchiladas, quesadillas and are deep-fried and folded in half to make Tex-Mex taco shells. Pieces of tortilla are fried to make tostaditas. They are a staple bread and are also used to eat off. In Spain, a thick omelette of potatoes, onion and often garlic, sometimes called a Spanish omelette, is also known as a tortilla.

### TORTILLAS

*Shred 2 cooked chicken breasts. Fry 1 chopped onion and add 2 chopped jalapeño chillies and 2 chopped tomatoes. Add chicken and cook for 5 minutes. Lightly fry 4 tortillas on each side; spread with 3 tablespoons re-fried beans, divide chicken among them and top with 1 tablespoon each of grated cheese and ready-made salsa. Wrap up the tortillas and serve. Serves 4.*

■ *See also* **Mexican food**

## treacle

The liquid collected at the end of the cane sugar refining process. Black treacle is the darkest and has a burnt, almost bitter taste. Light treacle (golden syrup), is the lightest and is sweet. In America, treacle is known as molasses, the darkest being blackstrap molasses; the lightest, light molasses. Treacle is used in baking: dark treacle adds flavour and colour; golden syrup is milder. Treacle puddings and tarts use golden syrup and a little dark treacle to get a balance of sweetness and flavour.

■ *See also* **sugar**

A cold British dessert made with sponge soaked with sherry, liqueur or fruit juice and layered with various combinations of fruit, custard and whipped cream. Though jelly is often added, it is not an original ingredient. The trifle started life as a simple cream concoction and didn't arrive at its present form until the eighteenth century. The word comes from *trufle*, an old French word meaning something of little importance. It is traditionally made in a cut glass dish or individual glass dishes and elaborately decorated.

### SHERRY TRIFLE

*Put 6 slices sponge cake in base of a dish; sprinkle with sherry. Lightly toast 100 g slivered almonds. Scatter over half the almonds, then some fresh raspberries. Pour over 500 ml cold egg custard. Beat 150 ml cream with 15 g sugar and spread over the custard. Stick remaining almonds into the cream and decorate with strawberries. Chill for 30 minutes. Serves 6.*

Generally the stomach of ruminants (cud-chewing animals) such as cows, sheep or ox, though pig's tripe is also eaten. Tripe is usually sold dressed (cleaned, partially cooked and white). There are four types, each with a distinctive texture. Blanket tripe is from the first stomach and is covered in villi; honeycomb tripe *(pictured)* is from the next stomach and has the texture of honeycomb; leaf or book tripe is covered in folds or leaves; and abomasum tripe, the least used, is covered in ridges.

Tripe can be boiled, braised or—not so usually—grilled. Though not eaten widely in the Anglo-Saxon countries, there are many good tripe recipes from southern Europe, the Middle East and Asia. In Turkey, tripe soup is an institution; tripe features in the French recipe, *tripes à la mode de Caen*; in Italy, there is *trippa all fiorentina;* and in the north of England, tripe and onions. It is used extensively in charcuterie to make sausages such as andouille and andouillettes.

**■ *See also* offal**

The fruiting body of a family of fungi that grow underground in a symbiotic relationship with the roots of certain trees. The best-known truffles are the prized and expensive black Périgord truffles of western France and the white truffles of Alba in northern Italy. Although truffles grow all around the world, only a few have the intensity of flavour that is prized for the table.

Truffles have long been synonymous with luxury, and are the most valuable of all fungi due to their increasing rarity, the labour-intensive methods of harvest (dogs and pigs are trained to sniff them out), and their exquisite aroma and flavour. A mere sliver of truffle is capable of impregnating foods with its heady, earthy aroma and flavour. Treat them simply. For example, store a truffle with your eggs for a few days, then make an earthy-scented omelette; do the same with rice prior to making a risotto; add shavings to a hot potato salad; or simply shave and spread on toasted sourdough sprinkled with olive oil. Fresh truffles are available seasonally. Use them within 1 week, or wrap in foil and freeze—use from the freezer without thawing. Truffles are also sold preserved or are used to flavour oil.

# truffle (chocolate)

A roughly shaped ball of rich chocolate paste smothered in a coating of cocoa powder is called a truffle. The paste is a ganache made from melted chocolate and butter or cream, sometimes flavoured with coffee, liqueurs or nuts. Truffles can also be coated in melted white or dark chocolate, nuts or chocolate shavings. They are named after the fungus, presumably because of the similarity in their appearances.

■ *See also* **ganache**

# tsatsiki

A simple, refreshing salad made from yoghurt, grated or chopped cucumber and garlic, popular in Greece and the Mediterranean. The Greek version has added mint and the Turkish version, called cacik, includes chopped dill. Tsatsiki is usually served as a dip with pitta bread, as part of a meze, or with fried fish and vegetables such as aubergine and courgettes.

*Also known as — cacik, tzatziki*

### TSATSIKI

*Peel and seed 1 Lebanese cucumber, then grate, lightly salt and put in a strainer to drain off the excess liquid. Combine with 375 g thick yoghurt, 1–2 crushed garlic cloves, 2 teaspoons lemon juice and 1 tablespoon finely chopped mint or dill. Season. Refrigerate for at least 1 hour. Serves 4.*

# tuile

A delicate, crisp, sweet biscuit, slightly curved at the edges to resemble its namesake, a (French) tile. Tuiles are characteristically made with ground almonds, but may also be flavoured with grated citrus rind or vanilla or decorated with flaked almonds. The curve is obtained by bending the warm biscuit over a rolling pin or a special tuile mould and leaving it briefly until the biscuit cools and stiffens. Tuiles can also be shaped into small cup-sized moulds to hold ice creams and sorbets by moulding them over the bottoms of glasses.

## BUYING

*Turkeys are sold in different sizes: the smaller ones weigh 2.5–3.5 kg and will feed 8–10 people; the largest weigh 9–11 kg and will feed up to 20. To calculate how big to buy allow 400 g per person.*

*Cuts of turkey include breast on the bone (sold in some countries as the buff), boned rolled breasts, turkey thighs and breasts, drumsticks and turkey meat for stir-frying.*

## COOKING

*If frozen, turkey needs to be thoroughly defrosted. This can take up to 3 days in the fridge, especially with a large bird and this must be done thoroughly. The turkey should be stuffed just before cooking it— never prepare it in advance and keep it in the fridge as the raw meat juices soak into the stuffing, which may not get sufficiently hot enough to kill off any bacteria when cooked. It is best to stuff the neck end only.*

*Turkeys benefit from basting (they need a long cooking time because of their size, which may cause their breast meat to dry out). You can do this by cooking them breast side down at the start; cover in foil or a piece of muslin soaked in butter; or add wine or stock to the roasting tin and spoon it over at intervals.*

A large flightless bird native to North America and Mexico. The centrepiece on the Thanksgiving table in America, and a popular Christmas dinner because it can feed so many people at once. In Mexico, turkeys are used to make mole and turkey meat has been used all over Europe and America since the sixteenth century. Despite its celebration food status, turkey is a good year-round alternative to chicken and other meats. It is relatively low in fat with a reasonable amount of protein and can be bought as cuts, as well as a whole bird.

Different varieties of turkey have different flavours, and some farming methods give a better flavoured meat than others. White feathered turkeys are the most common but Cambridge bronze and Norfolk black turkeys often have a better flavour as they are less intensively farmed. Turkeys can be bought fresh, frozen or as self-basting turkeys, which have had a butter or oil solution injected under their skin.

### Roasting

Roast for 20 minutes per 450 g at 170°C, then turn the oven off and let rest for 20 minutes in the oven. If your turkey is not stuffed, it will take 30 minutes longer. Make sure the turkey is thoroughly cooked—pull away a leg, if the juices run clear, the turkey is cooked.

Thanksgiving turkeys are traditionally served with mashed potato, sweet potato, succotash and cranberry sauce; Christmas turkeys with roast potatoes, Brussels sprouts and chestnuts, gravy, bread sauce, bacon rolls, chipolatas and cranberry sauce. As turkeys are relatively large birds, there is often plenty of meat left over— this can be used to make dishes in which one might normally use chicken.

see Middle Eastern food — **Turkey**

## Turkish delight

The Western name for a Turkish sweetmeat called *rahat lokum*, meaning 'rest for the throat'. The sweet is made by slowly boiling a mixture of syrup and cornflour, possibly with honey, fruit juice or mastic until gummy and gel-like. The mixture may be flavoured with mint, orange water or rose-water, or include nuts such as pistachios or almonds. The set mixture is cut into squares and rolled in icing sugar.

*Also known as — loucoum, loukoumia, rahat lokum*

# turnip

A relative of the cabbage, grown both for its root and the green tops, used as a spring vegetable. The turnip is one of the earliest cultivated European vegetables. They spread across the globe very early on, and appear in the cuisine of many countries: in Chinese and Japanese recipes, and as pickles in Korean and Middle Eastern cooking. In France they are eaten mostly when young. There are many varieties, long or rounded, white, tinged with green or purple, but all have white flesh.

Although turnips are usually relegated to ingredient status in soups and stews, they make excellent eating on their own. When young, grate them raw into salads; braise them; or make Chinese-style turnip cake. Older turnips can be roasted, which gives them a sweeter flavour. Turnip tops (greens) are boiled as for cabbage and served with butter. Turnips are also available salted and sun-dried in Asian shops. Store unwashed and refrigerated in a perforated plastic bag for up to 2 weeks.

***Turnips go with — baked ham, duck, garlic, honey, roast meat, sausages***

■ *See also* **navet**

### GLAZED TURNIPS

*Peel 4 turnips and cut them into quarters or trim 16 baby turnips. Boil for 8–10 minutes until tender but still firm, then drain well. Heat 2 tablespoons butter in a frying pan; add turnips, sprinkle on 1 tablespoon sugar and fry until turnips are golden and caramelized (be careful the sugar does not burn). Serve with roast meats or baked ham. Serves 4.*

# turnover

A circle or square of dough topped with a filling, then folded in half. The classic sweet fillings include apple *(pictured)*, jam or other fruit; savoury fillings can be mince meat or chicken. They are then baked or deep-fried and served as a snack, or the sweet ones for tea. Large savoury ones can be used for main meals. Very similar to the Cornish pasty.

# TVP

Stands for textured vegetable protein, a manufactured plant protein. The protein is extracted from vegetables, usually soya beans, which are made into a paste, then coloured and shaped to produce a product that has a similar texture to meat. TVP was originally marketed as a high-protein food for vegetarians but is increasingly used as an extender in processed foods such as sausages. TVP is sold in dried granules, which, when reconstituted, look and can be used like minced meat, or formed into a solid mass and shaped into 'steaks', or cubed and sold in tins or packets. TVP may be sold mixed with added flavourings to give it a meat-like flavour.

***Also known as — textured vegetable protein***

■ *See also* **seitan**

*From top: TVP 'mince', TVP 'chicken', rehydrated TVP 'mince'.*

# u-v

A native Jamaican member of the tangelo group of citrus fruit, whose parentage is the mandarin and the grapefruit. At home, its name is more kindly pronounced 'oo-gli'. It resembles a misshapen grapefruit with thick, baggy skin, which contains a fragrant, juicy and acid-sweet flesh. Treat as a grapefruit or orange—peel and eat in segments or use in compotes, sorbets *(pictured)* or ice creams.

## umeboshi

A small tart apricot, salted and dried by the Japanese as umeboshi, a name meaning 'dried ume', often erroneously called a Japanese plum. The ume was originally brought to ancient Japan from China. Samurai ate them to fight off battle fatigue and it was believed that they had medicinal, cleansing and curative powers.

Ume are picked before they ripen and soaked in brine and red shiso leaves until shrivelled and wrinkled. It is the shiso leaves that give the ume their characteristic deep-red hue. Umeboshi are used extensively in Japanese cuisine as a condiment, often served with rice or to make *bainiku*, a tart purée used in some sauces. Ume are also macerated in alcohol with rock sugar to make a liqueur, *umeshu*.

■ *See also* **Asian vegetables (shiso)**

## upside-down cake

A cake baked with a decorative pattern of caramelized fruit on the base, which becomes the top when turned out. The fruit may be fresh, such as bananas, or canned, usually pineapples with glacé cherries. Peaches, pears or dried fruits may also be used. Usually eaten as a pudding.

### PINEAPPLE UPSIDE-DOWN CAKE

*Pour 30 g melted butter over the base of a 20 cm baking tin and sprinkle with 2 tablespoons brown sugar. Arrange 440 g tin drained pineapple slices over base and decorate with glacé cherries. Beat 125 g butter and 225 g caster sugar until thick and creamy. Beat in 2 eggs, then add 280 g self-raising flour, 185 ml milk and 1 teaspoon vanilla extract. Beat on low speed until smooth, then pour over the base. Bake at 175 °C for 60 minutes. Leave in tin for 10 minutes, then turn out. Serve warm with custard. Serves 8.*

# vacherin

Vacherin is a speciality of Alsace, and is a cold dessert or cake consisting of several crisp meringue discs, layered with glacé or fresh fruit, whipped cream or ice cream. It is often highly decorated with piped whipped cream and crystallized flowers. Some vacherins are made from a solid base of meringue, which is then stacked with meringue rings and filled in the middle. The name of this dessert comes from a Swiss cheese of the same name, which it is thought to resemble.

# vanilla

## VANILLA ICE CREAM

*Beat 6 egg yolks with 110 g caster sugar. Heat 300 ml milk and 300 ml cream with a split vanilla pod until just boiling. Pour onto eggs and mix, then pour into pan and heat, stirring gently, without boiling, until thickened. Cool and remove pod. Churn in an ice-cream maker or pour into a freezerproof container and freeze. Stir hourly to break up any ice crystals (do this 3 or 4 times, or until smooth and thick), then freeze overnight. Serves 4.*

True vanilla comes from the pod of a climbing orchid vine native to Central America. The pods are picked when green, at which stage they have no flavour, then left to sweat and dry in the sun, causing them to shrivel, turn deep brown and acquire a light coating of small, white vanillin crystals. True vanilla is expensive, partly because of the labour-intensive methods of obtaining it and partly because the flowers are hand-pollinated on the one day of the year that they open.

Good-quality vanilla pods have a warm, caramel vanilla aroma and flavour, and should be soft, not hard and dry. Bury a pod in a jar of sugar and let the flavours infuse the sugar, or infuse the whole pod in hot milk and use for custards and ice cream. For extra flavour, use the tip of a knife to slice down the pod to allow some of the tiny, potently flavoured seeds to escape. Vanilla is sold as pods or distilled into pure vanilla extract (or essence). In both these forms, vanilla is quite expensive. Synthetic or imitation vanilla flavouring is now available and this must be labelled as such. It is cheaper and the flavour is inferior.

**Also known as — vanilla bean**

*Good-quality vanilla extract*

## STORAGE

*After use, wash the vanilla pod, dry it thoroughly and store wrapped in plastic in a cool, dry place. The pod can be used up to 4 times before it loses its flavour.*

**variety meats** — s'ee offal

The meat from unweaned or recently weaned male calves. The delicately flavoured flesh is finely grained, light pink to white with little marbling and fat. Traditionally veal is an expensive meat and the idea of killing an animal when it had not reached its full meat-producing potential is a luxury not available to many. Veal is used extensively in European cuisines, often as part of a dish along with other ingredients, in *blanquette de veau* or veal *paupiettes* (pieces of veal wrapped around a filling) for example. Veal is usually sold as escalopes; as roasting joints like leg and loin for use in braised dishes such as osso buco; and as chops. Common accompaniments include prosciutto or bacon and cheeses, which are melted on the meat, or sauces made with fortified wines such as Marsala and Madeira. Veal bones make very gelatinous stock.

**Veal goes with — anchovies, capers, lemon, sage, sour cream, spinach, tomato**

## WHITE OR PINK VEAL?

*Although white meat has always been highly prized by chefs, there is a moral issue that affects the consumer. Calves on a milk diet, and that have their movement restricted (a practice outlawed in many countries) have firm white flesh. Slightly older animals, sometimes grain or grass fed and reared in a more open environment, have pink meat. Let your conscience be your guide.*

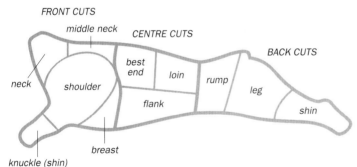

FRONT CUTS
middle neck
CENTRE CUTS
BACK CUTS
best end
loin
rump
neck
shoulder
leg
flank
shin
breast
knuckle (shin)

## CUTS OF VEAL

**Escalopes** — Also known as schnitzel, scaloppine and collop, a thin piece usually cut from the loin, leg or best end. Usually pan-fried, crumbed or stuffed and rolled.

**Leg and shin** — Used for roasting, either stuffed or on the bone. Veal shin (osso buco) is sliced and used for stews like osso buco.

**Shoulder** — Used for roasting and stuffing or diced.

**Loin** — Used as a loin roast, cut into chops or sold as a piece of fillet. Slices of fillet are medallions.

**Breast** — The belly of the calf, which is usually rolled and slow cooked or roasted.

**Best end** — The ribs, sold as individual rib chops or may be joined as one piece. With the bones removed used for escalopes.

## COOKING

*To prepare an escalope, cut the meat from a piece of leg, best end or loin into thin slices across the grain of the meat. Lay a slice flat on a chopping board, bring a mallet down flat on the meat, then in one continuous motion, slide the mallet from the centre outwards. Repeat several times. Use the mallet to evenly stretch and thin out the meat rather than pounding it.*

*Because of the lack of fat and marbling, veal should be cooked quickly, usually pan-fried with butter or olive oil, or slow cooked with liquid to prevent it from drying out.*

*Joints of veal may need to be larded or barded (see page 138) to help moisten the meat as it cooks.*

**See also  osso buco, saltimbocca**

## velouté sauce

One of the basic French white sauces, made with a butter and flour roux that is cooked until pale (blonde), then blended with a white stock, either veal, chicken or fish. The mixture is slow cooked until velvety in texture and sometimes further enriched with a liaison of egg yolks and cream. Velouté may also have other added flavourings such as saffron, tomato and fish stock. Some soups are also called veloutés.

■ *See also* **sauce, soup**

### VELOUTE SAUCE

*Melt 60 g butter in a saucepan. Blend in 60 g plain flour, cook and stir the roux over low heat until light blonde in colour. Remove from heat, then stir in 750 ml white stock, stirring until smooth. Return to the heat and stir until thickened. Simmer the sauce gently for 10 minutes, or until smooth and velvety. Season well. Makes 600 ml.*

## venison

The lean, dark-red and finely grained meat of any species of the European and American deer family. Young roe and red deer are considered the best flavoured, but this group also includes elk, reindeer, caribou, moose and antelope. Deer are considered wild, but today are usually farm bred. Hunting wild deer is now subject to regulations, mainly to control populations.

In cooking, the tenderloin from the saddle is cut into steaks and pan-fried. The haunch is usually roasted but can become tough and dry on overcooking, therefore it is larded or barded (see page 138) or cooked until slightly underdone. Venison may also be stewed, braised, made into salami, pâté and sausages. The meat may be marinated, though young venison is best not marinated as it loses its gamey flavour. Remove any fat before cooking. Venison is sold fresh, vacuum-packed or frozen.

*Venison goes with — black pepper, juniper berries, redcurrant jelly*

## verjuice

The unfermented juice of unripe grapes or crab apples. It was used extensively in medieval cooking and has had a revival in recent times as a light, delicate souring acid in place of vinegar and lemon juice in condiments and sauces, as well as being used to add a little sourness to meat dishes and for deglazing. Verjuice, which means 'green juice', is used in place of vinegar in the manufacture of Dijon mustard and in Iranian and Lebanese food. Verjuice is sold in bottles from some supermarkets and speciality food stores.

*Also known as — verjus*

Any number of green (*verte*) sauces, such as a mayonnaise or white sauce flavoured with fresh herbs, or made with the juice of blanched and puréed green vegetables or herbs such as parsley, watercress, chervil, tarragon or spinach. Traditionally served with fish or potato dishes.

***Also known as — sauce verte***

## Vichy carrots

Glossy, glazed carrots originally cooked in Vichy mineral water with sugar and butter. The dish is so called not only because the Bourbonnais area is famous for its spring waters, but also for its root vegetables.

***Also known as — carottes Vichy, carrots à la Vichy***

### VICHY CARROTS

*Peel 800 g young carrots and cut into thin rounds. Put in a shallow pan, just cover with water and add ½ teaspoon each salt and sugar and a knob of butter. Cover and cook over low heat until carrots are nearly tender, then remove the lid and boil until any remaining liquid evaporates. Serve sprinkled with finely chopped parsley and small knobs of butter. Serves 4.*

## vichyssoise

### VICHYSSOISE

*Melt 50 g butter and add 1 finely chopped onion, 3 sliced leeks and 1 finely chopped celery stalk. Cook over low heat until vegetables are very soft but not browned. Add 200 g diced potatoes and 750 ml chicken stock; bring to the boil. Simmer, covered, for 20 minutes, then purée in a blender. Stir in 220 ml cream; chill. Season and garnish with chives. Serves 6.*

A rich potato and leek soup thickened with cream and served chilled, created in New York in the 1920s by a French chef, Louis Diat, and named, nostalgically, after his birthplace, near Vichy. Vichyssoise is made by sautéeing mainly sliced leeks and diced potatoes in butter, which are then simmered in stock and sometimes wine. The cooked vegetables are puréed and chilled and served with added cream and chives to garnish. Vichyssoise can also be served hot.

## Victoria sandwich

A plain cake, named for the Queen who was fond of it, made by the creaming method, baked in two shallow tins, filled with jam and cream and dusted with icing sugar. Although not a true sponge—it contains a raising agent—it is sometimes called a Victoria sponge.

***Also known as — Victoria sandwich cake***

# Vietnamese food

A small Southeast Asian nation bordered to the north by China, to the west by Laos, and Cambodia to the south, Vietnam has survived colonization and the ravages of war culturally intact, and is culinarily diverse.

The fertile Red River delta to the north, and the Mekong River delta in the south, produce lush, fertile land, ideal for rice growing. Politically, Vietnam has been dominated by many cultures, principally China, who colonized it for 1,000 years. The Vietnamese adopted many Chinese practices and foods: chopsticks (the only nation in the region to use them), the wok, bean curd, noodles and some spices such as star anise. In the sixteenth century, Portuguese traders introduced foods such as potatoes and chillies from the New World, and the south of Vietnam uses spices from India introduced by traders over the years. French control lasted from 1858 for nearly 100 years, and the French influence is evident in many Vietnamese dishes and cooking methods, particularly in the south. Being served French bread with a curry is quite normal and French-influenced pastries such as brioche-like sweet breads are baked in the patisseries prevalent in many cities. It was fortuitous that the delicacy and subtlety of French cuisine matched so well with the indigenous diet.

*Rice paper rolls with prawns*

*Charcoal-grilled fish*

On the whole, Vietnamese flavours are light and delicate and fresh leaves, herbs, vegetables and roots are eaten in large quantities. *Nuoc nam (mam)*, a strong-smelling fermented fish sauce made from small fish, is ubiquitous in Vietnamese cooking. Other popular seasonings include shrimp paste, chillies, garlic, shallots, lemon grass, tamarind, lime juice, turmeric, ginger and galangal.

Fish and shellfish form a large part of the diet. Important catches include mackerel, tuna and sardines. Fresh squid is served with ginger and garlic. A popular dipping sauce, *nuoc cham*, is made by combining fish sauce with chilli, garlic, lime and sugar. Shrimps are made into shrimp paste, which can be both fresh and bottled. A particularly common snack is *chao tom*, shrimp paste wrapped around grilled sugar cane. Snacks like this are either made at home or bought from the multitude of street vendors. Noodle dishes, especially pho, are eaten throughout the day, but are a breakfast favourite. Noodles are often served in soups, based on the French consommé and include *pho bo*, made by pouring broth over noodles and strips of raw beef. Condiments such as bean sprouts, chillies, mint and coriander are added to taste.

*Sugar cane prawns—chao tom.*

A common practice dating from earliest times is to wrap food such as spring rolls, satay and pieces of meat and fish in a lettuce leaf with fresh herbs, and then dunk them into a spicy dipping sauce. Tea is the usual liquid taken with a meal.

*Vietnamese soup—pho bo.*

■ **See also** **pho**

A mixture of vinegar and oil, usually one part vinegar to three parts oil, which is whisked or mixed to form an unstable emulsion (it will separate when left to stand). Any oil and vinegar combination may be used as long as the flavours go well together. It may also be flavoured with mustard, garlic, herbs, spices or shallots. Vinaigrette is used to dress green salads and cold vegetable, meat and seafood dishes.

**Also known as — French dressing**

### COOKING

*Instead of using white wine vinegar, try balsamic (sparingly), red wine or sherry vinegars. Lemon, lime or verjuice may also replace the vinegar, but will need a pinch of sugar to temper them.*

*Extra virgin olive oil is considered the best oil to use though a good-quality vegetable or salad oil can be used in place of all or some of the olive oil.*

*Store the vinaigrette in a screw-top jar for ease—shake the jar to re-form the emulsion when you need it.*

Ingredients for making a vinaigrette.

### MAKING A VINAIGRETTE

1 Using a mortar and pestle, crush 1 small garlic clove with a little salt to form a smooth paste.

2 Add 1 tablespoon good-quality vinegar and ½ teaspoon Dijon mustard and mix well.

3 Gradually mix in 75 ml oil until a smooth emulsion is formed. Season with salt and pepper.

The large green leaves of the grape vine used in Middle Eastern and Greek cookery as food wrappers, mainly in dolmades, where they wrap a meat or rice mixture before the whole parcel is cooked in stock. They are also used to wrap small game birds or fish before braising or baking, and as garnish and decoration for cheese plates and salads. Buy fresh, or tinned in brine. Fresh leaves need blanching in hot water until soft enough to be pliable. Tinned vine leaves should be rinsed in cold water to remove the salty brine.

**Also known as — grape leaves**

# vinegar

From the French words *vin aigre*, meaning 'sour wine'. Originally the by-product of the fermentation process of wine or other alcohols, today many vinegars—balsamic for example—are purpose made. Vinegar has been used for thousands of years as a flavouring, pickling and preserving agent. Mixed with oil, it is used as a salad dressing or in marinades and in sauces as a souring agent.

### HERB-FLAVOURED VINEGAR
Wine vinegar flavoured with fresh herb sprigs such as tarragon and basil, garlic or chillies. Use in sauces, gravies and salad dressings. Tarragon vinegar is most common and is a base flavour in Béarnaise sauce.

### FRUIT-FLAVOURED VINEGARS
These include raspberry, blackcurrant, cherry and blueberry vinegar. Raspberry vinegar has a long history, and recipes that use it date back several centuries. Use these vinegars in salad dressings or with rich meats as they cut through the fat effectively.

### RICE VINEGAR
Made from fermented rice, the good-quality vinegars are aged. Rice vinegar from China varies in colour and flavour. The strongly flavoured black vinegar and a sweeter black version are used for braised dishes. Red rice vinegar is used as a condiment. Vinegar is most popular in Chinese Chiu Chow and Hakka cuisine; the milder white is used mainly in pickles. Japanese rice vinegar (*su*) comes in different strengths. Used for *sunomono* and sushi rice.

*Herb (rosemary and green peppercorns) vinegar*

*Cherry vinegar*

*Raspberry vinegar*

*Chinese rice vinegar*

*Japanese rice vinegar*

*Malt vinegar*

*Rice vinegar*

*Distilled vinegar*

*Cider vinegar*

### MALT VINEGAR
Brewed from malted barley, malt vinegar may be coloured brown with the addition of caramel and sold as brown malt vinegar, or left in its natural state and sold as light malt vinegar. Brown malt vinegar is used as a condiment, drizzled over fish and chips or for pickling. Spiced versions flavoured with pepper, allspice and chillies are also sold for pickling.

### DISTILLED VINEGAR
A clear vinegar, used for pickling, especially for white foods such as onions. Made from distilled malt vinegar or other grains.

### CIDER VINEGAR
A speciality of apple-growing areas, notably Normandy and parts of northern America, cider vinegar is distilled from apples. Used for pickles and chutneys and as a vinaigrette, it has a mild flavour and goes especially well with apples and tomatoes. It can also add flavour to dishes containing cider or apples. It is said to have health-giving and medicinal properties.

## OTHER VINEGARS

These can be made with any sugar or starch that can be fermented first to produce alcohol, then a vinegar. As well as wine, cider, malt and rice, vinegars can be made from ethyl alcohol (synthetic white vinegar), coconut milk, cane sugar, molasses, millet, sorghum, dates, stone fruit, citrus, bananas and palm wine.

*Coconut vinegar*

*Chardonnay vinegar*

*Balsamic vinegar*

*Champagne vinegar*

*Sherry vinegar*

*Red wine vinegar*

## BALSAMIC VINEGAR

Authentic balsamic vinegar, *aceto balsamico tradizionale di Modena*, comes from the Italian region of Modena, and is one of the most expensive liquids on earth. It is made by the solero method, blending from old to young (but at least 12 years old) material. It is made from the must (unfermented concentrated juice) of white grapes, and aged in wooden barrels for up to 50 years. Each bottle is signed and numbered. Cheaper balsamic vinegars, called *aceto balsamico di Modena*, are available and can be very good.

## WINE VINEGARS

Made from both red and white wine and champagne. The best and most expensive wine vinegars are made by the traditional Orleans method, where the vinegar is allowed to mature slowly in oak barrels. Commercial varieties use faster processes that don't give as good a flavour. Some wine vinegars are sold by grape variety, such as Cabernet Sauvignon, Rioja or Zinfandel. Use in vinaigrettes, in sauces and mustards. The red is good in marinades and the white in mayonnaise and hollandaise sauces.

## SHERRY VINEGAR

Made from young acidic sherry, which varies in strength and flavour. The vinegar is matured in oak sherry casks. Use in vinaigrettes and for deglazing or to give a flavour boost to casseroles. Good-quality sherry vinegar can be used on its own as a flavouring.

## PRODUCTION

*Originally a by-product of the wine-making industry, in some cases it still is. Champagne, wine or sherry that in its early life is deemed not quite good enough, is transformed into vinegar instead. The Orleans method by which many good-quality wine vinegars are made involves exposing the wine to a vinegar mother and leaving it to ferment slowly. It is then matured in oak barrels for 3 to 4 months.*

*In its most basic form, vinegar can be made by leaving wine to sour. At first, a grey film appears on top of the wine's surface, this then sinks to the bottom and forms a jelly-like layer, known as a 'vinegar mother'. The vinegar mother can then be given new wine, which it will transform into a weak vinegar by fermenting it. Commercial vinegar production using a mother is, however, a much more controlled process where time and temperature are carefully monitored to achieve the right flavour.*

*In vinegar production, mothers can be several years old. The benefit of the Orleans method shows up in the natural flavour and colour of vinegar as the vinegar is never heat treated or pasteurized. If you buy a bottle of vinegar made by the Orleans method and you do not use it quickly enough, it may start to produce its own mother—this can be used to make more vinegar or simply sieved out and thrown away.*

*Many commercial vinegars are made using bacterial cultures that ferment the wine and can take as little time as 24 hours to produce distilled vinegar.*

*See also  **balsamic vinegar***

# vitamins

Naturally occurring substances essential for proper functioning of the body. Food is the best and most natural source of vitamins, although some are destroyed during cooking, processing, or if the food is not fresh or exposed to light. Vitamin tablets cannot replace food and must be taken with food in order to be effective.

## SOME COMMON VITAMINS

**Vitamin A (retinol)**  Essential for night vision and healthy skin and mucous membranes. Found in dark-green and yellow vegetables and fruit, milk, eggs and liver.

**Vitamin B1 (thiamine)**  Maintains release and use of energy from carbohydrates. Found in pork, whole-grain products, legumes and nuts.

**Vitamin B2 (riboflavin)**  Enables growth of new body tissue, healthy skin and eyes. Found in milk, liver, kidneys, cheese and eggs.

**Vitamin B3 (niacin)**  Converts food into energy and maintains healthy skin. Main food sources include poultry, meats, fish, yeast extract, grains and vegetables.

**Vitamin B6 (pyridoxine)**  Aids food metabolism and formation of antibodies. Found in meat, bananas, legumes, avocado and dairy products.

**Vitamin B12 (cyanocobalamin)**  Allows formation of red blood cells, maintains a healthy nervous system and is needed for calcium absorption. Found in animal products such as eggs, liver, meat and fish.

**Vitamin C (ascorbic acid)**  Essential for iron absorption, healthy teeth and gums. Promotes cell renewal and healing of wounds. Found in fruit and vegetables, especially citrus fruit and kiwi fruit.

**Vitamin D**  For growth of bones and teeth. Formed naturally when skin is exposed to the sun but also found in egg yolks, liver, oily fish, margarine and eggs.

**Vitamin E (tocopherol)**  Protects cell walls from oxidizing, and thus ageing. Keeps red blood cells healthy. Found in grains and soya beans, leafy green vegetables and vegetable oils.

**Vitamin K**  For normal clotting of blood. Found in dark-green leafy vegetables, cabbage and cauliflower.

**Folic acid**  Helps in the formation of DNA and red blood cells. Important for women in pregnancy. Found in leaf and root vegetables, nuts, avocado and grains.

## COOKING

*Vitamins A, D, E and K are fat soluble and these are stored in the body until needed. These vitamins are not affected by heat and therefore remain in food during cooking. Other vitamins are water soluble—they are lost in boiling water and some are sensitive to air, heat or light (such as milk, which should be stored in a dark place) so need to be replenished daily. Although cooking can destroy some vitamins, losses are not huge (about 25 per cent). Shorter cooking times, steaming vegetables instead of boiling them, and using fresh produce will help reduce losses.*

# vol-au-vent

A round pastry shell filled with cooked chicken, fish, meat or vegetables in a hot, cream-based sauce. French in origin, the term means 'flying in the wind', which refers to the lightness of the pastry (puff or flaky). Vol-au-vents can be large or small *(bonchée)* and are served as an appetizer.

# W

## wafer

An unsweetened, thin, crisp biscuit, usually round or rectangular, made by cooking batter between two flat hot iron plates etched with a pattern on them. Wafers are traditionally served with ice cream and a sweet sauce, used to make biscuits *(pictured)* or curled to make ice-cream cones.

*Also known as — wafer biscuit, gaufrette*

## waffle

A crisp cake made by cooking batter on a special-purpose waffle iron, which gives the waffle a honeycombed pattern. The batter is poured into the heated base and the hinged top seals the batter, which is cooked until crisp and golden brown. Traditionally served hot with a sweet syrup, such as maple syrup, and butter, cream or ice cream. Belgium waffles are smaller and thicker and are often served sprinkled with icing sugar or served with strawberries or strawberry jam and cream.

## Waldorf salad

Diced apple, walnuts, celery or celeriac, dressed with mayonnaise and served on a bed of lettuce. The salad was named after the Waldorf Astoria Hotel in New York where it was created in the 1890s, though the use of walnuts may be a later addition of the twentieth century.

### WALDORF SALAD

*Lightly toast 40 g walnuts under a grill for 3–4 minutes. Reserve a few halves for decoration and roughly chop the remaining walnuts. Cut 2 cored red apples into very thin wedges and toss them in 2 teaspoons lemon juice. Add 1 diced celery stalk, the walnuts and 60 ml mayonnaise. Refrigerate for at least 2 hours. Serve on a bed of lettuce leaves and garnish with walnut halves. Serves 4.*

# walnut

The nut from a number of varieties of trees that belong to the same family as pecan and hickory nuts. These varieties vary from country to country, but include the English walnut (also called Persian); the black walnut, a strongly flavoured, oily nut; and the white (butternut) walnut. Fresh (wet) green walnuts can be eaten whole as their shells are still soft at this stage, or pickled. The mature nut has a hard shell, and the nut within is separated into two halves by an inedible papery membrane.

While they are mainly used in sweet dishes, such as cakes, biscuits, muffins and breads, walnuts also complement savoury dishes such as salads, stuffings, pasta sauces, pâtés and a French walnut soup. In the Middle East, half-ripe walnuts are preserved in sugar syrup. Pickled walnuts are made from green immature nuts pickled in a spiced vinegar and are served with meat or cheese. Walnuts can also be ground into a flour or pressed to produce a richly flavoured, but expensive, oil. Store walnuts in their shells for up to 3 months in a cool, dry place. Shelled nuts should be stored sealed and refrigerated for up to 6 months or frozen for 12 months.

***Walnuts go with — apple, cream cheese, pears, Roquefort***

## WALNUT TART

*Blind bake (see page 419) a 26 cm tart tin lined with sweet shortcrust pastry (see page 367). Whisk together 4 eggs with 225 g brown sugar, 170 g golden syrup, 55 g melted butter, 1 teaspoon vanilla extract and 2 tablespoons plain flour. Roughly chop half of 450 g walnut halves, scatter over base, pour filling over base, then arrange remaining walnuts over top. Bake at 200 °C for 10 minutes, then at 170 °C for 30–40 minutes. Serves 8.*

*Pickled walnuts*

■ *See also* **nuts**

# wasabi

Though often compared to horseradish, wasabi is, in fact, an unrelated herb. In Japan, it grows wild near freshwater streams, but it is also cultivated widely. Although all of the plant is used as food, it is the green root that is grated and eaten with sushi and sashimi, when it is sometimes mixed with soy sauce. Most of the so-called wasabi— in powder or paste form—available commercially is dyed horseradish. Real wasabi is expensive, and if seeking it, ask for *hon* (real) wasabi.

***Also known as — wasabe***

The walnut-sized corm of an aquatic plant native to Southeast Asia. It has a dark-brown skin and a crisp, juicy, white, mildly sweet flesh, which is eaten raw or cooked. Bought fresh or in tins, water chestnuts add texture to Asian cooking, especially in minced meat dishes, stir-fries, wontons or in sweet dishes. They are usually cooked quickly to retain their crisp texture, for which they are prized. In China, water chestnuts are sold by street vendors threaded onto skewers, either cold in summer or warm in winter. Canned chestnuts keep in a jar covered with water for up to 1 week (change the water daily). They can also be frozen. Water chestnut powder or flour is dried chestnut used as a thickener in Asian cooking.

Not to be confused with the Chinese water chestnut is another water chestnut but from a different family. Called bull's head or *ling kok* in Chinese, this starchy nut is similar to a potato in flavour and is cooked as a vegetable or used in pickles. Also related are the water caltrope of southern Europe and the singhara nut of Kashmir.

**Also known as — Chinese water chestnut**

An aquatic plant, a type of cress, that is both cultivated and found growing in the wild. Its dark-green leaves have a peppery, slightly pungent mustardy flavour and are used in salads, added to sandwiches and used as a garnish. Watercress may also be cooked in soups and sauces, although cooking destroys its potency. Buy dark leaves with no yellowing and use quickly. To store, stand stems in a bowl of water, cover with a plastic bag and refrigerate.

**Also known as — winter rocket**

### WATERCRESS SOUP

*Melt 30 g butter in a saucepan, add 1 chopped onion, 1 chopped leek and 2 peeled, chopped potatoes. Cook over low heat for 10 minutes without browning. Add 1.2 litres chicken stock; simmer for 10 minutes. Add 200 g washed, chopped watercress; simmer for 5 minutes. Purée, return to pan, stir in 150 ml milk; season. Serve with a sprig of watercress. Serves 4.*

A large fruit, round or oblong in shape—depending on the variety—native to Africa. Watermelon is so named because of its high water content of 92 to 95 per cent. Watermelons have sweet dark pink to red flesh, which contains seeds, usually coloured black, brown or white, although seedless varieties have been cultivated. Watermelon is best served lightly chilled and cut into wedges, but it can also be made into jam, sorbets or juiced. All parts are edible: the seeds may be dried, roasted and salted or the rind may be pickled.

It is difficult to tell if a watermelon is ripe but if buying whole, tap the fruit—it should sound hollow like a drum. The area where the melon rested on the ground should be pale yellow, not white or green. Wrap cut watermelon in clingfilm and refrigerate for up to a week, or store the whole melon in a cool dark place if it is too large to fit in the fridge.

■ *See also* **melon**

## WELSH RABBIT

*Melt 225 g grated Cheddar, 30 g butter and 60 ml beer in a small saucepan over low heat. Season well with 1 tablespoon dried mustard, a dash of Worcestershire sauce, salt and pepper. Spoon over 4 slices thick buttered toast and grill until bubbling and golden brown. Serves 4.*

There are many variations of this dish, and controversy pertaining to both its name and its exact ingredients is ongoing, but it is essentially a mixture of a cheesy white sauce or grated cheese, mixed with butter, mustard or Worcestershire sauce and beer or wine. The mixture may be grilled on toast or pre-melted and poured over toast. The question 'why a rabbit?' has never been answered satisfactorily, but reminds one of the Marx Brothers' question, 'why a duck?'. The alternative name, 'Welsh rarebit' was, perhaps, invented for those confused by the inexplicable rabbit.

## wheat

A valuable food grain and the staple food of many countries. There are many varieties, the most common being *triticum aestirum* or 'bread wheat', which accounts for 90 per cent of the world's production. This is refined into flour and used in baking or as a thickener. *Triticum durum* or 'durum wheat' is used in the production of dried pasta. A grain of wheat consists of an outer coating (bran), the embryo (wheat germ), and the endosperm, the floury part. During milling, the endosperm is ground into varying-sized particles to produce flour and semolina. Wheat is also made into burghul, puffed wheat (eaten as a breakfast cereal and used in confectionery), couscous and freekeh, used widely in Arabic cookery.

*Clockwise from front left: ears of wheat, wheat grains, wheat flour, wheat flakes.*

## FREEKEH

A grain made from roasted green wheat. The grains may be left whole or coarsely cracked. Freekeh can be used instead of rice, in salads such as tabbouleh, in stuffings or the flour is used in bread.

## PARTS OF WHEAT

**Wheat gluten** – In bread-making, gluten is important for its ability to stretch and entrap gas, resulting in a light, aerated bread. The largest amounts of gluten are found in durum wheat flour and hard wheat used for bread-making. Bread-making flour is called strong flour.

**Wheat starch** – A gluten-free flour consisting mainly of starch. Used as a thickener or mixed with tapioca starch to make dumpling wrappers.

**Wheat germ** – The embryo of the wheat grain is extracted and sold toasted or raw. If raw, store in the fridge as it will go rancid due to its high oil content. Add to breads or sprinkle on breakfast cereals.

**Wheat berries** – Whole, hulled grains. Soak overnight and cook for 1 hour, then serve as you would rice. The grains were traditionally used to make a type of porridge called 'frumenty'. In Italy, it is used to make a sweet tart called 'pastiera'.

**See also** **bran, bread, burghul, couscous, flour**

The ancestor of the domesticated pig, wild boar has been hunted for hundreds, maybe thousands of years. Today it is, on the whole, no longer wild, but farmed, in enclosed woodland, although Australian wild boar is sent regularly to Europe. The dark flesh has little fat and is denser and more flavoursome than pork, with which it can be substituted in recipes. Generally wild boar is preferred young and is best at 6 to 12 months. Use the meat in casseroles, roasts, serve as steaks or buy as sausages. The meat must be thoroughly cooked and is best served with spicy accompaniments such as cranberry sauce, apples, red wine, chestnuts or prunes.

■ *See also*  **pork**

*Wild boar casserole*

## COOKING

*Wild rice absorbs up to four times its own volume in liquid, so a little rice will go a long way.*

*Like brown rice, wild rice can take 40-60 minutes to cook, depending on whether you prefer a tender or more chewy texture.*

*Soaking wild rice overnight in cold water reduces the cooking time. The rice can then be boiled for about 20 minutes.*

*If mixing wild and white rice, cook them separately and then mix them.*

The seed of an aquatic grass that grows mainly in central and northern parts of America and southern Canada, but also in parts of Africa, Southeast Asia and China. Wild rice grows in lake and river marshes and was the principal foodstuff for the North American Indians who gathered it from their canoes by hand. Unlike rice, which is 'pearled' to remove the outer coat, wild rice is brown to green in colour as it retains its seed coat. It has a rich, nutty flavour and chewy texture and because it is quite expensive, it is often extended with brown or white rice—this also gives it added texture, colour and flavour. Wild rice may be served in salads, to accompany meats and makes a particularly good stuffing, especially for chicken or turkey.

**Wild rice goes with — poultry, seafood, turkey, vegetables, wild game**

**Also known as — Indian rice**

## WILD RICE SALAD

*Put 100 g wild rice in 250 ml boiling stock and add 1 tablespoon butter. Cook, covered, over very low heat for 1 hour. Cook 100 g basmati rice; drain, then mix with the wild rice, 2 cooked, chopped bacon rashers, 125 g currants, 60 g toasted slivered almonds, 30 g chopped parsley and 6 sliced spring onions; season. Drizzle with olive oil. Serves 4.*

# wine

An alcoholic drink made by the fermentation of sugar in grapes by natural yeasts. All grapes ferment, but only grapes from the European *Vitis vinifera* ferment naturally into wine, and it is the many varieties of this grape that are cultivated worldwide. Some wines bear the characteristics of a single grape (varietals) and/ or a single year (a vintage), while others are a combination of flavours (blends).

### ITALIAN CHIANTI

Tuscany and Piedmont produce some of Italy's greatest wines, with reds such as Barolo, Barbaresco and the controversial Chianti, now made to strict regulations allowing few, or even no, grapes to be added to the Sangiovese grapes.

### FRENCH BURGUNDY

One of the world's great wine areas, Burgundy produces excellent dry white Chablis and, in limited numbers, the finest red Pinot Noirs, with the best classified as *premiers* and *grands crus*.

### PORTUGUESE VINHO VERDE

Most wines come from the temperate north, with *vinhos verdes* (green wines), making up a large percentage. Though rarely exported, most *vinhos verdes* are red wines, as the 'green' refers not to the colour, but to the wine's acid youth. They are drunk in the year after harvest.

### FRENCH BORDEAUX

Bordeaux wines were classified in 1855 under the *grands crus classés*, with Châteaux Maragaux, Haut-Brion, Latour, Lafite-Rothschild and Mouton-Rothschild (elevated to the level in 1973) all *premiers crus*. The fact that the classification remains in use reflects the suitability of the *terroir* for growing Cabernet Sauvignon and the high standards of the châteaux.

### SPANISH RIOJA

Spain is one of Europe's largest wine producers, and Rioja is made on its northern border from Tempranillo grapes. The best whites are crisp and fresh, and the best reds fruity and wood-aged. Most are blended, though some *reservas* are single-vintage wines.

### FRENCH SAUTERNES

A late-picked Bordeaux dessert wine made mainly from Semillon and Sauvignon Blanc grapes, which have been infected with *Botrytis cinerea*, the 'noble rot' that gives them their honeyed sweetness. Great Sauternes can be aged for 20 to 30 years.

## CALIFORNIAN CHARDONNAY

The centre of America's wine industry, California produces some great Chardonnay, Cabernet Sauvignon and the particularly Californian Zinfandel wines. The finest tend to be those made from single varieties and in the cooler areas of the state, especially Napa Valley, Sonoma and Mendocino counties.

## AUSTRALIAN SHIRAZ

Shiraz grapes are traditionally popular with Australian wine-makers because they are so hardy in the Australian climate. Shiraz, along with fruity Chardonnay, are perhaps the most widely drunk of Australia's excellent wines, the best of which, both red and white, come from the cooler regions.

## FRENCH CHAMPAGNE

Made from red Pinot Noir and Meunier and white Chardonnay grapes, this is France's most northerly wine. Vintages are only made in exceptional years, and usually a little wine from previous harvests is added to a new one to maintain the champagne house's style.

## GERMAN RIESLING

Most of Germany's wines are cool-climate whites, particularly Riesling, as red wines do not flourish so far north. Wines are carefully categorized, from *Deutscher Tafelwein* (table wine) to *Qualitätswein* and *Qualitätswein mit Prädikat*, whose loftiest sub-categories of *Beerenausleses/Trockenbeerenausleses* are among the world's most prized wines.

## MATCHING WINE AND FOOD

*The more complex the wine, the simpler the food, and vice versa.*

*Light foods with light wines; strong foods with strong wines.*

*In a tasting menu, the finest wine may accompany the cheese course.*

*The sweetness of a dessert wine needs to be at least as sweet as the dessert it accompanies.*

*Make your own discoveries.*

## COOKING WITH WINE

*A little wine can add flavour, but don't be tempted to add more than the recipe suggests—too much does not improve the dish.*

*Wine used in cooking should be of a reasonable quality. Cheap wine will not add anything, but much of the character of expensive wine will be destroyed in the cooking process. Use wine you would consider drinking.*

*Wine in cooking should be used with care, it cannot be added at any time. If you want to add wine to a sauce, add it before the other liquids and boil off the alcohol for a few minutes so the dish does not taste too winey.*

*In uncooked dishes, wine should have a mellow flavour to complement the dish. In desserts such as syllabub or zabaglione, the flavour of the wine will dominate, so consider its aromatic qualities carefully.*

*Wine can be added to gravies and sauces to add a more complex flavour. A splash will do.*

*If using wine in marinades, bear in mind that as well as tenderizing the meat, the acidity will also begin to cook it, thus altering its appearance.*

# wonton

A Chinese speciality, wontons are made from dough wrappers stuffed with a filling of minced meat, vegetables or seafood. They may be boiled and served in a broth, either with or without noodles, or steamed or deep-fried and served as an appetizer with a dipping sauce.

The name wonton (or *huntun*) means 'swallowing clouds'. Wonton is the Cantonese name and *huntun* is the Mandarin name, both of which are derived from a similar word meaning 'chaos'. Wontons are traditionally served on the winter solstice (December 22) in northern China, the day on which winter arrives and ancestors are remembered. Originally a food for emperors, wontons are now a roadside snack to be enjoyed by everyone.

## WONTONS

*Mix 110 g minced prawns, 225 g minced pork, 6 finely chopped water chestnuts and 2 finely chopped spring onions. Stir in 2 teaspoons each soy sauce, rice wine and sesame oil, 1 teaspoon grated ginger and 1½ tablespoons cornflour; season. Put a teaspoon of filling in the centre of each wrapper and gather up the four corners to make a packet, then seal the edges with a little water. To cook, either drop the wontons in boiling water for 3–4 minutes or steam them in a steamer for 5 minutes. Serves 6.*

### Wonton wrappers

Wonton wrappers or skins are thinly rolled sheets of dough made from flour and eggs—the same dough used to make egg noodles. They are cut into squares. Both ready-made wrappers and wontons are available from Asian supermarkets. Store in their packets in the freezer for several months and defrost as needed.

# Worcestershire sauce

A thin piquant sauce used as a condiment or for seasoning meats, gravies, stews and soups, first made in the mid 1800s by the Lea and Perrins Company in Worcester, England. It is made by the same company to this day, from a 'secret' recipe that is rumoured to consist of vinegar, molasses, sugar, anchovies, tamarind, soy sauce, shallots, garlic, salt, sugar, spices and flavouring. It is an essential ingredient, together with tomato juice and Tabasco sauce, in the cocktail Bloody Mary, and is very popular as a table sauce in Japan.

***Also known as — Lea and Perrins' sauce, Worcester sauce***

## BLOODY MARY OYSTER SHOTS

*Into each large shot glass pour 20 ml vodka, 60 ml tomato juice, 10 ml lime juice and 3 drops Worcestershire sauce. Season with salt and pepper and a drop of Tabasco. Drop a freshly shucked oyster in each glass.*

**y a k i t o r i**

### YAKITORI

*Put 100 ml Japanese soy sauce, 2 tablespoons each mirin, vegetable oil, sake and sugar in a saucepan and bring to the boil, stirring. Turn off the heat and allow the marinade to cool. Cut 6 chicken thigh fillets into 4 cm pieces, thread the chicken onto skewers alternating with 3 cm pieces spring onion and place the skewers in half the cooled marinade. Turn to coat completely, then lift out and drain. Grill the chicken, turning and brushing with the remaining marinade. Boil the remaining marinade and serve as a dipping sauce. Makes 4 skewers.*

Japanese in origin and meaning 'grilled chicken', yakitori is made with pieces of chicken, sometimes interspersed with leek or spring onion, which are basted in a marinade and grilled over charcoals. Although chicken flesh is the mainstay of yakitori, other parts of the chicken may also be used, including the skin, wings and liver, or other ingredients such as beef tongue and ginkgo nuts. The food is served on skewers, often in pairs, and may be sprinkled with *shichimi*, a Japanese spice mix. Yakitori are served at *yakitoriya*, small street stands or restaurants.

**y a m**

The edible tubers of a tropical and subtropical climbing plant, and the staple food of many countries, particularly South and Central America, West Indies, Africa and the Pacific Islands. Strictly speaking, yams are the tubers of one family, but the word is often used loosely to encompass a range of other tropical roots such as sweet potato, taro and cassava. In the United States, sweet potatoes are called yams. There are many varieties and these vary in size, colour and shape. Some have a coarse skin, others smooth, while some may be pale, brown or purple in colour. The flesh colour also varies, from white to cream, yellow, pink or purple.

Yams are cooked as for potatoes, which they resemble in flavour, though they are more starchy and mealy. Yams must be cooked before eating to destroy the bitter toxic substance (dioscorine) that they contain. They may be boiled, puréed, baked, added to soups and stews and deep-fried. Store in a cool, dark and well-ventilated place.

# yeast

Living, naturally occurring, microscopic, single-celled fungi, which feed on carbohydrates, breathe air and give off carbon dioxide and alcohol. Yeast is used for bread and beer-making. When yeast is used for bread-making, it converts the natural sugars in the flour to bubbles of carbon dioxide, these are trapped by and stretch, as they expand, the elastic mesh formed by the gluten in the flour, causing the bread to rise. Baking kills the yeast and sets the dough; as the bread cools, air replaces the carbon dioxide. Yeast can be chilled, dried and frozen and re-activates when conditions return to normal, but it needs warmth and moisture to thrive. It is retarded by the use of excess sugar or salt so follow recipes carefully.

Wild yeasts are used to make sourdough breads, these are encouraged to grow on a piece of fermented dough or fruit and then used to leaven the bread dough they are incorporated into. Store fresh yeast in the fridge for up to 1 week or freeze for several months. Dried yeast will keep for about 1 year in a cool, dark place.

## BUYING

*Fresh yeast is sold as a compressed solid and should be moist, creamy grey in colour and smell pleasantly yeasty. Dried yeast is sold in granules or as an easy-blend yeast (that does not need to be mixed with water first). Dried yeast has twice the potency of fresh yeast. For every 15 g of fresh yeast, use 7 g dried yeast.*

*Easy-blend yeast*

## COOKING

**Fresh yeast** – *Crumble the yeast into a small glass bowl and add a little tepid water. Stir until yeast dissolves. To see if the yeast is active, add a teaspoon of flour and leave it to stand until a foam forms on the top. If no foam appears the yeast is dead.*

**Dried yeast** – *Sprinkle into a small glass bowl containing a little tepid water and leave to dissolve.*

**Easy-blend yeast** – *Sprinkle the yeast onto the flour. The yeast will be activated when you add the liquid.*

*Fresh yeast*

*Dried yeast*

## ACTIVATING YEAST

1 *Mix the fresh yeast with tepid water and 1 tablespoon flour until smooth.*

2 *Set aside for 5 minutes or until yeast is frothy (sponged).*

# yeast extract

Sold under such brand names as Marmite and Vegemite, yeast extract is a concentrated, thick, dark-brown substance with a salty taste and an intense flavour. Strictly speaking, it is not an extract, but is produced by allowing yeast to digest itself with its own enzymes. Its proteins are broken down by hydrolysis to form amino acids. The bitter yeasty flavour is filtered out and the liquid is boiled to form a thick mass. Other substances are added to flavour it, depending on the manufacturer. Yeast extract can be used to flavour savoury dishes and drinks, as a vitamin supplement and as a sandwich spread. It is an incomplete protein food and also contains amino acids and useful amounts of vitamins B1 and B2.

# yeeros — see kebab

## HOME-MADE YOGHURT

*Slowly bring 1 litre whole-fat milk to the boil. Cool to 45 °C. Stir in 2 tablespoons non-heat-treated fresh plain yoghurt or dried culture. Add 5 tablespoons skim milk powder, if desired, to make a thicker, creamier yoghurt. Cover, wrap in a thick cloth and set aside in a warm place at a constant temperature, between 40–46 °C, for 5–6 hours, or until set. Refrigerate. To make fruit yoghurt, stir in slightly crushed raspberries or strawberries; leave for 30 minutes, or stir through fruit poached in syrup. Makes 1¼ litres.*

Fermented and coagulated milk, which results when milk sugar (lactose) is converted to a lactic acid, producing a bacterial change. Yoghurt can occur naturally or be made commercially by adding active bacteria such as *lactobacillus bulgaricus* and *streptococcus thermophilus* to milk.

Yoghurt has been the staple food of Turkey, the Balkans, India, the Middle East and Central Asia for centuries. Yoghurt is usually made from cow's milk but can also use milk from the goat, sheep, mare, water buffalo, camel or yak.

In the Western world, yoghurt is usually eaten as a dessert or for breakfast but in the Middle East, Central Asia and India it is a much more important food and is eaten as an accompaniment to meals. Yoghurt can be drained and made into a type of cheese called labna; it is used as a medium for marinating and cooking meat (it also acts as a tenderizer), a tradition from areas where water was generally polluted; and is treated as a sauce in many meat and vegetable dishes.
**Also known as — yoghourt, yogurt**

## YOGHURT WITH AUBERGINES

*Cut 600 g peeled aubergines into cubes. Steam them in a colander over a saucepan of water or in a steamer for 10 minutes, or until cooked. Mash the aubergine with a fork and allow to cool. Combine 500 g plain yoghurt with 1 finely chopped spring onion, 1 crushed garlic clove, 1 tablespoon chopped mint and season well with cayenne pepper, salt and pepper. Fold the cooled aubergine into the yoghurt and garnish with extra mint leaves. Serve with bread. Serves 6.*

■ *See also* **labna**

## COOKING

*To make a thicker, creamier yoghurt, empty your yoghurt into a sieve lined with muslin and drain overnight. The longer you leave it to drain, the thicker it will become, until you can actually mould it into balls, called labna.*

*Yoghurt is more easily digested than milk and lower in fat than cream, with which it can be substituted in some recipes. However, yoghurt is unstable with heat so, to stop it separating, add a little cornflour before adding it to hot ingredients. Add the yoghurt at the last minute and do not allow it to boil.*

## Yorkshire pudding

A batter of egg, flour and milk, traditionally served with roast beef in the county of Yorkshire. Originally the batter was placed under spit roast beef to catch the meat drippings and juices and would cook in the heat of the fire. Either make in a large baking tray or individual round tins, and when cooked, serve at once or they will deflate. Yorkshire pudding is also eaten with jam or syrup and is used in other dishes such as toad in the hole.

### YORKSHIRE PUDDING

1   Put 125 g sifted flour and ¼ teaspoon salt in a bowl and make a well in the centre. Break in 2 eggs.

2   With a wooden spoon gradually beat in the eggs, drawing in the flour from the sides.

3   Add 290 ml milk and beat to a smooth batter. Set aside in the fridge for 30 minutes.

4   Heat 1 baking tray or 4 Yorkshire pudding tins filled with 4 tablespoons oil or dripping until smoking.

5   Pour in the batter. It should start to bubble at the edges.

6   Transfer to the oven and bake at 200°C for 15 minutes, or until puffed and golden and crisp around the edges.

## yule log

The traditional French Christmas cake (*bûche de Noël*), is, as its name suggests, shaped and decorated to resemble a log. Sponge cake is rolled into a log shape (swiss roll) and covered with chocolate or mocha butter cream, which is marked into ridges to resemble bark. It may be decorated with meringue mushrooms and chopped pistachios to resemble moss, with marzipan leaves and berries for holly and sprinkled with icing sugar to represent snow.

## yum cha — see dim sum

## zabaglione

A classic Italian dessert of warmed and whisked Marsala or wine, egg yolks and sugar beaten over hot water until it forms a light, foamy custard. Zabaglione is served as a dessert or as a sauce over fruit, cake, ice cream or pastries or it may be mixed with cream and frozen (*freddo*). Zabaglione is the anglicized form of the Italian word *zabaione*, which was adopted by the French as 'sabayon'.

■ *See also* **sabayon**

### ZABAGLIONE

*Place 4 egg yolks, 5 tablespoons Marsala and 4 tablespoons caster sugar in a bowl set over a saucepan of simmering water. Beat constantly with a wire whisk until the mixture has trebled in volume and is frothy. Pour into warmed glasses and serve immediately. Serves 4.*

## zahtar

A Middle Eastern—mainly Lebanese—spice mixture whose name also means thyme (a Mediterranean wild variety). Ingredients vary regionally, but it should contain, at least, dried thyme, dried and crushed sumac berries, sesame seeds and salt. It is used to flavour fried eggs and labna or sprinkled on bread.

*Also known as — za'atar, zaatar*

## zarzuela

A colourful Catalan seafood stew, whose seafood ingredients will vary seasonally, although it will usually include lobster, mussels, clams and monkfish. Two of the four essential Catalan sauces are used to make it: the soffritto of onion, olive oil and tomato, and the picada of pounded fried bread, almonds and garlic. Zarzuela is named after an operetta or musical comedy, probably because it is a symphony of taste, colour, shapes and texture.

■ *See also* **Spanish food**

## zedoary

A rhizome found growing in India and Southeast Asia, which bears a resemblance to turmeric (to which it is related) and ginger. The flesh is hard and orange and has a gingery mango flavour and musky aroma. Zedoary is sold fresh or dried *(pictured)* and is commonly used in Indian pickles. High in starch, the rhizomes may also be used to make a starch used in Indian cooking as a thickening agent. It is thought to purify the blood.

## zhug

A fiery relish from Yemen, similar to harissa, made with ground chillies with the addition of herbs and spices such as cardamom and caraway seeds, black pepper and coriander. Zhug is used to accompany grilled meats, poultry and fish, to flavour soups and stews and as a dip for bread. It is often eaten with a fenugreek paste called *hibeh*.
**Also known as — s'hug, houg**

■ *See also* **harissa**

### ZHUG

*Soak 4 dried chillies in water. In a mortar and pestle, grind 1 teaspoon each of black peppercorns and caraway seeds and 4 cardamom pods. Process 20 g coriander leaves, 2 tablespoons lemon juice, 8 garlic cloves, the chillies and 1 tablespoon oil. Add ground spices and blend to form a paste. Season well with salt.*

## zucchini — see courgette

## zuccotto

An Italian dessert whose shape is thought to have been inspired by the rounded roof of the famed Duomo cathedral in Florence. A round bowl is lined with sliced Madeira cake moistened with an alcohol such as maraschino or Marsala. The centre is filled with cream, candied orange or citron or almonds and hazelnuts and chopped chocolate, then topped with slices of cake to enclose the filling. The zuccotto is chilled until firm, then turned out and dusted with alternating segments of cocoa and icing sugar.

## zuppa inglese

Literally translated as 'English soup', an Italian cold pudding, similar to the English trifle, which is so smothered in custard that it looks like a soup. It is made with macaroons or sponge cake moistened with Marsala or rum, layered with custard, whipped cream and glacé fruit or toasted almonds. In some regions, melted chocolate may be folded through part of the custard for variation, while in others, it is topped with meringue. It is served chilled after refrigeration for several hours.

# kitchen equipment

Stocking a kitchen is a personal thing based on how much cooking, and what kind of cooking, you like to do. It is not always necessary to buy a whole set of knives unless you intend to use all of them—instead, it is better to have a few good ones that will last. Similarly, buy two or three good-quality saucepans and frying pans rather than a whole set of inferior ones as these will not give an even heat and may develop hot spots that burn every time you use them. Kitchen equipment, like chopping boards, bowls and ovenware, can be built up over time. Buy a few things at a time and make sure they are appropriate to the recipes you are using. Check that the equipment is efficient and comfortable to use rather than shiny, attractive and just for show.

## BASIC KNIVES

*Kitchen knives* – Buy the best you can afford. Make sure they are comfortable to hold and the handle and blade are well balanced. Put them in a block to keep them sharp—if they bash around against things in a drawer they will blunt quickly. You will need one **large knife** for chopping, one **medium knife** and one **small serrated knife** for fruit and tomatoes—if you can, find one with a pointed end that will easily pierce the skins. A serrated **bread knife** is used for slicing loaves. A flat-bladed knife is not a good substitute as it squashes the loaf rather than cuts it. Use a **steel** to keep all your knife edges sharp, and sharpen before every use. If you are planning on baking, then buy a **palette knife**. This has a long flexible blade for spreading and for turning items over, such as pancakes. They come in various sizes, but a medium (24 cm) blade is a good all-round option.

*Scissors* – **Kitchen scissors** should have tough blades, preferably with a serrated edge. The lower handle should be large enough to grip with three fingers. **Poultry shears** have a cutting point near the pivot for gripping bones as you cut them.

*Kitchen knives*

## SPECIALIST KNIVES

*Specialist knives* – These are needed if you plan on being more adventurous with your cooking. A **mezzaluna** is a double-handled knife with one or two curved blades, which are rocked from side to side to chop herbs. Its advantage is that it is quick and easy to use. Some come with a special board with a dip for holding the ingredient. An **oyster knife** is essential for opening oysters and other shellfish. Its short, flat blade with two cutting edges slides easily between shells. Your hand is protected by a disc of metal on the handle. Ordinary knives should not be used to open oysters, as it is very easy to cut yourself badly. If you are planning on doing any basic meat preparation, then a **boning knife** with a very strong, thin blade will help. The width of the blade means you make narrow cuts, even when the whole length of the blade is pushed into the meat. If you are planning on serving cheese often, buy a **cheese knife** with a curved forked end for picking up the cut pieces, otherwise a normal knife will do.

*Citrus zester and canelle knife* – These easily peel off zest in thin or thick shreds using a row of small holes or a deeper, V-shaped cutting edge.

*Mezzaluna*

*Saucepans*

## SAUCEPANS AND FRYING PANS

*Saucepans* – These should be good quality and the most expensive ones that you can afford. There is a huge range on the market but stainless steel with a sandwich base (stainless steel sandwiching a metal such as copper that conducts heat well) are a good bet for even heat distribution. Stainless steel is also non-reactive (it will not be affected by the use of an acid such as lemon juice). Choose pans with comfortable handles (check these do not heat up as the pan does) and lids that have a tight seal. You will need one large pan and a couple of smaller ones. A **pasta boiler** with a fitted drainer is useful for cooking pasta, as well as vegetables. If you heat up a lot of milk or soups, you may want a **milk pan,** which has a pouring lip.

*Frying pans* – Like saucepans, these should be good quality. Cast-iron ones are heavy but last a very long time. Non-stick ones have to be used with wooden or plastic implements but are easy to clean. An ovenproof handle is useful for making anything that needs to be finished in the oven or under a grill, such as a frittata.

## OVENWARE

*Ovenware* – These should be good quality and be able to be used on the stovetop and in the oven. **Casseroles** need to be heavy enough to absorb and retain heat and also need tight-fitting lids so as not to let any moisture escape. Cast-iron or enamelled ones (with cast-iron or steel underneath) are generally the best as they conduct heat well. You will need several sizes as it is important that the recipe fits the casserole—a small amount of stew will dry out in a large casserole. **Baking and gratin dishes** should be fully ovenproof and able to withstand high heat. Enamel, cast-iron and stoneware are good options. Choose ones that look nice enough to be used for serving. **Soufflé dishes and ramekins** should be made from ceramic, porcelain or glass (all are interchangeable) and, above all, be presentable for the table.

*Roasting tin* – Should be made from stainless steel or anodized aluminium so the tins can be used over a heat source without buckling. One with a rack is useful so meat and poultry can be roasted and the fat and juices collected underneath.

*Enamelled casseroles*

## GENERAL COOKING EQUIPMENT

*Chopping board* – An essential piece of equipment. There is endless debate as to whether wooden or polyethylene boards are more hygienic and views change on a daily basis. Whichever you choose, your board should be kept spotlessly clean.

*Graters* – These vary in shape, but the important part is the cutting edge, which should be very sharp. A **box grater** does not slip easily and is good for grating large quantities. A **Microplane®  grater** has very sharp blades and works well for smaller quantities as it can be held over a bowl or a dish of food.

*Potato masher* – Potato mashers work on all cooked vegetables. Old-style mashers with a cut grid often work better than those made of a wire coil.

*Tin opener* – It is worth buying a good-quality one that grips properly.

*Lemon squeezer* – Available in glass, ceramic, plastic and wood. The squeezers with a container underneath for collecting the juice are the most useful.

*Sieves* – These come in a range of different sizes. Larger **colanders** are best for draining. Round-bottomed **stainless steel sieves** have a coarse mesh suitable for sifting and puréeing and **nylon mesh sieves** are for fine sifting and puréeing.

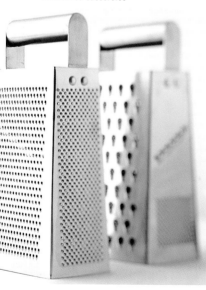

*Box graters*

## KITCHEN UTENSILS

*Spoons* - Useful for stirring, mixing and beating. **Wooden spoons** are good because they do not conduct heat, do not scratch and are non-reactive. Some spoons have a flat edge and corner to help you get into the side of a saucepan. **Metal spoons** are used for folding ingredients as their sharp edges cut easily through the mixture without squashing out air. A **perforated spoon** is useful for draining. **Ladles** are made for serving liquids and can also be used to measure— a 'ladleful' is used as a measuring term when adding stock to risotto.

*Pastry brush* - Made with either nylon or natural bristles, a pastry brush can be flat or round. Be careful when using nylon bristles with hot liquids as they may melt.

*Peeler* - A good peeler shaves only a thin skin off vegetables.

*Rubber spatula* - This can scrape a bowl completely clean and is particularly useful for removing food from food processors and blenders.

*Fish slice* - This needs enough flexibility to be able to slide under things.

*Wooden spoons*

## BAKING EQUIPMENT

*Bowls* - Glass ovenproof bowls or stainless steel bowls are useful for both whisking egg whites and melting chocolate, as well as all other mixing. A very large mixing bowl is invaluable for large quantities, and plastic bowls are a good non-breakable option—however, these are not good for egg white as they hold grease.

*Whisks* - These beat air into things or beat lumps out. **Balloon whisks** consist of loops of stainless steel joined by a handle. They range from large ones for egg white, through to small ones for sauces and dressings. **Rotary whisks** must be good quality to work efficiently, and they give slightly less volume than balloon whisks. **Flat whisks**, which consist of a wire coiled around a loop, are useful for whisking in saucepans or containers with flat bottoms or on flat plates.

*Cooling rack* - This is a raised wire rack for cooling cakes and pastries. Choose a large wire rack that can hold a large item or several small ones comfortably.

*Rolling pin* - This should be long enough to roll out a full sheet of pastry in one go, as this will ensure a smooth surface.

*Glass bowls*

## BAKEWARE

*Baking tins* - Buy good-quality bakeware. Bear in mind that black non-stick surfaces will brown baked goods faster than shiny metal ones so you might need to reduce oven temperatures. A **springform** tin can be used for cheesecakes, cakes and gateaux. The spring clip means the side can be gently eased away from more delicate textures. For loaves of bread, pound cakes or terrines, you will need a **loaf tin**. Buy one with welded non-leaking seams. Most recipes for breads and cakes will fit in an average 17 x 11 x 8 cm or 19 x 12 x 9 cm tin, despite the measurements given in the recipe. For quiches and tarts, buy a metal **tart tin** with a loose base so you can easily remove the tart. Recipes call for all sorts of sizes, but a 20 cm (serves 6) or 25 cm (serves 8) tin should fit most recipes. Individual **tartlet tins** are good for presentation if you do lots of entertaining.

*Pie dish* - A pie dish should have a good lip on it so you can stick the pastry down well, otherwise the pastry will slide down into the pie as it cooks.

*Baking sheet* - The most useful baking sheet is a heavy-duty flat one with a lip at one end. The flat sides mean you can easily slide things on and off.

*Tartlet tins*

*Bamboo steamer*

*Mortar and pestle*

*Metal measuring cups*

## ASIAN EQUIPMENT

*Wok* – Buy a carbon steel or pressed steel wok from your local Chinatown rather than expensive name brands as they conduct heat better. Season by rubbing it with salt and hot oil, then wipe it out after each use rather than washing it—this will build up a non-stick surface over time. Use with a **wok charn** for stir-frying. This is a shovel-like spatula ideal for tossing food around the curved side of the wok.

*Chopper/cleaver* – Used for chopping through bones, as well as an all-purpose knife. Buy a good heavy one for chopping and a lighter one for slicing.

*Metal or bamboo tongs* – Very useful for turning things over, or lifting things out of boiling liquids. Bamboo does not conduct heat.

*Clay pot* – Glazed on the inside and used for slow cooking as it heats up evenly all over. The lid is sloped and forces condensation back into the dish.

*Steamers* – Bamboo stackable steamers allow food to be cooked in steam. Steamed foods better retain the aromas and flavours that are lost during boiling.

## SPECIALIST EQUIPMENT

*Mortar and pestle* – A bowl (mortar) with a slightly rough surface and a crushing stick (pestle) that fits the curvature of the bowl and provides the second grinding surface. Very good for crushing seeds, spices and cloves of garlic.

*Salt and pepper mills (grinders)* – Buy a pepper mill with a steel grinding mechanism for efficiency and an adjustable grind. It should hold several tablespoons of peppercorns or will need refilling often. Salt should only be ground in a salt mill. This has a nylon grinder that will not corrode. The two are not interchangeable.

*Salad basket and spinner* – Very useful for drying salad—wet salad leaves dilute salad dressing. A salad basket is swung around (preferably outdoors) to shake any water off the leaves. A spinner is a basket turned by a handle or by pulling a string. The water is removed by centrifugal force and collected in an outer bowl.

*Mouli-legume* – This purées fruit and vegetables by forcing them through a flat metal sieve, removing any lumps or hard bits that can then be discarded. Food processors simply chop everything together.

## SCALES, MEASURING CUPS AND THERMOMETERS

*Scales* – You only need one set of scales. Choose one with both metric and imperial weights. A **balance scale** holds the weights on one side and the ingredients on the other. It can weigh very small amounts. An **electronic scale** has a digital display but is often less accurate for small weights under 30 g. **Spring weight scales** have a scale pan on top of a calibrated scale. Choose one with an adjustable tension screw as they will need adjusting to keep them true.

*Measuring jugs* – Plastic and glass jugs are best to use as you can read them easily. Choose one with the calibrations visible on both the inside and outside.

*Measuring cups* – Often used instead of scales for dry and liquid measures. Available in fractions and multiples of cup measures. Metal will last longer than plastic but make sure it is non-reactive for measuring acids such as lemon juice.

*Measuring spoons* – Available in sets ranging from ¼ teaspoon to 1 tablespoon. Dry measurements should be levelled off with a knife to be accurate.

*Thermometers* – These are essential for accurate oil measurements. An **oven thermometer** is used to ensure that the thermostat is registering accurately.

# kitchen terms

| | |
|---|---|
| *à la* | Means 'in the style of' in French. |
| *abats* | French for offal. |
| *absorption method* | A way of cooking rice by adding the exact amount of water and cooking with the lid on until all the water is absorbed and steam holes appear in the surface of the rice. |
| *aceto* | Italian for vinegar. |
| *acidulate, to* | To add acid (such as lemon juice or vinegar) to cooking or soaking water to stop fruit or vegetables from oxidizing and discolouring. |
| *acqua* | Italian for water. |
| *additive* | Something added to food to improve its keeping qualities, flavour, colour and texture. In the European Union, all additives are listed by E numbers or names on packaging unless they are natural and not required to be listed by law. |
| *adjust, to* | To taste before serving and then re-season if necessary. |
| *aerate* | To incorporate air into a mixture by sieving dry mixtures or whisking liquid mixtures (such as egg white or cream). |
| *affumicato* | Italian for smoked. |
| *aglio* | Italian for garlic. |
| *air dry, to* | To dry food, usually ham or fish, by hanging it in a flow of fresh air. |
| *al', all', alla* | Means 'in the style of' in Italian. |
| *al dente* | Italian term meaning 'to the tooth'—cooked but still retaining some bite—applied mainly to pasta. |
| *albedo* | American term for the white pith of citrus fruit. |
| *albumen* | Technical term for egg white. |
| *all-purpose flour* | American term for plain white flour that can be used for all types of baking. |
| *allumettes* | French for matchsticks, usually applied to the size of chopped potatoes and vegetables. |
| *altitude effects* | The effects on cooking at a high altitude, which drops the boiling point of water by 1°C for each 275 m. At very high altitudes, a pressure cooker is needed to cook successfully. |
| *amatriciana, all'* | With bacon, onions and tomatoes. |
| *ammonia* | A pungent gas. Overripe cheese and fish that are starting to go off smell of this. |
| *amuse gueule* | Meaning 'mouth pleaser' in French, this small appetizer is served before a meal. |
| *anticaking agent* | Something added to powdered food to stop it clumping together, usually a compound of magnesium, aluminium or sodium. Shown as an E number on packaging (E530-E578). |
| *antioxidant* | A preservation agent, such as vitamins C or E, that slows the reaction rate of food to oxygen. Shown as an E number on packaging (E300-E321). |
| *apéritif* | Drink taken before a meal to 'open' the appetite, such as champagne or sherry. |
| *appellation d'origine contrôlée* | French designation for a wine or foodstuff that guarantees its method of production and ingredients. |
| *appetizer* | Small items of food served before or at the start of a meal or with drinks. |
| *aromatics* | Ingredients, such as spices and herbs, that add aroma to food. |
| *arrosto* | Italian for roast. |
| *arroz* | Spanish and Portuguese for rice. |
| *artificial sweeteners* | Any sweetening product that does not contain sugars. |
| *asciutto* | Italian term that refers to pasta, gnocchi or rice drained of its cooking liquid. |
| *assiette* | French for plate, usually taken to mean a plated assortment of cheeses, meats or desserts. |

| | |
|---|---|
| **astringent** | An acidic or tannic solution (such as lemon juice or wine), which makes the skin of the mouth tighten up. |
| **au** | Means 'in the style of', 'in' or 'with' in French. |
| **au lait** | Means 'with milk' in French. |
| **back fat** | Hard pork fat from the back of a pig. |
| **bake** | To cook in an oven in dry heat, usually until browned on the outside. |
| **bake blind** | To bake a pastry case while it is unfilled to set the pastry. It is usually lined with baking paper or foil and filled with baking beads to stop the sides collapsing or the base from bubbling up. |
| **ballotine** | A stuffed roll of boned meat or poultry or a boned chicken tied into a round shape. |
| **bard, to** | To tie fat or fatty meat, such as bacon, over a lean joint or bird to stop it drying out as it cooks. The fat is removed before eating. |
| **baron of beef** | A very large joint consisting of two sirloins of beef connected by the backbone. |
| **barquette** | Boat-shaped tartlet tin. |
| **baste, to** | To spoon melted fat or liquid over food as it cooks to stop it drying out and to add flavour. |
| **bat out, to** | To flatten or pound meat until it is thinner. |
| **baton** | A stick of vegetable about 6 x 2 x 2 cm. |
| **batter** | A mixture of flour, milk and eggs used for pancakes and to coat food before frying. Also refers to soft cake, biscuit and scone mixtures. |
| **batterie de cuisine** | The necessary utensils with which to equip a kitchen. |
| **Baumé scale** | Density scale used to measure the concentration of sugar syrup. |
| **baveuse** | Meaning 'runny' in French, this refers to the consistency of egg when it has almost set but is still just liquid, such as the inside of an omelette before it is folded over. |
| **beard** | Also called a byssus, this is the hairy threads that mussels use to attach themselves to rocks. |
| **beat, to** | To incorporate air into a mixture with a spoon, fork or whisk. |
| **beurre manié** | Equal amounts of flour and butter made into a paste and whisked into a boiling liquid to thicken it without making lumps. |
| **beurre noisette** | French for browned butter. |
| **bianco** | Italian for white. |
| **bien cuit** | Meaning 'well-done' in French, this is usually used when referring to meat. |
| **bind, to** | To use a liquid to make dry ingredients stick together and hold their shape. |
| **blackened** | Meat or fish seared over a very high heat. This term is used in Cajun cooking. |
| **blanc** | A cooking liquid of water, flour and lemon juice that stops food from oxidizing and discolouring. |
| **blanch, to** | To cook in boiling water for a few minutes and then refresh in cold water. This keeps colour in vegetables and loosens tomato and fruit skins. Also refers to potato chips that are precooked in hot fat before being fully cooked—this improves their texture and colour. |
| **blanquette** | A white stew made with white stock thickened with egg and cream. |
| **blend, to** | To mix together well. |
| **bleu** | French for very rare meat (see blue). |
| **blood temperature** | Also called hand-hot and lukewarm, this is 37°C, and can be tested by dipping a finger into the liquid. When the finger feels the same in and out of the liquid, it has reached blood temperature. |
| **bloom** | The white coating that appears on cured meats and cheeses, which is a type of edible mould. Also refers to the white coating of sugar or fat that can appear on chocolate if incorrectly stored. |
| **blue** | Very rare meat, which is still raw in the centre. |
| **bocconcini** | Means 'mouthfuls' in Italian, but is usually applied to small balls of mozzarella. |
| **boil, to** | To cook in a liquid that is hot enough to produce enough steam bubbles to move the water. |
| **bone, to** | To remove bones from a bird or piece of meat leaving the flesh intact. |
| **bonne bouchée** | Meaning a 'good mouthful' in French, this is a small appetizer served before a meal. |
| **bonne femme** | Usually denotes something that is cooked in a simple way—'home cooking'. |
| **bordelaise, à la** | A French term for dishes with a wine sauce, often with bone marrow as a garnish. |

| | |
|---|---|
| **boscaiolo, al'** | An Italian term for 'forester style', meaning with mushrooms. |
| **bouillon** | A broth or unclarified stock. |
| **braise, to** | To cook slowly on a bed of chopped vegetables and with a little liquid in a covered pan. |
| **brine** | A strong saline solution (290–360 g salt per 1 litre water) used to preserve food. |
| **Brix scale** | A density scale used to measure sugar syrup by percentage weight of sugar. 100°Brix is water and 50°Brix is an equal amount of sugar dissolved in water. |
| **brochette** | A skewer of meat. |
| **brodo** | Italian for broth. |
| **broil** | American word for grill. |
| **broiler** | American word for a young chicken. |
| **broth** | The liquid in which meat, fish or vegetables and flavourings have been cooked. Also refers to a clear soup. |
| **brown, to** | To cook food until the outer surface caramelizes or a maillard reaction occurs (the reaction between a sugar and an amino acid, which causes food to brown). Browning does not mean cooking through. |
| **bruise, to** | To squash slightly. Used for aromatics like lemon grass so they give out their flavour more easily. |
| **brûlé(e), brûler, to** | To brown or caramelize under heat. The term is usually applied to sugar. |
| **brunoise** | Very small diced vegetables. |
| **butterfly chop** | A thick chop cut almost through horizontally and then opened out and flattened. |
| **cacciatora, alla** | An Italian term for 'hunter style', usually meaning with tomatoes and mushrooms. |
| **caffeine** | An organic compound found in coffee, tea, chocolate and cola nuts that acts as a stimulant. |
| **capsaicin** | The hot component (an irritant alkaloid) found in chillies. It is flavourless and odourless. |
| **caramelize, to** | To heat food until the sugars on the surface break down and form a brown coating, which may be sweet or savoury. |
| **caraque** | Flakes of chocolate made by pouring molten chocolate onto a surface, then scraping it off. |
| **carbohydrate** | An important source of energy in food. |
| **carne** | Italian, Spanish and Portuguese for meat. |
| **carte, à la** | A menu where each item is individually priced. |
| **cartouche** | A circle of buttered baking paper placed on the surface of a dish and used to keep food moist while it is cooking, or to stop a skin from forming when a dish is cooling. |
| **carve, to** | To cut slices of cooked meat from a large joint or from a bird. |
| **casalinga** | Means 'home-style' or 'home-made' in Italian. |
| **casserole, to** | To slowly cook a dish consisting of meat and/or vegetables on the stove or in the oven with a lid on tightly so that all the flavour and aroma is contained. |
| **caul** | Lacy fat used to wrap meat or balls of mince before cooking. It holds them together and bastes them as they cook. |
| **cephalopod** | A marine mollusc such as squid, cuttlefish or octopus that has tentacles growing from its head and often containing an ink sac within its body. |
| **charcuterie** | Cured meats, sausages and ready-prepared products such as pâtés and terrines made from a pig, though the term is used for other animals as well. |
| **chasseur, à la** | A French term for 'hunter style', usually meaning with onions and tomatoes. Often described simply as chasseur. |
| **chaud-froid** | Food that has been cooked, chilled and covered in a layer of aspic. |
| **chiffonade** | Finely shredded herbs made by rolling leaves, which are then sliced finely. |
| **chine, to** | To cut through the ribs of a joint close to the backbone so the backbone can be removed before carving to make carving easier. |
| **cholesterol** | A complex alcohol present in most body tissue and therefore animal products, which is essential for the normal function of nerves and cells. High levels of cholesterol may, however, be involved in the development of heart disease. |

| | |
|---|---|
| *chop* | A slice of meat with the bone from the vertebrae and part of the ribcage attached. |
| *civet* | A dark stew made from game and thickened with blood. |
| *clarify, to* | To skim or filter a liquid until it is clear, or to add beaten egg whites over heat, which then coagulate and trap any impurities. |
| *clouté* | Means studded—an onion clouté is studded with cloves. |
| *coating consistency* | A liquid that is thick enough to coat a food evenly without running off again. Test by pouring over the back of a spoon—a line drawn down the centre of the spoon should hold its shape. |
| *cocotte, en* | Eggs cooked in a small dish like a ramekin or cocotte. |
| *coddle, to* | To drop eggs in boiling water, then cook off the heat. |
| *cold smoke, to* | To smoke food at a low temperature (85°C), which gives it an airtight coating. |
| *cold-pressed oil* | Oil that is extracted by pressing but without being heated or having any chemicals added. Cold-pressed oils have a better flavour. |
| *collop* | A small slice of meat taken from a tender cut of meat such as a loin. |
| *concassée* | Meaning finely chopped, this term is usually used for peeled, seeded and chopped tomatoes. |
| *confit* | Meat or poultry cooked and preserved in its own fat. Also refers to preserved fruit. |
| *connective tissue* | A structural material in animals consisting usually of collagen, which is present around or in pieces of meat. It gives a gelatinous smooth texture to dishes that are cooked slowly. |
| *conserve* | A type of jam. |
| *cook out, to* | To cook something so that it no longer tastes raw. Usually used in relation to flour or spices. |
| *coral* | The eggs of a female lobster, which turn red when cooked and are used for flavouring sauces. Scallop roes are also sometimes called corals |
| *core, to* | To remove the inedible centres and seeds of fruits. Also refers to removing the blood vessels and tubes from a kidney. |
| *coulis* | A thick, sieved purée, usually of tomatoes or fruit. |
| *court bouillon* | A cooking liquid for fish made of water, vinegar, lemon juice, white wine and a bouquet garni. It may also include some vegetables. |
| *cover* | A place setting for one person. Restaurant capacities are measured in covers. |
| *cream, to* | To beat ingredients to incorporate air and make the mixture creamy in consistency. |
| *crimp, to* | To mark the edge of pastry or biscuits or to seal two layers of pastry together in a scalloped pattern. |
| *croquette* | Mashed potato, minced meat, fish or vegetables, or any other similar mixture, made into a paste, then formed into log shapes, which are crumbed and fried. |
| *croûte, en* | Enclosed in pastry before baking. |
| *crumb, to* | American term meaning to paner or cover in crumbs. |
| *crust* | A pastry case such as a pie crust, or the browned surface of baked goods such as bread or cakes. |
| *crustacean* | An aquatic animal, such as a crab or lobster with a hard external, segmented shell and soft body. |
| *cube, to* | To cut food into 2.5 cm cubes. Cubes are larger than dice. |
| *cuisine minceur* | Low-calorie cooking with little carbohydrate and fat. |
| *cuit(e)* | French for cooked. |
| *cup measure* | A volume measure used mainly in the USA and Australia based on a 235 ml cup in the USA, and a 250 ml cup in Australia. Both liquids and dry goods are measured in cups. |
| *curdle* | Describes when a liquid separates, usually curds and whey for milk; when oil separates out of mayonnaise; or when egg separates from cake mixtures. |
| *cure, to* | To preserve meat, poultry or fish by drying, smoking or salting. |
| *cut in, to* | To mix hard fat with flour by cutting it in using two knives until it is chopped into small pieces, each coated in flour. |
| *cutlet* | A piece of meat cut through the ribcage with the vertebrae and rib bone still attached. |
| *dariole* | A small (individual-sized) castle-shaped mould. |
| *deep-fry* | To fry something in oil. The food is completely immersed in the oil. |

| | |
|---|---|
| **deglaze (déglacer), to** | To loosen meat juices and flavours that may have stuck to the bottom of the pan when frying or roasting meat. A liquid is added to the hot pan and the pan is scraped and stirred. The liquid is then added to the dish or used to make gravy. |
| **degorge (dégorger), to** | To salt something like aubergine in order to make it give up any bitter liquid, or to soak meat or fish in water to get rid of any impurities. |
| **degrease (degraisser)** | To remove the oil from the surface of a dish by skimming or soaking it off with paper towel. |
| **dégustation** | A tasting or sampling, this term is usually applied to a menu in which you eat lots of small courses. |
| **déjeuner** | French for lunch. |
| **demersal** | A word used to describe flat fish. |
| **demi** | French for half. |
| **demi-deuil** | Means 'half-mourning' in French and is used for dishes that include white and black ingredients, with usually truffles as the black ingredient. |
| **demi-tasse** | A small cup, usually used to hold coffee. |
| **dépouiller, to** | To add cold liquid to a hot one so the scum and fat rise to the surface and can be skimmed off. |
| **desiccate, to** | To dry or dehydrate. Usually used to describe coconut. |
| **détrempe** | A mixture of flour and water used as a dough base. |
| **devein, to** | To remove the dark vein-like digestive tracts from prawns. |
| **devilled** | Food cooked in a strong-tasting sauce flavoured with a combination of ingredients such as Worcestershire sauce, Tabasco, mustard or chilli. Also known as (à la) diable and (alla) diavola. |
| **dextral** | A term used for flat fish that have two eyes on the right-hand side of the top side of their heads. |
| **dice** | Cut into small cubes. Dice are smaller than cubes. |
| **digestif/digestive** | French for a small drink taken after dinner. Digestifs are thought to aid digestion. |
| **dijonnaise, à la** | French term usually taken to mean 'with mustard' but can also mean 'with blackcurrants'. |
| **dolci** | Italian for sweets or desserts. |
| **doneness** | The point at which something is cooked through. |
| **doppio** | Means 'double' in Italian, but means 'strong' when applied to coffee. |
| **doria** | Dishes, usually fish, fried in butter and dressed with cucumber cooked in butter. |
| **dot, to** | To scatter or put small pieces of butter over the surface of food before cooking. |
| **double crust** | A pie with a bottom and top crust. |
| **dough** | A mixture of flour, liquid and other ingredients that form a pliable mixture used for making bread. |
| **draw, to** | To gut poultry and other birds. |
| **dredge, to** | To dust with a powder such as icing sugar or flour. |
| **dress, to** | Either to get game birds ready for cooking; to add a dressing; or to arrange cooked food attractively, as in dressed crab. |
| **dressing** | A mixture of oil and vinegar used to dress salads. |
| **drizzle, to** | To sprinkle liquid in a continuous stream. |
| **dropping consistency** | When a mixture such as cake mixture falls slowly off a spoon, that is, it won't run off or stay put. |
| **drupe** | Fruit with soft flesh and hard stones like plums and peaches. |
| **dry fry, to** | To cook food in a frying pan without any fat. |
| **dry roast, to** | To heat spices in a hot pan without oil to improve their flavour. |
| **Dubarry, à la/du** | Denotes a dish containing cauliflower. |
| **duchesse, à la** | A dish garnished with duchess potatoes. |
| **dust, to** | To sprinkle lightly with a powder such as icing sugar or cocoa. |
| **duxelles** | Chopped shallots or onions and chopped mushrooms sautéed in butter. |
| **egg wash** | A glaze used in baking made from eggs and water or milk. |
| **emulsion** | A stable suspension of fat in a liquid. This can be raw (mayonnaise) or cooked (hollandaise). |
| **entrée** | Originally the dish served between the fish and meat courses. In some countries, it now describes the main course; in others, the first course. |
| **essence** | Concentrated flavour derived from food, usually by macerating in alcohol. |

| | |
|---|---|
| *extract* | Concentrated flavour derived from foods, usually by distillation or evaporation. |
| *faggot* | Refers to a bundle when applied to herbs, or to a type of meatball. |
| *farce* | Stuffing or forcemeat. The stuffed item is described as 'farci'. |
| *farinaceous* | A starchy food. |
| *fat-free* | If labelled fat-free, food should have less than 0.5 g fat per 100 g. |
| *fécule* | A starch, such as potato starch, cornflour or arrowroot. |
| *feuilleté(e)* | Meaning flaky and used to describe pastries such as puff pastry. |
| *fillet* | A piece of boneless fish or meat. |
| *fillet, to* | To take the flesh off the bones of a fish, poultry or meat. |
| *fines herbes* | A mixture of finely chopped herbs, usually parsley, tarragon, chives and chervil. |
| *flambé (flamber), to* | Meaning 'to flame', this involves setting fire to alcohol in order to burn it off, leaving just the flavour behind. |
| *flan* | A round, straight-sided tart with a pastry, biscuit or sponge base and a precooked filling. Also refers to a caramel custard-like dessert from Spanish-speaking countries. |
| *flash point* | The point at which oil vapours will catch light but will not sustain burning. If oil gets this hot, it must be taken away from the source of heat immediately or it will reach fire point and burn. |
| *fleuron* | A crescent-shaped piece of puff pastry used as a garnish. |
| *florentine, à la* | Denotes the use of spinach, often with fish or eggs and topped with cheese sauce. Sometimes just the word 'florentine' is used. |
| *floury* | Used to describe food in which the flavour of flour has not been cooked out. Also refers to potatoes that have a fluffy texture when cooked. |
| *flute* | Indentations made to the sides of pastry either to help seal it together or for decoration. |
| *fold in, to* | To mix two things together using a gentle lifting and turning motion rather than stirring so as not to lose any trapped air bubbles. Used for cake mixtures and when adding flavourings to meringues. |
| *fond* | French for stock. Fond brun is brown stock and fond blanc is white stock. Often the type of meat from which the stock is made is also mentioned—fond blanc de volaille is chicken stock. |
| *forno, al* | Means 'baked' or 'cooked in the oven' in Italian. |
| *freddo* | Italian for cold. |
| *free-range* | Animals or birds that have access to open pasture. The meaning is interpreted in different ways by producers and free-range can be quite limited. |
| *French roast* | To roast poultry with a liquid, starting it breast side down to keep the meat moist. |
| *French, to* | To trim the meat away from the bones of chops or ribs leaving the bone exposed. |
| *friandises* | French for sweetmeats or confections served with petit fours, usually sweets such as peppermint creams or preserved fruits. |
| *fricassée* | A stew made from white meat, which is fried and then cooked in a white sauce such as velouté. |
| *froid* | French for cold. |
| *fry* | Technically, testicles of a lamb or calf, but may also be used for other offal. Also means baby fish. |
| *fry, to* | To seal the surface of food quickly by cooking it in hot fat. |
| *fumé* | French for smoked. |
| *fumet* | A strong-flavoured stock in which a fish has been poached. May also be used to describe mushroom or truffle-flavoured stocks. |
| *funghi* | Italian for mushrooms. |
| *galantine* | Boned poultry, fish or white meat, stuffed, rolled and pressed into a symmetrical shape before being cooked, chilled and glazed with aspic. Served cold cut into slices. |
| *gastronomy* | The study and knowledge of good food and wine. |
| *gastropod* | Single shelled (univalve) mollusc such as whelks and abalone. |
| *gaufrette* | A wafer, often very thin and fan shaped, shaped on a gaufrette iron, which leaves a waffled indentation. Curled gaufrettes can be used as ice cream cones. |
| *gelée, en* | Coated in aspic or garnished with aspic. |

| | |
|---|---|
| *giblets* | The neck, gizzard, liver and heart of poultry. Now not often sold in a package inside the chicken, but may be bought separately. |
| *gigot* | Refers to a leg of lamb or something that has a similar shape. |
| *gild, to* | To add a glaze of beaten egg or egg yolk before baking, giving the surface of the food a shiny, golden colour. |
| *glace* | A reduced meat stock or a glaze. |
| *glacé(e)* | Means frozen (iced) or glazed. |
| *glaze* | A coating that is applied to a precooked or cooked surface to make it shine or to help it colour when cooked, such as an egg wash for uncooked pastry and an apricot glaze for fruit tarts. |
| *glucose* | A type of sugar found in honey and corn syrup, which is generally used to help stop sucrose from crystallizing when making caramel and sweets. |
| *goujon* | A small piece of fried fish. The term is now also used for a piece of chicken breast meat. |
| *gourmand* | Someone who enjoys fine food—possibly too much. |
| *gourmet* | A connoisseur of fine food and drink; someone with a discriminating palate. When used in conjunction with food, it means good-quality food, skilfully prepared. |
| *grand-mère* | Used to denote home cooking or traditional country-style food. |
| *grate, to* | To finely shred something by rubbing it against a coarse or serrated edge. |
| *grease, to* | To coat a dish, tin or mould with cooking fat in order to stop the item being cooked from sticking. |
| *grecque, à la* | Means 'of Greek origin', and usually describes vegetables such as onions, mushrooms or leeks cooked in a mixture including olive oil and lemon juice. |
| *grind, to* | To break down ingredients such as spices and coffee beans into smaller pieces. |
| *halal* | Term given to meat killed and prepared under Muslim dietary laws. |
| *hand-hot* | 37°C—the temperature at which a liquid feels neither hot nor cold. Also known as blood temperature and lukewarm. |
| *hang, to* | To mature game or meat by hanging it in a cool, dry, airy place to allow flavour to develop. The length of time for hanging varies from days (game birds) to weeks (beef carcasses). |
| *hard boil, to* | To boil an egg until both the white and yolk are set (about 9–10 minutes from boiling). |
| *haunch* | Hindquarter of deer. |
| *haute cuisine* | Fine food prepared perfectly. |
| *hock* | The lower half of an animal's leg between the foot and lower limb. |
| *hors d'oeuvres* | Small dishes, both hot and cold, served at the start of a meal. Soup is not an hors d'oeuvre but a separate course on its own. |
| *hot smoke, to* | To smoke food at a temperature that also cooks the food. |
| *huitre* | French for oyster. |
| *hull, to* | To remove the stalks from berry fruit. |
| *ice, to* | To decorate or cover baked goods, such as cakes and biscuits, with icing. |
| *infuse, to* | To soak something in a hot or warm liquid (such as tea) in order to transfer flavour, colour and aroma to the liquid, which is later strained. |
| *insalata* | Italian for salad. |
| *involtini* | Italian for rolled pieces of meat or fish. |
| *irradiate, to* | To kill microorganisms and insects in foods like fruit, vegetables and cereals, or to prevent the sprouting of tubers or roots using ionizing radiation. It does not kill toxins or viruses. Irradiated foods do not, as yet, have to be labelled as such. |
| *jour, du* | Means 'of the day'. That is, a dish made for that particular day rather than available every day. |
| *jug, to* | To cook in a heavy earthenware jug, usually used to describe hare (jugged hare). |
| *julienne* | To cut food into fine sticks, thinner than matchsticks or shreds. |
| *jumbo* | Used to describe foods that are larger than normal. |
| *junk food* | Food that has lots of calories derived from sugar, starch and fat but little nutritional value. |
| *kernel* | The edible part of a stone or seed. Also used to describe corn. |

| | |
|---|---|
| **king, à la** | A dish with a sauce of cream, mushrooms and green peppers, often chicken based. |
| **kipper, to** | To preserve fish by salting and smoking. Also used to describe herring (known as 'kippers'). |
| **knead, to** | To mix a stiff dough by manipulating it by hand or with a mechanical dough hook in order to make it smooth. In bread-making, this also helps develop the gluten. |
| **knock back, to** | To knead gas bubbles out of a yeast-risen dough. |
| **knock up, to** | To separate the layers of puff pastry by running the back of the knife up the sides of the cut surface. |
| **lace, to** | To add extra spices, condiments and especially alcohol to a dish to make it more flavourful. |
| **lactic acid** | An acid formed when lactobacillus (bacteria) combines with lactose. It imparts a slightly sour flavour and helps in the preservation of food. It occurs naturally in yoghurt and in some salami. |
| **lard, to** | To thread strips of lard through a lean piece of meat in order to baste it as it cooks. |
| **lardons** | Short strips of pork fat or bacon. |
| **leavening agent** | A substance such as baking powder or yeast, which adds volume in the form of gas bubbles and lightens the texture of baked goods. |
| **liaison** | A thickening agent for a sauce, soup or stew made from eggs and cream, beurre manié or starches such as arrowroot. A liaison is added at the end of cooking. |
| **lights** | A butchery term for animal lungs. |
| **line, to** | To add a protective coating such as greaseproof paper (cake tins), strips of bacon (pâté), thin slices of cake (charlottes) to a dish in order to stop a filling sticking or to hold in a soft filling. |
| **lipids** | General term for fats and oils. |
| **liquidize** | To break down to a purée in a blender or food processor. |
| **lite (light)** | A term that simply means a food has less of something. It is used to describe things such as fat, flavour, colour, sugar, alcohol and calories and is governed by no regulations. For example, lite oil is light in flavour and colour, not fat or calories. |
| **loin** | Butchery term for the back portion of an animal comprising the last four vertebrae attached to the ribs and the ribless vertebrae along with all the attached meat. Can also be used to describe the same piece of meat without bones. |
| **low in fat, low fat** | Products labelled 'low in fat' in the USA and European Union guidelines must have less than half the fat of a full-fat version (exact levels are set by legislation). 'Low fat', however, can mean anything that has slightly less fat than its full fat-version, though European Union guidelines stipulate that fat content should be less than 5 g per 100 g and guidelines in the USA say it should be less than 3 g per 100 g. Other percentages of fat should actually be given, for example, 90 per cent fat-free. |
| **lute, to** | To seal the lid on a dish with a flour and water paste (luting) or to seal a pastry lid onto a pie dish with an extra strip of pastry. |
| **lyonnaise, à la** | Denotes a dish with onions. |
| **macédoine** | Small cubes or dice of mixed vegetables or fruit. |
| **macerate, to** | To soak food in a liquid so it absorbs the flavour of the liquid. Often used to describe soaking in alcohol and sugar syrup. |
| **maillard reaction** | The reaction between sugar and an amino acid, which makes food brown when it is cooked. |
| **maison** | Refers to a dish that is made on the premises from an original recipe. |
| **Marengo** | Veal or chicken cooked with tomatoes, onions, garlic, brandy and possibly mushrooms or crayfish. |
| **marinade** | A collection of wet flavourings in which foods are soaked so they take on flavour and, sometimes, to tenderize. Many marinades include an acid such as fruit juice (to tenderize the food) and an oil. |
| **marinate, to** | To soak food in a marinade. |
| **marquise** | A frozen dessert made by mixing sorbet with a liqueur and whipped cream, or a very smooth chocolate set dessert. |
| **Maryland** | Used to describe chicken pieces that have been crumbed and fried. In Australia, it refers to a leg and thigh portion of chicken. |
| **mask, to** | To cover a piece of cooked meat or fish with a layer of sauce or glaze. |

| | |
|---|---|
| **matelote** | A French fish stew generally made of freshwater fish. |
| **mature** | Food that has been kept in order to develop its flavour, such as cheese. |
| **medallion** | A small round piece of lean meat. |
| **mélange** | A mixture or blend. |
| **melt, to** | To turn food from a solid to a liquid state by heating it. |
| **menu** | A list of dishes available at a restaurant or café, usually with prices. |
| **meunière, à la** | A lightly floured food, usually fish, cooked in butter and garnished with lemon juice and parsley. |
| **mince** | Finely chopped meat. |
| **mirepoix** | Chopped vegetables on which pieces of meat are braised. They add flavour to the finished dish. |
| **mise en place** | To collect together, weigh and prepare the ingredients of a recipe before the actual assembling or cooking takes place. |
| **misto** | Italian for mixed. |
| **mix, to** | To combine and blend completely. |
| **mode, à la** | American term meaning served with a scoop of vanilla ice cream. |
| **mollusc** | A soft-bodied creature that has an internal or external shell. These include univalves, bivalves and cephalopods. Called mollusk in the USA. |
| **monter, to** | To add volume to an ingredient such as cream or egg white by whipping in air, or to add butter to a sauce at the end of cooking to make it shiny. |
| **Mornay, à la** | A dish with cheese sauce. |
| **mull, to** | To heat wine, beer or cider with spices and sugar. |
| **nage, à la** | Means 'swimming' in French and is an aromatic liquid (court bouillon) that crustaceans and shellfish can be cooked in. |
| **Nantua, à la** | Denotes the use of crayfish tails as a garnish. |
| **nap, to** | To coat a piece of food with a sauce. |
| **navarin** | A ragout of mutton, now usually lamb. |
| **niçoise, à la** | Meaning 'as prepared in Nice' and containing tomatoes, olives and garlic. It often refers to a niçoise salad. |
| **noisette** | A small round slice of meat from the loin or a small knob of butter. Also French for hazelnut. |
| **normande, à la** | Meaning 'in the style of Normandy'. Refers to either a dish with apples, cream and cider or Calvados, or a dish with a cream sauce and shellfish garnish. |
| **nouvelle cuisine** | A French term meaning 'new cooking'. This describes a culinary style that originated in the 1970s and consisted of small amounts of fresh food, arranged on a plate and garnished with reduced sauces. Vegetables were served just cooked and still crisp; butter, cream, eggs and flour were cut out of sauces and food was served undisguised by lavish garnishes. |
| **olio** | Italian for oil. |
| **oven-fry, to** | To dip food in flour and then brush with hot fat before baking. This term is used mainly in the USA. |
| **oyster** | The two small pieces of round flesh found on the back of a chicken just above where the thigh bone joins. Also refers to a bivalve mollusc. |
| **paillard** | A thin escalope of meat or poultry. |
| **pan-fry, to** | To fry in a frying pan in a small amount of fat. |
| **panada/panade** | A thick mixture, usually of flour, butter and milk or water used as the base of soufflés, quenelles and choux pastry. Sometimes eggs are also added. |
| **pan-broil, to** | To cook something in a frying pan without fat and to tip off any fat as it appears. This term is used in the USA. |
| **paner (pané), to** | To cover with flour, beaten egg and breadcrumbs prior to cooking. |
| **papillote, en** | Cooked wrapped in a paper parcel, which puffs up. Dishes cooked like this are served at the table. Papillote also describes the white paper frill used to decorate the tips of bones. |
| **parboil, to** | To half-cook something in boiling water. |
| **parch, to** | To dry roast |

**471**

| | |
|---|---|
| **pare, to** | To remove the thin outer layer of food using a knife with a short blade. |
| **Parmentier** | Denotes a dish containing potatoes. |
| **parmigiana, alla** | Means 'with Parmesan', either coated with or sprinkled with. |
| **pass, to** | To push food through a fine sieve. |
| **pâte** | French for pastry or the inside of cheese. |
| **pâté** | A cooked paste of meat, poultry or fish, either set in a terrine or cooked in pastry 'en croute'. |
| **pâte brisée** | Shortcrust pastry. |
| **pâte feuilletée** | Puff pastry. |
| **pâte sucrée** | Sweet shortcrust pastry. |
| **paupiette** | A stuffed, rolled piece of meat or fish. |
| **pavé** | Square-shaped. |
| **petit déjeuner** | French for breakfast. |
| **petits fours** | Bite-sized cakes and pastries. |
| **petits pois** | Small peas. |
| **pickle, to** | To preserve food in brine or acidic solutions such as vinegar. |
| **pinch** | As much of a powder, such as pepper, as can be held between a thumb and forefinger. |
| **pinion** | The wing tip of a bird. |
| **pipe, to** | To force a mixture through a nozzle, either smooth or patterned, in order to cover or decorate a surface or make an exact shape. |
| **piquer, to** | To make deep cuts into the surface of a piece of meat in order to insert pieces of garlic or herbs. |
| **pit** | The American word for a fruit stone. |
| **plank** | A piece of board with a groove around the edge, which is used to cook and serve fish or meat. |
| **plat du jour** | French for dish of the day. |
| **pluck** | The heart, lungs and liver of an animal. |
| **pluck, to** | To de-feather a bird. |
| **poach, to** | To cook gently in a barely simmering liquid. |
| **pod, to** | To take seeds, such as peas, out of their pod. |
| **point, à** | French for medium rare. |
| **poivre, au** | Denotes the use of coarsely crushed pepper. |
| **poloniase, à la** | Dishes such as cauliflower and asparagus that are sprinkled with chopped hard-boiled eggs, parsley, breadcrumbs and melted butter. |
| **polpettine** | Italian for meatballs. |
| **pot roast** | A joint of meat that has been browned with a little liquid in a sealed pan. |
| **poultry** | Domesticated birds bred for meat or eggs, including chicken, turkey, duck, goose, pigeon, pheasant, quail and guinea fowl. |
| **pousse-café** | A liqueur or brandy drunk after coffee. |
| **poussin** | A baby chicken. |
| **preserve** | A jam or marmalade. In the USA, preserves are chunkier than jams. |
| **primavera** | An Italian term that denotes the use of spring vegetables. |
| **prove, to** | To allow a yeasted dough to rise; also to heat a frying pan or wok with oil or salt and then rub the surface, thus filling in any minute marks with the mixture and making it non-stick. |
| **Provençale, à la** | Denotes the use of tomatoes, garlic and oil amongst other typical ingredients from Provence. |
| **pulp** | The flesh of fruit and vegetables or the matter left behind when fruit or vegetables have had all their juice extracted. |
| **purée** | A fine, soft, almost pourable paste made by processing or pounding food. |
| **rare** | A steak that has been cooked for a short time so it is still pink inside. |
| **ravigote butter** | Butter mixed with a paste of fresh herbs. Also called green butter. |
| **réchauffé(e)** | A reheated dish made with already-cooked food, such as shepherd's pie. |
| **reduce, to** | To boil a liquid in order to evaporate off water. This thickens the liquid and intensifies the flavour. |

**472**

| | |
|---|---|
| *reduction* | The concentrated liquid obtained by reducing. |
| *refresh, to* | To put just-cooked items into cold water in order to stop them cooking further. |
| *rehydrate, to* | To add water back to something that has been dehydrated. |
| *render, to* | To melt animal fat over low heat so that it separates out from any connective tissues. These go crispy and brown in the process. The fat is then strained to purify it. |
| *rest/relax, to* | To leave pastry in the fridge to allow the gluten, which will have been stretched during rolling, to contract again. Also means to leave batters until the starch cells in the flour have swelled through contact with the liquid; or to leave meat to let the juices settle back into the flesh before carving it. |
| *rigati/e* | When applied to pasta shapes, it means they are ridged on the outside. |
| *ristretto* | Italian for reduced. Used to describe sauces and stocks, as well as strong coffee. |
| *roast, to* | To cook in an oven at a high temperature without any covering in order to give a crisp, well-browned exterior and a just-cooked moist interior. Usually applied to meat, poultry or vegetables, though anything can be roasted. |
| *roe* | The eggs or sperm of fish or shellfish. Hard roes are eggs and soft roes (milt) are sperm. |
| *roll, to* | To make a dough or pastry thinner by compressing it between a rolling pin and work surface in a backwards and forwards rolling motion. |
| *rotisserie* | An oven or grill that cooks food while it rotates in front of the heat source. |
| *roux* | A mixture of flour and fat cooked together and then used as a thickening agent, such as in sauces and soups. A white roux is cooked until just a pale yellow; a blonde roux until it is a gold colour; and a brown roux until it is a darker golden brown. |
| *rub in, to* | To integrate hard fat into flour by rubbing the two together with your fingertips until the mixture resembles breadcrumbs. |
| *saddle* | A joint comprising the two joined loins of an animal. |
| *salmis* | A stew-like game dish made with the roasted breast of a game bird and a salmis sauce. |
| *sauter (sauté), to* | To shallow-fry in hot fat while shaking and tossing the pan. |
| *scald, to* | To pour over or immerse in boiling water for a short time in order to cook only the outer layer. Also, to bring milk almost to the boil; or to sterilize kitchen equipment with boiling water. |
| *scallop, to* | A way of decorating pastry edges by pushing the edge in with one finger while pushing the pastry on both sides of that piece in the opposite direction using the other thumb and finger. |
| *score, to* | To make a shallow cut with a knife without cutting all the way through. |
| *scramble, to* | To stir beaten eggs over heat, constantly mixing the cooked parts back into the uncooked parts. |
| *sear, to* | To brown the surface of meat in hot fat before fully cooking it. |
| *season, to* | To add flavour to something, usually salt and pepper, to bring out other flavours, or to smooth out the surface of a pan using hot oil or salt. |
| *sel* | French for salt. 'Sel marin' or 'sel de mer' is sea salt and 'gros sel' is rock salt. |
| *sell-by date* | The date by which food must be sold, known as the pull-date in the USA. The food is not necessarily inedible on this date, but will not last much longer. |
| *shank* | The front leg of beef, veal, lamb or pork. |
| *shelf life* | The length of time a product will stay fresh. |
| *shortening* | The fat used in baking. The term refers to the ability (shortening power) of the fat to allow the mixture to trap air bubbles and make it light. |
| *shred, to* | To cut food into very thin strips. |
| *shuck, to* | To open bivalves such as oysters or to remove the husks, shells or pods from seeds. |
| *sieve/sift, to* | To aerate and remove any lumps from a dry powder such as flour or icing sugar. |
| *sieze* | When melted chocolate turns into a lumpy mass because a tiny amount of liquid, usually condensed steam, drips into it. |
| *simmer, to* | To maintain a cooking liquid at a temperature just below boiling. |
| *singe, to* | To use a naked flame to remove hairs or small feathers from the skin of meat or poultry. |
| *skim, to* | To remove fat or scum from the surface of a liquid using a large spoon, ladle or skimmer. |

**473**

| | |
|---|---|
| *slake, to* | To mix a powder, such as cornflour, with a little liquid to form a paste in order for it then to be mixed into a larger amount of liquid without forming lumps. |
| *slow food* | A way of eating promoted by the Slow Food Society formed in Cuneo in Italy in 1986. The society promotes good cooking in the face of the advancement of fast food and junk food. |
| *slurry* | A term used in the USA referring to a mixture of flour and water, which is stirred into soups and sauces as a thickener. |
| *smother* | A term used in the USA that means to braise covered in a sauce or gravy in a covered pot, such as a smothered (Swiss) steak. |
| *soft boil, to* | To boil an egg until the white is just set and the yolk is runny (about 4–5 minutes from boiling). |
| *souse, to* | To pickle. |
| *sponge* | A bubbly, batter-like mixture made by mixing flour, yeast and a liquid and allowing it to stand for several hours. The first step in some bread-making recipes. |
| *steam, to* | To cook in the steam given off by boiling or simmering water. |
| *steep, to* | To infuse. |
| *stir-fry, to* | To cook pieces of food quickly in a wok using only a little oil and moving them around constantly. |
| *stud, to* | To insert flavourings such as whole cloves (into an onion) or slivers of garlic (into a piece of meat) into a piece of food at regular intervals. |
| *sweat, to* | To cook in fat over low heat without letting the food brown. |
| *tasse, en* | A French term meaning served in a cup, such as soups. |
| *tea-smoked* | Something smoked by heating tea, rice and sugar and suspending the food above it on a rack. |
| *temper, to* | To mix, blend, heat or knead something until it reaches the required consistency. Usually refers to tempering chocolate, which makes it glossy when it sets. |
| *tenderize, to* | To break down the tough fibres in flesh by mechanical (pounding), chemical (acid) or natural (hanging) means. |
| *tomalley* | The green-coloured liver of a lobster. |
| *top and tail, to* | To remove the stalks and tips from fruit and vegetables. |
| *torta* | Italian for cake, pie or tart; Spanish for cake, loaf or sandwich. |
| *toss, to* | To mix a dressing through food, usually a salad, so that it becomes coated. Also means to shake pieces of meat in flour to coat them; or to turn food in a pan by flipping it out of the pan, such as a pancake. |
| *tourte* | A flan or tart made with puff pastry. |
| *tranche* | French for a slice. |
| *trim, to* | To remove unwanted bits from meat or fish, or to cut something to a specific shape. |
| *truss, to* | To hold something, usually meat or poultry, in shape with string or skewers while it cooks. |
| *turn, to* | To shape vegetables, using a turning knife, into barrel shapes, or to carve mushroom caps with a decorative spiral pattern. |
| *UHT (ultra heat-treated)* | Liquid that has been heated and cooled to sterilize it without affecting the flavour too much. |
| *unleavened* | Made without any raising agents. |
| *Véronique* | A savoury dish, usually fish, decorated with white grapes. |
| *vigneron(ne)* | A wine grower. |
| *vitello* | Italian for veal. |
| *wet fish* | Fresh, uncooked fish. |
| *whip, to* | To incorporate air into something by beating it (cream, egg white) with a whisk or to form an emulsion by the same means (mayonnaise). |
| *zest* | The outer layer of citrus fruit, which is coloured and contains the essential oils. |
| *zuppa* | Italian for a thick soup. |

# cooking information

The conversion tables shown are an approximation of conversions—in reality, 1 oz = 28.35 g, but it is easier to call it 30 g as scales do not measure small enough amounts to conveniently use any measurements of less than 1 g.

## WEIGHTS

| Metric | Imperial | Metric | Imperial |
|---|---|---|---|
| 7 g | ¼ oz | 285 g | 10 oz |
| 15 g | ½ oz | 310 g | 11 oz |
| 20 g | ¾ oz | 340 g | 12 oz (¾ lb) |
| 30 g | 1 oz | 370 g | 13 oz |
| 55 g | 2 oz | 400 g | 14 oz |
| 85 g | 3 oz | 425 g | 15 oz |
| 110 g | 4 oz (¼ lb) | 450 g | 16 oz (1 lb) |
| 140 g | 5 oz | 560 g | 1¼ lb |
| 170 g | 6 oz | 900 g | 2 lb |
| 200 g | 7 oz | 1 kg | 2¼ lb |
| 225 g | 8 oz (½ lb) | 1.35 kg | 3 lb |
| 255 g | 9 oz | 1.8 kg | 4 lb |

## LIQUID MEASURES

| ml | fl oz | Other | ml | fl oz | Other |
|---|---|---|---|---|---|
| 5 ml | | 1 teaspoon | 250 ml | 9 fl oz | |
| 15 ml | | 1 tablespoon | 290 ml | 10 fl oz | ½ pint |
| 30 ml | 1 fl oz | 2 tablespoons | 400 ml | 14 fl oz | |
| 56 ml | 2 fl oz | | 425 ml | 15 fl oz | ¾ pint |
| 100 ml | 3½ fl oz | | 455 ml | 16 fl oz | (1 U.S. pint) |
| 150 ml | 5 fl oz | ¼ pint (1 gill) | 500 ml | 17 fl oz | |
| 190 ml | 6½ fl oz | ⅓ pint | 570 ml | 20 fl oz | 1 pint |
| 200 ml | 7 fl oz | | 1 litre | 35 fl oz | 1¾ pints |

## OVEN TEMPERATURES

| °C | °F | Gas mark | °C | °F | Gas mark |
|---|---|---|---|---|---|
| 70 | 150 | ¼ | 190 | 375 | 5 |
| 100 | 200 | ½ | 200 | 400 | 6 |
| 110 | 225 | ½ | 220 | 425 | 7 |
| 130 | 250 | 1 | 230 | 450 | 8 |
| 140 | 275 | 1 | 240 | 475 | 8 |
| 150 | 300 | 2 | 250 | 500 | 9 |
| 170 | 325 | 3 | 270 | 525 | 9 |
| 180 | 350 | 4 | 290 | 550 | 9 |

Cup measures are based on a U.S. cup (235 ml/8 fl oz). An Australian cup (250 ml/9 fl oz) may also be used in the same way without affecting most recipes. Tablespoon measures also vary between 15 and 20 ml, but the discrepancy is negligible.

## CUP CONVERSIONS

| Ingredients | Cup (U.S.) | Metric | Imperial |
|---|---|---|---|
| butter/margarine | 1 cup | 225 g | 8 oz |
| butter | 1 stick | 110 g | 4 oz |
| flour, sifted | 1 cup | 140 g | 5 oz |
| rice, cooked | 1 cup | 185 g | 6½ oz |
| rice, uncooked | 1 cup | 200 g | 7 oz |
| soft brown sugar | 1 cup | 170 g | 6 oz |
| sugar | 1 cup | 225 g | 8 oz |

## USEFUL MEASURES & APPROXIMATE CONVERSIONS

| Ingredients | Tablespoons | Metric | Imperial |
|---|---|---|---|
| breadcrumbs | 2 tablespoons | 30 g | 1 oz |
| cornflour | 1 tablespoon | 30 g | 1 oz |
| 1 egg white | 2 tablespoons | 30 ml | 1 fl oz |
| flour | 1 tablespoon | 30 g | 1 oz |
| gelatine, powdered | 4½ teaspoons or 6 leaves | 15 g | ½ oz |
| juice of 1 lemon | 4 tablespoons | 60 ml | 2 fl oz |
| juice of 1 lime | 2 tablespoons | 30 ml | 1 fl oz |
| sugar | 1 tablespoon | 30 g | 1 oz |

## FOOD POISONING

Hygiene and food safety are of paramount importance in the kitchen. Raw and cooked food may contain organisms that will multiply and become dangerous if the food is not treated correctly. All cooking and storage should be done with this in mind. Hands, utensils and surfaces should be kept scrupulously clean and food should be stored in its appropriate place (such as the fridge). Generally, fruit and vegetables should be washed.

The more common types of food poisoning are due to salmonella, listeria and staphylococcus. Rarer forms include botulism and ciguatera.

Salmonella are a group of bacteria present mainly in meat, poultry and eggs. Salmonella, which causes upset stomachs and fever, is curable with antibiotics. It may, however, cause more severe reactions in pregnant women, babies or the elderly. Salmonella can be killed by boiling or heating food to very high temperatures.

Listeria is also a bacteria and is mainly found in soft cheese, pâté and ready-made food. Human immune systems cope well with it, but if listeriosis does occur, it can kill. It is of particular risk to pregnant women.

Staphylococcus are organisms that can cause food poisoning. They are found in prepared foods such as meat pies that are not stored properly. They cause varying degrees of sickness but not fever and are untreatable. They can not be killed by heating.

Botulism is a rare but virulent form of food poisoning caused by the toxins secreted by an anaerobic organism that can only grow in sealed tins and jars, or in the centre of cured meats where there is no oxygen present. Botulism does not cause immediate sickness but damages the nervous system and it often kills. Botulism can be killed by boiling for a short time. Preservatives inhibit botulism growth.

Ciguatera is a rare form of poisoning contracted by eating reef fish that have been eating toxic plankton. It affects the nervous system and often kills. It is not destroyed by cooking.

This chart will help you to gauge how much of something to buy per head. The quantities are quite generous, but the more dishes you serve at once, the less you will need per person. The meat and fish quantities are for a single main course.

## QUANTITIES

| Ingredients | Quantities |
|---|---|
| Batter, pancake or crêpe | 110 g (flour quantity) makes about 12 crêpes. |
| Beef, fillet | 200 g per person. |
| Beef, joint off the bone | 200 g per person. |
| Beef, joint on the bone | 320 g per person. |
| Beef, steaks | 170–225 g each. Steaks with bones weigh more. |
| Beef and veal, cubed or sliced | 200–225 g each (trimmed weight). |
| Canapés | 4 to 5 canapés per head with drinks, 10 to 14 canapés per head if no other food is served. |
| Chicken, breasts | 1 breast each, but if sliced, 3 x 175 g breasts will feed 4 people. |
| Chicken, whole | 1 large (1.5 kg) chicken per 4 people for roasting, ¼ chicken per person for casseroles (two joints). |
| Fish, fillets | 180–200 g each. |
| Fish, whole (individual, such as trout) | 250–300 g each. |
| Fish, whole (large, such as salmon) | 350–400 g per person. |
| Lamb, chops | 2 per person. |
| Lamb, cubed or sliced | 225 g each (trimmed weight). |
| Lamb, cutlets | 3 to 4 each. |
| Lamb, leg or shoulder on the bone | 400–500 g per person. |
| Mince, all types | 170 g per person for hamburgers, pies etc, 110 g per person for chilli con carne and spaghetti Bolognese. |
| Pasta | 75 g per head for a small portion, 100 g for a normal portion, 150 g for a large portion. |
| Pastry, puff and flaky | 500 g pastry (made with 225 g flour) makes 1 millefeuille, 4 individual tarts or covers 1 pie. |
| Pastry, shortcrust and sweet | 225 g pastry (made with 170 g flour) lines a 20 cm tart tin, 325 g pastry (made with 225 g flour) lines a 25 cm tart tin. |
| Pork, chops | 1 x 175–225 g chop per person. |
| Pork, cubed or sliced | 200–225 g per person. |
| Pork, joint off the bone | 200 g per person. |
| Pork, joint on the bone | 320 g per person. |
| Potato | 110–185 g per head. |
| Prawns, shell on | 150 g per head as a starter and 300 g as a main. |
| Prawns, shelled | 85 g per head as a starter and 150 g as a main. |
| Rice | 55 g uncooked per head for boiled or fried rice. 30 g uncooked per head for risotto. |
| Soup | 300 ml per head as a starter and 500 ml as a main course. |

It is very important to store your food correctly and in the safest way possible to stop it becoming contaminated or to stop bacteria developing. As a general rule cooked food should be stored at the top of the fridge and raw food at the bottom.

## STORAGE

| Ingredients | In the fridge | Special requirements |
|---|---|---|
| Butter | Wrap tightly to stop it becoming tainted or going rancid. | Unsalted butter will not last as long as salted butter. |
| Dairy, such as milk and cream | Keep cartons and bottles closed as milk taints very easily. | |
| Eggs | Keep in the box in which they are sold as they easily taint from other smells in the fridge. | Do not store loose in the egg holes. |
| Fish | Put on a plate, cover with clingfilm and keep for as short a time as possible. | Gut fish before storage as ungutted fish go off quickly. |
| Fruit | Store in the salad compartment. Strong-smelling fruit like melon should be tightly wrapped if it is cut or it will taint other things. | Bananas and avocados should be stored in cool places but not the fridge, if possible. |
| Herbs | Store in their plastic bags or containers in the salad compartment or put large bunches in a jug of water. | Buy pot herbs if you can, as you often only need a few leaves out of each bunch. This way, you can pick them as you need them. |
| Meat | Remove from packaging, put on a plate and cover with clingfilm. | Store on the bottom shelf of the fridge so no blood can drip onto cooked food. |
| Poultry | If there are giblets included, remove them as soon as you get home. Unwrap the chicken, put it on a plate and cover with clingfilm. | Store on the bottom shelf of the fridge so no blood can drip onto cooked food. |
| Shellfish | Store in the salad compartment in a bowl and cover with a damp cloth. | Do not put in cold water if alive or they will drown. |
| Vegetables | Store in the salad compartment. | Root vegetables should be stored in the dark. |

## FREEZING

The most important thing when freezing food is to freeze it quickly. This means smaller ice crystals will form and these will be less damaging to the food—large ice crystals damage cell walls as they expand and when they defrost, moisture and nutrients are lost. Cover ice cream with greaseproof paper to stop the formation of ice crystals.

Wrap food in small portions so it freezes quickly. Make sure it is well wrapped, as any food, especially meat and fish, that comes into contact with freezing air will get 'freezer burn' (dry, discoloured patches).

Wet food and liquids should have a 2 cm gap between them and the lid of the box to allow for expansion.

Freezer temperature should be -20°C.

## DEFROSTING

Food should be defrosted slowly and thoroughly—this means in the fridge. Large joints and poultry should be given 2 days to defrost in the fridge. Food that has been wrapped in small portions can be quickly defrosted as needed.

## MICROWAVING

Always follow the instructions that come with your model of microwave. Some microwaves are also convection ovens and some have more power than others. A timing that is right for one oven may not work for another.

# index

# recipe index

# bibliography

Achaya, K. T. A Historical Dictionary of Indian Food. Oxford University Press, 1998.

Alexander, Stephanie. The Cook's Companion. Viking, 1996.

Andrews, Colman. Catalan Cuisine. Headline, 1996.

Ayto, John. The Diner's Dictionary Food and Drink from A to Z. Oxford University Press, 1993.

Bailey, Adrian. DK Pocket Encyclopedia. Cook's Ingredients. Dorling Kindersley, London, 1990.

Barker, Anthony. From A La Carte to Zucchini: An A to Z of Food and Cooking. Allen and Unwin, 1995.

Beard, James. James Beard's American Cookery. Little, Brown and Company, 1972.

Behr, Edward. The Art of Eating. No. 34: Gombo (Arcadian Food in Southwest Louisiana).

Bender, Arnold and David. Oxford Dictionary of Food and Nutrition. Oxford University Press, 1995.

Bharadwaj, Monisha. The Indian Kitchen. Kyle Cathie Limited, 1998.

Bhumichitr, Vatcharin. The Taste of Thailand. Pavillion Books, 1988.

Bhumichitr, Vatcharin. Thai Vegetarian Cooking. Pavillion Books, 1991.

Bissell, Frances. Sainsbury's Book of Food. Websters International Publishers, 1989.

Bloom, Carole. The International Dictionary of Desserts, Pastries and Confections. Hearst Books, 1995.

Brissenden, Rosemary. South East Asian Food. Penguin Books, 1996.

Brown, Erica. Provence Gastronomique. Conran Octopus, 1995.

Brown, Gordon, Classic Spirits of the World. Prion, 1995.

Brown, Linda. The Modern Cook's Handbook. Penguin Books, 1998.

Bruneteau, Jean Paul. Tukka. Angus and Robertson, 1996.

Carluccio, Antonio and Priscilla. Complete Italian Food. Quadrille Publishing Limited, 1997.

Chamberlain, Lesley. The Practical Encyclopedia of East European Cooking. Lorenz Books, 1999.

Christian, Glynn. Glynn Christian's Delicatessen Food Book. Good Food Retailing Publications, 1993.

Collister, Linda and Blake, Anthony. The Bread Book. Sedgewood Press, 1993.

Conran, Caroline and Terence and Hopkinson, Simon. The Conran Cookbook. Conran Octopus, 1997.

Cummings, Joe. World Food Thailand. Lonely Planet Publications Pty Ltd, 2000.

Danford, Randi, Feierabend, Peter and Chassman, Gary. Culinaria: The United States, Könemann, 1998.

David, Elizabeth. French Provincial Cooking. Penguin Books, 1970.

David, Elizabeth. Italian Food (revised edition). Penguin Books, 1989.

David, Elizabeth. Spices, Salt and Aromatics in the English Kitchen. Penguin Books, 1975.

Davidson, Alan. Mediterranean Seafood. Penguin Books, 1981.

Davidson, Alan. North Atlantic Seafood. Penguin Books, 1980.

Davidson, Alan. The Oxford Companion to Food. Oxford University Press, 1999.

Davidson, Alan. Seafood: A Connoisseur's Guide and Cookbook. Simon and Schuster, 1989.

Del Conte, Anna. The Classic Food of Northern Italy. Pavilion Books Limited, 1995.

Del Conte, Anna. Gastronomy of Italy. Prentice Hall Press, 1988.

Denny, Roz. The Real Food Handbook. Prion Books, 1999.

Dominé, André. Culinaria France. Könemann, 1999.

Dominé, André. Culinaria: Organic and Wholefoods. Könemann, 1997.

Dominé, André and Ditter, Michael. Culinaria: European Specialities (volume 2). Könemann, 1995.

Domingo, Xavier. The Taste of Spain. Flammarion, 1992.

Editors of Time-Life Books. The Good Cook: Beef and Veal. Time-Life Books B. V., 1978.

Editors of Time-Life Books. The Good Cook: Fish and Shellfish. Time-Life Books B. V., 1979.

Editors of Time-Life Books. The Good Cook: Game. Time-Life Books B. V., 1982.

Editors of Time-Life Books. The Good Cook: Lamb. Time-Life Books B. V., 1981.

Editors of Time-Life Books. The Good Cook: Pork. Time-Life Books B. V., 1979.

Editors of Time-Life Books. The Good Cook: Wine. Time-Life Books B.V., 1982.

Farmer, Fannie. Fannie Farmer's Classic American Cookbook. Papermac (Macmillan), 1982.

Fortin, François. The Visual Food Encyclopedia. Macmillan (USA), 1996.

Grigson, Jane. Charcuterie and French Pork Cookery. Penguin Books, 1970.

Grigson, Jane. Jane Grigson's Fruit Book. Penguin Books, 1983.

Grigson, Jane. Jane Grigson's Vegetable Book. Penguin Books, 1980.

Grigson, Sophie and Black, William. Fish. Headline Book Publishing, 1998.

Harbutt, Juliet. The World Encyclopedia of Cheese. Lorenz Books, 1998.

Harris, Jessica B. The Africa Cookbook: Tastes of a Continent. Simon and Schuster, 1998.

Harris, Valentina. Italian Regional Cookery. BBC Books, 1990.

Hazan, Marcella. The Essentials of Classic Italian Cooking. Macmillan, 1995.

Hemphill, Ian. Spice Notes. Pan Macmillan, 2000.

Herbst, Sharon Tyler. The New Food Lover's Companion (second edition). Barron's Educational Series, Inc., 1995.

Hom, Ken. Ken Hom's Asian Ingredients. Ten Speed Press, 1996.

Hsiung, Deh-Ta. The Chinese Kitchen. Kyle Cathie Limited, 1999.

Jaffrey, Madhur. A Taste of India. Pavillion Books Limited, 1985.

Johns, Pamela Sheldon. Italian Food Artisans: Traditions and Recipes. Chronicle Books, 2000.

Kennedy, Diana. The Art of Mexican Cooking. Bantam Books, 1989.

Kennedy, Diana. My Mexico. Potter, 1998.

Kremezi, Aglaia. Foods of Greece. Stewart, Tabori and Chang, 1993.

Larousse Gastronomique. Paul Hamlyn, 1992.

Leith, Prue and Waldegrave, Caroline. Leith's Cookery Bible. Bloomsbury, 1991.

Leonard, Jonathan Norton and the Editors of Time-Life Books. Foods of the World: Latin American Cooking. Time-Life Books, 1970.

Liddell, Caroline and Weir, Robin. Ices: The Definitive Guide. Grub Street, 1995.

McGee, Harold. On Food and Cooking: The Science and Lore of the Kitchen. Collier Books, 1984.

Mariani, John. The Dictionary of Italian Food and Drink. Broadway Books, 1998.

Marks, Gil. The World of Jewish Cooking. Simon and Schuster, 1996.

Masui, Kazuko and Yamada, Tomoko. French Cheeses. Dorling Kindersley, 1996.

Miller, Mark. The Great Chile Book. Ten Speed Press, 1991.

Millon, Marc and Kim. The Food Lover's Companion to France. Macmillan Travel, 1996.

Millon, Marc and Kim. The Food Lover's Companion to Italy. Little, Brown and Company (UK), 1996.

Millon, Marc and Kim. The Taste of Britain. Webb and Bower, 1985.

Mowe, Rosalind. Culinaria: Southeast Asian Specialties. Könemann, 1999.

Nakano, Koji and Howard, Lesley. Japanese Cooking. Sally Milner Publishing, 1991.

Nichols, Lourdes. The Complete Mexican Cookbook. Judy Piatkus (Publishers) Ltd 1996.

Ortiz, Elizabeth Lambert. Caribbean Cooking. Penguin Books, 1977.

Owen, Sri. The Rice Book. Transworld, 1993.

Passmore, Jacki. The Encyclopedia of Asian Food and Cooking. Doubleday, 1991.

Peterson, James. Essentials of Cooking. Artisan, 1999.

Powers, Jo Marie and Stewart, Anita. Northern Bounty: A Celebration of Canadian Cuisine. Random House of Canada, 1995.

Roden, Claudia. The Book of Jewish Food. Viking, 1997.

Roden, Claudia. The Food of Italy. Vintage, 1999.

Roden, Claudia. A New Book of Middle Eastern Food. Penguin, 1986.

Römer, Joachim and Ditter, Michael. Culinaria: European Specialities (volume 1). Konemann, 1995.

Root, Waverley. Food. Simon and Schuster, 1980.

Ross, Rosa Lo San. Beyond Bok Choy: A Cook's Guide to Asian Vegetables. Artisan, 1996

Schneider, Elizabeth. Uncommon Fruit and Vegetables: A Commonsense Guide. Harper and Row, 1986.

Sinclair, Charles. International Dictionary of Food and Cooking. Peter Collin Publishing Ltd 1998.

Solomon, Charmaine. Encyclopedia of Asian Food. William Heinemann, 1996.

Stasko, Nicolette. Oyster. Harper Collins, 2000.

Stobart, Tom. The Cook's Encyclopaedia. Grub Street, 1998.

Thompson, David. Classic Thai Cuisine. Simon and Schuster, 1993.

Toussaint-Samat, Maguelonne. History of Food. Blackwell, 1993.

Treuille, Eric and Ferrigno, Ursula. Bread. Dorling Kindersley, 1998.

Trewby, Mary. A Gourmet's Book of Herbs and Spices. Golden Press, 1989.

Tsuji, Shizuo. Japanese Cooking: A Simple Art. Kodansha International Limited, 1980.

van Aken, Norman. The Great Exotic Fruit Book. Ten Speed Press, 1995.

Vilmorin-Andrieux M. M. The Vegetable Garden. Ten Speed Press, undated.

Walden, Hilaire. North African Cooking. New Burlington Books, 1995.

Werle, Loukie. Australasian Ingredients. Gore and Osment, 1997.

Wolfert, Paula. Good Food From Morocco. John Murray, 1989.

Woodward, Sarah. Moorish Food. Kyle Cathie, 1998.

Yiu, Hannah. Easy Asian Vegetable Cooking. Oriental Merchant, undated.

Young, Grace. The Wisdom of the Chinese Kitchen. Simon and Schuster Editions, 1999.

## ACKNOWLEDGMENTS

The Publisher wishes to thank the following for all their help in making this book possible:
Antico's; Harry Black, Harry Black's Orchard; Fitzroy Boulting; Captain Torres; Bridgette Cox, CSIRO;
Demcos; Sue Dodd, Sydney Marketing Authority; Margaret Fulton; Herbies; Cath Kerry; Stefano Manfredi;
Barbara Santich; Carol Selva Rajah; Charmaine Solomon; Roman Sulovsky; Michael Symons; Tony Tan;
Tropical Fruit World, Duranbah.